MIKHAIL SHOLOKHOV AND HIS ART

Стараго міра—послѣдній сонъ:
Молодость—Доблесть—Вандея—Донъ.
—Марина Цвѣтаева

The Old World's Last Dream:
Youth—Valor—Vendée—The Don.
—Marina Tsvetaeva

MIKHAIL SHOLOKHOV AND HIS ART

HERMAN ERMOLAEV

PRINCETON UNIVERSITY PRESS

Published by Princeton University Press, 41 William Street,
Princeton, New Jersey
In the United Kingdom: Princeton University Press, Guildford, Surrey

Library of Congress Cataloging in Publication Data will be
found on the last printed page of this book

Publication of this book has been aided by a grant from the Paul Mellon
Fund of Princeton University Press

This book has been composed in Linotron Times Roman

Clothbound editions of Princeton University Press books
are printed on acid-free paper, and binding materials are
chosen for strength and durability

Printed in the United States of America by Princeton
University Press, Princeton, New Jersey

Designed by Laury A. Egan

To the memory of
Andrei Stepanovich Liubibogov
a Don Cossack

CONTENTS

LIST OF ILLUSTRATIONS

LIST OF TABLES

PREFACE

My interest in Mikhail Sholokhov goes back to the year 1938 when, as a secondary-school student, I read the first three volumes of *The Quiet Don*. I was struck by the impartiality with which the Civil War was portrayed. What Sholokhov wrote about this war was quite different from what one heard in school, read in the press, or saw in the movies. The novel appealed to me all the more since I was then living among the Don Cossacks. Scenes of the Civil War from *The Quiet Don* were evoked in my mind when, almost every day, I passed by the monument commemorating some sixty members of the local Red detachment who were sabered during their retreat by insurgent Cossacks in the spring of 1918.

The purpose of my study is to highlight important or little explored aspects of Sholokhov's works. I depart from the traditional method of presenting the author's life and work in a strictly chronological order. Instead, I concentrate on five selected subjects, allotting one chapter to each.

The first three chapters cover Sholokhov's life and work, his world outlook, and his literary style. Chapter I emphasizes those episodes from the author's life which had noticeable impact on his creative writing and which do not appear in the few existing studies on Sholokhov written in the West. The most informative of these studies, *Mikhail Sholokhov: A Critical Introduction*, by D. H. Stewart, came out in 1967. A considerable amount of information, particularly on Sholokhov's relationship with Stalin, became available later.

Chapter II discusses Sholokhov's views on life and traces their continuity and changes throughout his works. It shows how a one-sided commitment to Party ideology has led to the conceptual and creative deterioration of a gifted author.

Chapter III is central with respect to its location and its subject matter. Since literature is a verbal art, a detailed discussion of an author's language and imagery seems to me indispensable for a scholarly monograph. My aim is to define the peculiarities of Sholokhov's art and his place in literature. His style is compared to that of Tolstoi and six Soviet writers—Vsevolod Ivanov, Babel', Gladkov, Veselyi, Olesha, and Pasternak. I intend to demonstrate that Sholokhov is more an innovator than a traditionalist and a follower of Tolstoi. His main literary tool—the language—

differs a great deal from the language of the Russian nineteenth-century realists, but it has much in common with the Soviet ornamental prose of the 1920s. For the benefit of those who know Russian, about half of the stylistic illustrations are cited both in the original and in translation. I hope that the number of such samples will be sufficient to convey the flavor of the original and will not overload the text with transliterated phrases which are of no use to those who do not understand them.

Chapter IV deals with historical sources of *The Quiet Don*, an important subject that has received very little attention either in the Soviet Union or in the West. Soviet scholars are not in a position to explore this problem in depth. The results of such an exploration would reveal a far greater reliance by Sholokhov on the writings of White Russian émigrés than Soviet authorities would care to admit.

Chapter V examines a purely "Sholokhovian" problem, that of alleged plagiarism. It tests the validity of the contentions voiced by a certain anonymous Soviet critic, by Aleksandr Solzhenitsyn, and by Roi Medvedev that *The Quiet Don* was written by Fedor Kriukov (1870-1920) rather than by Sholokhov. Investigation of these contentions involves the use of evidence pertaining to Sholokhov's life, ideology, literary style, and historical sources of *The Quiet Don*. Thus Chapter V becomes a kind of knot that ties together the threads stretching from the preceding chapters.

Sholokhov is a controversial figure. He is extolled in the Soviet press, but despised by many intellectuals and writers. Because of his high official status, Soviet critical literature about him has degenerated into an unqualified praise of his personal, political, and artistic qualities. No original or objective evaluation of his art has been possible in the Soviet Union since the mid-1930s. It goes without saying that Sholokhov's political stance and his statements about fellow writers, especially his vicious remarks about Pasternak, Siniavskii, Daniel', and Solzhenitsyn, deserve condemnation. At the same time one should not overlook that it was Sholokhov who saved thousands of lives during the government-induced famine of 1932-1933. Risking his life, he persuaded Stalin to send grain to the starving Upper Don region.

Whatever one's attitude toward Sholokhov might be, *The Quiet Don* remains a remarkable work of the twentieth century. As an indication of its appeal to a select group of readers, I would like to refer to the results of a survey I have been conducting since 1966 among Princeton undergraduates in my yearly course on Soviet literature in translation. *The Quiet Don* proves to be on par with *Doctor Zhivago, The First Circle*, and *Cancer Ward*. Of course, my limited survey does not reflect the preferences of an average American reader. Yet the students I polled are a fairly heterogeneous body. They represent both sexes equally, come from different social and ethnic backgrounds, and concentrate in a wide variety of majors.

For greater clarity many events and publications are dated in accordance with both the New Style (the Gregorian calendar) and the Old Style (the Julian calendar). Pre-Revolutionary and White Russian publications adhered to the Old Style, which in the twentieth century runs thirteen days behind the Gregorian calendar. Single dates indicate the New Style.

The following translations are used for ranks and positions in the Cossack troops: prikaznyi = corporal, mladshii uriadnik = junior sergeant, starshii uriadnik = senior sergeant, vzvodnyi uriadnik = troop sergeant, vakhmistr = sergeant major, podkhorunzhii = sub-lieutenant, khorunzhii = second lieutenant, sotnik = lieutenant, pod''esaul = junior captain, esaul = captain, voiskovoi starshina = lieutenant colonel, polkovnik = colonel, general (of any rank) = general.

The word "ataman" means "headman." Every Don Cossack village, stanitsa, and district were governed by an ataman. The head of all the Don Cossacks was called voiskovoi (literally: army) or Don ataman.

My system of transliteration follows that of the Library of Congress, with some minor alterations. For example, I use "e" for both "e" and "ë." My transliterations are based on the "new," post-Revolutionary orthography regardless of the spelling used in the originals. The pre-Revolutionary spelling is retained only in the Russian text of the epigraph, in compliance with Marina Tsvetaeva's wish that her poems be published in the "old" orthography.

HERMAN ERMOLAEV

of California Press. These passages are excerpts from my article "The Role of Nature in *The Quiet Don*" published in *California Slavic Studies*, vol. 6, 1971. I thank the University of California Press for permission to reprint them, and I gratefully acknowledge permission granted by the editors of *Survey* to reprint, in chapter 2, passages from my article "Sholokhov Thirty Years After: *Virgin Soil Upturned*, II" which appeared in *Survey*, no. 36, April-June 1961.

I extend special thanks to the Princeton University Committee on Research in the Humanities and Social Sciences for its generous financial support of my research and for covering typing expenses.

My greatest debt is to my wife Tania. She took much time from her own research to edit and type the first version of my manuscript. She was my main adviser. Numerous improvements in content and style were made on her suggestions. Her moral support was invaluable.

MIKHAIL SHOLOKHOV AND HIS ART

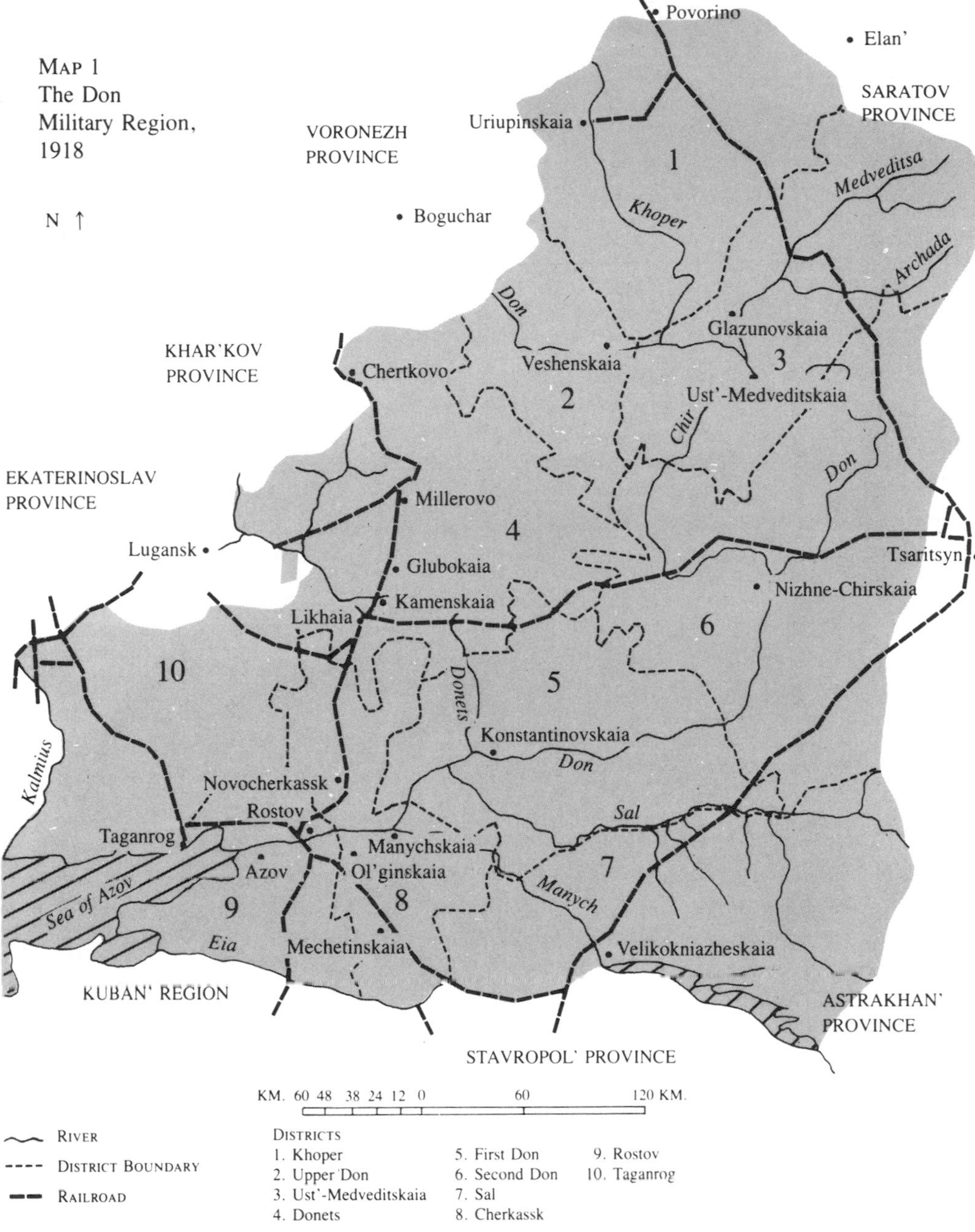

Map 1
The Don
Military Region,
1918
N ↑
VORONEZH PROVINCE
SARATOV PROVINCE
KHAR'KOV PROVINCE
EKATERINOSLAV PROVINCE
KUBAN' REGION
STAVROPOL' PROVINCE
ASTRAKHAN' PROVINCE
Povorino
Elan'
Uriupinskaia
Boguchar
Khoper
Medveditsa
Archada
Don
Glazunovskaia
Chertkovo
Veshenskaia
Ust'-Medveditskaia
Chir
Millerovo
Lugansk
Glubokaia
Kamenskaia
Likhaia
Tsaritsyn
Nizhne-Chirskaia
Donets
Konstantinovskaia
Kalmius
Novocherkassk
Rostov
Taganrog
Sal
Manychskaia
Azov
Ol'ginskaia
Manych
Sea of Azov
Eia
Mechetinskaia
Velikokniazheskaia
1
2
3
4
5
6
7
8
9
10
KM. 60 48 38 24 12 0 60 120 KM.
River
District Boundary
Railroad
Districts
1. Khoper
2. Upper Don
3. Ust'-Medveditskaia
4. Donets
5. First Don
6. Second Don
7. Sal
8. Cherkassk
9. Rostov
10. Taganrog

MAP 2
Area of the Upper Don Uprising, April 1 (14), 1919

CHAPTER I

LIFE AND WORK

Mikhail Sholokhov's place in Soviet literature is unique. A member of the Supreme Soviet since 1937, a delegate to all congresses of the Soviet Communist Party since 1939, a member of the Party's Central Committee since 1961, a member of the Presidium at the Twenty-Third through Twenty-Sixth Party Congresses (1966-1981), a Hero of Socialist Labor (1967, 1980), winner of Stalin and Lenin Prizes for literature (1941, 1960), Nobel Prize laureate (1965), a member of the Soviet Academy of Sciences (1939), recipient of honorary doctoral degrees from Saint Andrew's University in Scotland (1962) and from the Universities of Rostov and Leipzig (1965)—this record is unmatched by any other Soviet writer. The path to glory, however, was not an easy one. More than once the author's life and work were in jeopardy. Things have hardly been easier with his biography. Much important information about his life could not be published before and even after Stalin's death. Some factual accounts were periodically changed or omitted to bring them in line with the shifting political orientation. The study of Sholokhov's biography is further complicated by his reluctance to shed much light on his life and by the contradictory or questionable statements which he has a habit of making. The writing of even such a brief outline of Sholokhov's life as this one requires a more cautious and critical approach to the available information than would the writing of a longer biography of any other contemporary writer of his magnitude.

Born on May 24, 1905, in the village of Kruzhilin, near Veshenskaia stanitsa, in the Don Cossack Military Region, the creator of the greatest Cossack epic has no Cossack blood flowing in his veins. His father, Aleksandr Mikhailovich Sholokhov, was the son of a Russian merchant; and his mother, Anastasiia Danilovna Chernikova, came from Ukrainian peasant stock.[1] Aleksandr fell in love with Anastasiia in his parents' home in Veshenskaia, where she was employed as a maid. Aleksandr's parents objected to their son's marrying a maid, and the pregnant Anastasiia was married off to an elderly Cossack, whose name has never been disclosed. At the time of his birth, Sholokhov's mother must have been in her thirties, and his father was probably about the same age or older. According to

Sholokhov, his mother was either seventy or seventy-five in 1942,[2] and around 1950 the critic Isai Lezhnev wrote that Sholokhov's paternal grandfather came as an adolescent to the Don region from Riazan' Province "more than a hundred years ago."[3] Aleksandr was one of the oldest of his eight children. The age of Sholokhov's parents is of some interest because critics occasionally refer to them as very young when they met and because the writer Evgenii Popovkin quoted Sholokhov as saying, "My mother had quite a few of us. I was the youngest, the eighth." This phrase was printed in 1965 and 1966 but disappeared in 1973.[4] Whether there was a misunderstanding between Sholokhov and Popovkin or whether Anastasiia had any children before meeting Aleksandr remains unclear. In any event, Lezhnev states that Sholokhov was "the only son."[5] Having married a Cossack, Anastasiia legally became a Cossack woman and Sholokhov was born a Cossack. The author does not seem to have attached much significance to this fact. "I have never been a Cossack," he wrote in 1933.[6] Be that as it may, his legal Cossack status must have enabled him, particularly in his childhood, to learn more about the Cossack way of life than it was normally possible for young "outsiders" (*inogorodnie*), that is, the non-Cossack inhabitants of the Don region who had no economic rights or military obligations of the Cossacks. The Cossacks felt superior and antagonistic toward them.

In 1912, after the death of Anastasiia's husband, Aleksandr married her, and Sholokhov lost his Cossack status, becoming the son of a *meshchanin*, a member of the lower middle class. Aleksandr Mikhailovich, who finished only a parish church school, had no steady occupation. Changing jobs, he traded in cattle, grew grain crops, and worked as a clerk and manager in local stores. He wanted his son to get a good education and had apparently some money to pay for it. Prepared by a private tutor, Mikhail enrolled in 1912 in the elementary school in the village of Kargin, where his parents lived at that time. Beginning in 1914 or 1915, he attended a private secondary school in Moscow for two or three years, then studied in the town of Boguchar (Voronezh Province) and in Veshenskaia.[7] In 1918 the advancement of the German troops toward Boguchar and the outbreak of the Civil War put an end to Sholokhov's formal education. Having finished only four grades at the secondary school, he tried to fill his educational gaps by avid reading.

During the Civil War Sholokhov lived in the village of Pleshakov, where his father was manager of a steam grain mill, in the village of Rubezhnyi, and in Karginskaia stanitsa, formerly the village of Kargin.[8] For the greater part of the war this area was in or near the battle zone, particularly in the spring of 1919 during the anti-Bolshevik uprising of the Upper Don Cossacks. Of paramount importance was the fact that during almost the entire war Sholokhov lived in the territory held by the Whites. This must have been the chief reason why he, in his own words, described in *The Quiet Don* "the struggle of the Whites against the Reds, and not the struggle of the Reds against the Whites."[9] Sholokhov's sympathies were, however, on the Red side. He has stated that once the White Cossacks were looking for him as a Bolshevik and one of them hit his mother with a whip, asking her to reveal her son's hideout.[10]

In December 1919 the Red Army occupied the Upper Don territory, and Soviet rule was established there. Until October 1922 Sholokhov lived—almost uninterruptedly—in his native region, primarily in Karginskaia, working in various capacities for the new regime. He taught illiterate adults how to read and write, worked as a clerk in the Karginskaia Revolutionary Committee, joined a food-requisitioning detachment, completed a tax inspector's course in Rostov (February-April 1922), and served in special punitive units assigned to combat opposition in Soviet-held territory.[11] In 1922 Sholokhov was sent to Bukanovskaia (thirty-five miles from Veshenskaia) to supervise deliveries of food and to propagandize Soviet economic policy. In a conversation with young writers in 1967, he remarked that at the age of seventeen he had commanded a food-requisitioning detachment numbering 270 men.[12] The food-requisitioning policy, instituted in January 1919, demanded ruthless confiscation of grain and foodstuffs, leaving millions of peasants to starve and die. In March 1921 a less severe system of food taxation was introduced, but the consequences of the food-requisitioning policy and the drought in southern Russia in the summer of that year left 27 million people without bread.[13] The peasants hated the Soviet food workers intensely and resisted them by all possible means, including armed uprisings. Several large anti-Bolshevik detachments of armed Cossacks operated in the Upper Don region in 1920-1922. It was during Sholokhov's service in the food-requisitioning and punitive units that he took part in combat against the anti-Bolshevik partisans and went through some of the most trying experiences of his life. The struggle was conducted with extreme brutality. There were cases when the stomachs of the food workers were slit open and filled with grain, while the Soviet units resorted to summary executions of the partisans and of those who were accused of helping them. Apart from the dangers connected with regular fighting, Sholokhov was twice on the verge of being executed. According to a story that circulated in varying versions, he was taken prisoner in 1920 by the troops of the Ukrainian anarchist Nestor Makhno. His life was spared by Makhno's personal decision. At least three different reasons have been given to expain Makhno's magnanimity: Sholokhov's youth, the Ukrainian origin of his mother, and the intercession of an old Ukrainian woman.[14] Another time Sholokhov was sentenced to be shot for exceeding his authority. In his own words, he gave unspecified "rough treatment" to a person obliged to deliver a large quota of grain. After spending two days in confinement, he was given a suspended sentence of two years' imprisonment.[15] Furthermore, a source close to the writer reports that the sixteen-year-old Sholokhov, when working as food inspector in Bukanovskaia, was nearly killed by a kulak, Makar Dugin. Nothing is said about Sholokhov's manhandling of Dugin, and one can only wonder whether he might have been the man Sholokhov gave "the rough treatment."[16] What Sholokhov saw or did in the 1920-1922 period must have made a strong impression on him for the rest of his life. When the youngest of his four children, Mikhail, turned 18, the father wrote on the boy's photograph: "You now have the right to elect and be elected, but at your age I had the right to kill and be killed."[17]

The events of the 1920-1922 period provided themes for the majority of Sholokhov's early stories and found their way into part 8 of *The Quiet Don*. This period also saw the beginning of Sholokhov's literary career. In 1920 he wrote anonymous plays for amateur performances in the Karginskaia theater, where he was very popular as a comic actor. Two years later he wrote several short stories and made an unsuccessful attempt to have them printed in the journal *Ogonek* (*The Little Light*) and in journals and newspapers published by the Komsomol.[18] As of this writing, not a single play or story from the 1920-1922 period has been found anywhere.

In October 1922 Sholokhov went to Moscow in the hope of becoming a writer and continuing his education. The capital did not greet the young food inspector with open arms. His food-collecting skills were not needed and Moscow suffered from unemployment. To support himself, Sholokhov had to work as an unskilled laborer, longshoreman, stonemason, and accountant. At times he was without a job. His hope to enroll at a *rabfak*, a school that prepared workers and peasants for institutions of higher learning, was dashed. He was rejected because he lacked experience working in industry and had no recommendation from the Komsomol.[19] It may be appropriate to mention at this point that, contrary to occasional assertions in the Soviet and the Russian émigré press, Sholokhov had never been a member of the Komsomol—a fact that he repeatedly stressed in his interviews.[20] Nevertheless, in the early 1920s Sholokhov, like regular Komsomol members, fought for the Soviet regime and believed in Communism. In 1923, in Moscow, he joined the group of Komsomol writers called Molodaia gvardiia (The Young Guard). Together with them he attended seminars in creative writing conducted by experienced authors and critics. The Komsomol newspaper *Iunosheskaia pravda* (*The Youth Truth*) was the first publication to open its pages to him. His earliest published works, the so-called feuilletons "Ispytanie" ("The Test"), "Tri" ("The Three"), and "Revizor" ("The Inspector"), appeared in this newspaper on September 19, October 30, 1923, and April 12, 1924, respectively. "The Inspector" was published at the time when the newspaper was coming out under a new name, *Molodoi leninets* (*The Young Leninist*), given to it immediately after Lenin's death.

The feuilletons are the works of a literary apprentice. They reveal the comic element of Sholokhov's talent and his acquaintance with Gogol' and Chekhov. The aesthetic value of the feuilletons suffers from the fact that they have nothing to do with the typical Cossack milieu that the author knew well and could depict more vividly. Although one of the feuilletons, "The Inspector," has the Don region as its setting, there is not a trace of local color in its background or its characters. They are office workers, and speak a language bearing no resemblance to the racy Cossack dialect.

At the end of 1923 or at the beginning of 1924 Sholokhov left the capital for a trip to the Don country to marry Mariia Gromoslavskaia. He met her in 1922 when she worked as a statistician in his food inspector's office in Bukanovskaia. A teacher by profession, Mariia came from a well-to-do Cossack family. Before the Revolution her father, Petr Gromoslavskii, was a sexton and ataman in Bukanovskaia, but sided with the Reds during the Civil War. Soon after their wedding in Bukanovskaia the young Sholokhovs went to Moscow.[21]

At first the couple experienced great hardship in the capital. There were times when they did not have enough money for food. Literary work brought virtually no income, for prospective publishers were either rejecting Sholokhov's stories outright or delaying their publication. Thus the story "Prodkomissar" ("The Food Commissar") appeared in *Molodoi leninets* on February 14, 1925, although nine months earlier Sholokhov strongly urged the Komsomol writer Mark Kolosov to arrange its publication as soon as possible.[22]

The letter to Kolosov was written on the day Sholokhov left Moscow for the Don region. There, in Karginskaia, he continued writing stories and sending them to Moscow. What may be called a literary breakthrough came on December 14, 1924. On that day *Molodoi leninets* printed his story "Rodinka" ("The Birthmark"), set in the Don area, and the next year thirteen more stories came out either in this newspaper or in the Komsomol journals *Komsomoliia*, *Smena* (*The Relief*), and *Zhurnal krest'ianskoi molodezhi* (*The Journal of Peasant Youth*), and in the journals *Ogonek* and *Prozhektor* (*The Searchlight*). Some of the stories were also published in separate editions. The beginning of 1926 saw the appearance of the first collection of Sholokhov's stories under the title *Donskie rasskazy* (*The Don Stories*). Brought out by the publishing house Novaia Moskva (The New Moscow), this collection included the following eight stories:

"The Birthmark," "Shibalkovo semia" ("Shibalok's Seed"), "Predsedatel' Revvoensoveta respubliki" ("Chairman of the Revolutionary Military Council of the Republic"), "Bakhchevnik" ("The Watchman of the Melon Plots"), "Aleshkino serdtse" ("Aleshka's Heart"), "Dvukhmuzhniaia" ("A Woman Who Had Two Husbands"), "Pastukh" ("The Shepherd"), and "Kolovert' " ("The Whirlpool").

The significance of *The Don Stories* was greatly enhanced by the fact that Aleksandr Serafimovich (1863-1949) wrote an enthusiastic foreword to it. A representative of critical realism before the Revolution, Serafimovich joined the Bolshevik Party in 1919. After the publication of his novel *Zheleznyi potok* (*The Iron Flood*, 1924), he became one of the most celebrated authors in the Soviet Union. A Don Cossack by birth, Serafimovich was in an excellent position to give a critical evaluation of Sholokhov's stories. He was quick to point out the young author's superb knowledge of his subject and the faithful rendition of the rich and picturesque speech of the Don Cossacks. He also noted Sholokhov's sense of proportion as well as his ability to choose the most characteristic detail and to present life vividly, fully, and truthfully. Upon Serafimovich's request, Sholokhov visited him in 1925 in Moscow, and acquired in him a friend and admirer for many years to come.[23] Two years later Serafimovich's appreciation of Sholokhov's art was to play a crucial role in arranging for the publication of *The Quiet Don*.

Eight new stories by Sholokhov appeared in 1926, and toward the end of that year Novaia Moskva published the second collection of his stories entitled *Lazorevaia step'* (*The Tulip Steppe*). It contained twelve stories: "Lazorevaia step'," "Chuzhaia krov' " ("Alien Blood"), "Nakhalenok" ("The Shame Child"), "Smertnyi vrag" ("A Mortal Enemy"), "Kaloshi" ("Galoshes"), "Put'-dorozhen'ka" ("The Way and the Road"), "Prodkomissar" ("The Food Commissar"), "Iliukha" ("Iliukha"), "Krivaia stezhka" ("The Crooked Path"), "Batraki" ("The Farm Laborers"), "Chervotochina" ("Dry Rot"), "Semeinyi chelovek" ("A Family Man"). All these stories, except "Dry Rot," had been published before their inclusion in the collection. The stories "Zherebenok" ("The Foal") and "O Kolchake, krapive i prochem" ("About Kolchak, Nettles, and Other Things"), published in the first half of 1926, were not included.[24]

The standard translation of *Lazorevaia step'* is *The Azure Steppe*, both in the Soviet Union and the West. However, the word *lazorevyi* does not mean "azure" in the Don region. Above all, *lazorevyi* is associated with *lazorevyi tsvetok*, which means "tulip" in the Don Cossack dialect. In his works Sholokhov uses *lazorevyi* as synonymous with "red" or "yellow," the two main colors of wild tulips in the Don region. The only ambiguous case of its use is in the penultimate paragraph of the story "Lazorevaia step'.'' Whether Sholokhov here employs *lazorevyi* as the stock folkloric synonym of *lazurnyi* (azure), or whether he wants to convey the impression of red or yellow coloring is difficult to ascertain. In any event, the title *The Tulip Steppe*, featuring the Don Cossacks' favorite flower, is more appropriate for a collection of Don stories than *The Azure Steppe*.

By the time *The Tulip Steppe* came out Sholokhov virtually stopped writing short stories. Only three new stories—''Odin iazyk'' (''One Language''), ''Veter'' (''The Wind''), and ''Miagkotelyi'' (''Softhearted'')—were published in 1927. Sholokhov's stories proved to be quite popular. Several collections containing from two to ten stories were published between 1927 and 1932. Two of these collections were entitled *The Don Stories* (1929, 1930). The earlier, consisting of ten stories, was published in 250,000 copies in the *Roman-gazeta* series, that is, in the form of inexpensive paperback books intended to be as accessible as a newspaper. The largest collection of the period was brought out in 1931 by the Moscow Society of Writers. Titled *The Tulip Steppe: The Don Stories, 1923-1925*, it included nineteen stories and appeared in 5,500 copies. One of its stories, ''O Donprodkome i zlokliucheniiakh zamestitelia Donprodkomissara tovarishcha Ptitsyna'' (''About the Don Food Committee and the Misadventures of the Deputy Don Food Commissar Comrade Ptitsyn''), later dated 1923-1925, was published for the first time. With its appearance, the number of Sholokhov's published stories written in the twenties—the early stories, as they will be called in this study—reached twenty-six, not counting the three feuilletons. One more story, ''Obida'' (''The Offense''), written in 1925 or 1926, was published in 1962.

During the years 1926-1931 critical reaction to the early stories was on the whole favorable, though not as enthusiastic as Serafimovich's preface to the first collection of *The Don Stories*. Like Serafimovich, the reviewers praised Sholokhov's knowledge of Cossack life and the expressiveness of his language and imagery. But they also pointed out the defects in Sholokhov's ideology and his methods of characterization. Using typical sociological criteria of their time, the reviewers classified Sholokhov as a peasant writer who sees the world from the viewpoint of revolutionary peasantry, without paying due attention to the leading role of the working class. There are virtually no proletarians in his stories, the critics indicated. In the opinion of Aleksei Selivanovskii, a leading critic of the Russian Association of Proletarian Writers (RAPP), Sholokhov's characters do not realize that the only truth in the world is the truth of class struggle. Consequently, the characters experience a conflict between their inborn feeling of humaneness and the need for revolutionary cruelty.[25] Another of Sholokhov's shortcomings mentioned by the majority of reviewers was his black-and-white portrayal of characters. Political adversaries were predominantly depicted as villains, whereas friends were intentionally idealized.[26] The critics of the twenties did not regard the early stories as masterpieces. Some of the weaker stories appeared to the reviewer A. Pavlov to be naive and clumsy rough drafts, while Iosif Mashbits-Verov stated that, in terms of style, most of the stories were average. Nonetheless, he singled out "The Tulip Steppe," "A Family Man," and "Shibalok's Seed" as promising the great success that was realized in *The Quiet Don*.[27]

Indeed, there are several important features that the early stories share with *The Quiet Don*, as well as with other works by Sholokhov. Of the four basic ingredients of Sholokhov's mature art—the epic, the dramatic, the comic, and the lyrical—the first three had already manifested themselves in the stories. Like *The Quiet Don* and volume 1 of *Virgin Soil Upturned*, many of the early stories are filled with dramatic events. They are characterized by sharp conflicts, dynamic plots, and terse and meaningful dialogues. Their hallmark is a sociopolitical clash, at times within a family. Their usual denouement is a violent death.

In most stories political antagonism reaches a point at which killing is done with little or no compassion. This is true not only of lynchings and mass executions but also of killing the closest of kin. In "Dry Rot" a Komsomol member is beaten to death by his father and brother. A White Cossack officer from "The Whirlpool" considers it his duty to send his father and brother to death. The Red protagonist from "The Food Commissar" approves of the execution of his father as an enemy of the working people. A notable exception is "The Birthmark," where biological attachment proves to be stronger than political feud. The leader of anti-Soviet partisans shoots his son in combat, without being aware of the victim's identity. Minutes later the leader learns whom he killed and takes his own life.

The eighteen-year-old son from "The Birthmark" is one of the young people who are principal or important characters in half of the early stories. Their age, which the author unfailingly gives, ranges from fourteen to twenty. In all probability Sholokhov wanted to portray the experiences of his own age group during the Civil War and the first years of the Soviet rule. Yet his choice of the young characters is lopsided. Nearly all of them are staunch supporters of the Soviet regime, and the author tries to elicit sympathy for its aims by having his young protagonists either killed or savagely beaten by their enemies.

In several stories Sholokhov endeavors to evoke the reader's compassion for the murdered or executed adult Reds by making them fathers of infants or small children. Thus "The Whirlpool" contains a touching conversation between a condemned man and his six-year-old son. The emotional impact of the dialogue comes from the interplay between the naïveté of the boy's questions and the father's efforts to conceal his real situation.

In some stories children are orphaned by deaths resulting from nonpolitical causes. This is the case with "The Offense," one of Sholokhov's best stories. Its title reflects the feelings of a Cossack who had been robbed of his seed grain by a group of Ukrainians during the murderous famine of 1921-1922. Some time later the Cossack encounters accidentally one of the robbers, a widower, and kills him in revenge for the sufferings of his starving family of nine, for whom he is the sole provider. At the same time the Cossack takes along the Ukrainian's three-year-old son with an obvious intent to treat him as his own child.

The blend of ruthlessness and humaneness also appears in "The Foal," though under different circumstances. Here a White officer orders his Cossacks to stop firing at a Red cavalry man who is trying to rescue a drowning foal during a crossing of the Don. But the moment the foal is brought to safety the officer calmly shoots its rescuer. The story's message is clear: participants in the Civil War had no pity for one another but managed to retain compassion for animals.

The motif of man's cruelty to man runs through the majority of the early stories. Like *The Quiet Don* and volume 1 of *Virgin Soil Upturned*, they abound in scenes of violence filled with gory details. Male characters are perpetrators and victims of violent acts in about an equal proportion. The situation is different with respect to women. Their moral and physical torments are no less than those of men. Yet it is mainly the female representatives of hostile classes—wives of priests or of well-to-do men—who kill, abuse, or approve of murdering people. The women's limited participation in brutalities not only reflects their lesser role in political and social conflicts; it also bespeaks Sholokhov's emphasis on the woman as creator and preserver of life. His stories foreshadow *The Quiet Don* in representing mothers as the most attractive, humane, and noble characters. A mother is instinctively opposed to destruction of life. "I fed all of you from the same breast, I feel equally sorry for all of you," says the mother in "The Whirlpool" in reply to one of her sons' vow to show no mercy for his brothers.

Sholokhov's stories describe horrors and sufferings with the same epic calmness as do his novels. On a larger scale, the epic character of the stories is associated with their subject matter. Nearly all of them deal with events of the Civil War or the first years of the Soviet regime—the time of fateful historical upheavals that provided excellent epic material. This material was to receive a comprehensive treatment in *The Quiet Don*.

The lyrical vein, so prominent in descriptions of love and nature in Sholokhov's novels, is of little significance or artistic distinction in his stories. The author of the love story of Grigorii and Aksin'ia failed in his earlier works to impart to his descriptions of love even a modicum of depth or originality. The stories "Galoshes," "Iliukha," and "The Crooked Path," featuring romantic attachments, are among his weakest works. They are bland, superficial, and monotonous, and all deal with the same kind of unrequited love. On the other hand, Sholokhov demonstrated his lyrical potential in "Alien Blood" by a powerful and touching portrayal of paternal love emerging in an old Cossack for his political enemy.

Descriptions of nature in the stories are as a rule markedly inferior to those in the novels. Only occasionally does one come across a few paragraphs, such as the depiction of the spring in "Dry Rot," that foreshadow landscapes characteristic of Sholokhov's later works. Yet even the more effective descriptions of nature encountered in the stories lack that intense and intimate lyricism which bespeaks the unity of man and nature in some of the most memorable scenes in *The Quiet Don* and *Virgin Soil Upturned*.

The comic element plays a major role in several stories where the narrative is conducted in the form of *skaz*, that is, the story is told by a character in a way amply reproducing the linguistic idiosyncrasies of his ethnic, social, or professional milieu. Humorous and comic elements of such *skaz* stories as "About the Don Food Committee and the Misadventures of the Deputy Don Food Commissar Comrade Ptitsyn," "Chairman of the Military Revolutionary Council of the Republic," and "About Kolchak, Nettles, and Other Things" were to reappear in the figures of Prokhor Zykov in *The Quiet Don* and of old Shchukar' and Nagul'nov in *Virgin Soil Upturned*.

On the other hand, some *skaz* stories display patent propensity for black humor, which is well-nigh absent from the novels. Dreadful experiences and sights are occasionally described in distorted language in order to produce comic effect. Thus the narrator of "Chairman of the Military Revolutionary Council of the Republic," referring to the mutilated genitals of his dead comrade, says that "his sex had all been slashed with sabers to the point of disfigurement." In the story "About the Don Food Committee and the Misadventures of the Deputy Don Food Commissar Comrade Ptitsyn," morbid humor pervades the commissar's revelations about his methods of food requisitioning: "I'd, of course, stick my Mauser into his belly button with no pity and say in an anemic voice: 'There are ten bullets in this automatic; I'll kill you ten times over, I'll bury you ten times and dig you up back to the surface. Going to deliver?' " Behind this supposedly funny verbiage lies a grim reality: people are being robbed of their means of subsistence and, possibly, doomed to death from starvation. Whether Sholokhov deliberately employs here comic idiom to communicate the otherwise unpublishable truth about grain requisitioning is a moot question.

In any event, in *Virgin Soil Upturned* old Shchukar' is at times called upon to say some politically sensitive things in a form of comic chatter.

Already in his early works Sholokhov demonstrated considerable diversity in the use of *skaz*. There are *skaz* stories containing little or no comic element. One of them is "A Family Man," a gruesome tale by a Cossack of how he felt compelled to kill his two elder sons in order to save his other children. The narrator's earnest tone is here in full harmony with the gravity of his situation. By contrast, the narrator's amusing speech in "About Kolchak, Nettles, and Other Things" is consonant with the story of his troubles with emancipated women.

Of the early stories, "The Wind," published in the June 4, 1927, issue of *Molodoi leninets*, is particularly noteworthy. Its theme of pathological cruelty provoked by the feeling of humiliation and self-pity is unusual for Soviet literature. Because of its morbid and naturalistic aspects, unredeemed by any ideological merits, "The Wind" has never been reprinted in the Soviet Union and is virtually unknown. Nor has it ever been published in the West. The bulk of the story is told in the first person. The narrator is Khariton Turilin, a handsome, legless Cossack of about thirty years of age. His listener is a village teacher, Golovin, who has lost his way returning from a professional conference and has stopped at the Turilin's hut for the night. A lonely man, Turilin gladly talks to a stranger. He tells about his sufferings during the retreat of the White Cossack cavalry through the Sal District in the winter of 1920, when his frost-bitten legs were amputated and thrown out to the pigs. As the enemy advanced, the twenty-two-year-old cripple was abandoned by his superiors in spite of his plea that he be taken along. He falls into the hands of the Reds, who send him home in a cart transporting their soldiers ill with typhus. Upon his return to his native village, Turilin finds no close relatives except his sixteen-year-old sister Pelageia. Deeply hurt by the refusals of women to sleep with a cripple, Turilin asks Pelageia to take pity on him and live with him secretly. The girl refuses and appeals to his conscience. To Turilin, however, the question of conscience is irrelevant. Fate, he feels, has mistreated him so badly that he is entitled to some earthly pleasure. When his repeated pleas and threats fail, Turilin decides to resort to cunning and force. Six months later he rapes Pelageia after subduing her with charcoal fumes and tying her hands. But his expectations that the girl would agree to live with him after the incident do not materialize: "She made up her mind, the damned woman, and hardened like a bone. The bitch is dogged, just like her mother." Pelageia sells her share of the property and leaves for good.

Left alone, Turilin finds it easy to make a living. He writes letters for his illiterate fellow-villagers, and helps women to induce abortions. He gives his patients a mixture of water, corrosive sublimate, nitric acid, and gun powder. With particular delight he tells Golovin about the stomach pains of two girls whom he doctored to death. At this point the teacher interrupts Turilin, calling him scum and vermin. The cripple is dumbfounded. All he can do is inquire in a soft voice why the teacher says such things. Receiving no answer, Turilin feels offended and falls silent. Golovin, who has made his bed on the top of the cold brick stove, feels suffocated. "Tired, sluggish" lice crawl over his body, biting him "viciously and insatiably." Half an hour later he gets off the stove, saying that he is leaving. Turilin crawls out of his bed to see him off. Touching the teacher's knee with his hand, the cripple inquires whether he will get a pension if he applies for it. Golovin exits in silence.

Like the teacher's, the reader's attitude toward Turilin changes from sympathy to aversion. No matter how strongly the cripple feels wronged and humiliated, it is hard to accept his suffering as an excuse for his inhumanity. Nonetheless, one may find a piece of extenuating evidence in his mental constitution. He seems to possess a cast of mind incapable of distinguishing between good and evil. Somewhat naively, he takes for granted that everything that pleases him is right and permitted. This kind of mentality, complicated by megalomania, forms, in my view, the focal point of Solzhenitsyn's psychological portrayal of Stalin in *The First Circle*.

"The Wind" is a chilling story, both physically and spiritually. Its major incidents occur either in winter or in late fall (Pelageia's rape). A freezing wind blows when Turilin retreats with his unit, when Golovin is on his way home from the teachers' conference, during Turilin's telling of his story, and when Golovin leaves the cripple's hut. In the last instance, however, the wind is not only cold but "refreshing." This suggests a salubrious effect of nature on a human being sickened by the barbarity of his fellow man. Nature, Sholokhov seems to say, cannot be as cruel as people. He will emphatically reiterate this view in *The Quiet Don*. In a less pronounced manner he will remind the reader of Turilin when he describes Aksin'ia's rape by her father and Mit'ka Korshunov's proposition to his sister.

Similarities between the early stories and *The Quiet Don* prompted the critic Viktor Gura to derive the novel's plot from a combination of plots of several stories and to call *The Don Stories*, meaning the early stories, "an artistic Vorgeschichte of *The Quiet Don*." Sholokhov vigorously disagreed. The critic's assertion, he said in 1955, implied that *The Quiet Don* was pieced together "with the aid of scissors and glue." Such hodgepodge (*okroshka*) had nothing to do with the creative history of the novel.[28] However, in a 1975 interview Sholokhov stated that *The Quiet Don* "grew from *The Don Stories*."[29] It may appear that this statement contradicts the author's earlier contention. One may also suspect that the statement was meant, primarily or solely, as an indirect reply to the charges, revived in 1974 by Solzhenitsyn, that Sholokhov had plagiarized *The Quiet Don*. Whatever the motivations might be, I do not find any substantive contradiction between Sholokhov's statements, provided they are considered within the proper contexts. In 1955 Sholokhov rejected Gura's idea by pointing out that the three short stories—"The Crooked Path," "A Woman Who Had Two Husbands," and "The Tulip Steppe"—could not possibly form the basis for a complex plot of his four-volume epic. The 1975 statement was preceded by Sholokhov's telling his interviewers that his early stories were written in response to a compelling urge to portray the tragic and interesting time of the Civil War. Since *The Quiet Don* does essentially deal with the Civil War period, it does not seem incorrect to regard the novel as having "grown" from the early stories in the general sense of the word. This is apparently all that Sholokhov meant to say, for he did not bother to elaborate.

The creative history of *The Quiet Don* goes back to October 1925. By that time Sholokhov returned from Moscow to settle down permanently in the Don region and write a book on the role of the Cossacks in the Revolution. The book, entitled *Donshchina* (*The Don Country*), was to open with a description of the role played by the Cossack troops in General Lavr Kornilov's march on Petrograd in September 1917. Soon, however, it occurred to Sholokhov that the average reader had no knowledge of the Don Cossacks and would not understand why they took part in "the suppression of the Revolution." To introduce the reader to Cossack pre-Revolutionary life, Sholokhov moved the opening back to 1912. This decision greatly increased the scope of the project, and the author started feverishly collecting new material. Toward the end of 1926 he began to write what is now known as *The Quiet Don*.[30] There is another version of how the novel originated. At a public appearance in Rostov in the fall of 1928, Sholokhov reportedly said that at first he intended to write a short novel (*povest'*) about Fedor Podtelkov and Mikhail Krivoshlykov, the leaders of the Red Cossacks. When he came to the scene of the execution of Podtelkov and his men, he began to think that it would not be clear to the reader why the Cossacks who fought in World War I, the so-called front-line Cossacks, refused to participate in the execution. This concern generated the idea of writing a novel containing a broad portrayal of the war that would make clear the reasons for the solidarity between front-line Cossacks and front-line soldiers.[31] This version does not contradict in essence Sholokhov's published statements on the origins of *The Quiet Don*. The activities of Podtelkov and Krivoshlykov represent a major event in the Cossacks' participation in the Revolution. In the novel they are described in great detail. On the other hand, the theme of solidarity between the Cossacks and the soldiers is touched upon only lightly.

The initial work on what was to become *The Quiet Don* was done in Bukanovskaia and Karginskaia. In Karginskaia the author had to work in overcrowded living conditions, while in Bukanovskaia he could isolate himself for long hours in the study of his father-in-law. Two significant events of a personal nature occurred during this time: the death of Sholokhov's father and the birth of his first child, Svetlana. The birth of their daughter made it necessary for the young Sholokhovs to look for a new residence, separate from their relatives. In the fall of 1926 they moved to Veshenskaia. In 1919 this stanitsa formed the center of the Upper Don uprising that was to become the focal point of volume 3 of *The Quiet Don*. In the vicinity of Veshenskaia Sholokhov frequently interviewed Kharlampii Vasil'evich Ermakov, whom he had met before. Ermakov was probably the most important source of oral information to be incorporated in *The Quiet Don*. This former Cossack officer not only fought in World War I and the Civil War but also commanded an insurgent division during the Upper Don uprising. His military career and certain of his personal traits were utilized in the portrayal of Grigorii Melekhov.[32]

The collecting of materials and the principal work on the first three volumes of *The Quiet Don* were carried out in a conservative and predominantly anti-Soviet environment. An overwhelming majority of the Cossacks from the area where Sholokhov lived had served with the Whites. In 1923 Sholokhov's father-in-law apparently parted ways with the Soviet regime by again becoming a sexton. This step made Lezhnev characterize him as a "wavering, politically unstable person."[33] Very few facts are known about the colorful figure of Petr Gromoslavskii, but it is quite possible that he had something to do with the creation of *The Quiet Don*. Reported to be a writer of sorts, he could have been instrumental in supplying Sholokhov with printed sources, particularly with periodicals and books published by the Whites during the Civil War and in emigration.[34] Besides, the bulk of the work on the first three volumes of *The Quiet Don* was done during the period of the New Economic Policy (NEP), when many people, especially such conservative elements as the Cossacks, hoped that the Soviet regime would eventually abandon its Communist dogmas. The atmosphere of the NEP, the association with Gromoslavskii and former White Cossacks, and the reading of White sources could have diminished Sholokhov's earlier dedication to the Soviet regime. This might have contributed to the growth in *The Quiet Don* of an objectivity whose elements were already present in a number of his early stories.

In 1927 volume 1 of *The Quiet Don* was completed. There are three quite different accounts concerning the specific time of its completion and the circumstances of its publication. According to the earliest version, volume 1 was ready "late in the fall" or "toward the end" of 1927. The manuscript was sent to the monthly *Oktiabr'* (*October*) published by the All-Union and Moscow Associations of Proletarian Writers and printed by the publishing house Moskovskii rabochii (The Moscow Worker). The editorial board of the journal found the work devoid of any political immediacy and interest. At best it could be published only with drastic cuts. This verdict was passed on to the chief editor, who, fortunately for Sholokhov, happened to be Aleksandr Serafimovich. Upon reading the manuscript, the old Cossack disagreed with his colleagues and, with some effort, succeeded in persuading them to print volume 1 without extensive cuts.[35] It appeared in the first four issues of *Oktiabr'* for 1928.

Another version, advanced in 1960 by the writer Nikolai Trishin, a former chief editor of *Zhurnal krest'ianskoi molodezhi*, asserts that in June 1927 Sholokhov came to Moscow with a finished manuscript of volume 1 and took it to Goslitizdat (The State Publishing House for Artistic Literature). A month later it was rejected on the grounds that its author indulged in glorifying the Cossacks and idealizing their way of life. Then the manuscript was given to Serafimovich. With his enthusiastic evaluation it was forwarded to the publishing house Novaia Moskva and accepted there for publication as early as September 1927. In the same month Sholokhov returned to Veshenskaia to work on volume 2 of the novel.[36] A number of Soviet critics accepted Trishin's version, specifically its part pertaining to Goslitizdat.[37]

A third version comes from A. Stasevich, a former editor at Moskovskii rabochii. His account contravenes Trishin's assertion that Sholokhov submitted the manuscript of volume 1 to the State Publishing House in June 1927. Stasevich reproduces the text of Sholokhov's letter to Moskovskii rabochii dated July 22, 1927, in which the author speaks of "the delay in sending first parts of the novel" due to typing problems.[38] That Sholokhov was interested in having *The Quiet Don* published by Moskovskii rabochii is evident from his letter to Stasevich of April 3, 1927. In it he gave a brief description of the novel and inquired about the possibility of getting an advance. The publishing house agreed.

Stasevich reports, without documentation, that the manuscript of the "first parts" of *The Quiet Don* was received by Moskovskii rabochii at the end of 1927. While this might be correct, Stasevich offers a very vague explanation about the difficulties preceding the novel's publication. He says nothing about the rejection of the manuscript by the *Oktiabr'* editors and speaks merely of a delay caused by reorganizational problems in Moskovskii rabochii. He involves in these problems the then nonexisting publishing house Khudozhestvennaia literatura (Artistic Literature) and refers in uncertain terms to Serafimovich's help. It is possible that Stasevich deliberately glosses over the political reasons for the earlier rejection of *The Quiet Don*, since he wrote his article for the seventy-fifth anniversary of Sholokhov's birth.

Their factual discrepancies notwithstanding, all of the above accounts coincide in these two points: the actual writing of volume 1 took less than a year and it was Serafimovich who had the final say in arranging its publication. One can only speculate what the fate of *The Quiet Don* might have been had Serafimovich not come to its defense with his authority and prestige. Volume 2 must also have been written in a very brief period of time because it was serialized in the May-October issues of *Oktiabr'* for 1928. It may have required less time to write, because the author incorporated into it some portions of the manuscript originally intended for *The Don Country*. Sholokhov's estimations of the size of these portions were inconsistent, ranging from 3 to 7 printer's sheets.[39] It would mean a difference between some 50 and 115 printed pages, because a printer's sheet equals 16 pages. The writing of volume 2 also might have been further accelerated by the incorporation into it of slightly reworked excerpts from printed historical sources. This supposition may or may not be supported by Sholokhov's admission that the purely historical passages were the hardest for him to handle. They constrained his creative possibilities and compelled him "to bridle the imagination."[40] In any event, the actual writing of both volumes was probably done between the end of 1926 and the middle of 1928, or a month or two longer if the later portions of volume 2 were completed shortly before their serialization. By all standards this was a remarkable accomplishment.

The Quiet Don had an immediate and great success with the readers. Six book-form editions of volumes 1 and 2, a total of 45,000 copies of each volume, were printed in 1928-1929 by Moskovskii rabochii. Moreover, Moskovskii rabochii published 150,000 copies in its *Roman-gazeta* series. This publication began in July 1928 as a special event to mark the first anniversary of the founding of *Roman-gazeta*. The 150,000 copies were sold out quickly and *Roman-gazeta* issued a new large edition.[41] In view of the continuing demand, three more editions of 100,000 copies each were brought out in 1929-1931 by the State Publishing House. The writer Fedor Panferov called *The Quiet Don* the most important work published in *Oktiabr'*. Moskovskii rabochii, he stated, had received tens of thousands of letters from admiring readers of the novel.[42] Indeed, responding to a questionnaire put out by *Roman-gazeta*, the majority of its readers chose *The Quiet Don* as their favorite work from among some twenty-five titles printed in the early issues of that publication. These titles included Lev Tolstoi's *The Cossacks*, Henry Barbusse's *The Fire*, Dmitrii

Furmanov's *Chapaev*, and Maksim Gor'kii's *Childhood, My Universities*, and *The Artamonov Business*. Furthermore, *The Quiet Don* turned out to be the most popular work with every social group of readers polled by the *Roman-gazeta*, the groups being white-collar workers, workingmen, pupils and students, Red Army soldiers, peasants, and others.[43] The novel was also found to be the best-known literary work among proletarians entering technical colleges. Although *The Quiet Don* was not on the required reading list for the entrance examinations, the workers knew it better than any book actually on the list. Their judgment, according to an examiner, was well-nigh uniform, "A good work, but lacking Party orientation [*bespartiinoe*]!"[44] A certain Apresian, a workshop employee, said essentially the same thing, but with some elaborations: "People of all class categories like *The Quiet Don*. This raises many questions. There is some obliteration of class distinctions in the novel—the class enemy is not 'clobbered' and there is also no support for the Cossack poor. There is a great deal of what is valuable in *The Quiet Don*, but the sole defect that I pointed out spoils the novel—there is no clear-cut class approach in it."[45] Sholokhov admitted that Apresian had a point. He knew from letters, he said, that his novel was liked by diverse social groups. This resulted from the fact that he failed to draw "a clear-cut line of negation" and allowed his "pacifism" to slip in. His ideological shortcomings stemmed from "the influence of the petty-bourgeois milieu."[46] By that milieu Sholokhov obviously meant the Cossack environment in which he wrote *The Quiet Don*. He confessed that he was not content with the latter parts of the novel and wanted to revise them.

The reaction of literary critics to the first two volumes of *The Quiet Don* was much less favorable than that of the reading public. There were few critics, especially among the Party members, who gave Sholokhov high marks for his art and ideology. A reviewer for the journal *Na literaturnom postu* (*On Literary Guard*) spoke of the epic sweep in the portrayal of the Cossack way of life and found the depiction of Podtelkov and other Red Cossacks convincing.[47] For the drama critic Iu. Iuzovskii *The Quiet Don* was "a grandiose epic about people and their actions, about human passions, about toilers' sweat, about love and death, about war and revolution."[48] Vladimir Ermilov was the only leading proletarian critic who ventured to say that Sholokhov was a proletarian writer.[49]

Two other leading RAPP critics thought highly of *The Quiet Don* as a work of art, but were more restrained in their political assessment. Early in 1929 Aleksei Selivanovskii saw it appropriate to place *The Quiet Don* in the front ranks of proletarian literature and to call its author "*a peasant writer who had developed into a proletarian writer*." A few months later (probably because the serialization of volume 3 was discontinued for political reasons) the same critic admitted to having made an error. Sholokhov, he corrected himself, was "a peasant writer who *was developing* (not *had developed*) into a proletarian writer." Consequently, *The Quiet Don* did not belong to proletarian literature; it was merely drawing close to it.[50] Essentially the same opinion was expressed by Ivan Makar'ev. Although not everything was quite right in the description of social differentiation in Cossack villages, *The Quiet Don* remained "a most remarkable work of peasant literature."[51]

The views of Selivanovskii and Makar'ev can be considered as representative of the core of the RAPP leadership. A large group of important RAPP critics were, however, in disagreement with their top leaders. They felt that the leaders were too slow in bringing proletarian literature in line with the tempo of socialist construction and with the political goals of the time. The attitude of such critics toward *The Quiet Don* was predominantly negative. The principal faults of the novel, in their opinion, were the idealization of the lives of reactionary and well-to-do Cossacks, the depiction of the Whites as heroes motivated by lofty ideals, the presentation of the Bolsheviks as personally unattractive and cruel, the detached and objective portrayal of the struggle against counterrevolution, and the author's failure to reveal the machinery of class struggle. One of these critics, Sergei Dinamov, a functionary of the Communist Academy and chief editor of *Literaturnaia gazeta*, asserted that Sholokhov was not "an artist of the proletariat." Although he wanted to become such an artist, he could not conquer his attachment to the old way of life. Dinamov concluded that the author closely resembled Grigorii Melekhov, the protagonist of *The Quiet Don*, in being torn by internal contradictions.[52]

A great majority of proletarian critics and writers who took the floor at the second plenum of RAPP (September 1929) refused to recognize Sholokhov as a proletarian writer. One of the speakers, the Rostov writer Aleksandr Busygin, put strong emphasis on what he called Sholokhov's delight in portraying the life of the well-to-do Cossacks. This "idealization of the old Cossack way of life" touched a responsive chord in the hearts of the Cossacks to whom Busygin read *The Quiet Don*: "They listened very attentively and then said, 'Yes, it was a good life.' And their faces were sad—they used to have a good life, but now it's pretty bad."[53] Significantly, this was the reaction of the people from a village located in the Khoper District, where the Cossacks were less prosperous and more sympathetic to the Reds than in any other area of the Don Region.

The strongest attack on the novel came from the historian N. L. Ianchevskii. It was launched at a meeting of the Rostov Association of Proletarian Writers in the form of a lengthy report entitled "Reactionary Romanticism." The title referred to Sholokhov's sentimental romanticization of the people, nature, and folklore of the pre-Revolutionary Don. Ianchevskii's overall assessment of the novel virtually amounted to an indictment charging Sholokhov with political crimes punishable in the Soviet Union by death. *The Quiet Don*, the historian asserted, was "a work alien and hostile to the proletariat. . . . Quite deliberately Sholokhov propagates ideas under whose banner the kulak counterrevolution and the Don nobility, which has been thrown out of the country, fought here in the North Caucasus, in the Don region in particular."[54] Those who spoke after Ianchevskii rejected his extreme views as errors resulting from his "leftist" deviation. Nevertheless, the discussants reiterated many of Ianchevskii's accusations in a milder form and everyone made unflattering observations about Sholokhov's political orientation. They condemned his impartiality and humaneness as incompatible with proletarian literature, especially at a time when the kulaks were being liquidated.[55]

These critics were right in their own way. The objectivity of *The Quiet Don* did little to defend the Red terror, to propagate the official version of the Civil War, to justify, under the guise of class struggle, the destruction of millions of peasant lives during collectivization. Sholokhov, a member of RAPP, was clearly not a real proletarian writer. Even Serafimovich, praising the author of *The Quiet Don* for drawing an accurate picture of social differentiation among the Cossacks, found it necessary to give him a well-intentioned ideological warning. Sholokhov, he wrote in *Pravda*, was a highly original artist with an enormous potential. "And yet ruin is eagerly lying in wait for him." The day would come when the Cossack theme that Sholokhov knew so well from his childhood would be exhausted. "And if the young writer will not go into the thick of the proletariat. . . . If he will not be able to absorb the great teachings of Communism, to imbue his mind with it, the writer will be ruined."[56] It is a matter of speculation whether Serafimovich, an experienced author at the age of sixty-five, really believed in the beneficial effects of Communism on literary craft or whether he was simply giving advice to his protégé—make ideological adjustments or you will not be published. Whatever Serafimovich might have meant, there is no doubt that in order to survive both Sholokhov and his novel had to undergo changes. Many political deficiencies pointed out by the critics of *The Quiet Don* in 1928-1931 were eliminated by censors in subsequent editions of the novel.

Like his novel, Sholokhov too became the target of a vicious political attack. On September 8, 1929, the Rostov Komsomol newspaper *Bol'shevistskaia smena* (*The Bolshevik Relief*) printed an article, "Creators of Pure Literature," by a certain Nikolai Prokof'ev. He accused Sholokhov of being apolitical, of shunning public life, of interceding on behalf of the kulaks, of paying taxes for the former ataman of Bukanovskaia (his father-in-law?), of helping his disfranchised sister-in-law to regain her civic rights, and of failing to report to the press wrongdoings in the Veshenskaia Komsomol organization.[57] In a letter addressed to the editors of *Bol'shevistskaia smena, Molot* (*The Hammer*), and *Na pod''eme* (*On the Rise*), Sholokhov called Prokof'ev's charges false, expressed his agreement with the Party policy toward the kulaks, and demanded an investigation.[58] The investigation was conducted by the North Caucasus Association of Proletarian Writers. The report of its secretariat rejected all of Prokof'ev's charges as vile slander founded on rumors. At the same time the report touched upon the situation of Sholokhov's relatives. If the anonymous former ataman of Bukanovskaia mentioned in it was actually Petr Gromoslavskii, then one learns that Sholokhov paid no taxes for him, and his property was auctioned off for not delivering his grain quota. Sholokhov's sister-in-law was disfranchised for being the daughter of a former sexton. This decision was revoked in view of the fact that for several years she had earned her living as a schoolteacher and had no economic ties with her father. Sholokhov did not help her regain her civic rights. If she was disfranchised for simply being the daughter of a sexton, it would be safe to assume that her father suffered a stiffer punishment. A Cossack whom I designate as F.M.A. (he asked to remain anonymous) told me that in 1930 he had been present at an open Party meeting at which Sholokhov was given the status of Party candidate. During the meeting Sholokhov was asked whether or not he helped his father-in-law to return from exile. The answer was no. Other sources indicate that Petr Gromoslavskii was arrested in 1930 and released either early in 1931 or in 1932. His release is said to have been arranged by Sholokhov, who traveled to Siberia to talk to the local authorities.[59]

The bitterness and indignation with which Sholokhov reacted to Prokof'ev's attacks also typified his feelings about the rumors that he had plagiarized *The Quiet Don*. The rumors began to spread simultaneously with the serialization of the first two volumes in *Oktiabr'*. The main version, circulated in several variants, attributed the authorship of *The Quiet Don* to a White officer. The leadership of the Russian Association of Proletarian Writers came to Sholokhov's defense. It appointed five of the most influential figures of proletarian literature to deal with the case. Headed by Serafimovich and the top executive of RAPP, Leopol'd Averbakh, the five rejected, in a letter to *Pravda*, the plagiarism charges as an attempt by class enemies to slander a proletarian author. The writers and the public were asked to cooperate in exposing the slanderers so that they could be brought to trial. The signatories of the letter, however, did not present any concrete evidence for their conclusion. It was based on a reference to unidentified proletarian writers who allegedly were associated with Sholokhov for several years and who were familiar with his work on *The Quiet Don*, with the materials he used for it, and with the drafts of his manuscripts.[60] Whether Serafimovich and his associates actually read the manuscripts and rough drafts of *The Quiet Don*, as the critic Konstantin Priima claims, is by no means obvious from their letter.

Priima asserts that in mid-March 1929 Sholokhov brought to Moscow a suitcase full of his autographs. He gave them to the executive secretary of *Pravda*, who happened to be Lenin's sister Mariia Ul'ianova.[61] However, Priima's account raises several questions. It leads one to believe that Sholokhov had brought his autographs to *Pravda* before the Serafimovich commission was formed. Priima offers no explanation as to why a young non-Communist writer appealed to the Party's central newspaper, instead of to literary authorities. One is further puzzled by Priima's assertion that the Serafimovich commission was formed on the recommendation of *Pravda*'s editorial board. This does not seem to tally with the commission's statement that its letter was written "on behalf of the secretariat of the Russian Association of Proletarian Writers."

In 1930 the rumors of plagiarism were revived by the publication of a letter written in September 1917 by Leonid Andreev to Sergei Goloushev, an art critic and modest author. The letter spoke of Goloushev's sketch, "From the Quiet Don," in which he recorded his travel impressions of the Don region in 1917.[62] Before long, the rumors credited Goloushev with the authorship of *The Quiet Don*. Although the absurdity of these rumors was beyond doubt, Sholokhov complained bitterly about them to Serafimovich and asked him for advice as to what, if anything, he should do to prove that *The Quiet Don* was his.[63]

Sholokhov probably has never been accused of plagiarism in the Soviet press, though at least two critics did mention such accusations. According to Isai Lezhnev, plagiarism charges were printed in "a Rostov newspaper"—at first in three long articles under the heading "Unpublished Chapters from *The Quiet Don*" and then in Prokof'ev's article, "The Creators of Pure Literature." The editor of the newspaper was dismissed for disseminating slander.[64] This account is rife with errors. Lezhnev speaks of "one Rostov newspaper," but there should be two. By "Unpublished Chapters from *The Quiet Don*," he must have meant excerpts from the novel printed in *Molot* on November 18 and December 28, 1928, and November 30, 1929, while Prokof'ev's article, as we know, appeared in *Bol'shevistskaia smena*. The first two excerpts in *Molot*, which I read, are not accompanied by any comments on plagiarism. The third excerpt cannot contain any accusations of plagiarism because, like Prokof'ev's article, it appeared after Sholokhov had officially been cleared of such charges in *Pravda*. Furthermore, no editor was dismissed. It was the acting editor of

Bol'shevistskaia smena who, along with Prokof'ev, was reprimanded by Party authorities.[65] Lezhnev's errors can be explained by the extremely oppressive and secretive atmosphere of the 1940s, when he probably had no access to the original source materials. In his later study he deals at length with Prokof'ev's article without linking it to charges of plagiarism and without mentioning that such charges had been printed elsewhere.[66] Another reference to the appearance of accusations of plagiarism in the press was a vague statement by Veniamin Goffenshefer to the effect that "this monstrous slander of a Soviet writer has found its way even into a newspaper."[67] Whether the critic meant Prokof'ev's article is impossible to ascertain.

Prokof'ev may well be the only person specifically named as the one who spread the plagiarism charges. Others are referred to in the Soviet press as enemies, slanderers, and spiteful critics. Somewhat more concrete references single out the Trotskyites, the RAPP leaders, or simply RAPP people. Priima maintains that, in 1929-1930, the Trotskyites fabricated the charges of plagiarism because they had "sensed" that in volume 3 of *The Quiet Don* Sholokhov was going to reveal the atrocities they committed which subsequently caused the Upper Don uprising in 1919. Priima does not identify a single "Trotskyite," and cautiously uses the verb "sensed" because only parts of volume 3 were published in 1929-1930.[68] Neither in these parts nor in the entire volume 3 are the Trotskyites specifically blamed for any atrocities committed by the Reds. In holding the Trotskyites responsible for all the atrocities, Priima follows the official line of hushing up the cruelty of the Bolshevik regime.

Equally dubious are the assertions that rumors of plagiarism originated among the RAPP leaders out of their envy and malevolence.[69] No names, of course, are mentioned. And who could be named if even those RAPP leaders who were vilified and liquidated during the purges (Kirshon, Selivanovskii, Dmitrii Maznin), or imprisoned (Makar'ev), or expelled from the Party (Iurii Libedinskii) have been fully rehabilitated after Stalin's death, and if even Averbakh is no longer called an enemy of the people? And why would RAPP leaders invent accusations of plagiarism? It was in their journal that *The Quiet Don* was published. It was their commission that cleared Sholokhov of charges of plagiarism. The mythical RAPP leaders are used as convenient scapegoats to conceal the fact that in 1929-1930 many readers and writers had genuine doubts about Sholokhov's ability to write *The Quiet Don* because of his youth. It is possible that some RAPP leaders questioned Sholokhov's authorship of *The Quiet Don*, but this does not mean that they initiated or actively spread rumors about plagiarism. Doubts about the novel continue to exist among friends and foes of the Soviet regime. According to Anatolii Kuznetsov, competent writers and critics in Moscow have never believed that Sholokhov wrote *The Quiet Don*; and Louis Aragon called *Virgin Soil Upturned* Sholokhov's first novel.[70] In 1974 and 1975 the question of plagiarism was raised by Aleksandr Solzhenitsyn and Roi Medvedev. It will be treated in greater detail later in this study.

Simultaneously with political criticisms and accusations of plagiarism, Sholokhov had to cope with seemingly insurmountable obstacles to the publication of volume 3 of *The Quiet Don*. Twelve chapters of this volume appeared in the first three issues of *Oktiabr'* for 1929. At this point the serialization stopped. It could be that early in 1929 Sholokhov did not have enough materials ready to keep the serialization going. For example, the manuscript of chapter 8 was dated by him February 14, 1929.[71] By the fall of 1929 volume 3 was apparently close to being completed, but the author did not want to continue its serialization during that year. The reason, he said, was simple: "I will not be able to give the next installments because part 7 is not finished and part 6 is being partially reworked."[72] This decision might have been responsible for the fact that the editors of *Oktiabr'* and *Na pod''eme*, who had hitherto been announcing that the novel would be serialized in 1929, made it known in the November issues of their journals that volume 3 would be published in 1930. At about the same time Sholokhov was reported to be completing it.[73]

Late in 1929 or early in 1930 the editors of *Oktiabr'* must have received sizeable portions of volume 3. Their decision was not what Sholokhov would have liked to hear. "You probably already know," he wrote to Serafimovich on April 1, 1930, "that they would not publish part 6, and Fadeev (I received a letter from him the other day) suggests corrections that are completely unacceptable to me."[74] Sholokhov asked Serafimovich to read part 6 and give his opinion of it. By this time Sholokhov had been on the editorial board of *Oktiabr'* for several months, while Serafimovich continued to be its chief editor. But the old writer's association with the journal had most likely become all but nominal. Sholokhov's letter mentions that Serafimovich had been in the Kremlin hospital. Aleksandr Fadeev was probably the most influential person on the editorial board of *Oktiabr'*. It was he who became the acting editor of the journal when, beginning with its August 1930 issue, Serafimovich's name disappeared from the list of its editors. The July-September issues of *Oktiabr'* stopped mentioning *The Quiet Don* in the list of forthcoming publications. Serafimovich's reaction to Sholokhov's letter is unknown.

While the editors of *Oktiabr'* refused to resume the serialization of volume 3 of *The Quiet Don*, Sholokhov managed to publish twelve of its new chapters during the summer of 1930 in the journals *Krasnaia niva* (*The Red Cornfield*), *Ogonek*, *Na pod''eme*, and *Tridtsat' dnei* (*Thirty*

Days), and in a booklet, *Deviatnadtsataia godina* (*The Year 1919*). These publications proved to be invaluable for the textual study of the novel, since they contained passages that were either suppressed or revised in subsequent editions.

In the first half of 1931 the bulk of volume 3 must have been in the hands of the *Oktiabr'* editorial board. Headed by the well-known proletarian writer Fedor Panferov, the board included Sholokhov and such leading figures of RAPP as Vladimir Stavskii, Ermilov, and Makar'ev. Since March 1931 Fadeev's name was no longer among them, but there is little doubt that he was instrumental in the decision of the editorial board. The decision was even more unfavorable than the one made the year before. Upon learning about it, Sholokhov sent a telegram to Fadeev asking him to hand over a copy of part 6 to Maksim Gor'kii. A few days later, on June 6, 1931, he wrote Gor'kii a long letter. Some of the "orthodox" RAPP leaders, he stated in the letter, had accused him of justifying the Upper Don uprising because he wrote about the mistreatment of the Cossacks by the Reds. There were no exaggerations in his portrayal of the Red misdeeds, he claimed. If anything, he had "intentionally omitted such facts—which constituted the immediate cause of the uprising—as the shooting, without trial, of sixty-two old Cossacks in Migulinskaia stanitsa, or the shootings in Kazanskaia and Shumilinskaia stanitsas, where the number of the Cossacks who were shot (former elected village elders, holders of the Cross of St. George, sergeants major, honorary village judges, curators of schools, and other bourgeois and counterrevolutionaries on the village scale) has reached within six days the impressive figure of more than 400 men."[75] Part 6, Sholokhov continued, would be published only if he agreed to make substantial deletions, including some lyrical passages of which he was especially fond. Ten persons suggested excisions of ten different portions. Compliance with their suggestions would amount to cutting out three-fourths of the text. Sholokhov sent Gor'kii some, possibly closing, chapters of volume 3 and asked him for his opinion.

By that time Gor'kii had already read a part of the manuscript of volume 3 and his view of it is known from his letter to Fadeev of June 3, 1931. He considered *The Quiet Don* to be a work of "high merit," preferred volume 3 to volume 2, and thought that "Sholokhov was very gifted and could develop into a superb Soviet writer." Yet for Gor'kii Sholokhov was a "regional writer," still "biologically" attached to the traditional Cossack way of life and torn, like Grigorii Melekhov, between the old and the new.[76] A week after writing to Fadeev, Gor'kii made similar critical remarks on volume 3 in a conversation with young shock workers. At times, he said, Sholokhov failed to separate his views from those of Grigorii Melekhov with sufficient clarity. He expressed some typically "Cossack," regional aspirations and used local dialect excessively. Volume 3 belongs to regional literature.[77] Sholokhov recalled that some time later, during their meeting in Moscow, Gor'kii told him, "The book is well written and will come out without any abridgments."[78]

The editors of *Oktiabr'* were not the only people who attacked the manuscript of volume 3 of *The Quiet Don.* At the beginning of 1931 a prominent figure of the OGPU (security police, 1923-1934) told Sholokhov to his face: "Your *Quiet Don* is closer to the Whites than to us!"[79] According to Priima, who learned about this episode from Sholokhov in 1978, the OGPU man either read the manuscript or knew its content well, particularly chapter 39, describing "the monstrous repressions" conducted by a certain Malkin, who was to hold an important OGPU post in the early thirties. Priima does not disclose the identity of Sholokhov's attacker. He states, however, that this person considered himself close to literature and was a friend of Leopol'd Averbakh, secretary-general of RAPP. In all probability the anonymous VIP is Genrikh Iagoda, then assistant director of the OGPU and a relative of Averbakh. Whether the OGPU had anything to do with the delay in the publishing of volume 3 of *The Quiet Don* is difficult to ascertain. The fact remains that volume 3 did not appear in 1931, though its forthcoming publication in that year was consistently advertised in *Oktiabr'*.

Difficulties with volume 3 of *The Quiet Don* did not prevent Sholokhov from starting work on a new novel. The immediate impulse was provided by the massive collectivization of agriculture that got underway in the winter of 1929-1930. This momentous event and Sholokhov's first meeting with Stalin in January 1930, during which collectivization was discussed, made him direct his attention to the contemporary scene. "The conversation," he said, "was very profitable to me and encouraged me to put into practice new creative ideas."[80] The actual writing of the novel on collectivization probably began toward the end of 1930. In November 1931 the greater part of it was completed. Its title, *S krov'iu i potom* (*With Blood and Sweat*), symbolized the brutality and difficulty with which collectivization was carried out. A part of the manuscript was sent to *Novyi mir* (*New World*) in November or early December 1931. The journal demanded that the novel's title be changed and the sections describing the dispossession of kulak households be deleted.[81] At an informal meeting between the author and the local Party members in Veshenskaia the title was changed to *Virgin Soil Upturned.* The words of the title, in a slightly different grammatical form, came from chapter 21, where they, ironically, are spoken by an enemy of collective farming, Iakov Ostrovnov. Sholokhov refused to make the cuts demanded by *Novyi mir* and turned for help and advice to Stalin. Stalin, he recalled in 1955, read the novel's manuscript and said: "We were not afraid to dispossess the kulaks—why should we be afraid to write about it now! The novel ought to be printed."[82] And it was, in the January through September issues of *Novyi mir* for 1932.

There can be little doubt that Stalin ordered the publication of *Virgin Soil Upturned*. The only time when he was not directly credited with it was during de-Stalinization under Khrushchev. At that time the critics had to speak of "an intervention by the Party's Central Committee."[83]

By contrast, the question of how volume 3 of *The Quiet Don* was published is somewhat more complicated. The serialization of that volume was resumed and completed in *Oktiabr'* simultaneously with the serialization of *Virgin Soil Upturned*. Lezhnev and Lev Iakimenko assert that volume 3 was published thanks to Gor'kii's efforts, while Arkadii Airumian gives credit to Gor'kii and Serafimovich.[84] It is quite possible that Serafimovich interceded for Sholokhov in April 1930 and Gor'kii in June 1931. But had their efforts been successful, the serialization of volume 3 would probably have begun much sooner than it actually did. Besides, volume 3 was serialized with extensive cuts of a political nature, and Gor'kii was reportedly in favor of publishing it without abridgments. The Communist editors of *Oktiabr'* were obviously not inclined to heed every piece of advice coming from a non-Party writer, irrespective of his stature.

That Serafimovich, and probably Gor'kii, had little or nothing to do with the publication of volume 3 of *The Quiet Don* is evidenced from Sholokhov's letter to Serafimovich dated April 23, 1932. "In January I had arranged the publication of volume 3 of *The Quiet Don*," Sholokhov wrote, "but this arrangement did not turn out to be very solid and I won't be publishing it from May on (I'll give you the reasons when we meet)."[85] In fact, the double issue of *Oktiabr'* for May-June 1932 printed only a few excerpts from volume 3, those which had not been published in the preceding issues for technical reasons. The serialization was resumed in July. But what "arrangement" was Sholokhov speaking about? An editorial comment in *Komsomol'skaia pravda* and three later statements by Sholokhov may help to answer this question. The comment, appearing in connection with Sholokhov's address to his constituents in 1937, said, "When the enemies of the people who were active in literature had held up the publication of volume 3 of *The Quiet Don* for a year, comrade Stalin intervened personally and the book immediately went to press."[86] The statement, of course, may reflect the trend of picturing Stalin as a universal benefactor and it includes a typical lie of that time about "the enemies of the people."

The chief responsibility for holding up volume 3 must rest with the most influential editors of *Oktiabr'*—Fadeev, Panferov, Stavskii, Ermilov—none of whom has ever been branded "an enemy of the people." Yet the

Komsomol'skaia pravda comment cannot be simply dismissed because in the next sentence it gave correct information about Stalin's role in the publication of *Virgin Soil Upturned*. In 1941 Sholokhov himself said that the obstacles to the publication of volume 3 "were removed thanks to the attention and concern of the Party's Central Committee. . . ."[87] At this point the quotation is cut short and one is left wondering whether the author also mentioned Stalin. In 1967 Sholokhov confided to Priima: "In the polemics about *The Quiet Don* Stalin showed more tact and understanding than the orthodox leaders of RAPP who, as it is well known, delayed the publication of volume 3 of the novel for a year and a half."[88] It was not until the fall of 1972 that Sholokhov revealed some details about Stalin's role in the publication of volume 3. This time he told Priima about his meeting with Stalin at Gor'kii's country house near Moscow in July 1931. When he entered the drawing room, Sholokhov realized that Gor'kii and Stalin had just been discussing his novel. There followed a dialogue between Stalin and Sholokhov, during which Gor'kii kept silent, smoking cigarettes and burning matches. "Stalin," Sholokhov recalled, "started talking about volume 2 of *The Quiet Don*. . . . Then he asked where did I get the material pertaining to the excesses perpetrated by the Don Committee of the RKP(b) and revolutionary tribunals in the Upper Don region in 1919. I told him where. . . . 'Some people think,' Stalin said, 'that volume 3 of *The Quiet Don* would give great pleasure to the White Guard émigrés. What would you say to this?' . . . Then I replied: 'What pleasure for the Whites! A complete rout of the White forces in the Don and the Kuban' regions!' . . . In conclusion I. Stalin firmly said, 'We will publish volume 3 of the novel *The Quiet Don*!' "[89] All the available evidence indicates that Stalin or the Central Committee, with his blessings or tacit approval, backed the publication of volume 3 of *The Quiet Don*. Stalin's involvement with it, however, must have been much less pronounced than his involvement with *Virgin Soil Upturned*. Had he given an immediate and direct order to publish volume 3 of *The Quiet Don*, the editors of *Oktiabr'* would probably have serialized it a few months earlier without extensive cuts. In any event, it appears very likely that Sholokhov "arranged" the publication of volume 3 by appealing to the highest Party authorities and to Stalin personally. The dictator might have assumed—correctly—that volume 3 could be used against "Trotskyites" and other "enemies" by blaming them for all the atrocities that provoked the Upper Don uprising.

With the publication of *Virgin Soil Upturned* and volume 3 of *The Quiet Don* Sholokhov seemed to have become an established writer with a safe career ahead of him. He enjoyed the protection of the most powerful man in the Soviet Union. In November 1932 he became a full-fledged member of the Communist Party. His *Virgin Soil Upturned* supported collectivization and was a big political success. Following its serialization in *Novyi mir*, over a million copies of *Virgin Soil Upturned* were printed in various editions during the 1932-1935 period. The comparable figure for volume 3 of *The Quiet Don* was 320,000. *Virgin Soil Upturned* was unanimously hailed by Party critics as an exemplary work of socialist realism. It was favorably compared to *The Quiet Don*. Sholokhov was said to have overcome his earlier nonclass compassion and humanism. The critics were particularly eager to point out the descriptions that could serve as illustrations to Stalin's policy. In Makar'ev's view, *Virgin Soil Upturned* represented "the embodiment of the basic demands of socialist realism," such as an all-embracing portrayal of life, ideological saturation, simplicity and clarity of narrative, and plainness and terseness of expression. All these qualities, the critic claimed, were consistent with Party instructions concerning socialist realism and with "the demands made on art by Marx and Engels, Lenin and Stalin."[90] Dmitrii Maznin saw in the novel the most distinguishing features of socialist art—a negative attitude toward private property, advocacy of collective farming, and grouping of characters in accordance with their class interests.[91] The critic Nikolai Lesiuchevskii felt that Sholokhov affirmed "the universal historical significance of collectivization and the victory of the general Party line."[92] *Virgin Soil Upturned*, in Lesiuchevskii's eyes, was imbued with great Party spirit. It taught the masses how to remold the world by bringing to their attention the directives issued by the Party and Stalin.

Overshadowed by volume 1 of *Virgin Soil Upturned*, volume 3 of *The Quiet Don* received relatively little critical attention. On the other hand, the political success of *Virgin Soil Upturned* must have moved the critics to deal with volume 3 less severely than they did with the first two volumes. In a way *Virgin Soil Upturned* turned out to be a sort of a bone thrown to the Soviet regime to save *The Quiet Don*. The critic Galina Kolesnikova was happy to note that the class struggle, which was toned down in volumes 1 and 2 of *The Quiet Don*, flared up with full force in volume 3. She nonetheless took exception to the "objectivism" and "humanism" that the author displayed in presenting the Whites as personally more attractive than the Reds, and in showing that atrocities were committed by both sides. On the whole, however, volume 3, in Kolesnikova's estimation, was moving toward socialist realism and away from "objectivism."[93] Dmitrii Mirskii found volume 3 of *The Quiet Don* artistically superior to volume 1 because it was less heavily littered with provincialisms. Mirskii did not single out volume 3 in any other respect, but praised all three volumes for their full-blooded realism. The Civil War scenes and the portrayal of the class enemies from the inside, he contended, were the best of their kind in all of Soviet literature. The main shortcoming of the novel was, in Mirskii's words, its "political indistinctness," which, in the final analysis, "reflected the vacillations of the petty-bourgeois masses." In both of Sholokhov's novels Mirskii disapproved of some lyrical passages in which he correctly saw a constrast between eternal nature and the vanity of human struggle. Otherwise, *Virgin Soil Upturned* was to Mirskii "in every respect a tremendous step forward in comparison with *The Quiet Don*." Its strongest point was the presence of a dominant idea—the transformation of a village of small property owners into a socialist village—that gave unity to the novel's form and ideological content.[94]

It was hard to imagine in 1932 that during the next few years the author of *Virgin Soil Upturned* and Stalin's protégé would have to go through personal and creative trials that would be no less intense or dangerous than his previous experiences. But in the Soviet Union of the 1930s anything could happen to anyone. Political oppression and demands on literature were becoming increasingly stringent. Censors made substantial political and stylistic revisions in the 1933 edition of the first two volumes of *The Quiet Don*. Also there were some problems with volume 3. In 1967 Sholokhov told Priima that the leaders of RAPP who delayed its serialization in *Oktiabr'* "later tried to hinder its publication as a separate book."[95] Apart from their political dissatisfaction with volume 3, the former RAPP leaders might have been opposed to its book-form publication because many of the passages deleted from the *Oktiabr'* text would be included in the new edition. And, indeed, they were. There is no reliable information as to whether the former RAPP leaders put any obstacles in the way of the first book-form edition of volume 3. It was approved for publication on February 5, 1933, and its 15,000 copies must have come out early in 1933. Its appearance was recorded in *Knizhnaia letopis'* (*Book Annals*) for April of that year. Abramov and Gura mention a letter from Fadeev to Sholokhov dated August 27, 1933, and they say that it pertains to "the difficulties connected with the preparation of volume 3 of *The Quiet Don* for a separate publication."[96] Unless Fadeev wrote retrospectively about the first 1933 edition of volume 3, his letter should deal with one or both of the later 1933 editions of volume 3. One of them was approved for publication on July 19. The other—in the *Roman-gazeta* series—was printed in September. Both were published by Khudozhestvennaia literatura (Artistic Literature) and are identical with the first 1933 edition except for a few minor stylistic and compositional differences. Unfortunately, Abramov and Gura give no further information on the content of Fadeev's letter. To my knowledge, it still remains unpublished—one more indication that the Soviet authorities are not prepared to reveal the negative role Fadeev must have played in the publication history of *The Quiet Don*. In

1974, when the Council of Ministers established the Fadeev medal to be awarded annually for the best works on patriotic war themes, Sholokhov was the first to receive it for published portions of his unfinished novel, *Oni srazhalis' za rodinu* (*They Fought for Their Country*).

Sholokhov's most trying experiences in 1933 were associated not with literature but with agricultural upheaval. Brutal and compulsory methods of collectivization, the inherent inefficiency of Soviet collective farming, a lack of incentive on the part of collectivized peasants, and, above all, a reckless requisition of grain on governmental orders led in 1932-1933 to a widespread famine. It was particularly grave in the Ukraine and southern Russia, claiming millions of lives. To absolve themselves from any responsibility for the disaster, the Soviet rulers shifted all the blame on the so-called kulak sabotage—meaning such actions as agitation, hoarding of grain, absenteeism, stealing and damaging collective property—and on local Party officials who were said to be conniving at the sabotage. These charges were patently false if only because those who were branded kulaks had already been exiled in 1930.

An account of what happened in 1932-1933 in Veshenskaia was given to me by F.M.A., who at that time was an agricultural worker there. In 1932, he told me, collective farms in the Veshenskaia area were obligated to deliver to the state 960 kg. of wheat from a hectare (2.47 acres).[97] The actual crop was considerably smaller. A representative of the regional authorities ordered local officials to ensure the fulfillment of the grain-delivery plan regardless of the measures they might have to take. The local officials embarked upon a merciless confiscation of grain, accompanied by beatings and tortures. This resulted in famine and the growth of anti-Soviet and anticollectivization sentiments. The higher authorities began to look for scapegoats. The actions of the local Party officials were declared to be distorting Party directives and helping the kulaks and other counterrevolutionaries to undermine collective farming and to discredit the Soviet regime. A special court came to Veshenskaia to try its officials and sentenced three of them to death.

All these events gave Sholokhov a severe shock. His condition can be best seen from his letter written on February 13, 1933, to Petr Lugovoi, a close friend of his and the first secretary of the Veshenskaia *Raion* (County) Committee of the Communist Party from 1930 to 1945, excluding the period from the middle of 1932 to the middle of 1933. "The events in Veshenskaia have taken on a monstrous character," Sholokhov wrote, giving the names of the officials who were arrested and threatened with execution, while their families were deprived of food rations and doomed to "physical extermination" through starvation. "The old leadership," Sholokhov continued, "is being accused of sowing grain in a criminal and negligent manner, of ruining 20,000 hectares. We are accused of encouraging the plundering of grain, of helping to ruin the livestock. . . . Briefly, we all turned out to be counterrevolutionaries. . . . We must fight with all our fury and relentlessness to remove that undeserved black stain! I will speak about it in Moscow. . . .

"About three hundred members have already been expelled from the Party. This is before the purge. . . . The *raion* is headed toward a catastrophe. . . . What will happen in the spring I cannot picture even with my imagination as a writer. . . . I stopped writing. . . . What are we going to undertake?"[98]

A good question, considering the fact that apart from the sufferings of local Communists over two thousand households were expelled from collective farms for "sabotage" and over three thousand collective farmers were arrested by February 1933 in Veshenskaia *raion* alone. Many others had already died of starvation and those expelled from collective farms were deprived of their small personal plots and thus condemned to death.[99] The North Caucasus Party Committee felt, however, that the farmers were treated too softly. On March 21, 1933, a special reporter of its newspaper, *Molot*, launched a sharp attack on the Veshenskaia officials under the ominous title "The Veshenskaia Communists Are Conniving at the Kulak Sabotage." Things could only get worse.

We do not know whether Sholokhov made any appeals to the North Caucasus Party Committee. He must have known that such appeals would be futile. This committee, headed by Boris Sheboldaev, was but a tool in the hands of the Party's highest leadership, even if one of the most willing and cruel tools.[100] If Sholokhov was to have any hope of remedying the situation, he had to take the extremely dangerous step of addressing himself directly to Stalin, the principal architect of the disastrous policy in agriculture. Sholokhov wrote Stalin two letters concerning the conditions in the Upper Don region. What appears to be the first letter was dated April 16, 1933. In it Sholokhov asserted that the "excesses" committed by those in charge of grain procurement were not isolated instances but "*a method legitimized on the raion scale*." "Do you remember, Iosif Vissarionovich," the author asked, "the sketch 'In the Pacified Village' by Korolenko? Just such a 'disappearance' was applied not to three peasants suspected of stealing from a kulak, but to tens of thousands of collective farmers. And, as you see, this was done with a more extensive use of technical means and with a greater refinement."[101] It was probably in this letter that Sholokhov also described the condition of the starving people working in the fields: "Some are getting thin, they lie down right on the ploughed field like exhausted oxen. The half-dead are transported to the village."[102]

In conclusion Sholokhov asked for food aid to the Upper Don and for a dispatch to Veshenskaia of "genuine Communists" to conduct an impartial investigation and to expose "not only all those who employed the loathsome 'methods' of torture, beating, and abuse against collective farmers, but also those who inspired this."[103]

In a few days Sholokhov received a telegram from Stalin: "Thank you for the information. We shall do everything that is needed. Give the figures."[104] The author promptly mailed a letter containing the figures worked out in consultation with local Communists. Stalin responded with a telegram giving details on the distribution of grain aid and chiding Sholokhov for not communicating the requested aid figures by wire. About that time Stalin sent Sholokhov a written reply to his letters. The dictator admitted that the Party and Soviet officials did at times abuse their friends inadvertently and sink to sadism. Those guilty of such actions should be punished. The main point of Stalin's letter, however, was to give Sholokhov a political lecture. Stalin insisted that the author, while being concerned with the peasants, failed to see the other more important side of the coin. This was a quiet, outwardly harmless sabotage, a quiet war waged by "the esteemed grain growers" against the Soviet regime, threatening to leave the Red Army and factory workers without bread.[105] In spite of his political disagreement with Sholokhov, Stalin ordered that grain be sent to the Upper Don region. He did not do this out of compassion, but to bolster the authority of the Soviet regime and to enhance his own image as the benevolent "father of the people." Nonetheless, thousands of lives were saved. No one deserves more credit for this than Sholokhov. In terms of courage, loyalty to his friends, and concern for human misery, his appeal to Stalin may well be the noblest act of his life. It would be interesting to know if any other Soviet writer acted the way Sholokhov did.

Soon after the arrival of the grain a special commission of the Party's Central Committee came to Veshenskaia. It was headed by Matvei Shkiriatov, a leading figure in the Committee who was to become one of the most sinister hatchet men during the later purges. Sholokhov's importance was underscored by the fact that the commission, according to F.M.A., who witnessed its arrival, went to see the author first, not to the local authorities. The commission righted many wrongs and succeeded in freeing convicted officials, including those sentenced to death. On the other hand, the Party leaders of the North Caucasus Region who were directly responsible for the outrages went unpunished. It was only during the indiscriminate purges of the late thirties that Sheboldaev and his associates were liquidated on trumped-up charges.

Sholokhov's involvement with the 1932-1933 events resulted in a great loss of creative time. In what appears to be his second letter to Stalin, he stated: "I returned to life and my spirits picked up! Things were very bad before. My letter to you is the only thing I have written since last November. The last six months were lost as far as creative work is concerned. To make up for it, I will be working now with ten times as much energy as before."[106]

However, to carry out all the plans he had for the thirties, Sholokhov needed more than just energy. His immediate goal was to complete promptly volume 2 of *Virgin Soil Upturned* and volume 4 of *The Quiet Don*. In reality, the story of the writing of these volumes became one of continuous announcements by Sholokhov of projected completion dates and inability to deliver on time. The completion of *Virgin Soil Upturned*, for instance, was consecutively announced for 1934, the second half of 1935, the fall of 1935, and 1939.[107] In addition, the forthcoming publication of volume 2 of *Virgin Soil Upturned* was announced for 1933 in *Na pod''eme* and for 1934-1936 in *Novyi mir*. At one point the publishers of *Novyi mir* thought it necessary to respond to "the numerous inquiries from readers" with a special announcement that volume 2 of *Virgin Soil Upturned* would appear in their journal in the second half of 1935.[108] Some reasons for the delays might have been connected with the changes concerning the chronological framework of the novel. Early in 1933 the author intended to bring its action to the middle of 1932.[109] He obviously decided to avoid the politically sensitive events of the second half of 1932—the ruthless confiscation of grain and the outbreak of famine. A year later he chose not to go beyond the relatively uneventful year of 1931.[110] He was fully aware that this shift would be detrimental to the dramatic qualities of volume 2 of *Virgin Soil Upturned*. "Frankly," he said to a reporter, "there would be little room in it for the characters to prove themselves. It would be nice to place them in 1932! Here is where their personalities could be made to blossom! The way it is, I foresee that the second volume will be more boring than the first."[111]

Still unwilling to part with the critical year, Sholokhov started to write a play, set in the 1931-1932 period, about the life of collective farmers. The play was to be completed in 1935.[112] It probably remains unfinished. Likewise, nothing came of Sholokhov's desire to write a large political novel about *raionshchiki*, the local Party and government officials operating on the *raion* scale. These people carried out the collectivization and were later accused of indulging "the kulak sabotage." In order to portray the *raionshchiki* as full-blooded individuals, Sholokhov wanted to include the 1932-1933 "sabotage period" in the novel.[113] When the mass arrests of the *raionshchiki* began in 1937, he gave up his plan to write the novel.[114] There was no chance of publishing even relatively truthful accounts of village life, particularly of the 1932-1933 and 1937-1938 periods, and Sholokhov apparently was not willing to resort to gross distortions.

The impossibility of including the 1932-1933 events in volume 2 of *Virgin Soil Upturned* must have prompted Sholokhov to interrupt, by the middle of 1934, his simultaneous work on both novels and to concentrate on *The Quiet Don*. Both novels, according to him, were "almost finished" and he intended to send volume 4 of *The Quiet Don* to the publishers in mid-November or early December 1934.[115] The speed with which volume 4 of *The Quiet Don* and volume 2 of *Virgin Soil Upturned* were "almost finished" matched the remarkable speed with which the first two volumes of *The Quiet Don* had been written. But, as in the case with *Virgin Soil Upturned*, Sholokhov found it difficult to have *The Quiet Don* ready for publication by a previously specified time. In February and March 1935 he spoke of completing the novel in the early summer and of publishing it in the fall of that year.[116] On April 13, 1935, he notified Nikolai Nakoriakov, director of the publishing house Khudozhestvennaia literatura, that he was reworking the first half of volume 4 and could not predict the time of its completion. Furthermore, according to Nakoriakov, Sholokhov was careful not to "mess up" the novel's ending and reworked it six or seven times.[117] A year later Sholokhov wrote to Nakoriakov: "I am completing the last volume of *The Quiet Don*. . . . If no substantial corrections are needed, I will present the manuscript in May."[118] But corrections, perhaps of a political nature, were apparently required.

It was only in October 1936 that Sholokhov was able to announce the completion of volume 4 and his intention to send it to the publisher in about two months. He said he was still polishing it, rechecking certain points, and collecting additional materials for its ending.[119] Yet a year passed and only a few chapters of the novel appeared in various newspapers. By that time, however, *The Quiet Don* was completed beyond any doubt. "After twelve years of work *The Quiet Don* is finished," the opening sentence of Isaak Eksler's article announced in *Izvestiia* of December 31, 1937. "The last pages of volume 4 are lying on a round table in a small room in Sholokhov's house."[120] Indeed, part 7 of the novel was serialized, without interruption, in the November 1937-March 1938 issues of *Novyi mir*. But what happened to part 8, whose publication was delayed for two more years? This is something that the Soviet censors did not and do not want to disclose. Their aim is not to allow the appearance of any statements about the completion of *The Quiet Don* in 1936 or 1937. When reprinting Eksler's reminiscences about Sholokhov, which closely follow the text of his earlier articles, the censors, or Eksler at their suggestion, excised the opening sentence of his December 31, 1937, *Izvestiia* article and simply falsified Sholokhov's words which Eksler quoted in his article published on October 20, 1936. In that article Sholokhov was quoted as having said, in October 1936, "I can tell you that the fourth volume is finished at last." In the 1940 version of Eksler's reminiscences this statement was changed to "The fourth volume of *The Quiet Don* is not ready yet," and in the 1966 version it appeared in a more emphatic and emotional context: " 'But that's precisely the point—the fourth volume is not ready yet.' He uttered these words with some sort of irritation, swung his pipe and, a bit sadly, said slowly, with hesitations, that he was revising whole pieces again and again."[121] The last sentence was added in 1966. To cover up their alterations, the censors moved the time of Eksler's visit to Sholokhov from October to a hot summer. The year of the visit can still be deduced in the 1940 version, but not in the 1966 version.

What the censors most likely wanted to conceal was the role Stalin played in delaying the publication of volume 4 of *The Quiet Don*. Some light was shed on the subject by Petr Ivanovich Eremeev, an official in the Agitation and Propaganda Section of the Party Committee of the Rostov Province and a lecturer in Marxism-Leninism. According to the late Professor Marianna A. Poltoratskaia (Poltoratzky), who had been a faculty member of the University of Rostov, Eremeev told her that in the winter of 1938 Stalin, upon reading the manuscript of volume 4, called Sholokhov to Moscow and said to him, "Change the ending of the novel and show who Grigorii Melekhov is—a Red Cossack or a White-Guard scum."[122] Roi Medvedev also reports that Stalin was displeased with the ending and "asked when Sholokhov intended to bring his Grigorii round to the Bolshevik side."[123] In his 1967 interview with Priima, Sholokhov denied that Stalin put any political pressure on him during his work on *The Quiet Don*. He did, however, admit that there were disagreements between them about certain historical figures appearing in *The Quiet Don*, but he said that Stalin never interfered with his creative designs.[124] Sholokhov, of course, might have kept silent about the adverse effects of Stalin's interest in his work, all the more so because his statement about Stalin's noninterference with *The Quiet Don* was made in reply to what he called "idle fabrications of the bourgeois press." It is difficult, however, to imagine any other authority except Stalin's that could have delayed the serialization of part 8 for two years. On the other hand, had Stalin insisted on his wish to see Grigorii become a Red, part 8 would not have come out during his lifetime. Stalin did not need to give direct orders to prevent its publication. The mere knowledge of his dissatisfaction with the ending of the novel would make the editors of *Novyi mir* give up any idea of serializing part 8. At some point Stalin must have assented to Sholokhov's intentions for the work.

Needless to say, Sholokhov's refusal to comply with Stalin's wishes was an extraordinary act, particularly since it occurred during the worst period of the purges. Giving in to Stalin would have entailed a disregard for historical truth and for Grigorii's personal traits. The author would have ruined the ending of the novel and betrayed the principle of objectivity that he managed to maintain throughout *The Quiet Don* against overwhelming odds. Sholokhov could not but be aware that *The Quiet Don* might well become his only work that would ensure him a place in world literature. It had to be as free as possible from political distortions detrimental to its artistic qualities. The stakes were high, and Sholokhov was prepared to pay any price in terms of his career and safety. It might have been his last chance. In 1938 the future looked bleaker than the past. Sholokhov could easily imagine that for a long time to come he would have no opportunity to write the way he wanted. Moreover, he had every reason to believe that he would not survive the purges. Once again he had to live through experiences similar to those of the 1932-1933 period, and at one point his life was in more danger than during his 1920 confrontation with Makhno.

In 1937-1938 all top Party and Soviet officials and many Cossacks were arrested in Veshenskaia *raion*. Some of the local leaders were sent to the Butyrskaia prison in Moscow. This was very unusual treatment of local administrators, who as a rule were dealt with in their own *raions* or provinces. Even more unusual was the fact that Petr Krasiukov, one of the Veshenskaia administrators, was held in solitary confinement and that Lugovoi was at times interrogated by Nikolai Ezhov, head of the NKVD (security police, 1934-1943). It was, of course, only natural that all of them were charged with aiding the enemies, interrogated at night, beaten, abused, and starved. The transfer of Veshenskaia prisoners to Moscow and Ezhov's interest in them must have been connected with Sholokhov. Either the NKVD intended to discourage Sholokhov from defending them or, more likely, planned to frame him with the aid of their testimonies. Sholokhov, however, did not wait for this to happen. He went to Moscow, met with Ezhov, and got the prisoners released. One small detail needs to be added. When Lugovoi and Krasiukov were brought, separately, into Ezhov's office to confront Sholokhov, the first thing they did was to see if the author still had his belt on. Prisoners had their belts taken off, and they wondered if Sholokhov was under arrest.[125] Sholokhov is also said to have interceded on behalf of simple Cossacks. This information comes from the late artist Sergei Korol'kov, the illustrator of *The Quiet Don*, who emigrated from the Soviet Union during World War II. In or about 1952 he wrote my friend George Krugovoy that Sholokhov went to Ezhov and succeeded in freeing about a hundred of the Veshenskaia Cossacks who were likely to have been shot. Korol'kov met a few of these Cossacks.[126] There were apparently cases when Sholokhov was either unable or unwilling to help. A person who asked to be identified as G.G. told me that the author did not intercede for his friend Ianko Georgiadi, a Communist of Greek origin who was living in Moscow at the time of his arrest. During one of Sholokhov's visits to the capital, Georgiadi's wife went to see him to seek his help. As soon as Sholokhov saw the woman's tear-stained face, he realized the purpose of her visit and shut the door.[127]

There is no evidence that Sholokhov informed on anyone during the 1936-1939 purges. On the contrary, he reportedly prevented the arrest of Andrei Platonov.[128] Nor did he display more zeal in publicly condemning "enemies of the people" than did other writers. His signature, along with forty-odd signatures of his colleagues, appeared on a letter routinely demanding that "the spies" be shot.[129] On the other hand, in *Literaturnaia gazeta* of January 26, 1938, one can read individual condemnations of "the enemies" made by Platonov, Mirskii, Viktor Shklovskii, Isaak Babel', Iurii Olesha, Samuil Marshak, and twenty-seven other writers. They did their duty with varying degrees of diligence. Sholokhov, for some reason, was not among them.

A glimpse of what Sholokhov felt in 1937 or 1938 was provided by Korol'kov. Once, when Sholokhov came to Rostov, Korol'kov visited him in his hotel room and found him lying in bed, intoxicated. In the conversation that followed Sholokhov bitterly cursed the Soviet regime, accused it of destroying the Cossacks, and said that he feared he would be arrested.[130]

The fear was not unfounded. It was probably in the second half of 1938 that the NKVD began a large-scale operation against Sholokhov. Whether he incurred the wrath of the NKVD by his intervention on behalf of purge victims or whether the NKVD acted on instructions from above has not yet been disclosed. What we know about the NKVD scheme to liquidate Sholokhov comes primarily from an account published by the Soviet critic Lev Iakimenko. The people directly involved in the attempt to frame Sholokhov were a certain Grechukhin, head of the NKVD in the Rostov Province, and Ivan Pogorelov, a Party worker in Novocherkassk and a former member of the Cheka (security police, 1917-1922). At an unspecified date, Grechukhin summoned Pogorelov to his office and asked him whether he would be willing to carry out a very important assignment given to the Rostov NKVD by Stalin and Ezhov. Pogorelov readily agreed, even if it would cost him his life. Grechukhin smiled approvingly. According to absolutely reliable intelligence reports, he said, Sholokhov was preparing an uprising of the Don, Kuban', and Terek Cossacks against the Soviet regime. His known accomplices were his father-in-law, Lugovoi, Krasiukov, and Tikhon Logachev. The group had ties both at home and abroad. Pogorelov's mission would be to gain the trust of the group and to find out all the details about these connections. Pogorelov was promised a reward in the event of success and a bullet "without trial or investigation" should he divulge his mission.

Pogorelov took the latter alternative. He knew Sholokhov and his friends very well and believed in their innocence. But he did not dare to go to Veshenskaia to warn them for fear that Sholokhov, for some reason, would be killed upon his arrival there. It was only when Sholokhov and Lugovoi came to Rostov that Pogorelov was able to tell them about his mission. Then he went without permission to Moscow and tried without success to see Shkiriatov and Kaganovich. He left a detailed letter with the Party's Central Committee and headed for the Don region, where he went into hiding. In October 1938, upon their return to Veshenskaia, Sholokhov and Lugovoi began to receive anonymous letters. These letters said that the NKVD officials used all sorts of threats to extract from arrested Cossacks false confessions about the alleged counterrevolutionary activities of Sholokhov. The author and Lugovoi hurried to Moscow. The Politburo of the Party's Central Committee called a meeting to which many people from Veshenskaia and Rostov were summoned, including Pogorelov and Kogan, the deputy chief of the Rostov NKVD. Pogorelov spoke first and Sholokhov took the floor twice, demanding an end to the violent and slanderous actions of the NKVD. At this point Stalin asked Kogan whether he was given an assignment to defame Sholokhov and whether he gave any instructions to Pogorelov. Kogan replied that he had received such instructions from Grechukhin and that they were coordinated with Ezhov. Ezhov stood up and denied having any knowledge of these instructions. Sholokhov was guaranteed peace and safety.[131]

Another Soviet source devotes only a few lines to the plan to entrap Sholokhov, but it speaks in no uncertain terms about what awaited the author. "The murder of Sholokhov was being prepared. It was only thanks to his friends' selflessness . . . that his death was averted."[132]

Neither this source nor Iakimenko could, in 1964, throw light on the role played by Stalin in the NKVD case against Sholokhov. But in 1972 Priima was able to quote Sholokhov as having said, in 1969, that "Stalin looked closely into everything, and all the accusations against me were smashed to smithereens."[133] Stalin, of course, did not have to look closely into Sholokhov's case. As the prime mover behind the purges he knew very well how political charges were fabricated. Only a half-wit could believe that Sholokhov was preparing a huge Cossack uprising in collaboration with foreign agents. Stalin could have investigated the origins of the NKVD operation against Sholokhov, provided he initially knew nothing about it. But the question inevitably arises: Could the NKVD design a liquidation plan against such a figure as Sholokhov without Stalin's order or knowledge? The case against Sholokhov could hardly have been initiated by Grechukhin. Chief of a provincial section of the NKVD, he was unlikely to set out on his own to ruin a world-famous Communist writer who enjoyed Stalin's favor and who had enough influence to make Ezhov release his friends.[134] Grechukhin probably did not lie when he told Pogorelov that the "mission" concerning Sholokhov was given by Stalin and Ezhov. The two cooperated closely with each other. Ezhov regularly presented for Stalin's approval lists of important people whom he recommended for liquidation. Moreover, the arrests of prominent writers could hardly be made without Stalin's consent. It was he who decided against arresting Boris Pasternak and Olesha.[135] And it was he who in 1938 approved the arrest of the journalist Mikhail Kol'tsov. This, and more, was revealed in 1940 by Vasilii Ul'rikh, then president of the Military Collegium of the Supreme Court, in conversation with Kol'tsov's brother, the artist Boris Efimov: "Listen. Your brother was a well-known and popular man. He was a prominent public figure. Don't you understand that if he was arrested, it means that there was a special sanction for it?"[136]

In Stalin's eyes, Sholokhov was by no means a less significant writer than Olesha, Pasternak, or Kol'tsov. If, as seems logical, Stalin was the one who sanctioned the NKVD action against Sholokhov, then why did he do it? He might have been envious of Sholokhov's popularity, or annoyed by his interference with the NKVD activities, or angry about his refusal to change the ending of *The Quiet Don*. Or he might have been offended by the fact that all the recognition that his own military genius received in the entire novel was just a brief mention in the text and a footnote crudely attached to chapter 23 of part 7. By contrast, Lev Trotskii, his archenemy, was represented in volume 3 by his orders and even appeared in person, in the earliest edition. In short, a man like Stalin would have no difficulty finding a dozen reasons to liquidate his fellow-man. Yet it was he alone who could and did save Sholokhov's life at the Politburo meeting. By that time he could have changed his mind out of political as well as personal considerations. The great purge was being slowed down, and Ezhov was probably already marked for liquidation as a scapegoat and as one who knew too much. It was a good time for Stalin to further the impression that he disapproved of NKVD wrongdoings and did what he could to right them. Besides, it would be more difficult to justify before the Soviet people and the world the liquidation of the well-known Sholokhov than it would be of a military or a Party leader or a less-known writer. Stalin could have decided that the Party needed a young Soviet writer of Sholokhov's stature to enhance its own prestige as a creator of cultural values. Roi Medvedev reports that Stalin let Sholokhov go with the words, "Good working conditions must be created for the great Russian writer Sholokhov.'' Stalin needed an obedient literary great to replace the late Gor'kii.[137]

By saving the lives of Sholokhov and his comrades, Stalin also could have counted on making the author his loyal and sincere supporter. Indeed, this is just what Sholokhov appears to have become. During Stalin's lifetime he naturally could not avoid repeating platitudes of the dear-father-and-leader type. At times, however, he could have been less generous with his tributes. At the Eighteenth Party Congress Sholokhov spoke of ''the most profound human modesty of comrade Stalin.'' In a sickening dithyramb on the dictator's seventieth birthday, he said that Stalin had become ''the greatest of mankind.'' When Stalin died, the author eulogized him as ''the most humane of all people.''[138] These glorifications may look like parodies. They assert the exact opposite of what Stalin was. They are still embarrassing to the Soviets and are not reprinted in collections of Sholokhov's works. The titles of the articles containing the last two statements are omitted from scholarly bibliographical and biographical sources.[139] Yet Sholokhov seems to have had at least some admiration for Stalin, and his eulogies ring sincere, if exaggerated.

The reasons for this admiration can be both personal and political. Stalin made possible the publication of Sholokhov's works, granted his request for grain, and did not liquidate him in 1938. Stalin made a favorable impression on the author during their personal contact, which recalls the impression Nicholas I produced on Aleksandr Pushkin. ''Stalin,'' Sholokhov said in 1967, ''had always pleasantly struck me with his inner charm, profundity of thought, and propriety.''[140] Sholokhov, of course, needed more than his personal experiences to form an opinion of Stalin. He could not but know of the dictator's responsibility for the unprecedented terror and repression. But here the political element enters into the picture. From the time Sholokhov joined the Communist Party, he unconditionally committed himself to support every aspect of its policy at any given moment. To a Soviet Communist, Stalin was the incarnation of the Party's will and brain; he acted in the name of the Party. To praise Stalin was to praise the Party, the Soviet way of life. The intensity of ideological and political commitment in a totalitarian state requires one to disregard the errors and crimes of its leaders. If in the second half of the 1920s Sholokhov might have sympathized with the political neutrality of Grigorii Melekhov, he turned into a Mishka Koshevoi after joining the Party. Loyalty might well be one of his most distinguishing traits. He was loyal to his friends at the times when this virtue was in short supply, and he has apparently been loyal to his family. Perhaps his loyalty to Stalin had something to do with his refraining from publicly criticizing the dead leader under Khrushchev. He also might have felt that it was unwise to expose Stalin because such a policy would undermine the authority and prestige of the Party. Sholokhov seemed to be concerned with this point as late as 1970, when he tried to vindicate Stalin's role during World War II: "One should not distort or belittle Stalin's activity during that period. First, this is dishonest; second, it is harmful for the country, for the Soviet people."[141]

After Stalin's decision to spare him, Sholokhov was showered with honors bespeaking a steep rise in his official standing. At the end of November 1938 he was nominated for membership in the Soviet Academy of Sciences and became a full member on January 28, 1939. Three days later he was decorated with his first Order of Lenin. In March he participated as a delegate in the Eighteenth Party Congress. But his real success was in the field of literature. Part 8 of *The Quiet Don* was finally serialized in the double February-March issue of *Novyi mir* for 1940. The same year saw its publication in the *Roman-gazeta* series and in book form, a total of 500,000 copies. On March 15, 1941, Sholokhov was awarded for *The Quiet Don* the recently established Stalin Prize, which included 100,000 rubles in cash. The same year the first four-volume edition of the novel came out in one book.

The appearance of volume 4 of *The Quiet Don* was impatiently awaited by millions of readers. To many of them the novel was the greatest and most interesting work of Soviet literature. The critical reaction to the completion of the novel was enthusiastic. *The Quiet Don* was acclaimed as a real epic, a great ideological and artistic accomplishment by a writer of the new socialist type. David Zaslavskii claimed that volume 4 demonstrated the accuracy of Stalin's predictions regarding the development of military operations, while Iurii Lukin introduced the author to his readers as "a genuine pupil of Stalin."[142] Dissonant voices were few. The critic A. Bek contended that *The Quiet Don* did not belong to socialist literature, but was rather a culmination of the fellow-travelers' line in Soviet fiction.[143] Some critics believed that Sholokhov failed to present Koshevoi as a typical Bolshevik. Koshevoi appeared to them too shallow, artistically unconvincing, and lacking valid political and psychological motivations for his actions.[144] A few commentators felt that Sholokhov should have written more about Grigorii Melekhov's service with Budennyi's Red cavalry.

The fate of Grigorii presented a real challenge to the critics. They had to explain why this likeable protagonist ended his life as an adversary of the Bolsheviks. The denouement punctured the official myth that the middle Cossacks had at last sided with the Bolsheviks. One group of critics advanced the thesis that toward the end of the novel Grigorii ceased to be a typical social type. Goffenshefer, for instance, asserted that in part 8 Grigorii was no longer a seeker of social truth, but of personal peace. In Ermilov's opinion, Grigorii lost his right to be regarded as a tragic hero because the motivations for his actions had become too petty.[145] The other group of critics explained that Grigorii ended the way he did because he broke away from the people. This was for them the tragedy of a man with great potential who was prevented from finding the right path by his ideas and habits formed during tsarist times.[146] Soviet critics still have not reached a consensus on Grigorii's reasons for turning away from the Soviet regime.

On the second day of the Soviet-German war Sholokhov sent a telegram to the people's commissar of defense. He asked the commissar to put his Stalin Prize money into a defense fund and declared himself ready to defend "the socialist homeland and the great cause of Lenin and Stalin to the last drop of my blood."[147] His earliest contributions to the war effort were three sketches describing in a patriotic vein the response of the Don Cossacks to the German invasion and to Stalin's speech of July 3.[148] In August 1941, as a reporter for *Krasnaia zvezda* (*The Red Star*), Sholokhov came for a few days to General Ivan Konev's Nineteenth Army, fighting near Smolensk. What he saw and heard inspired him to write several sketches about the confidence, efficiency, and high spirits of the Red Army, as well as about what he believed to be an incipient demoralization of the German army. Three of these sketches (about the Germans) appeared in Soviet newspapers shortly after they had been written. Three others, originally intended for publication abroad, were printed only in 1965.[149] Sholokhov's next sketch, "Na iuge" ("In the South"), published in *Pravda* on February 28, 1942, described the demoralization of the Germans and their allies on the southern front. On June 22, 1942, the first anniversary of the war, *Pravda* published Sholokhov's story "Nauka nenavisti" ("The Science of Hatred"). The story was in full harmony with the intense propaganda of hatred for the Germans. Next day it appeared in *Krasnaia zvezda* and well over a million of its copies were issued in 1942 in pamphlet form. Soon after the appearance of the story Sholokhov met with Stalin. The dictator reportedly found that it was as timely and necessary for the current phase of the war as was Gor'kii's novel *The Mother* for the revolutionary movement.[150]

This success notwithstanding, "The Science of Hatred" was the last short piece published by Sholokhov during World War II. No more stories or sketches appeared over his signature. Explaining why he turned away from topical writing, Sholokhov confessed in 1949 that newspaper work was simply not for him. He said he lacked the ability to write quickly and trenchantly. He preferred to present his subject matter, not in the form of a sketch, but in a broader context, so that he could provoke thoughts in the reader's mind.[151] His war sketches are not among the writings that Sholokhov cares to keep in his memory. Asked by an interviewer whether he remembered his first reporting from the war, he replied: "Reporting?

No. But I remember how the stanitsa saw off its men to the front. I remember the tears, . . . the first rally.''[152] Indeed, it is impossible to forget the continuous wailing of crowds of women gathered on the banks of the Don River to bid farewell to their departing kinfolk. It is likewise impossible to forget the steamers packed with drinking, singing, and dancing Cossacks, trying to suppress their anxiety on their way to the front. But such scenes are not to be found in Sholokhov's sketches. Instead, they are full of jingoistic pronouncements by enthusiastic Cossacks and in one of them there appears a woman who claims she would handle a tank more efficiently than her husband.

It did not take long for the chief editor of *Krasnaia zvezda*, David Ortenberg, to realize that Sholokhov had serious difficulties with his newspaper assignments. The editor suggested that the author go to different sections of the front and write anything he wanted. Sholokhov agreed.[153] Not much is known about his visits to the front and it is not always easy to tell legend from the truth. Thus the story of how Sholokhov gave a volume of *War and Peace* to a group of soldiers fighting near Stalingrad enjoyed wide circulation in the Soviet press for at least twenty years. In a 1975 interview Sholokhov called this story ''an idle invention of some journalist.''[154]

During the war Sholokhov began to write a novel called *Oni srazhalis' za rodinu* (*They Fought for Their Country*). Whether this meant compliance with Stalin's wishes is not quite clear. In any event, when Stalin talked to Sholokhov about ''The Science of Hatred,'' the dictator said that it was time to start writing a novel about ''the holy, national war of liberation.''[155] The title Sholokhov chose for his novel suggests a somewhat less solemn and more intimate approach. His title, he later explained, meant that every soldier fought for what was to him his particular country—his home, his garden, his river, his beloved, his children. The word *rodina* in the novel's title should therefore not be capitalized.[156] The novel was projected as a trilogy. The first volume would cover the initial stage of the war, the second would deal with the battle of Stalingrad, and the third with the expulsion and defeat of the Germans.[157] Excerpts from the novel appeared almost simultaneously in *Pravda* and *Krasnaia zvezda* in May and November 1943 and in February and July 1944.[158] Numerous pamphlet-form editions were published in 1943-1945. All the excerpts deal with a Red Army unit engaged in bitter defensive fighting in the Upper Don region in July 1942.

This was also precisely the time when Sholokhov's archive was lost. There are at least four basic versions of how it happened.

1. Manuscripts of *The Quiet Don*, readers' letters about the novel, and various papers were either destroyed by German bombs that hit the author's

house or disappeared when the house was looted. (Sholokhov to Veniamin Vasil'ev, on June 9, 1947.)

2. Manuscripts, letters, and part of Sholokhov's library were taken to Stalingrad by an army truck in July 1942, stored in the city library, and subsequently destroyed in their entirety during the street fighting. The rest of the archive and the library perished later in Veshenskaia. (Lezhnev, based on information he received, possibly from Sholokhov, in or about 1949.)

3. "My entire archive . . . manuscripts of *The Don Stories, The Quiet Don*, and *Virgin Soil Upturned*, correspondence with Stalin and Gor'kii, and other valuable materials were handed over by me to the local archive for safekeeping. I hoped they would save them, but it turned out as if I had thrown them into an abyss. It is inconceivable how they lost that archive." (Sholokhov to Priima, April 1955.)

4. In the fall of 1941 Sholokhov came to Veshenskaia to evacuate his family to the east of the Volga River. At that time he handed over to the Veshenskaia NKVD office a box containing rough drafts of *The Quiet Don*, chapters from volume 2 of *Virgin Soil Upturned*, Stalin's letters and telegrams, his Stalin Prize certificate, and rare foreign editions of his works, for safekeeping. The swiftness of the German advance in July 1942 compelled the Veshenskaia authorities to retreat with such haste that they abandoned Sholokhov's archive, among others which they had, on one of the stanitsa's streets. (Anatolii Sofronov, 1961.)[159]

Versions one and two do not inspire much confidence. They arose during the time when the actual culprit could not be named. It could be that a part of Sholokhov's archive was destroyed by bombs or perished in Stalingrad, but that part certainly would not include the most important items the author wanted to preserve. These items are listed by him in version 3. This version reveals a great deal, though it still conceals the culprit in the euphemism "local archives." Version 4 dots the i's. It tells an essentially true story. In fact, in November 1941, when the Germans were moving on Rostov, Sholokhov came to Veshenskaia to take his family to the town of Nikolaevsk on the Volga. A few months later he would make the mistake of bringing his family back to Veshenskaia.[160] It was quite natural for the author to entrust his archive to the most powerful institution whose members would do their best to get out of Veshenskaia in case of a German threat. The only thing that Sholokhov failed to foresee was that these people would be much more concerned with their own safety than with his archive. The behavior of the Veshenskaia NKVD men was, however, not atypical. I know of a case where their colleagues fled from a Don stanitsa, leaving behind a heap of undestroyed documents that included files of their secret agents. Ironically, the Veshenskaia NKVD personnel did not have to run away in such a hurry. The stanitsa was never occupied by the Germans. To capture it, they would have to cross the Don, a potentially costly operation. In July 1942 Veshenskaia was not of strategic significance to the Germans because their main blow was directed southward.

There still exist divergences in later accounts concerning the disappearance of Sholokhov's archive. Some make no secret of the NKVD involvement; others go back to versions one and two. A great deal apparently depends on the individual writers and censors. Occasionally, the same author provides, or is compelled to provide, conflicting information. One 1975 article by Priima, for instance, puts the blame for the loss of the archive where it belongs. But his other 1975 article, which was intended for foreign consumption, speaks of "the local authorities."[161]

It is not known what efforts, if any, Sholokhov made to save or find his archive. In July 1942 he came to Veshenskaia for a rest that he needed after suffering a concussion in an airplane accident.[162] But in a very short time the front moved towards Veshenskaia and he began to evacuate his family. It was during the evacuation that his mother was killed in the family's yard by a German bomb.[163] Perhaps by that time the NKVD men had already left Veshenskaia or Sholokhov was too preoccupied with his family to care about his archive. He first took his family to Nikolaevsk, but two weeks later moved to the village of Dar'insk, near the town of Ural'sk in Kazakhstan. The family lived in Dar'insk, Kamyshin, and Moscow until the early spring of 1945 when Sholokhov brought them back to Veshenskaia. During all this time he continued visiting various sections of the front, and there is no evidence that he conducted any extensive search for his missing archive.

For five months Veshenskaia was the scene of trench warfare. Some parts of Sholokhov's manuscripts were used by the soldiers for rolling cigarettes, other parts were seen in the hands of local civilians, and still other parts were salvaged by officers, to be eventually returned to the author. Veshenskaia's authorities lived in villages some dozen miles away from the stanitsa and showed apparently little or no concern for Sholokhov's archives.[164] By that time Sholokhov's old friends from the local administration were no longer working in Veshenskaia.

As of now, only one officer, a commander of a tank brigade, is known to have returned to Sholokhov over a hundred pages of the manuscript of *The Quiet Don* in 1945.[165] In 1955 Sholokhov told Priima that Stalin's letter had been found in East Prussia, and then he stated: "The writer Vsevolod Vishnevskii, somewhere here, near our Dudarevka, in the front lines, intercepted by sheer coincidence about two hundred pages of the manuscript of the first volume of *The Quiet Don* and sent them to me.

Everything else perished without a trace.''[166] This statement is pure fancy. Dudarevka is about twenty-five miles from Veshenskaia, and Vishnevskii's published diaries prove beyond any doubt that during most of the war he lived in besieged Leningrad and had never been on the Don front.[167] Moreover, where are the two hundred pages of volume 1 of *The Quiet Don* that he is supposed to have intercepted? In 1968 Priima, as curator of the Sholokhov fund, received from the author 136 handwritten pages and 109 typed pages of *The Quiet Don*. These, Priima says, are the pages that were returned to Sholokhov by the commander of a tank brigade.[168] The articles by Sofronov and Priima dealing with this collection leave one with the impression that most, if not all, of its pages are from volumes 3 and 4.[169] There cannot be over two hundred pages of volume 1 among them. And how does Sholokhov's assertion that ''everything else perished'' tally with the reports that the tank brigade commander gave him over a hundred pages of the manuscript of *The Quiet Don*? There are too many incongruities in Sholokhov's statements to assume that he had been misquoted. Those who know him personally describe his memory, perhaps with some exaggeration, as ''mighty,'' ''unique,'' ''magnificent,'' or ''absolutely unusual and astounding.''[170] But somehow, at a certain point in his interview with Priima, his imagination must have gotten away with him.

I have never read about any portion of the manuscript of *Virgin Soil Upturned* as having been rescued. A sizeable number of handwritten and typed pages of Sholokhov's early stories can be found in the archive of the Institute of World Literature (IMLI) in Moscow. But these, in all probability, are the texts that the author had sent to the publishers in the mid-twenties.

The first years after the war Sholokhov was preoccupied primarily with *They Fought for Their Country*. Stalin is reported to have urged him to complete the novel quickly.[171] Already in September 1945 the author said he wrote many new chapters, some of which would probably be published in *Pravda* and *Krasnaia zvezda*.[172] It was, however, only in 1949 that four excerpts appeared simultaneously in *Stalingradskaia pravda* (*Stalingrad Truth*) and *Pravda*.[173] They continued the story of the fighting that was the subject of the 1943-1944 installments. At this point the narrative was getting too monotonous and the author had to switch to new characters and situations. The new scenes must have been already written. On August 5, 1949, *Stalingradskaia pravda* reported that Sholokhov ''had completed the first volume of the novel.''[174] But, from then on, work on the novel seemed to have gone in reverse. In March 1951 the author said that volume 1 was nearing completion, whereas in 1952 he spoke of working at the same time on the last volume of *Virgin Soil Upturned* and volume 1 of *They Fought for Their Country*.[175]

If Sholokhov was having difficulties with his war novel, he must have had no easier a time with his novel about collectivization. In the years 1946 to 1953 official optimism and the false idealization of Soviet life in fiction reached their peak. Publication of an even mildly realistic work on collectivization was out of the question. Moreover, volume 1 of *Virgin Soil Upturned* and *The Quiet Don* in its entirety had to undergo a thorough political and stylistic revision. Their bowdlerized versions appeared in 1952 and 1953, respectively.

On the other hand, Sholokhov became a more productive journalist than ever before. One of his pieces was a panegyrical obituary of Andrei Zhdanov, the enforcer of Stalin's literary policy in 1946-1948. There appears to be a streak of masochism in praising "our dear Andrei Aleksandrovich" for "the irreconcilability and mercilessness inherent in a genuine Bolshevik" with which he "fought against the shortcomings in our work."[176] This kind of "fighting," also conducted after Zhdanov's death, was precisely the reason why in the 1946-1953 period Sholokhov was unable to publish any new literary works save the four excerpts from *They Fought for Their Country*. These excerpts amounted to about fifty printed pages, less than one-third of the combined length of excerpts from the same novel published in 1943-1944. Sholokhov's political journalism of the 1946-1953 period is of the most vituperative and narrow-minded kind. Its main features are a condemnation of American leaders and foreign policy, coupled with an inordinate praise of the Soviet people, the Soviet regime, and, particularly, the Party. In terms of fabricating false accusations, Sholokhov the journalist rivals Andrei Vyshinskii, the prosecutor at the Moscow show trials of 1936-1938, but surpasses him in terms of virulence and personal insults. President Harry Truman, for example, is called "an American fascist in a white gown! [of the Ku Klux Klan]. . . . His eyes are as shameless and impudent as those of Hitler, Göring, and Himmler. He is the incarnation of human baseness in the past and in the present; he is the despicable bigot from the White House. . . ."[177]

Stalin's death prompted a revival of Sholokhov's literary activity. His immediate plans were to complete *Virgin Soil Upturned*. "Having put everything aside, I am now preparing the second volume of this novel for publication," he said in February 1954.[178] In April 1955 he said that in trying to write a good book he worked more slowly on volume 2 than he had on volume 1. Some chapters had been rewritten seven or ten times. There were still things to be done, including three last chapters with which he had continuous difficulty.[179] By the New Year he began to speak of sending the book to the printers in the first half of 1956 and then of resuming work on *They Fought for Their Country*.[180] In March 1958 he wrote that he had finished *Virgin Soil Upturned* and would complete volume 1 of *They Fought for Their Country* in the fall of that year.[181]

All these statements were in part supported by action. The year 1954 saw the appearance of several chapters of *Virgin Soil Upturned*.[182] From March 28, 1955, to February 12, 1960, the work was serialized in *Pravda* at irregular intervals. At the same time installments of varying size were printed in several publications, primarily journals. Yet the complete text was not published before January 1960.

An explanation for this delay was offered by Harrison Salisbury. According to Moscow literary circles, the publication of volume 2 was deferred for nearly two years because high officials in the Party propaganda apparatus objected to the ending—the suicide of its hero, Semen Davydov, imprisoned on false charges during the purges of the thirties. For a year Sholokhov would not yield. At the end of August 1959, Khrushchev visited him at Veshenskaia and invited him to join his party on a trip to the United States. Soon after his return to the Soviet Union (September 28), Sholokhov apparently gave in and *Pravda* began the serialization of the final section of his novel. In the United States Sholokhov denied having any trouble with the ending, and it is not certain what made him give in—the stimulus of the trip or a piece of advice given by Khrushchev.[183]

Sholokhov replied with a vigorous and nasty denial, contending that the published denouement (Davydov is killed by a former White officer) had been conceived in the course of his work on the novel's first volume.[184] This is impossible to verify. But we know that in the early thirties Sholokhov did not intend to include the 1932-1933 period of the so-called kulak sabotage in volume 2 of *Virgin Soil Upturned*. And this would be precisely the period when Davydov could be falsely accused of aiding the saboteurs and imprisoned. To reach the purges of 1936-1939 in *Virgin Soil Upturned*, Sholokhov would have to add more than one sequel to volume 1 and he did not plan to go beyond volume 2. Some insight into his later designs is provided by his statement to Priima in April 1955: "How the novel will end? It's hard to say. I am now pondering over the ending. I can definitely say one thing—the finale will be dramatic, there will be deaths." When Priima inquired whether Davydov would die, the author replied: "I can't say that. But it will be as life's truth commands. Those were harsh times, the struggle was to the death, and the victims were many."[185] This struggle, in Sholokhov's words, was the struggle "between two worlds," ending with the victory of collective farming and socialism. The above statements seem to indicate that if Davydov were to be among the victims, he would have to be killed by the outright enemies of the regime, such as former White officers. On the other hand, Davydov's imprisonment by the Soviet regime could also be blamed on "the enemies of the people'' who allegedly wormed their way into high Party and government positions. These were precisely the people whom Sholokhov in Stalin's time, and Priima in 1955, blamed for the repression of local Communists in 1933.[186]

It could well be that in 1955, as Sholokhov said, he was still ''pondering over the ending.'' He might have toyed with the idea of placing his characters in the 1932-1933 period, but it was probably not easy for him to make a firm decision. The political climate in 1955 was uncertain. Many aspects of Stalinism still persisted and Khrushchev had yet to consolidate his position as the new leader. But after Khrushchev's secret speech at the Twentieth Party Congress in February 1956, Sholokhov could have given serious thought to making Davydov's death that of a dedicated Communist innocently perishing under conditions generated by ''the cult of Stalin's personality.'' There is an indirect indication supporting this hypothesis—the interruption of the novel's serialization in *Pravda* from January 1956 to April 1957. This was by far the longest break in the entire history of the serialization. It occurred after seven excerpts had been published in the same newspaper in 1955 and one on January 1, 1956. Moreover, it occurred after Sholokhov had stated that volume 2 of the novel would go to press in the first half of 1956. It might be suggested that during this break Sholokhov was reworking the rest of the novel to adjust it to the ending culminating with Davydov's imprisonment.

In April 1957 three new excerpts appeared in *Pravda*, and a month later Sholokhov said that the ending of *Virgin Soil Upturned* would not go beyond the events of 1930.[187] It is not clear, however, why at this point the serialization of the novel in *Pravda* was held up again for more than a year, until May 25, 1958. In any event, if Sholokhov had the intention of placing his characters in the 1932-1933 period, he must have given up this plan before the summer of 1959. By April of that year, eighty percent of volume 2 had been published in *Pravda*. Yet the novel was still set in the summer of 1930 and the narrative was so slow and uneventful that a sudden jump into the dramatic 1932-1933 period would have ruined the work artistically. More than a few chapters would have been needed to portray the events that would lead to Davydov's imprisonment. Also, contrary to Salisbury's assertion, *Pravda* did not begin, but rather interrupted, the publication of the novel's final part after Sholokhov's return from the United States. Three excerpts appeared in *Pravda* in August 1959, two weeks before Khrushchev's visit to Sholokhov, but the next excerpt came out four months later. A fully satisfactory answer to the controversial question about the ending of *Virgin Soil Upturned* can, of course, be given only after an examination of the novel's rough drafts and manuscripts or on the basis of other solid evidence, neither of which is available at this time.

The earliest complete version of volume 2 of *Virgin Soil Upturned* was published in the Leningrad monthly *Neva* for July 1959 and January 1960. At about the same time it appeared in the journals *Oktiabr'* and *Don* and in the *Roman-gazeta* edition. In 1960 it was also brought out in four book-form editions combining both volumes and was included in two editions of Sholokhov's *Collected Works*. Altogether more than two and a half million copies of the complete text of volume 2 came out in 1959-1960. High by any standards, this figure is particularly impressive in view of the perennial shortage of paper in the Soviet Union.

The critical response was predictable. Volume 2 could not but be a great victory of socialist realism. The author was said to be looking at his characters through the eyes of the people and of the Party and revealing significant processes taking place in the life of the entire nation. In tune with Khrushchev's emphasis on the ties between the people and the Party, the critics lauded Sholokhov for showing how the Communists had gained the trust, respect, and affection of the people. The Communist characters, it was said, in their private lives displayed a new morality based on humaneness.[188] A few mild criticisms mentioned the excessive talkativeness of old Shchukar', the stiffness of a Party secretary, and the occasionally odd behavior of the village Communists, such as the shooting of cats by Razmetnov.[189] On April 22 (Lenin's birthday), 1960, Sholokhov was awarded the Lenin Prize for both volumes of *Virgin Soil Upturned*. He subsequently donated the financial component of the prize (75,000 rubles) to the construction of a school in Karginskaia.

The only other literary work Sholokhov managed to publish in a complete form after Stalin's death was the story "Sud'ba cheloveka" ("The Fate of a Man") printed in *Pravda* on December 31, 1956, and January 1, 1957. This New Year's gift, a blend of human drama and political propaganda, was warmly received by the critics as a work demonstrating the vitality, optimism, and moral and patriotic virtues of the average Soviet man.[190]

At one point Sholokhov seemed to have successfully resumed his work on *They Fought for Their Country*. The year 1954 saw the publication of what had come to be regarded as the novel's opening chapter, set in the spring of 1941.[191] But then began the familiar story of setting dates for completion and of not delivering on time. In the 1950s Sholokhov spent much time on *Virgin Soil Upturned*, but the situation did not improve significantly after its completion. In August 1960 the author signed a contract for the publication of his war novel with a Danish publisher and spoke of completing its first volume in November of that year.[192] His statements in January 1964 and October 1965 referred to the first volume as being in the process of completion.[193] In 1969 there appeared in the Western press reports that the Soviet authorities had held up the publication of the novel. The authorities were said to be dissatisfied with the depiction of the retreats of Soviet troops in 1941 and 1942. The portrayal of Stalin's political and military leadership appeared to be too critical to them. And they objected to the description of life in Soviet prison camps.[194]

A month later four excerpts from the novel appeared in four consecutive issues of *Pravda*, beginning with March 12. The excerpts are set in May-June 1941. Sensitive political issues are raised in the dialogues about Stalin's role during the 1936-1939 purges. One of the characters is a Red Army general who had spent four years in prisons and camps as a result of false charges leveled against him in 1937. What the characters say about Stalin, possibly in a censored version, is in conformity with the official view of him advanced under Brezhnev. Stalin shares the blame for the purges with his top NKVD officials, but is believed to have been misinformed and misled by them. He is given full credit for carrying out industrialization and collectivization. Life in prison camps is referred to only fleetingly. The 1969 excerpts constitute one-fourth of the entire published text of the novel. There can be little doubt that Sholokhov had more material ready for the printers. According to Zhores Medvedev, he was compelled to remove a chapter dealing with the NKVD's unlawful methods of investigation and with life in prison camps. Censors, Medvedev wrote, had been instructed not to pass anything about the camps. Sholokhov's attempts to see Brezhnev failed.[195]

That Sholokhov had difficulties with *Pravda* can be seen from the reply he gave in June 1969 to the question of whether he would continue the publication of his novel. "This does not depend on me," he said, frowning, "the editor of *Pravda* says that a newspaper is not a journal and it is not obliged to print everything in sequence."[196] Sholokhov must have felt deeply hurt by the editor's statement. He valued his long-time association with *Pravda*. When, during a hunting trip in the remote steppes of Kazakhstan, Sholokhov learned that he had been awarded the Nobel Prize for *The Quiet Don*, he refused to talk about it to any newsman, for he, as an old *Pravda* man (*pravdist*), would grant his first interview only to a *Pravda* reporter.[197] In September 1969 Sholokhov made another revealing remark. Noting that World War II memoirs of outstanding Soviet generals started to appear many years after the war, he commented: "This means that it's not so easy to write truthfully about the greatest of all the wars. The task of a writer is more complex than that of a memoir writer. I think a novel about the war will be written somewhat later."[198] It is very likely that the author was also speaking about the impossibility of portraying even limited truth in his own war novel.

In June 1970 Sholokhov, replying to a remark that readers were waiting for new chapters from *They Fought for Their Country*, said that his work on the novel was not progressing at the pace he would have liked. But then, he added, he was not in a hurry. Haste was dangerous at his age.[199] This reply, given for publication to a *Komsomol'skaia pravda* reporter, obviously does not tell the whole truth. In 1975 Sholokhov expressed the intention of getting busy with the novel in earnest as soon as the celebration of his seventieth birthday was over. He said that the completion of the novel was "not far off." He even hinted about what would happen to some of its characters.[200] However, no new fragments have come out since 1969. Can it be that Sholokhov is writing "for the drawer" hoping that "somewhat later" his war novel, or its parts, will be publishable?

The political climate has not been the only adversity interfering with Sholokhov's creative work. People constantly turn to him as a member of the Supreme Soviet with all sorts of problems and complaints. Many approach him for money. In a five-month period financial requests amounted to 1,600,000 rubles. One of them came from a newly wed couple who needed money to buy a cooperative apartment, the only thing they needed to obtain "full happiness." For the same reason a young man demanded cash for a Moskvich automobile. Such requests are particularly irritating to Sholokhov since they bespeak the materialistic aspirations of Soviet youth.[201] Much time is taken up by uninvited visitors. Although many reporters may not be very happy with his treatment of them,[202] Sholokhov appears to be more tolerant of chance visitors. In the late thirties, my friend Boris Bylinkin, then a teenager, once paid an unexpected visit to him in Veshenskaia together with two other persons. The author chatted amicably with them and showed them foreign editions of his works. Olga Andreyev Carlisle, a visitor from the West, was warmly received by Sholokhov in Moscow in 1960.[203] One visitor, in 1964, was greeted with particular affection, Grigorii Kondrat'evich Zhuravlev, a Don Cossack. For several years, in more than a hundred articles, he was glorified in the Soviet press as the sole survivor of some eighty Red Cossacks whose execution is portrayed in volume 2 of *The Quiet Don*. "The author of *The Quiet Don*," wrote Sholokhov's friend Petr Gavrilenko, "invited the hero of his wonderful book who had miraculously saved himself. They were photographed together. The writer gave Zhuravlev a copy of his novel *The Quiet Don* with a warm and cordial inscription."[204] Two years later Zhuravlev, in Gavrilenko's words, was exposed as a "pretender and adventurist who at one time had fled from the dispossession of the kulaks in the Don region to the Amur region."[205] It is a pity that Zhuravlev's story, with its numerous public engagements, receptions, and celebrations, will probably never become the subject of a play or a picaresque novel. Zhuravlev's performance eclipses that of Khlestakov. The latter's task was easier, for there was no KGB in Gogol''s time.

To get away from visitors must be one of the reasons why almost every year since the end of the war Sholokhov has made a trip to Kazakhstan, where in 1960 he built a house on the shore of the Ural River, near the town of Chapaev.[206] The other reason is his passion for hunting and fishing, which are also the favorite pastimes of his wife. Hunting and fishing must take more time from his writing now than they did at the time he worked on *The Quiet Don*. Intemperate drinking may be another cause of his low output after the war.

A decline in Sholokhov's literary production contrasts sharply with the increase in reprinting of his works in the Soviet Union. There were some 300 prewar editions numbering 15 million copies.[207] By January 1, 1980, almost 79 million copies were published in 974 editions. The printings of *Virgin Soil Upturned* totaled 16.5 million copies. The number of *The Quiet Don* copies is reported to be over 15 million.[208] To this should be added millions of copies published in 1980 in connection with the seventy-fifth anniversary of Sholokhov's birth.[209] The reprintings, however, do not bring as much in royalties as do new works. In 1971, at the Twenty-Fourth Party Congress, Sholokhov raised the question of changing the provisions of the copyright law which permits a situation to exist in which a book with "the highest ideological and artistic merits" brings the author progressively less money with each publication, until it is included in a collection of his works.[210] Whether Sholokhov had himself in mind is a moot question. Be that as it may, six editions of his *Collected Works* have been issued since 1956 for a total of some 2 million eight-volume sets.

In his speeches and journalistic writings Sholokhov has continued to propound the same hard Party line as he did in his obituary of Zhdanov. At the Twentieth Party Congress he thanked the Party for its firm ideological guidance of literature.[211] A Soviet writer, he said in 1970, must speak from any rostrum as a Communist, as an exponent of a revolutionary-humanistic view of the Party and the people.[212] He has been one of the most vicious attackers of liberal and free-thinking authors. Boris Pasternak was to him "a hermit crab" and "an internal émigré."[213] He spoke slightingly of *One Day in the Life of Ivan Denisovich* and called its author a Colorado beetle that eats Soviet bread but serves his Western bourgeois masters by secretly sending his writing abroad.[214] His most notorious remark concerned Andrei Siniavskii and Iulii Daniel' who, in February 1966, were sentenced to seven and five years in prison camps, respectively, for publishing their works of allegedly anti-Soviet content abroad. Incensed by those who thought that the sentences were too harsh, Sholokhov implied that had the two writers—"these rascals with black consciences, . . . these turncoats"—been caught during the twenties when one was tried, not in accordance with specific articles of law but "in accordance with the revolutionary sense of justice," they would have been shot.[215] Strangely enough, the solemn formula of "the revolutionary sense of justice" occurs in volume 2 (chapter 21) of *Virgin Soil Upturned* in an entirely different context. In a comic episode, which the critics were not enthusiastic about, the chairman of a village Soviet goes about the village shooting cats like "bandits," "in accordance with the revolutionary sense of justice."

Sholokhov's statement about the convicted writers cannot be justified, but, perhaps, it can be explained. Sholokhov is one of those on whom the purges of the thirties left an indelible imprint. The terrible experiences of 1938, Roi Medvedev believes, drastically changed his personality, breaking him morally and psychologically.[216] Sholokhov knew of so many people, among them his close Communist friends, who were falsely accused, tortured, or shot that Siniavskii and Daniel' could easily appear to him real enemies because they said a few unflattering things about Soviet life and had their works published in the West. This kind of mentality is peculiar not only to people like Sholokhov but to certain average Soviet citizens as well. Once I criticized the trial of Siniavskii and Daniel' in a conversation with a former Soviet citizen, who as a young woman was deported to Germany for forced labor, liberated by the Red Army, and then sent to Soviet prison camps. Her reaction was: "They got what they deserved. I spent several years in camps for nothing, but they at least did something."

With all his dedication to the regime, Sholokhov is one of the sharpest and boldest critics of Soviet conditions. An expert in agriculture, he has repeatedly spoken of the appalling mismanagement causing enormous losses in grain and livestock in collective farms.[217] Certainly, he blames individuals, not the system. But any impartial observer knows that the incredibly low productivity of collective farms and Soviet dependence on foreign grain are rooted in the Soviet organization of agriculture. Sholokhov is exasperated by seeing in rural *raion* centers hundreds of bureaucrats doing no productive work whatsoever. Indeed, he complains, "things are just like in a well-known saying, 'One is with a plough while seven are with spoons.' "[218] He is also bitter about the agricultural authorities who do nothing to combat the erosion of soil and drought.[219] At the Twenty-Third Party Congress he protested vigorously against the reckless pollution of the Volga River and Lake Baikal. Then he said: "I have, comrades, a personal problem. The quiet Don is perishing." The delegates began to applaud, expecting the author to say something amusing as he infallibly does in his speeches. But he went on to say that seven million cubic meters of industrial sewage were being dumped into the river every year. This contamination, coupled with certain fishing methods promoted by the Ministry of Fishing Industry, threatened the fish life in the Don with virtual extinction.[220]

Sholokhov's statements about life in the West represent the same mixture of realism and crude propaganda as do his statements about his own country. He does not conceal his admiration for the efficient farming and cattle breeding in Europe, Japan, and the United States. At the same time he did not hesitate to describe the United States to his Veshenskaia fellow-villagers as a land of contrasts where "next to millionaires there are masses of unemployed subsisting on banana peels."[221] This observation was made after the two-week trip to the United States with Khrushchev's party.

Some of Sholokhov's utterances on Soviet literature sound very much like those of Andrei Zhdanov at the First Congress of Soviet Writers. Soviet literature, the author declared in 1964, is "the most advanced literature in the world." It possesses an indisputable advantage over its Western counterpart, because it adheres to socialist realism and—the main thing—it is inspired by the ideology of Marxism-Leninism, which it propagates in artistic images.[222] On the other hand, no Soviet author has publicly said so many harsh words about his fellow-writers and about Soviet literature as Sholokhov. His speeches at writers' and Party congresses are known for their blunt criticism of the low quality of Soviet fiction and of the fact that the overwhelming majority of Soviet writers prefer to live in cities, especially Moscow and Leningrad, and do not care to know anything about the life of industrial workers, Party officials, or engineers, let alone rural life.[223] These criticisms describe the effects, not the cause. Sholokhov, naturally, cannot say that the deplorabe state of literature in the Soviet Union is above all created by his Party. Most of the Soviet writers live in cities, because cities are better supplied with goods and offer much more cultural and recreational opportunities than the long-neglected countryside. Every Soviet writer knows that if he were seriously to study the life of a factory worker or a collective farmer and describe it the way it really is, his work would not be printed. So why bother to "study life"? After all, socialist realism is not what one sees, but what one hears. By July 1981 membership in the Union of Soviet Writers had grown to 8,773.[224] This army of professional writers can exist only on governmental pay, and the Union's members enjoy a privileged status in terms of remuneration and social prestige. Perhaps all but a hundred of the Union members would be compelled to do something other than creative writing in the competitive West, but in the Soviet Union they can successfully produce fiction, knowing full well that what counts first is not knowledge of life or creative ability, but political conformity.

Sholokhov himself emphasized this scale of values in his speech to the delegates of the Twenty-Second Party Congress: "Like all of you, I am above all a Communist and only then a writer."[225] A Communist writer in the Soviet Union has to be particularly careful to adhere to the Party line. Had Sholokhov joined the Party in 1925, there would not have been *The Quiet Don* as we know it. About three-fourths of the novel was written before he became a Party member. During the work on volume 4 the newly fledged Communist in him was not yet strong enough to conquer the author of the three preceding volumes, and the novel was saved. But by that time the censors had already done considerable work on the first three volumes and on the early stories. And they were going to do much more on these and other works later.

Censorship of Sholokhov's works was of two basic types: political and puritanical. The majority of political corrections were aimed at presenting the Bolsheviks and their regime in the most advantageous light. This objective was accomplished primarily by deleting passages which might convey a negative impression of Bolshevik policy as well as the behavior, character, and appearance of individual Communists. Puritanical censorship eliminated what was judged to be out of tune with the moral or aesthetic education of Soviet citizens. In this case the censors dealt with a variety of things such as sex, offensive odors, gory details, foul language, unpleasant appearance, coarse manners, personal uncleanliness, and certain parts of the body. A good deal of censorship was done by the editors of publishing houses who examined Sholokhov's works before sending them to official censors for final approval. Thus the revision of the early stories between 1925 and 1932 was carried out chiefly by their editors rather than by official censors of Glavlit, an acronym for the Central Administration for Literary Affairs and Publishing Houses.

Printed and reprinted in various newspapers, journals, collections, and separate editions, the stories were exposed to the whims of dozens of editors. In several instances the earliest printed text differed more from the original than the subsequent editions. On the other hand, most of the stories escaped much tighter censorship between 1932 and 1956 because only five of them were reprinted during this period. The rest were deemed unworthy of publishing due to their relative objectivity and stark realism. The first collection of the early stories to appear after 1931 turned out to be volume 1 of the 1956-1960 edition of Sholokhov's *Collected Works* brought out by Molodaia gvardiia. The 1956 censors made several corrections pertaining to the Bolshevik leaders, but by and large their work amounted to choosing between several versions in which some of the stories came out during the 1925-1931 period. In most cases they steered a middle course, rejecting the heavily censored versions and accepting individual political and puritanical revisions. With a few exceptions, the texts of stories printed in 1956 have become standard for later editions.

The reader who wants to acquaint himself with the early texts should turn to the 1926 edition of *The Don Stories*. He should approach with caution the 1931 edition of *The Tulip Steppe*, which contains heavily distorted versions of "Aleshka's Heart," "A Woman Who Had Two Husbands," and "The Foal." The early stories are available in English in two volumes: *Tales from the Don* (Putnam, 1961; Knopf, 1962) and *One Man's Destiny and Other Stories, Articles, and Sketches, 1923-1963* (Putnam, Knopf, 1967). Altogether there are twenty-five stories and two feuilletons in these collections. Only two stories, "Galoshes" and "The Wind," and the feuilleton "The Inspector" are left out. The translator of both volumes is H. C. Stevens (pseudonym: Stephen Garry), who also translated *The Quiet Don* and *Virgin Soil Upturned*. His work is occasionally marred by serious errors. In the Soviet Union six identical stories were brought out by Progress Publishers in collections entitled *Early Stories* (1966) and *Stories* (1975). Both English and Soviet translations are based on the standard editions appearing since 1956.

Pre-1952 editions of *Virgin Soil Upturned* underwent only a minor political reworking and a moderate puritanical purge, resulting in the removal of half of the obscenities from the characters' speech. By contrast, a few sporadic editions for secondary-school students came out with lengthy cuts of a political nature and consistent excisions of obscenities and passages dealing with intimate relationships. The revised 1952 edition exemplifies the impact of the postwar policy on a work that was well-nigh beyond reproach in the 1930s. It turned out that the novel was in need of numerous corrections to improve the image of local Communists and to elicit more respect for Stalin. The censors also removed descriptions of lovemaking, gore, and other "dirty" details, and cleansed the narrative and dialogue of words and forms considered inappropriate or ungrammatical. The immediate reason for the linguistic purge was the publication of Stalin's brochure *Marxism and Problems of Linguistics* (1950). The censors proceeded from the dictator's statement that the grammar and vocabulary of modern Russian differ little from Pushkin's language and that any attempt to create a new language within a short period of time would disrupt communication among people. The Soviet literary lawgivers declared a merciless war on neologisms, jargon, dialecticisms, obscenities, and coarse words. All these elements, in their opinion, had an adverse effect on the power of literature to communicate the ideas of the Party and of Communism to the broad masses.

All political and nearly all puritanical revisions made in 1952 were rescinded in the 1957 edition of *Virgin Soil Upturned* included in Sholokhov's *Collected Works*. At the same time the official criticisms of "the personality cult" led to the deletion of several adulatory references to Stalin in the scene of the collective farmers' meeting at which the Gremiachii collective was named after him. This scene vanished altogether in the 1962 edition of *Collected Works* after Stalin had been attacked sharply at the Party's Twenty-Second Congress in the fall of 1961. The words "named after Stalin" were also gone from wherever they appeared in the designation of the Gremiachii collective farm in both volumes. Yet Stalin's name was preserved in less laudatory or neutral references. Subsequent editions of *Virgin Soil Upturned* followed the text printed in the 1962 edition of *Collected Works*. Exceptions are some of the 1970s editions (e.g., Moskovskii rabochii, 1971, 1975) which restored the scene of naming the Gremiachii collective farm after Stalin in the abbreviated version found in the 1956-1960 Molodaia gvardiia edition of *Collected Works*. The treatment of Stalin remains the main distinguishing mark between the post-1962 editions of the novel. If one wants to know more about Stalin, obscenities, and the Don Cossack dialect, one would be advised to read the 1932-1933 editions.

The first English translation of volume 1 of *Virgin Soil Upturned* was done by the Co-operative Publishing Society of Foreign Workers in the USSR. It appeared in 1934 as *The Soil Upturned*. Volume 1 is also available in identical English translations first published in 1935 in Great Britain and in the United States. The American edition bears the title *Seeds of Tomorrow*. Volume 2 came out both in England and America as *Harvest on the Don*, in 1960 and 1961, respectively. These translations are preferable to those brought out in the Soviet Union between 1956 and 1980. Entitled *Virgin Soil Upturned*, the Soviet translations are based on the revised 1952 version of the novel and include later excisions concerning Stalin.

The Quiet Don suffered much more from political censorship than either the early stories or *Virgin Soil Upturned*. While the 1928-1931 editions of the first two volumes show only sporadic political and puritanical revisions, the bulk of volume 3 received harsh treatment at the hands of the *Oktiabr'* editors in 1932. Its serialized version was mutilated by extensive omissions intended to play down Red brutalities that caused the Upper Don uprising. The first 1933 edition restored several lengthy excisions, but endorsed many shorter deletions and introduced two dozen additional corrections. In the same year the first two volumes were subjected to political, puritanical, and stylistic revision. Volume 2 became the principal victim of political intolerance. The greatest damage was done to the portrayal of Bunchuk and Anna. The censors' purpose was to strip their

1. From left to right: An interpreter, M. Sholokhov, and F. Shakhmagonov, Sholokhov's secretary. Prague, 1958

2. M. Sholokhov in Prague, 1958

3. M. Sholokhov after dinner, 1961

4. M. Sholokhov's house in Veshenskaia, 1961

5. The porch of M. Sholokhov's house

6. The Don and Veshenskaia, 1957. M. Sholokhov's house marked with a cross

7. A cove of the Don as seen from M. Sholokhov's garden

relationship of intimate, emotional, and romantic elements which would weaken Bunchuk's image as a steadfast Bolshevik. In part 5 the censors cut half of chapter 16 and expunged the whole of chapter 25. The 1935 edition reveals an intensive purge of obscenities. The prime targets were some eighty instances of *matiuki*—curses involving the use of the word "mother" in combination with the Russian equivalent of the all-too-familiar four-letter verb. Although the verb was never printed in the novel in full, about 60 percent of *matiuki* were banned. The censors of the 1936-1941 editions removed names of prominent purge victims. The 1945 edition, the first after the war, shows the influence of official nationalism. Its censored passages include unpatriotic and internationalist statements by Marx and Lenin. The 1946-1949 editions remained unchanged.

Then came the bowdlerized 1953 version. Some four hundred political corrections were made during the preparation of its text, three-fourths of them in volume 2. My estimate is very conservative, since identical or nearly identical corrections were counted as one. Not satisfied with the numerous deletions, the censors inserted passages stressing accomplishments of Lenin and Stalin and condemning the White movement. In making some three hundred puritanical revisions, the censors went as far as to remove hair from hands, legs, and chests of male characters. Political, puritanical, and hundreds of linguistic and stylistic emendations spelled the end of *The Quiet Don* as a historical and artistic work. The 1953 edition is known as Stalinist, though every volume of it was approved for publication and issued after the dictator's death. The 1955 edition for tenth graders (high-school seniors) rescinded a few of the 1953 political corrections, but made new excisions in passages about sex.

It was the text printed in the 1956-1960 Molodaia gvardiia edition of *Collected Works* that signaled a departure from the 1953 version. The 1956 editors rejected about three-fourths of the political and about nine-tenths of the puritanical revisions made in 1953. The 1956 text had served as a model for all editions until 1965, when the Rostov edition reinstated a dozen of the 1953 corrections connected with the 1917-1918 events. With minor alterations these corrections were incorporated into the 1965 text published in *Collected Works* marking Sholokhov's fiftieth birthday. A few more restorations appeared in the 1980 edition of *Collected Works*.

The number of unrestored political corrections made in *The Quiet Don* between 1928 and 1980 exceeds 250. The impact of all these corrections, ranging from one word to several pages, distorted to a considerable degree Sholokhov's original representation of the Red camp. That the novel still remains a fairly objective and remarkable work of art is first of all due to the fact that the portrayal of the Red camp occupies relatively little space in it. The censors, fortunately, showed more concern for friend than foe.

Scores of full-blooded Cossack characters were permitted to live the lives of normal human beings, while their Red adversaries were being depersonalized to meet the artificial standards of political and moral behavior. The second important reason for reducing the impact of censorial intrusion was Sholokhov's resistance to political insertions which are much more harmful to a work of art than deletions.

The available documentary evidence indicates that Sholokhov was of little help to the censors. He made some revisions in the first three volumes of *The Quiet Don*. Yet, as early as September 1932, he notified the editorial board of Khudozhestvennaia literatura that he "would make no further corrections, excisions, or additions" in his novel.[226] He insisted that in the first separate edition of volume 3 the board should restore an unspecified number of passages which had been high-handedly censored by the *Oktiabr'* editors. He also asked the board to reprint the first two volumes from the text of the 1929-1931 editions brought out by the State Publishing House.

It did not take much time for Sholokhov to learn that his requests and decisions carried no weight with the censors. The ink had hardly dried on his letter when his newly appointed censor-editor, Iurii Lukin, embarked on an extensive political pruning of *The Quiet Don* for its 1933 edition by Khudozhestvennaia literatura. Sholokhov had no choice but to accept Lukin's editing since it was performed in accordance with the Party's literary policy of the day. Shifts in this policy must have brought about all or most political changes made in *The Quiet Don* between 1933 and 1946 and particularly in the 1953 edition. In this edition Sholokhov's obligatory compliance with the authoritative political views was especially evident. A case in point: the revisions prompted by Stalin's statement about Sholokhov's portrayal of local Red leaders during the Civil War. "The prominent writer of our time Comrade Sholokhov has made in his *The Quiet Don* a number of blunders and outright erroneous assertions concerning Syrtsov, Podtelkov, Krivoshlykov, and others," Stalin wrote in a letter on July 9, 1929.[227] The letter was first published in 1949 and Sholokhov immediately wrote to the dictator asking him for a more detailed description of the alleged "errors." There was no reply.[228] Naturally, the censor-editor of the 1953 version, Kirill Potapov, played it safe with Stalin. He thoroughly revised the personal and political images of Podtelkov and expunged a few passages involving Krivoshlykov. He could do nothing about Syrtsov, whose name had already vanished from the novel.

That Sholokhov did not initiate all or most political corrections found in the 1953 version of *The Quiet Don* can be inferred from his letter of September 6, 1951, to Anatolii Kotov, director of Khudozhestvennaia literatura. In it Sholokhov complains about wasting his time on restoring the majority of Potapov's "castrating deletions." The author probably speaks here only of stylistic and, possibly, puritanical excisions, for he sees the root of the trouble in Potapov's lack of artistic taste, in his being a "very mediocre journalist."[229] Apparently Sholokhov was not in a position to protest against political revisions, especially those connected with Lenin and Stalin.

We do not know to which volume or volumes of *The Quiet Don* Sholokhov refers in his letter to Kotov. Nor are we able to tell what percentage of his restorations was accepted by the censor. An exceptionally high number of various corrections in the 1953 version suggests that Potapov disregarded the majority of these restorations.

The censor's disrespect for the author is manifest in Potapov's attempt to misrepresent Sholokhov's role in the preparation of the 1952 edition of *Virgin Soil Upturned*. The censor marked the page proof of this edition as "printed from the text newly examined and revised by the author." Sholokhov changed this designation to "examined and revised edition."[230] He obviously wanted to dissociate himself from the bowdlerization with which he had little or nothing to do. The censor endorsed the change. The 1952 version came out as "revised edition." The identical designation appeared in every volume of the 1953 edition of *The Quiet Don*. This seems to be the most Sholokhov could achieve to signal his noninvolvement in the mutilation of his works. He won a battle, but the censor won the war. The words "revised edition" were passed off as referring to the author's editorial work, and critics heaped praise on him for a job well-done.

Sholokhov undoubtedly took part in the preparation of the first edition of his *Collected Works*. Each volume of this edition was published as "revised by the author," and the great majority of revisions made in the bowdlerized versions of his novels were rescinded. However, the exact extent of Sholokhov's editorial effort is difficult to establish.

In sum, Sholokhov's participation in editing his works extended chiefly to reviewing censorial revisions. His ability to disagree with the censors varied, depending on the political climate of a given period. He could do very little between 1933 and 1954, but possessed noticeable authority during the preparation of his first edition of *Collected Works*. His own political and puritanical corrections must have been scarce. By and large he has remained faithful to his 1932 decision not to make any further revisions in *The Quiet Don* and, by implication, in *Virgin Soil Upturned*.

To get the best possible idea of the original text of *The Quiet Don*, volumes 1 and 2 should be read in their pre-1933 editions and volume 4 in its pre-1945 editions. No single edition of volume 3 is satisfactory. Its 1933, 1935, and 1936 editions are the most nearly complete and are clearly superior to the 1932 *Oktiabr'* version. Its chapters published in 1930 in various journals and the booklet *The Year 1919* present a good supplementary reading.

English translations of *The Quiet Don* are known under the titles *The Silent Don, And Quiet Flows the Don*, and *The Don Flows Home to the Sea*. The second title combines volumes 1 and 2; the third, volumes 3 and 4. All British and American editions of the novel use the same translation in which the original text is abridged by about twenty-five percent.[231] This also applies to the paperback editions published by the New American Library, which display the words "Complete and Unabridged" on the cover. English translations of *The Quiet Don* published in the Soviet Union in the 1960s and 1970s represent a revised and expanded version of the British-American editions. Soviet translations have a single title, *And Quiet Flows the Don*, and are divided into four volumes. Based on the 1956 and 1965 editions of *The Quiet Don*, the Soviet translations are more nearly complete than their British and American counterparts. Although this advantage and the improved translation make the Soviet editions preferable to the Western editions, they are still a far cry from the earliest texts of *The Quiet Don*. A new Soviet translation of *The Quiet Don*, by Robert Daglish, was announced in 1980. It is to be a part of an English language edition of Sholokhov's *Collected Works* prepared in Moscow by Progress Publishers.[232]

CHAPTER II
PHILOSOPHY OF LIFE AND IDEOLOGY

The Role of Nature

A clue to Sholokhov's view of life can be found in the closing paragraphs of volume 2 of *The Quiet Don*. They depict the grave of Valet, a Red soldier killed by the Cossacks. He was buried according to Christian practice, with his head to the west. In two weeks the small mound was overgrown with luxuriant and fragrant grasses. An old man set up at the head of the grave a little chapel with an affixed image of the Virgin and an inscription in Old Church Slavic: "In the years of strife and trouble, / Brother, judge not thy brother." The author goes on:

> The old man rode away and the chapel remained in the steppe to sadden the eyes of passers-by with its eternally mournful aspect, and to stir in their hearts a vague and sad longing.
>
> Later, in May, bustards fought around the chapel, beating out a little bare patch in the blue wormwood, crushing the green flush of ripening quitch grass; they fought for their hens, for the right to live, to love, to multiply. And after a while, right by the chapel, under a mound, in the shaggy shelter of the old wormwood, a hen bustard laid nine smoky-blue, speckled eggs and sat on them, warming them with her body and shielding them with her glossy wings (2:375).[1]

Here Sholokhov expounds a sort of pantheistic view of life as eternal. Christian teaching is cogenial neither with the spirit of man nor the laws of nature. It imbues man with dejection and is incompatible with the natural principle of fighting for the right to live, love, and procreate. Sholokhov does not deny that religion can have a mollifying effect on the behavior of true believers. One encounters in *The Quiet Don* old Cossacks who condemn on religious grounds looting and raping during the war (1:106, 262). On the other hand, the young Cossacks are presented as having lost their faith during World War I. If God existed, Grigorii Melekhov thinks, He would not have allowed such carnage to happen. Front-line soldiers, according to him, "have abolished God, leaving Him to old men and to women" (4:421). The opposing sides became even more embittered during the Civil War when the Reds openly preached atheism and the Whites who professed faith could not restrain themselves from acting contrary to Christian principles. A vivid example of this dichotomy is the mass execution of the Podtelkov men carried out at Easter. It is not difficult to discern Sholokhov's animosity toward organized religion. Priests appearing in his early stories—"Aleshka's Heart," "The Shame Child," and "The Way and the Road"—are greedy, callous, cruel, and dishonest. They are not much better in *The Quiet Don*. Next to a rather neutral description of a priest headed for the front at the beginning of World War I (1:321-322), Sholokhov draws markedly unpleasant portraits of two local priests. Father Pankratii is "a shrewish scandalmonger"; Father Vissarion, though "affable by nature," is said to have had syphilis and to be living with a mistress (1:115). The actual Father Vissarion, upon whom the fictional priest was modeled, was a well-educated person who owned a large library. The young Sholokhov borrowed many books from him and listened to his admonitions on the importance of good reading. In a 1975 interview the author spoke of Father Vissarion more kindly than he did in his novel: "And although I have always been and remain a confirmed atheist, I remember his lessons with gratitude. Father Vissarion had the reputation of being a talented priest, but he was more learned than his clerical status would imply."[2]

A question arises: Does the atheist Sholokhov apply the laws of struggle found in nature to human society? To a degree he does. The fight of the bustards at Valet's grave has something in common with the human fight in which Valet perished. At the same time one feels that the struggle in nature is presented as something more justified, spontaneous, and productive than human hostility. It is a struggle for the perpetuation of life. The biological stimuli of this struggle are more acceptable than the political and ideological motivations of human wars. In this respect the fight between the birds at Valet's grave acquires a particular significance, since the preceding chapter portrays the execution of the Podtelkov Cossacks.

In a number of important landscape descriptions associated with war, the emphasis is laid, not on the struggle in nature, but on its beauty and the abundance of vital forces in it. Nature is contrasted with man's actions and placed above him in a way reminiscent of Tolstoi's condemnation of war in "Sebastopol in May" through the juxtaposition of putrid corpses and a flowery vale. The cruel destruction of human lives during the Upper Don uprising takes place against the background of the spring "brilliant with unusual beauty" and the steppe "filled with inexpressible charm" (3:262). Detailed depictions of mutilated and decomposing bodies of the Cossacks killed in action give way to either a "quiet and tender" autumn landscape dominated by "the stern and silent beauty of the forest" (4:218), or to a page-long portrayal of the steppe in April, when, "made fecund by the spring, an invisible, almighty, and palpitating life was unfolding in the steppe'' and when ''hidden from the rapacious human eye, conjugal couples of birds and beasts, big and small, were mating in their secret steppe lairs'' (3:319).

As if the contrast between human self-destruction and the life-creating forces of nature were not sufficiently sharp, the author brings in ''the rapacious human eye,'' implying that indeed it is not birds and animals that are rapacious but man. This is not the only case of man's humiliation when compared to animals. Of Mishka Koshevoi, who observes the lives of horses, Sholokhov says that ''he gained a profound respect for their intelligence and their nonhuman nobility.'' The mating of horses, ''this primeval act, accomplished in primitive conditions, was so naturally wise and simple that it involuntarily aroused in Koshevoi's mind a comparison with human beings that was not in the latter's favor'' (3:61).[3] Man is degraded most profoundly before nature in a passage with sarcastic overtones describing the vigorous life in the steppe right after the burial of the old man Sashka, who was senselessly murdered by the Reds:

> On the earth which had just accepted the merry horselover and drunkard Sashka, life was still seething as furiously as ever. In the steppe that crept in a flood of green to the very edge of the orchard, and in the tangle of wild flax around the fence of the old threshing floor, one could hear the incessant pulsating call of the quail; gophers were whistling, bumblebees were humming, the grass rustled under the wind's caresses, the skylarks sang in the vibrating haze of the hot day, and confirming the grandeur of man in nature, from somewhere a long way off down the dry valley came the persistent, angry, and muffled rattle of a machine gun (4:47-48).

The machine gun is anonymous. It does not matter whether it belongs to the Whites or Reds. It is a symbol of human malice, arrogance, and destructiveness. A similar anonymity is found in the scene in which Grigorii Melekhov and Prokhor Zykov come across the dead body of a beautiful young woman (4:73-74). It is not stated who killed her. However, the earliest printed version of the scene contained a detailed account by Prokhor ascertaining that the woman, who had been retreating with the Reds, was caught, raped, and murdered by the pursuing Cossacks.[4] It was probably the author, not the censor, who removed this information in order to focus on cruelty and destructiveness per se. On the other hand, someone also deleted an episode that could be interpreted as a symbolic expression of the eternity of life and the oneness of the beauty of nature and man. We have in mind Grigorii's picking a large bouquet of immortelles and placing them on the face of the dead woman. He did it irrationally, "obeying an irresistible desire."

Life goes on regardless of whether the Whites kill the Reds or vice versa. The same indestructible life dominates the landscape in the scene of the atrocious murder of the Red commander Likhachev (3:196-197) and in the description of the grave of the executed Petr Melekhov, a White Cossack officer (4:194). There is no exaggeration in saying that if one wants to know Sholokhov's view of life, one should go to his graves. It is there that he transcends his ideological limitations and raises his art to the level of universality, treating the eternal subject of life and death with a purely human touch. This is also true of descriptions of graves and nature in his last completed and most orthodox work, volume 2 of *Virgin Soil Upturned*, particularly in the final scene.

Death for Sholokhov is first of all the extinction of a human being, not of a political friend or foe. In 1932 an important official in the government of the North Caucasus Region reproached the author for the manner in which he portrayed the death of Petr Melekhov. The reader, the official stated, should rejoice in the fact that a White bandit, a vermin, was shot. Yet the death of this inveterate counter-revolutionary is perceived by the reader through the eyes of his brother, also a counter-revolutionary. "Is this the way a proletarian writer should write?" the official demanded. "This is the way it came out!" Sholokhov replied. And, when the official left the room, he said to a friend: "He cannot or does not want to understand the most important thing in life and in the relations between people: death is death. Whether an enemy or one of our men dies, it is death all the same!"[5] It was the thought of the imminent death of a human being that ran through Sholokhov's mind during and after his visit to the imprisoned Cossack officer Aleksandr Senin, an episodic character in *The Quiet Don* and the prototype of Polovtsev in *Virgin Soil Upturned*. "I just came from the prison cell, where I talked to Senin," the author told his friends, "I talked to him, looked at him, and thought: soon this man will be no more. And Senin knows perfectly well that one of these days he will be shot."[6] The whole evening after the meeting with Senin, Sholokhov was engrossed in his thoughts and more reticent than usual.

The atheist Sholokhov views the sun as *the* life-generating force. He speaks of "life that repeats itself under the solar cycle" in *The Quiet Don* (3:196) and unequivocally calls the sun "the eternal source of life" in *They Fought for Their Country* (7:9). The sun is assigned a dominant role in a number of landscapes, especially those representing the vitality of nature. Thus a lengthy portrayal of a spring landscape brimming with life is capped with a respectful reference to "a proud and lofty sun" (3:284), and in all three novels we encounter natural scenes "haloed in sunlight" (3:319; 4:47; 6:264; 7:141).

Natural life under the sun proceeds parallel to human life. The belief in the unity of man and nature constitutes the main reason why Sholokhov's works, notably *The Quiet Don*, are permeated with analogies relating man's actions and inner experiences to the world of nature. Man, of course, has his own peculiarities not inherent in nature. He can readily surpass nature in cruelty and destructiveness. On the other hand, the complexity of his spiritual and emotional life is unknown to nature. After sabering four Red sailors in combat, Grigorii writhes in a fit of remorse on the rich black soil, imploring his subordinates to kill him. This eruption of feelings is contrasted with the insensitivity of the grass that "grows on the earth, indifferently accepting the sun and the rain" (3:267).

Nature also shows no compassion when a mortally wounded Cossack and the grief-stricken Natal'ia press themselves to "the unaffectionate earth" (1:356; 4:34, 146). Equally unconcerned is the River Don at the close of a chapter, where, after a detailed description of "the bitter-sweet life" of the village of Tatarskii with all its love, hate, and politics, the author observes that "glazed with the clear greenish-blue of autumn, the Don flowed on indifferently to the sea" (1:129).

The bond between man and nature is, however, more significant for Sholokhov than the difference between them, and this bond is not merely biological. For Sholokhov (as for Maksim Gor'kii) nature is the field of man's work. This is why Grigorii longs to plough the land instead of trampling wheat fields in the maneuvers of war (3:89-90). Life for Sholokhov, as for Pasternak, is a miracle, though not in the Christian sense. He simply marvels at natural life as such. Therefore he does not hesitate to characterize nature with such clichés as marvelous, enchanted, wonderful, magic, majestic, fantastic. These epithets are applied not so much in their banal, everyday sense but more in their literal meaning. They are used more frequently in the second half of *The Quiet Don* than in other works.

Since every form of life is a miracle, a man cannot force his artificial laws upon it. Iurii Zhivago ridicules attempts to reshape life as a lump of raw material, in accordance with political blueprints: "But life is never a material, a substance. Life, if you want to know, is the principle of uninterrupted self-renewal, it is eternally remolding, remaking, and transforming itself, and it is far beyond your or my silly theories about it."[7]

Sholokhov entertains a similar view when he asserts the impossibility of predicting the course of human life or of guiding it: "When swept out of its normal channel, life scatters into many branches. It is difficult to foresee which direction it will take in its treacherous and winding course.

Where today it trickles, like a rivulet over sandbanks, so shallow that its ugly shoals are visible, tomorrow it will flow rich and full'' (1:344). Elsewhere Sholokhov says, ''Life dictates its own unwritten laws to man'' (1:368), and numerous examples in *The Quiet Don* illustrate this point, including the confessions of the characters. Bitterly, Grigorii laughs about ''his queerly twisted life'' (1:377) and Anna Pogudko spends a long time ''thinking about her strange and drastically changed life'' (2:280).

Sholokhov is devoid of the officially optimistic view of life. The fates of his principal characters are bitter or tragic. For the most part Grigorii does not do what he wants, but what he is compelled to do, and he perishes. He is also involuntarily involved in the deaths of Natal'ia and Aksin'ia. Several principal characters meet a violent death in *Virgin Soil Upturned* as well. Grigorii's life is described as ''rich in sorrow and poor in joy'' (3:267), and that of Aksin'ia as ''long and poor in joy'' (4:15). Direct references to bitter, difficult, and joyless lives are made with regard to such different characters as Bunchuk (2:363), Grigorii's mother (4:304, 307), an Austrian soldier killed by Grigorii (1:261), and Iakov Ostrovnov's mother, whose ''life went on—like the life of everyone who lives—rich in long sorrows and poor in brief joys'' (6:19). To explain the hard lives of Sholokhov's characters exclusively in terms of social and economic conditions would be nearsighted. He treats life in its complexity and perceives its driving force—love—in a tragic context. ''The two sad friends and companions of almost every true love,'' he states in volume 2 of *Virgin Soil Upturned*, ''are separation and loss'' (6:313). This view is borne out in both of his novels.

The most significant love story in Sholokhov's works is that of Grigorii and Aksin'ia. It is a story of passion and unfulfilled hopes. The intensity of the characters' feelings is often depicted in traditional images derived from fire and heat. This is particularly true of Aksin'ia in volume 1, where at the beginning of their relationship the lovers ''ecstatically burned with one shameless flame'' (1:57). Of more interest, however, is the imagery drawn from the world of nature. This imagery attends the love story of Grigorii and Aksin'ia from its inception to the very end. The images associated with nature are used not only to convey the force of amorous obsession, but also the more subtle lyrical, dramatic, and tragic aspects of the love story. The central metaphor of this story is floral blooming, the symbol of love in folk poetry.

The first floral image to allude to the main feature of the budding relationship is the henbane. A tender agitating scent coming from Aksin'ia's hair makes Grigorii observe that it smells like henbane, ''a sort of white flower'' (1:35). The point here is that Grigorii calls henbane by a vernacular name, *durnop'ian*, that suggests intoxication. And the motif of love-intoxication permeates the next—and crucial—statement on the style of Aksin'ia's love: "A woman's belated love blooms, not like the scarlet flower of the tulip, but like that loco weed, the roadside henbane (1:52)." In addition to *durnop'ian*, the henbane is called here by a local term of *sobach'ia besila* that implies madness.

When Grigorii decides to break up his affair with Aksin'ia, her crushed love is symbolized by the chewed-up petals of the bindweed flower which he spits out, and by a field of flowering corn flattened by a herd of cattle (1:78, 94). But Grigorii soon leaves his wife for Aksin'ia, thinking of a happy life in the Kuban' region, "a welcoming land of blue skies, with Aksin'ia's passionate, late-flowering love, to boot" (1:162). The theme of hopeful dreaming has been added here to the leitmotif of blossoming.

The leitmotif is revived in volume 2, where Grigorii, continuing to love his unfaithful Aksin'ia, mistakes the scent of fallen leaves for "the fine intoxicating [*durnop'iannyi*] aroma" of her hair (2:44). Finally, in volume 3, after more than four years of separation, a reunion takes place on the shores of the Don, against a lyrical natural background in which "the poplars stood with their pale grey trunks in the water, rocking their naked boughs, and the willows, fluffy with blossoms—girls' earrings—luxuriantly rose over the water like thin wondrous green clouds" (3:307). This subtle watercolor harmonizes with the tender sadness of both characters and simultaneously represents a variation on the love and blooming theme which is developed further in Aksin'ia's observation that "a tree only blossoms once a year" and in Grigorii's question, "And you think ours has already blossomed?" (3:307).

Two pages later we learn that it has not. Aksin'ia's long-suppressed feelings burst out in streams of happy tears. The accumulation of feelings and their release are likened to the formation and downfall of an enormous block of snow which hangs over a cliff until it is dislodged by a gust of wind, and then plunges downward, crushing every bush in its way (3:310). In the case of Aksin'ia, the "gust of wind" happens to be Grigorii's tender greeting, and the avalanche of her reciprocal feelings turn out to be as destructive as the plunging block of snow. It is the night rendezvous with Grigorii, which Aksin'ia has arranged after their meeting, that induces Natal'ia to have an abortion, resulting in her death.

In the opening chapter of volume 4, Aksin'ia, on her way to Grigorii, is shown taking a rest surrounded by luxuriant late-spring vegetation. The languorous aroma of a lily of the valley—"already touched by mortal decay"—attracts her attention. Looking at the flower and inhaling its "mournful scent," Aksin'ia is unwittingly moved to tears (4:15). Then she falls asleep under a bush of eglantine and is gradually covered by its withering petals, shaken loose by the wind.

Both the dying lily and the fading bush of eglantine not only symbolize the approach of middle age for Aksin'ia but also introduce the motif of her impending death, which is enhanced by the presence of a cuckoo that "faintly and mournfully counted out someone's unspent years" (4:14).

Two years later, after various peripeties, Grigorii and Aksin'ia make an attempt to flee to the Kuban' region. The early motif of seeking happiness in this land of plenty is reiterated. The entire world seems to Aksin'ia exultant and bright. Her long-cherished hope of life with Grigorii seems to be coming true. When, during a halt, Grigorii lies down for a nap amid thick grass and flowers, Aksin'ia weaves a wreath of gay sweet-smelling flowers and lays it at his head (4:455). This wreath has a double meaning. As a wedding accessory it symbolizes a joyous union of the two characters; on the other hand, as a funeral accessory it indicates their imminent death. It is possible that the latter aspect is stressed by Aksin'ia's thrusting a few flowers of the prickly eglantine into the wreath, which can be taken as an allusion to the crown of thorns.

The death motif receives an added emphasis as soon as the fugitives resume their journey. As in folklore, nature foretells disaster. A bittern booms hollowly in the distance, the orchards look black and unfriendly in the mist, and the stillness of the night imbues Grigorii with anxiety and fear. A few lines later a Red soldier's bullet kills Aksin'ia. After burying her, Grigorii raises his head and sees "above him the black sky and the blindingly glittering black disk of the sun" (4:459). This black sun symbolizes more than the depth of Grigorii's grief. With Aksin'ia's death, he loses his will to live. Thus the sun—the generator of life in Sholokhov's view—has burned out for him.

The motif of blackness is immediately developed in the next and last chapter, which starts with a poignant comparison of the black barren steppe, scorched with fire, to the black life of Grigorii, whom death has deprived of everything dear to his heart (4:459-460).

In a few months Grigorii returns to surrender himself to the Soviet authorities. The cold sun in the concluding line of the novel emphasizes his alienation from the living world. The only thread left which ties him to life is his son, whose appearance in the final scene of the novel asserts the perpetuation of life. But Grigorii is already dead spiritually and is resigned to his physical destruction.

No doubt Grigorii will be shot. Not because Kharlampii Ermakov, Grigorii's prototype with respect to his military career, was executed in 1927, although, unlike Grigorii, he did not join anti-Bolshevik partisans in 1920-1921 and was in charge of a Red Army cavalry school from 1921 to 1924.[8] Nor because Fedor Melikhov, who commanded a small anti-Bolshevik detachment, was executed despite the fact that in accordance with the amnesty proclaimed in July 1921 he surrendered himself and his detachment to Soviet authorities.[9] Grigorii must die because Aksin'ia, his true love, is dead. He already knows of his end when he buries her, "firmly believing that they will not be parted for long" (4:459). This phrase announces his death. His execution by the Soviets is simply the most likely way his earthly existence will be terminated. Had he not lost his will to live when Aksin'ia died, Grigorii might have died in a different way or might even have survived. He might have escaped to the Kuban' region, for example, and lived there with the documents of the dead militiaman that he had in his possession. But this would not be an appropriate finale for Sholokhov's greatest love story.

For Grigorii the termination of is earthly life does not entail the end of his relationship with Aksin'ia. With his belief that they will not part for long, he expresses his confidence in the existence of some kind of afterlife. Does this mean that Grigorii, who lost his faith in God during World War I, could not reconcile himself with the loss of his love and was moved to view his and Aksin'ia's deaths in terms of resurrection and eternal life with which humans are believed to be endowed by God? Or did he always believe in a future life, regardless of his loss of faith in God's concern with peace and happiness? Whatever the answer might be, the belief in a life beyond the grave is professed by various other characters. Krivoshlykov is worried that he and Podtelkov may not recognize each other in the next world (2:362-363). The thought of meeting her husband after her death makes Dar'ia Melekhova happy (4:123). The Cossack Chumakov, who acts as an executioner in Fomin's detachment, is sure that he will be reunited with one of his comrades in the future life (4:437). And when the protagonist of "The Fate of a Man" goes to war, his wife prophetically tells him that they will no longer see each other in this world (7:598). All these references to the afterlife are made in extreme situations when the characters are close to their deaths and express strong feelings of love or friendship for each other. In this respect, Grigorii's thought of his impending reunion with Aksin'ia furnishes an additional proof that she was closer to his heart than Natal'ia.

As in the story of Grigorii and Aksin'ia, nature plays the dominant part in the descriptions of Grigorii's relationship with Natal'ia. These descriptions, however, are not marked by recurrent images of flowers and blossoms. Natural imagery associated with Natal'ia serves to underline the plight of a devoted but frustrated wife whose desperate actions run contrary to the basic laws of nature.

Abandoned by her husband and humiliated by her fellow-villagers, Natal'ia attempts to take her own life. The description of the suicide attempt is preceded by the portrayal of the Don liberating itself from winter ice.

The roar of the bumping floes merges with the ringing of the Easter bells (1:186). This scene not only creates an appropriate atmosphere for the arrival of the news that Natal'ia is near death, but also suggests the incompatibility of her action with Christian faith and—more importantly—with nature's coming to life in spring. This can be substantiated by the fact that the scene of Natal'ia cutting her throat is immediately followed by a repetition of the reference to the drifting floes and tolling church bells. The chapter ends with the observation that "the joyous, full-flowing, liberated Don was carrying its icy fetters away down to the Sea of Azov" (1:202). Here the indifference of joyous nature to Natal'ia underscores the unnatural character of her act.

Five years later the continuing coldness between Natal'ia and Grigorii is set off against a vigorous spring landscape, full of life-giving strength and fruitfulness, and eagerly awaiting the rain announced by distant thunderclaps (3:283-284). The fecundity of nature in this instance foreshadows, by means of contrast, the motif of Natal'ia's self-imposed infertility—her forthcoming abortion; the mention of faint thunderclaps is a prelude to the violent thunderstorm in volume 4.

During the thunderstorm Natal'ia curses the unfaithful Grigorii and implores God to punish him with death. Black thunderclouds, majestic and wild, burning white flashes of lightning, murmuring grass and bitter dust—all are in tune with the mood, posture, and action of the outraged woman (4:147). The subsequent rain reactivates the life-generating forces of nature. The steppe turns wonderfully green. At the same time Natal'ia makes the decision to kill the life within herself (4:149).

It is only in the last landscape associated with Grigorii and Natal'ia that nature appears in constructive harmony with the characters' wishes and actions. Grigorii, working in the field, suddenly experiences an urge to see his orphaned children. Natal'ia's last wish that he should take good care of them rings in his ears. On his way home he passes the stubble field full of rooks, with the old birds feeding the young ones (4:167). Until this episode the vitality of nature contrasted with Natal'ia's rejection of life, a tragic attitude for a woman who physically was "like a young apple tree in blossom—beautiful, healthy, strong" (4:156). This single blossom image is bestowed upon Natal'ia when she, on her deathbed, is seen through the eyes of Grigorii's mother.

Certain traits of Aksin'ia and Natal'ia are repeatedly mentioned in the novel to highlight differences between the two women. Aksin'ia's sensuality is accentuated by the use of the adjectives "avid," "shameless" and "wanton." At times these words occur in combinations, such as "shamelessly avid lips" (1:28) or "wantonly avid lips" (1:172; 2:44). Even Aksin'ia's beauty is described as "wanton" by a character and the author alike (3:56, 309). The outstanding feature of the bashful Natal'ia is her cleanliness, both physical and spiritual. No epithet characterizes her more aptly than "clean," and it figures prominently in the scene of her dying. Bleeding profusely from her abortion, she is worried not so much about her condition as about soiling the floor and "the clean bedding" with her blood (4:152). She asks for "a clean shift" and would like to be washed "clean" when she is dead (4:155). She wants her mother-in-law to dress her body in her green skirt—which Grigorii, she says, liked her to wear—and in her poplin jacket (4:155). Significantly, she means her light-blue jacket which she wore during her last meeting with Grigorii. It was then that her unfaithful husband displayed an unusual tenderness for her, being deeply touched by her "pure inner beauty" and her devotion to him (4:67-68).

This was the highest point in their relationship. Grigorii came to it gradually. His affection for Natal'ia grew out of his attachment to their children. And having become close to Natal'ia he found himself in a situation where he was willing to live with her and Aksin'ia, "loving each of them in a different way" (4:166). He would not abandon Natal'ia for Aksin'ia, as he did in volume 1. Thus Grigorii's love was bound to be divided between two women and diluted. The author was confronted with a situation that he could not allow to continue. Natal'ia had to disappear to make possible a complete reunion of Grigorii and Aksin'ia, and to allow the two lovers to give free reign to their feelings and dreams. Then their lives and hopes would be crushed to demonstrate the author's idea of the tragic predestination of a true love. Killing Natal'ia to achieve his ends, the author in a way redeemed himself by perpetuating her in the reader's memory. The description of her death belongs to the most moving and vivid passages in all of literature.

The third love story in *The Quiet Don* is the relationship between Bunchuk and Anna. Like the story of Grigorii and Aksin'ia, it asserts the supremacy of love and shows how the loss of the loved one affects the survivor. With the death of Anna, Bunchuk loses his will to live. He lapses into a state of complete indifference to everything, even to the Revolutionary cause. Memories of Anna haunt him until his death. As he is led to be shot, it seems that he is "looking forward to something unattainable and joyful" (2:366). He must have been imagining meeting Anna in the afterlife, without believing in its existence. Bunchuk's physical death is no less necessary than Natal'ia's. He cannot recover and go on living, because this would contradict the author's conception of a man who has lost his true love. Nor can he continue to exist in a state of prostration, because this would not be in agreement with the stereotyped image of a

Bolshevik. So the author thoughtfully puts him into the Podtelkov detachment to ensure a certain death for him.

Since the story of Bunchuk and Anna is set primarily in the city, nature is well-nigh absent from it, except for a few images tinged with sentimental romanticism. On the other hand, the bond between the two Bolsheviks has certain political implications not found in Grigorii's relations with his apolitical Cossack women. Apart from their feelings, Bunchuk and Anna are bound by their Marxist convictions. A Cossack and a Jewess, they are a living embodiment of Communist internationalism.

In *Virgin Soil Upturned* the realm of personal emotions is portrayed in the love experiences of Communists Davydov, Nagul'nov, and Razmetnov. Davydov is shown in relation to two women: the vain and dissolute Lushka, divorced wife of Nagul'nov, and the seventeen-year-old Varia, who drives oxen for the collective farm and embodies the purity and freshness of first love. The two love stories make an impression of stiffness and abruptness. Though Davydov's relationship with Lushka is described with humor and her portrait is vivid, the effect is spoiled by the author's desire to show how Davydov's association with an unworthy woman makes him neglect his duties as chairman of the collective farm. Their actual relations are relegated to the background and overshadowed by the judgment passed on them by the collective farmers and the Party secretary. In spite of his strong physical attraction to Lushka, Davydov's concern with his "authority" among the villagers makes him ask Lushka either to marry him or to break off the relationship. The proud woman scornfully rejects the suitor as a coward, and the relationship is cut short. And this is the way it must be for Davydov to remain the hero.

In the story of Davydov and Varia the devoted love of a selfless and innocent girl appears as a reward for Davydov, a compensation for what Lushka cannot give him. The beginning of the relationship is successfully portrayed in a gently humorous contrast between the calm, unconcerned Davydov and the loving girl who is longing for affection. But when Davydov responds to her love and decides to marry her, the relationship becomes unconvincing and artificial. Davydov's response is more rationalistic than emotional; he remains restrained and aloof. This aloofness may be partly attributed to Sholokhov's desire to underscore the chivalry and faithfulness of the working class in the realm of love, but his treatment is stiffly moralistic. It appears as if Sholokhov was in a hurry for Davydov to fall in love with Varia. Toward the end of the novel "at last it dawned on him that, without admitting it to himself, he had possibly loved this girl for a long time" (6:313). Yet, less than a month before, he intended to part with the girl, feeling that he was too old for her and not ready for serious love (6:110).

It was in connection with Davydov that the author expressed his concept of a true love, possibly out of a desire to stress that Davydov's love for Varia was precisely of this kind. The moment Davydov began to experience his "pure and unfathomable love," he felt that separation and loss, the two "companions of almost every true love," were reaching toward him (6:313). This is equivalent to the announcement of his impending death. A Communist protagonist, a hero of socialist realism, Davydov has to die because, in the author's view, he fell in love. Whether he should die in a Soviet prison or be killed by "the class enemy" appears to be a matter of finding the best way to liquidate him. Unlike Grigorii and Bunchuk, Varia survives the loss of her loved one. It would certainly be unrealistic and monotonous if both of the lovers invariably lost their lives in each case. It is enough that no real love has a happy ending in Sholokhov's works.

The description of the relationship between Makar Nagul'nov and Lushka begins with the breakup of their joint life. Because Makar loves Lushka he tolerates her promiscuity. This lasts until she embarrasses him politically by crying at the sight of her lover, Timofei Damaskov, being deported to the north as a son of a kulak. The depth of Nagul'nov's love is revealed to a greater degree in volume 2, where he comes in contact with Lushka during his hunt for the fugitive Timofei. Despite all his misogynistic tirades and superhuman self-possession, he appears as a suffering and magnanimous figure. A devoted revolutionary, he succeeds in controlling his emotions. Nonetheless, he realizes that it was precisely because of his and Davydov's preoccupation with political and administrative matters that Timofei outdid them in the business of love. If Lushka's hedonistic indulgence may appear excessive, the same can be said about the restraints that Nagul'nov and Davydov imposed upon themselves. Lushka is more than a lewd woman. She is full of *joie de vivre*, a quality that cannot but appeal to the author. Asked about his attitude toward Lushka, he cheerfully replied that he liked her.[10]

The only love story in *Virgin Soil Upturned* left unadulterated by social or political themes is Andrei Razmetnov's love for his wife, who committed suicide during the Civil War after having been raped and infected with venereal disease by the White Cossacks. The love is unfolded in moving reminiscences that strike a tragic undertone of irrevocability. These reminiscences run parallel to life in nature; in fact, they are provoked by a pair of pigeons that come to nest at Razmetnov's house. Razmetnov feeds them, and the sight of the male pigeon, who leaves all the food for its mate while circling about her, makes him recall his own courtship, marriage, separation and loss: "There arose in his mind the sorrowful image of the only one whom he had ever loved, more than life itself, it seemed, but not for long as he might have wished—the one from whom black death had parted him twelve years ago, perhaps on exactly such a glittering spring day'' (6:263).

Razmetnov goes to the graves of his wife and son and stands there with his grey head bowed low. At this point the author addresses the reader:

> Why did Andrei come here on this spring day that was radiant with the bright sun and brimming with awakening life? So that clutching his short strong fingers together and clenching his teeth, he could gaze with squinting eyes beyond the misty rim of the horizon as though trying to discern in the smoky haze his unforgotten youth, his short-lived happiness? Perhaps for this reason. Because the past which is dead but dear to the heart can always best be seen either from a cemetery or in the mute darkness of a sleepless night (6:264-265).

It is one of the key passages of the book. In it the author expresses anew his idea of the unity of man and nature. The bright spring day, teeming with life, symbolizes eternal renewal. The living, the dead, and nature form a single whole that cannot be destroyed or forgotten. The theme is underlined by the fact that the entire passage is repeated, virtually without change, at the very end of the novel, which may well be the place where Sholokhov chooses to reveal his innermost thoughts. Again Razmetnov stands at the grave and the same eternal nature surrounds him. These are the concluding lines of the novel:

> ''Not as I should, not neatly, have I kept your last abode, Evdokiia. . . .'' He bent down, picked up a dry clod of clay, rubbed it into dust in his palms, and in a voice already quite hollow said: ''And still I love you to this day, my unforgettable one, my only one for all my life. . . . You see, I don't have time. . . . We seldom see each other. . . . Forgive me, if you can, for all the evil I've done. . . . For all that hurt you . . . the dead.''
>
> He stood for a long time with bared head, as if listening and waiting for an answer; he stood motionless stooping like an old man. A warm wind blew in his face, a warm rain drizzled. . . . Beyond the Don sheet lightning flashed, and Razmetnov's stern and joyless eyes did not look downward any more, not at the caved-in edge of the grave so dear to him, but beyond the invisible rim of the horizon where half the sky, again and again, was illuminated by scarlet flames and where the last thunderstorm of the year, as majestic and violent as in a hot summer season, rumbled along, awakening dormant nature to life (6:383).

Thus the concluding passage strikes a deeply human note. Its effect, however, would not be so strong without chapter 21, containing Razmetnov's reminiscences and his first visit to the grave. It may well be that this chapter was written for the end of the novel. Chronologically, it does not belong to volume 2 at all; it is set in April, while the action in volume 2 begins in June. Yet the author placed it some hundred pages away from the ending so that the reader's impression of Razmetnov's love would still be fresh though not obtrusive.

The "majestic" thunderstorm in *Virgin Soil Upturned* and "the glittering world under the cold sun" in *The Quiet Don* are the very last words in the Russian texts of the novels. Their presence and position serve to accentuate the idea that above all man is a creation of nature rather than of the economic, social, and political environment. Human life in the broad sense, as an ingredient of natural life, is governed by love, procreation, and perpetual self-renewal. These forces constitute the core of life. There would be no political or social problems if humans ceased to be born. The inner lives of the anti-Bolshevik Melekhov and the Communist Razmetnov are shaped by basic natural forces. The difference in natural imagery associated with the two characters reflects no more than the difference in their situations. The "cold sun," as we have seen, symbolizes Grigorii's estrangement from earthly life. His single link to it is biological—his son—and only "for the time being." *The Quiet Don* ends in March, but there is no description or mention of the awakening of nature in the final scene. The author must have decided to keep natural imagery in tune with Grigorii's condition. In *Virgin Soil Upturned* the awakening of dormant autumnal nature by the thunderstorm corresponds to Razmetnov's awakening from his grief and his return to life. The thunderstorm, especially on a hot summer day, is a mighty stimulus to natural life. In *The Quiet Don* it makes the steppe turn "wonderfully green" (4:148). Razmetnov will not experience such a regeneration, of course. There will be no more true love in his life. And this will not be compensated for either by his activity as the new head of the local Party organization or by the life with his new wife.

The paramount significance that Sholokhov attaches to nature is further demonstrated by the fact that he frequently puts his landscapes in places where they are most likely to attract and hold the reader's attention, namely the beginnings and endings of the novel's divisions. Half of his early stories and many of their chapters or sections either begin or end with descriptions of nature, ranging from a brief sentence to a dozen lines. In *The Quiet Don* the first indication of the conceptual and structural importance of nature is given by the suggestive and symbolic title of the novel and by the epigraphs preceding volumes 1 and 3. The epigraphs consist of old Cossack songs about Father Don. In these songs natural processes occurring in the river are allegorically related to the Cossack past and to the momentous events of the novel: World War I, the Revolution, the Civil War, the Upper Don uprising of 1919, and the disappearance of the Cossacks as a distinct estate that formed in a unique environment during the course of centuries. Five of the novel's eight parts and over one-fourth of its chapters either begin or end with sketches of nature. The depiction of nature in the opening lines of a chapter often foreshadows its subject matter and tone, whereas nature appearing at the close of a chapter reveals the author's attitude toward its content.

Altogether there are about two hundred and fifty descriptions of nature in *The Quiet Don*, not counting those of less than two lines in length. Close to two hundred and fifty species from the animal and vegetable worlds appear in the novel, some of them (willow, poplars) as often as fifty times. Such abundance is eloquent testimony to the author's love and knowledge of nature, particularly that of his native Don country. This affection is expressed in the strongest terms at the end of a lengthy lyrical digression about the "dear" steppe: "Low I bow and as a son kiss your fresh earth, O you, Don steppe, soaked with unrusting Cossack blood!" (3:60). The patriotic theme of Cossack land and history is forcefully sounded in the metaphorical portrayal of "the mounds rising in wise silence, guarding the buried Cossack glory" (3:60), or in the old song about the heroic past of the free Cossacks (4:261). The Cossacks' devotion to their country is conveyed by the popular symbol of the bitter wormwood, which in foreign lands smells differently (2:107; 4:333, 447).

A sort of "Cossackization" of nature is evident in the fact that descriptions of nature are at times imbued with imagery associated with the Cossack way of life and folklore. One sees "the proud starry ways trodden by neither hoof nor foot," and "the moon—the Cossacks' little sun" (3:59). The Milky Way girdles the sky "like a silver-studded Cossack belt" (2:181), "lightning does trick-riding" (3:38), and the new moon and the easterly wind go "Cossacking" (1:366; 3:139). And faithful to folk poetry, Sholokhov uses *mesiats* for the moon; *luna* appears only once in all of his fiction (1:163).

The Upper Don uprising is presented as a movement kindred to the natural phenomena of the Cossack region. The *Vorgeschichte* of the uprising begins with a page-long portrayal of nature that, in the style of folk poetry, conveys the Cossacks' anxiety before the arrival of the Red Army and predicts war and destruction for them. A typical excerpt from it reads: "In the evenings, from behind the spears of the naked forest, the night lifted the enormous, red-hot shield of the moon. It glowed mistily with bloody reflections of war and fire over the still villages. And under its merciless, unfading light an indistinct anxiety was born in the hearts of people, and the animals fidgeted'' (3:107).

The Cossacks' anxiety increases when after the passage of the Red troops they expect the arrival of special punitive units. Here the condition of the Cossacks is compared to that of the snow-covered steppe which looks dead. In reality, the steppe is alive, because the winter rye planted in it in the fall will survive beneath the snow and sprout in the spring. When it is ripe, it will be cut down by the master and brought to the threshing floor (3:139-140). This passage can be taken as an allegory for the Upper Don uprising and the Cheka terror, for its earliest printed text contains the words ''rattling [*cheka*kaiushchie] blades of the mowing machine.''[11] One may add that winter rye can also symbolize the perpetual self-renewal of life. After threshing, grain will be planted again and a new cycle will start. Similarly, the life of the Cossacks will continue in spite of the bloody repression.

The main cause of the Cossack uprising is reflected in the behavior of the Don. Where its bed is wide the river flows quietly. But where ''the bed is narrow the imprisoned Don gnaws a deep channel for itself and swiftly drives its foamy, white-maned waves with a muffled roar'' (3:168). The same is true of the Cossacks: ''From the calm shallows of peaceful days life had fallen into a narrow channel. The Upper Don District started to seethe'' (3:168). The entire chapter goes on to describe the mounting unrest caused by arbitrary executions.

The beginning of the uprising is likened by a Cossack to the Don's freeing itself from its icy fetters (3:185). The rapidly growing scope of the uprising allows the author to speak of it as ''the wide flood'' that ''swelled, spread, and inundated'' the Upper Don District (3:197, 225). The ravaging effects of the uprising and the annihilation of the Cossacks and their own atrocities are summarized in a brief simile: ''Like an all-devouring steppe fire the uprising raged'' (3:261). This and all but one of the preceding references to nature in connection with the uprising appear at the very beginning of chapters and have a direct bearing on their content.

For what is regarded as a sociohistorical or epic novel, the part played by nature in *The Quiet Don* is exceptionally great. In its narrow function nature is introduced to lend to descriptions an air of reality or to provide a parallel or a contrast to human actions, conditions, and emotions. In its broader function nature serves to express the author's philosophy of life, accompanies the development of an event or relationship, and occupies strategic places in the novel's structure.

Compared with *The Quiet Don*, there are proportionately half as many descriptions of nature in *Virgin Soil Upturned*, and they occur much less frequently at the beginnings and endings of chapters. Nor does nature in

Virgin Soil Upturned participate in the plot to the same extent as it does in *The Quiet Don*. No relationships or events in *Virgin Soil Upturned* are portrayed with such a consistent and extensive use of natural imagery as are Grigorii's love stories or the origins and progress of the Upper Don uprising. Only Razmetnov's love story reveals a consistent, though not extensive, use of natural imagery, and the appearance of a wolf in three different landscapes may possibly be interpreted as a recurrent utilization of an animal image to hint at the anti-Soviet activities of Polovtsev. In the first instance, a grey she-wolf emerges as a metaphor of the night that comes from the east, leaving behind it the trail of "dusky shadows" (5:5). The metaphor presages the secret arrival of Polovtsev, a man with "a wolfish forehead" (5:8; 6:257). Moreover, it implies that in his struggle against collectivization—the struggle of dark against light, as the author sees it—Polovtsev represents the forces of darkness. In the second instance, a wolf appears in a nocturnal winter landscape in the beginning of a chapter and is shown walking in the steppe over the virgin snow (5:102). The appearance of the beast may be related to the passage in which Polovtsev slaughters sheep to prevent their being taken over by the collective farm. The episodic wolf seems to be the sole link connecting the winter landscape with the contents of the chapter. In the third instance, Makar Nagul'nov, walking in the steppe, frightens off a she-wolf that has recently whelped. The animal runs away from the man, her tail tucked between her legs and her black stretched dugs limply hanging under her sunken belly (5:280). The encounter is hardly accidental. It occurs just after Nagul'nov gave up the idea of committing suicide (because he was expelled from the Party) and firmly resolved to go on fighting the enemies of the Soviet regime. The wretched fleeing animal is symbolic of these enemies, with Polovtsev among them. Indeed, in the next chapter Nagul'nov puts to flight Polovtsev's men who attempted to seize grain stored on the collective farm. Furthermore, Polovtsev, like the she-wolf, has "a massive forehead" (5:88; 6:367), and Nagul'nov calls him and other enemies "wolves" (6:354).

The scene of Nagul'nov's encounter with the she-wolf is a part of the longest and in some ways unique depiction of nature in *Virgin Soil Upturned*. It is the sole place where nature takes on an epic quality as the historical cradle of the Cossacks. The focal point of the landscape is a burial mound, the grave of a Kuman prince killed in battle. The burial mount represents a symbolic link between the nomadic Kumans (*polovtsy*), who inhabited East European steppes from the eleventh to the thirteenth century, and the Don Cossacks, their successors in southern Russia. The warlike and freedom-loving spirit of both peoples is conveyed through the golden eagle hovering unchallenged over the steppe in search of prey. The description of its wings as "royal" (*tsarstvennye*) lends to the landscape an air of majesty, enhanced by the use of the old grammatical form *kryl* (wings) characteristic of an elevated style. The idea of an immutable nature that knows only seasonal changes underlies the assertion that neither winds, nor the sun, nor frost left any visible marks on the mound and it still "inviolably rules over the steppe as it did many hundreds of years ago" (5:278). An old legend ties the Kuman mound to the Cossack past. It tells that a wounded Cossack died at the foot of the mound, which from that time on became known as the Mound of Death. The legend is reinforced by the author's quoting a few lines from an old song about a mortally wounded Cossack and by his suggestion that this Cossack might have been the one who died at the foot of the mound (5:278). At this juncture the author projects the legendary Cossack past into the present by making Nagul'nov contemplate suicide while lying at the foot of the Mound of Death. But, unlike the legendary Cossack, Nagul'nov is not physically wounded, and he is able to recover from his moral humiliation. Two hours later he shows exceptional courage in defending granaries against a large crowd, his climactic action in volume 1. His heroism is perceived here as resulting not so much from his political devotion as from being a born Cossack. Such a conclusion is suggested by the two-page-long portrayal of the mound. Significantly, only the most daring Cossack character in the novel is brought into contact with the mound. And the mounds, as we know from *The Quiet Don*, are the guardians of "buried Cossack glory" (3:60).

An affinity with *The Quiet Don* is also seen in another landscape and in Nagul'nov's reflections on nature. Having left the mound, he walks through the late March steppe that is brimming with vigor and vitality: "A great life-generating work was in progress in the steppe. The grass was growing luxuriantly and birds and beasts were mating" (5:280). The phrases in this passage are either identical or nearly identical with those encountered in the similar description of the April steppe in *The Quiet Don* (3:319). Thinking of the limited time allowed by nature for the insemination of animals, plants, and the earth, Nagul'nov infers that man's promiscuity makes him "worse and filthier than the foulest animal!" (5:281). Mishka Koshevoi forms a similar opinion while observing the mating of horses (3:61).

Volume 2 of *Virgin Soil Upturned* has fewer obvious parallels with *The Quiet Don* than does volume 1. Its few lengthy descriptions of nature either are used to illustrate the triumph of collective farming or are associated with Davydov's personal experiences. The volume opens with a scene presenting the land as a breast-feeding mother and as promising a rich harvest. A field of winter wheat "sparkling with dewdrops" is contrasted with Iakov Ostrovnov, the enemy and saboteur, who looks like "a tired old horse" and who curses the Soviet regime in his powerless anger (6:6). The episode with Ostrovnov hammers home a political point at the expense of artistic economy. In volume 1 Ostrovnov has already cursed the Soviet regime with the same words, looking at the shoots of corn "threaded with trembling bugles of dew" (5:331). Elsewhere Davydov imagines how a large ploughed field would look in October when it is covered with winter wheat, the fruit of the collective farmers' hard toil (6:108). Even the burial mounds are seen through Davydov's eyes, reminding him of the storm-roused waves of the Baltic Sea (6:51).

Toward the end of the novel, however, one encounters natural scenes with philosophical messages akin to those found in *The Quiet Don*. In the penultimate chapter the life of the people and nature, represented by clouds floating over Gremiachii Log, passes on with "the same eternally majestic unhurried tread," regardless of what happens to individuals (6:359-360). The motif of the basic immutability of the natural order is reiterated in the last chapter. The same clouds, affected solely by seasonal changes, indifferently float over the same village and the fresh graves of Davydov and Nagul'nov, which are covered with feeble autumn grass (6:375). The description of the graves can be regarded as a prelude to the novel's climactic scene, which takes place at the grave of Razmetnov's wife. Thus in the last volume of *Virgin Soil Upturned* the author still professes his earlier and fundamental views on life and nature, though he injects a considerable dose of socialist realism into his landscapes and neglects to link them to Cossack history.

The use of landscapes in "The Science of Hatred" and "The Fate of a Man" is restricted by the fact that these stories are related by their protagonists. Nevertheless, both stories open with the author's descriptions of nature. In "The Science of Hatred" the central natural image is that of an oak tree hit by a German shell. With a gaping wound in its trunk, the tree comes to life in the spring. It continues to live, stretching its upper branches toward the sun and bathing its lower branches in a nameless river, whose "running water" suggests the folkloric "living water." The oak is patently symbolic of Russia. Crippled by the German invasion, the country survives by drawing upon its own sources of life. The country's ordeal and recovery are mirrored in the experiences of Lieutenant Gerasimov, who, in spite of his sufferings endured in German captivity, remains strong and hard as an oak (7:590). In "The Fate of a Man" nature is employed more subtly. The early spring in an empty steppe conveys the impression of gentle calmness and moves the author to contemplate clouds. The picture of serenity sets the stage for shocking the reader with a sharply contrasting account of violence, death, and grief to be told by the story's protagonist.

It is difficult to judge the role of nature in the unfinished novel *They Fought for Their Country*. However, one can mention the presence of the familiar motifs of nature's vitality and its indifference to human fighting and killing. The author speaks twice of a majestic equanimity which the blue skies retain during battles. He repeatedly uses the words "just like before" in references to birds and clouds, implying that the course of natural life is not affected by the fighting (7:90, 141). The triumph of natural vitality reveals itself also on the battlefield as soon as the fighting is interrupted. Grasses, flowers, birds, and insects resume their normal growth or activities, which the author calls "these smallest manifestations of the all-powerful life" (7:132).

The overall impression of landscapes in *They Fought for Their Country* is that they do not reveal any new aspects of Sholokhov the thinker or the artist. No description of nature in that novel equals the best landscapes in the two preceding novels in terms of conceptual significance, lyrical intensity, or aesthetic impact. Except for a few details, the nature scenes in *They Fought for Their Country* appear to be pale reflections of those in the earlier novels. At times the feeling of *déjà vu* is intensified by virtual repetitions of previously used phrases. Here are a few analogies with volume 1 of *Virgin Soil Upturned* taken from passages portraying the arrival of the spring: "a warm and wet wind came raiding in from the south" (5:193); "a thick and warm spring wind poured from the south" (7:5); "the large-grained snow began to sink with a rustle and a rumble" (5:193); "the last porous snow . . . began to sink in the gullies with a crunching sound" (7:5); "the sharp green sting of a blade of grass pushing aside last year's dead stubble reaches up to the sun" (5:194); "its [the blade's] pale-green stinglet pierced the rotten fabric of a maple leaf. . . . The blade of grass straightened . . . reaching up to the eternal source of life, the sun" (7:8-9).

Of course, one should not expect that descriptions of nature in *They Fought for Their Country* would be as vigorous, artistic, original, and significant as they were in *The Quiet Don*. By the time he started writing his third novel, Sholokhov might already have recorded his keenest observations of nature in earlier works and written himself out to some degree. Yet the contrast between natural scenes in the third novel, on the one hand, and the first two, on the other, is too great to be attributed exclusively to an exhaustion of talent. As it stands now, *They Fought for Their Country* is a work of shocking conceptual shallowness, and this could not but have an adverse effect on the artistic quality of its landscapes.

Beginning with *Virgin Soil Upturned*, aesthetic deterioration manifests itself to an even larger degree in the epic, dramatic, and realistic elements of Sholokhov's art. This decline will be illustrated elsewhere by comparing *The Quiet Don*, as the author's highest artistic achievement, with his subsequent works.

The Quiet Don and Tolstoi

The epic character of *The Quiet Don* stems from a predominantly dispassionate and broad portrayal of a nation at a crucial period of wars, revolutions, and drastic social and political changes that were to have far-reaching consequences for the entire world. If an epic is expected to convey a belief in the basic dignity of man and to be marked by a certain grandeur, heroism, patriotism, and violence, Sholokhov's novel has all of this in abundance. In its scope and in the significance of its subject matter *The Quiet Don* closely resembles *War and Peace*. If Tolstoi's epic is a monument to the Russian nobility, Sholokhov's is a monument to the Don Cossacks. *War and Peace*, however, immortalizes the triumph of both the Russian people and the nobility. The majority of Tolstoi's important characters survive. In the epilogue they appear as a large, closely knit family with numerous children. Not all of them are content with the situation in the victorious Russia. Some may oppose the government and suffer reprisals in the near future. But a century will pass before their descendants are uprooted and eliminated as a class. By contrast, in *The Quiet Don* nearly all the important characters die. Their violent deaths signify the end of the centuries-old existence of the Cossacks as a unique segment of Russia's population. This development gives the novel an air of somberness absent from Tolstoi's epic.

Because *The Quiet Don* focuses on the Don area and the Cossacks, a sizeable number of writers and critics have come to consider it a "regional" work. This view was expressed by such writers as Gor'kii, Aleksei Tolstoi, and Fadeev.[12] Members of the Committee on Stalin Prizes spoke late in 1940 of "the limitations of *The Quiet Don* resulting from the regional Cossack milieu depicted in it," and of the author's concomitant failure to show "the active people's force that led the Revolution."[13] Such assertions are debatable. The significance of *The Quiet Don* may well be regarded as exceeding its regional limitations. On several occasions Sholokhov goes beyond the Don territory to portray consequential events. He describes fighting in World War I and shows how the defeats and fatigue of Russian troops led to the disintegration of the tsarist army and to the February and October Revolutions. Furthermore, he portrays in great detail General Lavr Kornilov's movement, the political atmosphere in Petrograd on the eve of the Bolshevik seizure of power, and the disastrous retreat of the Whites in the winter of 1920 which culminated in the catastrophe at Novorossiisk. Many pages of the novel are devoted to momentous happenings of the Civil War that took place in the Don region. It will suffice to mention the formation of the White Volunteer Army, the first battles between the Reds and the Whites, the Cossack uprisings in the springs of 1918 and 1919, and the activities of the atamans Aleksei Kaledin and Petr Krasnov. The White Volunteer Army would have been defeated in 1918 had the Don Cossacks not rebelled against the Bolshevik regime in March of that year and formed a regular Don Army numbering 50,000 men four months later.[14] The Don Army of the same strength constituted more than half of General Denikin's White forces at the turning point of the Civil War in October 1919.[15] The Don Cossacks' casualties in that war reflect the degree of their participation in it and are much higher than their casualties in World War I. Thus Nagavskaia stanitsa, located in the middle Don area, lost 6 men with 30 wounded during the entire Great War, while 270 of its Cossacks were killed and 80 percent of its males were wounded within the first year of the Civil War. The Upper Don District, where 40 percent of those able to bear arms were killed during the Civil War, suffered the heaviest losses.[16] The Cossacks' involvement in the Civil War is in sharp contrast with the passivity of the bulk of the Russian population. The Bolsheviks' attempt to create an all-volunteer army of workers and peasants, as announced in the People's Commissars' Decree of January 15, 1918, ended in failure. On May 29, 1918, the All-Russian Central Executive Committee of the Soviets passed a decree establishing compulsory military service. The mobilization brought into the army thousands of reluctant soldiers, primarily peasants. The overwhelming majority of the draftees had no desire to fight for either side and readily laid down their arms as soon as the situation grew dangerous.[17] Sholokhov had in mind this type of soldier when he wrote about "morally unstable units consisting of newly mobilized Red Army men" who "surrendered by the thousands" (3:90). Draft evasion and desertion were largely responsible for the extremely low numerical strength of the warring sides. On the eve of the decisive battles of October and November 1919, the combined strength of the Reds and the Whites on the crucial southern front running from Kiev to Astrakhan' was approximately 250,000.[18]

Political and military events that occurred in the Don area during the Civil War and the extent of the Cossacks' participation in it had significant repercussions for all of Russia and seem to provide sufficient evidence for the contention that *The Quiet Don* is more than a purely "regional" work. The members of the Committee on Stalin Prizes were right, however, in asserting that Sholokhov did not show the people's leadership in the Revolution. But the reason for this omission was not the one that the Committee had in mind. Sholokhov did not overlook "the active people's force"; he simply did not write about something that did not exist. Yet the Committee members were less biased than Soviet critics of the 1960s and 1970s. To keep in line with the growing glorification of Sholokhov, the critics had to go in the opposite direction, closing their eyes to the actual content of *The Quiet Don* and seeing things that were not in it. A typical recent pronouncement describes Sholokhov's novels, above all *The Quiet Don*, as "the epic account of the greatest proletarian stage in the liberation movement of Russia."[19]

For all its historical value, *The Quiet Don* obviously lacks the philosophical complexity of *War and Peace*. Unlike Tolstoi, Sholokhov does not search for laws of history, or explore in depth the question of individual freedom and historical necessity, or probe into the meaning of human existence in a religious context. In terms of philosophy and ethics *The Quiet Don* does not go beyond viewing man in relationship to nature and beyond advocating common decency through the behavior of certain characters, chiefly Grigorii Melekhov. Clearly, a young, half-educated Sholokhov could not match the erudition and versatility of a rare genius who began his epic at the age of thirty-five. In Sholokhov's own words, "Tolstoi is unreachable."[20] What *The Quiet Don* essentially does is to present a wide river of life as it flows, and it is up to the reader to draw his own inferences about the complexities of human existence. If this method of presentation gives *The Quiet Don* any advantage over *War and Peace*, it might be the absence of such a character as Platon Karataev, who seems to be too obvious an illustration of the author's ideas. The moralistic trend is much less pronounced in *The Quiet Don* than in *War and Peace*, although Sholokhov, like Tolstoi, contends that "a work of art should infect emotionally and excite noble feelings, that is, educate."[21]

Tolstoi exerted considerable influence on the author of *The Quiet Don*. Nonetheless, it would be imprudent to view every similarity between that novel and Tolstoi's works as an unquestionable borrowing. Some similarities could be coincidental or resulting from the affinity of genre and subject matter. A few examples of what can be called Tolstoian traits in *The Quiet Don* will be listed, without trying to establish the degree of their derivativeness. To my knowledge, no specific statements by Sholokhov about his artistic ties with Tolstoi have appeared in print.

War and Peace and *The Quiet Don* combine the characteristics of family and historical novels. In both works family life unfolds against a broad historical background. In the spirit of Tolstoi, Sholokhov strips the war of its heroic veneer and exposes its senselessness and immorality. He presents the encounter between Kriuchkov's Cossacks and German cavalrymen, not as a heroic exploit on the part of the Cossacks, but as a clash of inexperienced men who are seized by fear and blindly mutilate one another and their horses until they ride away, morally crippled (1:286-287). Like Tolstoi, Sholokhov marks his characters with distinctive physical features, such as the fluffy curls on Aksin'ia's neck, Mit'ka Korshunov's cat's eyes, his father's freckled face and hands, Anikushka's hairless and womanish face, Prokhor Zykov's calflike eyes, Petr Melekhov's wheaten whiskers. At times Sholokhov's characters analyze their confused emotions or thoughts in a way reminiscent of the inner monologues of Tolstoi's characters. Evgenii Listnitskii's examination of his contradictory feelings about upper-class draft dodgers can serve as an example (2:98). An inner monologue may be followed by an authorial comment à la Tolstoi, containing a certain disclosure about the character. Thus Bunchuk's thoughts about the need to have friendly contacts with people are accompanied by the observation that "he thought so, deceiving himself and realizing that he was deceiving himself" (2:207). In her vitality and cheerfulness Duniashka resembles Natasha Rostova, and the passionate adulterous relationship of Grigorii and Aksin'ia parallels in some respects that of Vronskii and Anna. Some syntactical constructions seem to be modeled on Tolstoi's: "That which Aksin'ia awaited with anguish and joyous impatience; that which Grigorii was vaguely afraid of happened during the harvest" (1:206-207). In *Anna Karenina*: "That which for nearly a whole year had been the sole and exclusive desire of Vronskii's life, replacing all his former desires; that which for Anna had been an impossible, horrible, but all the more bewitching dream of happiness—that desire had been satisfied."[22]

The above quotations—the first referring to the birth of a child, the second to the sex act—bespeak not only syntactical identity but also the difference in the depth of psychological probing. Sholokhov limits himself to bare essentials. Had he been the author of the second quotation, he would probably have done without the participial phrase in its first half and without "but all the more bewitching" in the second. The perceptive comments on the intensity and interaction of feelings would have been absent. The difference between the two authors becomes increasingly evident if one turns to the paragraphs that follow the second quotation and to the scene of Grigorii's conquest of Aksin'ia (part 1, chap. 9). The quotation from Tolstoi opens a two-page-long chapter devoted in its entirety to the description of the immediate effects of Anna's fall. Vronskii feels like a murderer. Anna is overcome with feelings of guilt, shame, disgust, and horror. Tolstoi's moral position is apparent. Sholokhov is much briefer and concentrates on physical and external manifestations of emotions. Grigorii flings Aksin'ia over his arm the way "a wolf throws a slaughtered sheep across its back" (1:51-52). The word "slaughtered" may suggest that the seduction of Aksin'ia was a fateful event leading to her eventual ruin. However, the author appears to look approvingly at his lovers. Although she is "choking with the bitterness of repentance," Aksin'ia asks Grigorii not to carry her any farther because she will go of her own accord. Here the chapter ends, without anything being said about the mental state of the characters.

The next chapter tells of a drastic change in Aksin'ia's face caused by her passion. Oblivious to public reaction to her affair with Grigorii, she "held her happy but shameful head proud and high" (1:52)—"shameful" in the eyes of those who condemned her. As for the author, he seems to polemicize with Tolstoi's making his fallen Anna drop low "her head, once so proud and gay but now shameful" (8:177).

Tolstoi attaches so much significance to the psychical states of Anna and Vronskii after their union that he completely excludes all people and objects from their perceptions or thoughts. Neither of the lovers sees, smells, hears, or touches anything in the two-page-long chapter. And the author mentions in passing only three objects in their room: a sofa, a rug, and the floor. The seduction scene in *The Quiet Don* unfolds in well-defined surroundings. At one point Aksin'ia breathes the sour smell of Grigorii's sheepskin—a little detail typical for Sholokhov in that it reveals his cognizance of the outside world under any circumstances. In the four opening lines of the next chapter Aksin'ia's condition is metaphorically depicted with the aid of tangible imagery taken from the Cossack environment. Her love is associated with the blooming henbane and her passion is said to have branded her face. The subsequent lines return her to the real world of objects and people.

A significant difference between *The Quiet Don* and *War and Peace* lies in their authors' views of humanity. Tolstoi conveys a stronger belief in the basic nobility of human nature than does Sholokhov. Nowhere can this distinction be seen more clearly than in the extreme situations—the scenes of killing. When Tolstoi's characters kill their fellow-men, they suffer from an instinctive aversion. In the final stage of the Borodino battle all soldiers are horrified by realizing what they are doing to one another. Having beaten to death a man suspected of treason, a crowd of Muscovites begins to experience terror, remorse, and pity. French soldiers carrying out the execution of alleged arsonists are possessed with horror and know that they are committing a crime. Even the individuals who order the executions in cold blood are not devoid of humaneness. The dreadful Marshal Davout condemns alleged arsonists to death but saves Pierre because, after looking into each other's eyes, the two realize that they are both children of mankind and brothers. As a rule, Tolstoi's characters kill or condemn others to death only when they act as instruments of impersonal establishments such as a state or an army which compel man to act in a way contrary to his instinctive goodness and love for his neighbor. Davout orders the execution of the alleged arsonists because to him their lives are no more than numbers on the list compiled by his subordinates. Count Fedor Rastopchin, military governor of Moscow, calms his pangs of conscience over the lynching of a man suspected of treason with the argument that it was necessary for "the public good." This argument, the author remarks, is invariably used by man to justify his crimes against his fellow-man. Soldiers at Borodino are virtually absolved from any responsibility for the carnage since it was effected not by their own will but "at the will of Him who rules people and worlds" (6:298).

Tolstoi's optimistic view of human nature may appear unrealistic to the twentieth-century reader who witnessed genocide on an unprecedented scale. In his century the concept of killing for *le bien publique* assumed the proportions of mass killings for the good of mankind or a nation and became the most sinister feature of the totalitarian ideologies of Bolshevism and Nazism. Being a faithful account of its time, *The Quiet Don* could not avoid treating manslaughter in a new light and depicting human nature in terms different from those in *War and Peace* but more understandable to the modern reader.

The new kind of killer, the ideological one, is typified by Bunchuk. Committed through Marxism to revolutionary violence and inspired by Lenin's call for unleashing a civil war, he feels no compunction about destroying human lives in order to achieve the Communist millennium. During World War I he joins a machine-gun detachment so that he will get the best preparation for a civil war. That his skills are developed by shooting German proletarians is for him a matter of secondary importance. During the Civil War he dutifully executes the enemies of the Revolution to clear the ground for what he calls "a blooming garden" (2:300). But even Bunchuk finds it unbearable to hold his job for a long time as a leader of a firing squad of a Revolutionary tribunal. The reason for his quitting, however, is not that he becomes horrified by homicide as such, though he is aware that one cannot kill people without becoming "morally scarred" (2:300). He would easily go on shooting White officers, but he is upset by executions of plain Cossacks, these hard-working men with callous and bruised hands.

Such Cossacks were unhesitatingly executed by Mishka Koshevoi. He is more cruel than Bunchuk. He abuses his victims before killing them, has no qualms about murdering a harmless old man, burns Cossack villages, and shoots cattle running away from fire. If the meeting eyes of Pierre and Davout told them that they were brothers, Koshevoi's glance fixed upon a captive Cossack emitted different feelings. "With his blue eyes as cold as ice he would look at the Cossack and ask, 'Had enough fighting Soviet rule?' and would cut the prisoner down with his saber without waiting for an answer and without a glance at his face turning deathly pale. And he cut them down without mercy!'' (3:398).

Koshevoi is an example of how a rather good-natured fellow turned into a routine executioner. The son of a poor Cossack, he was effectively indoctrinated in elementary Marxism and willingly applied the Bolsheviks' terroristic methods in his war against the traditional Cossack way of life associated in his mind with plenitude and perfidy. There is no indication that he ever felt any horror or remorse during or after killing people, or that he was restrained by his comrades. On the contrary, his feelings and actions were in full harmony with Trotskii's order to give no quarter to any insurgent Cossack unless he deserted to the Reds with his weapons (3:395-396).

The Quiet Don has many more scenes of killing than *War and Peace*. The Bolsheviks are not the only cold-blooded, remorseless killers in Sholokhov's novel. There is the misanthrope Aleksei Uriupin, who, without any personal or political reason, misses no opportunity to kill a man. There are scenes of individual and mass executions of the Reds by insurgent Cossacks. There is Mit'ka Korshunov, the White counterpart of Koshevoi, who becomes an eager executioner in a punitive detachment. Yet history and the novel show a number of differences in the homicidal practices of the warring sides. In the Bolshevik camp homicide was a centrally organized activity justified by a definite ideology and directed toward definite social strata of the population or against any movement that opposed Bolshevik rule, such as spontaneous peasant uprisings. A genocidal order concerning the treatment of the Cossacks came from the very top of the Soviet regime. It was the directive of January 29, 1919, signed by Iakov Sverdlov, chairman of the All-Russian Central Executive Committee of the Soviets. The first paragraph of the directive instructed all important Party workers in Cossack regions ''to pursue massive terrorism against rich Cossacks and exterminate them to a man. To pursue massive terrorism without mercy against all Cossacks who had taken any part, directly or indirectly, in the struggle against Soviet power. It is necessary to take any measures against middle Cossacks which shall guarantee no further attempts on their part at new attacks on Soviet power.''[23]

The directive also ordered the confiscation of grain and agricultural produce, the settlement of poor Russian peasants on Cossack lands, and the shooting of anyone who did not surrender his arms to Soviet authorities. The terror was attended by acts of sacrilegious violence and mockery of the Cossacks' religious feelings. These subjects are barely touched upon in *The Quiet Don*. Perhaps Sholokhov did not want to arouse or intensify anti-Bolshevik sentiments in religious or non-Communist readers by describing in more detail the events which to him, an atheist and detractor of the clergy, were much less odious than acts of physical violence. The anti-religious violence was carried out with the blessings of the commanders of the Red Army. Here is an example from the book of the supreme commander of the Red forces in southern Russia: "Our gun layers flew in a particularly strong rage at the sight of the church dome proudly rising over the stanitsa. The dome became the target of a fervent shooting."[24]

It is inconceivable that the White generals would condone this kind of militant atheism. Nor did the White leaders ever issue such directives as Sverdlov's or order such things as "the Red Terror," an officially proclaimed measure involving summary shooting of hostages and anyone who could be termed a bourgeois or a counterrevolutionary. The executions on the part of the Whites were predominantly retaliative. Thus the execution of the Podtelkov men or the lynching of the Communist prisoners of the Serdobskii Regiment are first of all retributions for the murder of captured Cossack officers on Podtelkov's orders and for the mass shootings of the Upper Don Cossacks in the winter of 1919, which are described in Sholokhov's letter to Gor'kii of June 6, 1931, and shown, in part, in volume 3 of *The Quiet Don* (chaps. 22-24, 39). Likewise, Grigorii Melekhov views his order to kill twenty-seven Red prisoners as paying back in kind for the execution of his brother (3:214). Even Mit'ka Korshunov murders Koshevoi's family in retaliation for Koshevoi's sending his father to death, shooting his grandfather, and burning down his paternal home. Furthermore, Mit'ka's cruelty was inborn and then developed to monstrous proportions under the tutelage of the shabbiest elements of the White Army, "the scum of the officers—cocaine addicts, users of violence, and pillagers" (4:98)—whereas the "normal" Koshevoi was converted into a killer with the aid of an exemplary Bolshevik, Shtokman.

The Quiet Don also shows that individual opposition or protest against executions had a better chance to succeed in the White camp than in the Red. The novel offers no example where a manifestation of humaneness led to any positive results in the Red camp. A Cossack shocked by the killing of Kalmykov is told by Bunchuk that those who pity people like Kalmykov should be shot too (2:162). When Ivan Kotliarov voices a weak disagreement with the shooting of the Tatarskii Cossacks, Shtokman gives him a long lecture justifying the harshest treatment of the enemy. Underpinning Shtokman's arguments is Lenin's motto: "You can't make a revolution without dirtying your hands" (3:164). Grigorii Melekhov's attempt to prevent a summary execution of captured officers ends with Podtelkov's orally abusing him (2:251). On the other hand, serving with the Whites in 1918, Grigorii is able to act contrary to the growing practice of killing prisoners. As a result, he is demoted from squadron commander for softness (3:84). As commander of an insurgent division, he saves the lives of three Red commanders, acting against the recommendation of his chief of staff that the three be shot (4:136). Speaking for the detachment of Tatarskii Cossacks, Petr Melekhov refuses to take part in the execution of the Podtelkov men (2:365). When the insurgent Tatarskii Cossacks are about to kill Koshevoi, who had already sent to death several of their fellow-villagers, he is saved by the interference of a Cossack who appeals to the Christian ethics of the captors and states that they should not kill people as the Reds did (3:182).[25] Two months later Grigorii rides his horse to death trying to arrive at Tatarskii in time to prevent the lynching of Ivan Kotliarov and Koshevoi, mistakenly thinking that the latter is among the Communist prisoners of the Serdobskii Regiment. "There is blood between us, but we are not strangers, are we?" Grigorii thinks (3:321). The placing of an old friendship above political enmity is imbedded in traditional ethics. It is diametrically opposed to the ethical norms of the Bolsheviks. "If I'd happened to catch you that time, I'd have stretched you out nicely too!" Koshevoi says in the fall of 1920 when Grigorii reminds him of his having killed Petr (4:346).

The difference between the old and new attitudes toward homicide is illustrated, and probably not by accident, in two contrasting episodes. During the Russo-Turkish war of 1877-1878, the Cossack Grigorii Korshunov takes prisoner a Turkish officer, although the officer fires at him and resists physically. The Cossack spares the Turk because "he was a man too" (1:107). In 1919 Koshevoi kills Grigorii Korshunov—a frail Bible-reading man of seventy-six—in the course of an argument, remarking that "You, old devil, should have been packed off long before this!" (3:405). What can be regarded as a traditional view of killing people is held by the male members of the Melekhov family. Trained for war, these Cossacks accept killing in combat but abhor the murder of defenseless people. They do not want to have anything to do with Koshevoi or Mit'ka Korshunov (4:64, 102, 353). Yet the Melekhov family has to face the fact that Grigorii has developed into a highly efficient—virtually professional—killer in combat. He had to fight in three wars and excel in the art of killing people in order to survive. His reactions toward killing change. He goes through a brief period of excruciating torments of conscience over the unnecessary killing of an Austrian soldier in his first battle of World War I. In this Austrian he sees a human being. Their eyes meet before Grigorii deals him the mortal blow with his saber (1:260). As World War I goes on, Grigorii stops feeling pain for other men. But the killing of people leaves deep traces in him. He can no longer laugh as in former days and it is hard for him to look straight into the clear eyes of a child when he kisses one (2:49).

At the height of the Civil War Grigorii's continuous killing of people brings him to the point where he claims to have no pity left for anyone and to have become frightening to himself (3:285). No matter how harsh this admission may sound, it indicates that Grigorii remains human because he realizes that homicide has had devastating effects on his soul. This realization enhances the tragic nature of the situation in which he is placed by circumstances beyond his control. There is no way for him to get out of the war, and he is too honest, humane, and intelligent to justify his killing as a prerequisite for the advancement of a great cause.

The only time when Grigorii does not mind killing people and even feels delight in doing so is during his service with the Reds in 1920. Going into war against Poland, he wonders whether the Poles' skulls are stronger than those of the Austrians, Germans, and Russians (4:289). His heart leaps with joy when he splits in half the head of a White colonel (4:353). He is thrilled by killing the colonel because he hates officers for their having snubbed him as an ill-bred outsider. His eagerness to kill Poles stems from his determination to atone for his previous fighting against the Reds. Nonetheless, one is struck by the chilling cheerfulness with which he anticipates sabering Polish soldiers. Could Grigorii, who grows more sensitive after Natal'ia's death, have become so brutal? Or perhaps the author, while putting finishing touches on part 8, felt obliged or was encouraged to picture the Poles as an enemy deserving harsh treatment? It was the time when the Soviet Union had to justify its "liberation" of Western Belorussia and Western Ukraine from Polish domination. When, after his joining the Fomin detachment, Grigorii resumes his struggle against the Reds, he kills them, as he did before, without pity and without delight.

Formidable killer that he is, Grigorii is prevented from turning into a Bunchuk or a Koshevoi by his innate nobility and by the restraints of a traditional morality that values human life as such. In his abhorrence of killing defenseless people Grigorii Melekhov resembles Grigorii Korshunov. The identity of their names indicates their ethical kinship and continuity of tradition. Bunchuk and Koshevoi kill for the public good. Their kind of killing is criminal because it places the value of human life below social, economic, or political goals. Their kind of killing is highly arbitrary because it is impossible to achieve even a semblance of a consensus on what the public good should be. According to Tolstoi, a man who is not swayed by passion can never be certain about the essence of the public good. Conversely, a man who commits a capital crime has no doubt where this good lies (6:393). To justify his killing, such a man feels the need to profess the knowledge of the public good. Homicide for the public good can reach enormous proportions. Suffice it to mention the victims of such actions as collectivization, the purges of the thirties, the creation of a Gulag Archipelago, the deportation of nationalities accused of cooperation with the Germans. With their contempt for human life, Bunchuk and Koshevoi were among those who paved the way for these developments at the very beginning of the Bolshevik regime. The Bolshevik treatment of the Cossacks in *The Quiet Don* can be viewed as a prelude to subsequent genocidal actions in the Soviet Union.

Sholokhov may have a different opinion on this point. Yet, as the author of *The Quiet Don*, he appears more likely to condone the inevitable killing in combat by Grigorii Melekhov than the politically motivated destruction of people carried out by Bunchuk and Koshevoi. The main thing is that he dispassionately portrayed various kinds of killing and conveyed his concern for human life irrespective of his political leanings.

The most determined opposition to killing in *The Quiet Don* comes from the figure of the mother. She is the immediate source of life and has the strongest ties with it through her love and concern for her children. This predominantly biological attachment is less likely to be adversely affected by social, economic, or political considerations than any other form of human relationships. The mother is sacred for Sholokhov. Perhaps his affection for his own mother has something to do with it. He describes mothers with more warmth, sympathy, and respect than any other group of characters. Regardless of the political allegiances of their children, the mothers in *The Quiet Don* are united by the sameness of their emotions and actions. To accentuate the oneness of maternal feelings, Sholokhov places side by side two descriptions of grieving mothers whose sons were killed in war. One is the mother of an insurgent Cossack, the other of a Red soldier. With equal compassion Sholokhov portrays their unquenchable sorrow over the loss of those whom they had carried in their wombs and born in blood and agony (3:275-276). Neither of the two women cries for revenge. Nor does Grigorii's mother, who lost her elder son. Moreover, she reproves Grigorii for killing Red sailors (3:313). An old Cossack woman who lost three sons in the war saves the life of a Red soldier because as a mother she feels sorry for young people (4:31).

Maternal love is apt to elicit the most tender feelings in children. There is a moving scene depicting the mutual affection between Bunchuk and his mother (2:196-198). It is worth noting that the last time the reader saw Bunchuk was when he murdered Kalmykov. A stark contrast between a political executioner and a loving son is apparently intended to spotlight the complexity of Bunchuk's personality. The natural humaneness of Bunchuk's and Grigorii's mothers as well as of the old Cossack woman is fortified by their traditional religiosity. All three invoke the name of God in their pleas for protection and mercy. But with all their moral authority the mothers are unable to stop the destruction of human lives.

It can be said that in his portrayal of mothers Sholokhov follows the tradition of the Russian classics which presented the woman as morally superior to man. The tradition, however, has many individual variations. Tolstoi and Sholokhov tend to stress the woman's being the source of life more than did other writers except Gor'kii.[26] The two crucial phenomena for Tolstoi are birth and death. Birth is not only the act of creating life but also a stimulus to sublime spiritual uplifting. Sorrow caused by death and joy aroused by birth appear to Levin as "openings through which something higher became visible" (9:325). Confronted with death or birth, his soul soars to heights it had never experienced before. Three chapters covering Kitty's labor and delivery (part 7, chaps. 13-15) deal not so much with physical details of childbirth as with Levin's emotional responses to the great event. And throughout the three chapters the author makes the reader feel that it is not the father who has closest communion with the mysteries of life but the mother. In contrast to Tolstoi, Sholokhov is not inclined to raise the phenomenon of childbirth to a metaphysical plane. He devotes two pages to the description of Aksin'ia's labor and delivery and includes many more physical, at times gory, details of childbirth than does Tolstoi, but he refuses to go beyond the realm of empirical facts (1:207-208).

The Quiet Don is the only significant Russian novel that offers a comprehensive picture of the life of the common people and has a common man as the protagonist. It is, however, not the first literary work about the Cossacks. Two short novels, Gogol''s *Taras Bul'ba* (1835, 1842) and Tolstoi's *The Cossacks* (1863), are its remote predecessors. *The Quiet Don* does not seem to have any close ties with either of them. The portrayal of the Ukrainian Zaporozh'e Cossacks in *Taras Bul'ba* is vivid but too general and impressionistic. Gogol' shows little respect for historical facts. His chronology is a jumble. He initially sets the story in the fifteenth century and then, with the original characters alive and unaged, proceeds to describe events of the mid-seventeenth century. For his background information he relies less on historical writings than on Ukrainian historical and epic songs, and—above all—on his immense imagination. He employs hyperboles lavishly and unabashedly. The battles are described in a lofty epic style. The hero Taras weighs over 700 lbs. The novel is partisan and superpatriotic, its hallmark being a fierce dedication to Russia and to the Orthodox faith. Indeed, Gogol''s Ukrainian Cossacks of the sixteenth-seventeenth centuries are by far more pro-Russian than Sholokhov's Don Cossacks of the twentieth century.

What Sholokhov and Gogol' have in common are authorial digressions. Yet Sholokhov's digressions are on the whole less ecstatic than Gogol''s and—more importantly—they are couched in an earthly idiom and show an intimate knowledge of the subject matter. Gogol''s digressions are literary in style and betray a rather external familiarity with the subject matter. A case in point is his description of the mother whose son did not return from the war: "And for many a Cossack his old mother will weep, beating her withered breasts with her bony hands. Many a widow will be left behind in Glukhov, Nemirov, Chernigov, and other cities. She will, poor thing, run every day to the market place, stopping all the passersby, looking into the eyes of each one of them to see if the one dearest of all to her is among them. But many different troops will pass through the city, and never will the dearest one of all be among them."[27]

What Gogol' offers here is a conventional image of the bereft mother, with no new dimensions added. An air of solemnity is imparted to the style by the choice of the old, elevated word *persi* for *grudi* (breasts) and the use of the prefix *vz* instead of *za* in *vzrydat'* (weep, sob).

A comparable passage in *The Quiet Don* reads: "Turning over Beshniak's old clothes, his mother wept, shedding bitter and sparse tears. She sniffed the clothes, but only the last shirt, brought by Mishka Koshevoi, hid the smell of her son's sweat in its folds. Pressing her head to the shirt, the old woman swayed and dolefully lamented, patterning the dirty, stamped cotton shirt with her tears" (2:184).

Sholokhov communicates the mother's grief with the aid of concrete, fresh, and expressive details. The passage can hardly be called a lyrical digression. It is rather a restrained, measured, and unsentimental report. But even in his more personal, genuine digressions Sholokhov firmly stands on the ground of reality, his imagery losing nothing of its tangibility and concreteness. Typical in this respect is the apostrophe to a Cossack war widow, which precedes the passage about Beshniak's mother. In graphic and unsparing language the apostrophe reveals not only the widow's despair caused by personal loss, but also the impact her husband's death will have on her economic situation and health. The apostrophe ends with a dire prediction: "You yourself will have to do your own ploughing and harrowing, losing your breath from excessive strain. You will have . . . to lift heavy bundles of wheat on the pitchfork and you will feel that something is rending under your belly, and then you will writhe with pain and bleed, having covered yourself with your rags" (2:184). The portrayal is brutally specific and precise to the smallest detail. For "rags" Sholokhov uses the regional term *lokhuny*. The literary synonym *lokhmot'ia* would be out of place in the address to a plain Cossack woman. Sholokhov's *lokhuny* and Gogol''s *persi* symbolize the difference between a starkly realistic representation of contemporary life in *The Quiet Don* and a romantic and idealized version of the remote past in *Taras Bul'ba*.

In its portrayal of Cossack life *The Quiet Don* is much closer to *The Cossacks* than to *Taras Bul'ba*. This kinship can be largely explained by the fact that Tolstoi's novel is based on his keen observations of the Mountain Ridge (*grebenskie*) Cossacks during his stay in the Caucasus from June 1851 to January 1854. Furthermore, both authors make use of folk poetry and stories told by the Cossacks. At times there are striking similarities in detail. In both works the gait of Cossack women is called "smart" (*shchegolevataia*) and said to be peculiar to them.[28] The description of dead Russian officers in *The Quiet Don* cannot but evoke the sight of the dead Chechen in *The Cossacks*. Both authors delineate minute details pertaining to faces, limbs, positions, and clothes of the corpses. The details are so expressive that one can easily imagine what kind of people the dead ones were. A few lines from the passages in question will suffice to illustrate the similarities of the styles:

> The Cossacks stood silent and still around the dead man and looked at him. The brown body, with nothing on but wet blue pants which had turned dark and which were tightened by a belt over the sunken stomach, was slender and beautiful. The muscular arms lay straight alongside his ribs. The bluish, freshly shaven, round head with a clotted wound on its side was thrown back. . . . The thin lips, stretched at the corners and sticking out from under the trimmed red moustache, seemed to have formed a good-natured subtle smile.
>
> For quite a long time the Cossacks looked at the figure of a lieutenant, beautiful even after death. He lay on his back, his left hand was firmly pressed against his chest, his right hand was flung out with the handle of a revolver forever locked in it. . . . His blond curly head—the cap on it pushed back—pressed with its cheek to the earth as if caressing it, and his orange lips, touched by blue, were twisted mournfully and with bewilderment.[29]

Both *The Cossacks* and *The Quiet Don* feature the theme of the Cossacks' unity with nature. But here also lies a significant difference in the approach. Tolstoi looks at his Cossacks through the eyes of a largely autobiographical character, the nobleman Dimitrii Olenin, an outsider who left civilized society and intends to join a primitive natural life by marrying a Cossack girl. As a result, the author draws a too obvious and somewhat forced contrast between the naturalness of the Cossacks' life and the artificiality of the civilized world. The Cossacks' life is believed to be governed by exactly the same natural laws as the sun, grass, animals, and trees (3:270-271). In *The Quiet Don* the bond between man and nature is organically and unobtrusively integrated into the fabric of the novel and there is no assertion of an absolute unity between them. As an insider, Sholokhov focuses on Cossack life as such, without making it a testing ground for an intellectual's philosophical or moral views. No character in *The Quiet Don* resembles, even remotely, the intensely introspective Olenin, preoccupied with typically Tolstoian questions about life, goodness, and happiness.

The Quiet Don, like the rest of Sholokhov's works, is devoid of characters with searching minds who might be called intellectuals, or members of the upper stratum of the intelligentsia, to use the Russian designation. Sholokhov did not know this type of people when he wrote the bulk of *The Quiet Don* and he showed little desire of getting to know them even later. Only occasionally one meets in *The Quiet Don* a few representatives of the village intelligentsia, portrayed with a varying degree of sympathy. The intelligentsia above this level is mentioned only in passing and only unfavorably. The rustic, practical, and self-taught Sholokhov may harbor the same feelings toward people engaged in mental labor as do so many peasants, who look upon them as a leisure class shirking hard physical work. Another reason for Sholokhov's feelings can be traced back to the Bolshevik attitude toward the moral and humanistic values of the Russian intelligentsia. Its concern for human life was incompatible with the preaching and practicing of revolutionary violence. In justifying their terror, the Bolsheviks dubbed the intelligentsia *sliuniavaia*. Denoting "driveling" and connoting "a softy," this derogatory appellation derives from *raspustit' sliuni* (to drivel), a colloquialism for "to cry." It was precisely "the softheartedness" of the intelligentsia that moved Sholokhov to entitle one of his early stories "Zver' " ("The Beast"). In this story, published in 1925 as "The Food Commissar," the commissar Bodiagin approves the execution of his father for resisting the forcible requisition of grain. Soon thereafter the commissar sacrifices his life by engaging in a suicidal fight with insurgent Cossacks in order to save a child's life. Sholokhov described the gist of the story as follows: "I wanted to show that the man who killed his father in the name of the Revolution and who was considered 'a beast' (in the eyes of the *sliuniavaia* intelligentsia, of course) died because he saved the child."[30]

The same view of the intelligentsia is expressed by Shtokman. When Kotliarov voices his concern that the shooting of the Tatarskii Cossacks would turn their fellow-villagers away from the Soviet regime, Shtokman reproaches him for weakness: "You are a worker, lad, but you drivel like one of the intelligentsia" (3:164). Whether at this point the author shared the opinion of his character about the intelligentsia's "softheartedness" is a moot point. There is, however, no doubt concerning his feelings about the moral character of the intelligentsia. "The scum of the officers" with whom Mit'ka Korshunov serves in the punitive detachment are "the intelligentsia scoundrels'' (4:98). With a scorching contempt Sholokhov speaks of thousands of former tsarist officers who lived in the rear of the White Army and who used every trick they knew to avoid direct involvement in the Civil War. ''The majority of them represented the most repulsive kind of the so-called 'thinking intelligentsia' dressed up in a military uniform'' (3:43). At the same time Sholokhov openly admires the men of action and conviction, the relatively few ''honest and courageous'' officers who joined the White Army and were dying in battle or of typhus—a unique tribute paid to the enemy by a Soviet writer, a rare case where the quality of character is placed so emphatically above political allegiance.

This emphasis on individual integrity bespeaks Sholokhov's kinship to the Russian classics, particularly to Tolstoi. But, typically for Sholokhov, his seeker for morality is not an intellectual on the order of Prince Andrei, Pierre, or Levin, but a plain Cossack, Grigorii Melekhov. His search for *pravda*—encompassing here the concepts of truth and justice—is not nearly as complex as the quests of Tolstoi's leading characters, but it is conducted under more trying circumstances and is subject to stronger external influences. Wealthy and privileged, Tolstoi's characters had greater freedom to make their choices than did Grigorii. After a brief service in 1805, Prince Andrei was able to avoid active military involvement by taking a recruiting job under his father. By contrast, Grigorii was not allowed to transfer to the commissariat, although at the time of his request he had spent five years in combat and had been wounded or shell-shocked fourteen times (4:138). The internal moral struggle of Tolstoi's characters was not complicated by the necessity of choosing sides in a war, let alone a fratricidal civil war. For all their initial admiration for Napoleon, Prince Andrei and Pierre did everything they could to resist his invasion of their country, confident that their cause was right. On the other hand, Grigorii's search for truth was for the most time encumbered by his doubts as to whether he was fighting on the right side and by his being directly involved in killing people, no matter on which side he fought. Neither Prince Andrei, nor Pierre, nor Olenin had ever been in such a predicament. Moreover, Tolstoi magnanimously kept them from killing anyone, allowing them to search for moral values with consciences undisturbed by homicide. More can be said about the relationship between *The Quiet Don* and Tolstoi's works.[31] At this point, however, I would like to proceed with the discussion of Grigorii's search for truth.

Grigorii Melekhov

From its very beginning Grigorii's search for truth acquires a strong sociopolitical coloration because he has to choose between two different forms of government. His preferences are determined both by historical, social, and economic peculiarities of his native Cossack environment and by his personal traits, which are partly rooted in his environment and partly inherent in him as an individual. The weight of any single social or personal factor varies from one decision to another, with concern for justice taking, as a rule, precedence over all other considerations.

The long story of Grigorii's search for truth begins in the fall of 1914 with his first exposure to Bolshevik propaganda. Sensitive to social inequality and disturbed by "the monstrous absurdity of war," Grigorii turns out to be susceptible to the arguments picturing war as a struggle for the economic aims of capitalists and advocating the forcible replacement of all existing governments by the rule of the working people (1:369-371). His traditional concepts of the tsar, the country, and the military duty of the Cossacks are gradually destroyed. Yet Grigorii's Bolshevism is not translated into any action except for the incident when he breaks off a conversation with a member of the imperial family with the excuse that he feels the need to urinate (1:375). It seems improbable that the intelligent Grigorii would have acted in this ugly manner. The scene's appearance is possibly connected not so much with Grigorii's anger at the royal personage and his entourage—exploiters and warmongers—as with the author's own animosity toward the Russian monarchy and his somewhat stronger-than-average proclivity in his completed novels to pay heed to natural human needs. Grigorii's initial infatuation with Bolshevism does not last for more than two months. During his visit to Tatarskii the traditional military ethics of the Cossacks in him triumph over his Bolshevik leanings (2:45). He goes back to war still unreconciled to its senselessness but determined to fight as befits a Cossack.

This attitude prevails until after October 1917 when Grigorii's political thinking is strongly affected by the views of the Cossack separatist Efim Izvarin and the revolutionary Cossack Podtelkov. Podtelkov's idea of a freely elected Cossack government which would replace the traditional power of the atamans and generals proves to be more appealing to Grigorii's democratic disposition than Izvarin's project of creating a federative Cossack state in southern Russia in which the well-to-do Cossacks are to play a greater political role. Furthermore, Izvarin envisions the expulsion of all Ukrainian peasants from Cossack territory, whereas Grigorii is willing to share the land with those peasants who have lived in the Don region for a long time (2:191, 264).

It is under the influence of Podtelkov that Grigorii joins the troops of the Cossack Revolutionary Committee in the winter of 1918, when the overwhelming majority of the Cossacks watch the incipient civil war from the sidelines. At this time Grigorii admits to having "almost" accepted "the Red faith" (2:239). This faith, however, is soon shaken by his moral indignation at the massacre of the captive White Cossack officers on Podtelkov's orders. Wounded in the fighting against these officers, Grigorii "could neither forgive nor forget" their arbitrary execution (2:254). On his way to Tatarskii, he begins to reconsider his loyalty to the Bolsheviks and to wonder whether Izvarin is right. The past appears to him muddled and contradictory. He sees no clear path for him in the future. Weary of war, he would like to turn away from the world that is "seething with hatred, hostile, and incomprehensible" (2:255). His overriding desire is to return to a peaceful rustic life, plough the land, and tend cattle. Theoretically, he is still "for the Soviet power" (2:263), meaning the power of truly democratic soviets, not the nominal ones serving as a cover for Bolshevik dictatorship.

When in the spring of 1918 the Don Cossacks rise against Bolshevik rule, Grigorii, unlike Koshevoi and Valet, does not flee from Tatarskii to join the Red troops. He explains his decision to stay by an unwillingness to leave his wife and children (2:313). More important, however, is his implied reluctance to serve with the army that robs the Cossacks and rapes their women (2:319). On the other hand, he does not volunteer for the anti-Red detachment of his fellow-villagers when some old Cossacks protest against his election as the commander of the detachment because of his previous service with the Reds. This incident does not prevent him from joining the White Cossacks a week later in the operation against Podtelkov. His heated argument with the captured Podtelkov attests to his considerable shift in the direction of anti-Bolshevism and Cossack nationalism. He upbraids his former mentor for selling out the Cossacks to Moscow and to the Jews. What he has in mind is Podtelkov's role in the establishment of the Bolshevik form of government and his complete dependence on Bolshevik bayonets in keeping this unpopular government alive (2:370). This is not the situation he was looking forward to when he cast his lot with Podtelkov four months ago.

From May to December 1918 Grigorii serves with the White Cossacks commanding alternatingly a platoon and a squadron. At the beginning of his service he does not completely rule out the possibility of going over to the Reds (3:25). Neither he nor the author gives any satisfactory explanation for this vagueness that seems strange in view of Grigorii's recent castigation of Podtelkov. As the war progresses, Grigorii grows increasingly angry with the Bolsheviks. Like the rest of the Cossacks, he views them as invaders who took him away from the peaceful tilling of land. At times he thinks of the war in terms of a struggle between Russian peasants and Cossacks for the beloved land. With all his bitterness toward the Bolsheviks, Grigorii fights against them with a chivalry rare for the time.

He treats his prisoners humanely and takes no part in rampant pillaging of property belonging to the families of Red Army soldiers and those suspected of Bolshevik sympathies (3:83). A feeling of indifference about the course of the war overcomes Grigorii when he realizes that because of their strong desire for peace the Upper Don Cossacks will stop fighting with the arrival of winter. Indeed, at the turn of the year these poorly equipped men, demoralized by the intense cold and Bolshevik propaganda, abandon a large segment of the front along the northern borders of the Don Military Region. At the onset of the collapse Grigorii deserts his unit, nonchalantly thinking of rejoining his comrades when they pass by Tatarskii (3:97).

As the Red Army approaches Tatarskii, Grigorii and Petr decide, after much hesitation, to stay at home so that they can offer some protection to their wives and sister should the enemy soldiers attempt to rape them (3:112). What Grigorii sees and experiences during one month of Red occupation determines his choice of a warring side for the whole year. Twice he has to flee from Tatarskii to save his life. The first time a Red soldier attempts to murder him at a carousal just because he is an officer. It does not matter to the Reds that Grigorii holds the lowest officer's rank and that he received it exclusively for his valor in World War I. The second time Koshevoi enters his name on the list of enemies of the Soviet regime who are to be handed over to the Revolutionary tribunal for prompt trial and execution. This time Grigorii is to be liquidated for his perceptive views on the Bolsheviks which he expresses in an argument with his old friends, Kotliarov and Koshevoi, now the leading figures in the local Revolutionary committee. As a democrat, Grigorii is appalled by the emergence of a privileged stratum in the Bolshevik environment and wonders what will happen to equality when the Bolshevik rule is firmly established. The Bolshevik propaganda of equality is in his eyes just bait to catch ignorant folk. As a Cossack, he feels that his people have all the freedom and land they need and that the Bolshevik regime will bring them nothing but ruination. The government of the Russian Bolsheviks is as unappealing to his nationalist sentiments as the military rule over the Cossacks under the tsars: "Communists or generals—it's the same yoke on our necks" (3:152). Nevertheless, he sees a difference between the two. Bad as the generals were, "a lout becoming a lord is a hundred times worse" (3:153).

In the wake of his argument with Kotliarov and Koshevoi, Grigorii comes to the conclusion that he was foolish to search for a single universal truth. Such a truth does not exist. Different people have their own different truths, depending on their aspirations. The war appears to him as a conflict between the truth of the Russian peasants and the truth of the Cossacks. The peasants want Cossack land, the Cossacks defend it (3:156, 188). The war is thus a manifestation of the perennial human struggle for "a piece of bread, for a strip of land, for the right to live" (3:188). Here Grigorii applies the laws of nature to human society. The sentence expressing his thoughts on the human struggle bears a close semantical, lexical, and syntactical resemblance to the sentence describing the fighting bustards at the end of volume 2.

Grigorii's enthusiasm to fight the Red invaders reaches its peak in March 1919 when he madly gallops to Tatarskii to join the insurgent Cossacks. His fierce determination to drive the Reds out of the Don region springs from his indignation at the mass killing and pillaging of Cossacks by the invaders, from his attachment to "the rich Don earth *conquered* by Cossack blood," and from his justification of the Cossacks' right to extensive landownership: "We allowed the regiments of *stinking Russia* onto the Cossack lands. *They passed through it like the Germans through Poland, like the Cossacks through Prussia. Blood and devastation covered the steppe. . . . We are all the tsar's landowners. One Cossack allotment can go up to thirty-two acres. Protect your land!*" (3:188). The *Oktiabr'* editors deleted or replaced the italicized words and added the phrase "flaming with blind hatred" to the description of Grigorii's emotional state.[32] The addition was intended to play down humanitarian, patriotic, and economic motives for Grigorii's anti-Bolshevik sentiments by presenting them primarily as an outburst of irrational anger.

Yet even in its revised form the content of Grigorii's inner monologue during his ride to Tatarskii is at variance with his later statement to Koshevoi: "If the Red soldiers hadn't planned to kill me at that carousal, I might have not taken part in the uprising" (4:346). First printed in *Pravda* on December 31, 1939, as part of an excerpt from the novel, this statement implies that Grigorii's joining the insurgents resulted from his overreaction to an isolated incident, rather than from his opposition to the Bolshevik invasion as a whole. The statement is all the more incongruous because originally Grigorii did not attach much significance to the incident at the carousal. He returned to Tatarskii as soon as the Red troops left it and related the incident to Kotliarov and Koshevoi, adding that he did not regret his decision not to retreat with the Whites (3:137). But he had to flee from Tatarskii and welcome the insurrection after Koshevoi, Kotliarov, and Shtokman had decided to hand him over to the Revolutionary tribunal as an exceptionally dangerous enemy (3:164, 176-177). This decision played a far greater role in turning him away from the Reds than did the soldier's attempt to murder him. Nonetheless, it was secondary to his determination to defend the Cossack land and to free it from the Red terror. What the author, or the censor, allowed Grigorii to say in 1930 or even 1932 could not be reiterated in the late thirties or ever since.

The political orientation of the Upper Don insurgents appealed to Grigorii because they tried to steer a middle course between the Bolsheviks and the White generals. The insurgents advanced the slogan, "For Soviet power but against the commune, shooting, and pillaging" (3:197). They retained the use of the word "comrade" and replaced Revolutionary committees with soviets.[33] It was clear to Grigorii, however, that a position between the Reds and the Whites could not be maintained for a long time. The insurgents faced eventual destruction by the numerically superior enemy. Their sole hope for survival lay in uniting themselves with the Don Army that was now a part of the White forces commanded by General Anton Denikin. In June 1919 the Don Army fought its way to the insurgents.

Strange as it may seem, Grigorii wavers more during his participation in the uprising than during his subsequent service with the Don Army. Although he joins the uprising with great enthusiasm and becomes commander of an insurgent division, he almost immediately begins to wonder whether he is fighting on the right side and whether the Cossacks are not making a mistake by rising against the Russian people (3:217, 219, 235). These doubts appear to be somewhat unexpected and insufficiently motivated. They surface in Grigorii's fleeting thoughts, brief remarks, or in the frantic exclamations he shouts when writhing in a fit after sabering Red sailors (3:267). On occasion he also drops incredible half-serious hints that he might go over to the Reds (3:258; 4:87). Be that as it may, Grigorii does not display much devotion to the cause for which he is fighting. He grows indifferent to the outcome of the insurrection (3:349). Playing a leading part in the slaughter he considers senseless, Grigorii tries to escape from reality. For a while he seeks refuge in vodka, women, and his rekindled passion for Aksin'ia.

In spite of his doubts and contradictions, Grigorii invariably leads his Cossacks with great determination and skill. The only time he evades direct participation in battle is after his bitter clash with General Fitskhelaurov (4:96). The clash intensifies his long-standing antagonism toward generals and educated officers. He always felt that "the learned people" despised the common folk and manipulated them in their own interests. His antipathy to those whom he calls "the white-faced," "white-handed," "well-mannered and educated parasites" (3:349; 4:87) is the only one of his anti-White sentiments that is sufficiently developed by the author. It is possible that Grigorii's view of "the educated parasites" mirrors in some degree the author's own attitude toward the intelligentsia. Although Grigorii feels that he can no longer defend people like Fitskhelaurov, he is aware of his inability to reconcile the Cossacks with the Bolsheviks. Moreover, he knows that "deep in his heart he could not reconcile himself with them either" (4:96). With utmost clarity he sees the futility of the war. Yet there is no alternative for him but to continue fighting on the White side, and in the next battle he leads his division to a crushing victory, rendering a great service to General Sutulov (4:128). In the same chapter the author makes Grigorii utter, in a rather inconspicuous way, two sentences revealing a great deal about his ideological remoteness from the Bolsheviks. The sentences are addressed to Colonel Andreianov, Grigorii's chief of staff: "Yesterday . . . you, colonel, talked a lot of sense about the sort of systems that will have to be introduced into the army after we've beaten the Bolsheviks, so we can drive the Red infection out of the young people. I fully agreed with you, remember?" (4:136). The views Grigorii endorses must be ultra-conservative and resolutely anti-Bolshevik. Andreianov is a conceited nobleman, hating all plain Cossacks and soldiers for their "betrayal" in 1917 and believing that only his class can save Russia. Moreover, the boastful, garrulous, and cowardly colonel, who avoided front-line service as long as possible, represents the kind of people Grigorii despises most. That Grigorii agrees with such a man is a strong indication of his nonacceptance of the Bolshevik system. The Whites turn out to be the lesser evil for him.

By accident or not, Grigorii's conversation with Andreianov becomes the dividing line beyond which he stops vacillating and firmly sides with the Whites until the bitter end of Denikin's army. During the decisive Red offensive his main concern is not to fall into the hands of the enemy. Hardly recovered from typhus, he leaves Tatarskii to begin a tortuous retreat that terminates in Novorossiisk in March 1920. At times he hopes against hope that the Whites would still be able to turn the tide, and he even thinks of joining a regular white unit (4:251). Felled by a relapse of typhus, he would rather die on the road than cut short his journey and let himself be captured by the Reds (4:257). In Novorossiisk he tries hard to get on a ship evacuating the troops. Had there been a place for him on the ship, he would have sailed for the Crimea and probably there joined the Whites under General Petr Vrangel'. He would serve with Vrangel' until the final defeat and then sail from the Crimea toward foreign lands in November 1920. During the retreat he had already reckoned with the eventuality of emigration and was prepared to follow his White leaders into it (4:253-254).

The actual course of events took a different turn. Only the Volunteer Corps, the kernel of the White forces, was transported to the Crimea in its entirety, while the majority of the Cossacks were stranded in Novorossiisk. This development prompted General Vladimir Sidorin, commander of the Don Army, to accuse the Supreme Command of having betrayed the Cossacks. General Denikin denied the charge,[34] but most Cossacks felt the same way as Sidorin did. It was this bitterness at the

White command that moved Grigorii to remain in Novorossiisk and to surrender to the Reds rather than to continue the retreat toward Georgia (4:266, 276).

Taken prisoner by the Reds, Grigorii passed a special security screening and joined the First Cavalry Army commanded by Semen Budennyi. This was the time when the Bolshevik government was confronted with the imminent escalation of war with Poland and was eager to reinforce its cavalry with captive Cossacks. Even before the fall of Novorossiisk Lenin urged the Revolutionary Military Council of the Caucasus Front to prepare for the speediest transfer of as many troops as possible to the western front and to recruit prisoners in "the most vigorous manner [*arkhienergichno*]."[35] Although Grigorii's service with the Reds lasted for seven months, it is not described directly by the author. Everything that the reader is told about it comes from Grigorii and Prokhor in the form of brief accounts. In all probability Sholokhov shunned a more detailed portrayal of Grigorii's service with the Reds because in the late thirties such a portrayal could not be presented without an excessive and false idealization of the Red armed forces, especially the First Cavalry Army. No Red Army formation had been as persistently and auspiciously extolled in the Soviet periodical press, books, paintings, and songs as the First Cavalry. The chief reason for this glorification was Stalin, one of the First Cavalry's organizers and its honorary soldier. The First Cavalry proved to be an efficient fighting force, but it also knew defeats and demoralization, notably in the Polish campaign. To write about its negative aspects in the late thirties would be suicidal. Soviet history had already been rewritten, but even as early as 1924 the depiction of the First Cavalry in literature was a very sensitive matter. I am referring, of course, to Budennyi's savage attack on Isaak Babel' for the alleged slander of this "greatest instrument of the class struggle."[36] Sholokhov's decision to leave out Grigorii's service with Budennyi had more to do with the political atmosphere of the late thirties than with his 1949 assertion that it would have required an additional volume to present an appropriate portrayal of the First Cavalry, and that this would have damaged the structure of the novel.[37] The author did not have to devote the whole volume to this army. The point is that he passed over it altogether.

While the description of the military reverses and discipline problems of the First Cavalry was under a taboo, Sholokhov was also not in a position to say much about Grigorii's motives for fighting on the Red side or about his relations with the Communists in his unit unless he intended to end the novel with Grigorii's conversion to the Bolshevik faith. But neither the author nor his characters were interested in this kind of a happy ending. Although Grigorii was eager to serve the Soviet regime when he entered its army and although he became assistant regiment commander, he did not fight for the Bolshevik system, but for himself, for his right to return to his family and to Aksin'ia. As he saw it, he made a deal with the Soviet regime. He was to fight with the Reds until the end of the war, to make up for his fighting against them in the past (4:289-290). The Soviet regime, however, merely wanted to use his military skills in an emergency situation. His service became unbearable for him as soon as he noticed that the commissar and the Communists of his unit were keeping him under surveillance, fearing that he would betray them in battle (4:356). A vivid description of these nearsighted and callous Communists—the people who in Soviet fiction have to be presented as politically clairvoyant and responsible—would have been unpublishable. As victory over the Whites became certain, Grigorii was demobilized and sent home to be punished there for his role in the Upper Don uprising. The reason for the demobilization was clear to him: "I was no longer needed" (4:339). He used the same words at Novorossiisk to tell the Whites why they barred him from boarding the ship (4:266).

Discharged by the Reds, Grigorii returns home with the firm intention not to get involved in any struggle between the Soviet regime and its opponents. In his words, he is "fed up with everything, with the revolution and the counter-revolution" (4:347). All he wants is to live in peace with Aksin'ia and his children and till the land. His hopes, however, are immediately dashed by the vindictive policy of the Bolsheviks. Mishka Koshevoi, now his brother-in-law and chairman of the local Revolutionary committee, receives Grigorii with blind mistrust and tells him that he should be punished without leniency for his fighting against the Reds. Then Grigorii is subjected to an extensive interrogation by the Cheka about his role in the Upper Don uprising. There is no doubt in his mind that he will be arrested and, most likely, shot (4:365). The prospect of being shot appears to him as an unjust punishment in view of his honest service with the First Cavalry Army, and he decides not to let himself be arrested. When Koshevoi and other Bolsheviks are about to seize him, he flees from Tatarskii.

The flight marks Grigorii's final separation from the Bolshevik regime. The responsibility for the break rests with the Bolsheviks. They betrayed his trust by not taking into account his service in the First Cavalry and they made an enemy out of him by intending to take his life. The Bolsheviks let him down in a more reprehensible manner than did the Whites who did not have enough ships to evacuate all the troops from Novorossiisk. These two betrayals are the high points in Grigorii's political odyssey in volume 4. They justify his moral unacceptance of each of the warring sides and accentuate his tragedy of being compelled to take an active part in the mortal struggle between them.

The treacherous treatment of Grigorii by the Whites and the Reds stands in sharp contrast to the steadfast loyalty of the people close to him. This personal loyalty is not dictated by any political considerations. The individual must be a decent human being in the eyes of those who remain faithful to him in any adversity. Sholokhov places such a high value on personal loyalty that at the risk of overstating the obvious he uses the adjective *vernyi* (faithful, true) in connection with those who are devoted to Grigorii. He makes Aksin'ia say that her love for Grigorii is "true" (4:230). He refers twice to Prokhor as Grigorii's "faithful orderly" (4:231, 338). And even Grigorii's saber is said to have served him "faithfully" (4:229). To make sure that the reader does not miss the point, the author employs the word "faithful" three times within three consecutive pages. Significantly, these pages describe Grigorii's final preparations for his bitter retreat into the unknown with the defeated Whites in December 1919. At this critical juncture in his life the loyalty of those close to him is of particular value. The "faithful orderly" reappears in another critical situation—when Grigorii returns from his service with the Red cavalry and is met with Koshevoi's hostility. At this time Duniashka also displays an unshakeable loyalty to Grigorii in spite of her marriage to Koshevoi. She makes it possible for Grigorii to escape by warning him that her husband is about to arrest him. She saves Grigorii not only because he is her brother, but also because she believes that the punishment awaiting him after his arrest will be too severe. Later she helps him to carry out his plan of escaping with Aksin'ia, although her cooperation with "a bandit" is punishable by death. I cannot but think of the chasm separating Duniashka from Pavlik Morozov.

To avoid being captured by the Bolsheviks, Grigorii has no choice but to join a detachment of insurgent Cossacks under the command of Iakov Fomin. Although he joins Fomin without the enthusiasm he had at the beginning of the Upper Don uprising, Grigorii is no longer tormented by doubts as to whether he is fighting on the right side. For personal and political reasons he is vitally interested in overthrowing the Bolshevik regime. Victory over the Soviets would unite him with Aksin'ia and his children and free the Cossacks from the regime they hate because of the ruthless requisitioning of their grain. But the Cossacks are bled white in the Civil War, tired of fighting, and unarmed. It is also time for sowing, and Grigorii "with anxiety and bitterness" thinks that "they will probably not succeed in raising the Cossacks" (4:400). In spite of the unpromising situation and his decision to flee with Aksin'ia to the Kuban' region in the summer, Grigorii does not grow indifferent and does not seek refuge in vodka as he did during the Upper Don uprising. On the contrary, he vigorously reproaches Fomin for taking to drinking and for looting the families of Soviet employees. He is concerned with the reputation of the detachment: ''The people are beginning to talk badly of us'' (4:404). He is prepared to take half of the men away from Fomin and thus become commander of his own troop. He has no intention of surrendering even though only five men survived the rout of the Fomin detachment (4:419). But when Fomin manages to form a new detachment, Grigorii is no longer concerned with its condition. His aloofness is caused by the change in the attitude of the local population from friendly to hostile. The villagers now run away or hide from the partisans, knowing that many of the Cossacks who had previously welcomed Fomin were ''severely punished'' (euphemism for ''shot'') by the Revolutionary tribunal (4:441).

The Cossacks' alienation from the partisans compels Grigorii to speed up the realization of his plan concerning Aksin'ia. He terminates his armed struggle against the Bolsheviks with the single desire to start a new peaceful life with his beloved somewhere outside the Don region. Aksin'ia's death crushes him. The last months of Grigorii's life are marked by his complete mental alienation from the contemporary world. All his life is in the past and strictly personal. It is filled with painful reminiscences and dreams of Aksin'ia, his mother, and other relatives who are dead. His sole link to the living—the yearning for his children—is also intimate and biological. All he wants is to see once more his native village and his children. ''Then I can die,'' he thinks (at the age of thirty), revealing that he has no illusions about what awaits him in Tatarskii (4:461). Nothing matters any more. The most terrible thing in his life—the death of his beloved—has already happened. When the urge to see his children becomes overpowering, he goes to Tatarskii. The novel's last sentence says that his son and the home where he was born are ''all that was left in his life, all that for the time being made him akin to this earth and the whole . . . world.'' The Russian words for ''where he was born'' and ''made him akin'' are here, respectively, *rodnoi* and *rodnit'*, which at times are virtually untranslatable. They come from the root denoting birth and suggest a very close relationship. Sholokhov obviously chose them to emphasize that Grigorii's life was reduced to the feelings associated with the very essential of existence—with being born and giving birth. The use of *rodnoi* and *rodnit'* also enhances the emotional impact of the ending. The connection of these words with birth adds a touch of sadness to Grigorii's impending death.

In several ways the story of Grigorii's life may be viewed as questioning the soundness of Bolshevik theory and practice. The forces of nature informing his love for Aksin'ia and his attachment to his offspring and family proved to be more determinant for his behavior than economic or social conditions. Although he belonged to an economically privileged stratum, Grigorii was willing to share Cossack land with the peasants in the winter of 1918. But at the beginning of the Upper Don uprising he was fiercely determined to fight for it against the peasants. At this time Grigorii's martial temper ran high, but for the greater part of his long military career he was internally opposed to both World War I and the Civil War. Here lies another difference between him and the Bolsheviks who advocated the transformation of World War I into a civil war and viewed the latter as a means of seizing political power. Sholokhov, of course, could not express Grigorii's opposition to the Civil War by calling a spade a spade, especially after two references to the foolishness of that war—one of them representing the opinion of all the Cossacks, including Grigorii—had already been censored in 1933 (3:25, 82).[38] Hence in the passages showing Grigorii's desire to stay away from the senseless slaughter, the unnamed Civil War appears in the guise of such transparent designations as "what was going on around him" (3:254) or "what was taking place" (4:96). Grigorii's individualism, nonconformism, openmindedness, and personal quest for truth and justice distinguish him from a typical Bolshevik constrained in his thinking by dogmatic slogans and blindly following the dictates of his superiors.

It is difficult to ascertain the degree to which Grigorii is representative of the author's thoughts and feelings. As of now, Sholokhov has provided no evidence in the form of diaries, notes, or autobiographical sketches which could shed any light on the subject. One has to rely primarily on certain passages in *The Quiet Don* and on the author's rather scanty statements about his characters. The discussion of the role of nature in *The Quiet Don* has already shown that Grigorii's love for Aksin'ia illustrates the author's view on the supremacy of natural impulses in man. Furthermore, Sholokhov's treatment of nature gives a strong indication that he, like Grigorii, does not consider war to be the most sensible way of solving sociopolitical problems. When at the outbreak of the Upper Don uprising Grigorii justifies the war by virtually equating it with a natural fight for the right to live, the author probably disagrees with him. But what is the author's attitude when a few lines later Grigorii speaks to himself of driving the Reds out of the Don land "soaked with Cossack blood" (3:188)? These are precisely the words with which the author concludes his apostrophe to the Don steppe, the most personal and emotional digression in all of his writings (3:60). Does this connection suggest that the Cossack Grigorii Melekhov is after all not wrong in defending the land which the non-Cossack Sholokhov calls "my dear" (*rodimaia*) and which he kisses like a son? The decision is left to the reader. As usual, the author shuns an easy answer and complicates the dilemma by mingling pros and cons. Only in a few instances does he venture to state his position directly. When Grigorii discards his early Bolshevism in favor of the traditional Cossacks' code of behavior, the author calls the former "the great human truth" (2:45). Elsewhere he refers to the Cossacks withdrawing toward Novorossiisk as "the descendants of the free Cossacks, shamefully retreating after being defeated in an inglorious war against the Russian people" (4:261). One can question, of course, why the Cossacks' resistance to the oppression of the international-minded Bolshevism should be termed a war against the Russian people or why the Cossacks' retreat should be called shameful in view of the vast numerical and material superiority of their enemy. The author's political dicta seem to be intended to countervail undesirable inferences that the reader might draw from the predominantly objective narrative.

Sholokhov's recorded statements about Grigorii vary a great deal, their content frequently depending on the political climate of the time. His most valuable statement was made in the relatively free atmosphere of early 1929 before a large audience of Moscow factory workers: "Grigorii in my opinion is a kind of a symbol of the middle stratum of the Don Cossacks. Those who know the history of the Civil War in the Don region, and who know its course, also know that more than one Grigorii Melekhov and more than dozens of Grigorii Melekhovs vacillated until 1920, when an end was put to these vacillations. I am taking Grigorii as he is, as he actually was, therefore I show him vacillating, but I do not want to depart from historical truth."[39] A 1935 comment is quite different: "Melekhov's fate is very much his own, and in no way am I trying to represent in him the middle stratum of the Cossacks."[40] In 1935 Sholokhov obviously did not want to imply that the majority of the Cossacks remained at odds with the Bolshevik regime, as did Grigorii. The most he would do for his protagonist was to take him away from the Whites, but "not turn him into a Bolshevik. He is not a Bolshevik!"[41]

In December 1939 Sholokhov threw light on Grigorii's fate. "Remember Taras Bul'ba saying to Andrii, 'I begot you and I will kill you!'?"[42] he remarked, adding that the writer must tell the truth no matter how bitter it might be. Three months later the publication of the novel's ending showed that he did not change his mind. Moreover, unlike many critics, he refrained from any political denunciations of Grigorii that would justify the Bolsheviks' rough treatment of him in the last part of the novel.

In June 1947 Sholokhov described Grigorii in terms representing a hybrid between his 1929 and 1935 statements. He went so far as to assert that Grigorii personified the characteristic traits not only of "a certain stratum" of the Don, Kuban', and all other Cossacks, but also of the Russian peasantry as a whole. He did not elaborate which traits or which stratum he had in mind. At the same time he emphasized the uniqueness of Grigorii's fate by calling it "his own to a significant degree."[43] By doing so, Sholokhov killed two birds with one stone. One could not reproach him for implying that the majority of the Cossacks had the same anti-Bolshevik record as Grigorii, and he indicated that above all his protagonist was a fictional character, not a carbon copy of a certain sociopolitical type. This point was also implicit in his remarks made in 1951 in Bulgaria about people like Grigorii.

Reflecting the extreme politicization of literature by Zhdanovism, the Bulgarian remarks left much to be desired regarding their fidelity to the facts. Soviet power, Sholokhov said, led people of Grigorii's type "out of an impasse in which they found themselves. Some of them chose a complete break with Soviet reality, but the majority drew close to Soviet power. They served in the Soviet Army during the Fatherland War and are taking part in building up the national economy."[44] The main purpose of the pronouncement was a propagandistic glorification of the Soviet regime. What the Bulgarians heard had no relation to *The Quiet Don*, where the Soviet regime is shown doing its best to alienate and kill Grigorii, just as it did with people like him in real life. Kharlampii Ermakov, Platon Riabchikov, and Fedor Melikhov were shot long before they would have had a chance to serve in the Soviet Army during "the Fatherland War," that is, World War II. Sholokhov, however, made a loophole for himself in the above quotation. By saying that some people of Grigorii's type broke with the Soviets for good, he reserved for himself the right to claim that Grigorii was among them.

In the post-Stalin period Sholokhov has been as parsimonious with his comments on Grigorii as before. Nevertheless, he volunteered a few insights into his concept of Grigorii's tragedy. For him it is the tragedy of a seeker after truth who is trapped by the events of his time and lets the truth pass by. The truth is naturally with the Bolsheviks. Simultaneously, Sholokhov brought out the strictly personal aspects of Grigorii's tragedy and attacked the crude politicization of the novel's final scene in the film script written by the director Sergei Gerasimov. In the novel, he said, Grigorii acts as a father who has not seen his son for a long time. He encloses the boy in a strong, manlike embrace, causing him some pain. "But in the script Grigorii Melekhov puts Mishatka on his shoulder and walks somewhere uphill with him. A symbolic ending, so to speak: Grishka Melekhov goes up towards the gleaming heights of Communism. What may come out of it is a sort of frivolous poster instead of a picture of human tragedy."[45] In 1965 Sholokhov stated that a great deal of responsibility for this tragedy lay with Grigorii himself, though Koshevoi's "leftism" contributed to it. Yet in 1977 the author absolved Grigorii from any "guilt" for his tragedy by pointing to the complex interplay of historical, social, and political forces in the Don region.[46]

Sholokhov's comments on Grigorii's tragedy indicate that, at least in print, he talks about it in political terms. The tragic situation in which Grigorii finds himself at the end of the novel is for him a result of Grigorii's failure to join the Bolsheviks, the custodians of the genuine truth. This is the sole interpretation of Grigorii's tragedy found in Soviet sources. Its exponents differ only in the apportioning of "guilt" among those responsible for Grigorii's tragedy. Some put the blame primarily or entirely on Grigorii, while the others emphasize mistakes of the local Bolsheviks. The central government is, of course, beyond reproach. Apart from their primitive politicization of the very concept of tragedy, the Soviet interpreters of Grigorii's case proceed from the questionable premise that the Bolshevik regime is an incarnation of truth and justice. Any openminded student of that regime would rather tend to agree with Solzhenitsyn's identification of it with lies and violence. These were precisely the qualities that prevented Grigorii from accepting the Bolshevik regime throughout the greater part of the novel. The tragic flaw was not his political orientation, but his true love for Aksin'ia. This is how his tragedy is presented in *The Quiet Don*.[47]

Nearly all that Sholokhov said about Grigorii came in the form of replies to questions concerning the sociopolitical image of his protagonist. During a 1957 interview, however, he went beyond politics to volunteer what might well be his most revealing statement: "What the writer most of all needs—is to convey the movement of the human soul. I wanted to tell about this human charm through Grigorii Melekhov, but I did not quite succeed. Maybe I will succeed in the novel about those who fought for their country."[48]

In *The Quiet Don* the theme of human charm becomes a manifestation of redeeming qualities amidst cataclysm and bloodshed. It is up to the individual to preserve his humanity under trying conditions. Grigorii succeeds in doing so. The impact of historical forces upon him is formidable. They ruin his hopes for a peaceful life, entangle him in wars he considers senseless, and make him lose his belief in God and his pity for man. But they still prove powerless to destroy the grain of his soul—his inherent decency and his capacity for true love. In this sense Grigorii cannot be considered a victim of an inevitable historical process. Its victim is rather Koshevoi. It is he who loses a great deal of his original human charm.

The author's view of his characters may be reflected in what the characters say about one another. Two such opinions are of particular interest in connection with Grigorii and Koshevoi. Both are voiced toward the end of the novel and can be taken as summations. In official Soviet parlance Grigorii is a "bandit." The term carries the highest degree of opprobrium and is the only one allowed in the press to designate anti-Bolshevik partisans of all nationalities and times. But at least indirectly Sholokhov seems to question the applicability of this term to Grigorii. He makes Aksin'ia say to Mishatka that his father is not a bandit, but just an "unfortunate man" (4:456). Whether Aksin'ia speaks for the author is a moot question, but her judgment is not likely to pass unnoticed. By the same token, when Grigorii says to Koshevoi, "What scum [*svolochnoi*] you've become" (4:348), the reader may find it hard to disagree with Grigorii. All the more so since Grigorii expresses his opinion not so much with anger as with bewilderment at the stupid, hostile, and insulting way in which Koshevoi reacted to his return from service with the First Cavalry Army. The author's realism did not spare the sole Bolshevik character that was left alive for the duration of the novel's last volume. *Svolochnoi*, incidentally, is what the teacher Golovin called Turilin in "The Wind," when the latter told about his doctoring two pregnant girls to death.

THE DESCENT

Sholokhov's treatment of Grigorii and Koshevoi represents a kind of realism that is typical of *The Quiet Don*. Its core is an objective portrayal of opposites. It brings face to face conflicts occurring between and within historical movements, different social strata, and individuals. It is a realism of intense confrontation. Its courage and scope are unique in Soviet literature. The density of confrontation in *The Quiet Don* is felt more acutely than in the novels of Tolstoi or even of Dostoevskii. Revolutions and wars, especially a civil war, offer a multitude of diverse and sharp conflicts. Sholokhov focuses on them without either philosophizing very much or providing recipes for solutions.

The saturation of *The Quiet Don* with conflicts, clashes, and contradictions imparts to the novel the differentiae of a dramatic composition. Indeed, the novel is a blend of a historical drama and a tragedy of individual love. The author develops these themes in a series of highly dramatic situations, injecting dozens of pros and cons and shunning simplification. Thus Grigorii is put in a complicated and contradictory situation between Aksin'ia and Natal'ia. This intricate love triangle gives the author an opportunity to create a number of tense relationships and emotionally charged scenes. Among them are confrontations between Aksin'ia and Natal'ia, Grigorii and Stepan, Grigorii and Listnitskii, Petr and Stepan, and Aksin'ia and the old Melekhovs. In another case the author designs a delicate predicament for Grigorii's mother by making her live under the same roof with Koshevoi, the killer of her elder son and the husband of her only daughter.

Sholokhov's concern with the complexities of life is likewise seen in his reluctance to portray his characters only in black and white. In spite of all her love for Grigorii and her pride, Aksin'ia would be happy to remain Listnitskii's mistress after his marriage and, when rejected, begs him for a parting sexual favor (3:58-59). Implacable in his hostility toward Grigorii, Koshevoi is friendly and gentle with his son (4:300). Calculated cruelty coexists in Bunchuk with passionate irrational love. The human soul is a mystery, and its contrasting qualities may surface unexpectedly, surprising the reader accustomed to seeing a character in a different light. The usually quiet, restrained, and unaggressive Natal'ia bursts into a violent condemnation of the unfaithful Grigorii, imploring God to kill him (4:147). Shortly before her suicide, the promiscuous and cynical Dar'ia suddenly opens her eyes to the beauty of the surrounding world and regrets having lived her life without a single true love (4:123, 127). The unsentimental killer Chumakov turns out to be capable of displaying a touching humaneness toward his wounded comrade (4:435).

To portray both historical and individual conflicts and complexities effectively, the author of *The Quiet Don* needed more than desire and talent. He needed a strong will and a determination to overcome the formidable political obstacles that kept arising during his entire period of work on the novel. By and large he succeeded in realizing his objective. But what about his other works?

Virgin Soil Upturned deals with what was probably the most significant event in Soviet history between the Civil War and World War II. In the eyes of its opponents, collectivization of agriculture was a war of destruction unleashed by the Bolshevik regime against the peasants in order to reshape their life and labor in accordance with faulty ideological blueprints. Sholokhov, however, presents collectivization as a well-intentioned action in the best interests of the peasant masses. Unlike *The Quiet Don*, volume 1 of *Virgin Soil Upturned* was written "hot on the scent of events,"[49] and it was impossible for its author to place them in a historical perspective. This volume has the immediacy of an eyewitness report. The drama of the first five months of collectivization is re-created quite vividly. The dynamic events—such as stormy public meetings, the dispossession of the kulaks, the murder of Khoprov and his wife, the slaughter of cattle, the riot of the Cossack women, and the seizure of grain stored on the collective farm—follow each other in rapid succession, generating at times great tension and suspense. Relief is provided by the comic stories and mishaps of old Shchukar', a popular storyteller type, a born braggard, and an unfortunate wretch. The comic element is much stronger here than in *The Quiet Don*. Occasionally, it tends to degenerate into slapstick and windy eloquence.

Taken as a whole, volume 1 gives the official interpretation of events.

Its political high point is the weaving of Stalin's article "Dizzy with Success" into the fabric of the story. The article condemns the excesses committed during collectivization and appears to leave the peasant a choice between private and collective farming. Yet Sholokhov is fair enough to let some dissenting voices be heard. The truth is glimpsed when the foe Polovtsev calls Stalin's article "a despicable fraud and maneuver" (5:209) and when the friend Nagul'nov speaks of the compulsory nature of collectivization, arguing that the Soviet treatment of the peasants leaves them no alternative but to join collective farms (5:312). This sensitive theme is not developed any further.

Virgin Soil Upturned knows no full-blooded characters like Grigorii and Aksin'ia. Its principal female character, Lushka, is in a way a variation of Dar'ia Melekhova. Its protagonist, Semen Davydov, is rather flat. One of the twenty-five thousand industrial workers sent by the Party in 1929 to help organize collective farms, he is just a cog in the Party machine. He unquestioningly accepts any Party directive and shows no inclination for an independent evaluation of events. Like Bunchuk, he naively believes in the bright Communist future and stops at nothing to speed its arrival. Since the deportation of the so-called kulaks is regarded as a vital step toward the millennium, he feels and preaches no pity for their children, who are being sent together with their families to northern regions of Russia in midwinter. To him this treatment of the kulak children is perfectly justified because "the enemies" (unidentified) did not shed tears over the suffering of "our children" (5:62). Nor did enemies weep over his own sufferings when as a boy of nine he saw his mother turn to prostitution to feed her four children after her husband had been exiled to Siberia for taking part in a strike at his factory. Let us note that Bunchuk "almost choked" with hatred recalling a girl of twelve who became a prostitute after her father, a Petrograd worker, had been killed in World War I (2:154). It is somewhat unusual that Sholokhov's Communists single out survival through prostitution as one of the gravest ills caused by the callousness of the privileged classes, a callousness that justifies any kind of Bolshevik terror during and after the Revolution. Davydov does not indicate that the majority of the kulak families are sent to a sure death. On the contrary, he declares that the kulaks would certainly not die in exile and their children would be reeducated by the working class (5:62). The veil over the real fate of the exiled is cautiously lifted in the last chapter of volume 1. The fugitive Timofei Damaskov tells about his father's death in Kotlas, a region in northern Russia "from where there is no coming back" (5:333). Indeed, Kotlas "had been thickly settled by peasants when they were exiled in 1930 (one must realize that they had no roofs over their heads, but nobody is left to tell about it)."[50]

The two leading local Communists, Makar Nagul'nov and Andrei Razmetnov, are imbued with more life and individuality than Davydov. The secretary of the local Party cell, Makar is a colorful figure. A self-made fanatic and idealist, he has enough courage and honesty to be critical of "Dizzy with Success" (5:215). An impulsive but solemn extremist, he is obsessed with world revolution. His zeal to serve the Revolution goes far beyond the deportation of kulak children. In the name of the Revolution he declares himself prepared to machine-gun thousands of children, old men, and women (5:63). Razmetnov is different. A moderate man with a touch of gentleness and humor, he refuses to take further part in dispossessing the kulaks, out of pity for their children and out of disgust for a job which does not become a former soldier (5:61).

The scene of Razmetnov's refusal to participate in the eviction of the kulaks is significant in several ways. It brings to light the essential traits of the Communist characters. It shows the unlimited cruelty of which man is capable in acting for "the public good," however arbitrarily this concept may be defined by a narrow group of self-righteous tyrants. The deportation of the kulaks is a landmark in the history of terrorism. According to Solzhenitsyn, it was the first time—at least in modern history—that whole families were sent to destruction. The experiment "was subsequently repeated by Hitler with the Jews, and again by Stalin with the nationalities which were disloyal to him or suspected by him."[51] In looking back to Russian nineteenth-century literature, it is hard not to think of Ivan Karamazov's rejection of world harmony if the price of it is a single tearlet of one child tortured to death. Half a century later the heroes of socialist realism priced their brand of harmony above the tears of millions of children starved and frozen to death.

The three principal adversaries of the Bolsheviks are portrayed as having no lofty ideals. The most implacable and least selfish of the enemies is Aleksandr Polovtsev, a former Cossack captain. His immediate goal is the liberation of the Don and Russia from the oppressive and atheistic rule of the Bolsheviks through a Cossack uprising. His positive program is not clearly defined and appears to amount to the restoration of pre-Revolutionary order. He is not a separatist. His dedication to the Don land and Russia is sincere and seemingly unselfish. Ruthless, resourceful, and resolute, he emanates an awesome and somber power. To avoid a simplistic portrayal of this enemy, Sholokhov imbues him with two contrasting characteristics. Capable of slaughtering people and sheep in cold blood, he is touchingly fond of children and cats; in fact, he cannot stand children's tears (5:202). A comparison with Davydov and Nagul'nov suggests itself here. And it is not in their favor. Vatslav Liat'evskii, a former second lieutenant, projects the stereotyped image of a White Army officer as painted by official propaganda. A son of a landed nobleman, he opposes the Bolsheviks, with the sole purpose of regaining his class privileges and wealth. As a person, he is an antipode of Polovtsev. There is not a trace of the solemn stiffness and individual devotion to the cause in him. He is frivolous, occasionally reckless, and frankly cynical about the chances of overthrowing the Bolshevik regime. Although a villain, he elicits some admiration by his audacity, cheerfulness, and sense of humor. Iakov Ostrovnov is against the Soviet regime because it destroyed his dreams about becoming the richest man in the village. Yet his joining Polovtsev puts him in a delicate situation. As a collective farm manager, he is torn between the necessity of carrying out Polovtsev's instructions for sabotage, on the one hand, and his habit of doing his work to the best of his ability, on the other. His inner contradictions, however, never reach the same intensity as those of Grigorii Melekhov. He does not search for any truth. His orientation is firmly anti-Bolshevik, and only his fear of being arrested makes him regret his involvement with Polovtsev at the time when chances for success appear particularly dim.

During collectivization the struggle between the Communist organizers and their die-hard adversaries centered on winning the middle stratum of the peasantry to their respective sides. Hence the presence of a character symbolizing this stratum is of prime importance for any large work on collectivization. Through such a character the pros and cons of collectivization can be presented in a more comprehensive and objective manner than through the extremists of either side. However, it is precisely in the presentation of events through the eyes of a middle Cossack that *Virgin Soil Upturned* turned out to be as much a failure as *The Quiet Don* was a success. Kondrat Maidannikov, intended to personify a middle Cossack, is certainly not a Grigorii Melekhov. Clearly, Kondrat *is* a middle Cossack from the economic viewpoint. He also finds it very difficult to suppress his instinct for private ownership and is tormented by anxiety about the property and cattle which he voluntarily delivers to the collective farm. But his military record, political stability, frame of mind, and actions have little in common with those of the middle Cossack of the year 1930. He served only with the Red Army and joined the collective farm of his own free will. He "has long ceased to believe in God, he believes in the Communist Party that is leading the working people of the whole world to liberation, into a sky-blue future" (5:135). In volume 2 Kondrat is one of three Cossacks who apply for membership to the Party and who are accepted as candidates. That Kondrat's actions and attitudes are not typical of a middle-stratum Cossack can be seen from the behavior of the majority of his fellow-villagers, as well as from Davydov's admission that even the best collective farmers do not rush to join the Party because they "wait

. . . and see how things turn out with the collective farm'' (6:94). By choosing Kondrat to represent the middle Cossacks, Sholokhov avoided showing the full economic and emotional impact of collectivization on them. Whether this choice was his own is difficult to say. The whole truth about collectivization could not be revealed anyway. Given the political situation of the time, Sholokhov might well have done as much as was possible. This was not the case with volume 2.

In volume 2 Sholokhov abandoned any effort to become a chronicler of the collectivization. First of all, he drastically limited the chronological framework of the action. Volume 2 is set in two summer months of 1930. The time is too short for any sequence of momentous events. The village of Gremiachii Log appears as if cut off from the rest of the Soviet Union. Neither the echoes of continuing agrarian upheaval, nor the decisions of the Sixteenth Party Congress (June 26-July 13) concerning collectivization, nor even Stalin's speech at the Congress reach the village. The precise chronological dating which enhances the historicity of volume 1 is absent.

The striking feature of volume 2 is the abundance of static materials, consisting of a variety of narrative elements. Some of them are simple tales, told by characters about the events of the past. The subjects of others are contemporary occurrences narrated by the characters in the form of very short stories or anecdotes. Still others are actually episodes in the novel elaborated by the author and told as stories for their own sake. Such are the anecdotes about Nagul'nov listening to roosters crowing at night and Razmetnov shooting all the cats in the village to protect his pigeons. Almost all are characterized by their remoteness from the few dynamic events of the plot. They fill the space in a plotless book and they also illustrate Sholokhov's increased preoccupation with *skaz* and the comic element. This development is best evidenced by the frequent appearances of Shchukar'. He alone is allotted more space than the anti-Soviet forces.

These enemies are portrayed in the state of progressive moral degradation. Ostrovnov locks up his mother and lets her starve to death because she might inadvertently betray the hiding place of Polovtsev and Liat'evskii. The two officers are perpetually quarreling and insulting each other. When captured, Polovtsev readily betrays all his fellow-conspirators. He does it, not out of fear of torture or death, but because Sholokhov endows him with a rather strange interpretation of the officer's honor code which is reduced to the adage, ''you've lost, so you pay'' (6:380). This formula may apply to one's own life, but it hardly calls for sacrificing the lives of others by betraying them to the enemy. Another disputable point concerns the scope of the anti-Bolshevik conspiracy in the Don and Kuban' regions. Sholokhov speaks of over six hundred rank-and-file Cossacks and at least fifteen officers and generals, nine of them living in Moscow. The conspiracy is said to have been headed by a former Cossack lieutenant general who was in constant contact with military organizations of Russian émigrés (6:380). Not one of the generals is mentioned by name. It is debatable that the Cossacks, bled white during the Civil War, deported in large numbers at the beginning of collectivization, and virtually unarmed, were able or willing to stage a large-scale uprising. I have not come across any oral or printed source—Soviet or émigré—that would corroborate Sholokhov's information about the existence of a far-reaching conspiracy in the Don-Kuban' region. All we have are the reports that in 1929-1930 Aleksandr Senin (Polovtsev's prototype) was engaged in organizing "The Alliance for the Liberation of the Don" and worked out a plan for a rebellion.[52] Sholokhov might have exaggerated the dimensions of the conspiracy in order to justify, in retrospect, the repressive measures taken against the Cossacks during collectivization. According to his original design, "Polovtsev and Timofei would join a small band" in volume 2.[53] The statement does not seem to suggest that Polovtsev was going to get involved in any large-scale conspiracy or operations unless Sholokhov meant that he would join the "band" after an unsuccessful attempt to carry out some more ambitious plans. But the author said nothing of such plans.

Although in volume 2 Polovtsev and Liat'evskii are depicted in even darker colors than in volume 1, they are not prevented from displaying humanity on rare occasions. There is a scene of touching reconciliation between the two officers when Liat'evskii is leaving to take vengeance on an OGPU man who once kicked out his left eye during an interrogation (6:351-352). Thus the killing of this and another OGPU man looks like an act of retribution, especially since Liat'evskii does not kill their coachman. Here Sholokhov deviated from the precise re-creation of actual events. In reality, the prototypes of the two OGPU men were not killed.[54] There is nothing wrong with an artist's adapting the facts of life to his designs. However, the reader is entitled to wonder whether Sholokhov changed the facts solely for dramatic effect or whether he also took revenge upon the members of the institution that nearly destroyed him in 1938. At any rate, the two OGPU characters are not very attractive.

Sholokhov is impartial in describing the outward appearance of the enemies. Their faces are not stamped with the seal of vice. Moreover, Timofei is the most handsome man in the novel. The most memorable portrait of him is drawn, not when he is alive, but when he lies dead, killed by Nagul'nov: "Even in death he was handsome, this spoilt darling and a favorite of the womenfolk. A dark strand of hair fell over his clear white forehead not touched by suntan; his full face had not yet lost its faint rosiness; his curled-up upper lip, covered with a fluffy black moustache, was slightly raised, exposing his moist teeth; and a faint shadow of a surprised smile lingered on his blooming lips'' (6:153). The passage brings to mind Gogol''s description of the slain Andrii in *Taras Bul'ba*: ''Even in death he was beautiful. His manly face, which a while ago was filled with power and an irresistible charm for women, still evinced a marvelous beauty; his black brows, like somber velvet, set off his pale features.''[55]

Sholokhov might have thought of these lines when he wrote about the dead Timofei. There is a similarity between Andrii and Timofei in that love plays such an important part in bringing about their deaths. With regard to style, however, the two passages reveal the same differences that were noted earlier in comparing the excerpts from *The Quiet Don* and *Taras Bul'ba*. It is basically the difference between the romantic, conventional, and elevated imagery of Gogol' and the realistic, tangible, and earthy imagery of Sholokhov. The difference is only slightly diminished by the fact that the representation of the dead Timofei is not one of Sholokhov's earthiest descriptions, as can be seen from the presence of such conventional embellishments as the ''faint shadow'' or ''blooming lips.'' On the other hand, the portrait of the dead Timofei faithfully reflects Sholokhov's practice of sparing the faces of his beautiful characters from the wounds that caused their deaths. The faces of such people, dead or dying, enhance the message about man's destruction of beauty.

Timofei's face is the focal point of a lyrical and philosophical context. His wide-open eyes seem to be gazing ''with an exultant and silent amazement'' at the gentle changes in the sky brought about by the coming of dawn. The phrase is a lyrical variation on the theme of man and nature. It accentuates their beauty and contrasts the death of man with the birth of the day. It appeals to the reader's mind and imagination and elicits meditative, sensuous, and aesthetic responses. There is a poetic epilogue to Timofei's death. Lushka kneels before his body, bidding farewell in the style of folk poetry: ''You flew to me, my falcon, but you flew straight to your death'' (6:159). Timofei's death also leads to the triumph of common human feelings in Nagul'nov over his ideological obsession. Knowing that Lushka loves Timofei, Nagul'nov magnanimously allows her to say good-bye to her dead lover. It is Nagul'nov's own—unrequited—love for Lushka that moves him to commit a political crime. He saves her from being brought to trial as the accomplice of a ''bandit.''

When a group of Don writers, unhappy about Timofei's looks, wondered why a kulak's son should be so handsome even in death, Sholokhov replied with the question: ''And why cannot a kulak's son be handsome? What is it that Lushka loves him for?''[56] The rich, he explained, had always tried to marry their sons to the most beautiful women, breeding generations of handsome people.

Concerned with Timofei's appearance, the Don writers had no reason to worry about the political and ideological stance that Sholokhov took in volume 2 of *Virgin Soil Upturned*. The portrayal of the new life in it appeared to them "illuminated by unfading ideals of the Revolution."[57] Indeed, Sholokhov portrays events and characters in accordance with Party views, thus realizing in practice one of the cardinal tenets of socialist realism, its *partiinost'* (Party spirit). Life is shown in its historically determined movement toward socialism. The goals of the Party are identical with those of the masses. At this point *partiinost'* merges with *narodnost'* (national spirit), another pillar of socialist realism, which requires the portrayal of the most vital aspirations of the people as the Party sees them.

The Party itself is depicted as united and disciplined. Among its members there are no disagreements with the policy of its leaders, as was the case in volume 1, where Nagul'nov differed with Stalin. The Communist deviationists described in volume 1 are no longer in the Party. The only bad Communist in volume 2 is the chairman of a collective farm, who has fallen victim to his proprietary instincts. But this loss is more than compensated by the introduction of a new Party secretary, Ivan Nesterenko, an exemplary leader for a rural *raion* (county). He is an able Party organizer and an accomplished agricultural expert. The sphere of his activities is broad, ranging from leadership of local Party organizations down to concern for the verses displayed on posters in the collective-farm reading room. Nesterenko is demanding, but fair, open, friendly, warm. When he speaks to Davydov, the latter feels that "it was quite a long time since anyone of his Party superiors had talked to him with such friendliness, simplicity, and human kindness" (6:90).

Artistically, however, the Party secretary does not cut a convincing figure. Sholokhov's efforts to breathe life into him, to individualize him, seem futile. Even if Nesterenko wears a sumptuous Kuban' Cossack cap, challenges Davydov to a friendly wrestling match, suffers from malaria, has a creditable Civil War record and brown eyes, he still remains essentially the sum total of the virtues expected from a Party secretary of the late 1950s.

This contention can be corroborated by the somewhat puzzling publication background of chapter 8, entirely devoted to Nesterenko. Its text first appeared in *Pravda* on February 22 and 23, 1959, following installments published in that newspaper from March 28, 1955, to December 31, 1958, as unnumbered chapters. In the definitive version of volume 2 they formed chapters 9 through 21 consecutively.[58] It is likely that Sholokhov delayed Nesterenko's appearance as long as possible. The second half of the 1950s was a period of changes initiated by the volatile Khrushchev. It was therefore wise to make certain that the figure of an ideal

Communist leader is at least roughly in keeping with the latest image of him as cultivated by the Party hierarchy.

The trends of the period of de-Stalinization are further reflected in the author's attempt to present a more humane treatment of the people than the one that was habitual under Stalin's rule. The new attitude is particularly transparent in the handling of religious issues. The only means Davydov applies to persuade women to return to work on Sunday are his kindest words and most gallant manners (6:180-182). Needless to say, this episode is utterly untypical of anti-religious militancy of the time. There are many instances, however, where the author tries to discredit or ridicule religion.

Concentration on positive characters and developments led to the virtual hushing up of the unseemly aspects of the Soviet regime and of collectivization. There are merely a few critical observations and they are made not by the author but by the characters. The garrulous Shchukar' is allowed to say that the Soviet regime breeds quantities of fools (6:279). He also compares the dispossession of the kulaks with the skinning of dogs, alive and by the millions (6:204-205). A Cossack, Ustin Rykalin, fearlessly speaks to Davydov about the ruthless exploitation of collective farmers by career-minded Soviet and Party functionaries. Yet he absolves Moscow from any responsibility for the sins of the lower authorities (6:175-178).

The unbalanced presentation of life, the small chronological scope, and the abundance of marginal static material are the chief reasons why volume 2 of *Virgin Soil Upturned* is not a historical or epic work. Folklore has almost vanished, with the exception of the folk-narrative genre reflected in stories and anecdotes. Cossack songs, not only of the epic but even of the lyrical kind, are absent. The ethnic, regional element is scarce and subordinated to political and ideological concerns. As a book on collectivization, volume 2 is decidedly inferior to its predecessor. Though it lacks the balance and objectivity of *The Quiet Don*, volume 1 of *Virgin Soil Upturned* has a definite historical value. It could have become a part of an epic of collectivization had it been followed by one or more volumes of high caliber.

Since an objective portrayal of collectivization could not, and still cannot, be published in the Soviet Union, the appropriate question concerning volume 2 of *Virgin Soil Upturned* is whether Sholokhov did his best in the political climate of the time when he was writing the book. One of the ways to judge his performance is to compare his book with some contemporary works on identical or related subjects. Volume 2 of *Virgin Soil Upturned* presents the victory of the new agricultural system along with a vision of a bright future for the collectivized peasantry. The vision makes an impression of being a grotesque utopia when one reads about rural Russia of the 1950s and the early 1960s in Aleksandr Iashin's story "Rychagi" ("Levers," 1956) and Fedor Abramov's sketch "Vokrug da okolo" ("Around and About," 1962).[59] These works show the appalling poverty of collective farms and the highhanded control of them by incompetent Party bosses. The last thing the villagers would like to do is work in collective farms; while they love to cultivate their small personal plots. Sholokhov has always had a firsthand knowledge of what was going on in socialized agriculture. Nonetheless, in volume 2 of *Virgin Soil Upturned* he glosses over the hardships of the early stage of collective farming and refuses to notice the seeds of future deterioration. Not so Abramov. His chairman of the collective farm, aptly named "The New Life," remembers how the Party *raion* committee ordered him to carry out total collectivization within two days. He used political threats to fulfill the order and now he wonders whether present-day misery is not after all rooted in such methods. To him the history of collective farming is fraught with stupidities and crimes, particularly during the postwar period, "when year after year they scraped every single grain out of the *kolkhoz* barns."[60]

The last hundred pages of Gavriil Troepol'skii's novel *Chernozem* (*The Black Soil*, 1962) deal with the same events as volume 1 of *Virgin Soil Upturned*. The two works evince about the same degree of objectivity, except that Troepol'skii tells somewhat more about the Party directives to collectivize the peasants, regardless of their wishes, and is much more forceful in exposing Stalin's hypocrisy. A young Communist holds Stalin and the top leadership responsible for the wrong approach to collectivization and dares to speak of a dizziness from failure, rather than from success. Although such things could be printed only at the peak of de-Stalinization, Troepol'skii's willingness to bring up sensitive subjects compares favorably with Sholokhov's avoidance of them in volume 2 of *Virgin Soil Upturned*. The focus of Sergei Zalygin's short novel *Na Irtyshe* (*On the Irtysh River*, 1964) is not so much on the course of collectivization as on the issue of morality and humaneness. Set in March 1931, the story centers on a Siberian peasant whose sociopolitical profile resembles that of Kondrat Maidannikov. He belongs to the middle stratum of the peasantry; he fought against the Whites in the Civil War, joined a collective farm, and heroically tried to save its grain during a fire set by a "class enemy." But, unlike Kondrat, the Siberian is confronted with a critical choice. Either he delivers an extra amount of his grain to the collective farm—and by doing so dooms to starvation the arsonist's wife and children who found refuge in his home—or he and his family will be expropriated and deported like the kulaks. He unhesitatingly rejects the first alternative, demonstrating the triumph of individual conscience and compassion over state-inspired immorality and cruelty.

The comparison of volume 2 of *Virgin Soil Upturned* with its contemporary works shows that Sholokhov did not take advantage of the opportunities which had arisen during de-Stalinization. He turned away from the complexities of collectivization, concentrating instead on a Party-line portrayal of virtuous characters, inserted stories, and Shchukar''s chatter. The strongest sides of his talent—its epic, dramatic, and lyric qualities—were sacrificed to the lexical and comic aspects of *skaz* which, moreover, is frequently overdone and obtrusive.

Sholokhov's sketches and stories from the World War II period fit well into the mainstream of official propaganda. Seeing his supreme duty to be an agitational contributor to victory, the author does not mind telling half-truths, exaggerating, and hushing up. In this adherence to the formula ''the ends justify the means'' lies the unbridgeable difference between the doyen of Soviet letters and the pre-Revolutionary writer Lev Tolstoi. The two are literally worlds apart. Tolstoi placed truth above all other considerations. His ''Sebastopol in May,'' written at the height of the Crimean War, so strongly condemned the slaughter and was so frank about the Russian officers that an editor of the journal in which it was to appear excised one-third of its text to ensure its passage by the censors (2:441).

By no stretch of the imagination can one picture Tolstoi writing something like ''The Science of Hatred''—not only because Tolstoi would never teach hatred, but also because of his respect for truth. The protagonist of the story, Lieutenant Gerasimov, relates that during a Soviet offensive he saw the bodies of hundreds of women, old men, and children executed by the Germans (7:579). The offensive is supposed to have taken place at the very end of July or the beginning of August 1941, in the vicinity of the Ukrainian towns Skvira and Ruzhin. Although the Germans did commit all sorts of atrocities, it is improbable that they were engaged in mass shooting of Ukrainians in July 1941. Such executions were usually ordered as reprisals for the actions of Soviet partisans, and there were not many of them in the Ukraine in the summer of 1941, especially right behind the front lines. If the victims were Jews, then Sholokhov kept quiet about it, following the government's policy of toning down the fact that the entire Jewish population was subject to destruction under the German occupation. However, he let it be known that Jewish prisoners of war were shot (7:582). Before this disclosure he had Gerasimov come out with an amazing fabrication. The lieutenant claims to have seen, not far from Ruzhin, the body of a frail eleven-year-old girl with her bloodstained schoolbooks scattered around her. She was on her way to school when the Germans caught, raped, and killed her (7:579). In fact, no schools providing general education were open at that time. On the Soviet side the school year ended in June, and the Germans would not bother opening schools in the territory they had just occupied, not in the summer anyway. The blunder is all the more incredible since Gerasimov has a daughter of about the same age as the rape victim. This detail is still uncorrected. If we, like Sholokhov, expect an author to be true to life in the smallest detail, we should say that Gerasimov could not have been near Skvira or Ruzhin at the very end of July or early in August. At that time both these places were at least forty or fifty miles away from him and the distance was increasing every day. Late in July the Germans went on the offensive in this sector, forcing the Red Army to retreat beyond the Dnieper.[61]

Gerasimov tells basically a true story of the hard lot of Soviet prisoners of war. The Nazi treatment of them was indeed most barbaric and might have been the main reason why the Germans failed to defeat the Soviet Union. Of the five-odd million Soviet POWs about two-thirds perished.[62] But Gerasimov does not mention that the treatment of prisoners by the German front-line troops was much less harsh than in the POW camps in the rear. And he naturally does not say a word about the cases of Soviet troops slaughtering German prisoners, including the wounded.[63] The aim of the story was not to portray the war impartially, but to instill hatred and—no less importantly—to discourage Soviet soldiers from surrendering on the eve of the big enemy offensive in the summer of 1942.

"The Science of Hatred" and "The Fate of a Man" convey the wrong impression of the fate of the Red Army POWs upon their return to the Soviet side. Being taken prisoner was considered treason and most of those who returned went to special screening camps, prisons, or concentration camps. The treatment given Goncharov or Sokolov ("The Fate of a Man") upon their escape from German captivity and return to the Soviets is exceptional rather than typical. Solzhenitsyn is right in saying that Sholokhov has created the least incriminating case for Sokolov. He is taken prisoner unarmed and shell-shocked. He later escapes to the Soviet side, taking a German major as booty along with him. For this "fantastic, detective-story escape"[64] Sokolov is recommended for a medal. The standard procedure with fugitives from German captivity was to accuse them of being enemy spies and to punish them accordingly. Those who were cleared and readmitted into the army were sent to screening camps as soon as the war was over.[65] In "The Fate of a Man" Sholokhov portrayed the tragedy of a man who lost his entire family; yet he did not drop as much as a hint of the unprecedented tragedy of hundreds of thousands who exchanged Nazi captivity for the concentration camps of their own motherland.

It is in a way unfair to comment on *They Fought for Their Country*. The novel is far from being completed. With three-fourths of it published during the war and in 1949, it could not but be topical, propagandistic, and ultra-orthodox. The part of the novel treating Stalin and the purges appeared in 1969, after the best time to deal with these subjects had long since passed. Yet the printed text of the novel provides an insight into the ideological and artistic evolution of Sholokhov and should not be dismissed without a few remarks. Like volume 2 of *Virgin Soil Upturned*, the new novel concentrates on the positive, the trivial, and the comic. It is full of meaningless dialogues, with some characters trying hard to be funny. Such talk has little to do with the fact that the majority of characters are collective farmers and workers. Conversations between plain Cossacks in *The Quiet Don* were meaningful, sharp, witty, forceful. But the Cossacks were free to express conflicting views on any subject ranging from the intimate to the political. The characters in *They Fought for Their Country* have no disagreements about any significant issue; they unquestioningly accept the Soviet system, are satisfied with prewar life, and do their best to defend it. Such people no doubt existed. But there were also many others who asked themselves tormenting questions about their predicament. The Red Army soldiers fought not only for their country and against Hitler's tyranny. Willy-nilly they also fought for the preservation of Stalin's tyranny. Collectivization, famine, and the mass terror of the thirties were fresh in their memories. For millions, particularly before they could see Nazi atrocities for themselves, Stalin's regime was the primary enemy. If Sholokhov intends to continue his war novel with even a modest degree of objectivity, he will have to touch upon "a phenomenon totally unheard of in all world history: that several hundred thousand young men, aged twenty to thirty, took up arms against their Fatherland as allies of its most evil enemy."[66] Likewise he will have to portray the 1942 battles in a more realistic vein, shedding some light on events that resulted in the Germans' taking 1,653,000 prisoners during that year and in Stalin's issuing his draconian order no. 227.[67]

Focused on the successful fighting of Soviet soldiers, the description of battles in *They Fought for Their Country* is an end in itself. In *The Quiet Don* the question of who won a battle was frequently of secondary importance. It mattered more to show how the fighting effected moral and psychological changes in the characters or revealed the senselessness of war in comparison with the beauty and vitality of nature.

The principal figure in the 1969 installment, a Red Army general recently released from a Soviet concentration camp, belongs to those Communist diehards who preserved their total dedication to the regime regardless of what they experienced in the prisons and camps. The author has not yet disclosed the general's last name. We only know that he is the older brother of the agronomist Nikolai Strel'tsov. The two have different fathers. The general's first name and patronymic (Aleksandr Mikhailovich) are identical with those of Sholokhov's father, a possible indication of the author's predilection for this character. The patronymic may also be taken as an allusion to the first name of General Mikhail Lukin. He was to be the principal prototype of Aleksandr Mikhailovich, and Sholokhov interviewed him extensively in the spring of 1964.[68] Perhaps the author wanted to give his general a last name that would suggest his link with Lukin, but could not do so in the late 1960s, when experiences of people like Lukin were no longer publicized to demonstrate injustices resulting from "the cult of personality." General Lukin, severely wounded and unconscious, was captured by the Germans in 1941. Upon his return to the Soviet Union he spent five months under arrest and intensive interrogation. His account of these and some other experiences was welcome in 1964,[69] but became unpublishable in 1969 owing to the changing official view of Stalin. Furthermore, the Soviets should have learned from Russian émigré sources that Lukin, while in German captivity, maintained good relations with Andrei Vlasov and other generals of the Russian Liberation Army.[70] Thus there appear to be enough reasons why Sholokhov's original plans, as the critic Iurii Lukin put it, "underwent changes, and different material had to be used to create the figure of Strel'tsov, Sr."[71] As a result, not many characters in Soviet post-Stalin fiction can match Aleksandr Mikhailovich's persistent and enthusiastic praise of the dear Party. Such a person cannot be expected to provide perceptive insights into Soviet prewar developments, and he does not.

It is an old shepherd who reveals how the security police corrupted the common people by encouraging citizens to write political denunciations against one another, something that was unknown in pre-Revolutionary Russia (7:47). Once more Sholokhov shows little sympathy for the dreadful institution, this time through "the voice of the people." At the same time other characters suggest that during the purges the security police acted very much on its own. The Bolshevik system and the Party are thus exonerated from any responsibility for the terror. Even Stalin's role in it is greatly reduced by the characters' contentions that he must have been misled by the security police (7:19, 44). Stalin's innate cruelty is unveiled, however, in the general's comparison of his eyes with those of a tiger (7:40). To increase the similarity between the dictator and the beast, Sholokhov changed the color of Stalin's eyes from brown to yellow, incurring the displeasure of Soviet Georgians.[72] Solzhenitsyn too likened Stalin to a tiger, and more emphatically than did Sholokhov, but he seems to believe that Stalin's eyes were really yellow.[73]

A peculiar invocation of Stalin's authority occurs in what is an equally peculiar case of flagellation of the author of *The Quiet Don* by the author of *They Fought for Their Country*. The case springs from the predominantly objective portrayal of the White movement in *The Quiet Don*. To some early critics this portrayal represented a welcome departure from a stereotyped depiction of the Whites as downright villains. They spoke of Sholokhov's showing the personal, subjective honesty of the White generals, who acted in accordance with their class consciousness.[74] With the growth of ideological intolerance, Sholokhov's treatment of the generals had come to be regarded as lacking a clear-cut political delineation. The portrait of Kornilov, for instance, was said to have been suffering from "objectivism"; it could create the wrong impression that the actions of this "inveterate enemy" were motivated by his "subjective honesty."[75] Sholokhov apparently accepted the criticisms. In his third novel he called on Stalin to declare that Kornilov could not have been "subjectively honest" because "he went against the people" (7:40). The dictum was enthusiastically endorsed by Aleksandr Mikhailovich with the remark that it expressed "the truth in two words" (7:40).[76] What Stalin says about Kornilov in the novel he might have said to Sholokhov in one of their conversations, during which the interlocutors had voiced some differences of opinion concerning a few historical figures from *The Quiet Don*.[77] Be that as it may, in *They Fought for Their Country* Sholokhov the politician prevailed over Sholokhov the artist. There is something masochistic in his repudiation of the objectivity of *The Quiet Don*, a quality without which that novel could not have become a significant work of art. A creative person, Sholokhov must have felt that in renouncing his former open-mindedness he was committing an artistic betrayal. And he punished himself for it in a very painful manner—by voicing his self-criticism in a work of art and through the mouth of the most sinister figure in Russian history.

The recantation would not have been complete without covering the post-Kornilov period. Sholokhov reached into it by making his loyal Red Army general deliver a verbose diatribe against Denikin's Volunteer Army (7:38-39). The diatribe sticks out like a sore thumb. It has no obvious connection with the plot. It could be much shorter if it were intended to add to the political characterization of the general.

Sholokhov's road from *The Quiet Don* to *They Fought for Their Country* is marked by a progressive decline in the artistic value of his works and the amount of sociohistorical information that can be gleaned from them. The reasons are both external and personal. In response to increasing ideological pressures, an author had no alternative but to embellish Soviet life, keep silent about its dark sides, and simply lie. And nothing in Tolstoi's opinion is more detrimental to art than lying. Compliance with the cardinal demand of socialist realism to portray positive Soviet heroes produced such characters as Davydov, Nesterenko, and Aleksandr Mikhailovich, all falsely idealized. The happy choice of a non-Party Cossack as the protagonist of *The Quiet Don*, along with the author's refusal to transform him into a Bolshevik, saved the last two volumes of the novel from sinking to the level of volume 2 of *Virgin Soil Upturned* or *They Fought for Their Country*. In both of these works Sholokhov did more than submit himself to the political dictates of the time. He assumed the role of the standard bearer of socialist realism. The decrease in artistic quality of his works is in direct proportion to the increase of their propagandistic function. The artistic slide was accelerated by the discernible decline in his creative talent after it reached its fullest manifestation in the last volume of *The Quiet Don*. More about this subject will be said in the next chapter.

CHAPTER III

DETAILS OF STYLE AND STRUCTURE

THE BASIC RUSSIAN

In 1960 the Academy edition of *A History of Soviet Russian Literature* printed a facsimile of a handwritten page of *The Quiet Don*, containing 294 words from chapter 9 of volume 3.[1] There is every likelihood that the autograph, apparently written early in 1929, is a part of the fair copy of the manuscript. Aside from a few corrections in spelling and punctuation, its text appeared almost verbatim in the portion of the novel serialized in the March 1929 issue of *Oktiabr'* and in an excerpt published in an April 1929 issue of the fortnightly *Plamia* (*The Flame*).[2] Altogether twenty-eight emendations were made in the text of the autograph in the two journals and in subsequent publications of the novel. The length of the autograph equals one page in the 1948 edition, which has 1,470 pages. If we multiply 28 by 1,470, we get 41,160, the hypothetical total of grammatical and stylistic improvements made in *The Quiet Don* up to and including its 1956-1957 edition. After this edition corrections were exceptionally rare. Staggering as it may look, the figure 41,160 is not entirely unrealistic. The autograph represents a typical page of *The Quiet Don*. It comes from the middle of the novel and contains both authorial narrative and dialogue. It probably has more grammatical and stylistic inaccuracics than a comparable passage from volume 4, which was more carefully written, but fewer than a similar excerpt from volume 1, written at a time when the author's mastery of literary Russian left much to be desired.

Sixteen of the twenty-eight emendations pertain to punctuation, six to spelling, three to paragraphing, two to choice of words, and one to capitalization. Several major omissions of punctuation marks were not corrected either in *Oktiabr'* or *Plamia*. These phrases, for instance, were printed without a single comma: "Vyshe khutora, na vzgor'e, dostupnyi vsem vetram, stoial staryi vetriak" (On the top of the hillock above the village, open to all the winds, stood an old windmill) and "nashikh khutornykh, nikak, shest' podvod" (there are six carts with our villagers, I guess). Elementary rules of Russian punctuation call for setting off by commas the complementary words (*na vzgor'e*) and the detached attribute (*dostupnyi vsem vetram*) in the first sentence, and the parenthetical word (*nikak*) in the second. Violations of these rules and periodic omissions of commas in the sentences containing verbal adverbs and participial constructions were among the principal faults of Sholokhov's punctuation. This is particularly true of the early editions of his stories, the first three volumes of *The Quiet Don*, and volume 1 of *Virgin Soil Upturned*.

Two spelling corrections in the printed texts of the autograph can be dismissed as trivial. They involve replacement of colloquial forms with literary ones in a character's speech. Two others pertain to hyphenation of appositives and particles. Here Sholokhov erred in using a hyphen before the emphatic particle *zhe*. The last two misspellings—writing *presno pakhnushchaia* (fresh-smelling) as one word and leaving out the second *n* in *belostennye* (white-walled)—point to Sholokhov's deficient knowledge of basic grammar. The remaining corrections either eliminated obvious errors or increased the expressiveness of the narrative.

To gain a better understanding of Sholokhov's mishandling of literary Russian, a wider variety of samples ranging from grammatical errors to semantic absurdities will be examined. In listing the examples, the page number in parentheses will no longer refer to the 1975 edition of *Collected Works*, but to editions where inaccuracies cited are not corrected. The 1926 editions of *The Don Stories* and *The Tulip Steppe* (abbreviated respectively as *DS* and *TS*) will provide illustrations for the early stories, while examples from *The Quiet Don* (*QD*) and *Virgin Soil Upturned* (*VSU*) will be taken from their serialized versions in the journals *Oktiabr'* and *Novyi mir*.[3] All examples will come from the authorial narrative. Semantic errors will be translated as faithfully as possible into deliberately wrong English.

The following types of errors are among the most conspicuous:

1. Violations of spelling norms in the past passive participles or words of past passive participial origin. A. The use of one *n* instead of two. *DS: poserebrenym* (123)—silver-plated. *QD: ranenyi v nogu* (7, '28, 158)—wounded in the leg. *VSU: iz kamnia tesanaia, primorenyi* (1, '32, 38)—hewn out of stone, tired. B. The use of the double *n* instead of one *n*. *DS: kovannymi soldatskimi botinkami* (105)—with iron-shod soldier's shoes. *QD: putannye rasskazy* (1, '32, 30)—confused stories.

2. The use of the suffix *t*, instead of *nn*, in past passive participles formed from prefixed perfectives of the verbs *brat'* (take), *rvat'* (tear), and *drat'* (tear, flay). *QD: zadratoi* (2, '32, 22)—raised. *VSU: vobratykh* (1, '32, 42)—tucked in.

3. The use of an *n*, instead of a *b*, in the roots of prefixed imperfectives denoting various forms of "bending." *VSU: vyginaia . . . spinu* (1, '32, 57)—arching . . . her back. There are over sixty such forms in the early stories and *The Quiet Don*.

4. Ungrammatical case endings of nouns. *DS: teliaty* (134), nom. pl.

for *teliata* (calves). *TS: vshu* (3), acc. sing. for *vosh'* (louse). *QD: listov* (1, '28, 109), gen. pl. for *list'ev* (leaves of plants). *VSU: sharovarov* (1, '32, 68), gen. pl. for *sharovar* (trousers).

5. Substandard word formation. *DS: vzletyvaiut* (123) for *vzletaiut* (they fly up). *QD: ulozhivali* (8, '32, 9) for *ukladyvali* (they placed).

6. Miscellaneous misspellings. *DS: na stremianakh* (10) instead of *na stremenakh* (in his stirrups). *QD: portmonetom* (3, '28, 192) instead of *portmone* (purse). *VSU: iskussnogo* (1, '32, 47) instead of *iskusnogo* (expert).

7. The use of the particle *ne* where *ni* should have been used. *QD*: "otkuda ne voz'mis' " (1, '28, 148)—"out of the blue."

8. Ambiguity created by placing the direct object before the subject of the sentence when the direct object is a noun that has the same form in the nominative. *QD*: "glaza zastili slezy" (2, '28, 196)—"his eyes dimmed the tears."

9. Ungrammatical use of prepositions. Over thirty of these infelicities were corrected in the early stories and at least a hundred in *The Quiet Don*. Almost every correction involved the replacement of one preposition by another, producing over thirty varieties of such substitutions. More than fifty corrections concerned the preposition *nad* (above, over) that Sholokhov repeatedly employed instead of *vdol'* (along) and occasionally instead of *okolo, vozle* (near), *u* (by, at), *mimo* (by, past), *pod* (under), *po* (along), and *za* (beyond). *DS*: "nad pletniami sharkaiut nogi" (120)—"one can hear the shuffling of feet above the wattle fences." *QD*: "par visel nad potolkom" (1, '32, 14)—"steam hung over the ceiling." Second in frequency is the misuse of *pod* (under) in the combinations "idti pod sarai" and "byt' pod saraem," which literally mean "go under the shed" or "be under the shed." These expressions occur even in passages where the author means that people or objects are under the roof of the shed (*TS*, 133; *QD*, 1, '29, 77-78). Faulty use of *iz* and *na* accounts for incongruities like "s vedrami iz krinitsy idet" (*DS*, 147)—"she walks out of the well with the buckets" and "shashka . . . vzletela na vozdukh" (*QD*, 2, '32, 13)—"the saber . . . flew up onto the air."

10. Nonsensical phrases and sentences resulting from the author's misunderstanding of individual words. *DS*: "Aleksandr . . . vstal na koleni" (105)—"Aleksandr . . . got up on his knees." The author meant "kneeled," which in literary Russian is rendered by the idiom "stal na koleni."

As in early stories, the origins of absurd phrases in *The Quiet Don* can frequently be traced back to the author's confusion of words similar in sound or meaning. In the following examples such words will be given in pairs with the improper word given first.

Mochit'sia (urinate)—*omyvat'sia, oblivat'sia* (to be bathed in): "Pantelei . . . mochilsia goriachim potom" (1, '28, 126)—"Pantelei . . . urinated hot sweat." *Valiat'sia* (lie about)—*razvalit'sia* (sprawl): "Liza valialas'v kresle" (2, '28, 129)—"Liza lay about in the armchair." *Posmertnyi* (posthumous)—*poslednii* (last): "Dlia preobladaiushchei chasti ofitserskikh kadrov chin voiskovogo starshiny byl posmertnym" (6, '28, 91)—"For the greater number of regular officers the rank of lieutenant colonel had been awarded posthumously." The author wanted to say that the rank of lieutenant colonel was the highest that the Cossack officers would normally attain in the army. He could have done it by using *poslednii* instead of *posmertnyi*.

In a number of cases the author confused the same words in both his early stories and *The Quiet Don*. Here are a few examples. *Migat'* (blink)—*mel'kat'* (flash by): "Antoshka mignul bosymi piatkami" (*TS*, 91)—"Antoshka's bare heels blinked." "Dar'ia, mignuv podolom, vzbezhala na kryl'tso" (6, '28, 55)—"Having blinked with the hem of her skirt, Dar'ia ran up onto the porch." *Pitat'* (feed)—*vpityvat'* (absorb): "Peschanik zhadno pital rozovatuiu penu i krov' " (*Smena*, no. 11, 1925, p. 5)—"The sand greedily fed the pinkish foam and blood." "Zemlia pitala bogatuiu rosu" (4, '28, 133)—"The earth was feeding the heavy dew." In several instances *odet'* (dress) is incorrectly used for *nadet'* (put on), and the characters' glances are said to be *nenavistnye* (hated, hateful) instead of *nenavidiashchie* (hating, full of hatred). Particularly striking is the persistent substitution of *nemo* (silently) for *glukho* (hollow, muffled) to describe the dull sounds of voices, guns, thunder, horses' hoofs, steps, wheels, accordions, and crowing roosters. Altogether I could find about thirty such mistakes in the early stories, *The Quiet Don*, and *Virgin Soil Upturned*; there is one even in *They Fought for Their Country*: "nemo khlopali zenitki" (*Pravda*, November 15, 1943)—"the A. A. guns were thudding silently." This *nemo* is still uncorrected, as is another case in "The Offense" (1925 or 1926), first published in 1962.

The original number of cases of *nemo* was probably higher. The word *glukho* occurs, for example, about one hundred and fifty times in the earliest text of *The Quiet Don*. In many of these cases it could have been an editorial substitution for *nemo*.

11. Pleonasm. *TS: ladoni ruk* (158)—"palms of hands." *QD: stupni nog* (2, '28, 176)—"soles of feet."

12. Odd slips of pen. *QD*: "davno ne brityi rot" (4, '28, 148)—"mouth not shaven for a long time"; "svoi volosatye shirokie ladoni" (7, '28, 127)—"his large hairy palms."

Our examples of various stylistic irregularities expose only the tip of the iceberg. In every category listed here the number of examples could be multiplied many times, and there are numerous types of other errors. Measured by the standards of linguistic competence expected from a writer, the author of *The Don Stories, The Quiet Don*, and volume 1 of *Virgin Soil Upturned* was a semi-literate man.

The long process of stylistic revision of Sholokhov's writings varied with each individual work. In examining the style of the stories one should not overlook the fact that in the 1920s some of them underwent a more extensive pruning in their earlier than in their later editions. For the greater number of the stories a substantial revision, however, did not come until 1955-1956, when they were being prepared for inclusion in the first edition of *Collected Works*. This revision was quite thorough. Thus at least 250 corrections, counting changes in punctuation, were made in "Aleshka's Heart." Nonetheless, the 1956 versions of the early stories are closer to their original texts than the 1956 version of *The Quiet Don* is to its manuscript.

In terms of style, the earliest texts of *The Quiet Don* and *Virgin Soil Upturned* reproduce their respective manuscripts more faithfully than any of their subsequent editions. Yet certain corrections made in the serialized texts were rescinded in the first book-form editions—a good indication that these editions were set in type from manuscripts. The chief reason for the survival of so many errors in the serialized text of the first three volumes of *The Quiet Don* must be the editorial attitude toward the new literature of workers and peasants. The development of this literature was officially encouraged. It was expected to eclipse all nonproletarian literature by its artistry and ideological depth. Stylistic abnormalities of the new literature were looked upon less as a sign of illiteracy than as a manifestation of the earthy idiom of the toiling masses. This attitude is seen in the treatment of *The Quiet Don* in *Oktiabr'*, which was a stronghold of proletarian literature. Furthermore, the editing of the novel suffered from the obvious carelessness and incompetence of that journal's proofreaders. Their colleagues in *Novyi mir* did a markedly better job with volume 1 of *Virgin Soil Upturned*, considerably reducing the number of obvious errors. Volume 4 of *The Quiet Don* received still more editorial attention. It may be that Sholokhov had improved his grammar by that time. Yet his persistent repetition of certain errors already corrected in previous editions suggests that credit for the decrease in the number of mistakes in volume 4 must go as much to its proofreaders as to its author.

The major stylistic revisions of *The Quiet Don* took place in 1928-1929, 1933, 1953, and 1956. The first dealt with the earliest book-form editions of volumes 1 and 2. Their proofreaders concentrated on grave misspellings and also made a few corrections concerning dialecticisms, improper choice of words, and figures of speech. The scope of the 1933 revision, which affected the first three volumes, was much broader. Among its targets were phonetic spellings of dialecticisms in the characters' speech, certain local expressions in the author's narrative, syntax, paragraphing, redundance, ambiguities, prolixities, strained similes and metaphors, and misuse of prepositions. The hallmark of the 1953 revision was a mass expurgation of dialecticisms and supposedly coarse words from the speech of the author and characters alike. Simultaneously, numerous ungrammatical forms based on local pronunciation were corrected in the characters' language. Spurred by the campaign for purification of the language, the 1953 editors often went to extremes, causing enormous damage to the lexical texture of the novel. The prime objective of the 1956 editors was to repair this damage. They did it by rescinding about four-fifths of the corrections made in 1953. At the same time they caught remaining misspellings, replaced certain dialecticisms and colloquialisms by their literary equivalents, cut down the number of pleonasms, clarified the meanings of sentences containing misused words, and eliminated or simplified several metaphors. The singular contribution of the 1956 revision was the substitution of *pozadi* (behind) for *szadi* (behind) in about a hundred cases when *szadi* was used as both a preposition and an adverb, predominantly in phrases such as "He walked (sat) behind (them)." This replacement, however, is highly debatable. Works of both pre-Revolutionary and Soviet writers show the same use of *szadi* as Sholokhov's, and the dictionaries treat the two words as essentially synonymous. Of course, this does not apply to situations where *szadi* means "from behind" and *pozadi* means "in the past." A relatively small but not insignificant quantity of various stylistic emendations can be found in the single 1934 edition of volume 1, the deluxe 1935-1937 edition, and in the 1941, 1945, and 1955 editions. Stylistic changes after 1956 were marginal.

As a rule, the editorial work lacked consistency and thoroughness. For example, it took a quarter of a century to complete the replacement of *n* by *b* in the root of imperfective derivatives from the verb "to bend." It was only in 1953 that the literary form with *b* triumphed throughout the novel. Each volume still has its uncorrected "under the shed," while the preposition *nad* (above) has been preserved in several sentences not very different from some of those in which it was replaced by *vdol'* (along). There have been instances of faulty corrections. Particularly striking is the one in the sentence "Vengertsy uvideli kazakov i, brosiv orudie, poskakali" (1:318)—"The Hungarians saw the Cossacks and galloped away, leaving the gun behind." In 1935 the word *oruzhie* (weapons) was substituted for *orudie* (gun), probably on the assumption that the author meant here the common expression *brosat' oruzhie* (throw the weapons away). The verb *brosat'*, however, also means "leave, abandon," and this is precisely what Sholokhov had in mind. The lines that follow the sentence in question describe the fight between the fleeing Hungarians and pursuing Cossacks during which the Hungarians defend themselves with their weapons, killing one Cossack and wounding Grigorii. Incredible as it seems, twenty-seven out of the thirty-six post-1935 editions that I checked have the wrong word; this is most notably the case in recent editions. Some absurd or awkward phrases either have never been touched or have been revised only in one or two editions. No edition, except one published in 1964 by the Ministry of Defense, corrected the phrase "Prokhora, upavshego plashmia, rastoptannogo kopytami skakavshego szadi kazaka" (1:259)—"Prokhor, who fell flat and was crushed by the hoofs of the Cossack galloping behind him." Only the 1953 and 1955 editions deleted the simile in "sgorbias', kak cherepakha, . . . koriachilsia zheleznodorozhnik" (2:208)—"stooping like a turtle . . . the railroad man curved his back." A turtle cannot stoop, just as a living man cannot act like a dead one in the following sentence, which has never been corrected: " 'No-o-o-o' . . .—kak zadushennyi, zakhripel Podtelkov" (2:252)—" 'Oh . . . ,' Podtelkov wheezed as if he had been strangled to death."

Virgin Soil Upturned experienced a smaller number of stylistic revisions than did *The Quiet Don*. Most of its spelling errors were eliminated in 1932-1934, and, apart from sporadic corrections pertaining to dialecticisms and misused words, no significant changes occurred before 1952. The purpose and proportions of the 1952 revisions were identical with those in the 1953 edition of *The Quiet Don*. The undoing of the 1952 excesses was carried out in 1956-1957. Owing to the progress of de-Stalinization, it turned out to be more radical than the similar cleansing of *The Quiet Don* undertaken a few months earlier. The stylistic differences among published texts of volume 2 of *Virgin Soil Upturned* are negligible. The same applies to *They Fought for Their Country*. Sholokhov's command of grammar must have improved and the proofreaders must have been doing their job more expertly.

Dialecticisms

The abundance of stylistic infelicities in the young Sholokhov's works can be explained by the fact that his formal schooling terminated at the age of thirteen and that he lived most of the time among people speaking a variant of the Don Cossack dialect.[4] The literary Russian that he learned in school had little chance of survival in daily communication with the local people. Furthermore, living in the combat zone during the Civil War, serving with a food-requisitioning detachment, and fighting anti-Bolshevik partisans could scarcely have been propitious for the development of any linguistic culture in the young man. His reading of classics was apparently not enough to offset the impact of the local linguistic environment. It was this impact of his environment which caused him to use ungrammatical endings in the nominative plural, mishandle prepositions, use an *n* instead of a *b* in imperfective derivatives of *gnut'* (bend), and employ sub-standard forms of participles. It can be argued that dialectal forms should not be treated as sub-standard and that they ought to be able to occur freely in the author's speech. It appears to me, however, that a distinction should be made between dialecticisms like *vobratyi* (tucked in) or *stremem* (with river current) which deviate sharply from the accepted grammatical norms, and dialecticisms like *ozherelok* (collar) or *mosol* (bone) which are correctly spelled synonyms of their literary equivalents. Both kinds would be acceptable if the entire work were written in a dialect. But this would be an extreme case, and Sholokhov does not go that far. In his narrative he avoids many dialecticisms profusely used by his characters. Here belong words such as *isho* (still), *ide* (where), *moget* (he can), *zaraz* (now), and *zhiznia* (life). To him these words represent violations of the standard language which are too radical to be included into the authorial speech. Thus a critical opinion about Sholokhov's use of dialecticisms in his narrative depends upon one's own attitude toward his criteria for selecting them. In my view, his criteria were too liberal. There are too many dialecticisms in the early editions of his stories, the first three volumes of *The Quiet Don*, and volume 1 of *Virgin Soil Upturned*. Particularly undesirable among them are those representing distortions of grammatical norms. Whether Sholokhov deliberately used such dialecticisms cannot be ascertained in each individual case. The overall impression is that in many instances he must have been unaware that he was making serious grammatical errors, and he was certainly unaware that he was confusing words similar in sound or meaning.

The effect of dialecticisms on the readers of Sholokhov's works is twofold. On the one hand, dialecticisms hinder comprehension of the text. Not every reader can tell the meaning of *babaika* (oar), *kudlochit'* (pull at), or *triupkoi* (at a trot). Nor can one be expected to know the following dialectal connotations of such common words as *volochit'* (harrow), *rastriasat'* (divide), and *trus* (rabbit). On the other hand, the presence of dialecticisms contributes to the richness of local color. They are indispensable to the flavor of speech of the Cossack characters. They impart to the work a quality of authenticity, serve as a source for original imagery, and tend to strengthen the impression of the author's familiarity with his subject.

The function of dialecticisms can be illustrated with a few examples. Let us take the phrase "Ne tol'ko babu kveluiu i pustomiasuiu, a i iadrenykh karshevatykh atamantsev umel Stepan valit' s nog lovkim udarom v golovu'' (1:67)—''With a well-aimed blow to the head Stepan could knock down not only a weak and flabby woman, but also the big, snaglike men of the Atamanskii Regiment.'' Here Aksin'ia and the Cossacks of the Life-Guard Atamanskii Regiment are described by two vernacular words (*kveluiu, iadrenykh*) and two dialecticisms (*pustomiasuiu, karshevatykh*). Though not necessarily limited to the Don region, the use of dialecticisms is more limited geographically than the use of vernacular words. *Pustomiasaia*—listed in Vladimir Dal''s *Explanatory Dictionary of the Living Great-Russian Language*—literally means ''empty of meat'' and is applied to describe flabby people. Its picturesqueness increases if one imagines a watermelon which has little meat and is called *pustomiasyi* in the Don region. *Karshevatyi* is derived from *karsha*, a local equivalent of *koriaga* (snag). It calls to mind a snag with projecting boughs or roots, an image of sturdiness and danger. It would be hard to find a better epithet for the strong guardsmen.

One, of course, may find the use of *pustomiasyi* and *karshevatyi* esoteric and the use of *kvelyi* sub-standard. One may also question the appropriateness of the epithets ''weak'' and ''flabby'' for Aksin'ia. Is she not rather a picture of strength, with her ''steep back and compact shoulders'' and her ''breasts firm as those of a girl'' (1:27, 77)? And is not the appellation *baba* undignified for a woman?

This must have been the reasoning of editors who compressed the first part of Sholokhov's sentence to read ''Ne tol'ko sil'nuiu zhenshchinu, a i iadrenykh atamantsev'' (Not only a strong woman but also the big men of the Atamanskii Regiment). Here Sholokhov ceased to exist. Millions could have authored such a phrase. Apart from its vocabulary and imagery, the editors destroyed the rhythm, the word order, and the informativeness of the original sentence. In the original text the epithets ''weak and flabby'' are put after the word ''woman.'' The inversion is intended to attract more attention to them and to place them closer to ''big'' and ''snaglike,'' describing the Atamanskii Cossacks. The two pairs of contrasting epithets form the core of the sentence, bringing into sharp relief the difference between their referents. A distinct rhythmic change occurs in the original after the word *atamantsev*. The four epithets in the first part of the sentence, notably *pustomiasyi* and *karshevatyi*, are polysyllabic. Their pronunciation slows down the pace of the narrative, which is in tune with their descriptive function. As the author turns to Stepan, he accelerates the rhythm by resorting to short iambic words suited for communicating a swift, violent action. By renaming Aksin'ia a ''strong woman,'' the 1953 editors removed certain information about the Cossacks' view of a woman, namely that she is ''weak and flabby'' by definition. The original words convey this notion regardless of whether or not the author shares this view. The only justifiable emendation the 1953 editors made was the belated replacement of *valiat'* by *valit'*. The literary meaning of *valiat'* is "drag," or "roll," not "knock down." Otherwise the graphic, well-proportioned, and typically Sholokhovian sentence should have been left as it was. Except for *valiat'*, its original wording was restored in 1956.

The next example illustrates the use of dialecticisms in descriptions of emotions. As we remember, Aksin'ia's love for Grigorii was said to bloom "ne lazorevym alym tsvetom, a sobach'ei besiloi, durnop'ianom pridorozhnym" (1:52)—"not like the scarlet flower of the tulip, but like that loco weed, the roadside henbane." *Lazorevyi tsvet* is the local poetic name for *lazorevyi tsvetok* or simply *lazorevyi*, meaning a wild tulip. *Lazorevyi tsvetok* and *sobach'ia besila* (henbane) are strictly dialectal, not found in Dal''s *Dictionary*. *Durnop'ian* (henbane) belongs to the vernacular. The average reader cannot be expected to be familiar with *sobach'ia besila* or to perceive *lazorevyi* other than a synonym of *lazurnyi* (azure). Nonetheless, Sholokhov chooses to speak about Aksin'ia's love in the idiom of her region, employing a favorite device of folk poetry—a negative trope. The scarlet tulip symbolizes a fresh young love, possibly the first love. The image is associated with the spring, late April and early May, when wild tulips bloom in the steppes and on the slopes of ravines. By contrast, the belated, frenzied love of Aksin'ia is likened to the flowering henbane, a poisonous plant with a heavy scent. The 1953 editors excised *sobach'ia besila*, weakening the vividness, emphasis, and amphibrachic pattern of the sentence. Both words were restored in 1956.

Lazorevyi tsvetok figures prominently in the characters' speech as an endearing name for girls (1:71; 5:265), and it was applied to men as well (3:133). It is this flower that the author picked as the culminating image in his moving digression about the Cossacks' leaving their native villages before the arrival of the Reds in the winter of 1919. With heavy thoughts the Cossacks go into the unknown, and "maybe a tear, salty as blood," would fall on the hoof-gnawed road. "But what does it matter if the yellow tulip of parting will not grow on that spot in the spring?" (3:108.) It is probably impossible to find a more poetic and suggestive image to communicate the feelings of the people who may never return to their beloved land where the tulip flower has a singular aesthetic and emotional appeal. In "The Crooked Path" *lazorevyi tsvetok* appears in a somewhat strained trope depicting a "patch of blood that blossomed on the shirt like a tulip flower" (7:399). In several cases the single word *lazorevyi* functions as a color epithet. It indicates the reddish color of lightning (2:332) and of clouds lit by the rays of the setting sun (3:63). A light shining through a window was yellow like a tulip (*lazorevo zheltel*), but the 1933 editors must have found the analogy confusing, and they deleted it (1:377). In "lazorevaia smes' bab'ikh nariadov" (1:187)—"the tulip-colored blend of women's attire"—the epithet *lazorevaia* was supposed to convey the idea of the garments' being as multicolored as tulips. The 1953 editors replaced it with *pestraia* (motley), sacrificing picturesqueness to comprehensibility. The replacement appears to be justified since the intended meaning of *lazorevyi* was particularly difficult to grasp. This epithet becomes synaesthetic when Sholokhov says that the wheat straw strongly smells of "*lazorevyi* August" in the bitter February cold (5:102). The visual image of red or yellow tulips suggests the color of the August sun and the sensation of heat. The "*lazorevyi* August" may call up a train of associations, ranging from a harvesting scene in the sun-scorched Don steppe to a cooling swim in the Atlantic Ocean. English translations of *Virgin Soil Upturned* render the epithet in "*lazorevyi* August" as "azure" or "golden." The first overlooks its dialectal meaning; the second is probably as good as any. Yet "golden" is a hackneyed epithet, totally lacking freshness, originality, and suggestiveness—the hallmarks of genuine poetry. A "golden August" may be forgotten the next day, a "*lazorevyi* August" can be remembered for all of one's life.

This poetic image marked the last time Sholokhov employed *lazorevyi* in his own narrative. Its disappearance in later works is symptomatic of the change in his attitude toward dialecticisms, a change that must have occurred in 1933-1934. In March 1934 Sholokhov came out in support of Gor'kii's drive against littering Soviet fiction with local expressions. He readily admitted his own excessive use of dialecticisms and voiced a strong concern for the purity of language of literary works. In an uncompromising manner he attacked those critics and writers (Panferov, Serafimovich) who justified the use of dialecticisms or sloppy language as a faithful rendition of popular speech in a new literature.[5]

Beginning with volume 4 of *The Quiet Don*, Sholokhov studiously avoids dialecticisms in his own narrative. Among a handful of dialectal and vernacular words found in that volume are *imenie* (belongings), *kolodez'* (well), *moslakovatyi* (bony), *pikhat'* (push), *ugadat'* (recognize), *priginaias'* (bending down). They are all absent from later works. In contrast to the nearly universal references to women as *baby* in previous works, volume 2 of *Virgin Soil Upturned* has *zhenshchiny* in all but two or three cases—a strange upgrading, since both volumes of the novel are set in the same year. Occasionally, the language of the Cossack characters in volume 4 of *The Quiet Don* and in later works turns out to be more literary than the language of the author in the preceding works. In volumes 1 and 2 of *The Quiet Don* the author's regular word for "complain" was the dialecticism *zhalit'sia*. In volume 4 Duniashka, Dar'ia, and Grigorii employ its literary counterpart *zhalovat'sia* (4:121, 305, 424). If the author used to compare Aksin'ia's love to a blossoming *durnop'ian pridorozhnyi*, Dar'ia likens her life to a blooming *pridorozhnaia belena*, the standard designation for the roadside henbane (4:63). It is improbable that *zhalovat' sia* or *belena* belonged to the vocabulary of plain Cossacks. They certainly did not use these words in Sholokhov's earlier works (3:150; 7:253). The dialecticism *chizhelyi* (heavy) is another case in point. It was consistently used by characters in earlier works, but in volume 4 of *The Quiet Don* it is suddenly discarded in favor of the literary *tiazhelyi*. In volume 2 of *Virgin Soil Upturned* old Shchukar' refers to boiling water by the literary *kipiatok* (6:329). In volume 1 he used the dialecticism *var* (5:239), as did the author in "The Whirlpool" (7:364).[6] The vernacular *kochet* (rooster) is the word that the characters use everywhere (and the author almost everywhere) in volume 1 of *Virgin Soil Upturned*. In volume 2 the author shifts to the literary *petukh*, while the characters use it half the time. The change is all the more remarkable since the word "rooster" occurs in volume 2 over seventy times.

If Sholokhov's new attitude toward dialecticisms prompted him to use them more sparingly in his later works, the editors took care of reducing their number in his earlier writings. There was, however, no systematic or coordinated effort to purge his stories from dialecticisms between 1924 and 1931. Most of the editors did not seem to be concerned about them. The few exceptions were book-form editions of individual stories—such as *Aleshka's Heart* (1925), *The Red Guards* (i.e., "The Whirlpool," 1925), *A Woman Who Had Two Husbands* (1925), and *About Kolchak, Nettles, and Other Things* (1927?)—where a number of dialecticisms were replaced by their literary counterparts or, occasionally, omitted. For the most part these corrections were not incorporated into the principal collections of the early stories published between 1926 and 1932. The number of earlier corrections preserved in the 1956 editions appears to be small.

Although the 1956 editors of the early stories paid more attention to language and style than did the editors of *The Don Stories* (1926, 1929) or of *The Tulip Steppe* (1926, 1931), they proceeded rather cautiously with replacing dialecticisms in the authorial narrative and scarcely touched them in the speech of the characters. Thus in two stories narrated entirely by characters—"Shibalok's Seed" and "Chairman of the Revolutionary Military Council of the Republic"—the editors made about 160 emendations, including improvements in punctuation, but they replaced or excised only three dialecticisms: *sychas* (now), *snachalu* (at the beginning), and *posedat'* (mount).[7] Among the vernacular and dialectal words replaced in the author's speech in various stories are *otchekhvostivat'* (do something quickly), *pozhalit' sia* (complain), and *dobriachii* (kind). Now and then one encounters changes that in all probability are restorations based on the text of the manuscript. For example, a Cossack in "A Family Man" now says *skroz'* (through) instead of the literary *skvoz'* which he used in all previous editions of that story. Sholokhov was reported to have examined an unidentified number of manuscripts of his early stories before they were included in the 1956 editions of his *Collected Works*.[8] Unfortunately, we have no precise information as to which revisions were made by him and which by the editors. A few dialecticisms used by both the author and the characters were replaced by the 1962 editors of *Collected Works* in the stories that were not included in the 1956 editions. On balance, the early stories have retained proportionately more original dialecticisms than *The Quiet Don*. This happened not only because they went through fewer revisions, but also because the overwhelming majority of dialecticisms replaced in *The Quiet Don* before 1953 have remained unrestored.

The exact number of dialecticisms replaced before 1953 is difficult to determine. A great deal depends on one's definition of dialecticism and one's method of counting corrections. In my very conservative estimate, well over two hundred corrections affecting dialectal words were made before 1953. Multiple corrections of the same item counted as one. A large number of emendations, especially in 1928-1929 and 1933, dealt with phonetic dialecticisms. The characters' speech was filled with them, and the editors found it necessary to tone down the characteristics of local pronunciation by replacing words like *movo* (my), *ide* (where), *nadezha* (hope), and many others. In the authorial narrative the editors substituted literary equivalents for words like *mga* (mist), *titor* (churchwarden), and *tupik* (back of saber). The most frequently corrected dialecticism in the author's speech was *storchmia* (sticking out). In a dozen instances the 1933 editors replaced it by the colloquialism *torchmia*.

Morphological dialecticisms—words reflecting local inflection and word formation—underwent more careful editing in the author's narrative than in the language of the characters. Such sub-standard forms as *vobratyi* (tucked in), *izginat'* (bend), and *igraiuchis'* (playing) were wholly or partly replaced. The cleansing of the characters' language from morphological dialecticisms did not proceed beyond a random rectification of inflectional irregularities, except for a consistent replacement, in 1933, of adverbs *otsedova* (from here), *dokedova* (how long), and *pokedova* (for the present, while).

Little attention was paid to the characters' lexical dialecticisms—words whose structures were entirely or considerably different from those of their literary counterparts. Such words replaced in the characters' speech included *sem-ka* (well, why not), *koblo* (burrow), and *kosoi* (one-eyed). The last word belongs to the homonymous sub-group of lexical dialecticisms. Its second, standard, meaning is "squint-eyed." Replacement of homonymous dialecticisms in the authorial narrative occurred more frequently than in the characters' speech. It affected such words as *prokatit'* (take for a ride—elect), *putina* (fishing season—road), and *vykhod* (exit—cellar). Although *vykhod* is a regular word for cellar in the Don Cossacks' idiom, this is the only time I have encountered it in all of Sholokhov's writings. The author probably avoided using it because its basic meaning (exit) is so deeply engrained in the average reader's mind that he might be hard pressed to decipher its dialectal connotation.

Since the pre-1953 editing lacked strict consistency, many identical dialecticisms were replaced only in part. It also happened that local words, as well as other irregularities, corrected in an earlier edition would surface in their original form later. For example, some of the corrections made in the 1934 edition of volume 1 are found in the 1935 deluxe and in the 1939 Rostov editions, but not in the inexpensive editions of 1935, 1936, and 1938, although all but the Rostov edition were published by Khudozhestvennaia literatura in Moscow. The 1941 and subsequent editions accepted the 1934 corrections. Some dialecticisms eliminated in the serialized text of the novel were restored in later editions. Thus the local form *popoloz* (he started to crawl) was substituted for the literary *popolz* in Petr Melekhov's speech in 1928 (1:339). One can only guess how many corrections were made in the serialized text.

The 1953 revision encompassed all kinds of dialecticisms in the speech of both the author and the characters. Particularly conspicuous changes were made in the characters' phonetic and morphological dialecticisms. Literary forms appeared in place of such copiously used words as *isho* (still), *it'* (you see), *khuch'* (although), *entot* (that), *azhnik* (so that, even), *priidet* (he will come), and, sometimes, *zaraz* (now). At times corrections affected several words in a row. Thus Pantelei Melekhov's statement "V tserkvu azhnik stramno ittit' " became "V tserkov' azh sramno itti" (2:262)—"I'm even ashamed to go to the church." The following nine dialecticisms were replaced in Il'inichna's seventeen lines of advice to Natal'ia concerning her married life with Grigorii: *zhizniu* (life, acc. sing), *kakuiu chudu* (what an odd thing, acc. sing), *omorok* (fainting feat), *priidet, slez'mi* (tears, instr.), *it', schinat'sià* (going to), *okhvalivat'* (praise), and *isho* (4:148-149). There was no need to replace these words. Any Russian reader could understand them in context. Furthermore, two of them have shades of meaning absent from their literary counterparts. These are the two italicized words in the adjacent phrases: "ni razu ne *schinalas'* ukhodit'. Ia ne *okhvalivaiu* Grishku" (I was never once going to leave. I don't praise Grishka). In 1953 they were replaced by *sobiralas'* and *khvaliu*, respectively. As a result, the first phrase lost the sense of promptness conveyed by the structural similarity of *schinat'sia* and *nachinat'* (start), acquiring at the same time a tinge of procrastination easily associated with *sobirat'sia*. In the second phrase the neutral *khvaliu* is certainly not synonymous with *okhvalivaiu*. *Raskhvalivat'* (praise lavishly) could be a better choice. Even so, its prefix *raz* denotes intensification of action, while the prefix *o* in *okhvalivat'* indicates encompassment. Above all, the combination of the prefix *o* with a verb of praise produces a singularly novel effect since this prefix is an integral part of the verbs with opposite meaning: *okhaivat'* (smear) and *ogovarivat'* (slander).

Strictly speaking, *schinat'sia* and *okhvalivat'* are not translatable into literary Russian. At the same time they are indispensable for reproducing the racy popular speech as well as for enriching and invigorating the literary style. After all, literature is a verbal art. It is the author's talent for selecting and combining words that separates him from nonfiction writers. Of course, the use of fresh words is not enough to make a work original or artistic. It is not solely the well-chosen dialecticisms that make Il'inichna's advice to Natal'ia a good example of Sholokhov's masterful handling of the characters' language. The old woman's mentality and feelings are mirrored in all the elements of her speech—in its entire vocabulary, word order, and intonation. The Cossacks' dialogues are perhaps the strongest artistic feature of *The Quiet Don*. The authorial narrative is uneven. Many passages are brilliant, but many, particularly in the first three volumes, are marred by linguistic incongruities. The Cossack dialogue, on the contrary, is invariably superb. With his flair for drama, Sholokhov creates meaningful, emotionally charged conversations. The main thing, however, is that they sound admirably natural. Unlike any major Russian writer of the nineteenth or twentieth century, the author of *The Quiet Don* knows the dialect better than the literary language. He seems to hear his Cossacks talk and he records their speech effortlessly. It is the local idiom that contributes most to the expressiveness of their dialogue.

However severe and harmful, the 1953 purge did not affect all dialecticisms. Those left intact in the characters' speech included the frequently used *diuzhe* (much) and *troshki* (little), as well as many local terms pertaining to the Cossacks' way of life and to surrounding nature. As examples one can mention *kuren'* (house), *maidan* (square), and *levada* (grove). These types of dialecticisms also remained in the authorial narrative, although other varieties were purged from it more thoroughly than from the characters' speech.

Restoration of dialecticisms removed in 1953 began in the 1955 edition. Its scope, however, was very modest, and the restorations alternated with replacements of some words overlooked or spared in 1953. In 1956 well-nigh all of the 1953 corrections in the characters' language were reversed. Exceptions comprised primarily lexical dialecticisms, such as *zabivat'sia* (stop by), *klechatet'* (suffer), and *zatekat'sia* (be worn out with waiting). The treatment of the authorial dialecticisms was somewhat different. About one-fourth of them remained unrestored. Criteria for this failure to restore are not always clear. The 1956 editors restored such sub-standard forms as *tolkanut'sia* (collide) and *stukotet'* (knock), but refused to rehabilitate words like *posered'* (in the middle of) and *ogorozha* (fence). Often a given dialecticism was treated inconsistently. Thus the verb *nudit'sia* (feel uneasy) was reinstated in the speech of the author and the characters in some places (2:86, 314; 3:107), but was banned from the author's speech elsewhere (2:304). A certain consistency can, however, be discerned in the treatment of words which diverge semantically from standard Russian and of onomatops. A greater number of words like *gostit'* (be a guest—treat) and *glukhar'* (woodgrouse—bell) were not restored. The editors must have decided that dialectal meanings of these common words were quite different from the literary. By contrast, the meanings of onomatopoeic dialecticisms can easily be determined by their sounds, and that might have been the reason for their nearly total restoration. Typical examples from this numerous group are *brunzhat'* (buzz), *kvokhtat'* (cackle), and *chuliukan'e* (chirping).

While restoring the bulk of the dialecticisms banned three years before, the 1956 editors weeded out a number of those which during previous revisions had been spared or purged partially. The new pruning focused chiefly on the authorial narrative. The most conspicuous corrections made in it were replacements of *kolodez'* (well) by *kolodets*, and *suetno* (vainly) by *suetlivo* (hurriedly).

The fate of the following four dialecticisms in the authorial narrative merits special mention, particularly in the light of the 1953 and 1956 revisions: *vstrech'* (toward), *sboch'* (by, at the side of), *ugadat'* (recognize), and *siurtuk* (semi-military Cossack coat). *Vstrech'* is noteworthy because it occurred only in volume 3 of *The Quiet Don* (ten times) and in volume 1 of *Virgin Soil Upturned* (four times). Since both volumes were written about the same time, one can assume that there was a definite period in Sholokhov's life when he began to use *vstrech'*. Had he used it before, we would have certainly encountered this common word in some of the numerous publications of his early stories or in *The Quiet Don*, all of which know solely its literary counterpart—*navstrechu*. *Navstrechu* also occurs throughout volume 4 of *The Quiet Don*. Here, however, there is no way of telling whether it was an editorial substitution or the author's choice. In 1952-1953 *vstrech'* was replaced everywhere. It is no longer in *The Quiet Don*, but it was reinstated in two places in *Virgin Soil Upturned* (5:6, 194).

The story of *sboch'* illustrates Stalin's role in the 1952-1953 revisions of Sholokhov's novels. It also sheds light on the entire campaign for the purification of the Russian language conducted during the last years of the dictator's life. "In a conversation with me," Sholokhov said in 1955, "comrade Stalin also called my attention to the necessity of purging the language of my works of sub-standard, trashy words. Iosif Vissarionovich, for instance, took notice of the beginning of chapter 34 of *Virgin Soil Upturned*: 'At the side of the road stands a burial mound. . . .' [Sboch' dorogi mogil'nyi kurgan]. 'What kind of a word is *sboch'*?' asked comrade Stalin. 'We do not have it in the Russian language. There is the word *sboku* [by, at the side], there is *obochina* [edge, side]. These are full-bodied, resonant, and clear words.' The remarks made by I. V. Stalin, A. M. Gor'kii, and numerous readers concerning the purity of the language of *The Quiet Don* and *Virgin Soil Upturned* were taken by me into account during the revision of their texts."[9] Sholokhov did not say when his conversation with Stalin took place. But this did not matter much. Stalin's opinion on literary matters had been a law for many years, especially in the early 1950s, when he was hailed as a linguist of genius. The fate of *sboch'* was sealed. In all six instances in *Virgin Soil Upturned* and thirty instances in *The Quiet Don, sboch'* was replaced or, occasionally, deleted. Whether by design or accident, in nearly half of the cases its place was taken by *sboku*. These substitutions were as a rule awkward. The 1956 editors changed most of them to *sboku ot* (at the side of) or to other words. Four cases of *sboch'* in *The Quiet Don* and two in *Virgin Soil Upturned* were restored. One of the latter was in the sentence about the burial mound. If *sboch'* was to be reinstated anywhere, this was the most appropriate place to do so. Chapter 34, as we know, is the sole portion of the novel presenting the Cossacks in an epic perspective as successors to the Cumans. In "sboch' dorogi mogil'nyi kurgan" (5:277), the word *sboch'* does several things at once. It immediately brings local color to the narrative devoted to the Don countryside. A short, sharp word, it suggests the strength and swiftness of the Cossacks. A local term, it is the chief representative of the Cossack side in the four-word opening sentence in which the last two words represent the Cumans. The first word should be monosyllabic, so that the rhythm of the sentence may be maintained. The 1952 editors destroyed the rhythm by replacing *sboch'* by *sboku ot* (at the side of). The only appropriate monosyllabic preposition with a similar meaning is *u* (by, at), but *u* has no local flavor. Moreover, consisting as it does of only one sound, it would merge in pronunciation with the next word, upsetting the rhythm and balance of the sentence in question. In a word, *sboch'* appears to be irreplaceable here. No wonder it came back as soon as Stalin was gone. The dictator's death might also have been responsible for the preservation of *sboch'* in the early stories during their 1956 revision.

No lexical dialecticism was more frequently used by the author than *ugadat'*, the Don Cossacks' favorite word for "recognize," instead of the literary *uznat'*. There were at least 55 cases of *ugadat'* in the earlier editions of *The Quiet Don* and possibly more in the manuscript. The replacement history of *ugadat'* by *uznat'* in that novel is typical of the haphazard treatment of dialecticisms throughout the years. Two cases of *ugadat'* were replaced in 1933, 4 in the deluxe 1936 edition of volume 2, 24 in 1953, 15 in 1956, 10 have been left intact, and 2 of those replaced in 1953 were restored in 1956. A Soviet critic, speaking of the 1953 corrections, claimed that Sholokhov used *ugadat'* when the process of recognition was somewhat difficult, involving a degree of guessing.[10] This is not so. Before 1933 there were fewer than 10 *uznat'* in the novel. If the critic were correct, that would mean that in the other 55 cases the characters had difficulty recognizing each other, and this is clearly not logical. Incidentally, one of the original *uznat'* is in the sentence "Podtelkov . . . s trudom uznaet kazaka" (2:367)—"Podtelkov . . . with difficulty recognizes the Cossack." The goal of the 1953 and 1956 editors was to reduce the number of *ugadat'* used as a dialecticism. *The Quiet Don* was purged of it more drastically than any other work. All five cases of *ugadat'* in *Virgin Soil Upturned* went through its 1952 revision unscathed. One of them, however, was replaced in 1955 and two in 1957. Only half of the original *ugadat'* was replaced in the 1956 edition of the early stories.

A great confusion was created by the author's use of the word *siurtuk*. It means "frock coat" in the literary language, but in the local idiom it denotes a specific military-like coat worn by the Don Cossacks before the Revolution. The difference between the regular and the local frock coats was implied in the observation that the frock coat in which Stepan Astakhov returned from Germany was of a "city cut" (3:62). The frock coats worn by the city-bred characters, like the Bolsheviks Shtokman and Abramson (1:233; 2:199), could be of the same cut, while the local non-Cossack Valet is dressed in a regular coat (*pidzhak*), which was not part of Cossack attire (1:129, 152, 233).

In the early editions of the first three volumes of *The Quiet Don, siurtuki* (frock coats)—depending on their quality and condition—were worn by plain Cossacks in a variety of situations. The Cossacks wore them while cleaning chaff sheds, visiting their neighbors, getting married, attending village meetings, and even going to fight in the Civil War, when uniforms were in short supply. *Pidzhaki* (coats) or *kurtki* (jackets) worn by the Cossacks in volume 4 are either certain or likely substitutions for the original *siurtuki*, which were discarded during the serialization of that volume in *Novyi mir*.[11] Altogether there were at least thirty-four original *siurtuki* in *The Quiet Don*.

Thinking of the frock coat in conventional terms, the editors must have been puzzled at encountering that garment on a barefooted Cossack boy tending oxen or on Mishka Koshevoi when he goes fishing (2:333, 318). Nonetheless, it was not until 1936 that the purge of *siurtuki* at last commenced, with volume 2 of the deluxe edition. By 1953 one-third of *siurtuki* was replaced, mostly with *kurtki*. The high point of the purge occurred in the 1953 edition, where 14 *siurtuki* were changed to *pidzhaki* and 6 remained untouched. These were regular or military frock coats worn by officers, generals, political figures, and an old Galician (1:356). The 1956 editors also did nothing about the 6 *siurtuki*, but they rejected all *pidzhaki* introduced three years earlier. Ten characters exchanged them for *kurtki* and 4 put on their original *siurtuki*. Yet the *kurtki* did not last very long. Nine were taken off in the 1962 Rostov edition and the 10th in 1965, in the fourth edition of *Collected Works*. Eight characters donned their original *siurtuki* and 2—Shtokman and a Polish boy (1:233, 280)—their 1953 *pidzhaki*. Ironically, the person in charge of the 1962 Rostov edition was the same Kirill Potapov who had banned *siurtuki* from the 1953 edition. Potapov's undoing of his own work is indicative of the degree of editorial confusion caused by the *siurtuki*. A few more restorations of the original *siurtuki* occurred in the subsequent editions, but they were not approved in the 1965-1966 text of the novel published in the fourth edition of *Collected Works*. No changes in clothing were observed after 1966, but by that time some Cossacks serving in the Civil War formations managed to exchange their dress four or five times, ending up either in *pidzhaki* (3:105) or *siurtuki* (3:278). The record, however, was set up by Abramson. Between 1953 and 1966 he exchanged his *siurtuk* for a *pidzhak* and vice versa six times. Unlike Shtokman, he wears his original clothing at the present.

Altogether at least 15 *siurtuki* have disappeared from *The Quiet Don*, most of them without a good reason. Since the Cossacks did have their own kind of *siurtuki* that cannot be equated with *pidzhaki* or *kurtki*, the best solution would have been to explain the local meaning of the word *siurtuk* in a footnote or in an appended glossary. In cases where *siurtuki* were worn by the non-Cossack characters, the author should have been given the benefit of the doubt. The only justifiable replacements seem to be those affecting the *siurtuki* of the German soldiers, which were replaced by uniform coats (2:37) or, less felicitously, by jackets (3:19). And perhaps the Polish boy can wear a *pidzhak* instead of a small *siurtuk* (1:280).

In *Virgin Soil Upturned* the situation was complicated by the fact that Sholokhov extended the meaning of the word *siurtuk* to *pidzhak*. The extension reflected the Cossacks' habit of calling the Russian *pidzhak* by the name of their similar garment. It is therefore highly unlikely that the

Communist Davydov, a Leningrad factory worker, really wore a regular frock coat while carrying out collectivization in a Cossack village in 1930 (5:30, 325). No wonder Davydov's *siurtuk* was permanently replaced by *pidzhak* in 1945 and 1952. Six Cossacks lost their *siurtuki* in three stages: in 1945, 1952, and 1957. Of the two *siurtuki* left in the novel, one is a 1957 restoration and the other has never been removed. This bright blue garment is worn by a gypsy, before the Revolution. It has survived because it is long, as a real frock coat should be. Some Cossacks have been wearing *pidzhaki* since the first edition of *Virgin Soil Upturned*. No doubt the Cossacks of 1930 were not as frequently clad in their *siurtuki* as in the tsarist time. Nonetheless, it was strange to see Davydov dressed in a *siurtuk*, while the word *pidzhak* was repeatedly used in references to clothing confiscated from the well-to-do Cossacks who must have had *siurtuki* in their wardrobes (5:128-129). There are no *siurtuki* in volume 2 of *Virgin Soil Upturned*.

The erratic treatment of *siurtuki* in *The Quiet Don* suggests that its editors received little or no help from the author. The degree of Sholokhov's participation in the editing of his own works remains a mystery. Had he proofread them carefully and frequently, as the Soviet sources claim he had, he would have caught the glaring incongruity caused by the misunderstanding of the dialecticism *zagoit'sia* (heal). From the very beginning the editors mistook it for *zagnoit'sia* (fester). The case in point is a remark made by a Cossack woman to the effect that her husband's wounded leg has healed and he has sent her a message to bring him his horse (3:360). Out of forty-one editions I have checked, only six, from 1935 through 1941, have the right word. A similar blunder occurred in *Virgin Soil Upturned* with the dialecticism *pererub* (beam). In 1933 it was confused with cutover land because its root denotes chopping or cutting. Therefore in at least twenty-three editions Razmetnov's wife is said to have hanged herself not on the beam in the shed, but in the shed located on the beam (5:40).

The treatment of dialecticisms in *Virgin Soil Upturned* during the 1950s closely resembled their treatment in *The Quiet Don*. A mass purge in the bowdlerized 1952 version was followed by an intensive restoration in the first edition of *Collected Works* in 1957.[12] This restoration, however, had no effect on the high-school editions of 1958-1960 that continued to be modeled after the bowdlerized edition. The purge of dialecticisms in that edition was slightly less severe than in the 1953 edition of *The Quiet Don*, while the restoration rate in the 1957 edition of *Virgin Soil Upturned* was somewhat higher than in the 1956 text of *The Quiet Don*. Consequently, *Virgin Soil Upturned* has preserved proportionately more dialecticisms than *The Quiet Don*. Apart from the changes involving the characters' clothing in the first half of the 1960s, all but a few sporadic corrections affecting dialecticisms were made in both novels after 1956-1957.

Throughout the years *The Quiet Don* has lost hundreds of dialecticisms. Many more, however, were retained, and the novel still has a distinct dialectal coloration. It is up to the individual reader to judge whether it should have more or fewer dialecticisms in the authorial narrative. On the other hand, it is difficult to deny the fact that the injection of alien words and forms into the Cossack speech could not but impair its authenticity and attractiveness.

SIMILES

One of the most conspicuous features of Sholokhov's language is its figurativeness. My discussion of it will be centered on similes. Apart from metonymy, all principal figures of speech—metaphor, epithet, hyperbole, and simile—have their origins in the comparison of two things. Simile, being the most direct mode of comparison, can be regarded as the basic trope. To get a better glimpse of Sholokhov's artistic individuality, the use of similes in *The Quiet Don* will be compared to their use in *War and Peace* and the major works of six Soviet writers. Furthermore, the evolution of Sholokhov's style will be illustrated by changes in the employment of similes in all of his fiction. Since the interpretation of similes varies with each individual scholar, a few remarks about my approach are in order.

A simile is a figurative comparison of two things, concepts, actions, or states introduced by "like," "as," or other words indicating resemblance. That which is compared is called tenor; that to which the tenor is compared is called vehicle. It is the kind and degree of difference between the tenor and the vehicle that determines whether a comparison can be classified as a simile. For example, the sentence "John fights like Peter" is not a simile, but a literary comparison. No essential difference between John's way of fighting and Peter's is suggested. Conversely, the sentence "John fights like a tiger" is a simile. However ferociously John might fight, his way of fighting would still be quite different from that of a tiger. The figurative character of this simile is obviously enhanced by the fact that John and the tiger belong to different spheres of life. Nevertheless, not every comparison whose tenor and vehicle represent different spheres must automatically be designated as a simile. When Tolstoi says that the old Count Rostov's horse turned gray as did its master, he makes a literary rather than a figurative comparison. The process of aging affected man and animal in essentially the same manner.

Considerable difficulty may arise in distinguishing between similes and comparisons likening men to men. Some scholars seem to go as far as to limit simile to "the comparison of two things of different categories," arguing that "there is no simile if we compare *Gladstone* to *Disraeli*, the two not being sufficiently unlike. On the other hand there is a simile when we liken a *statesman* to a *fox*, the two being, in most respects, unlike."[13]

Such a criterion appears to be too sweeping and unrealistic. While it correctly accepts as a simile a figurative but trite comparison of a person with a fox, it would, for example, deny this classification to Tolstoi's imaginative likening of Anna Pavlovna's handling of her guests to the manner in which a spinning mill owner regulates the work of his spindles.[14] Selection of similes from man-to-man comparisons requires an individual approach which should be in agreement with general guidelines adopted by each researcher. As a rule, I include in the category of similes comparisons that refer to persons of different sexes, occupations, nationalities, or ages. If an adult is said to be crying like a child, I consider the phrase a simile. The differences between the crying of an adult and the crying of a child appear to be sufficient to lend to the comparison a certain degree of figurativeness. By the same token a Cossack's statement "Without arms I'm like a woman with her skirt pulled up. I'm naked" (3:138) contains enough figurativeness to qualify as a simile. I also treat as similes those phrases in which normal and healthy people are said to act as if they were drunk, blind, insane, ill, or stupid. However, a rather large group of comparisons connected by "as if" (*kak budto, kak by*) presents a real difficulty. Here are two examples from *War and Peace*: "Rostov pulled his arm out [of Denisov's grip] and looked at him directly and firmly and with such hatred as if Denisov had been his greatest enemy" (4:180) and "She passed between men who made way for her, and without looking directly at any one, but smiling at every one, as if courteously granting to each one of them the right to admire the beauty of her figure, her full shoulders, her breast and back . . . came up to Anna Pavlovna" (4:19). Whether or not such comparisons can be called similes depends, in my view, on the degree to which the situation described in the "as if" phrase corresponds to reality. Actually, Denisov was one of Rostov's best friends. Thus the essence of the first comparison lies in the fact that Rostov acted towards his friend the way he would be expected to act towards his enemy. The difference is substantial and the comparison can be regarded as a simile. In the second example there is a high degree of probability that Hélène consciously allowed people to admire the beauty of her body. No apparent or strong difference exists between the content of the "as if" phrase and the actual situation. The second example is, consequently, not a simile. The same is true of phrases in which the connective "as if" is used in the sense of "seem" or "pretend." In many comparisons introduced by "as if" the distinction between the literary and the figurative is virtually impossible to make. Selection of similes is thus bound to become a matter of strictly personal interpretations. Tolstoi's comparisons, with their subtle and prudently expressed insights into the workings of the human mind and heart, lend themselves less readily to classification than do the more direct comparisons in the works of Sholokhov and his contemporaries. As a result, fewer than one-fourth of Tolstoi's "as if" comparisons in the man-to-man group were classified as similes.

The study of similes is also complicated by the absence of any hard-and-fast rules for distinguishing between various figures of speech. For my investigation the interplay of simile and metaphor is important. Major ancient rhetoricians made no substantive distinction between the two tropes, though the Greek view was at variance with the Latin in ranking them. For Aristotle creation of a metaphor involved transfer of meaning on the basis of resemblance: "Metaphor is the application of the name of a thing to something else. . . . Making good metaphors depends on perceiving the likeness in things."[15] Aristotle called simile "a metaphor differing only by the addition of a word,"[16] i.e., an introductory word of comparison, such as "like" or "as." Quintilian's definition reversed the Aristotelian hierarchy: "On the whole metaphor is a shorter form of simile, while there is this further difference, that in the latter we compare some object to the thing which we wish to describe, whereas in the former this object is actually substituted for the thing."[17]

Modern scholars are inclined to treat simile and metaphor as distinct figures of speech. There is, however, no consensus on criteria for this differentiation. Marsh McCall distinguishes between the two figures primarily on formal grounds: simile is introduced by a connective and metaphor is not.[18] The same principle of classification is to be found in *The New Encyclopaedia Britannica* (1974) and *The Encyclopedia Americana* (1978).

Christine Brooke-Rose, with a reference to Quintilian, asserts that metaphor differs from simile "in that it replaces the word." Max Black, opposing this "substitution view," claims that "metaphorical statement is not a substitute for a formal comparison." Metaphor "creates the similarity" rather than "formulates some similarity antecedently existing."[19]

A great admirer of metaphor, Philip Wheelwright sees the difference between it and simile in "the quality of semantic transformation," in "the psychic depth at which the things of the world, whether actual or fancied, are transmuted by the cool heat of the imagination."[20] Wheelwright denies metaphorical status to Aeschylus' description of a harbor as "the step-mother of ships," for it came about "by analysis and labored comparison." On the other hand, Homer's reference to the wrathful Apollo—"His coming was like the night"—is a metaphor because it "stirs us emotionally as with a sudden revelation of half-guessed half-hidden mystery.''[21] Wheelwright brushes aside the most obvious index of simile, its connective, and makes an individual's perception the sole yardstick for distinguishing between simile and metaphor.

The last view to be brought up here is that of Michel Le Guern, who focuses on transfer of meaning. This transfer, he says, occurs in metaphor, but not in simile. For example, in the simile ''Jim is as stubborn as a mule'' both parts retain their proper meanings.[22] Le Guern's reasoning can be challenged with the aid of Aristotle's definitions of metaphor and simile. If, as Aristotle stated, the mark of metaphor is transfer of meaning and simile is essentially a metaphor, it is logical to infer that simile, too, involves transfer of meaning. Characteristically, Aristotle perceived ''the very little difference'' between simile and metaphor in the manner of expression; he said nothing about the absence of semantic transfer in simile. It may also be argued that the simile ''Jim is as stubborn as a mule'' contains transfer of meaning by implication. It is hard to avoid thinking of Jim in terms of a mule, especially since stubbornness is that animal's principal characteristic. At the same time it must be noted that simile suggests a weaker association between its components than metaphor.

For me metaphor tends to express identification of the tenor with the vehicle, while simile speaks of their likeness. The sentence ''Aksin'ia clenched her teeth, and her words—drops of rain on stone—fell scantly'' (1:348) is a metaphor because Aksin'ia's words are identified with raindrops. A metaphor thus presupposes a greater degree of figurativeness than a simile. The difference, however, is rather quantitative than qualitative. Actually, the tenor and the vehicle of a metaphor cannot be absolutely identical—Aksin'ia's words cannot be turned into drops of rain. One may say that metaphor involves comparison to the greatest possible extent, theoretically ad infinitum. Many metaphors can easily be transformed into similes by adding ''like'' or similar connectives. This explains why some scholars treat unlinked (asyndetic) metaphors of the above-cited kind as similes.[23] Even more scholars, notably the Russians, designate as negative similes the expressions of the type ''She is not a woman, but fire and smoke'' (1:299).[24] This type frequently occurs in folk poetry with the difference that its affirmative part is usually associated with people and the negative with the world of nature: ''It isn't the cuckoo bird that is cuckooing . . . it is a widow crying.'' In my opinion, such tropes are metaphors, for they state or imply an identity between tenor and vehicle, rather than a similarity. This is not to say that negative similies do not exist. They do, but they emphasize similarity and express it with the aid of appropriate connectives: Aksin'ia's love blooms ''not like the scarlet flower of the tulip, but like . . . the roadside henbane'' (1:52). Furthermore, there are asyndetic similes, ranging from lengthy parallels between man and nature to short simple phrases. The latter variety includes, for instance, the sentence describing Stepan's kicking prostrate Aksin'ia with his boots: "If you look at Stepan from a distance—the man is dancing the *kazachok* dance" (1:67). The second part of the sentence seems to emphasize less the identification of Stepan with a person dancing the *kazachok* than the similarity of their movements. The sentence therefore is closer to a simile than to a metaphor.

A special problem arises with figures of speech expressed by means of the instrumental case without a preposition. Russian scholarship regards such figures as either similes or the blending of simile and metaphor, a sort of transitional trope. In fact, the instrumental of comparison suggests a virtual identity between tenor and vehicle and is in this respect metaphoric. Figurative expressions in which the instrumental case could easily be replaced with the nominative preceded by the connective "like" will be treated here as similes. An elementary example is the sentence "Duniashka kozoi skaknula k vorotam" (1:29). In both Russian and English it can be rendered as "Duniashka leaped toward the gate like a goat" and be called a simile. The situation is not so clear in the sentence "Litso Bogatyreva chernoi lapoi ispiatnil gnev" (3:322). To translate this sentence as "Like a black paw, wrath splotched Bogatyrev's face" may not be the best solution because the original could be read as suggesting that the black paw is a part of wrath rather than a separate entity to which wrath is likened. It would therefore be better to consider the original sentence a plain metaphor and render it as "Wrath splotched Bogatyrev's face with its black paw."

Compound adjectives of the type *makovo-krasnyi* (poppy-red) and *molochno-belyi* (milky-white) are regarded here as epithets. On the other hand, figurative expressions featuring the adverbial use of the words like *molochno* or *sakharno* (sugarlike) are assigned to similes: "molochno blesteli zuby" (2:59)—"her teeth gleamed milkily"; "pod nogami sakharno pokhrupyval sneg" (3:131)—"the snow scrunched like sugar under their feet." Expressions containing hyperbolic images introduced by connectives equivalent to "like" or "as if" are also listed here as similes. It is the presence of these comparative connectives that provides justification for designating as hyperbolic similes (rather than hyperboles) such phrases as "Khristonia even sighed as if he were throwing a mountain off his shoulders" (2:331). Figurative expressions comparing the size of things by means of the preposition *s*—which in this use indicates approximation and hence likeness—are viewed by me as similes regardless of the degree of exaggeration contained in them: "golova . . . s pol'skoi kotel" (1:145)—

"his head . . . is as big as a field cauldron." I would not, however, object to calling this trope a hyperbole.

When the size or shape of the tenor is expressed by means of the preposition *v*—which in its literary use indicates an exact measurement—the figure is judged to be not a simile but a metaphor or a hyperbole, depending on the degree of identification or exaggeration suggested by it.

Included in my list of similes are expressions whose figurativeness has faded considerably or become hardly perceptible due to frequent use. Here belong clichés on the order of "fly like a bullet" and "pale as a sheet." An attempt to exclude such locutions would not help to gain a clearer idea of the author's use of similes. An individual researcher would be less arbitrary if he counted all clichés as similes than if he tried to decide whether a certain simile is already dead or still breathing.

All similes found in the works of Sholokhov and the seven writers to whom he is compared have been classified according to the spheres of life from which their tenors and vehicles had been drawn. While every student of similes is faced with the problem of their classification, the ways of ordering them vary a great deal, mirroring the views and aims of each individual. In one study the arrangement of similes in accordance with the meaning of their tenors produced five basic categories with 176 sections.[25] Professor Carl Proffer established twelve categories, classifying similes in *Dead Souls* with respect to the subject matter of their tenors and vehicles.[26] My study cannot go into such details, since it is not a monograph on similes. Moreover, a meticulous classification of the large number of similes collected for the study would obscure the general picture.

I limited myself to four basic categories, each corresponding to one of the following four spheres of life: man, animals, nature, and objects. Each category consists of four basic groups showing the numerical relationship between the tenors of the given category and the vehicles representing each of the four categories. Thus the first category demonstrates how often man is compared to man, to animals, to nature, and to objects. By analogy, the four groups of the second category show the number of times animals are likened to man, animals, nature, and objects. The first category includes everything directly associated with the world of man: parts and functions of the human body; mental, emotional, and health states; intellectual and physical activities; and so on. Among the words occurring in this category are heart, fairytale, joy, fever, reminiscences, war, childhood, song, chess game. The second category represents wild and domestic animals, reptiles, insects, birds, and fish, with their distinctive characteristics and habits expressed by words like mane, wing, beak, scale, fly, sting. The sources of the third category are inanimate nature and plants: heavenly bodies, sky, air, darkness, seasons, meteorological phenomena, bodies of water, forms of the earth's surface, trees, the steppe, vegetables. The fourth category encompasses a great variety of inanimate objects (or phenomena) such as localities, rooms, household articles, clothing, food, beverages, means of transportation, machines, musical instruments, toys, weapons, fuel, and ointments. Words like flame, spark, dust, field, and stone are listed in this category unless they are clearly associated with the realm of nature. Thus a ploughed field, dust in a room, a stone in a ring, or water on a goose are objects. It is the context that determines the classification of words which may belong to more than one category. An ordinary road is treated as an object; but if a long sad song is likened to a desolate steppe road overgrown with plantain, we have a comparison of man to nature (1:127). And if the road metaphorically stands for human life, it must be in the first category. Classification of words like eye, sweat, or blood depends on whether they refer to people or animals, with man getting the benefit of the doubt when neither is mentioned. Some words denoting sounds, such as howling or whistling, can be in any of our four categories. On the other hand, God and the devil, along with goblins and spirits, are put in separate categories.

Figures in my tables 1 and 3 show the relationships between the four basic categories and include what I call secondary tenors and vehicles. These are the second components of double (or balanced) similes on the order of "Thoughts scattered her sleep like wind scatters a haycock" (1:214). The secondary components here are "her sleep" in the tenor and "a haycock" in the vehicle, forming a man-to-object relationship. Some similes classified here as double do not contain both of their tenors or vehicles in the same sentence, but their missing member is either mentioned or clearly implied in the context. In some borderline cases the differentiation between a single and a double simile becomes a matter of personal opinion. Very seldom does one see a triple simile, as in the following phrase from *War and Peace*: "The noncommissioned officer ran up to the senior officer, and in a frightened whisper (just as at dinner the butler reports to the host that there is no more of the wine he asked for) said that there were no more charges" (6:267). The three relationships here are: noncom-butler, officer-host, and charges-wine. Two or more relationships are also found in unbalanced similes, that is, similes characterized by an uneven number of tenors and vehicles. There are four tenors and one vehicle in Sholokhov's simile "Infantry units, strings of carts, batteries, and hospitals crawled like caterpillars" (1:253). My table, however, reflects only two relationships: man to animal and object to animal. Two or more tenors or vehicles belonging to the same category are treated as one unless they are very different or unless the author singles them out by adding modifiers, connectives, or the conjunction "or." The phrase saying that after Anna's death Bunchuk looked at the world "like a man who was heavily intoxicated or one who had just recovered from a wasting illness" (2:338) may serve as an example. Figures for Sholokhov's works are based on their earliest printed texts or on the texts regarded to be the closest to the originals. All later changes made in the content or form of similes are disregarded. Therefore my figures include at least eighty-five similes—six of them double—that are no longer in *The Quiet Don*. Seventy-five percent of them vanished in 1933 and 1953. Causes of deletion were political, puritanical, and stylistic. Some of the victims were innocent; they just happened to be a part of larger passages removed for political reasons.

Soviet works compared to *The Quiet Don* with respect to similes are Vsevolod Ivanov's *Bronepoezd No. 14.69* (*Armored Train No. 14-69*, 1922), Fedor Gladkov's *Tsement* (*Cement*, 1925), Isaak Babel''s *Konarmiia* (*Red Cavalry*, 1926), Iurii Olesha's *Zavist'* (*Envy*, 1927), Artem Veselyi's *Piruiushchaia vesna* (*The Carousing Spring*, 1929), and Boris Pasternak's *Doctor Zhivago* (1957).[27] Although not written in the 1920s, *Doctor Zhivago* was included because its highly figurative language and its treatment of nature invite comparison with *The Quiet Don*. My standards for determining and categorizing similes are identical for all works. Another researcher might use different criteria and his findings would be different. Yet the resulting disparities, I believe, would be confined to details, while the overall conclusions would come close to those derived from the table below.

The Quiet Don contains three times as many similes as *War and Peace*, but the frequency of their use is proportionately about the same as in other Soviet works. Thus with regard to the figurativeness of its language *The Quiet Don* belongs to the mainstream of early Soviet literature which is marked by a strong penchant for what may be loosely termed ornamental style. At times the striving for figurativeness led to obtrusive repetitions of the same images, considerably increasing the number of tropes in a given work. To some extent this is true of *The Armored Train No. 14-69* and is quite characteristic of *Cement*.

An important source of tropes in *The Quiet Don* is found in its characters. They contribute 24 percent of its similes, counting doubles for two. This percentage is higher than the corresponding ratios in any of the works appearing in table 1, except for *Envy*. It can be partly attributed to the amount of dialogue in *The Quiet Don* and partly to the peculiarities of the Cossacks' speech. On the other hand, the characters of *War and Peace* provide only 15 percent of its similes. The obvious reasons for the low figure are twofold. Tolstoi's aristocrats, as educated people in general, curtail the use of figures in order not to make their speech sound affected. They are also less prone to use coarse or offensive comparisons than are

TABLE 1: Categories of the Similes in *The Quiet Don* and Works by Other Writers

Groups	*Quiet Don*	*War and Peace*	*Arm. Train*	*Cement*	*Red Cav.*	*Envy*	*Carous. Spring*	*Dr. Zhivago*
Man-man	552	348	45	159	56	74	96	182
Man-animal	392	91	27	132	30	16	106	32
Man-nature	274	63	36	41	18	11	88	76
Man-object	354	130	51	129	32	44	162	93
Man-God	3	3		4	2			1
Man-demons	7	3	1	3	1		7	
TOTAL	1582	638	160	468	139	145	459	384
Animal-man	17	5		3	2	2	6	8
Animal-animal	27	5	3	1	3		7	4
Animal-nature	16	2	1	2	1	1	3	7
Animal-object	43	6	4	7	6	3	5	10
Animal-demons	1							
TOTAL	104	18	8	13	12	6	21	29
Nature-man	44	10	4	2	5	4	11	67
Nature-animal	26		3	8	4		9	10
Nature-nature	37	6	3	25		2	8	30
Nature-object	82	12	7	25	18	4	18	82
Nature-God	1							
TOTAL	190	28	17	60	27	10	46	189
Object-man	31	15	8	12	8	6	20	25
Object-animal	36	5	1	29	1	14	16	7
Object-nature	60	10	7	19	7	15	20	16
Object-object	143	43	26	78	22	56	57	77
Object-God		1						
Object-demons				1				
TOTAL	270	74	42	139	38	91	113	125
God-man		3					1	2
God-animal					1		1	
TOTAL		3			1		2	2
SUM TOTAL	2146	761	227	680	217	252	641	729
Characters' similes	24%	15%	10%	17%	23%	71%	13%	20%

ABBREVIATIONS IN TABLES 1 AND 2

Quiet Don—The Quiet Don
Arm. Train—Armored Train No. 14-69
Red Cav.—Red Cavalry
Carous. Spring—The Carousing Spring
Dr. Zhivago—Doctor Zhivago

common people, who speak with greater spontaneity and with fewer inhibitions. Things are different, however, when characters happen to be endowed with creative imaginations. A case in point is Nikolai Kavalerov, the narrator of the first part of *Envy*. He is the source of virtually all the similes occurring in that part. Olesha admitted to having provided his hero with his own view of the world and with his own figures of speech. And although the second part of *Envy* is narrated by the author, the characters' share of its similes comes close to 45 percent. Nearly all of them are in the speech of Ivan Babichev, a character whose creative imagination seems to equal that of the author. A somewhat similar situation exists in *Doctor Zhivago*. Its protagonist—a poet and the author's mouthpiece—uses over one-third of the similes allotted to all the characters. His creativity helped to raise the characters' share of similes to one-fifth of their total number. The percentage would be higher if one were to include the poetry of Iurii Zhivago, comprising the last part of the novel.

In *Red Cavalry* the characters supply 23 percent of the similes. The figure is rather high, but it must be noted that two-thirds of the characters' similes occur in six *skaz* stories. Of greater significance is the fact that now and then Babel' makes his plain Cossack characters use somewhat florid and elaborate tropes that are out of tune with their way of speaking. The narrator of the story ''Salt,'' for example, says: ''After the expiration of the times when the night was relieved of its sentry duty and the drummers started to beat reveille on their red drums . . . I'm getting up from my resting place from which the sleep ran away like a wolf from a pack of villainous dogs'' (96). This kind of rhetoric does not occur in *The Quiet Don* or *War and Peace*. The characters' tropes in these novels are a part of their normal speech. Babel''s taking liberty with the speech of his characters illustrates his eminently subjective approach to life. He tends to create his tropes less for elucidating what he describes than for conveying his fanciful perceptions of it. Nor does he worry about his Kuban' Cossacks' speaking Russian exclusively, though half of these Cossacks speak Ukrainian in real life. Sholokhov, on the contrary, tries to reproduce the language of his characters with maximal lifelikeness. The Ukrainians and Kuban' Cossacks speak their native tongues in *The Quiet Don*, even though, judging by the editorial corrections, their speech did not always agree with standard Ukrainian. Discussing the language of the *Red Cavalry* characters, one should keep in mind that many of their incongruous expressions and Revolutionary shibboleths—often couched in an odd grammatical form—are introduced for comic effect. A ludicrous misuse of political terminology was a fairly common phenomenon among uneducated Bolshevik zealots. Sholokhov showed it in Nagul'nov, whose mentality and language resemble those of Nikita Balmashev, the narrator of Babel''s ''Treason.'' But, again,

Nagul'nov's speech is free from metaphorical excesses and it sounds more natural than Balmashev's.

The characters' share of similes in the three remaining works is 10 percent in *The Armored Train No. 14-69*, 13 percent in *The Carousing Spring*, and 16 percent in *Cement*. Part of the reason for the lower percentages is that the characters in these books—peasants, factory workers, and army officers—express themselves in a less figurative language than do the Cossacks. Although peasants with their old traditions of folk poetry and with their daily communion with nature and animals speak a more figurative language than educated officers or factory workers, their language is still somewhat less picturesque than that of the Cossacks. The Cossacks were not only tillers of the soil, but also warriors. Their long military service, their frequent participation in wars, their unique relationship to their horses, and many other things connected with the military side of their life gave rise to a kind of folk poetry and conversational tropes not found among the peasants. To bring out this specific figurativeness of the Cossacks' speech, an author must be thoroughly familiar with it and be willing to recognize his characters as an important source of tropes in his work. This recognition is not evident in *The Armored Train No. 14-69* and is rather half-hearted in *The Carousing Spring*. No quotas, of course, can be recommended for the characters' figures of speech. Yet the failure to make one's characters speak more vividly, while vigorously cultivating the figurativeness of one's own narrative, bespeaks immoderation and lack of balance. As for Gladkov, he probably could not have squeezed more similes from his proletarians than he did.

There exists a sharp difference between *The Quiet Don* and the other works regarding the participation of characters in the creation of double similes. In *The Quiet Don* 42 out of 97 doubles are supplied by its characters. In *War and Peace* it is 8 out of 71 doubles and 2 triples. This difference can be explained by the popularity of double similes with plain folk. Indeed, many everyday sayings represent this kind of simile. An author who faithfully renders popular speech is bound to introduce a certain number of doubles into his work. Double similes used by the characters of *The Quiet Don* can be simple rhymed sayings like "My s toboi, kak ryba s vodoi" (1:175), which literally means "You and I—we're as inseparable as fish and water." Or they may be fairly complex asyndetic phrases, like the following statement about Grigorii's previous association with the Reds: "He's a good fighter. . . . But we can't see the sun for the mist and we can't see his merits—his service with the Bolsheviks has obscured our sight!" (2:345). All but one of the characters' double similes belong to the first category, most of them being in the man-to-man and man-to-animal groups, where they outnumber the corresponding authorial similes by a 3 to 2 ratio.

The eight double similes used by the characters in *War and Peace* form a peculiar group. Except for Nikolai Rostov's cliché about playing cat and mouse, they deal with historical events or God or both. Two similes are patriotic statements by Russian priests concerning the War of 1812. In one of them God is asked to let the enemy be scattered before Russian troops "like dust before wind" (6:89). Count Rastopchin uses a simile to condemn Napoleon's treatment of Europe (5:338), while Napoleon uses one to present his plans for Europe in a positive light (6:294). The subject of the remaining similes is faith and morality. There is a touch of frivolity and blasphemy in Prince Vasilii Kuragin's telling Pierre that his unfaithful wife "is as innocent before you as Christ was before the Jews" (5:95). Conversely, there is gravity and concern in Bazdeev's words when he tries to convert the unbelieving Pierre. The mason says that Pierre is more foolish than a child "who, playing with the parts of an expertly made watch, would dare to say that because he does not understand what that watch is intended for, he does not believe in the master craftsman who made it" (5:80). Here the double simile plays the role of a Gospel parable. Elsewhere the religious Princess Mar'ia quotes Christ: "It is easier for a camel to pass through the eye of a needle than for a rich man to enter into the kingdom of Heaven" (4:127).

The above examples show that Tolstoi restricted his characters' use of double similes to solemn or earnest contexts, and put most of them into the mouths of secondary or episodic personages. Naturally, his principal characters—Pierre, Natasha, Prince Andrei—cannot be expected to be as fond of double similes as Sholokhov's Cossacks. Nonetheless, a total neglect of them on the part of the people who talk on a great variety of subjects may appear somewhat strange. Likewise, Platon Karataev, the embodiment of popular wisdom, could have injected one or two of these similes into his lively vernacular, but he did not.

The scarcity of double similes in the speech of characters in *War and Peace* is especially remarkable since Tolstoi uses them liberally in his own narrative, more often than Sholokhov. The twofold structure of these similes offers a writer a good opportunity to illustrate his philosophical points with greater effectiveness. Double similes and comparisons are Tolstoi's chief rhetorical devices in the exposition of his views on history. Their purpose is to bolster the thesis that historical events are not shaped by the will or designs of so-called great people. As a rule, Tolstoi's double similes are longer than Sholokhov's and their proportion in the man category of *War and Peace* (68 out of 73) is slightly higher than the corresponding figure in *The Quiet Don* (86 out of 97). Both these figures suggest that double similes tend to have man in their tenors more often than their single counterparts, and that it is more difficult and less common to form double similes with tenors other than man. There is, however, a telling difference between Tolstoi and Sholokhov in the distribution of these similes within the first category. In *War and Peace* 28 similes liken man to man, 7 man to animals, and 11 man to nature. The corresponding figures for *The Quiet Don* are 18, 39, and 22.

The percentage of double similes used by the characters in *The Quiet Don* is second only to that in *Envy*, where the personages use 75 percent of these similes (6 out of 8), thanks to the special status of Kavalerov and Ivan Babichev. *Cement* has one double simile in the characters' speech and none in the author's. This peculiar situation attests to Gladkov's penchant for setting up a single connection between tenor and vehicle. He appears to be averse to dividing the reader's attention between two points of resemblance. This may be one of the reasons why an unusually large group of *Cement* similes is expressed in the instrumental case, a form that leaves little room for elaborate or double comparison. It is the author's privilege to choose any form for his similes, but it is questionable whether he should pass his stylistic preferences onto those of his characters who must speak a different language. It looks strange that the proletarians of *Cement* were given only one double simile. As for other works, the characters received 4 out of 13 double similes in *Armored Train No. 14-69*, 5 out of 14 in *Red Cavalry*, 7 out of 42 in *The Carousing Spring*, and 5 out of 26 in *Doctor Zhivago*. The figures for the works of Ivanov and Babel' may not be large enough to draw any meaningful inferences, but it is evident that Pasternak and Veselyi were much less eager to share their double similes with their characters than was Sholokhov.

A vast majority of similes from each work examined here has man as tenor. However, the percentage of similes belonging to this human category and their distribution within it are by no means uniform. *War and Peace* has proportionately by far the heaviest concentration of its similes in the human category, especially in its man-to-man group. These two indexes mirror Tolstoi's intense preoccupation with human nature as well as his concern for verisimilitude, which is apt to weaken if man is compared to items from other categories. Like other Soviet works, *The Quiet Don* departs sharply from *War and Peace* with respect to the percentage of similes in the man-to-man group, but it comes closest to Tolstoi's epic regarding the percentage of similes in the entire human category.

There are, however, some marked distinctions between man-to-man similes in *War and Peace* and *The Quiet Don*. Tolstoi is eager to have in his vehicles the names of professions, occupations, or the general designation "man." Characters in *War and Peace* are likened to courtiers and carpenters, judges and jugglers, mathematicians and millers, surgeons and sorcerers, and many other professions, whose variety suggests the author's broad knowledge of life and his keen power of observation. On the other hand, the only people appearing in the corresponding function in *The Quiet Don* are a churchwarden, a defrocked priest, a bishop, a horse dealer, a hunter, and a prostitute. Tolstoi's favorite vehicle is "child." Some twenty-five times adults believe, blush, learn, look, play, smile, and—above all—cry or sob like children. No doubt Tolstoi's belief in children's purity and innocence played a major role in the emergence of these similes. Authorial child similes in *The Quiet Don* are about two-thirds as numerous as in *War and Peace*. They do not offer the same degree of insight into the child's behavior or its mind as Tolstoi's similes, but some may be remembered for evoking the image of a child amidst the horror of a massacre: "Two men were sabering a tall, manly captain. He was catching at the saber blades, and blood streamed from his slashed palms over his sleeves; he screamed like a child. . . ." (2:252). Elsewhere Sholokhov increases the suggestive power of a child simile by combining the motifs of the destruction and creation of life. Minutes before his execution Petr Melekhov feels that "life stirred forcefully within him like a baby under a woman's heart" (3:207).

In contrast with *War and Peace, The Quiet Don* has a large number of similes likening bodily, mental, and emotional reactions caused by non-physical factors to those resulting from a direct physical impact. Thus, hearing an order to halt, "Grigorii started at the shout as if he had been struck (*kak ot udara*)" (4:457). The nouns *udar* (blow) and *tolchok* (push) regularly occur in the vehicles of physical similes, as do past passive participles derived from the verb *bit'* (beat) and its prefixed forms. This kind of participle (often substantivized) is typical of everyday similes used in *The Quiet Don* by both the author and the characters. Here belong such expressions as "kak v vodu opushchennyi" (dejected; literally, as if immersed into water) and "stoiat' kak vkopannyi" (stand still, as if rooted to the ground; literally, as if dug in).

Vehicles in the form of past passive participles are virtually absent from *War and Peace*. At the same time Tolstoi avoids repeating identical or nearly identical similes, with the possible exception of those likening the crying of adults to the crying of children. Sholokhov is not so fastidious. Three times his characters squint one of their eyes as if taking aim (1:44, 232; 3:147) or wince as if they were in pain (1:257; 4:137, 407). Several times they act or feel as if they were drunk, in a dream, doing military exercises, or obeying a word of command. Such similes can be called self-comparing because they liken their agents to themselves. In *The Quiet Don* most of them are short. Their vehicles consist of one word, not counting prepositions. There are around a hundred self-comparing similes in *War and Peace*. Some have the same or similar vehicles as their counterparts in *The Quiet Don*, and some are as brief. Usually, Sholokhov's man-to-man similes are shorter and less elaborate than Tolstoi's. None of them even remotely resembles the eighty-odd-word comparison of Napoleon with a surgeon, illustrating the general's self-confidence (6:254). At the same time one can find in *The Quiet Don* a dozen similes bearing the stamp of Tolstoian style. One example describes Grigorii's interest in his surroundings after his recovery from typhus: "Occasionally, he would examine some household object which he had known since childhood: he would tensely move his eyebrows and look at it as though he were someone who had recently arrived from a strange, distant land and was seeing it all for the first time" (4:223). Whether Sholokhov followed Tolstoi here consciously or subconsciously is an unanswerable question.

Babel', Olesha, and Pasternak display a much stronger inclination to use as their vehicles the names of professions, occupations, famous people, and literary and biblical figures than does Sholokhov. This is particularly true of Babel'. A large proportion of his vehicles comes from the sphere of religion and includes words like "prophet," "priest," "nun," "apostle," and "Talmudist." Conversely, he seldom employs self-comparing similes. To a greater extent than Sholokhov, he is willing to stretch the point of resemblance between tenor and vehicle. To intensify an aesthetic effect in the portrayal of a colorful division commander, he does not mind suggesting that "his long legs resembled girls sheathed to their necks in shining riding boots" (40). To spice up religion with sex, he would say that a long "war" between the Catholic church and a painter, who was accused of decorating a church with sacrilegious frescoes, was "merciless like the passion of a Jesuit" (25). "Passion" and "passionate," as well as "fury" and "furious"—words with strong erotic and emotional overtones—repeatedly occur in *Red Cavalry* both in their literal and figurative senses, and, at times, in conjunction with religious concepts. Olesha's man-to-man similes are less flamboyant than Babel''s, but occasionally he goes farther than Sholokhov in likening things that are quite remote from each other. A fat, flabby woman, all tangled up in the intestines of animals, moves around her kitchen "tearing the guts apart with her elbows like a princess tearing up cobwebs" (35). A certain artificiality of the simile may be justified by authorial irony. Nevertheless, similes of this kind have a bookish flavor. They are virtually absent from *The Quiet Don*, where figures of speech are derived from the sphere of the author's personal observations. Babel' and Olesha show greater care in eschewing common, everyday similes than does Sholokhov. Pasternak occupies a middle position in this respect. His tropes are taken from all levels of life. Sophisticated philosophical similes coexist in *Doctor Zhivago* side by side with their most popular counterparts. At least twice one encounters such cliché vehicles as "kak rukoi snialo" (it has vanished as if by magic), "kak skvoz' zemliu provalilsia" (as if the earth swallowed him), and "as if he were beaten"; while "as if rooted to the ground" is repeated four times. Here a similarity with Sholokhov is obvious. On the other hand, Pasternak the poet is capable of creating similes that are probably the most imaginative and subtle of all the similes examined for this study. A remarkable thing about them is that they are fashioned from prosaic elements of daily life. One example will suffice. Before her attempt on Komarovskii's life, Lara is in a state of extreme excitement, barely standing on her feet: "Ona voshla, shagami rastalkivaia svoe plat'e, slovno perekhodia ego vbrod" (79)—"She entered pushing her dress aside at each step as if she were fording it." The English translator, apparently taken aback by Pasternak's imagination, substituted "a river" for "it." Next to Tolstoi, Pasternak has the largest number of similes with developed vehicles, and more often than any writer examined here he uses two vehicles separated by "or," as well as periods containing more than one simile.

Armored Train No. 14-69 and *The Carousing Spring* have a substantially smaller percentage of similes in the man-to-man group than *The Quiet Don*. The difference is not so great with respect to *Cement*, but one must keep in mind the repetitiveness of its imagery. In one-fourth of its man-to-man similes people look, behave, feel, and are treated as if they were persons of the opposite sex or were asleep, blind, ill, dead, or strangers to each other. Sholokhov's similes probe deeper into the human psyche than do those of Ivanov, Veselyi, and Gladkov; but all four writers are alike in keeping away from bookish imagery. All four, for example, avoid the names of historical or literary figures in their vehicles. A few exceptions can be found in *The Carousing Spring*. On the whole, however, its man-to-man similes have the same popular streak as Sholokhov's. Ivanov is at least as fond of self-comparing similes as Sholokhov, especially of those containing verbal predicates: "The old man was shaking his head as if he were going to break a hole in a dark wall" (104).

The importance of the man-to-animal similes in *The Quiet Don* is attested to by their number. It approaches four hundred, four times as high as the corresponding figure in *War and Peace*. The man-to-animal group is clearly the second largest in *The Quiet Don*, a status that it enjoys only in *The Carousing Spring*. In *War and Peace* it is a weak third, behind the man-to-man and man-to-object groups. This finding is at variance with the critic Andrei Saburov's assertion that "most often Tolstoi compares man with animals,"[28] which is not supported by any statistical evidence. Only *Cement* has a slightly higher percentage of man-to-animal similes than *The*

Quiet Don, both novels strongly differing from *Envy* and *Doctor Zhivago* whose man-to-animal groups encompass 6 or less percent of all their similes. The case of *Cement* illustrates the point that a frequent use of animal imagery is not necessarily contingent on a portrayal of the countryside. In every work the man-to-animal group has a higher percentage of the characters' similes than any other group, except a small man-to-devil group in *The Quiet Don*. The characters contribute about 18 percent of the man-to-animal similes in *War and Peace*, 41 percent in *The Quiet Don*, 40 percent in *Red Cavalry*, 37 percent in *Cement*, 28 percent in *The Carousing Spring*, 25 percent in *Armored Train No. 14-69*, and 56 percent in *Doctor Zhivago*. The last figure reflects Pasternak's restraint in likening man to animals in his own narrative.

As can be expected from the author of a Cossack epic, Sholokhov's favorite image in the man-to-animal group is that of a horse. There are many things people do like horses: walk, run, breathe, snort, chew, drink, wear themselves out, raise their heads, stamp their feet, distend their nostrils, twitch their ears, and so on. Occasionally, the horse is called upon to illustrate spiritual phenomena. A person persistently turning to the same thought is perceived as resembling a horse doing work characterized by continuous monotonous movement. Because her thoughts constantly revolve around Grigorii, Aksin'ia is compared to a blind horse that moves in circles, rotating a water wheel (3:310); and Grigorii mulling over his political predicament is "like a horse dragging a roller around a threshing floor" day in and day out (3:349).

The second place in the man-to-animal group of *The Quiet Don* belongs to the dog. There are at least 35 canine vehicles, 75 percent of them having been contributed by the characters. This is precisely the opposite of the situation with the horse similes, where the characters' share is a mere 25 percent. The disparity is due to the way the two animals are treated in life and to the popular manner of talking. Warriors and tillers of the soil value a dog far below a horse and show little concern for it. Comparisons with a dog are therefore predominantly negative, mirroring its plight and mistreatment. Popular dialogues are usually uninhibited and sprinkled with deprecatory or menacing remarks, particularly in the time of war and deprivation. Thus one character would threaten to beat the other up like a dog, or the dog would appear in similes referring to defecation, promiscuity, and barking, synonymous with lying. A character could also liken himself or someone else to a dog that is homeless, vicious, freezing, or hungry. An image of a hungry horse would be, of course, out of the question. A Cossack would rather go hungry himself than leave his horse unfed. His man-to-horse similes are chiefly neutral, favorable, or humorous. The dog, however, is treated evenhandedly by the author. He would simply observe that someone smells the air, eats snow, and shakes himself like a dog, or that one's look resembles that of a dog in its expression of devotion or sadness.

As in *The Quiet Don*, a large portion of the man-to-dog similes occurring in *War and Peace, Cement*, and *The Carousing Spring* belong to the characters and are used disparagingly. In each of these works, however, the proportion of the characters' similes in the man-to-dog sub-group is substantially lower than in *The Quiet Don*, ranging from 4 out of 12 in *The Carousing Spring* to 9 out of 15 in *Cement*. The high figures for *Cement* may look less impressive because its characters are prone to reiterate the same images—notably that of son of a bitch—and because the author tends to narrow his own figurative use of the dog's attributes to its vocal sounds. With dogs, fowl, and oxen appearing in one-third of *Cement*'s man-to-animal similes, it is hard to explain why there is only one man-to-horse simile in that novel. By contrast, *War and Peace* and *The Carousing Spring* liken humans to horses as frequently as to dogs and more frequently than to any other animal. Tolstoi's animal similes—seven of them comparing man to a horse—bespeak his prudence and perceptiveness. It is primarily his psychological insight into living creatures that enables him to form the kind of animal similes that is not found in *The Quiet Don* or the other works. Sholokhov may know horses as well as does Tolstoi. Nonetheless, he is not likely to relate man to a horse with the same degree of particularity as does Tolstoi in describing the jovial Murat. Upon joining Napoleon's army, Murat "had cheerfully resumed his familiar occupation, and—like a well-fed but not overfat horse that is still fit for the job—he felt himself in harness and began to prance in the shafts; having dressed himself up as brightly and expensively as possible, cheerful and contented, he galloped along the roads of Poland, without himself knowing where or why" (6:24).

Twenty-eight times Sholokhov and his characters liken man to the wolf. Over one-half of these similes are associated with Grigorii, developing the motif of the beastlike quality (*zverovatoe*) inherent in the Melekhov breed. The streak of fierceness is revealed in Grigorii's baring, clacking, or gnashing his teeth in a wolflike manner. His individualism and love for Aksin'ia lead to a break with his family, putting him in a situation which he describes as being "without corner, without home, just like a wolf of the ravines" (1:377). This simile establishes a direct spiritual kinship with his grandfather, who, after his marriage to a Turkish woman, "lived like a wolf" in seclusion at the very edge of the village (1:12). Observing changes caused in him by the Civil War, Grigorii's closest relatives say that his heart and complexion resemble those of a wolf (3:313; 4:63). During the war his spirit tosses like a hunted wolf in search of a way out of the political contradictions besetting him (3:188). A wolf cut off from land by high waters serves as the vehicle in Grigorii's simile referring to his situation on an island in the middle of the Don, where he and other survivors of the rout of Fomin's detachment find a temporary refuge (4:421). The author also sees some similarities between the survivors and wolves. After the rout the survivors walk towards the Don "in a wolflike fashion—in single file, stepping in each other's tracks" (4:412). Later, as they gallop away from militiamen, returning fire whenever the chasers come close, the survivors are said to be "fleeing like wolves pursued by borzois, occasionally snapping back and hardly stopping at all" (4:431).

The recurrent comparisons of the survivors with wolves raise the question of whether the author uses these animals as a means of political condemnation of Fomin's anti-Bolshevik struggle.[29] Although the wolf is a stock image of malice and predation in popular tropes, Sholokhov uses it as he does any other animal (except the jackal in the simile concerning the dishonorable officers from the intelligentsia), not for passing political judgments, but for illustrating phenomena of life. The two authorial similes comparing the Fomin men to wolves are meant to elucidate specific physical actions rather than discredit the characters politically. The sole negative comparison of the Fomin men with wolves comes from none other than their leader (4:405).

The depiction of Fomin's struggle against the Bolsheviks offers the only example of Sholokhov's consistent employment of animal similes to illustrate an enduring event throughout its development. Up to this point animal imagery served to add vividness to portrayals of individuals and, occasionally, to historical episodes. No integrated use of animal tropes can be found in the description of love stories, war, or the Upper Don uprising. The situation is different in *War and Peace* with regard to war. There the central historical event—Napoleon's invasion of Russia—is illustrated by fifteen man-to-animal similes focusing on crucial developments in the 1812 campaign. In a figurative sense the war is perceived as an encounter between a beast and a hunter. The dominant vehicles in the similes referring to the French army are the generic "beast" and "animal." The word "hunter" surfaces only in one of the similes (7:107), but it is implied in several. In a broad sense the hunter is the Russian army. As for historical figures, he personifies Kutuzov. "Like an experienced hunter," Kutuzov "knew that the beast was wounded" (7.129). Other animals to which the invading army is likened are an ape and a herd of cattle (self-destructive actions) and a mad dog (being killed).

About eighty different kinds of animals, including birds, insects, and fish, appear in the vehicles of man-to-animal similes in *The Quiet Don*, three times as many as in *War and Peace*. This figure does not include generic names, and various animals belonging to the same kind—horse, gelding, foal, mare, stallion—are counted as one. Nearly every animal comes from the immediate surroundings. There are no apes, lions, elephants, or boa constrictors—animals that appear in other works. Like similes with horses, dogs, and wolves in their vehicles, other animal similes bring up the points of resemblance that are either familiar to local people or that can be easily imagined by them. Some of the similes—like one comparing a prolific woman to a doe rabbit (1:229-230)—are quite simple and are also used by the characters (3:287). Others are more imaginative and complex: "Bunchuk smiled a bright, simple, childlike smile. It was strange to see it on his big gloomy face. It was as though a light-gray suckling hare, kicking and frolicking, dashed across an autumnal field that looked dreary from rainfalls" (2:13). This simile may appear somewhat farfetched. Nonetheless, it is realistic in the sense that Sholokhov purports to convey a more vivid impression of the tenor as it is, rather than to endow it with some bizarre qualities, a procedure often followed by Babel' in his animal and human similes alike. There is, for example, in Babel' a discernible desire to surprise the reader by attributing to a monk contrasting feline idiosyncrasies: "I see . . . your soul, gentle and pitiless as the soul of a cat" (9). Five more similes are intended to degrade religious figures and relics by imparting to them trivial or unpleasant animal characteristics. Thus in a church "the statues of Holy Mary studded with precious stones followed us on our way with their pupils as pink as those of mice" (10). Turning to flesh, Babel' looks for the same oxymoronic polarity: "Sashka's body blooming and stinking like the meat of a cow that has just been slaughtered. . . ." (113). The body of the promiscuous nurse may bear only a remote resemblance to the cow meat, and the likelihood of the meat's blooming and stinking at the same time is as low as that of all mice having pink eyes. Somewhat surprisingly, the author of *Red Cavalry* has not a single simile likening a man to a horse. Of course, he was not obliged to create such similes, and he has horses in tenors and vehicles of other similes. Still the absence of man-to-horse similes in *Red Cavalry* is symptomatic of a difference in the artistic visions of Babel' and Sholokhov. To a considerable extent it mirrors the differences in their environmental backgrounds.

Influences of milieu are likewise manifest in the vehicles of man-to-fowl similes in *The Quiet Don* and *Cement*. Sholokhov and his characters prefer roosters to hens and chickens in ten out of fifteen cases. Apart from purely physical actions, such as hopping, jumping, and running, people are said to resemble roosters in their nature—their pride, cockiness, courtship, and pugnacity. Sholokhov's Cossacks are more apt to feel a kinship with these qualities than do Gladkov's factory workers. In *Cement* merely two out of sixteen fowl similes compare man to a rooster.

A distinguishing feature of Sholokhov's avian similes is their important role in descriptions of singing. A connoisseur of Cossack singing, Sholokhov depicts it in picturesque detail. The voice of the second tenor shoots up like a bird (3:289; 4:260) or quivers "like a skylark soaring above the thawed April earth" (1:271). Among the similes pertaining to appearance or color one may single out those comparing black figures of the dead lying in the snow-covered steppe with a flock of rooks settled on a field (2:248; 3:93).

Many insect and fish similes are among the plainest in the animal group. Almost one-half of them occur in the characters' speech. Insects are regularly used in quantitative and auditory similes of the commonest type. Large numbers of people are compared to swarms of locusts or to midges, and human voices are related to the buzzing of bees or mosquitoes. On the other hand, bees can be found in a somewhat bookish and affected simile, uncharacteristic of Sholokhov: "For the last few days he had been under the sway of poetry, and his thoughts, like bees, were bringing someone else's melodious pain into the honeycombs of his memory" (3:50). This simile, referring to Evgenii Listnitskii, is no longer in the novel. As we conclude the discussion of animal similes, it would perhaps be relevant to cite a more typical example from the small piscine subgroup: "The carriage bounced feverishly on the bumpy road . . . the body swayed and the tightly sitting in-laws rubbed against each other like fish during spawning" (3:11).

The man-to-nature group includes the most imaginative, meaningful, and elaborate similes in *The Quiet Don*. At the base of these characteristics lies the authorial concept of the unity of man and nature which found its clearest expression in the recurrent juxtapositions of human and natural phenomena on existential, historical, and personal levels. Similes defining these connections with utmost forcefulness and vividness are those whose imagery is derived from inanimate nature and the vegetable kingdom. We have already seen a consistent employment of such similes throughout the love story of Grigorii and Aksin'ia. The heroine's feelings were likened to blossoming henbane, a field of corn flattened by a herd of cattle, and a plunging block of snow. Her hopes were associated with a bright spring landscape, while Grigorii's life after her death resembled a black steppe scorched with fire. Except for the first, these similes appear in the form of elaborate parallelisms. A special significance may possibly be attached to a short simile describing the emergence of Aksin'ia's love for Grigorii: "She was frightened by that new feeling which was pervading all of her, and in her thoughts she felt her way gropingly, cautiously, as though crossing the Don on the porous March ice'' (1:43). On the last page of the novel, as he goes home to surrender himself to the Bolsheviks, Grigorii crosses the Don ''on the blue, half-thawed, and pitted March ice.'' Whether by accident or not, this March ice points to a cause-and-effect relation between the birth of Aksin'ia's love and Grigorii's imminent death. He has no will to live because their love can no longer be fulfilled. Concomitantly, the March ice may suggest the frailty of human hopes, the reawakening of nature to start its eternal cycle, the brevity of man's life, the tragic character of a true love, and anything that some two thousand pages separating the two references to March ice may evoke in the individual reader. The causes and the progress of the Upper Don uprising are brought into sharp relief by a succession of natural similes involving the snow-covered steppe, the winter rye, the whirlpools and floods of the Don, and the steppe fires. These images, at times very elaborate and strikingly graphic, are as central to the portrayal of the Cossacks' revolt as are their animal counterparts in Tolstoi's description of the French invasion of Russia.

Man-to-nature similes constitute an organic component in the story of Grigorii's political vacillations. ''I'm roaming about like a snowstorm in the steppe,'' says he about his difficulties of grasping the political situation in the fall of 1917 (2:189). Toward the end of the novel Grigorii sums up his participation in the Civil War as follows: ''Since 1917 I have been walking on a winding path, reeling like a drunken man. . . . I strayed away from the Whites, but I didn't join up with the Reds, and floated like dung in an ice hole'' (4:355). This simile, in which nature is only a part of the picture, has already been applied to Grigorii by Ivan Kotliarov (3:154), who has also likened Grigorii to a weathercock that turns with the wind (3:153). Thus the story of Grigorii's vacillations exhibits not only a consistent use of natural similes in the movement of the plot, but also their interaction with similes from other groups.

Natural similes are one of Sholokhov's favorite tools for characterizing his personages. Dar'ia, for example, is thrice compared to a willow switch, the principal common points being ''supple, beautiful, and available'' (4:63).

The man-to-nature group is not free from stereotypes. Swiftly moving people are at times compared to a whirlwind, while blood, sweat, and tears flow in streams (*ruch'iami*). By and large, however, natural similes evince more originality and effort on the author's part than any other group. Significantly, the characters' share of the man-to-nature similes (about 15 percent) is substantially lower than their shares in other groups of the human category—an indication that natural similes are relatively difficult to form.

No work examined here likens people to nature by means of such extensive parallelisms and with such vivid natural detail (melting of snow, growth of winter rye) as does *The Quiet Don*. Sholokhov's intimate knowledge of nature must be one of the reasons why the number of plant similes in *The Quiet Don* is proportionately much higher than in *War and Peace, The Carousing Spring*, and *Doctor Zhivago*—works with sufficient numbers of natural similes to allow meaningful comparison. While 111 plant similes comprise 40 percent of the man-to-nature group in *The Quiet Don*, they number only 9 in *War and Peace*, 11 in *The Carousing Spring* and *Cement*, and 17 in *Doctor Zhivago*. Of course, Tolstoi and, to a lesser degree, Pasternak were more cautious than Sholokhov in drawing similarities between people and vegetation. Nonetheless, the difference is striking, especially since both writers are great admirers of nature. Some of Pasternak's plant similes, as we shall see, are of paramount significance. Veselyi's neglect of vegetable imagery is at least in part due to his emphasis on the elemental forces of the Revolution and war, which resulted in his use of images representing movement and violence. The situation is quite different in *The Armored Train No. 14-69*. Although this novel deals with war, three-fifths of its natural similes focus, not on actions, but on colors, qualities, and appearance. Herein lies a partial explanation of why Ivanov compares man to plants just a shade more often than to inanimate nature with its storms and hail. Generally speaking, Ivanov's and, especially, Veselyi's and Gladkov's natural similes tend to be more decorative and hyperbolic and less precise than Sholokhov's. "And their bodies were like granite in the mountains, like trees, like grasses," says Ivanov of his Red guerillas (80). "Impetuous days roared like furious rocks rushing down the mountains," writes Veselyi about the time of mass desertions from the front in 1917 (369). And in *Cement* the eyes of a perturbed woman "quivered like drops in the wind" (5:83). It would be wrong to assume that similar figures do not occur in *The Quiet Don*. Sholokhov did not escape from ornamental excesses characteristic of the literature of the time. Next to his plain, down-to-earth imagery, one encounters in *The Quiet Don* tropes that are affected and strained, as can be seen from the following double simile: "The time plaited the days like the wind plaits a horse's mane" (2:70).

In regard to the philosophical significance of its natural similes, *The Quiet Don* can be compared only to *Doctor Zhivago*. Both Sholokhov and Pasternak use them as indispensable instruments for conveying their world outlooks. But there is an important difference in the function of natural and other similes in their novels. Sholokhov relates man to surrounding nature, focusing on their biological affinities. On a philosophical level his natural similes are more significant than those referring to other spheres of existence. Pasternak relates man to the universe and he does it in religious terms. For him the universe is of divine origin. His similes, in conjunction with other tropes, express an organic interrelation between the basic components of the universe viewed in a Christian light. His natural and other similes act as equal partners, forming a single body of integrated diversities. The integration takes place on a symbolic level, which is also characteristic of the associative quality of Pasternak's poetry.

One way to begin a brief survey of the interrelation of various similes in *Doctor Zhivago* is to cite the following description of Lara: "Her spiritual charm made her incomparable. Her hands were as stunning as a sublime way of thinking" (46). Lara appears here as a manifest miracle of creation, a supreme union of physical and spiritual beauty. Moreover, she herself represents nature and its creativity. When she nurses the gravely ill Zhivago, he associates her with nature, thinking how good it was for him "to become a thing, a project, a product in her merciful, wonderful, beauty-lavishing hands!" (405.) Lara's hands thus become a symbol of the unity of creative, aesthetic, and ethical qualities revealed on a religious plane by the acts of mercy, self-denial, and generosity. The same qualities are attributed to a beautiful rowan tree feeding birds with its berries: "A living intimacy developed between the birds and the tree. As if the rowan tree . . . taking pity on the little birds, gave in, unbuttoned herself, and gave them her breast like a wet nurse to a baby" (363). The connection with Lara is underscored when Zhivago comes upon the rowan tree in the winter. At the sight of the tree holding out to him two of its branches covered with snow and frozen berries, he immediately remembers the large, white, and generous hands of Lara. Overwhelmed with emotion, he calls her "my little rowan tree, my flesh and blood" (385). Later, standing over Strel'nikov's body, he notices "small drops of blood that spurted aside and mixed with snow, forming red beads that resembled frozen rowan-tree berries" (476). Like Lara's hands, the rowan tree and its berries become symbols uniting the worlds of man and nature. In the case of Strel'nikov the berries may suggest his generosity, his close relationship with Lara and Zhivago, and, perhaps, an atonement for his political fanaticism and ruthlessness during his service with the Bolsheviks, although his suicide represents a grievous sin from a Christian viewpoint.

The theme of the religious unity of man and nature is overtly expressed in the simile stating that "the moonlit night was stunning like mercy or the gift of clairvoyance" (144). "Stunning" and "merciful" are precisely the words that characterize Lara. The night, then, equals her on the highest level of physical and spiritual beauty, and both are endowed with properties that are simultaneously human and divine. It could have been this heightened sense of equality between the human and the natural that induced

Pasternak, in all likelihood unconsciously, to compare nature to man almost as often as man to nature. A staggering 9 percent of all similes in *Doctor Zhivago* are personifications of nature, three for every two in *The Quiet Don*. A majority of Pasternak's personifications are, of course, not as lofty as the one with the moonlit night. In most cases natural objects are endowed with the abilities of ordinary people. But for Pasternak the ordinary is also divine and stunning. This is why an enormous blackish-crimson moon "first resembled a brick steam mill in Zybushino and then it turned yellow like the railway water tower at Biriuchi" (142). The simile does not aim at deromanticization or a deliberate "estrangement" (*ostranenie*) of the moon. It expresses the idea of a universal unity and equality. The prosaic structures in provincial towns are in the same class with the Queen of the Night. So are the stars and a lonely cow. The stars twinkled, and "threads of invisible sympathy stretched from them to the cow as if there were cattle yards in the other worlds where she was pitied" (143).

The last two similes occur in the passage where Pasternak voices his admiration for life with utmost enthusiasm. Characteristically, his enthusiasm embraces the entire universe, from household articles to planets. If in *The Quiet Don* man is associated primarily with surrounding nature, in *Doctor Zhivago* he is treated on a cosmic scale. Even in their most intimate moments Lara and Zhivago feel themselves to be a part of the universe (513). The unifying network of imagery is Christian, with charity, generosity, and self-sacrifice attributed to objects from various spheres of existence. The crowning image is to be found in the second part of the poem "Magdalene": "To embrace too many, Thou shalt stretch / Thy arms along the cross" (563). An association with Lara's hands and the rowan-tree branches is inescapable. It must be noted that the Christianity in *Doctor Zhivago* bears an imprint of Pasternak's personality and genius. It is less ascetic and more creativity-oriented than in its traditional interpretations.

The man-to-object group in *The Quiet Don* is proportionately about the same size as in *War and Peace* and *Red Cavalry*, larger than in *Doctor Zhivago*, and smaller than in four other works, notably in *The Carousing Spring* and *Armored Train No. 14-69*. With regard to their functions, the most conservative similes are found—not surprisingly—in *War and Peace*, where their role is mainly illustrative or argumentative, not decorative. Tolstoi's favorite image is that of a clock. It is used to elucidate the cause-and-effect relation in history (6:303); and it occurs several times in extended similes comparing the operation of the military machine with the work of a clock mechanism (4:348-349; 7:84, 103). On a personal plane Natasha aptly characterizes the stiff Boris Drubetskoi, saying that "he is so narrow, like a dining-room clock" (5:216). As in the case with natural similes,

Gladkov, Veselyi, and Ivanov are more willing to stretch figurative connections between man and objects than is Sholokhov. It must have been the quest for local color that inspired Gladkov to write that the eyes of a worker "were now cold and unblinking, silvery and gilded, like the Diesels" (6:57). In *The Carousing Spring* a one-eyed ex-policeman "dug into the peasants with his eye, lackluster as a rusty nail" (181). In *Armored Train No. 14-69* the eyes of a White ensign "looked lackluster and frayed, resembling rents in a dress" (100). It is somewhat easier to imagine the lackluster look of Grigorii's eyes at the moment of apprehension, when they "gleamed dully like splinters of anthracite" (2:55). Babel''s object similes display his customary audacity and whim. A bell ringer, lying on the floor of his desecrated church, lifted his head, and "his blue nose rose above him like a flag above a corpse" (114-115). *Envy* offers proportionately the largest collection of object similes, i.e., similes having objects either in the vehicle or the tenor. The latter variety comprises about 36 percent of all the similes in *Envy*, three times as high as the corresponding figure in *The Quiet Don*. Olesha not only exhibits an exceptional interest in the things around him; he communicates his impressions of them in delightfully fresh tropes, virtually without clichés or repetitions. In contrast to Babel''s, his similes are perceived as discoveries, rather than as inventions: "On his chest . . . was a scar. It was round and slightly raised like the imprint of a coin on wax" (26), or "I can't talk about it without my heart jumping like an egg in boiling water" (94). Both similes can serve as illustrations of Olesha's idea that the purpose of a trope lies in its suggesting similarities which the reader could have found himself.[30]

Some characteristics of Sholokhov's imagery can be brought to light by examining his use of objects in various similes outside of the man-to-object group. One would find, for example, that in his vehicles Sholokhov regularly employs images associated with fire, and that occasionally he compares fire to something else. His propensity for fire similes puts him in the same company as Veselyi and Gladkov and sets him poles apart from other writers. More often than anyone, Sholokhov likens plants with red leaves or fruits to fire. Thus in the fall "the bushes of sweetbriar stood as if enveloped in flames, and among their scanty leaves the red berries glowed like little tongues of fire" (4:218). Like Veselyi and Gladkov, he is among the few who see a similarity between fire and animals. In volume 3 Mishka Koshevoi burns down the houses of well-to-do Cossacks, and "against the slaty-black sky the ruddy flames fluffed up like a sparkling fox tail" (3:407). The rapid spreading of fire is suggested by the verb "fluffed up." The overall impression is that of terror and beauty.

A similar event is described in Babel''s story "Prishchepa," named after its protagonist, a Red Cossack who takes vengeance on his fellow-villagers for the murder of his parents. He winds up his destructive actions by setting fire to his own home. The simile with which Babel' describes the fire is indicative of the conceptual and stylistic differences between him and Sholokhov. It reads, "The fire shone like Sunday" (80). The vehicle is obviously less concrete and more suggestive than Sholokhov's "fox tail." At the same time both similes fit perfectly into their respective contexts. In *The Quiet Don* the down-to-earth image of a fox tail is a part of a dispassionate, strictly realistic narrative. The purpose of the image is to give a vivid and immediate sense of the beauty and destructiveness of fire. The fox tail is thus subordinated to fire. The significance of fire is greatly enhanced by its being the last episode in the volume wholly devoted to the Civil War. It becomes a symbol of war and destruction. In "Prishchepa" the emphasis is not on fire, but on Sunday, the Russian word for which is *voskresen'e*, literally meaning "resurrection." The Sunday, then, evokes, above all, light and joy associated with religious holidays, especially the Easter church service conducted by the light of candles held by the congregation. Thus the vehicle of Babel''s simile implies a sharp contrast not only with the fire it describes, but also with other acts of the protagonist—killing old women, hanging dogs, and defiling icons with excrement. The Sunday becomes the key image in the story, purported to produce a paradoxical effect by blending antipodal associations. To intensify the paradox, Babel' now and then speaks of the lowly Prishchepa in an elevated language. While Sholokhov's attitude toward Koshevoi is neutral, Babel''s treatment of Prishchepa is ironic. The same applies to many characters in his other stories.

Gladkov's similes involving fire and animals are rather pedestrian, on the order of "A flame flew up like a red bird" (4:81). Veselyi's similes are more imaginative, though somewhat strained and ornate. For example, "a camp fire stood like a big udder" (303). In *The Quiet Don* the identical tenor appears in a meaningful comparison connected with Il'inichna. Longing for Grigorii, she "looked out into the steppe where the mowers' campfire twinkled like a distant inaccessible little star" (4:308). In its sad, lyrical context the inaccessibility of the star suggests the futility of Il'inichna's hope to see her son again.

Sholokhov's object similes faithfully mirror one of the main traits of his talent—his extraordinary receptivity to sounds. This quality is evident in similes pertaining to a wide variety of sounds produced by shooting. Examination of such shot similes facilitates a comparison between Sholokhov and other writers, because all the works, with the exception of *Envy*, contain scenes of fighting. There are about thirty-five shot similes in *The Quiet Don*, most of them having the word "shot" or its equivalents as their tenors. There are merely five shot similes in *War and Peace*. Among the Soviet works the subtlest and largest set of shot similes (five) is to be found in *Doctor Zhivago*. Shot similes in *Red Cavalry* are limited to one indecorous platitude put into a character's mouth (151). In general, sound similes are virtually absent from Babel''s stories, a sign of his strong preference for visual imagery. Gladkov, on the contrary, is fond of auditory figures, but has only one simile involving shooting. Veselyi and Ivanov each have two shot similes. In comparison with other writers, Sholokhov displays a great diversity of imagery in his shot similes, although they are not as ingenious as Pasternak's.

Among shot similes appearing in *The Quiet Don*, but missing from the works of other writers, are stock comparisons of cannonades to such natural phenomena as thunder, a landslide, and subterranean rumbling. Nevertheless, some of these similes display a rather fresh and daring imagery, as in the following example: ''The chattering machine-gun fire bubbled up violently like a May cloudburst and trod over the forest floor'' (2:39). In other instances the sounds of shooting are likened to those made by insects, birds, or objects touching each other. One case offers a rare comparison of an auditory tenor with something other than a sound: ''They fired their revolvers and rifles point-blank, and the frosty wind put out the sound of shots like the sparks of a cigarette'' (3:100). The idea of the wind extinguishing the sounds of shots, as well as the sparks, fits eminently well into the context portraying an execution, a destruction of lives and hopes.

Another variety of similes that sets Sholokhov apart from his fellow writers is one where the tenor (man, animal, nature, or object) is perceived as if it were painted or drawn, or in some way made, fashioned, carved, chiseled, or cut out of something. *The Quiet Don* has about twenty such similes, but they are very rare or nonexistent in the works of other writers. There are, for instance, only two in *War and Peace*. A snow-covered barn in moonlight (5:318) and a distant forest on the horizon (6:258) are said to look as if hewn out of some precious stones. *The Quiet Don* may be represented by the following two examples: ''The grey beast [wolf] stood motionless as if carved out of rock'' (1:159) and ''The April days were fine and translucent as if made of glass'' (3:262).

Some significant idiosyncrasies of Sholokhov's similes are to be found in their forms. Below is a table showing the basic forms employed in *The Quiet Don* and other works. Looking at it, one should bear in mind that the number of forms in a given work is usually smaller than the number of its similes because one connective may combine more than one simile (double similes or similes with an uneven number of tenors or vehicles).

The outstanding feature of the similes in *The Quiet Don* is immediately apparent. Next to *Cement*, it has the highest percentage of similes expressed by means of the instrumental case and the lowest percentage of similes

TABLE 2: The Forms of the Similes in *The Quiet Don* and Works by Other Writers

Forms	*Quiet Don*	*War and Peace*	*Arm. Train*	*Cement*	*Red Cav.*	*Envy*	*Carous. Spring*	*Dr. Zhivago*
kak	908	375	118	223	153	137	282	365
instrumental	469	32	2	317	18	24	88	75
kak budto	21	112	2	3	5	8		2
kak by	7	28			3	6	1	25
budto	124	7	8	41		1	33	1
slovno	183	1	13	1		1	7	62
tochno	2	17	17	13	1	23	19	59
podobno, podobnyi	3	28				2	17	8
rovno	4						90	
chisto	24						1	1
adv. with *po*	83	2	4	27	2	4	4	8
adv. in *o*	57			26		1	2	2
comp. degree	25	3	3	6	4	1	16	9
prepositions	16	3		5	5	2	14	3
pokhozh, pokhodit'	30	8	36	12	9	19	20	20
tak	16	2		1	2	2		1
takoi-kakoi, tot-kotoryi	6	15	1					
asyndeton	9	13						
others	57	34	10	3	1	13	5	26
TOTAL	2044	680	214	678	203	244	599	667
Pre-positive vehicles	29%	19%	32%	17%	5%	12%	23%	16%
kak	44%	55%	55%	33%	75%	56%	47%	55%
instrumental	23%	5%	1%	47%	9%	10%	15%	11%

ABBREVIATIONS IN TABLES 1 AND 2

Quiet Don—The Quiet Don
Arm. Train—Armored Train No. 14-69
Red Cav.—Red Cavalry
Carous. Spring—The Carousing Spring
Dr. Zhivago—Doctor Zhivago

formed with the aid of the connective *kak* (like, as). The use of the instrumental in figurative expressions constitutes one of the main stylistic distinctions between pre-Revolutionary Russian prose and the Soviet prose of the twenties. Nowhere does this difference emerge with greater clarity than in a comparison of *War and Peace* with *The Quiet Don*. There are 32 instrumental similes in *War and Peace* and 469 in *The Quiet Don*. Moreover, Tolstoi's similes consist predominantly of common locutions such as ''zasnut' kamnem'' (fall asleep like a stone) or ''vertet'sia volchkom'' (spin like a top), and 22 percent of them are contributed by the characters. Sholokhov, on the other hand, allows his characters to contribute only 4.5 percent of his instrumental similes, much less than the corresponding figure in all other works, where it ranges from 7 percent in *The Carousing Spring* to 33 percent in *Red Cavalry*.

The prevalence of instrumental similes in *The Quiet Don* reflects the general trend toward ornamental prose and stylistic experimentation of the 1920s, when many writers felt an urge to create a new type of literature consonant with the atmosphere of the Revolutionary period. At the same time the adherence to the general trend did not prevent individuals from going their own ways in choosing their means of artistic expression, including the forms of their similes. There are, for example, hardly any instrumental similes in *Armored Train No. 14-69*. Their number is moderate in *Envy, Red Cavalry*, and *Doctor Zhivago*; substantial in *The Carousing Spring*, Konstantin Fedin's *Cities and Years* (1924), and Aleksandr Serafimovich's *The Iron Flood* (1924); high in *The Quiet Don*; and enormous in *Cement*. Not surprisingly, all these works, except for *Armored Train No. 14-69*, have a much higher percentage of instrumental similes than *War and Peace*. One may say, of course, that Tolstoi might have been more restrained in employing such similes than other pre-Revolutionary writers. Lacking pertinent statistical information, I can only note that the prose of Pushkin, Lermontov, Turgenev, Dostoevskii, Goncharov, Chekhov, Andreev, Bunin, Kuprin, or Belyi does not reveal the instrumental case to be a prominent form in their figurative language. Even Gogol' with his strong bent for comparisons has, according to Professor Proffer, only sixteen instrumental similes in both parts of *Dead Souls*.[31] A fairly frequent and, occasionally, daring use of these similes is encountered in Gor'kii's *Childhood*. Still, Gor'kii does not use them as frequently or as boldly as the authors of *The Carousing Spring, The Quiet Don*, and, especially, *Cement*. Aleksei Remizov liberally employs instrumental similes in some of his fairy tales, such as ''The Black Rooster.''[32] This is partly because Remizov writes in an ornamental style resembling that of oral folk literature, in which the instrumental is used to express metamorphosis or similarity. The practice harks back to the earliest period of Russian literature. *The Tale of Igor''s Campaign* is the most remarkable example.[33]

Tracing the history of instrumental similes throughout the entire Russian literature would require a separate study. What concerns us here is the specific use of such similes by Sholokhov within the general framework of his contemporary literature. It must have been the impact of certain works of the early 1920s, rather than that of Cossack folklore, that generated in the young author a fondness for the figurative use of the instrumental. Instrumental similes are much less visible in the local oral literature than in Gladkov's *Ognennyi kon'* (*The Fiery Steed*, 1922) and *Cement*, or Veselyi's early stories. One of the reasons for Sholokhov's enthusiastic adoption of the instrumental case for his similes could have been the brevity and dynamism of his expression. The use of the instrumental obviates the need for a connective and enhances the figurativeness of the language by virtually identifying the tenor and the vehicle.

Although the degree of figurativeness varies with each individual case, it still can be taken as a foundation for dividing instrumental similes into three basic types. First come similes in which the verb governing the instrumental is applied in the literal sense to both the tenor and the vehicle, as in the sentence ''Kraiukhoi zheltogo sotovogo meda lezhalo peschanoe vzgor'e'' (3:11)—''The sandy hillock lay like a large yellow slice of honeycomb.'' In the second type the verb is used literally with one part of the simile and figuratively with the other: ''Tek . . . patokoi svashen'kin zhurchlivyi golosok'' (1:72)—''The purling voice of the matchmaker flowed . . . like molasses.'' Here the degree of figurativeness is moderate. The flowing voice does not make an impression of a strained image. In some instances, however, Sholokhov stretches the connotative capacity of the verbs to the point of absurdity: ''Krupnyi sazan b'et cherez breden' zolochenym shtoporom'' (1:34)—''A large carp leaps over the dragnet like a gilded corkscrew.'' The simile compares the color and movement of the fish to those of a corkscrew when it is used to open a bottle. Yet the verb *b'et* (which here means ''leaps'') cannot be applied to the corkscrew except on the supernatural plane. The resulting incongruity must have caused the deletion of the vehicle in 1933. Even more affected and faulty is the simile ''Chernaia boroda ego plavilas' po zavshivevshei rubakhe zastyvshim chugunnym potokom'' (2:138), the exact translation of which is ''His black beard melted on his lice-ridden shirt like a stream of hardened cast iron.'' The entire simile was expunged in 1953 but restored (minus ''lice-ridden'') in 1956, leaving it up to the reader to imagine how a metal can be liquid and hard at the same time.

The third type encompasses similes in which the verb is applied figuratively to both the tenor and the vehicle: ''Vperedi rassypannoi radugoi tsveli bab'i zaveski'' (1:49)—''The women's aprons blossomed like a scattered rainbow before him.'' Similes of this and the second type can be more easily translated as metaphors than similes of the first type. Indeed, in the example cited above, ''like'' can be replacd by ''in,'' or the vehicle can be rendered as an appositive: ''The women's aprons—a scattered rainbow—blossomed before him.'' It is therefore possible to treat similes of the last two types as metaphors. I prefer to classify them as metaphoric similes. They make up about one-fourth of all the instrumental similes in *The Quiet Don*. It is a group in which connotative potentialities of verbs are stretched to the limit, creating a kind of imagery which was unthinkable in classic Russian literature.

Eighty percent of the instrumental similes in *The Quiet Don* describe, in about equal proportions, either action or appearance. The remaining 20 percent deal with sounds, feelings, emotional states, colors, smells, and other characteristics. In the action category a large group of similes involves movement, employing basic forms and derivatives of verbs like *idti* (go), *katit'sia* (roll), *padat'* (fall), *kruzhit'sia* (whirl), *tech'* (flow), *plyt'* (float), *polzti* (crawl). For the most part these verbs are used metaphorically, as in ''Snezhnym komom katilis' po gorodu slukhi'' (3:97)—''The rumors rolled through the city like a snowball.'' The dominant verbs in the similes illustrating appearance are *lezhat'* (lie) and *viset'* (hang). The former occurs some twenty times and is the most frequently used verb in all the instrumental similes. The two verbs are illustrated in the following examples: ''Zakhromal k liudskoi, obdiraia sosul'ki s borody, lezhavshei na vorotnike tulupa chernym bruskom'' (1:210)—''He limped toward the servants quarters, rubbing the icicles off his beard that lay like a black bar on the collar of his sheepskin coat,'' and ''Na lugu kiseinoi zanaves'iu visela moshka'' (3:20)—''Midges hung over the meadow like a muslin curtain.'' The verb ''hang'' introduces here not only a visual but also a quantitative similarity, suggested by the word ''curtain.'' Some thirty similes refer to color or brilliance. They feature verbs like *belet'* (appear white), *sverkat'* (glitter), *siiat'* (shine), and *iskrit'sia* (sparkle). A remarkable diversity of verbs is encountered in 35 sound similes. Out of 28 verbs employed in them only 3 are repeated: *zhurchat'* (purl), *zvenet'* (ring), and *lopnut'* (burst), which is used six times.

Altogether about 230 different verbs appear in the instrumental similes in *The Quiet Don*. Apart from clichés, most of these similes could be easily formed with the aid of standard connectives. Compared with two other avid users of instrumental similes—Veselyi and Gladkov—the author of *The Quiet Don* is rather conservative. In Veselyi's early stories the metaphoric variety of these similes serves as a major stylistic device for depicting the elemental character of the Revolution. Imagery is hyperbolic and drawn primarily from natural phenomena associated with movement, power, and violence. To convey the impetuousness of events, Veselyi employs brief similes, frequently without a verb. Fourteen similes in the story "Fiery Rivers" have no verbs, a number greater than in *The Quiet Don*. Typical similes of this kind portray the impulsiveness and daredevilry of revolutionary sailors: "Shouts like rain, curses like hail, work like a downpour" (62) or "On to Orenburg like a storm. Across Transcaucasia like thunder. Along the Volga like wolves" (66). The original wordings of the last three similes—"Na Orenburg burei. Po Zakavkaz'iu grozoi. Po Volge volkom"—offer a sample of verbal instrumentation, with inner rhyme and syntactical symmetry. Moreover, each simile forms, in both sets, a separate paragraph, and the margins of the paragraphs are arranged in a definite slanted pattern. There are no such extremes in *The Quiet Don*.

Cement is the only work in which there are more instrumental similes than those formed with the principal connective *kak* (like, as). Compared to *The Quiet Don*, Gladkov's novel has proportionately about the same number of instrumental similes illustrating action and appearance, fewer similes pertaining to color, feelings, and state of mind, and no olfactory similes. On the other hand, nearly fifty of *Cement*'s sound similes are expressed by means of the instrumental case, many more than in *The Quiet Don*. Auditory imagery is an essential part of Gladkov's bombastic style. His penchant for loudness and eccentricity produces similes of the type "Solntse gremit barabanom" (1:91)—"The sun thunders like a drum," which is put into the mouth of a semi-literate character. Gladkov's use of odd figurative connotations must be an important reason why the number of different verbs occurring in instrumental similes is proportionately somewhat larger in *Cement* than in *The Quiet Don*. On the other hand, Gladkov reemploys the tenors and vehicles of these similes with a far greater frequency than does Sholokhov. A metal worker, for example, is likened five times to a block of anthracite and three times to a black or stone idol (1:81-83; 2:75, 80). Like Veselyi, Gladkov is more inclined than is Sholokhov to lend his prose a "dynamic" quality by leaving out verbs from his instrumental similes. The number of such omissions in *Cement* is almost double the number in *The Quiet Don*.

Although instrumental similes in *Red Cavalry, Envy*, and *Doctor Zhivago* are on the whole more numerous and daring than in pre-Revolutionary prose, they do not display any characteristics that would require more than a few remarks. A number of similes formed in these three works with the aid of *kak* and other connectives would normally be put into the instrumental by the author of *The Quiet Don*. This applies in particular to similes with verbs denoting color, shine and glitter, motion, and position. Apparently for the sake of freshness, Babel' and, especially, Olesha take much greater care to avoid clichés than Pasternak, who, like Sholokhov, unabashedly employs popular instrumental similes side by side with his original tropes.

An examination of instrumental similes in various works permits us to make a few generalizations about the sources of their imagery. Compared to other forms of similes, the instrumental group exhibits a sharp decrease in the use of human images in its tenors and vehicles. In *The Quiet Don*, for instance, similes with human tenors comprise close to 75 percent of all its similes and only 52 percent of its instrumental similes. Vehicles show an even more drastic decline. While around 30 percent of all similes in *The Quiet Don* have human images as their vehicles, the corresponding figure for its instrumental similes is a mere 6 percent. The main cause of the discrepancy lies in the very nature of instrumental similes, in their organic brevity that precludes lengthy elaborations. In common use these similes seldom establish more than one simple connection between the tenor and the vehicle. The essential brevity is likewise preserved in instrumental similes containing two or more points of analogy. In such similes the noun-vehicle is normally modified by one or two adjectives, rather than by subordinate clauses. As an example we may cite the simile ''Pod ukhom ego bol'shim chernym shmelem gudel Pantelei Prokof'evich'' (1:87)—''Pantelei Prokof'evich droned on into his ear like a big black bumblebee''—where the two adjectives add the idea of size and color to that of sound. Illustration of more complex things, such as mental and emotional states, would be likely to require longer vehicles, especially if an author—Tolstoi, for instance—tends to make relatively extensive comparisons. It is particularly difficult to form instrumental similes with human vehicles. Man is too versatile to be as readily associated with one principal characteristic as a whirlwind is with speed, a stone with sinking, or a kite with ferocity—to name just a few favorite images of instrumental similes. The difficulty increases tenfold when man is likened to man. Merely 4 similes of this kind are put into the instrumental case in *The Quiet Don*; there are hardly any in the other works except for *Cement*, which has 22. However, 9 of these repeat the same images in their vehicles and some are formed in a highly arbitrary manner. It is, for instance, unnatural to say ''Gleb pobezhal gorbunom'' (3:77) or ''Ona sama prishla nagoi devchonkoi'' (4:61). In a word-for-word translation these phrases read ''Gleb took off like a hunchback'' (the author meant Gleb was running bent low) and ''She came to him of her own will like a naked girl.'' Typical man-to-man similes expressed by means of the instrumental case can be exemplified by the following phrases from *The Quiet Don*: ''Zhivet barynei'' (3:68) and ''Khoziainom poshel v ambar'' (3:88), meaning, respectively, ''She's living like a lady'' and ''He went into the barn as if he were its master.'' The scarcity of human imagery in instrumental similes sharply contrasts with the abundance of images derived from the worlds of nature and objects. In every work examined here the percentage of objects in tenors of its instrumental similes is much higher than the percentage of objects in tenors of all its similes, and the same is true of natural images in vehicles.

The second distinctive form of *The Quiet Don* similes consists of an adverb with the prefix *po*. This form has no exact equivalent in English and can normally be rendered with "like" and a noun. Thus the simile "Shel, po-bych'i ugnuv golovu" (1:53) can be translated as "He walked lowering his head like an ox." The number of adverbial similes with *po* found in *The Quiet Don* (over 80) appears impressive in comparison with their scantiness in all other works except *Cement*. Commonly used in spoken language, the *po* similes are simple, short, and as unlikely to suggest complex relations as are instrumental similes. The great majority of their tenors comes from the human category, while animal imagery prevails in their vehicles. Their largest groups are man-to-man and man-to-animal, numbering, respectively, about 30 and 40 in *The Quiet Don* and 10 and 15 in *Cement*. Many analogues in the man-to-man group involve sex and age, that is, situations in which man acts like a woman (*po-bab'i*) and an adult like a child (*po-detski*). The notable paucity of imagery drawn from nature and objects is mainly due to the limited possibility of deriving adverbs with *po* from words denoting objects and natural phenomena. Besides, the *po* similes frequently involve physical action, which is hard to illustrate with the aid of inanimate objects.

The third noteworthy variety of *The Quiet Don* similes is formed with adverbs of manner ending in *o*, as in "Ruch'isto zhurchal golos svakhi Vasilisy" (3:211)—"The matchmaker Vasilisa's voice purled like a brook." The figurative use of these adverbs creates a certain stylistic complication because it substantivizes the adverb in the sense that its meaning becomes equivalent to that of a noun preceded by the connective "like." The resulting awkwardness is the probable reason why many writers are reluctant to form similes with adverbs ending in *o*. There are virtually no such similes in all but two of the eight works examined here. *The Quiet Don* has fifty-seven of them and *Cement* twenty-six. Their presence is also felt in Evgenii Zamiatin's *We*. Stylistic awkwardness may appear trivial if adverbs ending in *o* are common words on the order of *ugol'no* (like coal) or *svintsovo* (like lead) that can also be used as first parts of typical compound epithets; but it is rather disturbing to see odd neologisms such as *vzryvno* (like explosions) or *strunno* (like strings), which are recurrently employed in *Cement*. Gladkov's adverbial vehicles are as a rule more audacious than Sholokhov's, reaching at times the ultimate in studied mannerism: "Saraino plastalis' labazy" (1:98)—"The grain shops stretched like sheds.'' Judging by their use in *The Quiet Don* and *Cement*, the similes with adverbs ending in *o* draw their imagery primarily from the spheres of man and objects, the latter being a decidedly dominant source for vehicles in both works. The adverbs ending in *o* appear to be well suited for the illustration of various relations. They refer chiefly to action, color, and appearance in *The Quiet Don*, and to sound and appearance in *Cement*. Products of a bold stylistic experimentation, these similes are wisely kept out of the characters' speech by both Sholokhov and Gladkov.

Altogether *The Quiet Don* has about forty different forms for its similes, more than any other work examined here. *Doctor Zhivago* takes a close second. Table 2 shows all of Sholokhov's favorite forms as well as some of those he uses least. *Kak* (like, as) is the most frequently used connective in *The Quiet Don*, occurring in about 45 percent of the similes. This is a rather low percentage. All other works, except *Cement*, show a higher proportion of *kak* similes. Moreover, around 37 percent of the *kak* similes in *The Quiet Don* are contributed by the characters, considerably more than in any other work. Sholokhov's relative moderation in the use of *kak* can be attributed in part to his predilection for the instrumental case and the connectives *slovno* (as if, like) and *budto* (as if). The highest percentage of *kak* is found in *Red Cavalry*. Like the English connective ''like,'' *kak* introduces the vehicle in the most direct and forceful manner, and Babel' eagerly exploits this quality in his efforts to stun the reader with the bizarre originality of his imagery. As a result, he employs no more than ten other forms, almost one-third the number in *Envy*. One may further point to such individual peculiarities as the nearly total neglect of *tochno* (as if, like) by Sholokhov; Ivanov's predilection for *pokhozhii* (similar), which harmonizes with his static, descriptive manner; Tolstoi's preference for *kak budto* (as if) and *podobnyi* (similar), which tend to express similarity somewhat less emphatically than most other connectives; Veselyi's attachment to the colloquial *rovno* (just like), which enhances the popular strain in his works; and the use of the vernacular *chisto* (just like) in *The Quiet Don*, where it occurs exclusively in the characters' speech. On the other hand, Sholokhov hardly ever lets his characters use *slovno* and he seldom employs it in the man-to-animal group.

The last point to be discussed here with regard to the structure of similes is the position of their vehicles. Depending on whether they follow or precede the tenor, vehicles are divided into post-positive and pre-positive. Placing the vehicle before the tenor helps to bring the image into sharper relief, as in the sentence ''Like a flash of zigzag lightning, a brief recollection cut through his thoughts'' (1:158). In this example we have what I shall call an absolute pre-positive vehicle, because it precedes the tenor and its modifiers. An important variety of pre-positive vehicles is one in which the vehicle is put between the words describing the tenor's properties or mode of action. Comparison thus becomes focused on individual qualifiers that in most cases turn out to be adjectives: "Starukha . . . zhevala korichnevymi i sukhimi, kak vishnevaia kora, gubami" (3:237). Similes of this kind defy an exact rendition of their word order in English. Hence the above example must be translated as "The old woman . . . chewed her lips brown and dry as the cherry-tree bark." Medial vehicles, as I shall call them, are also found in the double similes: "Shtokman . . . tochil, kak cherv' drevesinu, nekhitrye poniatiia i navyki" (1:156)—"Shtokman . . . ate into their simple ideas and customs like a worm into wood." As a rule, pre-positive vehicles are employed consciously as a stylistic device. They occur more frequently in literary works than in ordinary speech. Indeed, in every work examined here the number of pre-positive vehicles in the characters' language is minimal compared to their number in the authorial narrative.

The use of pre-positive vehicles varies a great deal with each individual writer. These vehicles account for roughly 32 percent of all vehicles in *The Armored Train No. 14-69*, 30 percent in *The Quiet Don*, 23 percent in *The Carousing Spring*, 20 percent in *War and Peace*, 16-17 percent in *Cement* and *Doctor Zhivago*, 12 percent in *Envy*, and 5 percent in *Red Cavalry*. Nevertheless, there is a unifying factor behind these figures. In each work the proportion of pre-positive vehicles among its instrumental similes is very high, ranging from some 22 percent in *Red Cavalry* to 31 percent in *Cement* and 53 percent in *The Quiet Don*. The same applies to similes with vehicles consisting of adverbs ending in *o*. Around 54 percent of them in *Cement* and 45 percent in *The Quiet Don* have pre-positive vehicles, all of which—like their counterparts in instrumental similes—are of the absolute variety. By contrast, positions of vehicles in other similes show considerable dependence on the purely individual taste of the writer. A case in point are similes connected by *kak*.

Pre-positive vehicles account for over 20 percent of all *kak* similes in *The Quiet Don* and *The Carousing Spring*, 45 percent in *Armored Train No. 14-69*, and only 1.5 percent in *Cement*. Gladkov is simply adamant about having hardly any pre-positive vehicles unless they appear in the instrumental case or as adverbs ending in *o*. The high number of pre-positive vehicles in Ivanov's short novel is indicative less of his stylistic daring than of his descriptive manner, for three-fourths of his pre-positive vehicles introduced by *kak* are medial and refer primarily to adjectival modifiers of the tenor. In *The Quiet Don* two-thirds of the pre-positive vehicles with *kak* are medial. Their presence, however, is not overly conspicuous, due to the size of the novel and to the large number of absolute vehicles. Some 13 percent of *kak* similes in *War and Peace* have prepositive vehicles, three-fourths of them absolute. Tolstoi must have strongly believed that beginning his similes with an illustration was an effective way to stir the reader's imagination and make him more receptive to the author's ideas. This may explain Tolstoi's liking of absolute vehicles in his lengthy asyndetic similes of an argumentative nature.

Until now *The Quiet Don* has been treated as a single entity, and its similes have been compared to those in the works of other writers. Our next step is to survey the use of similes in separate volumes of *The Quiet Don* and in the rest of Sholokhov's writings. The basic statistical data are given in tables 3 and 4, where the heading ''Early Stories'' covers three feuilletons and twenty-seven short stories, including ''The Wind,'' which is all that has ever been published of Sholokhov's short fiction written during the 1920s. The data also include similes that had been censored.

All of Sholokhov's works contain large numbers of similes. In proportion to the size of individual works, the highest concentration of similes is found in ''One Language,'' ''Galoshes,'' ''The Crooked Path,'' and ''The Fate of a Man'' among the stories, and in volumes 1 and 3 of *The Quiet Don* among the novels. As a whole, *The Quiet Don* has a slightly higher concentration of similes than the early stories. However, its first three volumes, containing, respectively, 612, 532, and 605 similes each, sharply contrast with the last volume, numbering merely 397 similes. More importantly, only 57 percent of all the similes in volume 4 belong to the author as against the median of 80 percent in the first three volumes. Corresponding figures are 76 percent for the early stories, 64 and 38 percent, respectively, for volumes 1 and 2 of *Virgin Soil Upturned*, and 48 percent for *They Fought for Their Country*. Almost all similes in ''The Science of Hatred'' and ''The Fate of a Man'' come from their protagonists. Keeping in mind that volume 1 of *Virgin Soil Upturned* was written between volumes 3 and 4 of *The Quiet Don* and that four-fifths of *They Fought for Their Country* came out before volume 2 of *Virgin Soil Upturned*, one can speak of a steady decline in the authorial use of similes beginning with volume 1 of *Virgin Soil Upturned*. There appear to be several causes of this development. One is the exhaustion of the author's imagination. The number of similes Sholokhov poured out in his early stories and the first three volumes of *The Quiet Don* would normally suffice for three novels of the size of *War and Peace*. It must have been increasingly difficult to create fresh figures of speech, particularly in *Virgin Soil Upturned*, because it depicts the same land and people as *The Quiet Don*. Furthermore, the prose of the thirties turned away from the metaphorical exuberance of the twenties, and Sholokhov, approving of this trend, exhibited more restraint in the use of figurative language. In volume 4 of *The Quiet Don* one may

TABLE 3: Categories of the Similes in M. Sholokhov's Works

Groups	*Quiet Don*	Early Stories	*VSU 1*	*VSU 2*	"Sci. of Hatred"	"Fate of a Man"	*They Fought*
Man-man	552	85	106	187	8	17	92
Man-animal	392	98	120	128	2	16	49
Man-nature	274	55	45	43	1	17	20
Man-object	354	87	75	91	3	14	58
Man-God	3		1	2		1	2
Man-devil	7	2	1	5	1	2	2
TOTAL	1582	327	348	456	15	67	223
Animal-man	17	4	4	13			5
Animal-animal	27	9	10	9			
Animal-nature	16	6	2	5			2
Animal-object	43	7	15	1			5
Animal-devil	1						
TOTAL	104	26	31	28			12
Nature-man	44	22	6	3			6
Nature-animal	26	9	5	1			1
Nature-nature	37	13	11	7		1	7
Nature-object	82	17	17	9		2	14
Nature-God	1						
TOTAL	190	61	39	20		3	28
Object-man	31	19	5	8			12
Object-animal	36	17	6	3		1	4
Object-nature	60	8	5	4	2		11
Object-object	143	27	19	24	2	1	24
Object-God							
Object-devil							
TOTAL	270	71	35	39	4	2	51
SUM TOTAL	2146	485	453	543	19	72	314
Characters' similes	24%	24%	36%	62%	74%	89%	52%

ABBREVIATIONS IN TABLES 3 AND 4

Quiet Don—The Quiet Don
VSU 1—Virgin Soil Upturned, vol. 1
VSU 2—Virgin Soil Upturned, vol. 2
"Sci. of Hatred"—"The Science of Hatred"
"Fate of a Man"—"The Fate of a Man"
They Fought—They Fought for Their Country

miss the ornamental brilliance of its predecessors, but one receives more satisfaction from its deeper psychological insights. In terms of aesthetic preference, the choice between the first three volumes of *The Quiet Don* and the last volume is like the choice between Pasternak's early and late poetry. What disappoints the reader is not so much the quantitative shrinking of authorial similes as progressive repetition, from work to work, of identical or similar vehicles, a repetition that reaches an uncomfortable level in *They Fought for Their Country* and volume 2 of *Virgin Soil Upturned*.

The dearth of fresh imagery in these works can also be partly attributed to Sholokhov's not being in a position to describe his characters and events with the same degree of frankness and fullness as in *The Quiet Don*. He curtailed his own narrative and, as was noted in the preceding chapter, filled the space with meaningless dialogues and various tales and anecdotes told by the characters. The result was a steep increase in the characters' similes. While Shchukar' uses about twenty-five similes in the first volume of *Virgin Soil Upturned*, he employs a hundred of them in the second. Many of these similes are put into his mouth with the obvious intent of producing a comic effect. They are not used here as aptly as are their counterparts in *The Quiet Don*. Many of Shchukar''s similes are also identical with or akin to those used in earlier works. Despite these shortcomings, Shchukar''s similes retain the peculiar flavor of the Don dialect and are superior to their rather bland and commonplace counterparts in the speech of the Red Army soldiers in *They Fought for Their Country* and "The Science of Hatred." On the other hand, the hero of "The Fate of a Man" is endowed with a lively imagination which allows him to create some apt lyrical similes.

The growing role of his characters in creating similes and, to a greater degree, the general trend toward stylistic conservatism produced significant changes in Sholokhov's use of instrumental similes.

The highest concentration of instrumental similes is found in the early stories and volume 1 of *The Quiet Don*, where they comprise, respectively, 30 and 32 percent of all the similes. Moreover, in the authorial narrative, instrumental similes outnumber similes formed with *kak* by a dozen in the early stories and by more than forty in volume 1 of *The Quiet Don*. Such a preponderance of instrumental similes does not occur in any of Sholokhov's later writings, and this can be taken as an indication that the years from 1925 through 1928 were the time when his predilection for the ornamental style found its strongest expression. The figurative language in the early stories is somewhat more audacious than that in volume 1 of *The Quiet Don*. The stories have proportionately more instrumental similes of the type "I snova tishina raspletalas' v khate nezrimoi kruzhevnoi

TABLE 4: The Forms of the Similes in M. Sholokhov's Works

Forms	*Quiet Don*	Early Stories	*VSU 1*	*VSU 2*	"Sci. of Hatred"	"Fate of a Man"	*They Fought*
kak	908	176	244	313	13	43	160
instrumental	469	139	66	33	1		24
kak budto	21	5	2	11		2	4
kak by	7			4			7
budto	124	26	16	31		13	20
slovno	183	45	31	33	3	5	38
tochno	2	1					1
podobno, podobnyi	3		2	1			1
rovno	4	8					
chisto	24	1	5	3			
adv. with *po*	83	24	16	24	1		12
adv. in *o*	57	4	9	4	1	1	4
comp. degree	25	7	13	18		1	2
prepositions	16	3	4	5			5
pokhozh, pokhodit'	30	11	4	8			5
tak	16	1	2	3			
takoi-kakoi, tot-kotoryi	6		1	1			
asyndeton	9		4				
others	57	10	10	21		3	16
TOTAL	2044	461	429	513	19	68	299
Pre-positive vehicles	29%	22%	23%	11%	21%	14%	17%
kak	44%	38%	57%	61%	68%	63%	54%
instrumental	23%	30%	15%	6%	5%	0%	8%

ABBREVIATIONS IN TABLES 3 AND 4

Quiet Don—The Quiet Don
VSU 1—Virgin Soil Upturned, vol. 1
VSU 2—Virgin Soil Upturned, vol. 2
"Sci. of Hatred"—"The Science of Hatred"
"Fate of a Man"—"The Fate of a Man"
They Fought—They Fought for Their Country

pautinoi'' (7:545)—''And again the silence sprawled in the hut like an invisible lacy cobweb.'' Volume 2 of *The Quiet Don* marks the beginning of the quantitative decrease of instrumental similes, although their number in it is still very high: about 23 percent. The corresponding figure for volume 3 is only slightly lower, but in subsequent writings the situation changes rather rapidly. The proportion of instrumental similes goes down to 15 percent in volume 1 of *Virgin Soil Upturned*, to 12 percent in volume 4 of *The Quiet Don*, to 8 percent in *They Fought for Their Country*, and to 6 percent in volume 2 of *Virgin Soil Upturned*. It is in the instrumental similes of the last two books that the scarcity of new imagery reveals itself with particular clarity. Most of these similes are copies or slight variations of those seen in Sholokhov's earlier writings.

The history of similes formed with adverbs ending in *o*—another manifestation of Sholokhov's ornamental style—closely resembles that of the instrumental similes. The strongest concentration of these similes is found in the first three volumes of *The Quiet Don*, where they average 17 per volume. Their number diminishes in every subsequent work, falling to 3 in volume 2 of *Virgin Soil Upturned*. The only noteworthy difference between the adverbial and instrumental similes is that the former were hardly used in the early stories.

Metaphors, Epithets, and Colors

Further discussion of Sholokhov's stylistic peculiarities requires a few remarks on his use of metaphors, epithets, and color. In conformity with the ornamental trend of the 1920s, the metaphors of the early stories and *The Quiet Don* display a high degree of figurativeness and daring. Many metaphors are expressed by verbs whose figurative use would be limited or eschewed altogether in the classical Russian prose of the nineteenth century. This applies to basic forms and derivatives of such verbs as *tsvesti* (bloom), *pleskat'sia* (drip), *bryzgat'* (spurt), *tech'* (flow). Some of these verbs figure prominently in the works of Sholokhov's contemporaries. A day blooming with the sun, heat, or twilight is a recurrent image in Boris Pil'niak's *The Naked Year* (1921), while *pleskat'sia* forms the main metaphor in the same author's ''Rasplesnutoe vremia'' (''The Spilled Time''), written in 1924. *Red Cavalry* abounds in metaphors involving verbs associated with flowing.

The connotations of Sholokhov's verbal metaphors are at times quite elusive, defying an adequate translation into English. Here is an example with *pleskat'sia*. A description of a Cossack cavalry attack against Red infantrymen ends with the words ''Tikho zapleskalas' rubka'' (2:307), meaning that the sabering of the Reds commenced in relative silence after the shooting had stopped. The verb *zapleskalas'* suggests, however, more than a mere beginning of the slaughter. It may evoke the movement and color of waves resembling movements of the cavalrymen and the color of their flying sabers. In addition, some idea of the sound of the blows may be conveyed through the onomatopoeic root *plesk* (splash). The metaphor proposes no clear-cut relation, leaving it to the individual reader to imagine any connections between sabering and splashing.

An additional insight into the nature and variety of Sholokhov's verbal metaphors can be gained by examining predicates employed with the subject *tishina* (silence, stillness). Since it is not easy to portray the state or actions of this abstract noun, the range of metaphors applied to it can be taken as an index of authorial ingenuity and daring. Verbs used metaphorically with *tishina* in the early stories and/or *The Quiet Don* are: *zvenet'* (ring), *raspletat'sia* (untwine), *raspleskat'sia* (spill), *zastyvat'* (freeze), *tsepenet'* (grow torpid, freeze), *drozhat'* (tremble), *lech'* (lie down), *styt'* (get cold, freeze), *gudet'* (drone), *baiukat'sia* (drowse), *navisat'* (hang over), *pastis'* (pasture), *pokoit'sia* (rest), *kisnut'* (turn sour, mope), *raspast'sia* (break up), *lopnut'* (burst), *repat'sia* (crack), *treskat'sia* (crack), *kopit'sia* (gather, accumulate), *poloskat'sia* (splash), *zret'* (ripen), *osedat'* (settle), *prosteret'sia* (stretch), *zakhriasnut'* (harden), *pristyt'* (freeze), *vo ves' rost vstat'* (stand up straight), *rasprosteret'sia* (stretch out), *mertvet'* (be dead silent), *tkat'sia* (weave), *priast'sia* (spin). This variety looks especially impressive if one considers that *War and Peace* contains no verbal metaphors with *tishina* except in the common idiom *votsarilas' tishina* (silence fell), and that the combined total of such metaphors in *Red Cavalry, Cement, Doctor Zhivago, The Naked Year*, Olesha's *Envy* and *Three Fat Men*, and Serafimovich's *The Iron Flood* is about the same as in Sholokhov's early stories and three times smaller than in *The Quiet Don*. Although a number of Sholokhov's silence metaphors may appear affected, the majority of them are rather apt and innovative.

These qualities, however, are not evident in Sholokhov's later works. In point of fact, original silence metaphors cease to occur in the last hundred pages of volume 3 of *The Quiet Don*, where the clichés "stoiala tishina" (there was a silence) or "ustanovilas' tishina" (a silence set in) supplant more imaginative variations. Later works contain almost no verbal usages with *tishina* other than these two clichés and an equally bland combination "tishina dlilas' " (silence lasted). The disappearance of silence metaphors attests to the dwindling of Sholokhov's ability to create new tropes and to his deliberate departure from an ornamental style.

One of Sholokhov's pet tropes is what can be called the genitive metaphor. Its core consists of two nouns, one of which is simply a noun in the genitive case expressing possession. The expressiveness of such metaphors is frequently intensified by adding adjectival or participial modifiers to their tenors and vehicles. Some genitive metaphors in *The Quiet Don* resemble those in *Red Cavalry* and *Cement*, whose authors use them about as often as Sholokhov. The style and setting of *Red Cavalry* are called to mind when one sees ''zakatnuiu rozovost' lysiny'' (1:269) of a Polish landlord; that is, his bald head the color of a pink sunset. On the other hand, vehicles of Sholokhov's genitive metaphors show a greater morphological diversity than Babel''s, notably in the use of forms characteristic of popular speech. For example, Babel''s phrase ''Gedali . . . obvivaet menia shelkovymi remniami svoikh dymchatykh glaz'' (37)—''Gedali . . . winds the silk straps of his smoke-colored eyes around me'' is intensely metaphorical; yet it has no unusual lexical forms. Had Sholokhov written a similar phrase, he might have enhanced its figurativeness and novelty by discarding the common adjective *shelkovye* (silk) in favor of a rare collective noun *shelkov'e* (approximately: silk), and by modifying it with the adjective *remennoe*, derived from *remen'* (strap). He might have done this by analogy with his phrases ''na serom shelkov'e pyli'' (1:38) and ''sinee shelkov'e vozhzhei'' (1:122), which mean ''in the gray silk of dust'' and ''the blue silk of the reins.'' An affinity with Gladkov can be exemplified by ''goluboi liven' klinkov'' (1:318)—''a blue torrent of blades'' of attacking Cossacks, which is reminiscent of ''goriashchii liven' shtykov'' (5:101)—''a burning torrent of bayonets'' in *Cement*.

As with his other tropes, Sholokhov visibly reduced his use of genitive metaphors in volume 4 of *The Quiet Don* and his later works. No ''torrent of blades'' appears, for example, in the description of a cavalry charge: ''In the dim light of the sun their blue blades glittered over their heads'' (4:409).

The simplification of style involved more than authorial restraint. It required periodic editorial excisions of particularly fanciful metaphors, mainly in the first two volumes of *The Quiet Don*.

We turn now to epithets and will use this loose term here to designate adjectival and participial modifiers employed in a figurative sense. The phrases ''besstydnoe polymia'' (1:57)—''a shameless flame'' and ''natselovannaia volnami gal'ka'' (1:11)—''pebble kissed by water'' may serve as examples. Our definition should, of course, be taken with a grain of salt. It is often impossible to decide whether a given adjectival modifier can be classified as an epithet. It may also be argued that figurative participles can be treated as metaphors.

The variety and nature of Sholokhov's epithets can be judged by their use with the word *tishina* in all of his works.[34] A large group of his epithets modifying *tishina* may be called emotive. They attribute to it feelings and moods experienced by the characters during periods of silence. Thus the epithet *nelovkaia* (awkward) is used several times to describe a silence that set in after people broke off their conversations, feeling ill at ease. Elsewhere *velichavaia i strogaia* (majestic and stern) silence descends over the steppe as the Cossacks, sensing the solemnity of impending death, gaze at the advancing Reds (3:75). Other emotive epithets used with *tishina* are *gustaia* (thick, oppressive), *nastorozhennaia* (watchful), *nudnaia* (dreary), *zastoinaia* (stagnant), *napugannaia* (frightened), *dremotnaia* (drowsy), *nedozrevshaia* (unripe), *napriazhennaia* (tense), *sklepannaia molchaniem* (riveted by silence), *stylaia* (cold), *mertvaia* (dead), *glukhaia* (profound), *poteriannaia* (disconcerted), *vymorochnaia* (desolate), *tugo natianutaia* (tightly stretched), *pustynnaia* (deserted), *tiazhkaia* (heavy), *gnetushchaia* (oppressive), *tiagostnaia* (painful), *nekhoroshaia* (unpleasant), *zloveshchaia* (ominous), *strashnaia* (frightening), *tiazhelovataia* (rather heavy), *rasteriannaia i nedoumevaiushchaia* (confused and puzzled), *nedobraia* (unfriendly), *predgrozovaia* (presaging a storm), *obmanchivaia* (deceptive).

Mertvaia (dead) and *glukhaia* (in the sense of "absolute") are also used to characterize silence in nature. At the same time the grandeur and purity of nature are transmitted through the images of *velikaia* (great), *blagostnaia* (blissful), and *blazhennaia* (blessed) silence. Stillness described by these epithets reigns over the land when there is no fighting and shooting (4:38, 436; 7:131). In like manner, *khoroshaia* (benign) and *laskovaia* (gentle) silence envelops nature as soon as shooting stops (4:24, 39). Other epithets pointing to attractive or anthropomorphized features of natural silence include *baiukaiushchaia* (lulling), *dremnaia* (drowsy), *mirnaia* (peaceful), *sladkaia* (sweet), *miagkaia* (gentle), *sonnaia* (sleepy), *ne striakhnuvshaia dremoty* (still drowsy), *sonlivaia* (somnolent), *skazochnaia* (fairy-tale, magic), *zacharovannaia* (enchanted), *umirotvorennaia* (placid), *grustnaia* (sad), *zadumchivaia* (pensive). Several epithets emphasize the profundity of silence in nature: *pustaia* (empty), *nemaia* (mute), *pustozvuchnaia* (soundless), *pustynnaia* (desolate), *kladbishchenskaia* (graveyard-), *glubokaia* (deep), *nerushimaia* (unbreakable), *nemotnaia* (mute), *bezzhiznennaia* (lifeless). Silence that makes an impression of being easy to break is called *khrupkaia* (fragile) and *lomkaia* (brittle). A predominantly aesthetic perception of silence accounts for epithets suggestive of delicate craftsmanship: *tonko vypriadennaia* (fine-spun) and *granenaia*. In the context in which it appears, the last word, meaning "cut" or "faceted," defies a precise translation into English. In some instances silence is described by epithets characterizing motion, density, temperature, humidity, or sound conductivity of the air. These epithets are *shelkovo shelestiashchaia* (rustling like silk), *tiaguchaia* (viscous), *nepronitsaemaia* (impenetrable), *dremuchaia* (dense), *prozrachnaia* (transparent), *znoinaia* (hot), *moroznaia* (frosty), *pyl'naia* (dusty), *tumannaia* (misty), *vlazhnaia* (damp), *gulkaia* (resonant). Finally, the epithets *temnovataia* (darkish), *sirenevaia* (lilac), *siniaia* (blue), and *chernaia* (black) reflect the author's perception of silence through color.

Sholokhov's fondness for figurative modifiers is evidenced by the fact that the number of different epithets applied to "silence" in *The Quiet Don* is almost double their combined number in the following works taken together: *War and Peace, The Naked Year, Red Cavalry, Cement, The Iron Flood, Three Fat Men, Envy*, and *Doctor Zhivago*. Gladkov and Pil'niak, however, use epithets with "silence" about as frequently as Sholokhov. At least four of these epithets—*pustynnaia* (desolate), *znoinaia* (hot), *pustaia* (empty), and *chernaia* (black)—occur in both *The Naked Year* and *The Quiet Don*. Epithets in the early stories and *The Quiet Don* are more "ornamental" than in later works. It is primarily in the former that we encounter the more affected descriptions of silence, like *khrupkaia* (fragile), *nedozrevshaia* (unripe), or *tiaguchaia* (viscous). In *The Quiet Don* one could find the atrocious combination "bezzvuchno drebezzhashchaia tishina" (soundlessly rattling silence) that was supposed to reflect the anxiety of the Cossacks who had been assembled to be told about the declaration of war (1:273). The epithet was changed to *zastyvshaia* (frozen) in 1953 and to *napriazhennaia* (tense) in 1956. Beginning with volume 1 of *Virgin Soil Upturned*, epithets describing "silence" become increasingly repetitious, although new varieties are occasionally found in this and later works.

A distinctive characteristic of Sholokhov's use of epithets is his consistent employment of the participle *razdavlennyi* (crushed) in the figurative sense. A great admirer of physical labor, he attaches this word to hands battered by hard work. In *The Quiet Don* such are the hands of Natal'ia (1:73), of local non-Cossack Communists (3:330), and of Grigorii's mother (4:304). Natal'ia's father also had such hands in the original text (3:149). In *Virgin Soil Upturned* the blacksmith Shalyi displays battered hands (5:153; 6:300). In a more conventional application, *razdavlennyi* describes people in a state of acute suffering. The merchant Mokhov is crushed by shame (1:129), a Belorussian by his sudden misfortune (1:254), and Nikolai Strel'tsov by his grief and jealousy (7:8). "Crushed by her grief" or "anguish" are the key words characterizing Natal'ia when she is abandoned by Grigorii and humiliated by Aksin'ia (1:349, 350). *Razdavlennyi* is the word describing Evgenii Listnitskii crushed by his memories (2:100), a Cossack widow worn out by fatigue (2:184), and Grigorii's hostility swept away by his brother's pathetic smile (3:24). The use of *razdavlennyi* in the last example is somewhat awkward since it is hard to imagine how a pathetic smile can "crush" something, even figuratively.

Among nonfigurative adjectival modifiers one may single out the word *nevniatnyi*, the basic meanings of which are "indistinct," "vague," and "unintelligible." *Nevniatnyi* is a standard literary word, regularly used by many writers as different as Pushkin and Gladkov. What is unusual about it in Sholokhov's works is the frequency and diversity of its application. Symptomatic of Sholokhov's sensitivity to sounds, *nevniatnyi* and its adverbial form *nevniatno* are among his favorite words. Apart from the routine use of *nevniatnyi* for description of unintelligible sounds, Sholokhov—more often than other authors—employs it to convey indistinctness of smells, outlines, and feelings. He speaks, for instance, of "nevniatnyi, kak aromat sena, zapakh devich'ego tela" (3:399)—"the faint, haylike scent of the girl's body"; of "nevniatnoi, tonko vypriadennoi niti gorizonta" (3:26)—"the vague, fine-spun thread of the horizon"; and of "nevniatnuiu gorech' sozhaleniia" (3:29)—"intangible bitterness of regret." The use of *nevniatnyi* reaches its peak in volumes 2 and 3 of *The Quiet Don* and goes down almost to zero in *They Fought for Their Country*. Simultaneously, beginning with volume 1 of *Virgin Soil Upturned* (except in its first paragraph), Sholokhov restricts the function of *nevniatnyi* to a description of sounds.

A number of Sholokhov's epithets and plain attributes strike the reader with their peculiar structure, giving rise to a belief that some of these words must have been coined by the author. For example, the critic Veniamin Vasil'ev lists the following words as neologisms: *drozhlivyi* (jittery, jumpy), *izlomistyi* (zigzag), *izmorshchinennyi* (wrinkled all over), *izrytvlennyi* (rutted), *izuzorennyi* (decorated with designs), *nastalennyi* (hardened with steel), *obzernennyi* (turned into grains, beads), *rezuchii* (sharp), *zvonistyi* (ringing).[35] In fact, all these words but the last two can be found in Vladimir Dal''s *Dictionary* in identical or almost identical form, while *rezuchii* is given in *Slovar' russkikh donskikh govorov* (*The Dictionary of the Russian Don Dialects*, 1975-1976) and is used by a Cossack character in "The Wind." Sholokhov cannot be credited, therefore, with the creation of most of these words, even though he endows them with new connotations in his figurative use of them. A case in point is the epithet *nastalennyi* that can be easily mistaken for a neologism. It is derived from the verb *nastalit'*, meaning "to weld steel" onto an object, particularly an axe. In *The Quiet Don* the epithet *nastalennyi* serves to portray the hard gaze of Bunchuk (2:161), the angry look of an insurgent Cossack commander (3:260), and a clear, firm voice of a captain, giving a command (1:289). Elsewhere the author employs the verb *nastalit'* to emphasize the stern expression of an old Cossack's eyes (1:262), and Nagul'nov uses the expression *nastalit' serdtse* in reference to a man who wants to make his heart hard like steel (5:33). If the realist Sholokhov allows Nagul'nov to use *nastalit'*, it is a good indication that this verb occurs in the speech of ordinary Cossacks. The same is probably true of most or all of the words listed by Vasil'ev as Sholokhov's creations. A more controversial list of Sholokhov's "neologisms" was made up by the critic S. A. Koltakov.[36] Although it mistakenly includes such common words as *sin'* (the blue) and *klykastyi* (with big fangs), the list also contains words of hard-to-establish origin like *besperepletnyi* (unbound) and *zrachkastyi* (with big pupils), neither of which is in Dal''s *Dictionary*. The best way to determine whether these and other disputable words were actually created by Sholokhov would be to undertake a close study of the idiom spoken in the Veshenskaia area. As of now, Sholokhov appears to have been interested more in expanding connotations of existing words than in coining neologisms.

In trying to communicate his impressions of people and the outside world as precisely as possible, Sholokhov continually employs compound adjectives.[37] A large number of these adjectives denote color. In some of them both components designate nothing but color, as in "izzhelta-krasnyi sazan" (1:18)—"yellowish-red carp"; in others one of the components consists of a word denoting an object whose color is merely one of its characteristics, as in "svintsovo-serye tuchi" (3:368)—"leaden-gray clouds." The latter combinations imply a certain degree of figurativeness and can be regarded as epithets. As for one-word color adjectives, Sholokhov predominantly employs them in the literal, purely descriptive, function. This also applies to "black" and "light-blue" or "blue" (*goluboi*), but with the difference that these words are used symbolically more often than other color adjectives.

The figurative use of "black" in Sholokhov bespeaks a strong influence of popular tradition in which this color symbolizes distressful or reprehensible aspects of life. Black rumor, anguish, infirmity, news, joylessness, days, reputation, pride, death, thoughts, and disgrace are typical combinations occurring in *The Quiet Don* and, to lesser extent, in other works. The symbolic role of *goluboi* (translated here as "blue") is more subtle, versatile, and original. Sholokhov associates with this color a clear, sunlit day, suggestive of beauty, purity, and joy which are offered to man by Mother Nature. But, with the exception of childhood, man fails to take advantage of the offer. He turns his life into a succession of self-inflicted sufferings and frustrated hopes. His sad existence is only occasionally brightened by nostalgic flashbacks into the *goluboi* period of his early life.[38] Thus episodes from Grigorii's childhood enter into his war reminiscences "tonkoi goluboi priad'iu" (2:49)—"like a fine blue thread," or "golubym solnechnym dnem" (3:261)—"like a blue sunny day," stirring the feelings of love and sadness in him. Sentimental recollections of childhood are equally dear to Nikolai Strel'tsov in *They Fought for Their*

Country. In a moment of grief he recalls his past, his youth that vanished in "the blue haze" of the distant horizon (7:30).

Goluboi implies hope and dreams of happiness when Grigorii plans to leave with Aksin'ia for "the welcoming blue land" of the Kuban' Cossacks (1:162), and when Kondrat Maidannikov thinks that the Communist Party will lead all the working people of the world into "the sky-blue future" (5:135). Sholokhov, of course, does not say what happened to Kondrat's dreams of mass happiness, but he repeatedly shows how his other characters' aspirations for individual happiness are frustrated by separation and loss. *Goluboi* is the color of the outer world on the day Razmetnov sees his wife for the last time (5:37). When Cossack recruits leave their native land in a troop train, their sad thoughts and the vagueness of their future are communicated by the lyrical image of "a distant . . . thread of forest, blue, pensive and inaccessible, like a faintly shining evening star" (1:223). Elements of remoteness and inaccessibility often appear in conjunction with *goluboi*, affirming the grandeur of nature and suggesting the futility of human aspirations.

In scenes of violent death, the joyfulness and tenderness implicit in *goluboi* are contrasted to this ultimate of human cruelty—man's depriving his brother of enjoying the dearest gift of nature. In "The Offense" a child, having just witnessed the murder of his father, howls "Daddy! . . . Daddy! " into the calm steppe "enveloped in a blue twilight" (7:436). In *The Quiet Don* a young Ukrainian, his skull fractured in a fight with the Cossacks, will no longer walk on "the merry blue earth" (1:137). A mortally wounded Cossack falls from his horse with his hands wide open as if he were trying to embrace "the distant, blue horizon" (1:319). Doomed to a violent death, Ivan Kotliarov sees the ridges of cretaceous mountains looming in the distance like "a blue apparition" (3:335). In the same paragraph, "in the boundless blue [*sineve*] of the skies, inaccessibly high," Kotliarov also notices a little, swiftly floating cloud, its opal shadow reflected in the distant bend of the Don. This is Sholokhov's way of saying that "life's but a walking shadow," and here he is at his best. In the entire paragraph not a word is said about the illusiveness of human hopes, or about the thoughts and feelings of a doomed man. All that the reader is supposed to know about them is told in the unique language of nature imagery.

Some of Sholokhov's landscapes resemble those of Impressionist painters. His concern with the effect of light would occasionally cause him to portray the same subject in different colors just as it appears to his eyes at different times of the day. Such is a description of a block of snow: "Glittering like sugar in the sun, blue in twilight, pale-lilac in the mornings, and pink at sunrise" (3:310). In a similar vein Sholokhov depicts different appearances of the same object during the four seasons. Here belong the colorful representations of a copse in *The Quiet Don* (3:388-389) and the familiar burial mound in *Virgin Soil Upturned* (5:277-278). A somewhat curious case of different coloring of the same object involves lightning when it functions as a vehicle in instrumental similes. Lightning takes on the color of the tenor: "Beloi molniei vspykhivalo kipenno-goriuchee operen'e kryl'ev [strepeta]" (3:318-319)—"Bright, foam-colored wings [of the bustard] flashed like white lightning"; "Kot mel'kal po ogurechnym griadkam . . . ryzhei molniei" (6:272)—"The cat flashed through the beds of cucumbers . . . like ginger lightning"; "[Okun'] sverknul zelenoi molniei" (7:36)—"[The perch] flashed like green lightning."

Although no other part of speech denoting color is used as often as the adjective, an unusually large number of color verbs, adverbs, and nouns are found in Sholokhov's works. Each of these groups is sprinkled with fresh, eye-catching words. Along with everyday verbs like *belet'* (appear white) or *zelenet'* (appear green), one sees the rare *rzhavet'* (appear rusty) *belesit'sia* (appear whitish), *sizet'* (appear blue-gray), *vyzheltit'sia* (bloom yellow), *puntsovet'* (appear crimson). Sholokhov's rendition of color by means of adverbs is an equally rare phenomenon. It is virtually impossible to convey the literal meaning of color adverbs in English. In most cases they become adjectives in translation. As an example may serve *sine* (blue), Sholokhov's favorite color adverb: "V glazakh Stepana sine popykhivali iskry nepriiazni" (3:66)—"Blue sparks of hostility flickered in Stepan's eyes." In addition to *sine*, Sholokhov employs *alo* (scarlet), *rozovo* (rosily), *zhelto* (yellow), *rdiano* (red), and *lazorevo* (color of yellow tulip). Color nouns are particularly prominent in Sholokhov, thanks to a high frequency of their appearance and an impressive variety of their forms. Standard nouns like *belizna* (whiteness) or *zheltizna* (yellowness) alternate with such popular forms as *bel'*, *belen'*, *beles'* (whiteness), *zhelten'*, *prozhelten'*, *zhelch'* (yellowness), *ryzheven'*, *ryzhina* (redness, ginger), *goluben'* ([light] blueness), *krasnina* (redness), *siz'* (bluish grayness), *sin'* (blueness).[39] There are four equivalents of *chernota* (blackness) in *The Quiet Don: chern'*, *ischern'*, *chernina, chernet'* (a noun!). This may be a record number of vernacular synonyms of a color noun for any work of Russian fiction.

It is difficult to conceive of a work which has more words denoting color than *The Quiet Don*. It contains about three thousand of them, counting compound color adjectives as just one adjective and disregarding words referring to brightness, like "pale," "light," "dim," "dark." The nine hundred color words in volume 1 mark the peak in Sholokhov's usage of color. Their number continues to be high in all of his subsequent works, most of them occurring in the authorial narrative.

Sholokhov's palette is exceptionally rich. Around sixty various hues can be registered in his early stories and over one hundred in *The Quiet Don*. These figures include all words indicating color, such as *dymchatyi* (smoky), *izumrudnyi* (emerald), and "tsveta linialoi zaiach'ei shkurki" (1:375)—"the color of a faded hare's skin." In his lavish use of color Sholokhov is comparable to Babel'. But there are some telling dissimilarities between the two authors. Being more subjective, Babel' tends to treat the outer world like a coloring picture, rather than like a tableau with its own colors. He is more apt to project his ideas and emotions into his verbal painting and he has a stronger predilection for bright colors than does Sholokhov. In *Red Cavalry* the percentage of color words denoting the four basic colors (red, yellow, green, and blue) is significantly higher than in Sholokhov's early stories or *The Quiet Don*.[40] At the same time *Red Cavalry* has hardly any compound color adjectives, a sign that Babel', unlike Sholokhov, is not concerned with a careful representation of various shadings. And, in stark contrast to Sholokhov, Babel' employs no color words other than those of the standard Russian.

Sholokhov's language and imagery are so peculiar that it would be sufficient to examine a single sentence as a review of what was said about them in this and preceding sections (as well as in the preceding chapter): "Ne lazorevym alym tsvetom, a sobach'ei besiloi, durnop'ianom pridorozhnym tsvetet pozdniaia bab'ia liubov' " (1:52)—"A woman's belated love blooms, not like the scarlet flower of the tulip, but like that loco weed, the roadside henbane."

Some twenty characteristics of Sholokhov's style can be seen in this sentence. It has a distinct local coloration. *Lazorevyi* (tulip, red) and *sobach'ia besila* (henbane) are common words of the Don dialect. The poetic quality of the sentence is rooted in the popular figurative conception of love as flowers in bloom. An affinity with folk poetry can be seen in the choice of *lazorevyi tsvet* (instead of *lazorevyi tsvetok*) and in the use of a negative trope. A master in portraying conflicts and polarities, Sholokhov builds his statement on two contrasting images. As a merciless realist, he refuses to idealize his favorite heroine through linking her love to the pure, romantic image of a blooming tulip. His emphasis is on Aksin'ia's passion and sensuality, on the madness and intoxication suggested by dialectal names for henbane. The sentence is characteristic of Sholokhov because it speaks of love, the cornerstone of his philosophy of life, and because its imagery comes from the world of nature. As with many other statements relating man to nature, the sentence is placed at the beginning of a chapter to foreshadow its content. The sentence resembles an adage, a generalizing observation about human beings which Sholokhov periodically makes in his fiction. The popular, somewhat coarse adjective *babii* (woman's) is the word that Sholokhov strongly prefers to its normal counterpart *zhenskii* in *The Quiet Don* and in volume 1 of *Virgin Soil Upturned*. The markedly Sholokhovian character of the sentence is signaled by its being an instrumental simile with a pre-positive vehicle and by its containing a color adjective and the verb *tsvesti* (bloom). The use of coordinate parts of the sentence for intensification (*lazorevym alym*) or contrast (*alym tsvetom—sobach'ei besiloi*) is a device that Sholokhov likes to employ in his lyrically tinged passages. The amphibrachic rhythm of the sentence can also be related to such passages since their rhythmical patterns involve a liberal use of trisyllabic units. Finally, a word order with the noun subject closing a rather long sentence is not entirely alien to Sholokhov's syntax in his somewhat elevated passages. The best example of it is the ending of volume 2 of *Virgin Soil Upturned*. And one may wonder whether his reading Sholokhov might have influenced Solzhenitsyn in choosing the same construction in the description of the castle of the Holy Grail at the end of chapter 42 in *The First Circle*.

One or more characteristic traits of the sentence in question from *The Quiet Don* can be found in sentences written by other authors. But none of their sentences would combine all the peculiarities of Sholokhov's sentence. He is the only one who could have written it.

Structure of the Works

Although innovative linguistically, Sholokhov is rather a traditionalist with respect to the structural aspects of his works. In his completed novels incidents are arranged in chronological order; the basic unity of the plot is sustained through the presence of one central character and through the succession of occurrences springing from major historical events—war, revolution, or collectivization of agriculture. *The Quiet Don* exhibits a much greater consistency in maintaining the connection between its protagonist and historical situations than does *Virgin Soil Upturned*, whose volume 2 is set in a relatively uneventful period.

Yet *The Quiet Don* is not devoid of structural defects. A case in point is volume 2. It lacks the strong unifying role of a central character and contains some loosely connected scenes. One of the reasons for these flaws lies in Sholokhov's less-than-perfect blending of the constituent parts of the volume: sections written as the text of *The Quiet Don* and those borrowed from the manuscript of *The Don Country*, an unfinished earlier work that began with the description of the Kornilov movement. But, above all, Sholokhov spread himself too thin, trying to cover a multiplicity of Revolutionary events in different parts of Russia. Grigorii Melekhov could witness all but a few of these events, and his presence in the volume was drastically reduced. The rest of the historical scenes either went unattended by major characters or required the involvement of people like Kotliarov, Bunchuk, and Podtelkov, who, due to their ideological lopsidedness, were unable to look at the events as critically as Grigorii. By comparison, the author of *War and Peace* created three full-blooded male characters—Prince Andrei, Pierre, and Nikolai Rostov—and made them take part in a variety of historical events without stretching the reader's credibility. The first two are also people of great intelligence and sensitivity, a factor that contributed to the presentation of events on the appropriate philosophical plane.

Trying to give a broad picture of the Revolution, Sholokhov overpopulated volume 2 with a multitude of new characters and names. Their combined total is in the neighborhood of 650, including all identifiable individuals who either appear in person or are mentioned by name (or otherwise) in the authorial narrative, the characters' speech, and various documents. The number of new characters in volume 2 is about 200 higher than in volumes 1 and 3 and about 300 higher than in volume 4.

The episodic role of the new characters in volume 2 is manifested in the fact that merely a dozen of them reappeared in the flesh in one or both of the subsequent volumes. The presence of hundreds of ephemeral personages increased the fragmentation of the narrative and impeded an effective unfolding of the plot. In volume 3 Sholokhov avoided repetition of these flaws by introducing fewer new characters, by focusing on a single event (the Upper Don uprising), and by reinstating Grigorii as the central unifying character. Unity of the plot was achieved, even though the number of new characters remained substantial and all but a few of them were not deemed important enough to be admitted into volume 4. In this volume Sholokhov also managed to maintain the unity of the plot. He became increasingly circumspect about adding new characters and concentrated on the inner life of Grigorii and the people close to him.

Sholokhov's skill in handling plot can be exemplified by examining the first two chapters of *The Quiet Don*. Chapter 1 functions as an exposition. In sketching Grigorii's family background, it discloses the origins of his individualism, courage, and capacity for love. These qualities will determine his behavior throughout the entire novel. In chapter 2, while they are returning from fishing, Pantelei Melekhov angrily warns Grigorii not to court Aksin'ia. The warning foreshadows complications, especially since Grigorii shows no intention of heeding it. In the second part of the chapter Grigorii takes the catch, a carp, to the merchant Mokhov to earn some money for tobacco. On his way he encounters several Cossacks, some of whom will play an important role in the novel. Accompanied by one of them, Mit'ka Korshunov, Grigorii enters Mokhov's house. This gives

Mit'ka the chance to meet the merchant's daughter Elizaveta and to seduce her a hundred pages later. Thus in one chapter the author manages to introduce the reader to several characters, to suggest a possibility of true love, and to prepare the ground for an ordinary affair that is going to have vulgar repercussions. All this is accomplished through a natural sequence of incidents, in an eminently believable manner. A skillful use of detail is noteworthy, particularly in the case of the carp, where the fish becomes the immediate cause of Grigorii's visit to Mokhov.

The carp may also be called upon to illustrate changes in Sholokhov's narrative emphasis. In *The Quiet Don* the scene of angling for carp takes up one and a half pages consisting of an alternation of a dynamic narrative and spicy dialogue. A similar scene in *They Fought for Their Country* consumes five pages filled with copious detail about the process of fishing and with empty talk between Nikolai Strel'tsov and his half brother, who makes vain attempts to be witty (7:51-56). Here Sholokhov the fisherman overshadows Sholokhov the novelist, producing a worthy sequel to Sergei Aksakov's "Carp," a section in his *Notes about Angling for Fish* (1847).

Sholokhov seldom resorts to devices aimed at creating or heightening suspense. His real-life incidents are often so dramatic in themselves that he may feel no need for an added tension to keep his reader on tenterhooks. Among the devices he occasionally uses to arouse suspense or curiosity is suggesting what will happen, but without giving any specific information about things to come. Such predictions may take a form of dramatic irony. When Grigorii thinks that the war is over for him, the readers are told that he will be in for a lot more fighting (4:349). In other instances the author or the characters announce that something has already happened, but the reader is kept in the dark for a while about the nature or the particulars of the occurrence. One has to read fifteen pages to learn that Mit'ka's words "Natal'ia is dying" referred to her attempted suicide (1:188). At times Sholokhov breaks off the portrayal of a situation at a tense point. He does it, for example, in the scene of a chance encounter between Grigorii and Stepan at the moment when the latter is coming toward his rival "with his big, heavy fists firmly pressed to his chest" (1:195). Here the narrative was broken off to keep the reader in the state of expectancy. In other passages the main purpose of interruptions may be to provide a temporary relief from the horrors of violence. Thus in volume 3 of *The Quiet Don* a page-long chapter is inserted between chapters 54 and 56, which portray the massacre of captured Communists. The inserted chapter contains nothing but a matter-of-fact account of cooperation between insurgent Cossacks and the Don Army in the spring of 1919. It could be easily attached to chapter 53, which describes the establishment of the contact between the insurgents and the Don Army, or it could form the beginning of what is now chapter 57, which is devoted exclusively to a survey of the situation on the southern front.

The buildup of suspense may also be interrupted out of philosophical considerations. In volume 2 of *Virgin Soil Upturned*, chapters dealing with anti-Soviet conspirators are placed at the very beginning and near the end of the book. This arrangement serves to accentuate the contrast between the opposing forces and to concentrate action and suspense closer to the climax—the killing of Davydov and Nagul'nov in chapter 29, the last in the novel. The author, however, avoided a progressive building up of tension. The first part of chapter 28 describes the slow pace of life in Gremiachii Log and its typical everyday happenings. The purpose of this description is to emphasize the immutability of a basic, primarily biological, life that goes on undisturbed by the bitter internecine struggle for socioeconomic or ideological causes. At the same time the presentation of a settled everyday life may connote the stability of the new social order, in contrast to the futile and feeble attempts of the conspirators to destroy it.

There are some noteworthy differences in the length of chapters in *The Quiet Don*. Chapter 55 is not the only minichapter in volume 3. Chapters 26 and 29 are even shorter, taking up less than one page. Neither is inserted to provide a relief from horrors. Chapter 26, dealing with Grigorii, is injected into a narrative concerned chiefly with Koshevoi. It shows how Grigorii avoided being arrested by Koshevoi and Shtokman on the eve of the Upper Don uprising. Neither of the two Reds appears in it. The author apparently did not want to combine chapter 26 with chapter 28, which concentrates on Grigorii's reaction to the news about the outbreak of the uprising. Inclusion of pre-uprising material in chapter 28 might have weakened the effect of Grigorii's response to the news. The subject of chapter 29 is the return of Koshevoi to the Red camp after his escape from Tatarskii, where he was nearly killed by insurgent Cossacks. Since these incidents were described in detail in chapter 27, the episode of Koshevoi's return to the Reds would seem to form its logical conclusion. Yet Sholokhov wedged this episode between Grigorii's return to the rebellious Tatarskii and the beginning of his activities as an insurgent commander. By so doing the author might have wanted to alternate scenes from the Red and White camps. More likely, however, he intended to accentuate the difference between Grigorii and Koshevoi by drawing attention to unusually short chapters portraying sharply contrasting situations in which two former friends found themselves during the events that were to have a lasting effect on their personal relationship and political allegiance.

The function of the minichapter 9 in part 3 is clear. This chapter follows the description of the skirmish between the Cossacks and German cavalrymen and represents an authorial digression which condemns war in a Tolstoian manner and degrades the courage of the Cossack Koz'ma Kriuchkov, the first private in the entire Russian army to receive the Cross of St. George in World War I.

Beginning with volume 1 of *Virgin Soil Upturned*, chapters become increasingly longer. Their length reaches its peak in volume 2, where the average chapter is two and a half times longer than in volume 1 of *The Quiet Don*. Slowing down of the narrative pace must have had something to do with it. As his style was turning descriptive, Sholokhov displayed more willingness to take a character through various situations in one long chapter. Thus the twenty-page chapter 6 of part 8 of *The Quiet Don* includes the following sections pertaining to Grigorii's return from Budennyi's Cavalry Army: Grigorii on the road in a cart driven by a young Cossack widow who makes advances toward him; Grigorii's conversations with Koshevoi, Prokhor, and Aksin'ia in Tatarskii; Grigorii's drinking with Prokhor and his heated argument with Koshevoi. Had Sholokhov dealt with these incidents ten years earlier, he would probably have split them into two or three chapters. The increasing garrulousness of the characters was another contributing factor to the lengthening of chapters, notably in volume 2 of *Virgin Soil Upturned*. Here forty pages are allotted to chapters 22 and 23 describing a loquacious Party meeting. Chapters are not yet numbered or clearly marked in *They Fought for Their Country*, but a potential chapter featuring the verbose Red Army general may run to thirty pages.

In direct contrast with *The Quiet Don*, the chapters in volume 4 of *War and Peace* are significantly shorter than in volume 1. On the whole the length of an average chapter in Sholokhov's epic is greater than in Tolstoi's. There are no real minichapters in *War and Peace*, however.

Plot Errors

It must be well-nigh impossible for authors of vast epics to avoid discrepancies, ambiguities, and errors connected with the purely fictional aspect of the narrative, let alone historical, military, geographical, and other inaccuracies. In *War and Peace*, for example, Natasha is 13 years old on her name day (September 8) in 1805 (4:54), 15 at the beginning of 1806, and 16 in 1809 (5:14, 210). The chain on the little icon given to Prince Andrei by his sister is made of silver in one instance and of gold in the other (4:146, 397). For some reason an officer calls Denisov captain when the latter is a major (5:146, 148). The Polish Count Willarski enters Pierre's room "with the same official and solemn air with which Dolokhov's second had called on him" (5:84). There is, however, no previous mention that Dolokhov's second (Nikolai Rostov) had called on Pierre. All the arrangements for the duel between Pierre and Dolokhov were made by Rostov and Nesvitskii (Pierre's second).

In *The Quiet Don* the young Sholokhov was bound to make more such plot-connected mistakes than the mature author of *War and Peace*. For instance, Antip Brekhovich, who was supposed to have been captured and executed by the Reds in chapter 33 of volume 3, suddenly reappeared in the flesh in chapters 51 and 56. The oversight was corrected in 1936 through an insertion of a phrase indicating that Antip saved himself from the Reds by hiding in a ravine (3:207). A few more plot-connected slips were caught at various times,[41] but some have remained undetected or underwent faulty emendation. During the preparation of the 1953 edition someone noticed a glaring discrepancy between the date of Grigorii's first injury in August 1914 (Old Style) and the time of his finding a diary on the body of a dead Cossack. According to the notification of his squadron commander, dated August 18, Grigorii was killed (he turned out to be wounded) on the night of August 16 near the town of Kamenka-Strumilova. Yet the last entry in the dead Cossack's diary, which Grigorii found before being wounded, is dated September 5 (1:308, 336). Without much ado the editors, or Sholokhov, if he was consulted, moved both dates in the commander's notification ahead exactly by one month. This only aggravated the problem. It created a conflict with the contents of chapters 12, 13, and 20, which describe the engagements around Kamenka-Strumilova. From the description of the fighting, which is said to have begun on August 15 (1:308), it follows that Grigorii was wounded on or about August 16 for the first time, and on or about August 21 for the second time. Soon thereafter he was evacuated to an eye hospital in Moscow. The editors left all this information intact. They either failed to notice it or, more likely, resolved not to tamper with it because of its factual nature. Indeed, several battles were fought in August 1914 near Kamenka-Strumilova, and one of the units engaged there was the Twelfth Don Cossack Regiment in which Grigorii served. The editors could have changed the dating in the dead Cossack's diary, but this procedure would have required a partial revision of its text in order to fit it into a new chronological framework. No one seemed willing to do the job. It was much easier to make the squadron commander invent fighting outside Kamenka-Strumilova at a time when this town was far behind the front lines. Simultaneously, the editors overlooked a serious error in the commander's notification: Grigorii was wounded, not at night, as it states, but at noon (1:318-319).

A number of inaccuracies and ambiguities have remained undetected to this day. It is questionable that Grigorii could have arrived in the Veshenskaia area on the night of November 4 (1:376) if he was discharged from the eye hospital at the end of October and then spent about ten days in another hospital in Moscow (1:373). It is not clear why Grigorii told Aksin'ia that he would like to ride to Tatarskii to see how his fellow-villagers defend it (3:387). At this time Tatarskii was occupied by the Reds, and its Cossacks entrenched themselves opposite it on the left bank of the Don (3:374, 388). One is puzzled why Mit'ka Korshunov's eyes turn from yellow to green in volume 1 (1:19, 181), stay green throughout volumes 2 and 3, and regain their original yellow color in the last volume (4:98, 99). Grigorii Bogatyrev (3:295, 327) is called Petr in volume 4, because his first name is confused with that of the aviator Bogatyrev (4:262, 270). Kharlampii Ermakov uses a wrong diminutive in reference to Pavel Kudinov, calling him Iliushka instead of Pashka (3:258). Although Ermakov is under the influence of alcohol, the misuse of the diminutive is hardly meant to illustrate his condition. To my knowledge, only three editions avoided this mistake. The 1975 and 1980 editions of *Collected Works* replaced Iliushka with Pashka, and the 1975 Sovremennik (Contemporary) edition omitted the first name altogether. The 1978 deluxe edition, marking the fiftieth anniversary of the publication of *The Quiet Don*, has Iliushka. The Junior Captain Polkovnikov is occasionally called lieutenant (1:352) or captain (1:258) by the author. Ivan Atarshchikov, a junior captain (2:96, 102), is mentioned as a lieutenant (2:169), while the rank of Efim Izvarin changes back and forth from lieutenant (2:185, 292) to junior captain (2:238). Mishka Koshevoi entered Grigorii as a junior captain on his list of the enemies of the Soviet regime (3:174) at a time when Grigorii, who was never to advance to this rank, was merely a second lieutenant, two grades below a junior captain (3:84; 4:138). Since Koshevoi must have known Grigorii's rank, his error stems, in all probability, from the fact that his list of enemies was hastily added to the original text, causing the author or the editors to lose sight of Grigorii's actual rank.[42] The error spilled over into the Soviet film adaptation of *The Quiet Don* (1957-1958) in which Grigorii wears the insignia of a junior captain.

A few minor points in the plot may evoke bewilderment. Grigorii gets out of fierce fighting with his cheek severely cut by a saber stroke (3:215). Although the wound must have left a conspicuous scar, the author never mentions it. A character named Emel'ian appears out of the blue to order the Melekhovs to provide horses and a carriage to transport munitions for the Red Army (3:155). It is not immediately clear that this Emel'ian, long absent from the novel, may be the former coachman of the merchant Mokhov and an active supporter of the Reds.

In his later works Sholokhov committed noticeably fewer plot errors than in *The Quiet Don*, though one discrepancy in *They Fought for Their Country* is rather conspicuous. In the first 1943 installment of this novel

Nikolai Strel'tsov spoke of his having two children who lived with his mother because his wife left him in June 1941 (7:60). However, an installment published in 1969 presents a different picture: in June 1941 Strel'tsov's mother had been dead for nine years (7:30) and he has only one child. Nonetheless, he still continues to have two children in the passage that was originally published in 1943. The only difference is that they are now living with his mother-in-law.

Sholokhov's Place in Literature

In the conclusion of this chapter it may be appropriate to define Sholokhov's place in literature with respect to style. His central work, *The Quiet Don*, belongs to the Soviet ornamental prose of the 1920s, which was distinguished, above all, by the liberal use of tropes.[43] There exist two basic varieties of this prose. Some writers, like Babel' and Olesha, concentrated on creating fresh and striking figures of speech. Otherwise their authorial narrative remained markedly traditional, as far as the literary character of the language is concerned. Their vocabulary comes from the standard Russian, their diction is clear and correct. Other writers, like Gladkov and Veselyi, while flooding their works with tropes, seasoned their authorial speech with vernacular and experimented with syntax. Sholokhov stood closer to this group. This can be seen in his predilection for dialecticisms, his fondness for similes expressed by means of the instrumental case and adverbs ending in *o*, his syntactical inversions, and his clipped sentences without verbs. In the use of dialecticisms he went further than any major Soviet writer of the 1920s; in the use of instrumental similes he is rivaled only by Gladkov, who might have had a greater influence on the style of *The Quiet Don* than any other contemporary writer.

What sets Sholokhov apart from all practitioners of ornamental prose is the creation of an epic, something that not many authors seem to be able or willing to write. And the fact that his epic was written in ornamental style distinguishes Sholokhov from Tolstoi, giving him a unique place in all literature. The chief difference between *War and Peace* and *The Quiet Don* lies in the style: in vocabulary, figures of speech, and syntax. This difference overshadows similarities such as a chronological arrangement of events, attention to detail, and occasional use of certain "Tolstoian" locutions and methods of description. The author of *The Quiet Don* is an innovator rather than a traditionalist. It is no wonder that his writing appeared affected, coarse, and opaque to such a fastidious stylist as Ivan Bunin, an outstanding continuer of "classical" Russian realism in the twentieth century. Reading the first volume of *The Quiet Don* in 1941, Bunin called Sholokhov a "very talented man." Yet he found "not a single simple word'' in the book and had a hard time reading it owing to ''the twists of language and a multitude of local words.''[44]

Bunin's assertion about the total lack of simplicity in *The Quiet Don* is too sweeping, but his annoyance with dialecticisms is understandable. Nevertheless, Sholokhov's fondness for regionalisms was not without a redeeming feature. The vernacular was needed to impart more freshness and raciness to the literary Russian. Colorful popular idiom had not been entirely neglected in Russian fiction. It occurs, for example, in Nikolai Leskov's *skaz* stories and in Remizov's stylized fairytales. But it is seldom encountered in the authorial narrative of the major Russian works of the nineteenth and early twentieth centuries. Thus Sholokhov, in spite of his excessive use of dialecticisms, still played a pioneering role in invigorating the vocabulary of Russian fiction. This process is no less desirable now than it was in the 1920s. Campaigns for the ''purification'' of language under Stalin and the isolation of most members of the Soviet literary profession in Moscow and Leningrad contributed to making the language of a typical Soviet writer flat and stereotyped. One fighter for the revitalization of literary Russian is Solzhenitsyn. He regularly introduces popular expressions into his works. He does it, however, more prudently than Sholokhov. He studied Dal''s *Dictionary* to enrich his vocabulary and he appears to employ popular locutions from different parts of the country. This procedure allows him to select the wisest and raciest samples of popular speech, notably proverbs; but it cannot generate the unique local flavor or the spontaneity in the use of vernacular that are peculiar to the authorial narrative of *The Quiet Don*.

CHAPTER IV
HISTORICAL SOURCES OF *THE QUIET DON*

As in *War and Peace*, the historical outline in *The Quiet Don* could not have been drawn without resorting to a variety of sources. But if Tolstoi, writing his epic half a century after Napoleon's invasion of Russia, had to rely chiefly on printed sources, Sholokhov was in a position to use printed sources, oral accounts, and his own observations in approximately equal proportion. The present study will address itself primarily to printed sources, for they can be identified with certainty or probability. On the other hand, it is frequently impossible to tell whether a given description has its origin in oral information supplied to the author or in his own experiences. The study of the three types of sources is further complicated by the fact that the reticent Sholokhov has said very little about them.

The use of printed sources in *The Quiet Don* is irregular. It is least frequent in volume 1, the bulk of which is devoted to the peace-time life of the Don Cossacks. It is most frequent in volume 2, which deals with World War I, the Revolution, and the beginning of the Civil War. Many events of this volume take place outside the Upper Don region, and Sholokhov had to use published materials for their portrayal. This reliance on printed sources decreases in volume 3, which focuses on the Upper Don uprising. Sholokhov personally witnessed this event and he could have heard much about it from its participants. Printed accounts of the uprising at the time of his writing volume 3 were scarce and sketchy. Volume 4 reveals only a sparse use of printed sources. It pays more attention to the personal lives of the characters than do volumes 2 and 3, and descriptions of its major historical events—the link-up of the Don Army with insurgent Cossacks, the retreat of the White Cossacks toward Novorossiisk, and operations of the Fomin detachment—are based partly on the oral stories of participants and partly on what the author could have seen himself.

VOLUME 1

Borrowings from printed sources for volume 1 seem to be sporadic and limited to information concerning large military operations at the beginning of World War I. For example, the phrase "The Twelfth Cavalry Division under the command of General Kaledin was advancing in front of the Brusilov's Eighth Army" (1:287) could have been taken, with minor alteration, from volume 2 of General Anton Denikin's *Ocherki russkoi smuty* (*The Russian Turmoil*),[1] which served as an important source for volume 2 of *The Quiet Don*. But there are no further analogies between volume 1 and the general's memoirs. Indeed, the sentence that follows the above quotation not only is absent from Denikin, but also gives wrong information. Sholokhov writes that the Eleventh Cavalry Division was advancing to the left of the Twelfth Cavalry Division. Just the opposite was the case. The Eleventh Division belonged to the Third Russian Army that was advancing westward to the north of the Eighth Army. General remarks on the advance of the Eleventh Divison toward Leshniuv, Stanislavchik, Radzivillov, Brody, and Kamenka-Strumilova (1:287, 308) might have come from a printed source, whereas the detailed descriptions of the fighting of the Twelfth Don Cossack Regiment suggest Sholokhov's indebtedness to oral accounts of those Cossacks who fought there.

The Twelfth Regiment was manned by the Cossacks from the Upper Don region. Sholokhov could easily have met some of them, particularly Kharlampii Ermakov, in the 1920s. There is no way of determining the extent to which Sholokhov as an artist reworked their oral accounts, but it is possible to ascertain that he reproduced faithfully a number of facts pertaining to the Twelfth Regiment on the eve and at the beginning of the war. The regiment, as Sholokhov writes, belonged to the Eleventh Cavalry Division and was stationed in Radzivillov, near the Austrian frontier. The declaration of war found the regiment taking part in maneuvers in the vicinity of the town of Rovno. The regimental commander was Colonel Vasilii Maksimovich Kaledin (1:253). Sholokhov probably knew that he was the elder brother of General Aleksei Kaledin, commander of the Twelfth Cavalry Division (until February 1915) and the future ataman of the Don Cossacks.[2] One of the squadron commanders in the Twelfth Regiment was Junior Captain Polkovnikov (1:250).

The authenticity of all these details is corroborated by the writer Ivan Sagatskii, whose father served with the Twelfth Regiment before and during World War I. Sagatskii says, however, that Georgii Polkovnikov's rank in the Twelfth Regiment was that of a captain. In 1917 Polkovnikov was to become the last commander of the Petrograd Military District under the Provisional Government. He was shot by the Bolsheviks during the Civil War.[3] A Soviet source gives an additional detail: Captain Polkovnikov served with the Twelfth Regiment until July 1914, at which point he was transferred to the staff of the Eleventh Cavalry Division.[4] This means that he could not have led the charge of the Fourth Squadron of the Twelfth

Regiment in the battle for the town of Leshniuv on July 26 (August 8), 1914,[5] nor could he have fought with this squadron near Kamenka-Strumilova three weeks later, as he does in *The Quiet Don* (1:258, 336).

The rape of the maid Frania and Grigorii's saving the life of the commander of the Ninth Dragoon Regiment (1:242, 352) are among the stories that are grounded in reality. Captain Tsygankov of the Twelfth Regiment recorded them in his reminiscences, which he read to a group of officers in the winter of 1917-1918. One of his listeners was Sviatoslav Golubintsev, who believes that Tsygankov served as the prototype for Captain Kalmykov in *The Quiet Don*.[6] Be that as it may, the names of both captains are derived from the names of nationalities well known in the Don region: Gypsies and Kalmyks. As for the commander of the Ninth Dragoon Regiment, the historian Sergei Semanov established that his real name was Kuz'min-Korovaev, not Gustav Grozberg (1:352). Sholokhov either did not know this fact or deliberately chose to use a German name in order to allude to the large number of ethnic Germans in the Russian army, as the critic Petr Palievskii suggests.[7] The name fon (von) Divid occurs in the Cossack Uriupin's reference to the commander of the Eleventh Cavalry Division (1:355). Actually, the commander's name was De-Vitt.[8] The Cossack simplified it to a more familiar name. Sholokhov was probably not aware of this change; simplified forms of proper names, reflecting the Cossacks' way of pronouncing them, occur sporadically in his own narrative.

In the novel Uriupin speaks of fon Divid's thanking the Cossacks for recapturing a Russian battery from the Hungarian hussars (1:355). He has in mind the attack of the Fourth Squadron near Kamenka-Strumilova, in which Grigorii was wounded by a saber stroke and left unconscious on the battlefield (1:319). In all probability it was this encounter that Captain Tsygankov related to his fellow-officers, although in his story the battery was reportedly saved, not by the Cossacks, but by a squadron of the Eleventh Iziumskii Hussar Regiment.[9] It is difficult to ascertain whether the successful assault was actually made by the Cossacks or whether Sholokhov substituted them for the hussars out of artistic considerations.

For his minute description of the encounter between four Cossacks and a German mounted patrol to the west of Kal'variia, near the East Prussian border (1:281-285), Sholokhov is reported to have drawn primarily on oral information given to him by one of the participants, the Cossack Mikhail Ivankov of Karginskaia stanitsa.[10] The encounter was widely publicized in Russia as a heroic exploit of the Cossacks. One of them, Corporal Koz'ma (Kuz'ma) Kriuchkov, became a national hero. Accounts of the fighting vary a great deal with respect to individual details. Even stories written down as told by Kriuchkov show considerable differences. In one such story related to a fellow-Cossack, Kriuchkov emphasizes his defensive actions, saying nothing about the losses he inflicted upon the enemy. On the other hand, a newspaper and a jingoistic booklet quote Kriuchkov as saying that the Cossacks sent the Germans in flight and that he killed eleven of them.[11] The tone and content of Sholokhov's description of the encounter are closer to those of the story told by Kriuchkov to his fellow-Cossack, although there are several factual discrepancies between them. The main peculiarity of Sholokhov's version is that the Germans appear as dragoons armed with sabers *and* lances. This looks like an error. It was the uhlans who were equipped with both swords and lances. Kriuchkov was probably right in calling his adversaries uhlans.[12]

Sholokhov's intent to play down Kriuchkov's heroism reveals itself in the assertion that Kriuchkov had spent the rest of the war at the divisional staff headquarters, where he received three more Crosses of St. George without having seen any action (1:286). A Cossack who knew Kriuchkov personally admits that many people believe such stories. Kriuchkov, according to him, had served at divisional headquarters for only a brief period of time. He returned to his regiment voluntarily, ending the war as a platoon sergeant.[13]

Sholokhov is specific with respect to the locality where the fighting between the four Cossacks and the Germans occurred. He mentions places such as the small town of Pelikalie and the Aleksandrovskii farmstead, which can probably be found only on special maps. He might have heard these names from Ivankov. He also designates other Russian troops stationed in the area. There are references to the Third Infantry Corps and the 108th Infantry Regiment (1:275). However, the name of this regiment is Saratovskii, not Glebovskii.[14]

A curious discrepancy involves the surname of one of the four Cossacks. In all of the Soviet editions he is Astakhov. In the English translation of *The Quiet Don* published in Great Britain and the United States he is called Mrykhin (Mrikhin). Professor D. H. Stewart noticed the difference, suggesting that the English translation was made from a typescript that antedated the one used for the Soviet editions. The change, he thinks, was probably made by Sholokhov himself, "since Mrikhin was his prewar tutor."[15] There is, however, no evidence that the tutor, or any other Mrykhin, was among the four Cossacks—Astakhov, Kriuchkov, Ivankov, and Shchegol'kov.[16] Either Ivankov gave Sholokhov a wrong name (which is unlikely) or the author himself replaced Astakhov with Mrykhin (a common name in the Upper Don region) in order to remove any possibility of the reader's confusing him with Stepan Astakhov. In this case he might have changed his mind later for the sake of historical accuracy.

It is difficult, if not impossible, to find the sources used by Sholokhov for the descriptions of battles in which Lieutenant Evgenii Listnitskii took part in August-September 1914. It is also not quite clear where Listnitskii fought. He departed for the front from Petrograd in a train going to Warsaw. At his destination he encountered a local Belorussian peasant and a field hospital that is said to have been transferred from the southwestern front (1:321-322, 325). All this suggests that he must have arrived somewhere on the western front.

On the other hand, there are strong indications that Listnitskii came to the southwestern front. Even the presence of the Belorussian peasant can be seen as evidence of this. Sholokhov appears to have had a strange idea that the western Ukraine (Volyn') had a fairly large Belorussian population. For this reason a "tall, gray-haired Belorussian" is portrayed as an inhabitant of the Volynian village of Berestechko, located near the Austrian border (1:254). Actually, the Belorussians comprised less than one percent of the population in the entire Volyn' Province and must have been particularly scarce in its southwestern part where Berestechko and Radzivillov are located.[17] Furthermore, at the same time that he encounters the Belorussian, Listnitskii also meets a few wounded Cossacks of the Twelfth Don Cossack Regiment, which at that time was fighting in Galicia (1:325). Then the author tells us that the division in which Listnitskii served was given an order to cross the Styr' River and to take the enemy from the rear (1:327). At this time only the southern stretch of the river was near or in the combat zone. This means that Listnitskii's unit must have been deployed in the middle section of the southwestern front, probably to the north or northwest of Brody, where the Twelfth Don Cossack Regiment was fighting.

Indirect evidence in support of this assertion may be provided by a tentative identification of Listnitskii's regiment and its peacetime station. Although Sholokhov gives no information on these points, one may suggest that he placed Listnitskii in the Fifteenth Don Cossack Regiment. In volume 2 he writes that the regiment in which Listnitskii had once served belonged to the First Don Cossack Division and that during the advance of Kornilov's troops on Petrograd this regiment arrived at the town of Narva on August 28 (September 10), 1917 (2:145). According to a historical source, the only regiment of the First Division that arrived at Narva was the Fifteenth.[18] In fact, the First Don Cossack Division was composed of the Ninth, Tenth, Thirteenth, and Fifteenth Don Cossack Regiments and its peacetime station was the Zamost'e-Tomashov area in the Volyn' Province.[19] Thus the Twelfth and Fifteenth Don Cossack Regiments could not have fought far from each other. It is perhaps not accidental that on its march to the front the Twelfth Regiment encounters a unit identified by a character as the Ninth Don Cossack Regiment (1:254).

We next see Listnitskii taking part in a large cavalry attack "on the southwestern front in the area of Shevel' " on August 29 (September 11), 1914 (1:360-361). However, neither "Shevel' " nor the names of the villages mentioned earlier in connection with Listnitskii's service at the front could have been found on available maps. This adds to the uncertainty as to whether or not Sholokhov used published materials for the portrayal of battles in which Listnitskii fought. Be that as it may, individual episodes of these engagements are represented with such vivid detail that their sources can hardly be anything other than firsthand accounts enriched by the author's imagination.

Volume 2

The whole of the long chapter 3 of part 4 is devoted to an abortive Russian offensive against Kovel' and Vladimir Volynskii in October 1916. Clearly, Sholokhov used published materials here. He depicts operations of large formations, giving the correct numbers and names of Russian divisions and regiments and precise or only slightly changed names of localities. The area of the fighting can be seen on maps in part 5 of *Strategicheskii ocherk voiny 1914-1918 gg*. (*The Strategic Study of the War of 1914-1918*, 1920). This part covers operations up to October 1916, and one wonders whether Sholokhov used part 6, which could not be obtained. Individual episodes of the offensive, such as the fraternization between Valet and a German soldier or the graphic description of dead Russian officers, must have their origins in oral accounts and in the author's imagination.

If Sholokhov meticulously copied the numbers and names of Russian regiments employed in the battle for Kovel' and Vladimir Volynskii, he was less careful with designating a regiment in a fictional situation. After his desertion from the front, Bunchuk is said to have obtained papers bearing the name of a private of the 441st Orshanskii Regiment (2:25). The correct name of the 441st Regiment was Tverskii.[20]

Chapter 4 mentions some of Grigorii's war experiences from 1915 to November 1916. It is possible that here the author follows Kharlampii Ermakov's military career. Two points need clarification in this account. In one instance Grigorii remembers how in May (June) 1916 his regiment had broken through the front near Lutsk together with other troops of the Brusilov army (2:48). This was the Eighth Army, commanded at that time not by General Aleksei Brusilov, but by Aleksei Kaledin, the future Don ataman. In the second instance Grigorii recalls how he saved the life of the wounded Stepan Astakhov in the battle near the East Prussian town of Stallupönen (2:46-48). Sholokhov gives no date for this incident, but, to judge by the sequence of Grigorii's reminiscences, it must have occurred after July 1915. However, there could have been no fighting in the area of Stallupönen after the Russians had been driven out of East Prussia in mid-February 1915. I do not know whether the Twelfth Don Cossack Regiment went to East Prussia from Galicia and fought near Stallupönen in mid-November 1914 or in February 1915. If it did, Grigorii could not have been with it in November because he was on leave in Tatarskii at that time (1:376). If Sholokhov meant the fighting to have taken place in February 1915, he would have given some indication of the winter weather or landscape in his two-page portrayal of the battle. Yet his references to nature are so uncharacteristically vague that one gets the impression of his not being sure what season he is dealing with. To judge by the fact that Stepan tries to hide his uniform in a bush, one may conclude that the scene is set in any season but winter. Perhaps the author chose the East Prussian setting to dramatize the situation in which the wounded Stepan found himself. He faced certain death, for, as Sholokhov says, the Germans took no Cossack prisoner in East Prussia at that time, avenging the destruction of their towns by Cossack troops.[21]

Several clearly identifiable sources were used for the description of the Kornilov movement in chapters 11 through 20 of part 4. In chapter 11 a character recapitulates the main points of the memorandum that General Lavr Kornilov presented to the Provisional Government in response to his appointment as supreme commander-in-chief (2:101). The entire passage, numbering fifty-four words (from "in the memorandum" to "before the law"), was copied from Denikin's *The Russian Turmoil* with only two alterations: "Russia" was changed to "country" and the verb "indicated" was replaced by "insisted on" in the phrase "indicated the necessity of the following vital measures."[22] The purpose of the latter change was to impute dictatorial aspirations to Kornilov. Sholokhov must have copied in a hurry since he overlooked an obvious misprint in Denikin's book—the use of the word *zamkom* (instr. sing. for "lock") instead of *zakonom* (inst. sing. for "law"). As a result, the earliest edition of the novel contained the phrase "and the establishment of their [military committees'] responsibility before the lock." Because the phrase testified to Kornilov's respect for law, it has vanished from the novel since 1953, as have statements about Kornilov's proposal to use capital punishment for only "the most serious crimes, primarily military," and his advocacy of "revolutionary" courts-martial.

Chapter 12 offers a few examples of how information borrowed from printed sources is incorporated into a dialogue. In a conversation between the officers Kalmykov and Evgenii Listnitskii, the former says that "our Third Corps is being held in reserve on the Rumanian front" (2:116). This is a virtual verbatim reproduction of a phrase from General Aleksandr

Lukomskii's "Iz vospominanii" ("Reminiscences," 1922). The same applies to Listnitskii's assertion that "the Cossacks would not even think about the possibility of Kornilov's dismissal," and to Kalmykov's enthusiastic account of Kornilov's arrival at the Winter Palace with a squadron of his faithful Turkmen (*tekintsy*) and machine guns placed in automobiles (2:117, 118).[23]

Just before telling this story, Kalmykov read to Listnitskii the telegram which Mikhail Rodzianko sent to Kornilov on behalf of the "Conference of Public Figures" held in Moscow in August 1917. Sholokhov must have extracted all sixty-five words of the telegram from *The Russian Turmoil*. He might also have seen the text of the telegram in Evgenii Martynov's book *Kornilov* (1927). However, Martynov does not mention that the telegram was signed by Rodzianko, a fact which is noted in both *The Russian Turmoil* and *The Quiet Don*.[24] Either Denikin or Lukomskii could have provided material for Kalmykov's remarks about his being sent to Petrograd with secret instructions to put himself at the disposition of the Officers' Union (2:116-117).[25] This organization was to form officers' detachments for combatting Bolshevik attempts to seize power through an armed insurrection. The officers, Denikin writes, were dispatched to Petrograd under the pretext of studying bombing. This is precisely what Bunchuk says to himself about Kalmykov somewhat later (2:155).[26]

Lukomskii is the primary source of chapter 13, which portrays his role at the beginning of the Kornilov movement. The dependence on his "Reminiscences" is striking. At one point thirty-seven words spoken by him are borrowed without a single alteration, while Kornilov's reply to them loses merely four marginal words out of forty-five (2:120-121).[27] Some descriptive authorial passages contain phrases resembling those found in *The Russian Turmoil*. Thus, in a paragraph describing arrivals of various people at General Headquarters in Mogilev, Kornilov is said to have been viewed by the officers as "the banner of the restoration of Russia" (2:123). In Denikin's book Kornilov is "the banner of the counter-revolution for some, and the banner of the salvation of the motherland for others."[28] Next to the passages with clearly identifiable sources, one can find a number of paragraphs whose origin requires further investigation. This, for instance, is the case with several lines portraying the appearance of fon Vizin, assistant to the commissar of the Provisional Government at General Headquarters, who entered the room as Kornilov and Lukomskii were finishing their private conversation (2:121).

The first half of chapter 14 presents a picture of the enthusiastic welcome Kornilov received upon his arrival at the Aleksandrovskii Station in Moscow. According to Viktor Gura, the source for this description of the arrival ceremonies is a detailed report on Kornilov published in the Moscow newspaper *Russkoe slovo* (*Russian Word*) on August 15 (28), 1917. This is a debatable assertion, since the more likely source appears to be an equally detailed account of the general's arrival found in Martynov's *Kornilov*. There is strong evidence that Sholokhov used this book for the description of some other events, and the scene of Kornilov's arrival in *The Quiet Don* evinces more textual similarities with Martynov's account than with the newspaper report. For example, the report makes no mention of the Turkmen's forming "two lines" in front of Kornilov's railway coach, and, more importantly, it says nothing about well-dressed women showering Kornilov with flowers (2:124-125).[29] At one point, however, Sholokhov and the newspaper identify a French colonel as a "military attaché," while Martynov calls him a "military agent." One can only speculate as to whether this is a coincidence or a sign that Sholokhov also read *Russkoe slovo*.

The second half of chapter 14 is taken up by a conversation between Kornilov and Kaledin, ataman of the Don Cossacks, during the Moscow State Conference. It is not possible to speak of a specific source for this scene. The conversation was private and neither general left any extensive information about it. Kaledin gave a brief report on it to the Don Cossack Parliament (*Voiskovoi Krug*) in September 1917, without citing a word of direct discourse.[30] Thus Sholokhov must have composed a two-page dialogue on the basis of what he knew from secondary sources about the views and personalities of the generals. Compared with his slavish copying of conversations between Lukomskii and Kornilov in the preceding chapter, this was a drastic change of technique. The reason for the about-face was political. Sholokhov intended to create the impression that Kornilov and Kaledin had organized a far-reaching conspiracy to crush the Bolshevik movement and to force the Provisional Government to accept their demands concerning the reorganization of the Russian army. The generals' own words had to justify the author's conclusion that "from now on the threads of a great conspiracy stretched out like a black spider web . . . throughout the Cossack lands from end to end" (2:128).

To achieve his goal, Sholokhov mixed truth with fabrication. What Kornilov says in the novel about the indecisiveness of the Provisional Government, the demoralization of the Russian army, and the urgent need to establish discipline has parallels in works by Denikin, Lukomskii, and Martynov.[31] When Kaledin expresses his agreement with Kornilov's ideas, one might think that Sholokhov had read *Kornilov* or volume 2 of *Donskaia letopis'* (*The Don Chronicle*).[32] Yet Sholokhov goes too far in making the generals agree on large-scale cooperation in carrying out conspiratorial designs (2:127). There exists no evidence that Kaledin cooperated with Kornilov when the latter ordered troops to move on Petrograd some ten days later. Accusations of mutiny brought against Kaledin by the Provisional Government proved to be false.[33]

Equally spurious is Kornilov's threat "I shall not hesitate to lay the front open" (2:127). This is supposed to demonstrate that the general was prepared to commit treason in order to pressure the Provisional Government into acceptance of his program. Actually, at the Moscow State Conference, Kornilov spoke of the dangerous situation on the Riga front, warning that it could lead to the capture of Petrograd by the enemy. Somewhat later the Bolsheviks used this statement to make "a preposterous charge that Kornilov had intentionally surrendered Riga to the Germans."[34]

The historical unsoundness of the Kornilov-Kaledin dialogue in *The Quiet Don* is further enhanced by factual inaccuracies. Sholokhov has the generals meet on August 14 (27) in the Bol'shoi Theater, where the State Conference was held (2:126). In reality, they met in Kornilov's train on August 13 (26).[35] Sholokhov also errs in saying that the meeting occurred an hour before Kaledin was to announce "The Declaration of the Twelve Cossack Military Regions" (2:128), since the announcement took place on August 14 (27). It is improbable that Kornilov would invite Kaledin and others to visit him "after the session" for a further discussion of their cooperation (2:127). According to Kaledin, he had only one meeting with Kornilov.[36] There was hardly any time for a second meeting.[37]

The subject of chapters 15 through 18 is the Kornilov "mutiny": an abortive attempt to occupy Petrograd which ended with the arrest of its principal organizers by the Provisional Government. To place his descriptions of the movements and moods of Kornilov's troops in their historical context, Sholokhov turns to several printed sources. Here, more often than in other sections of his novel, he introduces historical documents. The first of them is Kornilov's appeal to the people of Russia, announcing his break with the Provisional Government (2:131-132). Its text must have been quoted from Lukomskii's "Reminiscences."[38] The source of the next document, the telegram sent by Kornilov to Kaledin on August 29 (September 11), is probably Martynov (2:142).[39] The telegram was prompted by reports that Kaledin had cabled an ultimatum to the Provisional Government, threatening to cut off supplies to Moscow should Kornilov's program be rejected. The reports turned out to be wrong. Since Sholokhov gives no information on the background of Kornilov's telegram, the reader of *The Quiet Don* is left with the impression that Kaledin was actively involved in the Kornilov "mutiny."

There can be little doubt that Sholokhov is indebted to Martynov for the text of the telegram which General Ivan Romanovskii sent on August 27 (September 9) to the commander of the Third Cavalry Corps and to the commanders of three divisions, including the so-called Native Division, which was manned by members of national minorities from the Caucasus. It is hardly accidental that the authors of *Kornilov* and *The Quiet Don* introduce the text of the telegram with an identical phrase: "a copy of the following telegram from the staff of the northern front" (2:145).[40] However, the recipient of the telegram in *The Quiet Don* is not General Aleksandr Krymov, as in *Kornilov*, but Prince Bagration. The discrepancy might be due to Sholokhov's oversight or to his belief that Bagration should also have received the telegram. Indeed, Sholokhov refers to Bagration as the "commander of the Native Division" (2:145), that is, as one of the persons to whom the telegram was addressed.[41]

The text of Romanovskii's telegram is followed by a paragraph concerning Bagration's telegram to Kornilov. This telegram deals with Kerenskii's order to bring all the troops that were advancing on Petrograd back to their original stations. Simultaneously, Bagration communicated that "the division's troop trains have been held up on the way between the Gachki junction and the Oredezh station because the railroad, in compliance with the Provisional Government's instructions, would not hand out any staffs [a symbol of authorization to proceed]" (2:145). Sholokhov borrowed this phrase from Martynov with only two alterations. He transposed the words "the Oredezh station" and "the Gachki junction" and did not enclose the phrase in quotation marks. In the next sentence he again turned to Martynov for the text of Kornilov's reply to Bagration's telegram (2:145).[42]

The last document used in the section under discussion is Kornilov's appeal to the Cossacks dated August 28 (September 10), 1917, which Kalmykov reads to a Cossack meeting (2:156-157). Apart from a corrected misprint and occasional differences in punctuation, the language of the appeal in *The Quiet Don* is identical to that printed in *The Don Chronicle*.[43] The text of the appeal in this collection, and in the novel, is complete. Other sources that Sholokhov is known to have used for his description of the Kornilov movement either ignore the appeal or cite only excerpts from it.

Every one of the six editions of *The Quiet Don* brought out in 1929 by the publishing house Moskovskii rabochii (The Moscow Worker) contains in chapter 17 a facsimile of a map showing the distribution of Kornilov's troops on the road to Petrograd. It must have been based on Denikin's hand-drawn plan, which is reproduced in his book under the caption "Troop Trains of Gen. Krymov en route to Petrograd on August 29, 1917."[44] Sholokhov's map has the same title, the same legend, and the same number of places as Denikin's plan. But the writer gives a wrong date in the caption (August 18) and fails to differentiate between two formations to the south of the town of Dno. The first discrepancy must have been due to an oversight, while the second could have been caused by an unclear printing of symbols in Denikin's book.

Denikin's plan must also have been the source for Sholokhov's debatable assertion that the First Don Cossack Division was moved up to Petrograd along the Revel' (Tallin)-Vezenberg-Narva railway (2:145), i.e., in an easterly direction along the Gulf of Finland. This is the route indicated by symbols on Denikin's plan. Strange as it may seem, the general was probably wrong. Another general, Martynov, who carefully studied movements of Kornilov's troops, says that only one regiment of the First Division was sent to Narva—by mistake. And it was sent, not from Revel', but from Pskov. The bulk of the division was assembled in the Pskov area and was moved north along the Pskov-Luga-Petrograd and the Dno-Petrograd railways.[45]

General Petr Krasnov's article "On the Inner Front" was the principal source for Sholokhov's portrayal of the confusion, frustration, and delays experienced by Kornilov's troops on their way to Petrograd. The first six paragraphs of chapter 17 follow closely the wording of selected passages from chapters 4 and 5 of Krasnov's article.[46] Some phrases, however, appear to be lifted from Martynov; for example, "Mounted Ingush patrols penetrated up to the Somrino station" (2:144).[47]

Martynov might also have been a source for the opening paragraphs of chapter 18, which contain general remarks about the failure of the Kornilov movement and about a delicate mission of General Alekseev to arrest Kornilov and his associates (2:162-163).[48] On the other hand, it was definitely Lukomskii who provided information for a more detailed portrayal of the conference that Kornilov held with his staff members to determine a course of action. Apparently because of its importance, Kornilov's verdict is quoted word for word: "Further resistance would be both foolish and criminal" (2:163).[49] There are signs that Sholokhov handled the historical aspect of chapter 18 somewhat carelessly. He mistakenly asserts that General Alekseev was appointed supreme commander-in-chief to succeed Kornilov (2:163). In fact, Alekseev refused the offer of the position. Kornilov was replaced by Kerenskii, and Alekseev served briefly as the latter's chief of staff. In the last paragraph of the chapter Sholokhov speaks of the Kornilov movement's coming to "an inglorious end" in Bykhov. Unless the reader is familiar with the history of the Kornilov movement, he will see no connection between it and the small provincial town whose name has not been mentioned before. Sholokhov failed to say that ten days after their arrest in Mogilev, Kornilov and his associates had been transferred to Bykhov, about thirty miles south of Mogilev.

Chapter 20 may be regarded as an epilogue to the Kornilov movement. It describes the stay of Kornilov and his followers in the Bykhov prison, ending with the flight of the last five prisoners when their lives are threatened by an approaching Red detachment. The beginning of the chapter, portraying the prisoners' daily routine, is based on the firsthand accounts of Lukomskii and Denikin (2:170).[50] A small detail indicates that Denikin might have been Sholokhov's favorite source here. In both *The Quiet Don* and *The Russian Turmoil* Kornilov and his associates are said to have been held in a girls' high school that was converted into a prison (2:170). In Lukomskii's ''Reminiscences'' it is an old Catholic monastery that serves as a makeshift prison.[51]

The rest of the chapter manifests an outright reliance on Denikin. The closest borrowings are to be found in the text of Kornilov's letter to the new supreme commander-in-chief, General Nikolai Dukhonin (2:171-172),[52] and in the characters' direct speech. A case in point is an oral report given to Kornilov by Colonel Kusonskii, a messenger from General Headquarters: ''In four hours Krylenko will arrive in Mogilev, which General Headquarters will surrender without resistance. General Dukhonin has instructed me to *inform* you that all prisoners must leave Bykhov *at once*'' (2:173). Except for the two italicized words, which are synonymous with the words given by Denikin, Sholokhov copied Kusonskii's report verbatim, and a few lines below he took down Kornilov's order to the prison commandant word for word: ''Release the generals immediately. The Turkmen must be ready to leave by midnight. I am going with the regiment'' (2:173).[53]

Haste was probably the main reason why Sholokhov committed at least two factual errors in chapter 20 in passages based on Denikin's book. One error is the assertion that Kornilov wrote a letter to several powerful bankers asking them to help the families of the officers who had participated in his movement (2:170). According to Denikin, the author of the letter was General Alekseev. The other error is the statement that Dukhonin ''immediately'' canceled his order to have the prisoners sent off by train to the Don region (2:172). In Denikin's book he did it several hours later.[54]

The last chapter of part 4 relates the story of the Twelfth Don Cossack Regiment from its retreat on the Rumanian front up to its return to the Don region. The story was probably written on the basis of oral accounts. Those who are familiar with the regiment's journey through the Ukraine do not question the overall accuracy of Sholokhov's story except for one episode: the execution of the regimental adjutant Chirkovskii, sentenced to death by the Cossacks themselves and shot by a Cossack and a Red Guard sailor at a Ukrainian station (2:180). Sviatoslav Golubintsev, who was with the regiment from the beginning to the end of its journey, claims that none of its officers were mistreated or killed by the Cossacks. Golubintsev made friends with the regimental adjutant, Lieutenant Cherkesov, and said good-bye to him in the Don region. Ivan Sagatskii, who heard about the regiment's journey home from its commander and another senior officer, also dismisses, as Sholokhov's invention, the sentencing and execution of the adjutant.[55]

A rather extensive use of printed historical sources in part 4 allows one to make a few remarks about Sholokhov's adaptation of them for his political and artistic purposes, particularly in the representation of the Kornilov movement. Almost all of these sources were authored by White émigrés who sympathized with Kornilov's aims and/or took part in his movement. The White sources offered, and still offer, a more authoritative picture of the movement than their Soviet counterparts, and it was only logical that Sholokhov turned to them for factual historical material. I do not know how Sholokhov managed to read these books, but they must have been much more readily available in the 1920s than at the present. A good deal of what their authors wrote about the Kornilov movement was not deemed unprintable as late as 1928. In that year the Leningrad publishing house Krasnaia gazeta (Red Gazette) brought out a collection entitled *Miatezh Kornilova: Iz belykh memuarov* (*Kornilov's Rebellion: From White Memoirs*), which included long extracts from Denikin's *The Russian Turmoil* and Krasnov's "On the Inner Front." The collection must have come out when Sholokhov had already completed part 4 of *The Quiet Don*.

No doubt Sholokhov's views on the Kornilov movement were closer to those of the Bolsheviks than to those of the generals. This is the chief reason why his borrowings from the generals' writings underwent certain political modifications. For example, if Lukomskii quotes Kornilov as saying "I am not seeking anything for myself and I do not want anything. All I want is to save Russia and I shall unquestioningly obey the Provisional Government when it is cleansed and strengthened," Sholokhov changes the quotation to read "As for the Provisional Government . . . well, we shall see about it. . . . I am not seeking anything for myself. . . . To save Russia . . . to save it regardless of anything, at all cost!" (2:122.)[56] A clear expression of unselfish and overriding concern for Russia is transformed into vague, elliptical phrases implying threats to the Provisional Government and presenting Kornilov as an assertive and reckless individual. This characterization provides justification for putting into his mouth the threat to open the front in order to force the Provisional Government into acceptance of his recommendations for a reorganization of the Russian army. In another instance Sholokhov faithfully follows Lukomskii in reproducing Kornilov's description of the Bolsheviks as traitors who deserve to be hanged (2:122), but he refrains from quoting or paraphrasing Kornilov's statement about the Bolsheviks' and Lenin's cooperation with the Germans.

This collaboration must have been the main cause of Kornilov's hatred for the Bolsheviks, for in his eyes the Germans were Russia's "primordial enemy."[57]

Elsewhere Sholokhov altered a phrase from *The Russian Turmoil* to stress the involvement of the upper stratum of the Russian bourgeoisie in the Kornilov movement. Denikin writes that in the Bykhov prison Kornilov received 40,000 rubles from Moscow, possibly in response to Alekseev's call to leading financiers to assist the families of the officers arrested in connection with the Kornilov movement. In *The Quiet Don* the bankers "promptly sent some tens of thousands of rubles, fearing embarrassing disclosures" (2:170). This phrase is designed to imply an active and generous support of Kornilov by financial magnates. With this aim in mind, Sholokhov chooses to omit the fact that the money arrived after a long delay and that it could barely cover the most urgent needs.[58]

As an artist, Sholokhov faced the task of transforming the matter-of-fact accounts of his printed sources into imaginative prose. He did this using the standard devices of a fiction writer. Much more often than the authors of his sources he would take notice of immediate surroundings, or describe outward appearances, faces, postures, actions, manners of speaking, and movements of individuals, or dramatize situations by converting indirect discourse into dialogue. A good example of this fictionalization is his rendition of the initial stage of the conversation between Kornilov and Lukomskii concerning the purpose of transferring cavalry formations from the southwestern front (2:120). In Lukomskii's "Reminiscences" this part of the conversation is reported in the form of indirect discourse in three consecutive paragraphs.[59] Sholokhov transformed the indirect discourse into a dialogue and interspersed it with descriptions of the characters' faces, bodily movements, and their manner of speaking, as well as with references to pieces of furniture. Now and then, one may question the verisimilitude of some such details. For example, it looks very strange that Kornilov, answering a question, would be "touching Lukomskii's knee with his hand." At this point relations between the two generals were strictly formal. Lukomskii had not yet been let in on Kornilov's secret plans. Apart from these considerations, touching a peer's knee could hardly have been a custom among tsarist generals. No less preposterous is Kornilov's "twisting a metal button" on Kaledin's tunic during their confidential exchange (2:127).

Occasionally, Sholokhov develops his insertions into long passages. A case in point is the second half of chapter 16. It is devoted primarily to the conversation between Kornilov and Romanovskii, during which the former tries to catch a butterfly and then relates a dream that he had the night before. The chapter ends with a landscape featuring the micalike surface of the Dnieper and hazy fields (2:143). The author apparently invented the whole passage in order to present Kornilov not only as a historical figure but also as a human being.

Part 5 of *The Quiet Don* deals with the initial stage of the Civil War in the Don region. It introduces new historical figures and describes political and military events in detail. Historical material for these descriptions came from Soviet and White sources in about equal proportions. The first nine chapters cover the period from the late fall of 1917 up to the negotiations between the Red Cossack delegation and the Don Government in January 1918. The central historical figure in this section is Fedor Podtelkov, the leader of the Red Cossacks; the focal event is the battle for Rostov. In this section we encounter a new source, the brochure *Orly revoliutsii* (*Eagles of the Revolution*, 1920) by the political functionary Aron Frenkel', which contains a reprint of Podtelkov's autobiography. From it Sholokhov might have borrowed information about Podtelkov's birthplace and his latest residence (2:190).[60] However, Podtelkov tells much more about the location of his native village in the novel than he does in his autobiography. The probable cause of this topographical precision is that Podtelkov's birthplace is located not far from Pleshakov, where Sholokhov lived.

The text of Podtelkov's address at a meeting in Kamenskaia has its origin in Frenkel''s brochure, although it might have come into the novel via M. Korchin's book *The Battle for the Soviets in the Don Region* (1947), where it is reprinted verbatim (2:224-225).[61] This strongly pro-Bolshevik address was inserted in the novel in 1953, probably by the editors. The language of the address is too literary, and Sholokhov in all likelihood would have made changes in it. Moreover, this is not the address that Podtelkov delivered in Kamenskaia. Frenkel' states that the text of the address given in his brochure represents a typical example of Podtelkov's speeches to the Cossacks. Actually, Podtelkov's address in Kamenskaia was quite different. A. Mandel'shtam, a Moscow Bolshevik who heard Podtelkov's address in Kamenskaia, called it "very much confused and quite cowardly."[62] It must be said that throughout his brochure Frenkel' tends to overemphasize Podtelkov's ties with the Bolsheviks, while glossing over his political flaws.

Two serious political shortcomings of Podtelkov—his objection to sharing the Cossack land with the peasants and his refusal to supply arms to the Red miners (2:192, 242-243)—must have appeared in the novel as a result of Sholokhov's reading *Notes about the Civil War* (1924-1933), by Vladimir Antonov-Ovseenko, and *How the Revolution Was Fought* (1925-1926), by Nikolai Kakurin.[63] In 1953 the censors deleted Podtelkov's arguments against allotting the Cossack land to the peasants and shifted the responsibility for keeping arms from the miners to an anonymous member of the Cossack Revolutionary Committee. Both of these revisions have been retained in all subsequent editions.

The description of how the White Volunteer Army came into being was probably based on what Denikin said about it in *The Russian Turmoil*. Some of Sholokhov's phrases sound like Denikin's (2:193).[64] Nonetheless, Sholokhov tries to discredit the anti-Bolshevik forces by suggesting, among other things, that there were people who joined the Whites because of "higher pay." According to Denikin, the White recruiting organization had only 400 rubles in November 1917. There must have been several printed sources on which Sholokhov relied for his portrayal of the battle for Rostov. One of them appears to be *Eagles of the Revolution*. For instance, phrases about the Cossacks' refusal to move beyond Aksaiskaia stanitsa, the formation of the so-called patchwork detachments by General Alekseev, and the duration and bitterness of the fighting (2:194, 212) have visible lexical parallels in Frenkel''s brochure.[65]

The second half of chapter 8 depicts a stormy session at the Congress of the Front-Line Cossacks in Kamenskaia on January 10 (23), 1918. It is difficult to pinpoint any specific oral or printed source for this depiction. A possible exception is the last paragraph, in which Khristonia relates how the chairman of the Kamenskaia draft board resisted arrest (2:224). This episode is mentioned by Antonov-Ovseenko.[66] One of the passionate anti-Kaledin speeches was delivered at the Congress by a miners' delegate whom Sholokhov identified as Sergei Syrtsov, a prominent Bolshevik leader in the Don region (2:219). One wonders whether the author confused Syrtsov with Efim Shchadenko, another leading Bolshevik from that area. A Red Cossack who attended the Congress and Syrtsov himself state that the speaker for the miners was Shchadenko.[67] Syrtsov's name disappeared from the novel in 1936 and he himself was liquidated two years later.

In the second half of chapter 9, Sholokhov describes negotiations between the Don Government delegation and members of the Don Cossack Military Revolutionary Committee in Kamenskaia. The author must have used more than one printed source for his description of these negotiations. However, the only likely source that I was able to find is an article entitled " 'Parity,' " by Georgii Ianov, a former member of the Don Government. Some of Sholokhov's details pertaining to the arrival of the Government delegation and to its negotiations are identical with those found in " 'Parity' " (2:225).[68] On the other hand, Sholokhov is more specific about the names of speakers and the contents of their speeches. Also, he differs slightly from Ianov in listing the names of the Don Government delegates as well as the names of the delegates of the Cossack Revolutionary Committee who were sent to Novocherkassk after the negotiations in Kamenskaia. In the latter case Ianov gives six names, Sholokhov seven. The seventh member—S. Kudinov—might have been added from F. G. Kosov's record of the negotiations in Novocherkassk, the seat of the Don Government.[69]

The journey of the Revolutionary Committee's delegates to Novocherkassk and their reception there are depicted in the first half of chapter 10. The abundance of detail and dialogue in these scenes leaves little doubt that the author's imagination played a decisive part in creating them. The situation is different in the second half of the chapter, where the portrayal of the negotiations between the Don Government and the delegation of the revolutionary Cossacks reveals a reliance on identifiable printed sources. The text of the ultimatum presented by the Cossack Revolutionary Committee to the Don Government was probably copied from Antonov-Ovseenko's *Notes about the Civil War* (2:229-230).[70] The greater part of Sholokhov's depiction of the debates that followed the presentation of the ultimatum must have been based on Kosov's record. One of Podtelkov's statements contains several sentences identical with those cited by Kosov (2:233).[71] However, Sholokhov the politician injected into Podtelkov's statement a few phrases which portray the Don Government as unpopular and responsible for unleashing the Civil War. At the same time he discarded the words "We are Cossacks, not Bolsheviks" from Podtelkov's reply to one of Kaledin's questions (2:231).[72] The elimination of this self-characterization concealed Podtelkov's aloofness from the Bolsheviks. Actually, Podtelkov and his closest associate, Mikhail Krivoshlykov, were populists who advocated the equality of all working Cossacks under their own government. Frenkel' admits that Podtelkov and Krivoshlykov never called themselves Communists and toward the end of their lives referred to themselves as left-wing Socialist Revolutionaries.[73]

In addition to Kosov's record, a recognizable source for Sholokhov's portrayal of the Novocherkassk negotiations is Ianov's " 'Parity.' " From this article Sholokhov took almost verbatim the vehement denunciation of Podtelkov by Junior Captain Shein, along with the characterization of the captain as one who had risen from the ranks and held four crosses of the Order of St. George (2:234).[74] Among other borrowings from Ianov are Podtelkov's demand for the resignation of the Don Government, beginning with the words "You're laughing now," and Kaledin's reply to Podtelkov, beginning with "You said that if we hand over power to you" (2:233, 235).[75] Sholokhov transferred all twenty-eight words of Kaledin's reply without any changes, but he substituted colloquialisms for several literary expressions in the language of Podtelkov and Shein. He did the same thing to Kosov's renditions of Podtelkov's language.

Another example of an artistic transformation of factual material can be seen in the treatment of Ianov's phrase "Podtelkov quickly, almost in one breath, drank glass after glass of water without stopping.''[76] The fictionalized version of this phrase reads: ''With a smile, Podtelkov reached for the decanter, poured himself another glass of water, and drank quickly. He was parched with thirst. It looked as if he were pouring clear water, which covered the sides of the decanter with bubbles, over a big fire that was burning inside of him'' (2:231).[77]

At the beginning of chapter 11, Sholokhov cites the two-page response of the Don Government to the demands of the Cossack Revolutionary Committee which he copied from Antonov-Ovseenko's *Notes about the Civil War* (2:235-237).[78] This work is also the source of the next two paragraphs dealing with the military operations of the White partisan detachment commanded by Captain Vasilii Chernetsov.[79]

Chapter 12 portrays in copious detail the fighting between the Chernetsov partisans and the Red Cossacks near the railroad station of Glubokaia, the capture of Chernetsov, and the massacre of the White prisoners on Podtelkov's orders. I was unable to discern any specific sources which Sholokhov might have used for his description of these events. It appears that he relied a great deal on oral stories from participants, one of whom might have been Kharlampii Ermakov. Like Grigorii Melekhov, he served with the Red Cossacks at the beginning of the Civil War. Furthermore, Sholokhov resorted to poetic license, notably in the controversial scene of Podtelkov's killing of the captured Chernetsov. The author's version of the killing is quite different from the versions found in both Red and White descriptions of this incident. Sholokhov certainly read in Antonov-Ovseenko's book the reports by Syrtsov and the Cossack Revolutionary Committee. According to these reports, some forty captured officers and cadets were killed by their escort when they attempted to escape. At the same time Chernetsov tried to shoot Podtelkov, but the latter cut him down with his saber.[80] In all likelihood Sholokhov was also familiar with the more detailed description of Chernetsov's end in *The Don Chronicle*. He could have learned from it that Chernetsov, who had been wounded in the leg, was put on horseback by his captors and rode side by side with Podtelkov. The Red Cossacks abused their prisoners and Podtelkov threatened to do Chernetsov in. At an opportune moment Chernetsov hit Podtelkov in the face with his fist and shouted to the prisoners, ''Our men are coming! Forward!'' The prisoners ran in different directions. Some of those who escaped told how Podtelkov cut down Chernetsov with his saber; others said that Chernetsov killed Podtelkov.[81]

In *The Quiet Don* the two adversaries confront each other not on horseback but on foot. In a heated exchange Chernetsov calls Podtelkov a betrayer of the Cossacks and threatens him with retribution. Podtelkov cuts his enemy down and gives the command to kill all the prisoners

(2:252). The author seems to have dismounted the two foes in order to heighten the tension by making them meet each other face to face. More significant, however, is the fact that the killing of Chernetsov and his men looks more like a murder in *The Quiet Don* than in the White accounts. Whether Sholokhov based his version on an unknown source or whether he intended to stress the cruelty of the Civil War by depicting the slaughter of White prisoners as an act of unprovoked violence is a matter of speculation. In any event, Podtelkov's order to cut down the prisoners detracts from his image as a Revolutionary hero.

This explains why the censors of the 1953 edition of the novel saw it necessary to present Podtelkov's killing of Chernetsov as an act of self-defense. In their version Chernetsov tries to shoot Podtelkov by suddenly drawing a concealed revolver, which misfires. This incident, however, was not invented by the censors. It had, for instance, been mentioned in an article by Nikolai Turoverov, a former Chernetsov partisan, in the book *The Don on Fire* (1927) by Dan. Delert, and in an article by Dmitrii Pototskii, a White general. In the last account it is Podtelkov himself who tells about the incident.[82] Sholokhov might not have seen the two articles by the White Russian émigrés, but he most likely read Delert's book published in Rostov. To the great disappointment of hard-line Soviet critics, Sholokhov restored his original version in 1956. The restoration was essential for the plot of the novel, for Podtelkov's slaughter of Chernetsov and the other prisoners was an important reason why Grigorii Melekhov turned away from the Reds.

The material for the opening paragraphs of chapter 15 came from Antonov-Ovseenko's book. Sholokhov copied from it the text of the telegram sent to Antonov-Ovseenko by the Don Cossack Military Revolutionary Committee on January 19 (February 1). The telegram, announcing the recognition of the central Soviet Government, was signed by Krivoshlykov and six other members of the Cossack Revolutionary Committee (2:272).[83] The names of Antonov-Ovseenko and of all six of the signatories have been missing from the novel since 1941. Antonov-Ovseenko was liquidated no later than 1939 as an "enemy of the people." The signatories might have been found guilty by association, or the names of some of them might have come to be considered unprintable for other reasons. However, it is hard to find a cause of the removal of Krivoshlykov's signature. He has always been treated as a Revolutionary hero and his name has not been purged from other passages in the novel. Although Antonov-Ovseenko has long been "posthumously rehabilitated," his name is still being kept out of the novel.

Sholokhov is also indebted to Antonov-Ovseenko for information about operations of the Red troops led by Rudol'f Sivers and about the insurrection of the workers in the Baltic Works in Taganrog. The author, for example, copied precisely the figures of material losses suffered by Sivers in the fight against Colonel Aleksandr Kutepov near the station of Neklinovka: one cannon, twenty-four machine guns, and one armored car (2:273).[84]

The greater part of chapter 15 is devoted to the last day in Ataman Kaledin's life. Since Sholokhov relied here on at least two publications, one should be particularly careful in determining which source was used for each individual passage. The narrative about Kaledin begins with the information that on January 28 (February 10) Kornilov sent Kaledin a telegram saying that the Volunteer Army would abandon Rostov and move into the Kuban' region (2:273). The information could have been taken from Denikin's *The Russian Turmoil*, or Ianov's " 'Parity,' " or Nikolai Mel'nikov's "Aleksei Maksimovich Kaledin." Ianov and, especially, Denikin seem to be the principal sources. Words about "abandoning Rostov" occur only in Ianov's article, and it is only in Denikin's account that Kaledin opens the session by reading telegrams from Alekseev and Kornilov. In Ianov's article Kaledin reads Kornilov's telegram after making a few remarks on the military situation, and in Mel'nikov's article he reads it toward the end of the session. Denikin is also the only one who gives the date on which Kornilov sent his telegram.[85]

The next phrase—"At 9 a.m. on the 29th an extraordinary session of the Don Government was convened in the Ataman's Palace"—may be a variation of a similar phrase in either Ianov's or Mel'nikov's articles. By coincidence or not, the first word in the expression "extraordinary session" (*ekstrennoe soveshchanie*) is identical with the first word used by Mel'nikov (*ekstrennoe zasedanie*), while the second word is identical with the second word used by Ianov (*srochnoe soveshchanie*). Both Mel'nikov and Ianov say that the session was held in the Ataman's Palace. There are two things in Ianov's favor, however. First, he gives the precise hour of the meeting, while Mel'nikov does not. Second, there is no conclusive evidence that Sholokhov drew upon Mel'nikov's article in the subsequent portrayal of Kaledin's last day.

In *The Quiet Don* Kaledin reports that all he has for the defense of the Don region and Novocherkassk is 147 bayonets (2:273). This phrase is based on Denikin's account. One finds in it lexical similarities and the same number of bayonets. In contrast, Ianov speaks of "100-150 bayonets." Kaledin concludes his report with a forty-six-word statement beginning with "The situation is hopeless" and ending with "I am resigning as ataman of the Don Cossacks" (2:274). Except for the insertion of a preposition, the statement is taken verbatim from Denikin.[86]

This statement is followed by a conversation among the members of the

Don Government in the course of which they offer their resignations, decide to turn over their power to the City Duma, and schedule a meeting with representatives of the Duma for 4 p.m. (2:274). All these items are mentioned in Ianov's and Mel'nikov's articles, and Ianov again emerges as Sholokhov's more likely source. Several of Sholokhov's words are identical with Ianov's and—more importantly—both authors speak of the City Duma, whereas Mel'nikov refers to the City Council (*gorodskaia uprava*).[87]

Sholokhov clearly relied on Denikin in reproducing Kaledin's admonition to the members of the Don Government. In the novel the ataman says: "Gentlemen, be brief. Time is pressing. You know Russia has perished because of too much talk. I declare a recess for half an hour. Talk things over and . . . let us finish this as soon as possible" (2:275). The first three sentences are borrowed word for word from *The Russian Turmoil*.[88] Mel'nikov's version of Kaledin's admonition also contains the words "Russia has perished because of too much talk," but the rest of it is different. Ianov's version contains no mention of Kaledin's admonition. However, Sholokhov must have taken Kaledin's words about the recess from Ianov.[89]

When Sholokhov used *The Russian Turmoil* to copy the first three sentences of Kaledin's admonition, he reached the point where he had taken from Denikin practically everything that he said about Kaledin's last day. When he had to choose among Denikin, Ianov, and Mel'nikov (if he had read Mel'nikov), Sholokhov invariably preferred the general as his source. He might have been impressed by the clarity and conciseness of Denikin's account. On the other hand, he went far beyond Denikin's brief statement that Kaledin ended his life by shooting himself through the heart. He wrote two pages about the incidents immediately preceding and following the ataman's death. The principal (possibly the only) source for these pages was Ianov's eyewitness account in his " 'Parity.' " Some phrases were borrowed almost word for word. Here is one example. Ianov: "On the cot lay a 'Colt.' On the back of the chair a field jacket hung neatly. A wristwatch was on the small table." Sholokhov: "On the cot lay a Colt. . . . Near the cot a field jacket was neatly hung on the back of the chair, and a wristwatch was on the small table" (2:276).[90]

In many places Sholokhov enlivens Ianov's matter-of-fact reporting by dramatizing situations and adding various details. For example, all Ianov says about the reaction of a Don Government member to Kaledin's death is: "Turning his face to the window, G. I. Karev sobbed." Sholokhov expanded it to "Karev was hunched over the window, his fingers clutching its gilt knob. His shoulder blades were moving convulsively under his coat; every now and then he shuddered violently. The hollow animal-like wailing of an adult nearly knocked Bogaevskii off his feet'' (2:276).[91] The author of *The Quiet Don* also added a not-too-subtle symbol—the cawing of crows—which suggests that Kaledin and his cause were doomed (2:274, 277).

Historical events that immediately follow Kaledin's suicide are depicted in chapter 18. Sholokhov must have written it, especially the first page, with the aid of several printed sources. The beginning sentence of the chapter—''After Kaledin's death Novocherkasskaia stanitsa handed over authority to the Campaign Ataman of the Don Military Region, General Nazarov''—is almost identical to the one found in Konstantin Kakliugin's article on Nazarov in *The Don Chronicle*. The second sentence says that on February 4 (17) the Don Cossack Parliament elected Nazarov ataman of the Don Cossacks (2:283). This information probably comes from General Isaak Bykadorov's reminiscences of Nazarov published together with Kakliugin's article. Bykadorov must also have been the source for the characterization of Nazarov as ''a vigorous and ebullient general'' and, particularly, for the observation that, sensing an inevitable defeat by the Bolsheviks, the general ''would sit leaning on his arm, holding his hand against his forehead, as though lost in painful meditation'' (2:284).[92] Sholokhov probably had *The Russian Turmoil* before him when he wrote that Nazarov had proclaimed mobilization of the Cossacks from seventeen to fifty-five years of age (2:283). The same figures may also be found in V. Volin's *The Don and the Volunteer Army* (1919), but Sholokhov is not likely to have read it.[93]

Sholokhov appears to have turned to at least two sources for his description of the arrival of the Sixth Don Cossack Regiment in Novocherkassk and its subsequent refusal to fight against the Bolsheviks. Some details, like the full name of the regiment and the names of places where it had skirmishes with the Reds on its way to the Don region, were probably taken from Antonov-Ovseenko. At the same time Sholokhov obviously made use of Lukomskii. For example, it is hardly coincidental that the phrases ''The regiment was given a ceremonial welcome. After a public service in Cathedral Square. . . .'' (2:284) also occur in the general's ''Reminiscences.''[94]

The likely source for the description of the retreat of the Volunteer Army from Rostov is Denikin. One finds in his book the same details about the White troops and refugees as in *The Quiet Don*: a long train of carts, diversity of clothes and uniforms, women wading through the snow in high-heeled shoes, General Alekseev riding in a carriage, and Colonel Kutepov, formerly commander of the Preobrazhenskii Regiment, his cap on the back of his head (2:285-286).[95] At times Sholokhov appears to have used other sources along with *The Russian Turmoil*. This can be seen in the sentence "On the morning of the 9th, Captain Chernov's detachment, pressed by Sivers and fired upon by the Cossacks of Gnilovskaia stanitsa, entered Rostov" (2:284). Nearly every word of this sentence seems to have been borrowed from Denikin's book, with the notable exception of "Captain Chernov." Denikin has General Cherepov instead of Chernov.[96] It is hard to believe that Sholokhov would have made two mistakes while adapting a single sentence. Moreover, Captain Chernov did actually exist. His detachment fought near Rostov, in the sector commanded by General Aleksandr Cherepov.[97]

The second part of chapter 18 deals with the situation of the Whites after leaving Rostov. The opening sentence—"By March 11 the Volunteer Army was concentrated in the area of Ol'ginskaia stanitsa" (2:288)—was probably taken from Lukomskii. However, Sholokhov must have put in the wrong month because of an oversight. In Lukomskii's "Reminiscences" Kornilov "concentrated the Volunteer Army in the area of Ol'ginskaia stanitsa on February 10 (23)."[98] In the next sentence Sholokhov says that in Ol'ginskaia Kornilov waited for the arrival of Campaign Ataman Petr Popov, who had left Novocherkassk with a detachment "numbering about sixteen hundred cavalrymen, five cannons, and forty machine guns." Since Lukomskii does not mention the number of machine guns and gives somewhat different figures for men and cannons, one may assume that Sholokhov's information could have come from Denikin. The only discrepancy is that the general has "1,500 men."[99] The difference in the number is, of course, insignificant, but the word "cavalrymen" (*sabli*) as a substitution for Denikin's "men" (*boitsy*) represents a factual error. In his article entitled "From the History of the Liberation of the Don," General Popov wrote that half of his 1,500 Cossacks had been infantrymen.[100] Had Sholokhov been familiar with Popov's article or had he read Lukomskii attentively, he would not have written that Popov arrived in Ol'ginskaia on March 13 (26). Again, he errs by precisely one month, although Lukomskii, from whom he obviously borrowed details about Popov's arrival, has here "February 13 (26)."[101]

The central event of the second half of chapter 18 is a conference in Ol'ginskaia at which the leaders of the Volunteer Army and General Popov discuss the question of whether their forces should move into the steppes of the Sal District or march to the Kuban' region. Sholokhov's primary source for his description of the conference is a detailed firsthand account in Lukomskii's "Reminiscences." Many phrases were transferred into the novel verbatim or with slight changes. This is, for example, true of Popov's arguments for remaining in the Don region (2:289-290) and of Alekseev's statement supporting the movement into the Kuban' region: "It will be easier for us to break through the Bolshevik ring in that direction and to join forces with the detachment that is operating outside Ekaterinodar'' (2:291).[102] There is, however, a big formal difference between Lukomskii's text and that of Sholokhov. In most cases the general chooses indirect discourse as a vehicle for reporting what was said at the conference. The writer, on the other hand, puts words into the mouths of his characters, creating a lively dialogue.

It is likely that the penultimate paragraph of chapter 18 represents a condensed version of what Denikin wrote about Kornilov's decision in Mechetinskaia (2:292-293).[103] In this stanitsa Kornilov received the unfavorable reports about the Sal District, summoned the commanders of the fighting units, and announced his decision to proceed toward the Kuban' region. This episode is not described by Lukomskii because by that time he had left the army on a mission.

The second half of chapter 18 offers a good example of how Sholokhov fictionalizes his printed sources. It is possible to single out several phrases and passages that he added to factual information to make his narrative more vivid. What enables us to point out these additions with confidence is General Popov's unpublished letter containing his comments regarding Sholokhov's portrayal of his visit to Ol'ginskaia.

The description of the visit begins with the announcement that ''Popov, accompanied by his chief of staff Colonel Sidorin and several Cossack officers of his escort, rode into Ol'ginskaia on the morning of the 13th'' (2:288). The pertinent passage from Popov's letter reads: ''Sholokhov invented this trip without a shadow of truth. In the first place, I made two trips on the same day: the first time I went alone and the second time I took Col. Sidorin, my chief of staff, along with me. Both when alone and when with Sidorin, I went in a sledge, without an escort.''[104]

By inventing a mounted escort, Sholokhov obtained a number of characters needed for the creation of fictional scenes, and he put these people to work right after his announcement of Popov's arrival. He showed how Popov was being helped off his horse by his orderly, ''a young Cossack with black forelock, a dark face, and eyes as sharp as a lapwing's''; how another orderly, ''an elderly and bowlegged cavalryman,'' took care of the horses; how the young orderly struck up a conversation with a red-cheeked maid, ''wearing big galoshes over her bare feet''; and how the girl reacted to his remarks, while walking ''through a puddle to the barn.'' We also see General Sergei Markov standing by the window and ''watching the Cossack orderlies tending the horses and exchanging pleasantries with the maid'' (2:288-289).

The fictional entourage reappears at the end of the chapter when Popov is about to leave Ol'ginskaia. One of the escorting officers is identified as Izvarin, a Cossack separatist who had once served with Grigorii Melekhov.

3.

Знакомое, там я был действующим лицом. Это описание моей поездки 13/II из ст. Старочеркасской в ст. Ольгинскую на свидание с генер. Корниловым.

Здесь все — от начала до конца — сплошное вранье; нет ни одного слова правды.

Быть может это право романиста? Мне вспоминается хороший донской писатель Тренев, к-рый тоже писал между прочим о Степном Походе так же, как Шолохов, и у него было тоже сплошное вранье...

Возможно, что это требовалось „моментом", даже было, по соображениям конъюнктурным, нужно было изобразить „весьма горькими" пленицей...

Вот и в романе Краснова — „От Двуглавого орла к красному знамени" — тоже написано обо мне небылицы, но там то, само собою понятно, — автору нужно было „все" „так изобразить" по соображениям иного характера, хотя, к слову, от исторической правды никогда не любил.

Возвращусь к моей поездке в ст. Ольгинскую.

Шолохов эту поездку выдумал без тени правды. Во-первых, я в один и тот же день ездил 2 раза: в первый раз один, а во второй — я взял с собою ген. Сидорина, моего начальника Штаба. Ездил и один и с Сидориным на санях и без конвоя.

Что я говорил или предлагал ген. Корнилову, Шолохов не мог не знать: это было напечатано в журнале „Донская Волна" и в воспоминаниях ген. Лукомского, чем Шолохов пользовался.

Excerpt from General P. Popov's letter to S. Pahomov, 1952

4. Во второй раз я показал по просьбѣ ген. Корнилова на Воен. Совѣтѣ старших войск начальников, чтобы повторить мое предложеніе — остаться Добр. Арм. на Дону, а не ходить на Кубань за мыльными пузырями.

Ген. Корнилов вполнѣ раздѣлял мой план, но на Воен. Совѣтѣ накануне вопрос этот обсуждался, и было выработано рѣшеніе на основаніи "неправильной" информаціи (относительно конных заводов зимовников), почему генер. Корнилов, который из-за этого [illegible] рѣшеніе, хотѣл показать, какіе мотивы побуждали его на этот раз...

Шолохов совершенно искажает картину Военнаго Совѣта, ничего не сказал о моем планѣ, назвал лиц на Совѣтѣ не присутствовавших, не отмѣтил, что против моего предложенія возражал один ген. Алексеев и т.д.

Резюмируя совѣщаніе, ген. Корнилов твердо и опредѣленно указал, что рѣшеніе его то, к-рое было предложено мною: Доб. Арм. остается на Дону, наносит, по-указанію намѣченному, удар на Торговую, поворачивает фронт на Тихорѣцкую, а я с моими партизанами одновременно наношу удар на Великокняжескую и поворачиваю фронт на Царицын...

Ночью я выѣхал в хут. Арпачин, куда должны были прибыть из Степного мои партизаны, чтобы на утро переформировать свой отряд и приступить к выполненію моей задачи на Великокняжескую.

Но... на слѣдующій день, по настоянію генер. Алексеева и генер. Корнилова [illegible], было собрано еще раз Воен. Совѣт, на этот раз без меня. Генер. Корнилов сдѣлал "уступку" ген. Алексееву, и Добр. Армія пошла на Кубань.

Когда Добр. Армія ушла уже верст на 80–100, [illegible] Я никогда не помню никаких [illegible]

Говоря о моем неприсутствіи на Воен. Совѣщаніи Шолохов открыто пишет: "он (т.е. я) [illegible] 'инспектор' [illegible] [illegible] на [illegible] [illegible]..." Это то же ложь: на [illegible] 5-ой [illegible] не было, к-рого не было, и [illegible]

Izvarin and Sidorin exchange a few words, while the orderlies talk about the maid in a sexual context. When Popov comes out into the yard, one of the orderlies helps him to find his stirrup. And then "waving his simple Cossack whip, Popov put his horse into a trot, and behind him, standing in the stirrups and leaning a little forward, came the Cossack orderlies, Sidorin, and the officers" (2:292).

Despite his liberal insertions of fictional passages, Sholokhov cannot be said to have invented everything concerning Popov's trip to Ol'ginskaia, as the general contends. The author might have really believed that Popov made only one trip and that he had a mounted escort. This assumption can be supported by examining sources that Sholokhov used for the description of the conference in Ol'ginskaia. In Lukomskii's "Reminiscences" he read that the conference started at noon on February 13 (26) and that Popov had arrived with Sidorin, his chief of staff, sometime before the beginning of the conference.[105] Lukomskii makes no mention of Popov's coming to Ol'ginskaia twice. Nor does Denikin, in whose book Popov and Sidorin come to Ol'ginskaia in the evening.[106] Consequently, Sholokhov had no choice but to describe only one of Popov's trips. All he could do was to choose between Lukomskii's and Denikin's designations of the time at which Popov was said to have arrived in Ol'ginskaia. He followed Lukomskii, probably because his account of the events in Ol'ginskaia is much more detailed than Denikin's. Incidentally, Denikin is not wrong about the time of Popov's arrival. He refers to the ataman's second trip to Ol'ginskaia, while Lukomskii writes of his first trip.

Sholokhov could not have known about this difference unless he had read Popov's article "From the History of the Liberation of the Don" (1918), but there is no evidence that he did. For this reason he also could not have known that Lukomskii was apparently mistaken in saying that Popov *and* Sidorin arrived in Ol'ginskaia before noon and that the conference was scheduled for 12:00 that day. According to Popov, he made his first trip to Ol'ginskaia (from Starocherkasskaia) in the morning; for the second trip he and Sidorin set out for Ol'ginskaia at four in the afternoon. Furthermore, Popov does not say anything about his having attended any large conference during his first visit to Ol'ginskaia, either in the morning or at noon. He refers merely to his conversations with Alekseev and Kornilov, adding that the latter scheduled a "general conference" for 6:00 p.m.[107] Popov's version must be correct. It was written within a few months after his trips to Ol'ginskaia, and it is corroborated in part by Denikin's statement that the ataman *and* Sidorin arrived in Ol'ginskaia in the evening.

Sholokhov is responsible for inventing a mounted escort and for putting Popov on horseback. Neither Lukomskii nor Denikin mentions these details. The generals also do not specify the means of conveyance that Popov used. They merely say that he "arrived" (*priekhal*) in Ol'ginskaia. Sholokhov could have easily assumed that the campaign ataman of the Don Cossacks would not come to a top-level conference in a sledge and without an escort commensurate with his rank and position. In addition to this, there was no way that Sholokhov could have established that Popov rode in a sledge, since this fact was not revealed in print.

Another fictional detail that Popov singles out in his letter is the description of his hand: "He held out a fat [*miasistuiu*] white hand with a gold ring, deeply embedded in the flesh of the index finger" (2:290). Visibly displeased, the general comments: "Speaking of my feeling at ease at the council of war, Sholokhov paints this picture: 'he (that is I) held out a fat white hand *with a gold ring on the index finger*. . . .' This is a lie: there was no fat white hand, just like there was no 'gold ring on the finger.' I have never worn any rings."[108]

A number of Popov's objections concern the factual aspects of Sholokhov's presentation: "Sholokhov has completely distorted the picture of the council of war. He said nothing about my plan, gave the names of persons who were not present at the council, failed to note that Gen. Alekseev was the only one who objected to my proposal, etc."[109]

The general is not quite right. Sholokhov allotted him a whole page to state his views at the conference. Indeed, his plan is presented in the novel in more detail than in Lukomskii and Denikin combined. This plan, according to Lukomskii, encountered opposition not only from Alekseev but also from Romanovskii. Sholokhov borrowed this information (2:291), but it is hard to ascertain whether it is correct. Here we have Popov's word against Lukomskii's. We may only add that Denikin was completely on Alekseev's side.[110] Sholokhov made at least one error in giving the names of those who were present at the conference. He took the names from Lukomskii, overlooking the fact that Denikin did not attend the conference due to illness.[111]

A weak point of Popov's criticism is that he attributed to Sholokhov several inaccuracies which resulted, not from the author's disregard for historical truth, but from his reliance on Lukomskii. Popov probably did not reread Lukomskii's "Reminiscences" at the time he wrote his letter about Sholokhov. This is regrettable, especially since in the same letter Popov notes that Sholokhov used Lukomskii as a source for the description of the Ol'ginskaia conference. On the other hand, Popov is probably wrong in saying that Sholokhov must have read his 1918 article "From the History of the Liberation of the Don."

Historical passages in chapter 19 deal with the capture of Novocherkassk by the Red Cossacks under the command of Nikolai Golubov, with his breaking up of the session of the Don Cossack Parliament, and with the arrest of Ataman Nazarov. There is no doubt that a map in Antonov-Ovseenko's book supplied Sholokhov with all the dates and places pertaining to Golubov's march on the Cossack capital (2:293), while articles by Bykadorov and Nikolai Duvakin (assistant to Ataman Nazarov) appear to have provided material for the description of the last day's activities of the Parliament. For example, information about the dispatch of Captain Sivolobov to Golubov to negotiate the surrender of Novocherkassk might have come from Duvakin; and the scene of the dispersal of the Parliament might have its origin in the Bykadorov article (2:294). Thus Nazarov's question "How do you dare to interrupt a session of the Parliament?" is identical in Bykadorov's article and in *The Quiet Don*. At the same time Sholokhov might have used a document entitled "The Fourth Parliament" to introduce a brief talk between Golubov and a member of the Parliament (2:294).[112]

One place in chapter 19 offers an example of how Sholokhov sprinkles his fictional narrative with passages borrowed from historical sources. Describing activities of the fictional character, Bunchuk, the author says that "At Sivers' headquarters a Revolutionary tribunal had been organized to mete out summary justice to captured White Guards. Bunchuk worked for a day in the court. . . ." (2:295.) The first sentence has an unmistakable similarity to one found in Antonov-Ovseenko's *Notes about the Civil War*.[113]

Apart from a brief political and military survey, the whole of chapter 20 is devoted to Bunchuk. The content of the survey reminds one of a few paragraphs in Frenkel''s *Eagles of the Revolution*. One phrase—"At the end of March detachments of Ukrainian Red Guards driven back by the Haidamaks and the Germans began to arrive in Rostov"—seems to be patterned on a similar phrase in Frenkel' (2:301).[114]

The subject of chapter 21 is the insurrection of the Upper Don Cossacks caused by the unruly behavior of the retreating Reds. It seems that the bulk of the chapter is written on the basis of oral accounts and personal observations. I was unable to find a specific printed source. The insurrection is described in an article printed in *Donskaia volna* (*The Don Wave*), but there is no indication that Sholokhov used it.[115]

Oral accounts and, possibly, personal observations provided material for the creation of the colorful adventurer Fedor Likhovidov, the newly elected ataman of Karginskaia stanitsa, in the first half of chapter 24.

After the portrayal of local happenings in chapters 22 through 25, Sholokhov turns to larger events in chapter 26. His outline of the political situation in the Don region in April 1918 coincides with Frenkel''s assessment of it in *Eagles of the Revolution*. However, there is a discrepancy in dating the convocation of the First Congress of the Soviets of the Don Republic. According to Frenkel', the Congress convened in mid-April (New Style); according to Sholokhov, at the end of April (2:339).[116]

The bulk of chapter 26 and the next four chapters are devoted to the so-called Podtelkov expedition. This was the ill-fated march of a Red Cossack detachment into the northern part of the Don region in the hope of enlisting the Cossacks of the Khoper and the Ust'-Medveditskaia Districts in the Red Army. The detachment set out from Rostov under the command of Podtelkov, then chairman of the Council of the People's Commissars of the Don Soviet Republic. Frenkel' went with the detachment as a political instructor and later gave a detailed account of its march in *Eagles of the Revolution*. This brochure was to become the basic source for Sholokhov's portrayal of the Podtelkov expedition. Numerous passages and phrases in *The Quiet Don* have obvious parallels in *Eagles of the Revolution*. This applies to such items as the creation of the Extraordinary Mobilization Commission and the departure of the Red detachment (2:339), the reception of the expedition by the local population (2:343, 348-349), the encirclement of the detachment by the White Cossacks and its surrender (2:351-352), the congeniality between the prisoners and their captors right after the surrender—they exchange triple kisses in observance of the Russian Easter custom (2:353), the disarmament of the prisoners (2:354-355), and the escape of a Red machine gunner who took the breechlock of his gun along with him (2:355).[117]

At this point Frenkel' also escaped, and the rest of his story dealing with the trial and execution of the Podtelkov men is based on secondhand information provided, in part, by Sergei Syrtsov. Thus Sholokhov might be indebted to this Bolshevik leader for certain details pertaining to the execution. Among them may be the role of the officer Spiridonov in carrying out the execution (2:365, 367), attempts by Podtelkov and Krivoshlykov to encourage their condemned comrades (2:369), Podtelkov's "last word" before his death (2:370), and the hanging of him and Krivoshlykov by two masked officers (2:371).[118] On the other hand, Sholokhov might have heard about these and other episodes from the Cossacks of Karginskaia stanitsa who took part in the capture of Podtelkov and witnessed his execution. Kharlampii Ermakov is also reported to have been present at the hanging of Podtelkov.[119] Finally, Sholokhov extracted from Frenkel' two relevant documents: the resolution by elected judges condemning all members of the Podtelkov detachment to death and the list containing the names of the seventy-six condemned men (2:358-361).[120]

Despite his dependence on Frenkel' for factual material, Sholokhov displayed much freedom and imagination in creating his own artistic version of the Podtelkov expedition. The author was more daring in adapting

Frenkel''s material than he was in dealing with the information provided by Lukomskii, Denikin, or Ianov. He felt more at ease with Podtelkov and his Cossacks in the Don steppes than with Kornilov at General Headquarters or with Kaledin in the Ataman's Palace. He was more restrained in altering the polished speech of generals as quoted by Denikin than in changing the Cossack language in Frenkel''s rendition. In *The Quiet Don* Podtelkov speaks a much racier idiom than in *Eagles of the Revolution*. The difference can be illustrated by comparing two versions of Podtelkov's ten-line reply to the doubts voiced by his comrades with regard to the situation in the northern districts. In Frenkel''s brochure Podtelkov expresses himself smoothly and grammatically. He even resorts to such stock terms of political jargon as "the White Cossack bands" and "the waves of the counter-revolution." In *The Quiet Don* he speaks in the vernacular, using coarse locutions as well as dialectal and ungrammatical forms, like *poperedi* (ahead of) and *ne bois'* (don't be afraid). Frenkel' and Sholokhov are also far apart in their renditions of Podtelkov's intonation and sentence structure. Frenkel' introduces Podtelkov's reply with the remark that he spoke "all flaring up with excitement." Yet his Podtelkov produces three long, listless declarative sentences, without a trace of agitation. Sholokhov does not comment on the way Podtelkov spoke. He makes him answer a specific question with a barrage of short, emotionally charged sentences, eight of which are exclamatory and one interrogative (2:346).[121]

To dramatize his narrative, Sholokhov frequently uses direct discourse or dialogue in passages where Frenkel' limits himself to plain reporting. A master of dialogue, Sholokhov is not content with reshaping Frenkel''s prose into lively conversations. He invents numerous dialogues unrelated to Frenkel''s material. A case in point is a page of earthy talk between two members of the Podtelkov detachment (2:341-342). Furthermore, Sholokhov evolves from his imagination several tense, powerful scenes that could not have been witnessed by Frenkel'. One thinks of the closed conference of elected judges deciding the fate of the Podtelkov men and the last sleepless night of the condemned prisoners (2:356-364). In the latter instance Sholokhov might have drawn in part from his own experience—his two days of confinement before his death sentence for the mistreatment of a "kulak" was commuted. And, of course, Sholokhov takes full advantage of Frenkel''s references to natural phenomena. He not only mentions rain on the day before the surrender of the Red detachment, but also represents nature as foreshadowing a dismal end to the Podtelkov expedition. Chapter 28, in which the Reds are captured and condemned, begins with a skyscape featuring heavy clouds, approaching darkness, and orange sheet lightning "quivering like the wing of a wounded bird." Down on the earth, "the mournful glimmers of the fading daylight" were lurking in the folds of the ravines, and grasses "gave off an inexpressible odor of decay" (2:350).

One of Sholokhov's additions turned out to be a political liability. It was a page portraying Podtelkov's mistress, Zinka, a buxom girl who traveled with the detachment under the guise of a nurse. Krivoshlykov and Zinka hated each other intensely, and Krivoshlykov demanded from Podtelkov that "the whore" be thrown off the train (2:340). In 1953 the censors sided with Krivoshlykov. Zinka has vanished from the novel altogether, and the image of the Revolutionary hero is no longer tarnished by an unworthy connection. It is difficult to ascertain whether Zinka was a real person. Her presence suggests that Sholokhov might have heard something about Podtelkov's relations with women. Podtelkov's intimate life, however, matters less than Sholokhov's determination to portray the Revolutionary hero as a human being with vices as well as virtues.

For the sake of objectivity, Sholokhov was highly selective in using Frenkel''s brochure. He rejected those items which could be perceived as propagandistic overstatements. One of them was Podtelkov's talk about the superiority of the Red Guards over the Cossacks, which contained the following phrases: "As for fighting, they [the Cossacks] are good for nothing. The Red Guards are much more courageous than the Cossacks. . . . Any Red Guard would defeat any Cossack in an open combat."[122] This is not the impression one gets from reading *The Quiet Don*. Suffice it to mention that in the engagement near the station of Likhaia "the Red Guards were retreating in panic" under a frontal attack by the Chernetsov Cossacks (2:237). This episode comes from Antonov-Ovseenko, who speaks of "wild panic" and adds that the defeated Red Guard detachments had to be sent home, to Moscow and Khar'kov, for the replacement of casualties.[123] Sholokhov's impartiality in the treatment of Podtelkov can be judged by the censors' reaction to it. In 1953 they made about forty political revisions pertaining to Podtelkov. Over one-third of these revisions, including the longest deletions, have not been rescinded.

Sholokhov's objectivity is also seen in his depiction of the enemy. The White camp is represented in part 5 more even-handedly than in part 4. Sholokhov's borrowings from the White sources are not free from antagonistic insertions. His portrayal of the retreating Volunteer Army may serve as an example: "It [the column] stretched across the Don like a fat black snake; then, twisting, it crawled toward Aksai" (2:284-285). The corresponding sentence in Denikin's book contains no degrading imagery: "A dark ribbon stretched over the flat, snow-covered field."[124] On the other hand, part 5 has no direct authorial condemnation of the White cause, as was the case with the Kornilov movement in part 4. Nor do the generals act like conspirators in part 5. They are presented as open and selfless opponents of the Bolshevik rule. The dispassionate portrayal of the Ol'ginskaia conference suggests the author's respect for the professional expertise and personal qualities of the Volunteer Army's leaders. The main factor in eliciting this respect must have been the memoirs by Denikin and Lukomskii. Sholokhov also must have been grateful to these generals for providing him with important material for his novel. Perhaps a token of his gratitude can be seen in his description of Denikin's eyes as "intelligent," a characteristic that a Soviet writer did not have to show (2:288).

Volume 3

With respect to its subject matter and sources, volume 3 may be divided into two parts. The first part, consisting of chapters 1 through 14, covers the period of Ataman Petr Krasnov's rule. Chapters dealing with Krasnov's activities alternate with those portraying fictional characters. The primary printed source for the descriptions of historical events is the ataman's memoirs, entitled "Vsevelikoe Voisko Donskoe" ("The Grand Army of the Don," 1922). The title refers to the independent state of the Don Cossacks formed under Krasnov. The second part of volume 3 depicts the occupation of the Veshenskaia area by the Reds and—mainly—the uprising of the Upper Don Cossacks in the spring of 1919. Sholokhov's attention is focused on Grigorii Melekhov's participation in the uprising. Oral accounts of insurgent Cossacks and the author's own observations must have provided the basic material for the creation of numerous scenes connected with the uprising.

Sholokhov's dependence on Krasnov becomes apparent from the very beginning—from passages in chapter 1 which describe the work of the so-called Parliament for the Salvation of the Don that was in session from April 28 (May 11) to May 5 (18), 1918. The content of Krasnov's speech at a session of the Parliament, the date he was elected ataman of the Don Cossacks, the number of votes cast for and against him, the characterization of the laws he proposed, the acceptance of the new flag and emblem for the Don Cossack state, and Krasnov's joke about the possibility of changing new laws—all these items were borrowed from "The Grand Army of the Don," at times verbatim (3:17-18).[125] However, a few details do not seem to have been taken from Krasnov. For example, Sholokhov says that the resolution on the wearing of shoulder straps and all insignia of military rank had been proposed by Georgii Ianov, chairman of the Parliament (3:17). This resolution is mentioned by both Krasnov and Ianov, but neither reveals the name of its author.[126]

The whole of chapter 4 is based on Krasnov's memoirs. The chapter opens with the portrayal of a meeting between political and military leaders of the Don state and senior commanders of the Volunteer Army in Manychskaia stanitsa on May 15 (28). The tone and content of the dialogue between Denikin and Krasnov faithfully reflects the latter's account of the meeting (3:39-41).[127] There are also some striking similarities in the descriptive passages, for example, in the portrait of General Alekseev.

At the same time Sholokhov does not restrict himself to copying or paraphrasing Krasnov. Thus he enlarges his portrait of Alekseev by showing the general's swollen veined eyelids, his fine wrinkles, his yellowish short hair, and other physical signs of age and exhaustion. Moreover, he makes Afrikan Bogaevskii watch Alekseev with "acute compassion" and think how terribly he had aged (3:39-40). These details are absent from Krasnov's account.[128] Similarly, Sholokhov must have invented some portions of the dialogue. In *The Quiet Don* Denikin calls Krasnov "a provincial Napoleon. . . . Not a smart man, you know." Answering Denikin, Romanovskii characterizes the ataman as "a brigadier general intoxicated with a monarch's power" (3:42). This exchange is not found in either Krasnov's or Denikin's account of the meeting in Manychskaia.[129]

In the next paragraph Sholokhov is indebted to Krasnov for the description of strained relations between the Volunteer Army and the Don Cossacks after the Manychskaia conference. It is also likely that Sholokhov had the ataman's memoirs before him when he wrote about the officers who hid from the Civil War in Rostov and Novocherkassk, while courageous and selfless members of the officer corps were dying in battles (3:42-43).[130] The sentiments of the Don ataman and the Soviet writer are in this case identical.

The second half of chapter 4 is devoted to Krasnov's relations with the Germans. Sholokhov's depiction of the visit of three German majors to Novocherkassk is a close paraphrase of what Krasnov wrote about it (3:43-44).[131] Like Krasnov, Sholokhov reports the conversation between the ataman and the German officers in the form of indirect discourse. However, in two instances Sholokhov attributes certain statements to individual officers, while Krasnov attributes them to "the German command" or its "representatives." With the obvious intent of exposing Krasnov's ties with the Germans as fully as possible, Sholokhov included in the novel the complete text of the ataman's letter to the German emperor. The text of this long letter must have come from "The Grand Army of the Don" (3:44-46).[132] The same source provided material for the concluding paragraphs of chapter 4. Here Sholokhov relates that the letter was used by Krasnov's adversaries to accuse him of selling himself to the Germans. One also learns that General Aleksandr Cheriachukin, one of Krasnov's messengers to Germany, was taken by the Germans to the western front, where he observed the power of the Krupp artillery (3:46).[133]

Parts of chapters 11 and 14 deal with the arrival of two Allied missions in Novocherkassk. Here Sholokhov drew liberally upon Krasnov's memoirs for information about such things as the names of French and British officers, the reception of the missions in Novocherkassk, and the visits of the Allied officers to the front in the company of Krasnov.[134] In one place Sholokhov transferred verbatim 130 words from the speech that the ataman gave at the reception of the first mission. The extract begins with the words "they await your help" and ends with "all our dreams and hopes" (3:98-99). Likewise, Sholokhov made no changes in the following statement by Captain Bond: "I propose a toast to the great country of Russia and I should like to hear in this hall your beautiful old anthem. We shall not pay attention to the words; I should just like to hear the music" (3:99).[135]

In a few places Sholokhov inserted disparaging passages which have no analogies in Krasnov's memoirs. He comments that the Allied "ambassadors" were greeted in Novocherkassk with "excessive servility and obeisance" (3:98). His description of the banquet in honor of the first mission closes with the phrase "One of the distinguished guests was so overcome by emotion that in the simplicity of his soul he burst into tears, pushing his beard into a napkin lavishly smeared with caviar" (3:100). "A drunkard's face" is a distinctive mark in Sholokhov's portrait of Konstantin Mamontov, suggesting that the Cossack general had a weakness for alcohol (3:102). In fact, Mamontov "did not drink himself and did not like drunkards."[136]

There are several discrepancies between accounts given by Krasnov and by Sholokhov of the same incidents. For example, in *The Quiet Don* "everyone rose, emptying their glasses" as the band struck up the old Russian anthem "God Save the Tsar" at the banquet in the Ataman's Palace (3:100). In Krasnov's memoirs "everyone rose and stood motionless as though in prayer." [137] It is impossible to ascertain whether Sholokhov overlooked or distorted this sentence. Elsewhere he describes the inspection of the Gundorovskii Regiment as occurring during the trip of the second Allied mission to the front in January 1919 (3:114). Actually, the inspection, during which Krasnov exchanged kisses with nearly half of the regiment, took place on November 28 (December 11), 1918, when the ataman visited the front with the members of the first Allied mission.[138] The reason for Sholokhov's transposition of this episode is unclear.

Occasionally, Sholokhov brings in details that are not contained in Krasnov's memoirs. The episode of the flight of General Matvei Ivanov, the commander of the northern front of the Don Army, from Veshenskaia to Karginskaia may serve as an example. In Sholokhov's version Ivanov leaves Veshenskaia with General Zambrzhitskii, his chief of staff. "Their car got stuck in the snow, Zambrzhitskii's wife bit her lips till the blood came, and the children howled. . . . On December 22 Ivanov's adjutant arrived from Karginskaia to Veshenskaia and, laughing to himself, collected the things the commander had left behind'' (3:102). Krasnov simply says that Ivanov had to move his headquarters to Karginskaia because it could not function in Veshenskaia in the presence of the rebellious Twenty-eighth Regiment.[139] At this point Sholokhov also differs from Krasnov with respect to chronology. In *The Quiet Don* General Ivanov is said to have left Veshenskaia four days before the Twenty-eighth Regiment entered it. Krasnov must be correct. General Ivanov could not have left Veshenskaia on or before December 22 (January 4), as Sholokhov reports, for Krasnov's order to move the headquarters of the northern front from Veshenskaia to Karginskaia is dated January 8 (21), 1919. The rebellious Twenty-eighth Regiment was at that time already in Veshenskaia.[140]

In chapter 14 Sholokhov expanded Krasnov's accounts about the punitive troops that had been sent against the Twenty-eighth Regiment and about the ataman's journey to Karginskaia with Allied officers on January 6 (19), 1919 (3:113, 114-115).[141] He revealed, for example, that Krasnov and the officers warmed themselves and drank tea in the house of Levochkin, a wealthy Karginskaia merchant. Clearly, Sholokhov was able to add such details because he had lived in Karginskaia.

In his borrowings from Krasnov, Sholokhov adhered strictly to the ataman's dating of events in accordance with the Old Style. This practice was at odds with his partial use of the New Style in volume 2. The discordance was made worse by editorial intervention in 1953, when some dates pertaining to the Krasnov period were converted to the New Style. Thus the editors introduced the New Style in passages dealing with Krasnov's relations with the Germans (3:43-46), but left the Old Style intact in chapters portraying the activity of the Parliament for the Salvation of the Don and the second visit of the Allied mission to Novocherkassk. Moreover, the editors replaced the correct date of the arrival of this mission—December 28 (Old Style)—with a wrong one (3:102). These inconsistencies have not been eliminated in subsequent editions.

Kharlampii Ermakov must have been an important oral source for the description of the Upper Don uprising, especially of incidents involving Grigorii Melekhov. In the mid-1920s Ermakov lived in the village of Bazki, just across the Don from Veshenskaia. Sholokhov's indebtedness to him can be seen from the author's own words:

''Dear Comrade Ermakov,

''It is necessary for me to get from you some additional information concerning the 1919 epoch.

''I hope you will be so kind as to give me this information upon my arrival from Moscow. I am planning to visit you in May or June of this year. This information pertains to details of the Upper Don uprising.''[142]

Unfortunately, it is nearly impossible to tell exactly what information Sholokhov received from Ermakov. The author does not say much about it. All we know from him is that Ermakov had told him about ''the terrible fighting with the sailors near the village of Klimovka.''[143] This is the engagement in which Grigorii sabered four Red sailors and then went into nervous shock (3:263-267).

One way of determining what Sholokhov might have borrowed from Ermakov is to compare passages about Grigorii with descriptions of Ermakov's participation in the Upper Don uprising by Pavel Kudinov. The former commander-in-chief of the insurgent Cossacks and an important character in volume 3 of *The Quiet Don*, Kudinov wrote a long article entitled ''The Uprising of the Upper Don Cossacks in 1919.'' It was serialized in a Cossack émigré journal in March-July 1931, shortly before the delayed publication of volume 3 of *The Quiet Don*. In all probability Sholokhov did not use Kudinov's article for his novel.

The portrayal of Grigorii's first encounter with the Reds after he joined the insurgent Cossacks has several analogies with Kudinov's account of Ermakov's actions at the beginning of the uprising. In both the novel and the article, the enemy is a Red punitive detachment led by the commissar Likhachev. The overconfident commissar rides in front of his detachment with a small group of soldiers. He does not lose his head when the Cossacks ambush him near the village of Tokin. In the ensuing skirmish he is wounded and taken prisoner (3:191-194).[144] Even some small divergences confirm that Sholokhov and Kudinov deal with the same incidents. In *The Quiet Don* Likhachev is wounded in the right shoulder and only three soldiers from his escort flee from the Cossacks. In Kudinov's article Likhachev is wounded in the left shoulder and all but two Reds manage to escape.

Some differences might have arisen out of Sholokhov's considerations as a writer of fiction. For example, in the novel Likhachev is captured by a Cossack patrol commanded by Grigorii. At this point Grigorii does not hold a high commanding post among the insurgents. He serves in the Tatarskii squadron under his brother Petr. Sholokhov might have wanted to show that, as in 1918, the Tatarskii Cossacks trusted Petr more than Grigorii, because they still remembered Grigorii's service with the Reds. In Kudinov's article Likhachev is taken prisoner by a group of Cossacks with whom Ermakov just happened to be at that time. According to Kudinov, Ermakov was in charge of a relatively large detachment numbering some 400 Cossacks.

One also encounters divergences of a factual nature. In *The Quiet Don*

Grigorii, now a regimental commander, sets out against Likhachev's forces on March 7 (20). The Reds retreat toward the village of Chukarin without fighting, and at the end of the day Grigorii takes Karginskaia in a swift attack (3:212-213). In Kudinov's version Ermakov engages the Reds on the night of March 1 (14), right after the capture of Likhachev. The Reds offer some resistance. Their artillery fires from Chukarin. The Cossacks drive them out of Chukarin and Tokin and pursue them in the direction of Karginskaia. However, the Reds receive reinforcements and manage to hold Karginskaia for the time being.[145]

Discrepancies of this kind are inevitable. As time went on, it was becoming increasingly difficult to collect detailed information about isolated incidents of the uprising. This task must have been especially hard for Sholokhov. He had to rely on Ermakov's memory and his willingness to talk about the event which was branded a counter-revolutionary crime and for which Ermakov eventually paid with his head. I do not know whether Kudinov consulted any reliable documents while writing his story of the uprising. He seems to have depended a good deal on his own recollections. Some minor points in his account do not coincide exactly with those found in the pertinent documents.

Further similarities and differences between Sholokhov and Kudinov concern insurgent forces and their commanders. Both Grigorii and Ermakov are in command of the First Insurgent Division, with headquarters in Karginskaia (3:227, 250). On the other hand, the sectors of the front Sholokhov assigns to the Second and Third Divisions are different from those indicated on a map drawn by Kudinov. Merkulov, commander of the Second Division, is a master sergeant in *The Quiet Don* and a lieutenant in Kudinov's article. The Special Brigade is designated as the Sixth by Sholokhov and as the First by Kudinov.[146] Both Kudinov and Sholokhov say that the First Division was the last to cross the Don when the insurgents were forced to give up the territory on the right bank of the river (3:373-374). However, there is a small discrepancy in dating the retreat. According to Kudinov, he ordered the retreat in the evening of May 11 (24) and all insurgent troops were evacuated from the right bank by the morning of May 12 (25).[147] Sholokhov dates the beginning of the retreat May 22, apparently using the New Style (3:355). In all of the above-mentioned divergences, Kudinov's information appears to be more authoritative than Sholokhov's.

In chapter 38 Sholokhov describes a conference at Kudinov's headquarters on March 18 (31), where Grigorii meets Lieutenant Colonel Georgidze, chief of the operations department. It is impossible to establish whether there was a conference on that date. Kudinov makes no mention of it in his article. Be that as it may, more important for us is his assertion that he had never had someone like Georgidze on his staff.[148] Sholokhov must have invented this character for political reasons. The presence of Georgidze at Kudinov's headquarters suggests cooperation between the insurgents and the White Army. It casts aspersions on the popular and spontaneous character of the Cossack uprising by linking it to a figure symbolizing the old regime.

Several chapters of volume 3 descibe the events connected with the voluntary surrender of the Red Serdobskii Regiment to the insurgent Cossacks. In contrast, Kudinov devotes one paragraph to the surrender of the regiment and one paragraph to the service of its former members with the insurgents. In both the novel and the article, the Serdobskii Regiment rebels against the Bolsheviks in Ust'-Khoperskaia stanitsa, but the similarity ends here. Kudinov claims to have received the telegram about the surrender of the regiment on March 28 (April 10).[149] Sholokhov dated the surrender April 15 (28) in his narrative (3:298, 301) and April 2 (15) in Kudinov's letter to Grigorii (3:320). The latter date made no sense at all, for Grigorii received the letter on April 22 (May 5), the day his division began its offensive from Karginskaia (3:320).[150] The letter was written shortly after the surrender of the Serdobskii Regiment and must have been delivered to Grigorii a few hours later.

Sholokhov was equally erratic about the strength of the rebellious regiment. It numbered "eleven hundred" in the authorial narrative and "about five hundred" in the words of its commander (3:294, 302). The inconsistency was corrected in 1933 by making the commander raise his figure to "about twelve hundred." Kudinov gives no information on this point, but the commander of the Red Ninth Army reported that 380 Serdobskii soldiers had gone over to the enemy.[151] However, this figure may be too low.

In the novel, only 194 former Serdobskii soldiers are allowed to fight on the Cossack side in a special battalion, and they are thrown into the battle on the day of their surrender. The greater number—over eight hundred—are treated as prisoners of war (3:325-326). According to Kudinov, the entire Serdobskii Regiment joined the Cossacks. However, it entered the fighting, not on the day of its surrender, but on April 8 (21).

Sholokhov errs slightly in giving the surname of the commander of the Serdobskii Regiment as Voronovskii. It must be Vranovskii, as in Kudinov's article.[152] Also the name of the unit in which Vranovskii is said to have once served cannot be the 117th Liubomirskii Rifle Regiment. Such a regiment did not exist. There was a 117th Iaroslavskii Infantry Regiment.[153] On the other hand, Sholokhov gives correctly the ranks of Vranovskii and his assistant Volkov, in the tsarist army (3:294).[154] It would be interesting to know the source of his information.

The same applies to documents coming from the insurgent camp: a correspondence between Kudinov's headquarters and Grigorii Melekhov (3:214-215), an appeal of the insurgents' District Council to the Cossack population (3:226), and Kudinov's letters to Grigorii Bogaterev and Grigorii Melekhov about the surrender of the Serdobskii Regiment (3:295-296, 320). Kudinov's article contains no mention of these documents. Whether Sholokhov composed them himself or copied them from a private collection or from state archives remains a mystery. It can only be noted that the tone and content of Kudinov's statements about the Serdobskii soldiers in his letters to Bogaterev and Melekhov are not quite the same as in his article. In the letters Kudinov speaks of the soldiers slightingly and callously. He does not say that they will join the Cossacks as a separate formation. Rather, he states that the Serdobskii soldiers will be distributed in twos and threes among the Cossack squadrons (3:296). In the article he refers to the Serdobskii soldiers as a regiment fighting against the Reds under Vranovskii's command. He calls them "valiant" and is clearly in sympathy with them.

Sholokhov and Kudinov mention several identical facts concerning the establishment of a liaison between the insurgents and the Don Government in Novocherkassk. An airplane with two officers of the Don Army lands near the village of Singin. One of the officers is Petr Bogatyrev, a native of Singin (3:326-328).[155] The date of the landing varies slightly: April 20 (May 3) in *The Quiet Don* and April 15 (28) in Kudinov's article. But in both cases the airplane arrives at noon (3:326).[156] The correct day of the arrival might be April 26 (May 9) which is given in a report by General Ivanov, who had dispatched the two Don Army officers to the insurgents.[157] It is therefore likely that Sholokhov based his dating on oral accounts of the local Cossacks.

The number of identifiable printed sources Sholokhov used in connection with the Upper Don uprising is small, reflecting the scarcity of such materials. A heavy reliance on Krasnov's memoirs is evident at the beginning of chapter 57 in the description of a plan drawn up by the Don Army command concerning a link-up with the insurgents. Sholokhov copied or paraphrased closely Krasnov's information about the strength, quality, and distribution of the opposing troops, the direction of the intended blow, and the aims of the offensive. There are only two deviations from the ataman's account. Sholokhov added 150 machine guns to the armament of the striking force of the Don Army and converted its famous Gundorovskii Georgievskii Regiment into two regiments: the Gundorovskii and the Georgievskii (3:343-344).[158]

A page later Sholokhov challenged Nikolai Kakurin's figures pertaining to the Upper Don uprising. He did it in a footnote containing a lengthy excerpt from Kakurin's book *How the Revolution Was Fought*. In Kakurin's opinion, the insurgents numbered 15,000 men and had several machine guns. According to Sholokhov, in April-May the insurgent forces consisted of 30,000 to 35,000 Cossacks possessing 25 cannons and about 100 machine guns. Kudinov places the strength of the insurgents at 25,000 men on April 29 (May 12), and the figures provided by Trotskii and Grigor'ev are also closer to Sholokhov's than to Kakurin's.[159] Sholokhov's footnote is no longer in the novel. It disappeared in 1937. The censors might have learned that Kakurin had been sentenced to ten years in prison in 1932,[160] and that his interpretations of certain Civil War events turned out to be at variance with the falsification of history inspired by Stalin in the 1930s.

Lev Trotskii's *How the Revolution Armed Itself* was another Soviet source that Sholokhov used in connection with the Upper Don uprising. He copied two documents from it: the article entitled "The Uprising in the Rear" and the order to the expeditionary forces of May 25, 1919 (3:352, 395-396).[161] Both documents were written by Trotskii, though this fact is not readily recognizable from the text of *The Quiet Don*. The novel gives only one lead to the authorship of "The Uprising in the Rear." It is Kudinov's remark that the article appeared in "the newspaper entitled *On the Road* for the twelfth of this month" (3:351).[162] There is no clue as to the authorship of the order to the expeditionary forces in most editions of *The Quiet Don*. This, however, was not the case in the novel's original text. Here Kudinov spoke of the order as "Trotskii's" and Sholokhov designated it as issued by "the chairman of the Revolutionary Military Council of the Republic," that is, Trotskii (3:395). But this is not widely known, for the first piece of information was deleted in 1933 and the second in 1937.

Both of Trotskii's documents play an important role in the novel. The article is discussed by the insurgent leaders and it makes Grigorii think of an affinity between Denikin and the insurgent Cossacks (3:352-354). The order inspires Mishka Koshevoi to fight and to treat the insurgents with the utmost ruthlessness (3:397-398). Needless to say, Sholokhov ran a great risk by publishing both documents three years after Trotskii's exile from the Soviet Union. And the presence of Trotskii's writings in *The Quiet Don* could easily have cost Sholokhov his life during the 1936-1939 purges. Why, then, did the censors fail to remove the heretical texts from the novel? They apparently felt that the deletion of the two conspicuous documents would arouse undesirable curiosity concerning the reasons for their sudden disappearance. The censors must have preferred to excise the designation of Trotskii's post from the text of his order in the hope that future generations of Soviet readers would have no way of establishing the identity of the order's author. Time proved them correct. Reading Trotskii was a capital crime under Stalin, and Trotskii's writings still remain inaccessible to the average Soviet citizen. Even the historian Sergei Semanov does not know who the author of the order to the expeditionary forces was.[163]

The original text of what is now chapter 57 contained a scene of Trotskii's visit to the station of Chertkovo early in May 1919. The dating of the event in the novel might have been based on the fact that Trotskii's article "Our Southern Front" was written in Chertkovo on May 11.[164] But the description of his visit to Chertkovo must have followed oral accounts. Trotskii was shown addressing Red troops at the station, urging them to fight mercilessly and courageously against the insurgent Cossacks and other enemies of the Revolution. In the middle of the speech a machine gun started to fire somewhere outside Chertkovo and a rumor spread that the Cossacks were about to attack the town. Although it was over thirty miles to the front lines of the insurgent Cossacks, wild panic broke out. Trotskii finished his speech in a hurry and left Chertkovo in his train (3:346). Deleted in 1933, this unflattering portrayal of Trotskii was restored in the 1980 edition of *Collected Works*.

Oral accounts must have been an important source for Sholokhov's information about the Red troops employed against the insurgent Cossacks. His reliance on such accounts is seen in his occasional factual inaccuracies. Had he, for example, consulted a reliable printed source, he would not have referred repeatedly to the Fifth Zaamurskii Regiment as the Fourth (3:188, 198, 238).[165] He is correct in saying that a brigade of the Thirty-third Division was transferred to the insurgent front in May, but it is questionable that it fought against Grigorii Melekhov's division for several days on the right bank of the Don (3:347, 397). According to Kudinov, the insurgents evacuated the right bank by the morning of May 12 (25), and they did it three days earlier in *The Quiet Don* (3:355, 373). Documentary evidence indicates that the Second Brigade of the Thirty-third Division could not have been used against the insurgents before May 25.[166]

The chronology of the Upper Don uprising leaves much to be desired in *The Quiet Don*. Originally, Sholokhov adhered to the Old Style in dealing with the Red occupation of the Upper Don region and with the greater part of the uprising. Then, beginning with chapter 57, he switched to the New Style, regardless of whether he was depicting the Red or the White camp. The confusion increased in the 1953 edition, where a few dates were changed from the Old Style to the New Style at random. The 1955 edition either eliminated these changes without restoring the original dates (3:320) or left them intact (3:168, 298). In some cases the 1955 editors demonstrated a lack of confidence in Sholokhov's chronology by replacing his precise dates with approximate ones. Thus February 25 (Old Style) became "the last days of February" in the reference to the time

Koshevoi went to Veshenskaia to inquire about the meeting of the local Communist group (3:179). The editors of the 1956 *Collected Works* rejected this change and preferred not to date Koshevoi's trip at all. The decision was ill-advised. February 25 was the only date in the novel marking precisely the beginning of the Upper Don uprising and it was merely a day ahead of the corresponding date given by Kudinov and Grigor'ev.[167] Otherwise the 1956 editors preserved the 1953 and 1955 revisions concerning dates of the Upper Don uprising. As a result, erratic dating continues to exist in the novel to this day.

Volume 4

The first five chapters of part 7 cover the last stage of the Upper Don uprising—the fighting on the left bank of the Don and the link-up of the insurgents with the group of the Don Army commanded by General Aleksandr Sekretev. The only printed source that Sholokhov is certain to have used here is Krasnov's memoirs, "The Grand Army of the Don." At the very beginning of chapter 1 he describes the concentration of the striking force on the Donets front with the purpose of breaking through the Red lines and effecting a link-up with the insurgent Cossacks. This information comes from page 312 of Krasnov's memoirs and it had already been used in chapter 57 of volume 3. But there is a difference in Sholokhov's comments. In volume 3 he says that the concentration of the striking force was in the process of being completed by the middle of May (3:343). In volume 4 he writes that the plan for assembling the striking force had been almost completely put into effect by the end of May. The second date is a serious error. The concentration of the striking force must have been carried out much earlier, for its breakthrough took place on May 11 (24).

In the opening lines of chapter 5 Sholokhov mistakenly dates this event June 10 (New Style) and says that Sekretev's troops established contact with the insurgents on the third day after the breakthrough. Actually, the link-up occurred on May 25 (June 7), two weeks after Sekretev had pierced through the enemy lines at the Donets. Sholokhov must have been poorly informed about Sekretev's forces and the circumstances of their march, which covered some 180 miles. He writes that Sekretev's group had 3,000 men, 6 cannons, and 18 machine guns at the beginning of its attack (4:40). These figures are at variance with the ones furnished by Maksim Buguraev, colonel of the Don artillery, who took part in Sekretev's march as a battery commander. According to Buguraev, Sekretev's group had six four-gun batteries, and it consisted of two divisions and one brigade. Their total manpower should have been twice as large as Sholokhov thought it was.[168]

Furthermore, Sholokhov neglected to mention that the composition and immediate aims of Sekretev's group were not identical with those of the striking force he described in chapter 57 of volume 3 and in chapter 1 of volume 4. This striking force was to be assembled in accordance with the plan worked out by General Sviatoslav Denisov, and it was to start its offensive on February 5-6 (18-19). But no attack was launched at that time, possibly because of the resignations of Krasnov and Denisov on February 2 (15).[169]

Sholokhov's factual errors connected with the Upper Don uprising must have resulted from his excessive trust in his own memory and in the oral accounts of others. He failed to take advantage of the available printed sources. He could have obtained the correct dates of the beginning and the end of Sekretev's march from Trotskii's book or from Kakurin's. Both of these books he definitely had in his possession.[170]

Sholokhov's mistake in dating Sekretev's breakthrough reappears in the scene of a conference at Kudinov's headquarters held on or about May 20 (June 2).[171] Here a Don Army officer who has just arrived in an airplane reports that any day Sekretev's group might start its attack on the Donets front and march to link up with the insurgents (4:29). The officer speaks in the future tense about events that happened nine days before.

Kharlampii Ermakov could have been a source for the depiction of the battle between the insurgents and the Reds who landed at the left bank of the Don, near Veshenskaia (4:17-26). Grigorii Melekhov's troops play a decisive part in the defeat of the enemy. A similar description of the rout of the Red landing force by elements of Ermakov's division can be found in Kudinov.[172]

Much of part 7 is devoted to Grigorii's service with the Don Army. In general, this service was patterned on that of Ermakov. However, it is impossible to tell which of its numerous episodes have origins in Ermakov's oral accounts and which in Sholokhov's imagination. The description of some events unrelated to Grigorii might have been based on Sholokhov's own experiences or on stories told him by eyewitnesses. A case in point is the visit of General Vladimir Sidorin, the commander of the Don Army, to Tatarskii in July 1919, during his trip to the front through recently liberated territory. The immediate sources for the portrayal of this event must have been oral accounts of those who witnessed Sidorin's arrival at Pleshakov. Sholokhov was also in Pleshakov at that time, but his father prohibited him from attending the welcoming ceremony.[173] Since there are other accounts of Sidorin's trip to liberated territories, his visit to Tatarskii allows one to take a closer look at Sholokhov's reshaping of oral information for political purposes.

In *The Quiet Don* a prominent member of Sidorin's entourage is a British colonel. He accompanies the Don Army commander "on orders from

General Briggs, chief of the British Military Mission in the Caucasus,'' and studies the mood of the Cossacks and the situation at the front (4:109). The colonel is presented as a cross between a spy and an imperialist. He conceals his knowledge of Russian and takes delight in the thought of Russia's being bled white in the Civil War and ceasing to be a threat to Britain's possessions in the East (4:109-110). In fact, there was no British colonel with Sidorin. Of the three British officers who accompanied the general, two were majors and one was a captain. H.N.H. Williamson, one of the majors, wrote in his memoirs that he had joined Sidorin's party by accident, for ''any effort on the part of individuals [British officers] to take a strong line or to visit the front to study the conditions was severely squashed by Mission Headquarters Staff.''[174] The captain was the sole British officer who spoke Russian in Sidorin's party, and all three British officers joined it at the time when the British Mission was headed by General H. C. Holman, who had replaced Briggs in the early summer of 1919.[175] Of course, Sholokhov could not have known all these details, and he was free to create a fictional character to his liking. Nonetheless, he could have refrained from producing a crude political stereotype.

The description of Sidorin's visit to Tatarskii includes the scene of his decorating Dar'ia Melekhova and other widows of the Cossacks killed during the beginning of the Upper Don uprising. The scene goes back to a real event. Soviet sources report that the author utilized here the story of Mariia Drozdova, a member of the family in whose house the Sholokhovs had lived in Pleshakov. The widow of a Cossack officer, Drozdova killed the defenseless prisoner Ivan Serdinov with a bayonet, believing that he had been responsible for the death of her husband.[176] In the novel Dar'ia shoots Ivan Kotliarov under identical circumstances (3:340-341). On the other hand, it follows from the narrative that Dar'ia and the other women are awarded medals exclusively for their massacre of the Communist prisoners (4:111). This may not be entirely true. It is possible that the Pleshakov women also distinguished themselves through some other, albeit not very palatable, actions. H.N.H. Williamson mentions, for example, a village ''where, during the insurrection, the women themselves, itching to repay a few debts, had caught the commissars as they tried to flee and murdered them with farm tools and kitchen knives.''[177] One cannot ascertain whether the author means Pleshakov, and he says nothing about the women receiving any decorations. Be that as it may, Williamson's version of the terrible revenge is likely to be closer to the truth than what the British colonel hears from Sidorin in the novel: ''We are rewarding women who showed exceptional courage in fighting the Bolsheviks. . . . In revenge for the deaths of their husbands these widows destroyed a whole detachment of local Communists'' (4:112-113). When the colonel inquires whether these women took part in the battle under the same conditions as the men, Sidorin replies yes. Sholokhov appears to have gone too far in trying to represent the enemy general as a brazen-faced liar.

Political bias against the White generals and their British allies might have been responsible for Sholokhov's assertion that during the evacuation from Novorossiisk "the staff of the Volunteer Army prudently betook themselves to the British dreadnought *The Emperor of India*" (4:264). This phrase stresses the ties between the White movement and the foreign interventionists and implies selfishness and cowardice on the part of the White command. The source of the phrase is unknown and its factual value is questionable. Denikin reports that he and his staff, as well as the staffs of the Don Army and the Don ataman, embarked on Russian ships, as did General Kutepov, commander of the Volunteer Corps. All these commanders left Novorossiisk at the last moment.[178] Strictly speaking, Sholokhov is also incorrect in using the appellation "Volunteer Army" when he describes the situation in March 1920. The Volunteer Army had been reorganized into the Volunteer Corps some three months before.

An extensive use of printed material is manifest in chapters 20 and 23, which contain surveys of the military situation in the summer and fall of 1919. Both chapters show lengthy borrowings from Kakurin's *How the Revolution Was Fought*, comprising as much as half of the text in chapter 20. Phrases pertaining to the deployment, strength, names, and operations of the Red and White formations are frequently taken down word for word. A twenty-seven-word sentence beginning with "In the reserve of the striking force" and closing with "the Saratov fortified sector" may serve as an example (4:188).[179] There was no question of acknowledging such borrowings irrespective of Sholokhov's wishes. By the time chapters 20 and 23 were serialized in the January 1938 issue of *Novyi mir*, Kakurin had already died (in prison or in a camp) and his writings were banned. Only Sholokhov could say whether he was aware of these facts.

In spite of his slavish copying, Sholokhov managed to make a mess of Kakurin's presentation of the Red command's plans relating to the destruction of the White forces on the southern front in August 1919. There were three plans. The first belonged to Ioakim Vatsetis, commander-in-chief of the Red Army until July 1919. It proposed that the main blow be delivered on the western and northwestern part of the front through Khar'kov and the Donets Basin in the direction of Rostov. The second plan was spelled out in the directive of July 23 issued by Sergei Kamenev, the new commander-in-chief. Kamenev ordered that the main attack be mounted in the eastern sector of the front through the Don region. The third plan was worked out by Vladimir Egor'ev, commander of the southern front. It also provided for the offensive to be launched through the Don territory, though it suggested a different organization and deployment of the striking force. In chapter 20 Sholokhov united elements of all three plans into one.

As a result, the reader of *The Quiet Don* is confronted with a medley consisting of elements of mutually exclusive strategies. He is told, for instance, that "the all-out offensive was timed to start between August 1 and 10," but he does not know that this date refers to Vatsetis' plan, not to Kamenev's, as is implied by the novel's text (4:188).[180]

Sholokhov's mishandling of Kakurin's material is all the more striking, since each of the three plans is discussed by Kakurin under a separate heading. It must be noted, however, that Sholokhov was not in a position to present a plan separately or to name its architect. At the time of the serialization of chapters 20 and 23, Vatsetis was already in jail awaiting execution, and the history of the Civil War was rewritten to satisfy Stalin's megalomania.

Both chapters were affected by these developments. In chapter 20 Kamenev's plan was attributed to Trotskii. It was characterized as "defeatist" because it called for the striking force to advance through the Don region, where the hostile Cossacks stopped it by fierce resistance. In chapter 23 Vatsetis' plan was ascribed to Stalin. He was said to have saved the southern front by insisting that the offensive must be launched through Khar'kov and the Donets Basin, areas with sympathetic populations and better roads. The proof of Stalin's strategic talent was furnished in the form of a footnote containing a long excerpt from his memorandum of October 15 to Lenin in which he laid down the advantages of attacking through the Donets Basin.

The idea of presenting Stalin as the author of the plan devised by Vatsetis was not new. Symptomatic of his rapid rise to power, the plan had already appeared in 1929 in Kliment Voroshilov's book *Stalin and the Red Army*. A laudatory excerpt from it, including Stalin's memorandum to Lenin, was hurriedly incorporated into the page proofs of volume 3 of *The Civil War, 1918-1921* (1930).[181] In all likelihood the portion of Stalin's memorandum printed in *The Quiet Don* was taken, not from this book, but from one of the 1937 editions of *Stalin and the Red Army*.[182] It is difficult to say whether Sholokhov or the censors introduced in the novel Stalin's name and memorandum and criticism of Trotskii. In any case, the additions were inevitable tributes to the falsification of history. Stalin not only did not work out the plan of an attack through the Donets Basin, but, like all other members of the Politburo except Trotskii, initially endorsed Kamenev's plan. By contrast, Trotskii vigorously opposed the adoption of this plan and, as a sign of protest, proffered his resignation from the Politburo and from the chairmanship of the Revolutionary Military Council of the Republic.[183] The vilification of Trotskii, the glorification of Stalin, and the text of his memorandum to Lenin were all deleted from the novel in 1956. On the other hand, no revisions have been made in Sholokhov's treatment of the three different plans as one, and his indebtedness to Kakurin still remains unacknowledged. This raises the controversial question of how much factual material can be borrowed by a fiction writer without identifying the source.

If Sholokhov used any printed materials in writing part 8 of *The Quiet Don*, they are not readily discernible. Except for the initial pages of chapter 1, part 8 is set in the Upper Don region and deals with local developments of 1920-1922. The most significant of them is the armed struggle of the anti-Bolshevik partisans. Sholokhov portrays it through operations of a detachment commanded by Iakov Fomin. The choice of this detachment must have been largely determined by Sholokhov's personal observations and experiences. In 1919 he lived for a few months in the village of Rubezhnyi, Fomin's birthplace. He says that during that time he frequently discussed political subjects with Fomin.[184] In 1921-1922 Sholokhov participated in skirmishes against Fomin's partisans. He also must have heard a good deal about their activities from the local population. Naturally, facts related by word of mouth can be easily distorted, and there is no way of telling whether every episode in the descriptions of Fomin's detachment reflects what really happened even if the author wanted to remain true to life. Local press might have provided additional information on Fomin. One thing is clear, however: Sholokhov could not have used Kharlampii Ermakov as a source for his portrayal of Grigorii Melekhov's association with Fomin. Ermakov did not serve in Fomin's detachment and lived outside the Don region during its existence.[185]

The rebellion of Fomin and his squadron is characteristic of the last stage in the Cossacks' armed struggle against the Bolshevik regime. The regime's active opponents at this time were those who had sided with it during the Civil War, but who had grown increasingly indignant over the continuation of its food-requisitioning and terroristic policies after the war. It is the service record of such men in the Red Army that Sholokhov hushes up in order to play down the sincerity and intensity of their disillusionment with the Bolshevik rule. He does not reveal that Fomin once commanded a Red regiment. Nor is the reader informed that I. Vakulin, a friend of Fomin's who rose against the Bolsheviks in the Ust'-Medveditskaia District in December 1920, had served as a regimental commander in the elite Twenty-third Division and received the Order of the Red Banner. The majority of Vakulin's insurgent unit were former members of the Twenty-third Division.[186] Instead of these facts, which he must have known, Sholokhov mentions that Fomin and Vakulin served in the rebellious Mironov's corps when it surrendered to Budennyi's cavalry (4:372). This politically unfavorable remark refers to Mironov's unauthorized attempt to march his Red Cossack troops to the front against Denikin in the summer of 1919.[187]

Sholokhov is correct in indicating that Fomin and his squadron rebelled in March 1921 and that the defeat of his detachment and his death occurred in March 1922.[188] However, he failed to coordinate the time of Grigorii's joining Fomin's detachment with the beginning of the rebellion. Grigorii returns to Tatarskii late in the fall of 1920 (4:331), probably at the end of November. Before joining Fomin, he spends a week in Tatarskii (Friday-Thursday) and then lives three weeks in one village and "more than a month" in another as a fugitive (4:381-382). This adds up to two and a half months at the most and means that Grigorii joined Fomin about the middle of February, roughly a month before the outbreak of the rebellion.

In volume 4 Sholokhov uses the New Style consistently, irrespective of whether he deals with the Reds or the Whites. December 12, 1919, the date the Tatarskii Cossacks set for their evacuation in the face of the advancing Reds, may serve as an example. Official reports issued by both warring sides show that the first half of December (New Style) was the time when the Bolsheviks captured Veshenskaia, crossed the Don, and fought in the area of Karginskaia.[189]

Sholokhov used much less printed material for volume 4 than for volumes 2 and 3, and he virtually avoided drawing upon White sources. The chief reason for this disparity must have been the political climate of the time. The adulteration of history and the ban on most Soviet and White historians precluded any extensive or meaningful use of historical materials.

The treatment of printed historical sources in *The Quiet Don* differs significantly from that in *War and Peace*. In *The Quiet Don* the function of historical passages is primarily informational. Above all, Sholokhov acquaints the reader with important events that affected the lives of his characters. Unlike Tolstoi, he has no unifying philosophy of history which would illuminate events from a definite viewpoint. Of course, Sholokhov has his own concept of life as a biological process of perpetual self-renewal, but this philosophy is expressed mainly in descriptions of nature and the people close to it, not in the representations of historical figures. In *War and Peace* Napoleon and Kutuzov illustrate the author's views on the individual's role in history, on free will, on national character, on methods of warfare, and on ethical issues. Tolstoi did not simply copy or paraphrase historical materials pertaining to the two characters. He reshaped them to highlight his philosophy of life and history. Napoleon and Kutuzov are inseparable parts of an integrated plot. This cannot be said about Kornilov, Denikin, Lukomskii, or Krasnov in *The Quiet Don*. Their connection with the plot is rather tenuous.

It would be wrong to reproach Sholokhov for not having created such impressive, contrasting figures as Napoleon and Kutuzov. Whom could he have chosen to play the role of the Red counterpart to Denikin, especially at the time of writing volume 4, when any Soviet leader could have been purged at any moment? Be that as it may, historical materials are not as successfully integrated in *The Quiet Don* as in *War and Peace*, and the reasons for this shortcoming are not merely political. Sholokhov did not feel at home with historical materials and had problems with their artistic organization. He made no secret of it: "From my viewpoint, the historical-descriptive aspect of the novel turned out to be more difficult to handle and more unsuccessful than any other aspect. This chronological-historical sphere is alien to me."[190] This aloofness may partially explain Sholokhov's extensive copying of historical information and his factual errors. Similarly, it may account for his failure to check the accuracy of historical passages and to correct mistakes. His indifferent, irresponsible attitude is at odds with his statement about the necessity of exercising extreme care in the treatment of facts: "Any error, even the smallest one, does not escape the reader's attention. . . . When the writer sins against truth even in the smallest detail, he elicits mistrust in the reader."[191] At the same time he was apparently unaware of his own mistakes in *The Quiet Don*, saying that "not a single military specialist ever found any kind of error or inaccuracies in my work."[192]

Although Sholokhov did not succeed in integrating historical passages into the plot or in avoiding factual errors, he managed to re-create the historical climate of a fateful period by portraying the pressure of historical developments on his characters. This was his achievement as an artist, especially in volume 4, where he had to refrain from portraying the most important historical figures. On the other hand, his extensive use of printed historical materials in volume 2 and the first half of volume 3 provides useful background information for the reader and helps the author to draw a fairly objective picture of the White movement. Finally, the use of historical materials proves to be of great significance in studying the controversial question of who actually wrote *The Quiet Don*.

CHAPTER V

THE QUESTION OF PLAGIARISM

The number of people questioning Sholokhov's authorship of *The Quiet Don* has always been great. It includes writers, literary scholars, critics, and average readers. The last group must have been especially numerous in the late 1920s and the early 1930s. Millions who knew the period and events described in *The Quiet Don* from personal experience were still alive at that time. Thousands could not help but wonder how Sholokhov managed to represent so faithfully a multiplicity of situations of which, owing to his youth and non-Cossack background, he had no personal knowledge. Such doubts created exceptionally favorable conditions for the spreading of allegations that Sholokhov was not the real author of *The Quiet Don*. Since no suggestions or charges of plagiarism were allowed to be printed, they circulated by word of mouth, developing into a sort of a legend that had a great variety of versions.

Some of these versions were printed in the Russian émigré press. Thus in May 1930 a Paris newspaper reported a "sudden 'discovery' " made in Soviet literary circles. The supposition allegedly surfaced there that the real author of *The Quiet Don* was a White officer from the Caucasus who, at an unspecified time, had been shot by the Cheka. Sholokhov, who was said to have served with the Cheka, appropriated the victim's papers which included the manuscript of *The Quiet Don*. The officer's mother sent a letter to the State Publishing House, claiming that *The Quiet Don* was written by her missing son. Sholokhov was confronted by the old woman and subsequently proved his innocence before a Comrades' Court.[1]

Several other versions of the plagiarism were reported in letters to the editor of *Novoe russkoe slovo* (*The New Russian Word*). These letters were written in the fall of 1974 in response to the publication of D.'s book *Stremia "Tikhogo Dona": Zagadki romana* (*The Current of "The Quiet Don": Riddles of the Novel*). For the most part the letters came from former Soviet citizens who had heard allegations of Sholokhov's plagiarism in the Soviet Union during the twenties or thirties. According to one version, Sholokhov availed himself of the diaries of a White officer, who had left them with Petr Gromoslavskii, Sholokhov's future father-in-law. A second version has it that the author of *The Quiet Don* was a White officer killed in 1919 in combat near Veshenskaia. In a horse-drawn train captured by the Reds, Sholokhov found the officer's suitcase containing the manuscript of *The Quiet Don*. When Sholokhov was about to publish it under his own name, the officer's widow sued him for plagiarism and the publication of the novel was temporarily halted. In a third version, Sholokhov received either the diaries or the manuscript from the widow of an officer who was killed in action. A fourth version attributes the authorship to a White officer who died in a hospital. The manuscript, which he had with him at the time of his death, disappeared and turned up later in Sholokhov's hands.[2] A fifth version, printed in another newspaper, speaks of an officer who was hiding from Soviet authorities. Unable to publish the novel under his own name, he gave the manuscript to Sholokhov.[3]

The contradictory nature of the above examples does not allow one to treat them other than as hearsay allegations. Yet they cannot be simply dismissed as gossip. There may be a grain of truth in them, for one should not rule out the possibility that Sholokhov could have taken advantage of some kind of written materials formerly belonging to a White Cossack officer. We have, however, no reliable information about either the quantity of such materials or the manner in which Sholokhov might have utilized them. Unsubstantiated stories involving a White officer cannot therefore be used against Sholokhov as evidence of his alleged plagiarism.

The same applies to general statements coming from literary circles. A case in point is a statement by the Rostov writer Aleksandr Busygin, a leader of regional organizations of proletarian writers at the time of the publication of the first three volumes of *The Quiet Don*. In 1928 or 1929 Busygin reportedly expressed doubts that Sholokhov had authored the novel. "The Rostov writers' organization," he said, "has evidence that the author of *The Quiet Don* is another person, who comes from a class alien to us. Our writers' organization is looking into the matter now."[4] The person who gave this information claims that he had heard it directly from Busygin. The statement must have been made before March 29, 1929, when *Pravda* published the letter of the Serafimovich commission equating allegations of plagiarism against Sholokhov with slander spread by enemies of the proletarian dictatorship. No literary organization would investigate any charges against Sholokhov after this verdict. Busygin's statement indicates that some of these charges might have been presented in writing. But, again, there is no way of knowing whether they contained enough evidence to prove Sholokhov guilty. In all probability Busygin's statement was not motivated by any ill feelings toward Sholokhov. The two writers appear to have been on friendly terms. In 1941 Busygin was killed in the war. Sholokhov wrote an introduction to the 1952 volume of his works and remembered him warmly at a 1955 conference of young Don writers.[5]

Another literary figure from the Don region who questioned the young Sholokhov's ability to create *The Quiet Don* was Aleksandr Listopadov, a prominent collector and student of the Don Cossacks' songs. In 1938 he expressed his doubts to the musician Mikhail Gol'dshtein, adding that Gor'kii knew about Sholokhov's plagiarism but was afraid to speak up.[6]

A revival of rumors of plagiarism occurred in connection with the awarding of the Nobel Prize for Literature to Sholokhov in 1965. Andrei Voznesenskii recited a poem containing a thinly veiled allusion to the laureate: "A superclassic and satrap, / Shame on you, dear. / You cribbed one novel, / But couldn't crib another."[7] The only thing that is not clear is what "another" refers to here: *Virgin Soil Upturned* or *They Fought for Their Country*.

The ink had hardly dried on Voznesenskii's poem when fresh fuel—a story told by Professor Alexei Yakushev—was added to the plagiarism controversy. His story in a nutshell is as follows. At the beginning of 1968 a woman living in Leningrad wrote a letter to Aleksandr Tvardovskii, the chief editor of *Novyi mir*. She said that her brother, a White officer, had written the story of his participation in the Civil War, particularly in the Upper Don uprising. There existed several manuscripts of his work. Early in the 1920s the officer was arrested by the Soviet security police. Shortly before his execution he disclosed the whereabouts of one copy of his manuscript to a fellow-prisoner, a priest. The priest betrayed the location of the manuscript to his police or court interrogator, who happened to be Sholokhov. Later the woman found parts of her brother's manuscript, together with variants and rough drafts. Except for minor changes, these materials turned out to be essentially the same as parts of *The Quiet Don*. The woman asked *Novyi mir* to help her in opening an official investigation. At Tvardovskii's suggestion she handed over all her materials to the procurator in Leningrad, with the purpose of starting formal proceedings. In a short while Tvardovskii visited the woman in Leningrad. She looked visibly frightened and said she was not in a position to talk about the matter. Tvardovskii went to the procurator and asked for permission to examine the materials turned in by the woman. The procurator told him that the case was closed and advised him to mind his own business. A few days before this episode, Sholokhov had been reportedly seen at the procurator's office in a state of excitement.[8]

Professor Yakushev heard this story first from Tvardovskii's assistant, Aleksandr Mar'iamov, and then from Tvardovskii himself. He also read a copy of the woman's letter. I have no reason to doubt the integrity of Professor Yakushev, whom I know personally. Nevertheless, I subscribe to the opinion that the story he heard "does not, in the absence of independent investigation, constitute proof of plagiarism."[9] There is also no concrete evidence that Sholokhov served in the security police.

Unfortunately, no official inquiry, impartial or biased, into the authorship of *The Quiet Don* has been possible in the Soviet Union since 1929. The verdict of the Serafimovich commission has been considered final, with no right to appeal it. This intransigence hurts both those who believe in Sholokhov's authorship and those who question it. Soviet rulers must have feared that Sholokhov's involvement in any open inquiry would be either insulting or dangerous for him. At the same time the reluctance to deal squarely with the issue of plagiarism reinforces the view that Sholokhov must be guilty. And, because of his political reputation, many people would like to believe that he stole *The Quiet Don*.

Although the official Soviet policy precluded an open investigation of charges of plagiarism, it did not succeed in achieving total suppression of clandestine individual efforts to establish the authorship of *The Quiet Don*. Naturally, those who conduct this type of "illegal" research have no access to potentially incriminating evidence that still might be in the hands of the state. Nonetheless, scholarly work focusing on textual analysis of Sholokhov's writings can be done. It is possible to define stylistic and ideological peculiarities of *The Quiet Don* and compare them with those of Sholokhov's early stories and *Virgin Soil Upturned*, or with those found in the works of another writer who can be regarded as the likely author of the controversial epic. As of now, two studies exploring these issues have reached the West: *The Current of "The Quiet Don"* by D. and *Problems in the Literary Biography of Mikhail Sholokhov* by Roi Medvedev.[10] There is little doubt that their appearance was timed to coincide with the seventieth anniversary of Sholokhov's birth.

The Current of "The Quiet Don" is connected with Solzhenitsyn, who kept in touch with its author in Russia. Just before his arrest, in February 1974, Solzhenitsyn finished microfilming the book's manuscript.[11] As a precautionary measure he preferred not to reveal the name of its author. He designated him by the letter "D*" (I use D.) and characterized him as "a first-rate literary scholar," who died before completing his work. No doubt Solzhenitsyn attached great importance to D.'s study. He not only arranged its prompt publication but also wrote a preface and supplied an addendum that includes his brief biographical sketch about the Don Cossack writer Fedor Kriukov (1870-1920).

Although D.'s study is incomplete, its published portions, numbering some 150 pages, offer enough evidence to evaluate the quality and results of his research. D.'s central thesis states that the printed version of *The Quiet Don* consists of two entirely different texts. One belongs to the novel's real author, presumably Fedor Kriukov; the other is contributed by the coauthor, Sholokhov.[12] The author's text can be identified by its poetry, masterly use of folk idiom, precise and graphic re-creation of the ethnic milieu, and conceptual and artistic unity. By contrast, the coauthor's text is flat. It bespeaks lack of professional fluency and literacy and smacks of journalese. The coauthor's handling of the vital Cossack dialect is inept, resulting in the creation of labored, artificial dialogues. When the coauthor attempts to imitate the author in descriptions of nature or environment, he produces sections that are stylistically ludicrous and unrelated to the plot. Likewise alien to the original text are the coauthor's insertions of political passages with pro-Soviet content. On the other hand, the coauthor eliminated a number of ideologically unacceptable chapters, creating visible gaps in the narrative. All these changes notwithstanding, the novel still retains that "cohesion of ideas" (Tolstoi's term) which manifests itself, not in direct authorial pronouncements, but in the totality of artistic representation (16-19).

The textual analysis which underlies D.'s conclusions is often unconvincing, contradictory, or demonstrably faulty. Since I have already published a review article on D.'s book, I shall limit myself to citing a few of the most representative examples supporting my opinion. In what can be regarded as D.'s central finding, he claims that more than 95 percent of the first two volumes belong to the author (20).[13] This figure is invalidated by D.'s own statement that eleven chapters dealing with Bunchuk in part 5 were written by the coauthor (59). These chapters alone comprise about 20 percent of volume 2. D.'s overlooking the fact that Bunchuk is absent from one of these chapters (chap. 21) is insignificant, since he also fails to notice that chapters 19, 20, and the original chapter 25 deal with Bunchuk and Anna. The three chapters cannot be assigned to the author, for, according to D., Anna was invented by the coauthor (113). Consequently, at least thirteen chapters of volume 2 should be treated as the coauthor's, leaving the author with no more than 75 percent of its text. This figure is subject to further reduction, for D. ascribes to the coauthor large portions of chapter 1 (part 4), which also deals with Bunchuk (53-57). Conversely, the author's percentage can be slightly raised, thanks to yet another discrepancy in D.'s calculations. Among the eleven chapters attributed to the coauthor are chapters 4 and 17, parts of which are treated by D. elsewhere as characteristic of the author's ideas (51-53). Furthermore, one is puzzled by D.'s inclusion of chapter 30 in the eleven chapters. This chapter portrays the execution of Podtelkov men and contains some of the most powerful scenes in the novel. These scenes could have been created only by a gifted artist, not by the hapless coauthor. Besides, merely twenty-five lines of chapter 30 are allotted to Bunchuk.

One may agree with D. that the chapters with Bunchuk are on the whole artistically inferior to the large segments of the novel which he attributes to the author. Nonetheless, one does not have to share his view that most of the chapters on Bunchuk were written by the coauthor. The author, too, might have portrayed people like Bunchuk, Anna, and the factory workers less vividly than the Cossacks because he was not so well acquainted with the city as with his native countryside. The presence of a single author is suggested by the fact that the chapters with Bunchuk bear the same stylistic peculiarities as the entire novel. One may point to the metaphoric use of verbs like *lopat'sia* (burst), *teplit'sia* (glimmer), and *lokhmatit'sia* (become tousled), to similes expressed by means of the instrumental case or by past passive participles of verbs denoting skilled or artistic work ("cut out," "carved"), and to linguistic infelicities betraying a half-educated writer. One may also refer to the repetition of identical syntactical patterns and to the use of the epithet *goluboi* (blue) in scenes of violent death to enhance the theme of human cruelty.

In a number of instances where D. attributes certain passages to the author he can be proved wrong by citing historical sources used in writing the novel. For example, chapter 4 of volume 3 cannot belong completely to the author, as D. maintains (20), for it is largely based on materials drawn from General Krasnov's memoirs published in 1922. Nor can any portion of chapter 20, part 7, be regarded as Kriukov's, for the bulk of its text was copied from Kakurin's book *How the Revolution Was Fought* (1925-1926).[14]

D.'s favorite method is to look for inconsistencies, contradictions, and lacunae caused by the coauthor's tampering with the original text. More often than not, D.'s inferences are questionable or wrong. The figure of Bunchuk crushed by Anna's death to the point of complete indifference to his cause and to his comrades represents for D. an utterly improbable transformation of the stalwart Bolshevik at the coauthor's hands (59). Also, Grigorii's surrender to the Bolsheviks at the end of the novel is perceived by D. as a manifestation of weakness incompatible with Grigorii's character (147). D. fails to notice that the cases of Bunchuk and Grigorii reflect the author's belief in the supreme significance of love and in the devastating consequences of the loss of the beloved. In search of missing links, D. concludes that the novel must have contained chapters describing the life of the Steppe detachment. The author could not have omitted this theme "because of its connection with the theme of the Upper Don uprising" (78). The Steppe detachment existed from February 12 (25) to May 5 (18), 1918, until the decision of the Don Cossack Parliament to establish a regular Don Army.[15] Activities of the Steppe detachment cannot therefore be linked with the Upper Don uprising that started almost a year later. As an example of "classical incoherence" resulting from the coauthor's haphazard revisions, D. points out the discrepancy he sees between the opening lines of chapters 1 and 32 of volume 3. Chapter 1 tells us that when the Red forces were being driven out from the Don region in April 1918, the Khoper Cossacks (*khopertsy*), almost to a man, went with the Reds.[16] In chapter 32 we read that one of the stanitsas participating in the Upper Don uprising was Ust'-Khoperskaia. How could it happen, D. demands, that the Khoper Cossacks joined the rebellion when they were said to have retreated with the Reds? (138.) The answer is that the word *khopertsy* designates Cossacks of the Khoper District, not of Ust'-Khoperskaia stanitsa. This stanitsa belonged originally to the Ust'-Medveditskaia District and was included in the newly formed Upper Don District in the spring of 1918. Ust'-Khoperskaia, the home stanitsa of Ataman Kaledin, was a leader in armed uprisings against the Bolshevik rule.

D.'s study is rife with errors pertaining to the history and geography of the Don region and to the plot of *The Quiet Don*.[17] Some of the errors, like those involving the age or ranks of the characters, are inconsequential; others, like the treatment of the Cossack Bunchuk as an "outsider" and a lower-middle-class citizen (51) or the assertion that Grigorii did not want to take prisoners (126), led to faulty arguments and inferences. Solzhenitsyn says that D. wrote his study with interruptions and was seriously ill during the last months of his work. This must have affected the quality of his research. D.'s weakness, however, is his proclivity toward a highly speculative approach to the subject, a tendency to see things that do not exist.

D.'s failure to support his thesis by means of convincing textual analysis is coupled with his unacceptable explanation of the existence of some parts of *The Quiet Don* in 1917. In an excerpt from his "Detective Chapter," D. speaks of a sketch "From the Quiet Don" which the art critic Sergei Goloushev offered to Leonid Andreev for publication in the newspaper *Russkaia volia* (*The Russian Freedom*) in September 1917. Hazarding some of his strangest conjectures, D. avers that Goloushev "clearly did not write and could not have written" such a sketch (163). D., as Solzhenitsyn explains in a note, was to reveal that the sketch offered by Goloushev was none other than chapters from a novel which Kriukov was working on. Goloushev could have received the chapters from Serafimovich (168). As a matter of fact, Goloushev did write the sketch in question and published it under his pseudonym, Sergei Glagol'.[18]

Discussion of D.'s study can hardly be complete without an examination of the main points of Solzhenitsyn's preface to it. What D. attempted to demonstrate through textual analysis Solzhenitsyn proposes in the form of questions that arise in minds of many who find it impossible to accept

Sholokhov as the author of *The Quiet Don*. In Solzhenitsyn's opinion, Sholokhov's limited life experience and meager education were obviously insufficient for the creation of a novel featuring a broad portrayal of various layers of pre-Revolutionary society in the Don region. Nor was Sholokhov capable of providing a deep insight into the psychology of this society (5).

In response to this argument one might say that Sholokhov grew up in the environment described in *The Quiet Don*. He spent several years of his childhood in the home of a Cossack (to whom his mother was married) and then lived almost uninterruptedly in the Don region, side by side with the Cossack families before and during the publication of the novel. Marrying a Cossack woman from a large family provided him with additional sources of information about the Cossacks. He could certainly learn a great deal from his father-in-law. *The Quiet Don* focuses on the middle stratum of the Cossacks typified by the Melekhov family. Certain details about the pre-Revolutionary mode of life of such Cossacks could have been learned during the first years of the Soviet regime. Although Soviet rule destroyed their military and administrative setup, the Cossacks still retained some pre-Revolutionary aspects of their family life. During the NEP period they continued to till their individual plots of land, ride their horses, go to church, have their traditional weddings and funerals, sing their songs, and preserve their old-time mentality. Naturally, the elements of traditional life were not as strongly manifested during the NEP as in tsarist times, but they were there and Sholokhov could have observed them until their virtual disappearance in the wake of collectivization and the 1932-1933 famine. Sholokhov's own observations, combined with stories he might have heard about local teachers, students, merchants, and priests, were probably sufficient to enable him to draw a rather limited picture of the village intelligentsia found in *The Quiet Don*. Talks with his mother, who once served as a maid in an estate of a Don landowner, could have helped him to describe the Listnitskiis. However, in dealing with these people the author reveals a weak grasp of the psychology and ethics of the upper class, as well as his ignorance of the officer's honor code. It is unthinkable that Lieutenant Evgenii Listnitskii would take no action after being severely beaten by the Corporal Grigorii Melekhov. "This is an incident that an officer and nobleman like Listnitskii could not easily forget," says Dmitrii Mirskii.[19] Colonel Maksim Buguraev told me that Listnitskii should have tried his best to kill Grigorii. I agree with D. that Listnitskii's report about Bunchuk's Revolutionary activities, which he sends to the divisional staff (2:15-16), sounds unnaturally servile in the place where the officer expresses his devotion to his country and the monarch (57). One also encounters in Listnitskii's speech words and forms that a person of his time and upbringing could not have used. Thus in the early editions of the novel he spoke of being a part of "their collective" (2:98) or used the informal pronoun *ty* (thou) when addressing his father in a letter (1:321). A young writer like Sholokhov is more apt to make all of the above mistakes than an author who is supposed to be closely acquainted with various strata of the Don society.

Solzhenitsyn wonders how Sholokhov was able to depict World War I and the Civil War with such knowledge and vividness if he took no part in the former and was merely fourteen when the latter ended (6). It can be suggested that for his depiction of World War I Sholokhov could have used oral accounts by its participants, printed sources, and his own experiences from fighting anti-Bolshevik partisans during his service in the food-requisitioning detachment and in special punitive units. The Cossack Ivankov, for example, told him about the encounter between Kriuchkov's troop and the German cavalrymen. Descriptions of battles with unerring listings of names and numbers of Russian units could have been based only on published or archival materials. Skirmishes with anti-Bolshevik partisans can, of course, stand no quantitative comparison with the Great War's battles in terms of men and weapons. Nevertheless, fighting the partisans, Sholokhov experienced the emotions of a man engaged in deadly combat, and he could have projected them into battle scenes of World War I. Thus, to represent the war that he had never seen, Sholokhov could have drawn upon sources similar to those used by Tolstoi in *War and Peace* and Solzhenitsyn in *August 1914*.

For his portrayal of the Civil War Sholokhov had one more source: his personal observations. He lived in the center of the Upper Don uprising, in or near the combat zone. He might have witnessed some fighting, and he certainly saw the troops of both sides and the situation in Cossack villages. Many episodes, particularly in volumes 3 and 4, could go back to these observations. Local Cossacks, especially Kharlampii Ermakov, enriched his knowledge of the uprising with their firsthand accounts. Actually, the Civil War for Sholokhov ended when he was seventeen, rather than fourteen. The active resistance of the anti-Bolshevik partisans, which can be regarded as the last phase of the Civil War, continued in the Upper Don region into 1922. Scenes of the Civil War outside the Upper Don region were as a rule created with the aid of Russian émigré or Soviet sources identified in the preceding chapter. Sholokhov's scanty education and his lack of life experience at the time of the writing of *The Quiet Don* could have been in part compensated for by characteristic attributes of a very gifted author: lively imagination, impressionability, keenness of observation, and a good memory. The presence of these qualities explains why descriptions of separate battles are usually impressive. On the other hand, general accounts of military operations are not free from serious factual errors. The creator of *The Quiet Don* was not as competent a historian as Solzhenitsyn suggests. This is one more point in favor of Sholokhov's authorship of the novel.

For Solzhenitsyn *The Quiet Don* is a work of "artistic force attainable only by an experienced master after many attempts" (6). Yet, he says, the "best" volume 1 and the "magnificent" volume 2 had each, supposedly, taken just one year to write. Volume 3 was submitted less than a year after the appearance of volume 2, and only the intervention of censorship interrupted the astoundingly rapid pace of the novel's publication. Assuming that Sholokhov is a genius, Solzhenitsyn continues, one is hard put to explain why he, since 1929, has not created anything matching either the high quality of the first two volumes or the speed with which they were written. There is a sudden change between volumes 2 and 3. *Virgin Soil Upturned* is patently inferior in the aesthetic respect to *The Quiet Don* and shows a different perception of the world (6, 8-9).

First of all, it is difficult to share Solzhenitsyn's view that *The Quiet Don* could have been written only by an experienced master. It is precisely its first two volumes which contain so many grammatical and stylistic irregularities that their authorship can be attributed to none other than a relatively inexperienced, half-educated, but exceptionally talented writer. This inference suggests itself with particular clarity after reading the novel's earliest printed text in *Oktiabr'*. Preference for individual volumes of *The Quiet Don* is a matter of taste. Nevertheless, it is strange that Solzhenitsyn considers volume 2 "magnificent" and obviously thinks it artistically superior to the last two volumes. Fragmentary and overcrowded with characters, volume 2 bears the stamp of inexperience and haste to a greater degree than any other volume. Solzhenitsyn is not specific about the "sudden change" he sees between volumes 2 and 3, although he undoubtedly means a rapid artistic decline. Actually, volume 3 was written in the same style as the first two. Stylistic differences between volume 4 and its predecessors are largely due to Gor'kii's campaign against dialecticisms, Sholokhov's own wish to moderate his earlier metaphoric exhuberance, and a more careful editing by proofreaders. On the whole, however, volume 4 constitutes an integral part of the novel, in both style and ideas.

Although *Virgin Soil Upturned* differs from *The Quiet Don* in terms of craftsmanship and political orientation, one should not discount the possibility of Sholokhov's being able to author both of these novels. As was noted in chapter 2 of this study, the increased stringency of ideological control, Sholokhov's joining the Communist Party, and his becoming a "classic" of socialist realism made it impossible for him to produce a significant work of art. Sholokhov was not the only prominent writer who failed to surpass his achievements of the 1920s in his later published works. It is also true of Fedin, Leonov, Olesha, Vsevolod Ivanov, and Babel'. At least Sholokhov managed to maintain his artistic and philosophical standards in the last volume of *The Quiet Don*. Furthermore, some descriptions of nature and the brutally vivid portrayal of Khoprov's murder in volume 1 of *Virgin Soil Upturned* could probably have been written only by the author of *The Quiet Don*. Even volume 2 of *Virgin Soil Upturned* shows conceptual and artistic ties with *The Quiet Don* in passages dealing with Razmetnov's true love for his dead wife. And in both volumes of *Virgin Soil Upturned* the Cossack dialogue retains its genuine ring, though it is degraded by what Solzhenitsyn calls "Shchukar"s strained and coarse humor" (9). The overall inferiority of Sholokhov's works written after *The Quiet Don* may be explained partly by an exhaustion of his creativity. He saturated his epic with artistic images to the degree that it was hard for him not to repeat himself in his later writings.

The first three volumes of *The Quiet Don* must have been written with astounding speed, though over a somewhat longer period of time than indicated by Solzhenitsyn. Volume 2 included an undetermined number of pages from *The Don Country*, which Sholokhov began to write in 1925, and volume 3 could hardly have been submitted in finished form in less than a year after the publication of volume 2. Volume 3 was probably not complete when its first twelve chapters appeared in the January-March issues of *Oktiabr'* for 1929. Sholokhov seems to have written these chapters shortly before their serialization. For example, the manuscript of chapter 8 printed in the March issue of the journal is dated February 14, 1929. Volume 3, or the bulk of it, must have been completed by 1930, also a remarkable achievement. To write as rapidly as he did, the author of the first three volumes of *The Quiet Don* must have had talent, great capacity for work, and time. I believe that the young Sholokhov did possess the first two qualities. Also, in 1926-1929 he probably had more time for writing than in later years, when he would be beset by uninvited visitors and burdened with extraneous obligations as a high-ranking Party figure and member of the Supreme Soviet. Furthermore, after beginning his work on *The Quiet Don*, Sholokhov all but stopped writing short stories. A weighty argument in Sholokhov's favor is that he demonstrated his ability for exceptionally quick writing by completing volume 1 of *Virgin Soil Upturned* within the space of one and a half years. Work on its sequel and volume 4 must have proceeded at the same pace, for in the middle of 1934 Sholokhov claimed that both these books were nearly finished. This accomplishment is especially remarkable, since volume 4 of *The Quiet Don* is about a hundred pages longer than either of the first two volumes and since Sholokhov was compelled to interrupt his literary work for six months in connection with the 1932-1933 famine and the persecution of local Communists. Publication of the final volume of *The Quiet Don* must have been delayed for years, due to the political climate of the 1930s and to Stalin's intervention into the fate of Grigorii Melekhov.

Solzhenitsyn contends that over the years Sholokhov has given his consent to political and stylistic revisions of *The Quiet Don*. Particularly striking is his toleration of the massive replacement of picturesque Don idioms by inexpressive everyday words in the 1953 edition. This is not the behavior of the mother "who preferred to give up her child rather than to have it divided in two" (9).

My impression is different. Sholokhov made some corrections in the early editions of the first three volumes of *The Quiet Don*. Yet, as we know, in September 1932 he notified the publishing house Khudozhestvennaia literatura (Artistic Literature) that he would not make any further revisions. His stance mattered little, however. Given its political objectivity, *The Quiet Don* had to be subjected to periodic censorship. Sholokhov could do nothing about it. The best example of this is the 1953 edition. Had Sholokhov voluntarily assented to the innumerable revisions made in this edition, he would not have rescinded the great majority of them three years later. If he seems to have shown lack of concern over the 1953 mutilations, it is not because he was not the author of *The Quiet Don* but because of the political climate of the time and of a personal problem. People close to him maintain that in the 1950s he was suffering from acute alcoholism and was remarkably indifferent to the text of his works.[20] This statement, however, is too general. In 1951 Sholokhov was upset about the incompetent editing of the forthcoming 1953 version of *The Quiet Don*, and in September 1953 he asked Khudozhestvennaia literatura when this edition would be coming out.[21] He was definitely not indifferent to the 1956-1960 edition of his *Collected Works*. Over many years he evinced no more than a marginal cooperation with censorship. He hardly made any political additions to *The Quiet Don* and seems to have accepted only unavoidable cuts and changes. This is why many readers of even the 1956 text of *The Quiet Don* continue to wonder how such an impartial work could have been published in the Soviet Union. As for the style, Sholokhov must have welcomed elimination of his numerous grammatical errors and excessive dialecticisms. He might have disagreed with many puritanical corrections, but could do nothing about it. The inability of the Soviet writer to see his work published in the form he considers to be the best was demonstrated by Solzhenitsyn himself. In 1963-1964, in the hope of having *The First Circle* accepted by *Novyi mir*, he made substantial revisions in its original text.[22] Among other things, he removed nine chapters with strong political coloration and changed the main line of the plot. In the original version Volodin makes a telephone call to the American Embassy in Moscow to warn the ambassador of the Soviet agents' arrangement to receive the secret of the atomic bomb in New York.

The likely author of *The Quiet Don*, according to Solzhenitsyn, is Fedor Kriukov, though it is possible that the novel might have been written by an unknown genius from the Don region who perished during the 1920-1922 liquidation of those who fought against the Reds (192).[23] In December 1974, at a press conference in Stockholm, Solzhenitsyn emphatically reiterated his views on the authorship of *The Quiet Don*, adding that a book of such low artistic merit as *Virgin Soil Upturned* could have been written by Sholokhov's father-in-law.[24]

In contrast to Solzhenitsyn, who did not present any concrete evidence in support of Kriukov's authorship, Roi Medvedev offers his arguments in Kriukov's favor in considerable detail. The idea of Kriukov's being the real author of *The Quiet Don* is not new. Medvedev speaks of its appearance in 1937-1938, but it must have occurred to some people even earlier. For example, Aleksandr Listopadov expressed his belief in the possibility of Kriukov's authorship to Mikhail Gol'dshtein in 1938. It is, however, inconceivable that the distinguished folklorist, who knew Kriukov personally, did not think of this possibility during or shortly after the publication of the first two volumes of *The Quiet Don*. Indeed, such thoughts were entertained at that time by several educated persons who wrote to General Petr Popov asking him for his opinion.[25] Like other advocates of Kriukov's authorship, Medvedev believes that he has found ample support for his hypothesis in Kriukov's origin, life, and works. A brief biographical profile of Kriukov is therefore in order.

Kriukov was a Cossack by birth, a well-educated man, and a genuine Don writer. He was the elder son of the ataman of Glazunovskaia stanitsa in the Ust'-Medveditskaia District. His father, a literate and well-to-do man, sold a large piece of land to pay for his son's higher education. Upon his graduation from the Petersburg Institute of History and Philology, Kriukov taught history and geography in secondary schools in Orel and Nizhnii Novgorod. He began writing when he was a student, showing great interest in the old Cossack mode of life. Two of his sketches on this subject were published in 1892. His first work of fiction, the story "Kazachka" ("A Cossack Woman"), appeared in 1896 in the liberal journal *Russkoe bogatstvo* (*The Russian Wealth*). In 1906 he was elected deputy to the First State Duma from the Don Military Region. He was one of the leaders of the People's Socialist Party and his views may be characterized as those of a liberal populist. In protest against the dissolution of the First Duma, he signed the Vyborg appeal (1906), calling on Russian citizens to resist the draft and to stop paying taxes. The signature cost him three months in prison. Barred from teaching, he served for some time as a librarian in the Petersburg Mining Institute and then devoted himself completely to literary work. He is known as an author of numerous stories, sketches, and essays. Many of them deal with the Don region, revealing Kriukov's close acquaintance with the Cossacks' customs, language, history, economics, and social stratification. As befits a true Cossack author, Kriukov knew well the local songs and was an excellent singer. A great number of his writings were printed in *Russkoe bogatstvo*. Although Kriukov was a prolific author held in high esteem by Gor'kii, Serafimovich, and Korolenko, he was relatively unknown to the average reader. This situation was in part due to the fact that merely two collections of his writings have ever been published. The first, *Kazatskie motivy* (*Cossack Themes*, 1907), did not sell well; the second was volume 1 of his *Rasskazy* (*Stories*, 1914), but publication of further volumes was apparently cut short by the beginning of World War I. During the Revolution and the Civil War Kriukov took a strongly anti-Bolshevik stance. In the spring of 1918 he was arrested by the Bolsheviks, and it was only by coincidence that he escaped being shot. Later he served as secretary of the Don Cossack Parliament and edited the official newspaper of the Don Government, entitled *Donskie vedomosti* (*The Don News*). During the disastrous retreat of the Whites he died of typhus or pleurisy on February 20 (March 4), 1920, in or near Novokorsunskaia stanitsa in the Kuban' region.[26] Because of his opposition to the Bolsheviks, only one of his writings is known to have been reprinted in the Soviet Union. His name is occasionally mentioned in journals or scholarly publications, but a 1965 attempt at a partial rehabilitation of his image by a Don writer, Vladimir Molozhavenko, was met with a vicious rebuff rife with factual distortions.[27] Other endeavors to rehabilitate Kriukov or to have his writings published proved futile.[28]

Roi Medvedev's first study on the authorship of *The Quiet Don* was written shortly after the publication of D.'s *The Current of "The Quiet Don."* Zhores Medvedev reports that the manuscript of his brother's study began to circulate in *samizdat* in the winter of 1974-1975 under the title *Zagadki tvorcheskoi biografii Mikhaila Sholokhova* (*Riddles of Mikhail Sholokhov's Creative Biography*). This manuscript, or its enlarged version, came out in French translation in the summer of 1975 as *Qui a écrit "le Don paisible"?*[29] In the spring of 1977 Roi Medvedev published an article, "The Riddles Grow: *A Propos* Two Review Articles," in response to my reviews of *The Current of "The Quiet Don"* and *Qui a écrit "le Don paisible"?*[30] Soon thereafter there appeared in Great Britain Medvedev's book entitled in English translation *Problems in the Literary Biography of Mikhail Sholokhov* (1977). It represents an expanded and revised version of *Qui a écrit "le Don paisible"?* Among other things, Medvedev added a new chapter that deals with Soviet writings published on the occasion of the seventieth anniversary of Sholokhov's birth. My discussion of Medvedev's views will be centered on *Problems in the Literary Biography of Mikhail Sholokhov*. At the same time I will take into account that some of the opinions expressed by him in this study were modified or elaborated in his article "The Riddles Grow," which was written somewhat later.

Medvedev's analysis proceeds from the concept that a literary work reflects a multifaceted image of its author. It is possible, therefore, to extrapolate from the text a large number of distinguishing features relating to the author's life, philosophy, political and social ideas, artistic peculiarities, knowledge of the subject matter, attitude toward the characters, and so on. In *The Quiet Don* Medvedev sees fifty or sixty main distinguishing features. Only five or six of them can, in his opinion, be attributed to the young Sholokhov, the author of *The Don Stories*, while the mature Kriukov can be entitled to forty or forty-five.[31] But since Kriukov's score is below 100 percent, Medvedev finds it premature to draw conclusions (109). Medvedev, of course, does not number the points he assigns to Kriukov or to Sholokhov, but the amount of evidence he adduces in favor of each author corresponds to his ratings. The evidence can be divided roughly into three categories: biographical, ideological, and stylistic. Each of the categories will be taken up in the above order.

In the biographical category the emphasis is placed on Kriukov's life experiences, which are supposedly mirrored in *The Quiet Don*. Compared with the other categories, the biographical category presents a more tangible kind of evidence which, in some instances, can be accepted or rejected by references to established facts. This applies, for example, to Kriukov's military and political activities between 1914 and 1920. Medvedev contends that "all the events occurring at the front and described in *The Quiet Don* Kryukov could have seen with his own eyes" (91). In particular, Medvedev means the events of August and September 1914 described in volume 1 and "a picture of the front in October 1916" given in volume 2 (91). To buttress his inference, Medvedev asserts that Kriukov "spent August and September 1914 mainly at the front in the Caucasus" as a newspaper reporter (91), that he returned several times to the front with an ambulance unit, and that he was summoned for service as an officer in the summer or fall of 1916. In fact, Kriukov could have witnessed none of the Great War's events portrayed in *The Quiet Don*. Fortunately for us, during that war he published a sufficient number of topical sketches to allow us to trace his whereabouts and activities with a great degree of certainty. During the first three months of the war he lived primarily in Glazunovskaia and Petrograd. His sketches sent to the Moscow newspaper *Russkie vedomosti* (*Russian News*) in September-October are revealingly entitled "In the Deep Rear." In November, when Turkey entered the war, he went to the Caucasus. There he joined the Third Hospital of the State Duma. The entire journey to the front turned out to be quite long. Kriukov arrived in the battle zone only in February 1915 and stayed there about two weeks, working with the State Duma's hospital in the Kars region.[32] With that same unit he spent several weeks in the Galician sector of the front in the winter of 1916. His stay coincided with a lull in the fighting caused by a period of bad roads. The hospital unit was stationed about four miles behind the front lines, and Kriukov made only occasional visits to the trenches.[33] I could find no evidence of Kriukov's making additional trips to the front with or without an ambulance unit. Furthermore, his regular contributions to *Russkie vedomosti* for the rest of 1916 show beyond any doubt that Kriukov was neither called up as an officer in the summer or fall of that year nor served at the front in October.[34] It is also doubtful that he could have been an officer anyway. In peacetime he was exempt from military service because of his nearsightedness.[35]

The question of Kriukov's rank and military experience arises again when Medvedev suggests that Kriukov served in the Don Army as an artillery officer and that he used his new combat experience to depict engagements of the Veshenskii Regiment described in chapters 8 through 10 of volume 3 (95). Kriukov indeed saw some action in May-June 1918. He took part in the uprising of the Ust'-Medveditskaia Cossacks and joined a unit commanded by Lieutenant Colonel A. V. Golubintsev. The unit did not belong to the Don Army, however. In June 1918 Kriukov suffered a slight concussion from an artillery shell.[36]

Neither Golubintsev nor biographical information about Kriukov published in the November 18 (December 1), 1918, issue of the Rostov journal *Donskaia volna* (*The Don Wave*) makes any mention of Kriukov's having ever served as an artillery officer. If he had, it would have been noted by at least one of these sources. Kriukov probably left Golubintsev's unit soon after suffering the concussion. I have found no evidence indicating that he fought for any prolonged period of time. In any case, he could not have stayed in the army after having been elected secretary of the Don Cossack Parliament in August 1918. The election precluded his participation in many events described in chapters 8 through 10 because these chapters cover the entire second half of 1918. Even in his military involvement in 1918, Kriukov was not as close geographically to the battle area of the Veshenskii Regiment in chapter 8 as Medvedev maintains. Kriukov fought and suffered the concussion near Archadinskaia in the Ust'-Medveditskaia District, while the Veshenskii Regiment saw action in the vicinity of Durnovskaia in the Khoper District (3:73). The two stanitsas are some eighty miles apart as the crow flies, not a short distance considering the condition of the roads.

A further debatable point is Medvedev's parallel between the battles for Ust'-Medveditskaia described in chapter 11 of part 7 and the fighting in the same area in the fall of 1919 during which Kriukov fought in the ranks of the Ust'-Medveditskaia home guard. Medvedev does not date the earlier battle, but he links it to Kriukov's participation in the fighting of the fall of 1919 (95-96). The earlier battle occurred in June 1919, when combined forces of the Don Army and the Upper Don insurgents were swiftly driving the Reds out of the Don region. At that time Kriukov was still in Novocherkassk. The fighting he took part in during the fall of 1919 was a dogged defensive battle.

Thus Kriukov appears to have taken no part in—nor even witnessed—a single battle with which Medvedev links him. This seriously weakens Medvedev's position, for, in his opinion, personal military experiences are indispensable for creating superb martial scenes. He does not think that creative imagination and oral or written accounts of fighting are sufficient for portraying war on the level found in *The Quiet Don*. By the same token, the authors of *War and Peace* and *August 1914* could not have given their powerful descriptions of battles without having been involved in actual combat (41-42). It seems that by Medvedev's own standards Kriukov's military experience would be insufficient to produce the great variety of battle scenes encountered in *The Quiet Don*. His military qualifications in this respect are on a par with Sholokhov's. Kriukov knew more than Sholokhov about World War I, but less about the details of the Upper Don uprising. Altogether, he might have spent less time in close proximity to the battle zone than did Sholokhov. The hypothesis of Kriukov's authorship is further undermined by the fact that no battle in *The Quiet Don* closely resembles any in which he took part.

Medvedev gives much weight to Kriukov's opportunities to witness historical events as secretary of the Don Cossack Parliament. Kriukov, Medvedev believes, "could have seen with his own eyes the negotiations between the Military Government headed by the Don Cossack Ataman and the Regional Military Revolutionary Committee, the collapse of the government and the Assembly, the suicide of the Don Cossack Ataman Kaledin, the start of the formation of the Volunteer Army on the Don, the retreat from Novocherkassk of the active-service Ataman Popov, his negotiations with Kornilov and Alekseyev, as well as many other events described in the second book of *The Quiet Don*" (93).

These events cover the period from January 15 (28), 1918 (negotiations in Novocherkassk), to February 13 (26), 1918 (Popov's negotiations with Kornilov), the time when Kriukov lived in the Ust'-Medveditskaia District, mainly in Glazunovskaia.[37] Medvedev's errors must stem in part from his belief that Kriukov was secretary of the Don Cossack Parliament "in 1917-1918" (17), instead of from August 1918 to November 1919.[38] Medvedev overlooks the possibility that the abovementioned historical events, as well as a few others (42), did not have to be witnessed to be depicted in *The Quiet Don*. Its author could, and did, take them from published accounts by participants. Nearly all of these sources came out after Kriukov's death. Medvedev seems to overestimate the importance of personal experiences for an author writing an epic on contemporary events. At the same time he underplays the role of creative imagination and the possibility of using written and oral sources. The author of *The Quiet Don*, whoever he might be, could not have seen all the events that Medvedev suggests he witnessed. In "The Riddles Grow" Medvedev expresses a more guarded view about Kriukov's chances of having personal acquaintance with the military and political events described in *The Quiet Don*. He still suggests, however, that "Krjukov was far more likely than Šoloxov to have been a first-hand observer of the most important events described in *The Quiet Don*."[39]

Medvedev's supposition that Kriukov worked on a novel comparable to *The Quiet Don* rests on statements by Molozhavenko, the literary scholar B. N. Dvinianinov, and the Don writer Prokhor Shkuratov. Molozhavenko says that Kriukov began to write a big novel about the Cossacks before World War I (18). Dvinianinov dates the writing 1917-1918, when Kriukov lived in Glazunovskaia (80). Neither of these statements is documented and their credibility is somewhat lessened by factual errors in their respective contexts. Molozhavenko, for example, asserts that before World War I collections of Kriukov's stories "were coming out one after another," while Dvinianinov maintains that Kriukov "in 1919 went over to the White Guard camp for good."[40] Actually, Kriukov was firmly on the White side in 1918, if not earlier. In the spring of 1918 he wrote a poem in prose, "Rodimyi krai" ("My Native Land"), enthusiastically welcoming the Cossacks' uprising against Bolshevik rule as a fight for freedom, honor, and the native land.[41]

Shkuratov, who knew Kriukov personally, remembers having seen in the Ust'-Medveditskaia newspaper *Spolokh* (*The Alarm*) Kriukov's statement that he had just completed the first volume of his new novel, *The Quiet Don*. There is no indication as to when Shkuratov could have seen the newspaper, which also, he says, contained seven letters from Korolenko to Kriukov. In one of them Korolenko urged Kriukov to continue writing about the Don region (98). This is probably a reference to Korolenko's letter of November 11 (23), 1898, written in reply to Kriukov's doubts about his ability to handle themes other than those pertaining to the Don region. Korolenko's letter can be found in the November 18 (December

1), 1918, issue of *Donskaia volna*. A large part of this issue was devoted to Kriukov in connection with the twenty-fifth anniversary of his literary activity. Of course, Korolenko's letter could have been published elsewhere, and possibly in the fall of 1918. On November 10 (23), 1918, Ust'-Medveditskaia stanitsa organized a big celebration of Kriukov's jubilee. The author was present, accepting congratulations from some twenty delegations. The account of this celebration is given in *Donskaia volna* for December 9 (22), 1918. Neither this account nor any item on Kriukov in the November 18 (December 1) issue of the same journal says anything about his writing a novel dealing with the Don Cossacks. This is not to say that Shkuratov could not have read about it elsewhere, but his information ought not to be treated as absolutely reliable. Medvedev admits that, at the age of eighty, Shkuratov could occasionally give different versions of the same event (98).

A more concrete piece of information about Kriukov's plans was given by Petr Margushin, who in 1919 belonged to the editorial staff of *Donskie vedomosti*. Several times Kriukov spoke to Margushin of his new novel portraying the occupation of the Don by the Bolsheviks. In order to learn more details about the circumstances under which the occupation took place and about the Bolshevik terror in occupied areas, Kriukov, in the late spring of 1919, sent Margushin on a fact-finding mission to those stanitsas which had suffered most from Bolshevik atrocities in the preceding winter. Kriukov intended to use Margushin's findings for his novel.[42]

Margushin's firsthand account sheds light on a few important points. It appears that in the spring of 1919 Kriukov's novel must have been in its initial stage. The author might not yet have decided upon its title, for he did not mention it to Margushin. Since Kriukov planned to write about the Bolshevik occupation of the Don, he might not have included in his prospective novel an earlier period that is covered in volume 1 of *The Quiet Don*. Given his particular interest in the Bolshevik rule and its repercussions, Kriukov would possibly have put more emphasis on history and less on family life than we see in *The Quiet Don*. It is unthinkable that a person like Kriukov would forego writing about the Civil War in the Don region. If we assume that he started working on a novel in 1919, or a year earlier, two questions must be answered. One concerns the amount of time Kriukov had for writing his novel; the other is about its setting.

The bulk of volume 3 and the first four chapters of part 7 deal with the Upper Don uprising, covering the time from March to June 1919. During this period Kriukov served in Novocherkassk as secretary of the Don Cossack Parliament. When the news of the uprising reached the Parliament's presidium, he drafted an appeal encouraging the insurgents.[43] Inspired by the successful offensive of the Don Army, he left for Glazunovskaia around June 1 (14).[44] He arrived in his native stanitsa shortly after its liberation from the Reds and must have stayed there for at least a month, since two decrees of the Don Cossack Parliament dated July 1 (14) do not bear his signature.[45] At some later point he made a trip to Novocherkassk, returning to Glazunovskaia in August or early September. At this time the Reds were advancing toward the stanitsa. Kriukov felt dispirited, saying that "everything was lost." He promptly left Glazunovskaia, never to return.[46]

I could not find any evidence about Kriukov's visiting the Veshenskaia area between June and September 1919 to collect material about the Upper Don uprising. Even if he had gone to Veshenskaia, he could not, during a short visit, have obtained the kind of detailed information which underlies the description of the uprising in *The Quiet Don*. Nor did he have much time for writing. From Glazunovskaia he went to Ust'-Medveditskaia, where he joined the local home guard unit late in September or early in October 1919.[47] About a month later he arrived in Novocherkassk and took part in meetings of the Don Cossack Parliament until at least mid-December. At this time there occurred his widely publicized conflict with Professor Efim Tarasov, head of the Don Information Section. Tarasov accused him, as head of the Don Press Section, of refusing to supply the Information Section with the paper needed for printing bulletins for the army and the general public. Tarasov called him a Bolshevik and claimed that paper was being used for printing various literary works, including Kriukov's own "useless stories." The author proved Tarasov wrong and the latter was fired.[48] Before the seizure of Novocherkassk by the Reds (January 7, 1920), Kriukov joined the ill-fated retreat of the Whites. No doubt he was unable to write much during the last two months of his life. He was retreating under the most miserable conditions and, to make it worse, he fell ill with typhus. Apart from his inability to give a comprehensive picture of the Upper Don uprising, Kriukov, as Medvedev admits, could not have portrayed the evacuation of the Whites from Novorossiisk in part 7, nor could he have written the whole of part 8. The evacuation and events depicted in part 8 occurred after his death.

The setting of *The Quiet Don* can be used as a strong argument against Kriukov's authorship of the novel. Its author would have needed an intimate knowledge of Veshenskaia and the neighboring stanitsas and villages. With the exception of the estate Iasenovka (Iagodnoe), all these places appear in the novel under their real names, often accompanied by detailed descriptions of localities. The sole fictitious place is Tatarskii, which combines characteristics of several local villages. Moreover, a number of characters in *The Quiet Don* are modeled upon real people who lived in or near the places where Sholokhov lived. The best known of them is Kharlampii Ermakov. Grigorii Melekhov inherited his military record, the "Turkish" blood, and certain personal traits. The kinship between Grigorii and his prototype was periodically explored by Soviet scholars in interviews with Ermakov's daughter Pelageia (namesake of Grigorii's daughter) and some older Cossacks.[49] A noteworthy testimony came from a White Cossack officer, Evgenii Kovalev, who in the summer of 1919 served with Ermakov in a Don Army brigade manned by the Upper Don Cossacks. Kovalev found so much affinity between Ermakov and Grigorii with respect to appearance and daring that he wrote an article entitled "Kharlampii Ermakov, the Hero of *The Quiet Don*." In the same brigade Kovalev met "quite a few personages from Sholokhov's *The Quiet Don* who actually existed."[50] Neither Kovalev nor the émigré Cossack journal that printed his article can be suspected of fabricating parallels between real people and the characters from *The Quiet Don* in order to justify Sholokhov's claim to its authorship.

Several prototypes come from the village of Pleshakov, where Sholokhov's father served as manager of a steam grain mill. At least three of them worked in the mill: Ivan Alekseevich Serdinov, David Babichev, and Valentin. They appear as Ivan Alekseevich Kotliarov, Davydka, and Valet in the novel. Serdinov, the first chairman of the Elanskaia Revolutionary Committee, was captured by the White Cossacks, marched through the villages in a column of Communist prisoners, and was killed by Mariia Drozdova, the widow of a White Cossack officer. Kotliarov was killed by Dar'ia Melekhova under similar circumstances. The three Shumilin brothers, nicknamed Shamili, resemble the Kovalev brothers who lived in Karginskaia. The merchants Ozerov and Levochkin from the same stanitsa can be recognized in the figures of Mokhov and Atepin. All these analogies had been established before rumors of plagiarism were revived in connection with the awarding of the Nobel Prize to Sholokhov.[51] The analogies therefore were likely to have resulted from scholarly investigations rather than from attempts to collect evidence in support of Sholokhov's authorship of *The Quiet Don*.

This cannot be said of the markedly intensified search for prototypes that followed the appearance of D.'s and Medvedev's studies. Organized by Soviet authorities, the search was intended to look like a spontaneous action of local enthusiasts prompted by the seventieth anniversary of Sholokhov's birth. It was not literary scholars but teachers and students of the Veshenskaia secondary school who were chosen to conduct the research. Their findings were published in the Rostov monthly, *Don*. No doubt Sholokhov wholeheartedly approved of this undertaking. He readily helped researchers with bits of pertinent information.[52] One can only wonder why it had taken the local enthusiasts so long to organize such an exciting investigation.

The secondary-school team visited places where Sholokhov had resided. Interviewing their inhabitants, the researchers obtained additional information about the already known prototypes and found a few new ones. They reported, for example, that in Pleshakov the Sholokhovs rented two rooms in the house belonging to the Drozdov family. This Cossack family served in some ways as a model for the portrayal of the Melekhov family. The appearance, political attitudes, and fate of Petr Melekhov are said to be similar to those of the officer Pavel Drozdov, while the character and the prewar life of Grigorii are believed to resemble those of Pavel's brother Aleksei.[53] The Communist Petr Semiglazov, whom Grigorii kills in combat in chapter 37 of volume 3, turned out to be patterned after Petr Semiglasov. His picture can be seen in a museum in Bokovskaia.[54] Several prototypes were found for characters of the early stories. Aleksei Kramskov, the prototype of Aleshka in "Aleshka's Heart," is still living in Karginskaia.[55]

In addition to the secondary-school team's findings, *Don* printed a detailed account of how the life and death of Ivan Serdinov are mirrored in Ivan Kotliarov.[56] The author of the article is Serdinov's son. The article could easily have been written much earlier, for example in 1965, when Serdinov, Jr., attended the celebration of Sholokhov's sixtieth birthday.[57]

It is possible that Serdinov, Jr., and interviewers from the Veshenskaia secondary school tended to focus on similarities rather than on differences between the novel's characters and their prototypes. It is also possible that the older informants, some of them in their eighties or nineties, might not have had the clearest recollections of the remote past. Nonetheless, it is undeniable that *The Quiet Don* is deeply rooted in an area with which Kriukov seems to have had no lasting contact. I do not know Kriukov's life well enough to assert that he had never been to Veshenskaia. If he had, it must have been for a brief time, not sufficient for getting to know well the numerous individuals who served as models for secondary and tertiary characters of *The Quiet Don*. Kriukov's fiction, essays, and travel sketches provide no evidence of his interest in Veshenskaia. His stories dealing with the Cossacks are as a rule set in or around Glazunovskaia. His contemporaries had no difficulty in identifying their characters with local inhabitants.[58] Had Kriukov started writing a novel before or during the Revolution, he would almost certainly have set it in his native Ust'-Medveditskaia District.

Medvedev's ideological argumentation singles out *The Quiet Don* from among Sholokhov's writings chiefly in terms of political objectivity, humanism, and attitude toward the non-Cossack population of the Don region, the so-called outsiders. While Medvedev is correct about the special position of *The Quiet Don*, his evidence against Sholokhov's authorship is open to question. His key statements on the important issue of the relationship between Sholokhov's early stories and *The Quiet Don* are too sweeping: "The *Tales of the Don* are utterly subjective. They have no trace of that calm objectivity and ostensibly dispassionate attitude which we have determined as a typical feature of *The Quiet Don*" (72); "The main heroes of the *Tales of the Don* are Young Communists, grain-requisitioners, the representatives of the new order. In the *Tales* there is no admiration for the Cossacks and their way of life. Only on one or two occasions do we encounter Red Cossacks. Otherwise the Cossacks are enemies, bitter and vicious enemies" (63).

True, Sholokhov's political sympathies in the majority of his early stories are on the Soviet side, though there are not one or two, but ten stories depicting Red Cossacks. Two of these Cossacks serve in responsible positions as food commissars. The viciousness and atrocities of the White Cossacks are shown not only in the early stories but also in *The Quiet Don*. A real distinction between the stories and the novel lies in the portrayal of the Red terror. In the stories one encounters only isolated cases of Red violence, primarily involving harsh treatment of those who refused to comply with the forced requisition of grain. There are no scenes of the organized Red terror which was largely responsible for the retaliatory brutality of the White Cossacks. This omission was due in part to the strong pro-Soviet feelings of the young Sholokhov. On the other hand, no Soviet author, in the 1920s or later, would have been allowed to publish a short story about the Red terror. The very genre of the short story requires concentration on a single theme, and the censor would not approve of a story featuring Red atrocities. Bits of Red terror can be interspersed in a larger work, provided they are attributed to the "right" individuals, such as Trotskyites, and matched or overshadowed by the enemy's barbarity. This is the way the Red terror in the Don region is treated in Iurii Trifonov's novel *Starik* (*The Old Man*, 1978). A more objective depiction of Red violence in volume 3 of *The Quiet Don* ran, as we know, into nearly insurmountable obstacles and had to be toned down.

A number of the early stories—notably "Alien Blood," "The Offense," "The Wind," "The Crooked Path," and "Galoshes"—are objective, nonpolitical, and focused on purely human problems. It is precisely for these reasons that "The Wind" has not yet been reprinted and that "The Offense" was published for the first time only in 1962. In all five of the stories the characters act in accordance with the dictates of their hearts or physical impulses. In some other stories the personal element coexists with the political. "Aleshka's Heart," for instance, is patently pro-Soviet, but its title signifies the inborn kindness of its protagonist. The White Cossacks are shown as brutes in "A Family Man," yet the story accentuates not a political conflict but the personal drama of a father who takes part in the killing of his two sons in order to save his other seven children. In the politically biased story "The Whirlpool" the execution of Red Cossacks is followed by the description of a whelping she-wolf. As so often in *The Quiet Don*, this sequence implies a contrast between the self-destructive acts of human beings and the creative biological forces of nature.

Thus the early stories cannot be regarded as ideologically monolithic. Some of their salient features disturbed Soviet critics of the 1920s and the early 1930s. When serious criticism of Sholokhov was still printable, *The Little Soviet Encyclopedia* gave the following evaluation of his *oeuvre*: "Sholokhov wrote a number of works that are ideologically close to proletarian literature ('A Mortal Enemy,' 'Dry Rot'); however, more characteristic for him are those works where class awareness is replaced by general humaneness. Biologism—love for everything 'living,' the urge to propagate the species, and so forth—takes precedence over class criterion ('Shibalok's Seed,' 'A Family Man,' 'The Foal,' and others). The same idea is expressed in the central character of *The Quiet Don*, Grigorii Melekhov."[59] Medvedev also cites a part of this evaluation, but he treats it merely as a reference to occasional similarities between the early stories and *The Quiet Don* (63).

One may challenge Medvedev's view by pointing out that *The Quiet Don* represents a further development of objective, universal, and "biological" elements of the early stories, rather than of their topical and political aspects. This development was possible because the bulk of *The Quiet Don*, as mentioned in chapter 1, was written in a conservative, essentially anti-Soviet milieu at a time when many people believed in the stability of the NEP, seeing in it a sensible return to the old ways of life. The impact of the "petty-bourgeois" environment was cited by Sholokhov as the cause of ideological defects in *The Quiet Don*. The use of émigré sources must have contributed to the impartial portrayal of the White camp.

Medvedev observes that most of the early stories were written in 1924-1925 in the same surroundings as *The Quiet Don*, but their ideological orientation is that of a Komsomol member.[60] This observation ignores the fact that the first three volumes of the novel were created primarily in 1926-1929, when most of the stories had already been written. Sholokhov's political commitment during this period should not necessarily have been as strong as in 1924-1925, when his thinking was affected by his association with the Young Guard group in Moscow in 1923-1924. Upon his return to the Don region, Sholokhov's political enthusiasm might have gradually declined, sinking to its lowest level during the last years of the NEP. This supposition can be corroborated indirectly by the publication dates of his stories. The majority of his biased stories, such as "The Shepherd," "The Food Commissar," "The Way and the Road," and "A Woman Who Had Two Husbands," came out in 1925, while the more objective and neutral stories, such as "The Offense," "Alien Blood," and "The Wind," were published in 1926-1927 or later. Not every story fits into this pattern, and some stories may have longer intervals than others between the time of writing and the time of publication. Even so, the general picture emerging from the examination of all the publication dates suggests that, as time went on, Sholokhov's stories became increasingly dispassionate. One reason for Sholokhov's objectivity in *The Quiet Don* might be associated with the peculiarities of his creative mind. As a man endowed with great talent, he might have felt the ability to create a significant work of art. His intuition could have told him that to realize his potential he would have to forego ideological bias and represent the complexities of life as impartially as possible. And he did what he could, to the point of rejecting Stalin's idea on the fate of Grigorii Melekhov.

Yet *The Quiet Don* is not devoid of direct authorial support for the Bolshevik cause. The author calls Communist teaching "a great human truth" (2:45); he asserts that Red soldiers fight insurgent Cossacks for the liberation of the working people, for Soviet power and Communism (3:276), while the Cossacks wage "an inglorious war against the Russian people" (4:261). Proponents of the author-coauthor hypothesis would be inclined, with Medvedev, to regard such declarations as Sholokhov's political insertions into the original text. But if it were so, one is entitled to ask why Sholokhov failed to delete from the same original those numerous phrases which, in Medvedev's words, "*no Communist author could have in any way written*."[61]

The presence of blunt political pronouncements in the predominantly objective narrative of *The Quiet Don* can be explained by the tension between Sholokhov the artist and Sholokhov the ideologist. The artist had to portray life as it was. When Sholokhov, for example, wrote about the Upper Don uprising, he did not have to invent the Red terror, the Cossacks' love for their native Don country, and their determination to fight for it and for their own lives. Since he understood and shared the Cossacks' attachment to their land, he was able to compose a moving digression about the "dear steppe" (3:59-60). He could graphically present Grigorii's reasons and enthusiasm for fighting the Bolsheviks at the beginning of the Upper Don uprising when he was galloping madly to join the insurgents (3:188). Thoughts, sentiments, actions, and condition of the insurgents could be conveyed in concrete artistic images embodying real situations. On the other hand, there existed no facts of life which would demonstrate that Communism is "a great human truth," that it brings liberation to the working people, that it puts an end to all wars. The Communist invasion of the Don region brought oppression and terrorism. This was the reality, and Sholokhov represented it in artistic images. At the same time he had the choice of either writing about "the great human truth" in the form of abstract definitions or of fabricating scenes that would illustrate the greatness of "the truth." He elected the first alternative. He probably did so not only because it was a lesser evil, but also because he continued to believe in Communist ideology. Yet his belief at the time of writing *The Quiet Don* must not have been as strong as before, and he was unwilling to articulate it in propagandistic images as he did in many of his early stories.

It is easy to accept Medvedev's overall view of striking disparities between *The Quiet Don* and Sholokhov's later works with respect to his philosophy and treatment of sensitive subjects. In *Virgin Soil Upturned*, Medvedev states, Sholokhov rejects the philosophy of general humanism characteristic of *The Quiet Don* and takes a political stance determined by a consideration of class struggle (151). In contrast to a straightforward treatment of complex issues in *The Quiet Don*, "The Fate of a Man" eschews the exploration of such crucial questions as to why millions of Soviet soldiers were taken prisoner and why Stalin abandoned them and punished them as traitors (161). *They Fought for Their Country* offers a distorted and oversimplified idea of the purges, while Sholokhov's speeches and topical writing are normally "dogmatic and reactionary" (165, 166). My difference with Medvedev lies in determining the origins of these developments. To him they signify the possibility that their author could not have written *The Quiet Don*. To me they are deplorable results of the political climate in the Soviet Union and of Sholokhov's degeneration as the standard-bearer of socialist realism. This was discussed in chapter 2 of this study.

Two important ideological features of *The Quiet Don* are, for Medvedev, the hostility toward outsiders and "the Cossack version of working-class populism," which envisions the establishment of popular self-rule within the framework of a united Russia (43). Both these features, Medvedev contends, are incompatible with Sholokhov's "publicly voiced opinions" as well as with his being a young Communist and outsider; but they may reflect the philosophical credo of the Cossack populist Kriukov (182). Although Kriukov seems to have favored autonomy of the type outlined by Medvedev, one can only speculate as to whether or not Kriukov's concept of it coincides with that of the author of *The Quiet Don*. The novel does not advocate any single clear-cut idea on the Cossack self-government. It simply offers a variety of views expressed by such different people as Izvarin, Podtelkov, General Krasnov, and the radical Cossacks, who stood for a completely independent Don region ruled by the soviets without Bolsheviks (3:259-260). Sholokhov could have presented all these views as historical facts, irrespective of his attitude toward them.

There is no reason why he could not have treated the Cossacks' hostility toward the outsiders in like fashion. It is debatable whether the author of *The Quiet Don* shows any personal dislike for the outsiders. Medvedev and D., for example, point to the unsympathetic portrait of Sergei Mokhov, but his vices stem less from his being an outsider than from his unscrupulousness as a merchant. In any event, the author hardly approves of the Cossack cockiness and pugnacity which provoked such savage fighting with the Ukrainians at Mokhov's steam mill (1:134-139).

Moreover, there is no conclusive evidence that Kriukov nurtured any animosity toward the outsiders. A passage from his sketch "New Things" cited by Medvedev speaks of the Cossacks' antagonism toward the outsiders who laid claim to the Cossack land (182). However, in this quotation Kriukov reproduces ideas of an average Cossack rather than his own. He attributes them to an old man attending the Cossack Congress in Novocherkassk in the spring of 1917.[62] At this time and during the Civil War, Kriukov must have disliked the aggressive, pro-Bolshevik type of outsiders, not outsiders per se. In 1915 he described movingly the anxieties of an outsider couple from Glazunovskaia whose son was drafted into the army. Notes of compassion sound in his words about the estrangement of a young outsider in Cossack surroundings.[63] Although Kriukov was a Cossack patriot, he appears to have been free from national or social prejudices. With heartfelt sympathy he wrote about a Jewish nurse, the first member of the hospital unit of the State Duma to die of typhus. He called her "the daughter of a people with curtailed rights."[64]

There are no valid grounds for Medvedev's suggestion that the opposition to "the senseless imperialist war" and "a scornful picture of Krasnov" in *The Quiet Don* are to be associated with Kriukov rather than with Sholokhov (43). In fact, Kriukov's attitude toward World War I was firmly patriotic. At the beginning of the war he wanted the young people of Glazunovskaia to march through its streets carrying banners and singing the national anthem. He regularly went to see off the Cossacks leaving for war, prayed with crowds, and made farewell speeches. He was sensitive to suffering caused by the war, but saw no alternative to fighting and deplored the disintegration of the Russian army in 1917.[65] We do not know whether Kriukov despised Krasnov. If he did, he might not have agreed to serve as secretary of the Don Cossack Parliament when Krasnov was the Don ataman. It is important to note that *The Quiet Don* contains no mention of the two sessions of the Parliament (fall of 1918 and winter of 1919) at which Kriukov had the chance to observe Krasnov's activities as the Don ataman. By contrast, several pages of the novel are devoted to the Parliament for the Salvation of the Don (spring of 1918) that elected Krasnov ataman of the Don Cossacks.[66] Kriukov was not a member of this Parliament. Opinions about Krasnov's portrait in *The Quiet Don* may vary; the general himself deemed it accurate.[67]

Medvedev's main literary arguments for Kriukov's authorship of *The Quiet Don* are based on his evaluation of the artistic merits of Sholokhov's early stories and on a comparison of excerpts from *The Quiet Don* with those from Kriukov's works. Medvedev readily admits that many of Sholokhov's stories offer genuine Cossack speech, numerous original metaphors, some aptly drawn landscapes, and terseness of expression in depiction of tense situations and the characters' feelings (60-61, 65). Nonetheless, these qualities cannot provide for him a satisfactory explanation for "the enormous unfilled gap" that separates the stories from *The Quiet Don* (67). Medvedev is particularly interested in comparing descriptions of nature in Kriukov's writings and *The Quiet Don*. After citing several lengthy landscapes, he expresses the belief that if *The Quiet Don* had been published anonymously in the late 1920s, many critics would have named Kriukov as the most likely author of the greater part of the novel (109).

A strong support for this hypothesis can be found, for example, in the following passage from Kriukov's long story "Zyb' " ("Ripples," 1909):

> The stanitsa was wrapped in fresh April twilight. The whitewashed walls of the huts merged into one vague long line, *but the black roofs were sharply silhouetted against the rose-colored glass of the fading sunset*. In the damp and resonant air, in the invisible cold heights, the anxious quick cry of wild geese rang out. They flew over the stanitsa to where *the lakes that overflowed the meadow lay motionless like murky mirrors* among the groves of trees. For a moment the inaccessible voices of the wild expanse resounded *like tinkling silver*; they amazed the vigilant ear, and melted away, like the path of a falling star.
>
> The earth, warmed during the day, exuded a humid warmth, a scent of old drying manure, and the sticky aroma of the first young verdure.[68]

The first italicized phrase reminds the reader of those figurative and literary expressions in *The Quiet Don* which present sharp outlines of people and objects against the background of the sky, as well as of the lavish use of color and the metaphorical combinations of two nouns formed by means of the genitive case. The second and third phrases are instrumental similes; one of them describes voices as "silver" and uses the epithet *zybkii* (unsteady), translated here as "tinkling." These three features, especially the first, are characteristic of *The Quiet Don*. The entire passage resembles the novel's landscapes in that nature is perceived simultaneously with the senses of sight, hearing, and smell. Analogies between landscapes in Kriukov's writings and in *The Quiet Don* can be attributed to the fact that their authors grew up in similar countryside surroundings, had a keen eye for natural phenomena, and occasionally employed kindred images. At the same time there are striking stylistic differences between the two writers. Kriukov's style is more emotional and subjective. He feels strong compassion for the poor, the humiliated, the unfortunate. He transmits his feelings in lyrical passages like this one from "Ripples":

> And for a long time in the stifling silence of their hut, in the grey darkness, both Terpug and his mother silently wept. There were no words, no complaints, but the whole soul was crying: Why? Why are we so wretched? . . . All the mute poverty of the cramped hut, each rotting corner, each corroded worm-holed door post asked with anguish: Why? . . . Helplessly their thoughts tossed about in an impasse: There is nothing you can do. . . . The burning wrong, the endless despair. . . . There is nothing you can do.[69]

Such sentimentalities are absent from *The Quiet Don*, as is the lofty, temperamental diction that Kriukov chooses at times to convey his enthusiasm:

> Oh, the beauty and intoxication of fighting, the fascination of risk and mad impetuous movement, the stunning display of force and daring! . . . The innocent vanity and joy of the fighter before the women whose amazed glances crown him with silent praise! . . . How many bruises Terpug had endured for their sake![70]

The three excerpts cited above reveal a prominent stylistic feature that sets Kriukov's works apart from *The Quiet Don*: the absence of dialecticisms. There are hardly any local words in Kriukov's authorial narrative. Very seldom one encounters in it words like *ugadat'* (recognize), *kochet* (rooster), *bok* (side of the river), or *ogorozha* (fence), the meanings of which are immediately clear. It is not uncommon to see the author of *The Quiet Don* use dialectal words and forms where Kriukov uses their literary equivalents. Furthermore, the extensive use of dialecticisms is characteristic not only of *The Quiet Don*, but also of the early stories and volume 1 of *Virgin Soil Upturned*. Of course, the total number of local words in the author's speech in *The Quiet Don* is substantially larger than in the early stories; but this is not surprising, given the size of the novel and the fact that seven stories and one feuilleton are entirely or predominantly narrated by the characters. A considerable number of identical dialecticisms can be found in both the stories and in *The Quiet Don*. Among them are: *brekhat'* (lie), *brunzhat'* (buzz), *chapigi* (handles of a plough), *chikiliat'* (limp), *moskliaven'kii* (skinny), *nastoburchit'* (raise), *peredom* (ahead, first), *pikhat'* (push), *podsmyknut'* (pull up), *posered'* (in the middle of), *rasteleshit'sia* (strip to the skin), *sboch'* (by, at the side of), *shumet'* (shout), *tiankii* (clingy, thick), *var* (boiling water), *zhalit'sia* (complain). The presence of these and many other dialecticisms calls into question Medvedev's assertion that the stories "contain absolutely no Don Cossack dialect, not of the kind that permeates *The Quiet Don*" (62). Medvedev refers here to the authorial narrative, not to the Cossack speech, which is full of dialecticisms in the novel as well as in the stories.

In addition to dialecticisms, *The Quiet Don* shares with the early stories and other works of Sholokhov hundreds of identical or nearly identical expressions and figures of speech. For instance, in *The Quiet Don* Kornilov's eyes look "dimmed, gray, as if strewn with ashes" (2:163). In "Dry Rot" the dark eyes of a Cossack "smoldered dimly, like pieces of coal under ashes" (7:487). In "The Fate of a Man" Sokolov's eyes look "as if sprinkled with ashes" (7:594). Many recurrent images are vehicles in simple instrumental similes expressing power and swiftness. These vehicles include the words "wind," "whirlwind," "wave," "kite," and "lightning." The frequent use of instrumental similes in *The Quiet Don* and the early stories is another indication of a close relationship between these works. Especially remarkable is the kinship between the stories and the novel's first volume. Roughly one-third of their similes are in the instrumental case. One hundred and eighty-seven instrumental similes in volume 1 comprise 40 percent of their total number in the novel; the frequency of their occurrence in that volume is about twice as high as in "Ripples," which has twenty-two instrumental similes, possibly more than any other work by Kriukov.

Strong evidence for Sholokhov's authorship is the multitude of grammatical, semantic, syntactical, and punctuation errors found in the earliest editions of his stories, in the first three volumes of *The Quiet Don*, and, to a lesser extent, in volume 1 of *Virgin Soil Upturned*. Writings of the well-educated pedagogue Kriukov are practically devoid of such defects. His deviations from the standard Russian, however scarce they might be, betray the influence of his native Cossack idiom. In a few cases he spells the local word *levad* (grove) phonetically as *livad* and quite regularly puts the preposition *pod* (under) directly before the noun *sarai* (shed) in phrases like "lezhat' pod saraem" (lie under the shed). A more precise wording would be "lezhat' pod navesom saraia" (lie under the overhang of the shed).

An affinity between *The Quiet Don*, the early stories, and volume 1 of

Virgin Soil Upturned is further seen in the virtual absence of the words *pozadi* (behind) and *tochno* (like, as if) from the authorial narrative in the earliest editions of these works. I found merely two cases of *pozadi* in the stories and none in volumes 1, 2, or 3 of *The Quiet Don* or in volume 1 of *Virgin Soil Upturned*. Except for a rare use of the colloquial *nazadi* (behind), one encounters only *szadi* (behind) regardless of whether it functions as an adverb or as a preposition. In Kriukov's writings there appears to be one instance of *pozadi* for every two instances of *szadi*. In all of Sholokhov's fiction only four similes are formed by the connective *tochno*. The corresponding figure for Kriukov's writings which I have read is 130. He consistently uses *tochno* in his fiction. There are nine cases of it in "Kazachka" ("A Cossack Woman," 1896), eleven in "K istochniku istselenii" ("To Healing Waters," 1904), twenty-two in "Shkval" ("The Squall," 1909), and nine in "V kamere No. 380" ("In Cell No. 380," 1910), a short story of twenty-five pages. If Kriukov were the author of *The Quiet Don*, what would the reason be for his employing *tochno* in merely two similes out of two thousand?

Some significant differences between *The Quiet Don* and Kriukov's writings are apparent at first sight. Kriukov's stories are written in a smooth literary language; they have few examples of inversions and "clipped" sentences without verbs. Their figures of speech are less daring and more precise. Kriukov as the historian and ethnographer is strongly felt in his fiction. His stories are more descriptive and static than Sholokhov's. He lacks the flair for creating dramatic, well-developed plots. His characters are apt to engage in lengthy, at times tedious, conversations. His own narrative is not as terse as that of the author of *The Quiet Don*. Some of the above differences can be illustrated by comparing the handling of similar scenes in Kriukov's stories and in *The Quiet Don*.[71]

A variety of factual errors in *The Quiet Don* can be cited here as the final argument against Kriukov's authorship of the novel. These are the errors that Kriukov could not, or was not likely to, have committed. It is out of the question that he would have called Kaledin (2:123), Nazarov (2:283), and Bogaevskii (3:344) *nakaznye* (appointed) atamans. These atamans were not appointed but elected, a fact of tremendous significance for the Don Cossacks. For nearly two hundred years, since the time when Peter the Great put an end to Cossack independence, the ataman of all the Don Cossacks had no longer been elected by the Cossack Parliament but was appointed by the tsar. The first thing the Don Cossacks did after the February Revolution was to restore the historical function of the Parliament to elect the ataman. General Kaledin was the first ataman to be elected in this manner on June 18 (July 1), 1917. The author of *The Quiet Don* must have associated the term *nakaznyi* with "chief" and applied it to appointed and elected atamans alike. Only a person who was quite young in 1917-1919 and did not learn much of Cossack history later could have made this blunder. The blunder is also found in the characters' speech. Kudinov refers to Bogaevskii as an appointed ataman (3:394) and old Melekhov does the same with Krasnov (4:108). Neither character can be blamed for the error. A Cossack officer and commander of insurgent Cossacks, Kudinov certainly knew that Bogaevskii had been elected, while Melekhov was a member of the Parliament that elected Krasnov. The same error occurs in "The Whirlpool" (7:375), linking the early stories to *The Quiet Don.*

A weak knowledge of Cossack history accounts for calling Count Mikhail Grabbe, the last appointed ataman, a baron (4:131) and for giving the name Vasilii to Kondrattii Bulavin, the famous Don ataman who fought against Peter the Great (1:153). Kriukov would not have made these errors. As a matter of fact, he wrote "Kondratii Bulavin" in an ethnographic sketch.[72] In his sketches from the World War I period, Kriukov consistently refers to Petersburg by its new name, Petrograd, while the author of *The Quiet Don* and his characters fail to notice the change at times (1:324, 358). Kriukov knew, of course, that the headquarters of the Russian army was at Mogilev in Belorussia, not in Moldavia (2:143). He also knew better than to use the Russian surname Stolypin for the East Prussian town of Stallupönen, which in Russian is either Shtallupenen or Stalliupenen or Stalupenen (1:68; 2:46). No doubt Kriukov was sufficiently familiar with etiquette not to allow a well-dressed man to have his bowler on in the presence of ladies in a respectable restaurant on Nevskii Avenue in the summer of 1917 (2:115).

Several inaccuracies pertaining to military service indicate that the author of *The Quiet Don* could hardly have been an officer, or even a private, in the White Army, particularly in the Cossack units. No Cossack officer or private would call a sub-lieutenant (*podkhorunzhii*) an officer, as the author of *The Quiet Don* repeatedly does (4:98, 172, 359). For some reason Kriukov also calls a sub-lieutenant an officer in "Ofitsersha" ("The Officer's Wife," 1912), but he probably would not have done so after serving in Cossack units during the Civil War. The author of *The Quiet Don* is unaware of the distinction between *chin* and *zvanie*. Dictionaries give "rank" for both of these words; yet in the tsarist and White armies the word *zvanie* applied to the nonofficers and the word *chin* to officers, except in the expression *nizhnie chiny* (the ranks). In the Cossack troops the highest *zvanie* was that of a sub-lieutenant, while the lowest *chin* was that of a second lieutenant (*khorunzhii*). The author of *The Quiet Don* is therefore wrong in applying the word *chin* to a sub-lieutenant (3:227). Speaking to his superior, Captain Listnitskii should have said "Sir!" instead of "Colonel!" (2:100). Similarly, a Cossack should have addressed his officer by rank, not by the word "commander," in the summer of 1917 (2:132). Finally, the name for the trail of the gun carriage (3:252) is *khobot* (trunk, trail), not *khvost* (tail).

There is no way of telling how many of these military errors could have been made by Kriukov. One can merely suggest that he would have shown more knowledge and prudence than the author of *The Quiet Don*. On the other hand, all of these errors could have easily come from Sholokhov's pen. There are similar mistakes in his other works. In "Dry Rot" he has a Cossack say that during World War I his squadron was commanded by a lieutenant colonel (7:482). It is impossible that a person of such high rank would have led a squadron at the time when losses in officers were very heavy. Moreover, as Colonel Maksim Buguraev told me, lieutenant colonels did not command squadrons even in peacetime. A Cossack regiment normally had two lieutenant colonels, serving as assistants to the regimental commander. In "The Whirlpool" a colonel designated his rank by drawing stars on his tunic, something he should not have done because a colonel's shoulder straps had no stars on them. In *Virgin Soil Upturned* it is Captain Polovtsev, a regular Cossack officer, who states that the rank of *podporuchik* (second lieutenant in infantry or artillery) is equivalent to sub-lieutenant in the Cossack troops (5:165).

This error and a few others mentioned in the three preceding paragraphs were corrected between 1933 and 1954. Most errors, however, have remained, including those concerning elected atamans, sub-lieutenants, and Stallupönen. I asked a recent émigré writer from the Soviet Union how it is possible that critics like Iurii Lukin, who has been editing Sholokhov's works since the early thirties, are so uninformed about their subject matter. All they care about, the writer replied, is the prestige they enjoy from being Sholokhov's editors. In a way we should be thankful to these editors for allowing us to see more of the original text of *The Quiet Don*.

In summary, there is enough evidence to rule Kriukov out as the likely author of *The Quiet Don*. The novel is set in an area unfamiliar to him; he could not have had enough time to write volumes 3 and 4; the majority of the important historical sources used for the novel came out after his death; stylistic differences between his writings and *The Quiet Don* are much greater than similarities; and he could not have committed the multitude of grammatical, syntactical, and factual errors found in *The Quiet Don*. Conversely, there is sufficient evidence to conclude that the novel was written by Sholokhov. It is set in the area where he lived, and many of its characters have prototypes among the people whom he knew or observed. For the description of events that he did not witness personally, Sholokhov relied upon oral accounts and published materials. He had the time to write all four volumes of the novel and he demonstrated that he could write with remarkable speed. His modest education and the haste with which he wrote the first three volumes are responsible for the inordinate number and variety of errors encountered in the early editions of *The Quiet Don*. Ideological differences between *The Quiet Don* and other works by Sholokhov can be explained by the circumstances in which the epic's first three volumes were written and by the author's determination and ability to create a significant and, consequently, objective work of art. Furthermore, the objectivity of *The Quiet Don* was in a way prefigured by the objectivity of some of the early stories. *The Quiet Don* is markedly superior to the rest of Sholokhov's writings, but the artistic inferiority of *Virgin Soil Upturned* and later works was unavoidable, due to the increasing stringency of political controls, Sholokhov's becoming a hard-line Party writer, a certain exhaustion of his artistic capabilities, and his drinking problem. The artistic disparity between *The Quiet Don* and the early stories is great, but the main reason for it appears to be the rapid growth of Sholokhov's craftsmanship. The gap between the best of the early stories and the first two volumes of *The Quiet Don* is, relatively speaking, not as wide as that between the best stories and the inane, imitative feuilletons written two or three years earlier. The kinship between *The Quiet Don* and the rest of Sholokhov's works is revealed in the hundreds of identical or nearly identical images, similar landscapes, and basically the same attitude toward love and nature. The early stories, *The Quiet Don*, and volume 1 of *Virgin Soil Upturned* are further united by a liberal use of dialecticisms and numerous, frequently identical, grammatical irregularities. *The Quiet Don* must have been written by a young, half-educated Don author who was influenced by the Soviet ornamental prose of the 1920s. Sholokhov fits this description.

In spite of all the evidence in Sholokhov's favor, not everyone would be willing to dismiss Kriukov as the possible author of *The Quiet Don* unless the question of plagiarism were investigated by a computer. Fortunately, such an investigation has been conducted by a team of Swedish and Norwegian scholars since the fall of 1975. As of now, only preliminary results have been published. They were obtained from the analysis of a relatively small number of excerpts from *The Quiet Don*, Kriukov's stories, Sholokhov's early stories, and volume 1 of *Virgin Soil Upturned*. The findings show that Sholokhov's works are significantly closer to *The Quiet Don* in terms of sentence length, the distribution of parts of speech in sentences, and the richness of vocabulary than are Kriukov's.[73] Particularly revealing are the data on the commonest part-of-speech combinations at the beginnings and the ends of sentences. In view of the heavy stylistic and political revisions of Sholokhov's works, selection of passages for a computer study must be made with great care. The Swedish-Norwegian team should have used the earliest text of *The Quiet Don*, instead of the 1956 edition. An analysis of the earliest text would probably have revealed a bigger difference between *The Quiet Don* and Kriukov's works.

In his article "The Riddles Grow," Medvedev stated that he had previously exaggerated Kriukov's role in the creation of *The Quiet Don*. He readily conceded that the bulk of volumes 2, 3, and 4 was written by Sholokhov.[74] On the other hand, Medvedev reaffirmed his adherence to the author-coauthor hypothesis, suggesting that volume 1 was written by Kriukov before 1920 and fell into Sholokhov's hands "in an almost finished form."[75] That volume 1 displays characteristic traits of Sholokhov's style is, in Medvedev's view, due to Sholokhov's work on its original text. Sholokhov, Medvedev maintains, was not "a mere copyist," but a kind of creative editor. More talented than the well-educated Kriukov, he was able to improve greatly the artistic quality of "a fair text."[76] This does not convince me. Volume 1, with its numerous dialecticisms, grammatical and stylistic errors, metaphorical exuberance, and instrumental similes, diverges more sharply from Kriukov's writings than any other volume of *The Quiet Don*. To make something so Sholokhovian as volume 1 of *The Quiet Don* out of a typical Kriukovian text would be tantamount to a virtual rewriting of the entire volume, to creating an original work with respect to vocabulary and style. Although many readers seem to think of volume 1 as the best in the novel, it is the volume where the linguistic inexperience of the author manifests itself with utmost clarity. The hand of a young, developing author is also evident in the fact that the descriptions of nature in volume 1 are shorter and less impressive than in the last two volumes. The landscapes in volume 1 are similar to those in the early stories.

It may be noted that a number of prominent émigré Cossacks had no doubts about Sholokhov's authorship of *The Quiet Don*. In 1945 General Petr Krasnov, former Don ataman and a prolific author, told the writer Boris Shiriaev that Sholokhov was "an exceptional writer of enormous talent." The main thing was that he "*wrote the truth*" in *The Quiet Don*.[77] General Petr Popov, former campaign ataman, thought that the language of *The Quiet Don* could not have been Kriukov's. The novel was written by a beginning author, a non-Cossack who lived in the Don region and studied the Cossack way of life. Boris Bogaevskii, a son of the last Don ataman in Russia and editor of *Rodimyi krai*, wrote a favorable outline of Sholokhov's life and work, treating him as the author of *The Quiet Don*. Furthermore, Kriukov's adopted son Petr, a writer and Cossack nationalist, is reported never to have raised the question of his father's having written *The Quiet Don*.[78] Sholokhov himself denied categorically any link with Kriukov: "I do not know and I have never read the writer F. D. Kriukov."[79]

Although D. and Medvedev failed to present convincing evidence in support of Kriukov's authorship of *The Quiet Don*, their writings activated the study of Sholokhov's works and resurrected, so to speak, the writer Fedor Kriukov. In the West, the Swedish-Norwegian computer study has already revealed some important details about the vocabulary and sentence structure of both of these writers. In the Soviet Union, contributions vary in form and value. The first Soviet reaction to the revival of the authorship controversy was the interview given by Konstantin Simonov to the Moscow correspondent of the West German magazine *Der Spiegel*. Simonov spoke of D.'s book, limiting himself to general but sensible arguments in favor of Sholokhov.[80] The choice of Simonov to rebut D. was, of course, not accidental. He happened to be in France when D.'s study came out. He is rather well known abroad from the time of World War II, when the Western democracies were allied with the Soviet Union. Moreover, his statements acquire an extra measure of impartiality because of Sholokhov's open enmity toward him. In 1951 Sholokhov took him to task for defending the use of pseudonyms by Soviet writers, and sharply criticized the quality of his writings at the Second Congress of Soviet Writers.[81]

Except for the Simonov interview, Soviet authorities prefer to marshal their counter-arguments in articles and books, without mentioning D. or Medvedev. Thus a few valid parallels between *The Quiet Don* and the early stories are drawn by the Don writer Anatolii Kalinin in an article representing an obvious reply to *The Current of "The Quiet Don."*[82] Most of the article, however, is filled with empty rhetoric and sickening praise of Sholokhov as man and artist. New details about prototypes for the characters from *The Quiet Don* and the early stories are reported in the familiar articles by the Veshenskaia teachers and Serdinov, Jr. In his book *"The Quiet Don"—Literature and History* (1977), Sergei Semanov gives pertinent information about certain historical figures and events described in *The Quiet Don*. In all likelihood the appearance of Semanov's book was prompted by an intent to demonstrate Sholokhov's competence as a historian. This consideration as well as Semanov's own unfamiliarity with certain events account for the fact that most of Sholokhov's historical errors are not mentioned. Semanov also wrote a script for a documentary film based on *The Quiet Don*. Among other things, the viewer is expected to see the novel's geographical settings and photographs reflecting the Cossacks' life in peace and war.[83] It is hard to imagine that this unusual film, whose shooting began in April 1980, is entirely unrelated to the question of who wrote *The Quiet Don*.

The defense of Sholokhov's authorship of *The Quiet Don* was undoubtedly a prime consideration in publishing *"The Quiet Don": The Novel's Messages* (Rostov, 1979), a collection of articles and miscellaneous items. This book includes the article by the Veshenskaia teachers about prototypes of Sholokhov's characters as well as an abridged translation of Geir Kjetsaa's article "Storms on the Quiet Don." Published originally in *Scando-Slavica* (no. 22, 1976), this article reports preliminary results obtained by Swedish and Norwegian scholars in their computer analysis of several excerpts from the works of Sholokhov and Kriukov. Two previously unpublished and valuable items in the Rostov collection are letters by Sholokhov: one to Ermakov and the other to the publishing house Khudozhestvennaia literatura. It is quite possible that Viktor Gura's book *How "The Quiet Don" Was Created* (1980) is in part a reply to D. and Medvedev. Without polemicizing with them, Gura puts special emphasis on the facts that speak for Sholokhov's authorship of *The Quiet Don*.

At this writing, nearly all demonstrable borrowings on Sholokhov's part come from published historical materials. In some instances he simply copied information. It is up to each individual to decide whether a writer who reproduces well-nigh verbatim several passages from Kakurin's book, or quotes thirty-seven words of direct discourse from Lukomskii's memoirs, or copies 130 words from Krasnov's address, can be charged with plagiarism. Perhaps Sholokhov should have avoided such lengthy appropriations, especially in his military surveys. On the other hand, one can understand his desire to render as faithfully as possible the speech of historical figures whose mode of expression was quite different from his own.

No evidence has so far been presented to show that Sholokhov utilized someone else's imaginative work for writing *The Quiet Don*; that the epic's characters, plot, situations, dialogues, imagery, and descriptions of nature were taken from a manuscript of a known or unknown author. Sholokhov might have had in his hands certain unpublished materials which contained more than purely historical information, and he might have used them in some way for the fictional parts of *The Quiet Don*. But unless we have an authentic manuscript of another writer and are able to ascertain the extent of Sholokhov's borrowings from it, all talk about his theft of *The Quiet Don*, or parts of it, will remain within the realm of conjecture. The burden of proof falls heavily on those who question his authorship of the epic. Their task, formidable as it is, is further complicated by the reluctance of Soviet authorities to release any materials that they regard as potentially injurious to Sholokhov's official image, especially those that may add fuel to the plagiarism controversy. Yet the attitude of Soviet authorities should not necessarily be construed as a policy of covering up a definite case of plagiarism. Until there is convincing proof to the contrary, Sholokhov ought to be treated as the sole author of *The Quiet Don*.

NOTES

Chapter I

1. Mikhail Sholokhov, autobiographical note, *Lazorevaia step': Donskie rasskazy, 1923-1925* (Moscow: Moskovskoe tovarishchestvo pisatelei, 1931), p. 13, and "Schast'ia tebe, ukrainskii narod!" *Radians'ka Ukraina*, October 31, 1954 (reprinted in Mikhail Sholokhov, *Sobranie sochinenii*, 8 vols. [Moscow: Khudozhestvennaia literatura, 1956-1960]), 8:387.

2. Sholokhov's statement in a 1943 interview with a representative of VOKS (All-Union Society for Cultural Relations with Foreign Countries), *Sobranie sochinenii*, 8:382. In his "Pis'mo amerikanskim druz'iam" (1943), Sholokhov speaks, in the same context, of "my seventy-year old mother" (*Sobranie sochinenii*, 8:173). It could be that he preferred to use here a round figure.

3. I. Lezhnev, *Put' Sholokhova: Tvorcheskaia biografiia* (Moscow, 1958), p. 19. The words "more than a hundred years ago" reappear without comment or acknowledgment in Viktor Petelin, *Mikhail Sholokhov: Ocherk zhizni i tvorchestva* (Moscow, 1974), p. 7.

4. Evgenii Popovkin, "Obaianie talanta," *Moskva*, no. 5 (1965), p. 178, in Mikhail Andriasov, comp., *Mikhail Aleksandrovich Sholokhov* (Moscow, 1966), p. 233, and in Mikhail Andriasov, comp. and ed., *Slovo o Sholokhove* (Moscow, 1973), p. 413. This phrase is omitted in Petelin, *Mikhail Sholokhov*, p. 7.

5. *Put' Sholokhova*, p. 21.

6. Letter to M. I. Grineva (Kuznetsova) [December 28, 1933], Gosudarstvennaia ordena Lenina biblioteka SSSR imeni V. I. Lenina, *Zapiski otdela rukopisei*, vol. 29 (Moscow, 1967), p. 264. The letter is dated by the postoffice stamp put on its envelope in Veshenskaia.

7. There are some differences in Soviet accounts of Sholokhov's educational record. Cf. Lezhnev, *Put' Sholokhova*, pp. 24-25; V. V. Gura and F. A. Abramov, *M. A. Sholokhov: Seminarii*, 2d ed. enl. (Leningrad, 1962), pp. 164-165.

8. A. Palshkov, "Molodoi Sholokhov (Po novym materialam)," *Don*, no. 8 (1964), pp. 161-162. Gura and Abramov (*M. A. Sholokhov*, p. 165) and Lezhnev (*Put' Sholokhova*, p. 25) give slightly different dates or places. Palshkov offers a more detailed account of Sholokhov's life during the 1918-1922 period.

9. Quoted in "Beseda Mikh. Sholokhova s chitateliami," *Na pod''eme* (Rostov-on-Don), no. 6 (1930), p. 172. The title refers to Sholokhov's public appearance in the Workers' Palace in Rostov-on-Don at the end of May 1930.

10. Interview with a representative of VOKS, *Sobranie sochinenii*, 8:382.

11. Mikhail Obukhov, "Vstrechi s Sholokhovym (20-30-e gody)," in V. A. Kovalev and A. I. Khvatov, eds., *Tvorchestvo Mikhaila Sholokhova: Stat'i, soobshcheniia, bibliografiia* (Leningrad, 1975), pp. 291, 295; Palshkov, "Molodoi Sholokhov," pp. 163-166, 169-171; Gura and Abramov, *M. A. Sholokhov*, p. 165; Lezhnev, *Put' Sholokhova*, pp. 29-30.

12. Mikhail Andriasov, *Veshenskie byli* (Moscow, 1975), p. 166; Valerii Ganichev, "Vsegda s molodezh'iu," in Andriasov, ed., *Slovo o Sholokhove*, p. 170. In a later article Ganichev states that Sholokhov's detachment numbered 216 men ("Molodye literatory i Sholokhov," *Molodaia gvardiia*, no. 4 [1975], p. 37).

13. M. P. Kim, ed., *Istoriia SSSR: Epokha sotsializma (1917-1957 gg.)*, (Moscow, 1958), p. 262. Soviet sources tend to hush up or minimize the role of the food-requisitioning policy in causing famine.

14. K. Potapov, " 'Tikhii Don' Mikhaila Sholokhova," in Mikhail Sholokhov, *Tikhii Don*, rev. ed. (Moscow: Khudozhestvennaia literatura, 1953), vol. 4, p. 450; Konstantin Priima, "Veshenskie vstrechi: K tvorcheskoi istorii sholokhovskikh proizvedenii," *Pod''em* (Voronezh), no. 5 (1962), p. 148; Mikhail Andriasov, "Syn tikhogo Dona," in Andriasov, comp., *Mikhail Aleksandrovich Sholokhov*, p. 49. Priima's sources indicate that Sholokhov was captured by the Makhno men in May 1921. Our dating rests on the following evidence: in *The Quiet Don* (vol. 4, part 8, chap. 5) Sholokhov speaks of the Makhno raid into the Upper Don region as having occurred in the fall of 1920; the raid and related events are set in September 1920 in the second part of Sholokhov's story "Put'-dorozhen'ka" ("The Way and the Road"); the raid is described in Soviet publications and archival materials which date back to the fall of 1920 (Palshkov, "Molodoi Sholokhov," p. 163).

15. Popovkin, "Obaianie talanta," *Moskva*, pp. 178-179, in Andriasov, comp. *Mikhail Aleksandrovich Sholokhov*, p. 235, and in Andriasov, comp. and ed., *Slovo o Sholokhove*, pp. 414-415; Anatolii Sofronov, "Bessmertnik," *Ogonek*, no. 31 (July 26, 1964), p. 10, and *Sholokhovskoe* (Moscow, 1975), p. 54. Sholokhov's age at the time of the episode is given as seventeen by Popovkin and as fifteen or sixteen by Sofronov. Recounting the episode in his article "Moguchee techenie" (*Moskva*, no. 4 [1975], p. 18), Sofronov made a significant revision. Sholokhov is quoted as saying that he was captured, sentenced to death, and released by the Makhno men. There is no mention of any "kulak." Sofronov (or the censors) must have decided that the story of Sholokhov's cruelty might tarnish his official image. The situation is somewhat ironic since both *Sholokhovskoe* and the April 1975 issue of the monthly *Moskva* were approved for publication almost the same day.

16. Petr Chukarin, "Stranitsy zhizni," in A. M. Suichmezov, comp. and ed., *Nash Sholokhov: Slovo o velikom zemliake* (Rostov-on-Don, 1975), p. 127. Journalist Chukarin is Sholokhov's former secretary.

17. Quoted in Mikhail Kovalev, " 'Kazhdaia travka po-svoemu rastet . . . ,' " *Donbass* (Donetsk), no. 3 (May-June 1975), p. 134.

18. Lezhnev, *Put' Sholokhova*, pp. 29, 32; Palshkov, "Molodoi Sholokhov,"

pp. 164-165; Petr Baikal'skii, "Mnenie odnostanichnika," *Molot* (Rostov-on-Don), October 14, 1928.

19. Lezhnev, *Put' Sholokhova*, p. 41.

20. Konstantin Priima, "Sholokhov v Veshkakh," *Sovetskii Kazakhstan*, no. 5 (1955), p. 75; Ganichev, "Vsegda s molodezh'iu," p. 165.

21. Gura and Abramov state that Mikhail and Mariia were married on January 11 and came to Moscow in February (*M. A. Sholokhov*, p. 168). Lezhnev, giving the same date of the marriage, says that the couple left for Moscow two or three days after the wedding ("Molodoi Sholokhov," *God tridtsat' vos'moi*, no. 21 [1955], p. 324). There is an unconfirmed report that Sholokhov and Mariia, on the insistence of her father, were secretly married in the church. Local authorities quickly learned about the event, and Sholokhov was expelled from the Komsomol. See U. M., Letter to the editor, *Novoe russkoe slovo* (New York), September 18, 1974.

22. Letter to Kolosov, May 24, 1924, in Viktor Gura, "Vechno zhivoe slovo (Novye materialy o M. Sholokhove)," *Voprosy literatury*, no. 4 (1965), pp. 5-6.

23. R. Khigerovich, *Put' pisatelia: Zhizn' i tvorchestvo A. Serafimovicha* (Moscow, 1956), pp. 293-296; Gura and Abramov, *M. A. Sholokhov*, p. 169. According to Lezhnev, Sholokhov came to Serafimovich to show him his first writings as early as 1923 (*Put' Sholokhova*, p. 42).

24. There is some conflicting information about the earliest publication of the story "About Kolchak, Nettles, and Other Things." Two sources indicate that it appeared originally in *Krest'ianskii zhurnal*, no. 5 (May 1926). See *Russkie sovetskie pisateli prozaiki: Biobibliograficheskii ukazatel'*, vol. 6, part 2, ed. V. V. Serebriakova (Moscow, 1969), p. 161; Bibliography, in Mikhail Sholokhov, *Sobranie sochinenii*, 8 vols. (Moscow: Pravda, 1975), 8:402. A third source makes no mention of *Krest'ianskii zhurnal*, stating that the story was first published separately by Gosizdat in 1925. See Notes, in Sholokhov, *Sobranie sochinenii* (1956-1960), 1:348. It is possible that the book-form edition of the story appeared in 1927, as reported in *Russkie sovetskie pisateli prozaiki* (p. 10). There was probably only one book-form edition, and, to judge from a copy that I have, it must have been undated. In any case, the author of the Notes is mistaken in saying that "About Kolchak, Nettles, and Other Things" was included in the 1926 edition of *The Tulip Steppe*.

25. A. Selivanovskii, "Mikhail Sholokhov (Vmesto predisloviia)," in Mikhail Sholokhov, *Donskie rasskazy* (Moscow: Moskovskii rabochii, *Roman-gazeta*, no. 16, 1929), p. 3, and in *Lazorevaia step'* (1931), p. 5. See also A. Pavlov, review of *Donskie rasskazy* (*Roman-gazeta*, 1929), *Na literaturnom postu*, no. 24 (December 1929), pp. 55-56. Striking ideological and stylistic similarities between the above-cited articles lead to the conclusion that A. Pavlov is the pseudonym of Aleksei Pavlovich Selivanovskii.

26. A. Reviakin, review of *Donskie rasskazy* (1926), *Oktiabr'*, no. 5 (1926), p. 148; Viktor Iakerin, review of *Donskie rasskazy* (1926), *Novyi mir*, no. 5 (1926), p. 187; Selivanovskii, "Mikhail Sholokhov," *Roman-gazeta*, p. 3, and *Lazorevaia step'* (1931), pp. 6-7.

27. I. Mashbits-Verov, "Mikhail Sholokhov," in N. F. Nikitina, ed., *Mikhail Sholokhov* (Moscow, 1931), p. 145. This article was originally published in *Novyi mir*, no. 10 (1928), pp. 225-236. See also Selivanovskii, "Mikhail Sholokhov," *Roman-gazeta*, p. 4, and *Lazorevaia step'* (1931), pp. 7-8.

28. Priima, "Sholokhov v Veshkakh," p. 76; V. V. Gura, "Donskie rasskazy M. Sholokhova—predistoriia 'Tikhogo Dona,' " in Vologodskii pedagogicheskii institut, *Uchenye zapiski*, vol. 7 (filologicheskii) (Vologda, 1950), pp. 162-174. This article contains a number of valid observations on similarities between the early stories and *The Quiet Don*. On the other hand, Gura draws dubious parallels, attempting to prove that the early stories constitute "an ideological Vorgeschichte of *The Quiet Don*" (pp. 140-162).

29. Quoted in Sergei Balat'ev and Il'ia Estrin, "Aprel', 1975 god," *Literaturnaia Rossiia*, May 23, 1975.

30. I. Eksler, "V gostiakh u Sholokhova," *Izvestiia*, December 31, 1937, and "Kak sozdavalsia 'Tikhii Don,' " *ibid.*, June 12, 1940; Lezhnev, *Put' Sholokhova*, pp. 84-85; L. Iakimenko, *Tvorchestvo M. A. Sholokhova* (Moscow, 1964), p. 89.

31. Obukhov, "Vstrechi s Sholokhovym," pp. 286-287.

32. Eksler, "Kak sozdavalsia. . . ," *Izvestiia*, June 12, 1940; Lezhnev, *Put' Sholokhova*, pp. 344-348; Priima, "Veshenskie vstrechi," pp. 149-150; Aleksandr Bobrov, "Veshentsy," *Literaturnaia Rossiia*, May 23, 1975. Lezhnev erroneously gives Ermakov's first name as Evlampii.

33. *Put' Sholokhova*, p. 33.

34. Assertions that Gromoslavskii was a writer can be found in Roy A. Medvedev, *Problems in the Literary Biography of Mikhail Sholokhov*, trans. A.D.P. Briggs (Cambridge, 1977), p. 59; "Press-konferentsiia A. I. Solzhenitsyna. Stokgol'm 12 dekabria 1974 g.," *Novoe russkoe slovo*, January 25, 1975.

35. Lezhnev, *Put' Sholokhova*, p. 109; Khigerovich, *Put' pisatelia*, pp. 297-298; Gura and Abramov, *M. A. Sholokhov*, p. 172; Iakimenko, *Tvorchestvo M. A. Sholokhova*, pp. 118-119; A. S. Serafimovich, *Sbornik neopublikovannykh proizvedenii i materialov*, comp. Iu. A. Krasovskii, and ed. A. A. Volkov (Moscow, 1958), pp. 503, 577-578; Valentin Osipov, "Nastavnik—znachit drug," *Smena*, no. 10 (May 1975), pp. 10, 11.

36. Nikolai Trishin, "U istokov," *Komsomol'skaia pravda*, May 22, 1960. Occasionally, Trishin speaks of part 1 of *The Quiet Don*, meaning volume 1.

37. See, e.g., L. Vol'pe, "Primechaniia," in Mikhail Sholokhov, *Sobranie sochinenii*, 8 vols. to date (Moscow: Khudozhestvennaia literatura, 1965-), 2:409; A. Khvatov, *Khudozhestvennyi mir Sholokhova* (Moscow, 1970), p. 26; Ark. Airumian, " '. . . Za Sholokhova stoial goroi,' " *Ogonek*, no. 21 (May 24, 1975), p. 11. Two factual errors in Trishin's version might generate some doubt about the reliability of his memory. Instead of Gosizdat (The State Publishing House) he speaks of Goslitizdat, which came into being only in 1930, and the manuscript with Serafimovich's approval should have been sent, not to Novaia Moskva, but to Moskovskii rabochii. However, it is easy to make such errors. For example, Sholokhov is quoted as saying that the first collection of his stories was published

by Moskovskii rabochii. He meant Novaia Moskva (A. Larionov, "Smysl bor'by: Beseda s M. A. Sholokhovym," *Komsomol'skaia pravda*, June 24, 1970.)

38. A. Stasevich, "Tak eto bylo. . . ," *Komsomol'skaia pravda*, May 24, 1980. According to Sholokhov's original plans, *The Quiet Don* must have consisted of nine parts. The words "first parts" probably refer to what is now volume 1, or the bulk of it. The earliest text of the novel, published serially in *Oktiabr'*, was divided only into parts. The division into volumes and parts appeared in the first separate edition, in 1928. Sholokhov's letter of July 22, 1927, was written in Veshenskaia, and this raises a question about the chronological accuracy of Trishin's statement that from June to about September 20, 1927, Sholokhov worked in Moscow as the editor of the literary section of *Zhurnal krest'ianskoi moledezhi* ("U istokov"). The accuracy of this statement appears all the more dubious since Sholokhov's letter is a reply to a letter from Moskovskii rabochii sent to Veshenskaia some time before July 22.

39. Cf. Iakimenko, *Tvorchestvo M. A. Sholokhova*, p. 89; Eksler, "V gostiakh . . . ," *Izvestiia*, December 31, 1937, and "Kak sozdavalsia. . . ," *ibid.*, June 12, 1940. An attempt to determine the extent of borrowing from *The Don Country* is made in Michael Klimenko, *The World of Young Sholokhov: Vision of Violence* (North Quincy, Mass.: Christopher Publishing House, 1972), pp. 66-114.

40. Quoted in Eksler, "V gostiakh. . . ," *Izvestiia*, December 31, 1937.

41. Evg. Levitskaia, "Opyt izucheniia chitatel'skikh interesov (Po dannym chitatelei 'Roman-gazety')," *Na literaturnom postu*, no. 2 (January 1929), p. 46. The new large edition must have come out in 300,000 copies. The figure 30,000 in the printed text of Levitskaia's report is an obvious misprint, as is her figure 15,000 referring to the size of the first *Roman-gazeta* printing, which numbered 150,000 copies (*Roman-gazeta*, no. 7, 1928, p. 3). Levitskaia must have spoken of volume 1, but there is every reason to believe that volume 2 was published in *Roman-gazeta* in about the same number of copies as volume 1. Evgeniia Levitskaia, then a senior consultant for Moskovskii rabochii, read and recommended for publication the manuscript of volume 1 of *The Quiet Don*. Sholokhov dedicated "The Fate of a Man" to her. For details see Aleksei Ulesov, "Istoriia odnogo posviashcheniia," *Izvestiia*, October 7, 1959. Somewhat different figures for the 1928-1929 publications of *The Quiet Don* are given in K. I. Priima, "Mirovoe znachenie 'Tikhogo Dona,' " *Don*, no. 7 (1978), p. 9. Priima probably errs in stating that *Roman-gazeta* printed 250,000 copies between July 1928 and the beginning of 1929, i.e., 200,000 copies fewer than the figure given by Levitskaia for the comparable period. He is certainly wrong in asserting that the first book-form edition of volume 1, in June 1928, was printed in 50,000 (instead of 10,000) copies. He is likewise mistaken in saying that "in 1929 Moskovskii rabochii published six mass editions of *The Quiet Don* (vol. 1 and vol. 2)." Two editions of volume 1 appeared in 1928, and none of the six editions (each of which numbered 5,000 or 10,000 copies) can be called "a mass edition." Priima does not disclose the source of his information; mine is taken from publication facts printed in the books in question.

42. "Pisateli o 'tolstykh zhurnalakh,' " *Na literaturnom postu*, no. 24 (December 1928), p. 59.

43. Levitskaia, "Opyt izucheniia. . . ," pp. 46, 47.

44. Quoted in "Beseda Mikh. Sholokhova. . . ," *Na pod''eme*, no. 6 (1930), p. 172.

45. Quoted *ibid.*, p. 171.

46. Quoted *ibid.*, p. 172.

47. N. N., "Po zhurnalam," *Na literaturnom postu*, no. 8 (April 1928), p. 3, and no. 15-16 (August 1928), p. 101. *Na literaturnom postu* (1926-1932) was a critical and theoretical journal of the All-Union and the Russian Associations of Proletarian Writers. RAPP was the principal organization of proletarian writers, whose leadership insisted that proletarian literature portray life in accordance with Marxist social and historical teachings, with particular emphasis on dialectical contradictions in human experience.

48. Quoted in "Na vechere Sholokhova i Svetlova," *Molot*, December 11, 1928.

49. V. Ermilov, "O tvorcheskom litse proletarskoi literatury," in L. Averbakh, ed., *Tvorcheskie puti proletarskoi literatury: Vtoroi sbornik statei* (Moscow-Leningrad, 1929), p. 184.

50. Cf. A. Selivanovskii, " 'Tikhii Don,' " *Na literaturnom postu*, no. 10 (May 1929), pp. 55, 56, and "Na styke s krest'ianskoi literaturoi," *Oktiabr'*, no. 10 (1929), p. 185.

51. I. Makar'ev, "Na podstupakh k ovladeniiu metodom," *Na pod''eme*, no. 4-5 (1931), p. 112.

52. S. Dinamov, " 'Tikhii Don' Mikh. Sholokhova," *Krasnaia nov'*, no. 8 (1929), p. 219, also pp. 213, 215, 217-218; M. Maizel', "O 'Tikhom Done' i odnom kritike," *Zvezda*, no. 8 (1929), pp. 195-197; L. Toom, "Kulak i bedniak v literature," *Molodaia gvardiia*, no. 15 (August 1929), pp. 66-67.

53. Quoted in Lidiia Toom, *Na krutom perelome: Stat'i* (Moscow, 1930), p. 94.

54. N. L. Ianchevskii, "Reaktsionnaia romantika," *Na pod''eme*, no. 12 (1930), p. 130.

55. "Preniia po dokladu N. Ianchevskogo," *ibid.*, pp. 155-182. More details on Ianchevskii's report and its reception can be found in D. H. Stewart, *Mikhail Sholokhov: A Critical Introduction* (Ann Arbor, Mich.: University of Michigan Press, 1967), pp. 232-235. For a survey of Soviet critical views on *The Quiet Don* see Richard Hallet, "Soviet Criticism of *Tikhiy Don*, 1928-1940," *The Slavonic and East European Review* (London), vol. 46, no. 106 (January 1968), pp. 60-74.

56. A. Serafimovich, " 'Tikhii Don,' " *Pravda*, April 19, 1928.

57. Pravlenie Sev.-Kav. assotsiatsii proletarskikh pisatelei (SKAPP), "Protiv klevety na proletarskogo pisatelia," *Molot*, November 5, 1929, and *Na pod''eme*, no. 11 (1929), pp. 99-100.

58. *Na pod''eme*, no. 10 (1929), pp. 94-95. The letter, written early in October 1929, was published in *Bol'shevistskaia smena*, October 6, 1929 (Gura and Abramov, *M. A. Sholokhov*, p. 175). On Sholokhov's reaction to Prokof'ev's attack see also his letter to Aleksandr Fadeev (?) dated October 3, 1929 (Gura and Abramov, p. 175). In Lezhnev's *Put' Sholokhova* (p. 219) the addressee is given as Aleksandr Busygin, a Rostov writer. In Khvatov's *Khudozhestvennyi mir Sho-*

lokhova (p. 30) the addressee is Fadeev. This is probably correct because the letter was written in Rostov at a time when Fadeev lived in Moscow.

59. Medvedev, *Problems*, p. 59. All these assertions need further checking. It is noteworthy that F.M.A.'s account of the Party meeting coincides in detail with its description in M. Teslia, "Pisatel', kommunist, obshchestvennyi deiatel'," *Don*, no. 4 (1975), p. 172. Teslia, a former Party boss of the Rostov Province, says, of course, nothing about Gromoslavskii.

60. Serafimovich et al., "Pis'mo v redaktsiiu," *Pravda*, March 29, 1929. The other signers of the letter were Fadeev, the playwright Vladimir Kirshon, and the prose writer Vladimir Stavskii, an intransigent Stalinist. Since Averbakh and Kirshon were liquidated during the purges, the critics avoided mentioning their names in connection with the letter even after Stalin's death. Both names are missing from Lezhnev's *Put' Sholokhova*, 1958 (p. 215), and Averbakh's name is omitted from Gura and Abramov, *M. A. Sholokhov*, 1962, p. 174. Averbakh has not yet been completely rehabilitated.

61. "Mirovoe znachenie 'Tikhogo Dona,' " *Don*, no. 7 (1978), p. 10.

62. D. L. Andreev and V. E. Beklemisheva, eds., *Rekviem* (Moscow, 1930), pp. 134-136.

63. Letter to Serafimovich, April 1, 1930, in Khigerovich, *Put' pisatelia*, p. 300. Khigerovich erroneously asserts that this letter prompted Serafimovich to draft the collective letter to *Pravda*. The collective letter, as we know, was published on March 29, 1929. Goloushev's sketch appeared in *Narodnyi vestnik*, September 24 and 28 [Old Style?], 1917. There is no connection between it and *The Quiet Don*. See Medvedev, *Problems*, pp. 141-142.

64. I. Lezhnev, *Mikhail Sholokhov: Kritiko-biograficheskii ocherk* (Moscow, 1941), p. 8, and *Mikhail Sholokhov* (Leningrad, 1948), p. 12.

65. Vl. Ivanov, "Postanovlenie kraikoma VKP (b)," *Molot*, November 5, 1929, and *Na pod''eme*, no. 11 (1929), p. 100.

66. Lezhnev, *Put' Sholokhova*, pp. 214-218.

67. V. Goffenshefer, *Mikhail Sholokhov: Kriticheskii ocherk* (Moscow, 1941), p. 15.

68. Konstantin Priima, "Gordost' sovetskoi i mirovoi literatury," *Inostrannaia literatura*, no. 5 (1975), p. 203, and "Mirovoe znachenie 'Tikhogo Dona,' " pp. 13, 17. Sergei Syrtsov, a leading Bolshevik in the Don region during the Civil War, is the only person (besides Trotskii) whom Priima mentions by name as one of those responsible for the mass repression of the Cossacks in the winter of 1919. However, Priima justly refrains from calling him a Trotskyite. Trotskii and Syrtsov were greatly responsible for the repression of the Cossacks, but the main directive for the brutal treatment of the Cossacks came from Iakov Sverdlov. See Sergei Starikov and Roy Medvedev, *Philip Mironov and the Russian Civil War*, trans. Guy Daniels (New York: Alfred A. Knopf, 1978), pp. 110-115.

69. F. A. Abramov and V. V. Gura, *M. A. Sholokhov: Seminarii* (Leningrad, 1958), pp. 18-19; Gura and Abramov, *M. A. Sholokhov* (1962), p. 19; Khigerovich, *Put' pisatelia*, p. 299; Obukhov, "Vstrechi s Sholokhovym," p. 290.

70. "Sholokhov's Claim Doubted Again," *Daily Telegraph* (London), Septem-

ber 3, 1974; "*L'Express* va plus loin avec Aragon" (an interview), *L'Express*, September 20-26, 1971, p. 71.

71. A. Sofronov, "Nad bestsennymi rukopisiami 'Tikhogo Dona,' " *Ogonek*, no. 16 (April 16, 1961), p. 29.

72. Letter to Fadeev (?), October 3, 1929. Quoted in Gura and Abramov, *M. A. Sholokhov* (1962), p. 175. At that time Sholokhov planned to split volume 3 in parts 6 and 7, with part 6 ending somewhere around the present chapter 28. See V. Gura, *Kak sozdavalsia "Tikhii Don": Tvorcheskaia istoriia romana M. Sholokhova* (Moscow, 1980), p. 146.

73. "Protiv klevety na proletarskogo pisatelia," *Molot*, November 5, 1929, and *Na pod''eme*, no. 11 (1929), p. 100.

74. Quoted in Iakimenko, *Tvorchestvo M. A. Sholokhova*, p. 129. The quotation is cut short at this point and the reader does not know whether Sholokhov specified the corrections suggested to him. Other critics (or censors) omit the phrase involving Fadeev. See, e.g., Khigerovich, *Put' pisatelia*, p. 299; Khvatov, *Khudozhestvennyi mir Sholokhova*, p. 32.

75. Quoted in *Literaturnoe nasledstvo*, vol. 70 (Moscow, 1963), p. 696. The dimensions of the Red terror against the Cossacks can also be illustrated by the fact that "merely along the route of the 8th Army [which passed through the Veshenskaia area] the tribunals shot more than 8,000 persons 'for the good of the social revolution' " (Starikov and Medvedev, *Philip Mironov*, p. 148). In his letter to Gor'kii, Sholokhov refers to volume 3 of *The Quiet Don* as part 6.

76. Gura, *Kak sozdavalsia "Tikhii Don,"* pp. 159-160, and *Zhizn' i tvorchestvo M. A. Sholokhova*, 2d ed., rev. and enl. (Moscow, 1960), p. 62. Embarrassment over Fadeev's negative role in the publication of volume 3 of *The Quiet Don* might have been the main reason why his correspondence with Gor'kii was not included in vol. 70 of *Literaturnoe nasledstvo*, devoted to Gor'kii's correspondence with Soviet writers.

77. Gura, *Zhizn' i tvorchestvo M. A. Sholokhova*, p. 63; Maksim Gor'kii, *Sobranie sochinenii v tridtsati tomakh*, vol. 26 (Moscow, 1953), p. 69.

78. Quoted in *Literaturnoe nasledstvo*, vol. 70, p. 698.

79. Quoted in Priima, "Mirovoe znachenie 'Tikhogo Dona,' " p. 17.

80. Quoted in I. Lezhnev, "O prototipakh geroev 'Podniatoi tseliny,' " *Neva*, no. 2 (May 1955), p. 158.

81. Gura, *Kak sozdavalsia "Tikhii Don,"* p. 158; Priima, "Sholokhov v Veshkakh," *Sovetskii Kazakhstan*, no. 5 (1955), pp. 81-82.

82. Quoted in "Sholokhov v Veshkakh," p. 82, and Konstantin Priima, *"Tikhii Don" srazhaetsia*, 2d ed., rev. and enl. (Moscow, 1975), p. 454. For Stalin's role in the publication of *Virgin Soil Upturned* see also "Rech' doblestnogo patriota: Pisatel' Mikhail Sholokhov na sobranii Novocherkasskogo izbiratel'nogo okruga," *Komsomol'skaia pravda*, December 1, 1937; Anatolii Sofronov, "V gostiakh u Sholokhova," in Andriasov, comp. and ed., *Slovo o Sholokhove*, p. 462.

83. V. V. Gura, "Osnovnye zadachi izucheniia tvorchestva M. A. Sholokhova," in B. A. Larin, ed., *Mikhail Sholokhov: Sbornik statei* (Leningrad, 1956), p. 122, and Gura, *Zhizn' i tvorchestvo M. A. Sholokhova*, p. 157.

84. Lezhnev, *Put' Sholokhova*, p. 231; Iakimenko, *Tvorchestvo M. A. Sholokhova*, p. 135; Airumian, " '. . . Za Sholokhova stoial goroi,' " *Ogonek*, no. 21 (1975), p. 12.

85. Sholokhov, *Sobranie sochinenii* (1975), 8:37. To my knowledge, this letter has not yet been published in its entirety.

86. "Rech' doblestnogo patriota," *Komsomol'skaia pravda*, December 1, 1937.

87. Quoted in Gura and Abramov, *M. A. Sholokhov* (1962), p. 330.

88. Quoted in Priima, *"Tikhii Don" srazhaetsia*, p. 453.

89. Quoted in Priima, "Mirovoe znachenie 'Tikhogo Dona,' " p. 18.

90. I. Makar'ev, "K proshlomu net vozvrata: O romane M. Sholokhova 'Podniataia tselina,' " *God shestnadtsatyi*, no. 2 (1933), p. 482.

91. Dm. Maznin, " 'Podniataia tselina' i tak nazyvaemoe 'novatorstvo,' " *Krasnaia nov'*, no. 5 (1933), pp. 205, 217.

92. N. Lesiuchevskii, " 'Podniataia tselina,' " *Literaturnyi sovremennik*, no. 4 (1933), p. 130.

93. Galina Kolesnikova, " 'Tikhii Don,' " *Oktiabr'*, no. 2 (1933), pp. 212-215.

94. D. Mirskii, "Mikhail Sholokhov," *Literaturnaia gazeta*, July 24, 1934. This article contains an unusually high number of inaccuracies. Mirskii consistently misspells the names Melekhov and Listnitskii, refers to volumes of *The Quiet Don* as parts, gives the wrong time for Listnitskii's return from the Denikin Army, and calls Valet's grave Podtelkov's grave.

95. Quoted in Priima, *"Tikhii Don" srazhaetsia*, p. 453. Sholokhov has in mind *former* leaders of RAPP, for this organization was liquidated in April 1932.

96. Gura and Abramov, *M. A. Sholokhov* (1962), p. 181. In the next line the authors erroneously state that the first book-form edition of volume 3 came out on August 27, 1933.

97. In 1931 Sholokhov wrote that 960 kg. (60 poods) of wheat from a hectare could be harvested in the Veshenskaia area only during bumper crops in ideal weather conditions. Since Veshenskaia lies in the drought zone, Sholokhov thought that its inhabitants should concentrate on cattle breeding. See "Za perestroiku," *Sobranie sochinenii* (1975), 8:31.

98. Quoted in Priima, "Sholokhov v Veshkakh," pp. 72-73; N. Mar, "U beregov tikhogo Dona. . . ," *Literaturnaia gazeta*, March 17, 1962; Iakimenko, *Tvorchestvo M. A. Sholokhova*, pp. 138-139. Iakimenko erroneously dates the letter May 13, 1933, and Gura and Abramov place it in January of that year (*M. A. Sholokhov* [1962], p. 180). Neither of the above sources quotes the letter in full. Some of its lines are still considered unpublishable. Significantly, Priima accompanied his publication of the letter with the explanation that he had found it (along with two copies of Sholokhov's letters to Stalin and two telegrams from Stalin to Sholokhov) among Lugovoi's papers left in a barn belonging to an old Cossack woman. Actually, he received the letter from Lugovoi and wanted to protect him from unpleasant consequences. The cover-up was exposed by Iakimenko (*Tvorchestvo*, p. 139), who pretended not to know why Priima had concealed his true source.

99. Priima, "Sholokhov v Veshkakh," p. 73; A. Bakharev, "Veshenskii kudesnik," *Don*, no. 5 (1965), p. 91.

100. In 1932 Sheboldaev and Stalin's henchman Lazar' Kaganovich deported entire villages from the Kuban' region to northern Russia on the theory that all villagers must be punished for the hostile actions of their kulak neighbors. See Roy A. Medvedev, *Let History Judge: The Origins and Consequences of Stalinism*, trans. Colleen Taylor, ed. David Joravsky and Georges Haupt (New York: Alfred A. Knopf, 1972), p. 399. The leading role of Stalin and the Party's Central Committee in "combating the sabotage" was stressed by Sheboldaev in his speech at a high-level Party meeting in Rostov at the end of January 1933. See "Pravdivaia kniga, prizyvaiushchaia k bditel'nosti," *Literaturnaia gazeta*, February 17, 1933.

101. Quoted in N. S. Khrushchev, *Vysokoe prizvanie literatury i iskusstva* (Moscow, 1963), p. 191. Excerpts from the letter were made known for the first time by Khrushchev on March 8, 1963, at a meeting with Soviet writers and artists. To my knowledge, the letter has not yet been published in full. In the Korolenko sketch (1911), the peasants are severely beaten by police and remain cripples for life. The word "disappearance" is a literal translation of *ischeznovenie*, which the peasants use in the sketch instead of *istiazanie* (torture).

102. Quoted in Bakharev, "Veshenskii kudesnik," p. 91. Aleksandr Bakharev, a Rostov writer, does not give the date of the letter.

103. Quoted in Khrushchev, *Vysokoe prizvanie*, p. 191. A possibility that Sholokhov was not the only signatory to the letter is raised by his words "A group of Party workers from northern *raions* of the Don region wrote a letter to Comrade Stalin, asking him to investigate the wrong actions of the regional leaders and give food aid to a number of *raions*" ("O prostom slove," *Pravda*, December 23, 1939). There is, however, no doubt that the letter was written by Sholokhov.

104. Quoted in "O prostom slove." Priima dates the arrival of the telegram April 16, 1933 ("Sholokhov v Veshkakh," p. 74), apparently confusing it with the date of Sholokhov's first letter to Stalin. Andrei Plotkin, then chairman of the Veshenskaia collective farm, says that the telegram came at the end of March (" 'Na ogonek' k Sholokhovu," in Andriasov, comp., *Mikhail Aleksandrovich Sholokhov*, p. 227). This may be a slip of memory. In all probability the telegram arrived in April.

105. Khrushchev, *Vysokoe prizvanie*, p. 192. Khrushchev quotes such excerpts to demonstrate Stalin's callousness and arrogance. At the same time he fails to mention the positive action Stalin took in response to Sholokhov's letters.

106. Quoted in Bakharev, "Veshenskii kudesnik," p. 91. It may be noted that since "last November" Sholokhov wrote at least one letter (to Lugovoi, on February 13, 1933).

107. "V rabote 'Tikhii Don' i 'Podniataia tselina': Beseda s tov. M. Sholokhovym," *Literaturnaia gazeta*, February 6, 1934; N. Smirnov, "Vziatoe iz zhizni," *Molodaia gvardiia*, no. 10 (1973), p. 211; Dir [Mikhail Rogov], "Razgovor s Sholokhovym," *Izvestiia*, March 10, 1935; "Posledniaia kniga 'Podniatoi tseliny,' " *Pravda*, January 1, 1939.

108. *Novyi mir*, no. 5 (1935), reverse of the title page.

109. A. Kut, "Vtoraia chast' 'Podniatoi tseliny,' " *Vecherniaia Moskva*, March 1, 1933.

110. Quoted in "V rabote. . . ," *Literaturnaia gazeta*, February 6, 1934.

111. Quoted in Dir, "Razgovor. . . ," *Izvestiia*, March 10, 1935.

112. "P'esa o kolkhoze: Mikhail Sholokhov o svoikh blizhaishikh tvorcheskikh planakh," *Komsomol'skaia pravda*, June 29, 1934. See also V. Ketlinskaia, "Mikhail Sholokhov," *ibid.*, August 17, 1934; Dir, "Razgovor. . . ," *Izvestiia*, March 10, 1935.

113. Dir, "Razgovor. . . ." See also Eksler, "V gostiakh. . . ," *Izvestiia*, December 31, 1937.

114. Isaak Eksler, "Veshenskie byli," in Andriasov, comp., *Mikhail Aleksandrovich Sholokhov*, p. 301.

115. "P'esa o kolkhoze," *Komsomol'skaia pravda*, June 29, 1934.

116. G. Ryklin, "Nad chem rabotaet Mikhail Sholokhov," *Pravda*, February 27, 1935; Dir, "Razgovor. . . ," *Izvestiia*, March 10, 1935.

117. A. Less, "Izdatel' i pisatel'," *Moskva*, no. 4 (1962), pp. 178-179. At this time Sholokhov did not intend to serialize volume 4 in a journal. He wanted to publish it in book form. Nonetheless, in 1935 and 1936, the editors of *Oktiabr'* continued to print advertisements saying that volume 4 would be serialized. Sholokhov was one of the editors.

118. Quoted from the letter of April 3, 1936, in Gura and Abramov, *M. A. Sholokhov* (1962), p. 189.

119. I. Eksler, "U Sholokhova," *Izvestiia*, October 20, 1936.

120. Eksler, "V gostiakh. . . ," *Izvestiia*, December 31, 1937. Eksler, a reporter for *Izvestiia*, visited Sholokhov on the eve of 1938.

121. Cf. I. Eksler, "U Sholokhova," *Izvestiia*, October 20, 1936; "V stanitse Veshenskoi," in S. G. Lipshits, ed., *Mikhail Sholokhov: Literaturno-kriticheskii sbornik* (Rostov-on-Don, 1940), p. 130; and "Veshenskie byli," in Andriasov, comp., *Mikhail Aleksandrovich Sholokhov* (1966), p. 302.

122. Told to me by Dr. Poltoratskaia. The conversation between her and Eremeev took place in the Soviet Union sometime before World War II.

123. Medvedev, *Problems*, p. 129.

124. Priima, *"Tikhii Don" srazhaetsia*, p. 453.

125. All information about the arrests of the Veshenskaia administrators is taken from Iakimenko, *Tvorchestvo M. A. Sholokhova*, pp. 144, 146; and B. Chelyshev, " 'I torite dorozhki. . . ,' " *Molodaia gvardiia*, no. 5 (1965), pp. 169-170. Chelyshev's account is based on his interview with Krasiukov's wife.

126. Professor George Krugovoy's letter to me, April 7, 1972.

127. Interview with G.G., February 19, 1977. The episode was told to G.G. by Georgiadi's wife.

128. Viktor Nekrasov, "Tsari i literatura," *Novoe russkoe slovo*, July 16, 1978.

129. "Ne dadim zhit'ia vragam Sovetskogo Soiuza," *Literaturnaia gazeta*, June 15, 1937. The letter was prompted by the trial of Marshal Mikhail Tukhachevskii and other military leaders.

130. Krugovoy's letter to me, April 7, 1972.

131. Iakimenko, *Tvorchestvo M. A. Sholokhova*, pp. 146-150. Iakimenko's account is based on information given to him by Pogorelov. As a result of the post-Khrushchev policy of saying as little as possible about the purges of the 1930s, the account is reduced by half in the second (1970) and the third (1977) editions of *Tvorchestvo*.

132. A. Sofronov, "Bessmertnik," *Ogonek*, no. 31 (July 26, 1964), p. 10. Sofronov erroneously gives Pogorelov's first name as Grigorii and the year of the plot against Sholokhov as 1937. The entire account of the event is missing from the 1975 reprint of Sofronov's article in his *Sholokhovskoe*, p. 54.

133. *"Tikhii Don" srazhaetsia* (Rostov-on-Don, 1972), p. 431; also 2d ed. (1975), p. 454. According to Priima, the attempts to slander Sholokhov were made in 1938.

134. That Grechukhin was hardly in a position to initiate a frame-up of Sholokhov can be corroborated indirectly by the following episode. In the early or mid-1930s an ambitious prosecuting attorney from Rostov attempted to indict Sholokhov on charges of using hired labor for the construction of his house in Veshenskaia. To protect the author's reputation, the higher authorities ordered the prosecuting attorney to drop the charges. The attorney attributed his fiasco to the fact that he was known only in the Soviet Union, while Sholokhov was known throughout the world. The episode was told to me by a lawyer from Rostov Province.

135. Medvedev, *Let History Judge*, pp. 294, 309.

136. Quoted in N. Beliaev, comp., *Mikhail Kol'tsov, kakim on byl* (Moscow, 1965), p. 76.

137. Roy A. Medvedev, "The Riddles Grow: *A Propos* Two Review Articles," *Slavic and East European Journal*, vol. 21, no. 1 (Spring 1977), p. 111. According to Medvedev, Sholokhov was arrested in the summer of 1938 and freed after a long conversation with Stalin, which took place in the presence of Ezhov. In the light of information provided by Pogorelov, Lugovoi, and Krasiukov's wife, the statement about Sholokhov's arrest in the summer of 1938 is debatable (unless the arrest has always been a state secret which could not be disclosed even at the peak of de-Stalinization).

138. "Rech' t. Sholokhova," *Literaturnaia gazeta*, March 20, 1939; M. Sholokhov, "Otets trudiashchikhsia mira," *Pravda*, December 20, 1949, and "Proshchai, otets!" *ibid.*, March 8, 1953.

139. Cf. Abramov and Gura, *M. A. Sholokhov* (1958), pp. 168, 170, and Gura and Abramov, *M. A. Sholokhov* (1962), pp. 203, 205. See also *Russkie sovetskie pisateli prozaiki: Biobibliograficheskii ukazatel'*, vol. 6, part 2 ("M. A. Sholokhov," pp. 3-163) (Moscow, 1969), p. 161. Also omitted is "O prostom slove" (*Pravda*, December 23, 1939), written on the occasion of Stalin's sixtieth birthday.

140. Quoted in Priima, *"Tikhii Don" srazhaetsia* (1975), p. 453.

141. Quoted in Larionov, "Smysl bor'by," *Komsomol'skaia pravda*, June 24, 1970.

142. D. Zaslavskii, "Konets Grigoriia Melekhova," *Pravda*, March 23, 1940; Iu. Lukin, "Vstupitel'naia stat'ia," in Mikhail Sholokhov, *Tikhii Don* (Moscow: Khudozhestvennaia literatura, 1941), p. xv.

143. Gura and Abramov, *M. A. Sholokhov* (1962), p. 59.

144. M. Charnyi, "Burnye gody 'Tikhogo Dona,' " *Oktiabr'*, no. 9 (1940), p. 171; P. Gromov, "Grigorii Melekhov i Mikhail Koshevoi," *Literaturnaia gazeta*, October 6, 1940.

145. V. Goffenshefer, " 'Tikhii Don' zakonchen," in Lipshits, ed., *Mikhail Sholokhov*, p. 37; V. Ermilov, "O 'Tikhom Done' i o tragedii," *Literaturnaia gazeta*, August 11, 1940. See also Charnyi, "Burnye gody. . . ," p. 171; A. Leites, "Bez 'schastlivoi razviazki,' " *Literaturnaia gazeta*, September 8, 1940.

146. Iu. Lukin, "V 1940 godu," in Lipshits, ed., *Mikhail Sholokhov*, p. 21; V. Shcherbina, " 'Tikhii Don' M. Sholokhova," *Novyi mir*, no. 4 (1941), pp. 197, 212-213.

147. Quoted in Abramov and Gura, *A. M. Sholokhov* (1958), p. 163. The entire text of the telegram is omitted from the 1962 edition of this book (p. 197). The last words, beginning with "and the great," are not included in the 1980 edition of *Sobranie sochinenii* (vol. 8, p. 83). Had Sholokhov mentioned just "the great cause of Lenin," the entire text of his telegram would have been printable at any time.

148. M. Sholokhov, "Na Donu," *Pravda*, July 4, 1941; "V stanitse Veshenskoi," *ibid.*, July 6, 1941; and "V kazach'ikh kolkhozakh," *Krasnaia zvezda*, July 31, 1941.

149. M. Sholokhov, "Na smolenskom napravlenii," *Krasnaia zvezda*, August 29, 1941; "Gnusnost'," *ibid.*, September 6, 1941; "Voennoplennye," *Pravda*, November 2, 1941; "Pervye vstrechi," *Literaturnaia gazeta*, April 20, 1965; "Liudi Krasnoi Armii," *Sovetskii voin*, no. 8 (1965); and "Po puti k frontu," *Izvestiia*, October 17, 1965. The last three sketches can also be found in *Literaturnoe nasledstvo*, vol. 72, book 1 (Moscow, 1966), pp. 33-50. The original title of the first sketch was different, possibly mentioning General Konev or his army. On August 28, 1941, Stalin prohibited the mention of Konev's name in *Krasnaia zvezda* because foreign reporters who had read previous accounts of the general's offensive operation tended to exaggerate its significance. See D. Ortenberg, *Vremia ne vlastno: Pisateli na fronte* (Moscow, 1975), pp. 72, 342.

150. Chukarin, "Stranitsy zhizni," in Suichmezov, comp. and ed., *Nash Sholokhov*, pp. 130-131.

151. Lezhnev, *Put' Sholokhova*, p. 383.

152. Quoted in Larionov, "Smysl bor'by," *Komsomol'skaia pravda*, June 24, 1970.

153. Ortenberg, *Vremia ne vlastno*, p. 74.

154. Quoted in Vitalii Zaseev, "U Sholokhova, v Veshenskoi," *V mire knig*, no. 5 (1975), p. 16. The story was originally told to Priima by a Cossack, Vasilii Griaznov. See "Sholokhov v Veshkakh," *Sovetskii Kazakhstan*, no. 5 (1955), pp. 69-70.

155. Quoted in Chukarin, "Stranitsy zhizni," p. 131.

156. Mikhail [sic] Korsunov, "Vstrechi s Sholokhovym," *Prostor* (Alma-Ata), no. 5 (1975), p. 105. Soviet spelling rules require that the word *rodina* be capitalized

if it denotes the Soviet Union. The editors regularly capitalize it in the title of Sholokhov's novel. Korsunov's first name is Nikolai, not Mikhail.

157. Abramov and Gura, *M. A. Sholokhov* (1958), p. 168; Gura, *Zhizn' i tvorchestvo M. A. Sholokhova*, p. 233.

158. Mikhail Sholokhov, *Oni srazhalis' za rodinu, Pravda*, May 5-8, November 4, 14, 15, 17, 1943; February 12-14, July 3, 1944.

159. V. G. Vasil'ev, *O "Tikhom Done" M. Sholokhova* (Cheliabinsk, 1963), pp. 4, 201; Lezhnev, *Put' Sholokhova*, p. 403; Priima, "Sholokhov v Veshkakh," p. 82; Sofronov, "Nad bestsennymi rukopisiami. . . ," *Ogonek*, no. 16 (1961), p. 28. Sofronov dates the German advance towards Veshenskaia June 1942, instead of July 1942.

160. This happened in May 1942, according to Lezhnev (*Put' Sholokhova*, p. 403), and in July 1942, according to Gura and Abramov (*M. A. Sholokhov* [1962], p. 198).

161. Cf. Priima, "Gordost' sovetskoi. . . ," *Inostrannaia literatura*, no. 5 (1975), p. 204, and "Autograph Pages from 'The Quiet Don,' " *Soviet Literature* (Moscow), no. 10 (1975), p. 184. Sofronov reiterates his 1961 version in *Sholokhovskoe* (1975), p. 41, but says elsewhere that the rough draft of the entire volume 2 of *Virgin Soil Upturned* "burnt, as it is well known, in the house destroyed by fascist bombs" ("Moguchee techenie," *Moskva*, no. 4 [1975], p. 14). Accounts based on versions one and two can be found in Petelin, *Mikhail Sholokhov*, p. 264; V. Litvinov, "Narodnyi pisatel'," *V mire knig*, no. 5 (1975), p. 12; Khvatov, *Khudozhestvennyi mir Sholokhova*, 3d ed. (Moscow, 1978), p. 261.

162. Sholokhov's letter to Andrei Plotkin [1945], in Boris Chelyshev, "Rodnoe i blizkoe," *Don*, no. 6 (1975), p. 162; Lezhnev, *Put' Sholokhova*, p. 402. Sofronov mistakenly asserts that Sholokhov was at the front when his mother was killed ("Bessmertnik," *Ogonek*, no. 31 [1964], p. 10).

163. The event is dated July 10 by Gura and Abramov (*M. A. Sholokhov* [1962], p. 198) and July 13 by Lezhnev (*Put' Sholokhova*, p. 403). There is also a discrepancy concerning the time of the first evacuation of Sholokhov's family. Lezhnev says it occurred on October 16, 1941, when the Germans captured Rostov (*ibid.*, p. 402). Abramov and Gura date the evacuation November 1941 (*M. A. Sholokhov* [1962], p. 197). This is probably correct, especially since Rostov was captured, not on October 16, but November 23.

164. Sofronov, "Bessmertnik," pp. 10-12. This information is based on accounts of several officers who fought in the Veshenskaia area.

165. Sofronov, "Nad bestsennymi rukopisiami. . . ," *Ogonek*, no. 16 (1961), pp. 28, 31; Priima, "Gordost' sovetskoi. . . ," *Inostrannaia literatura*, no. 5 (1975), p. 204, and "Autograph Pages. . . ," *Soviet Literature*, no. 10 (1975), p. 184.

166. Quoted in Priima, "Sholokhov v Veshkakh," p. 82. In 1962 Priima quoted this statement with additional details: "Our intelligence captured a woman spying for the Germans and found my manuscript in her possession. All attempts by

Vsevolod Vishnevskii to trace the whereabouts of my archive proved futile'' (''Veshenskie vstrechi,'' *Pod''em*, no. 5 [1962], p. 159).

167. Vsevolod Vishnevskii, *Sobranie sochinenii*, 6 vols. (Moscow, 1954-1961), 3:532-749, 4:7-69.

168. ''Gordost' sovetskoi. . . ,'' p. 204. In ''Autograph Pages . . .'' Priima gives slightly different figures: 143 handwritten and 110 typed pages (p. 183). According to an editorial footnote to this article, the handwritten pages of *The Quiet Don* were given, on Sholokhov's instructions, to the Pushkin House of the Leningrad branch of the Soviet Academy of Sciences (p. 184).

169. Sofronov, ''Nad bestsennymi rukopisiami. . . ,'' pp. 26-31; Priima, ''Autograph Pages. . . ,'' pp. 183-189. In the collection in question the beginning of part 8 is dated December 17, 1938. This indicates that we have here a late version of part 8. The preceding version of part 8, as we know, was completed a year earlier.

170. Spas Popov, ''Donskie vstrechi,'' *Oktiabr'*, no. 5 (1975), p. 219; F. Biriukov, *Khudozhestvennye otkrytiia Mikhaila Sholokhova* (Moscow, 1976), p. 10; Andriasov, *Veshenskie byli*, p. 122; Petr Lugovoi, ''U istokov 'Podniatoi tseliny,' '' *Literaturnaia gazeta*, March 12, 1975.

171. Viktor Petelin, *Gumanizm Sholokhova* (Moscow, 1965), p. 481.

172. Gura and Abramov, *M. A. Sholokhov* (1962), p. 200.

173. *Oni srazhalis' za Rodinu, Pravda*, July 28-30, August 1, 1949.

174. Quoted in Abramov and Gura, *M. A. Sholokhov* (1958), p. 167.

175. Gura and Abramov, *M. A. Sholokhov* (1962), p. 204.

176. M. Sholokhov, ''Skorb' nasha muzhestvenna,'' *Pravda*, September 2, 1948.

177. M. Sholokhov, ''Ne uiti palacham ot suda narodov!'' *Pravda*, September 24, 1951. This article was, charitably, not translated for a collection of Sholokhov's writings entitled *One Man's Destiny and Other Stories, Articles, and Sketches, 1923-1963*, trans. H. C. Stevens (London: Putnam, 1967). This collection also omitted several pages of attacks on ''the American imperialism'' and warmongering from the articles ''A Word on Our Country'' (1948) and ''Light and Darkness'' (1949), which was translated as ''Sunlight and Shadow.''

178. ''Vstrecha izbiratelei s M. A. Sholokhovym,'' *Literaturnaia gazeta*, February 27, 1954.

179. Priima, ''Sholokhov v Veshkakh,'' p. 83.

180. Evg. Liufanov, ''U Mikhaila Sholokhova,'' *Literaturnaia gazeta*, January 1, 1956.

181. ''Pis'mo Mikhaila Sholokhova l'vovskim studentam,'' *Komsomol'skaia pravda*, March 17, 1958.

182. They were published in *Literaturnaia gazeta*, March 9, 1954; *Ogonek*, no. 15 (April 11), pp. 2-5; no. 16 (April 18), pp. 13-16; no. 17 (April 25), pp. 10-12; no. 21 (May 23), pp. 4-7; no. 23 (June 6, 1954), pp. 12-16. For subsequent publications of excerpts from volume 2 of *Virgin Soil Upturned*, consult Gura and Abramov, *M. A. Sholokhov* (1962), pp. 343-344, or *Russkie sovetskie pisateli prozaiki*, vol. 6, part 2 (1969), p. 161.

183. Harrison E. Salisbury, "Khrushchev Bid to Sholokhov Follows a Dispute over Novel," *The New York Times*, September 1, 1959, p. 1, and "Sholokhov Novel Has a New Ending," *ibid.*, February 18, 1960, p. 5.

184. M. Sholokhov, "O malen'kom mal'chike Garry i bol'shom mistere Solsberi," *Pravda*, March 1, 1960.

185. Quoted in Priima, "Sholokhov v Veshkakh," p. 83. In his later references to this statement Priima says that it was made in February 1955 (*"Tikhii Don" srazhaetsia* [1972], p. 427, and [1975], p. 450). However, references to the time of the year in "Sholokhov v Veshkakh" clearly indicate that Priima interviewed the author in April (pp. 76, 81). It is also very unlikely that Priima would have erred in an article written immediately after his conversation with Sholokhov.

186. Sholokhov, "O prostom slove," *Pravda*, December 23, 1939; Priima, "Sholokhov v Veshkakh," p. 73.

187. M. Sholokhov, "Vyravniat' shag s partiei, s narodom," *Pravda*, May 19, 1957.

188. L. Iakimenko, "Chelovechnost', narodnost', masterstvo," *Znamia*, no. 4 (1960), pp. 209-212; A. Kalinin, "Borozdoi podniatoi tseliny," *Literatura i zhizn'*, February 17, 1960.

189. Iakimenko, "Chelovechnost'. . . ," pp. 223-224; Viktor Pankov, "Na strezhne zhizni," *Znamia*, no. 5 (1960), p. 185.

190. "Geroi nashei literatury" (editorial), *Literaturnaia gazeta*, February 14, 1957; Efim Permitin, "Russkii kharakter," *ibid.*, March 21, 1957; D. Nikolaev, "Sud'ba chelovecheskaia, sud'ba narodnaia," *Znamia*, no. 4 (1957), pp. 209-212.

191. *Leningradskii al'manakh*, no. 8 (1954), pp. 3-9, and *Literaturnaia gazeta*, October 23, 1954.

192. "Datskii izdatel' v gostiakh u M. A. Sholokhova," *Trud*, August 27, 1960.

193. Petr Iashchenko, "Shkol'niki u Mikhaila Sholokhova," *Literaturnaia gazeta*, February 1, 1964; Korsunov, "Vstrechi. . . ," *Prostor*, no. 5 (1975), p. 105.

194. "Soviet Said to Ban Novel by Sholokhov," *The New York Times*, February 8, 1969, p. 5.

195. Zhores A. Medvedev, *Desiat' let posle "Odnogo dnia Ivana Denisovicha,"* rev. ed. (London: Macmillan, 1973), pp. 137-138.

196. Quoted in Korsunov, "Vstrechi. . . ," *Prostor*, no. 6 (1975), p. 99.

197. *Ibid.*, no. 5, pp. 101, 102.

198. Quoted *ibid.*, no. 6, p. 103.

199. Larionov, "Smysl bor'by," *Komsomol'skaia pravda*, June 24, 1970.

200. Viktor Petelin, *Rodnye sud'by*, 2d ed. enl. (Moscow, 1976), pp. 139-140; A. Sofronov, "Veshenskaia v tsvetu," *Ogonek*, no. 21 (May 24, 1975), p. 17.

201. Korsunov, "Vstrechi. . . ," no. 6, p. 99.

202. Eksler, "V stanitse Veshenskoi," in Lipshits, ed., *Mikhail Sholokhov*, p. 140.

203. Olga Andreyev Carlisle, *Voices in the Snow: Encounters with Russian Writers* (New York: Random House, 1962), pp. 50-62.

204. Petr Gavrilenko, *S Sholokhovym na okhote: Ocherki* (Alma-Ata, 1965), p. 74.

205. Petr Gavrilenko, *Sholokhov sredi druzei: Ocherki*, 3d ed., rev. and enl. (Alma-Ata, 1975), p. 71. For more details on Zhuravlev see Konstantin Priima, "Za chest' bezymiannogo geroia 'Tikhogo Dona,' " *Literaturnaia gazeta*, March 25, 1970.

206. Gavrilenko, *Sholokhov sredi druzei*, pp. 42, 111.

207. Eksler, "Veshenskie byli," in Andriasov, comp., *Mikhail Aleksandrovich Sholokhov*, p. 310.

208. "Gordost' sovetskoi literatury," *Izvestiia*, May 24, 1980.

209. "Na vsekh iazykakh," *Komsomol'skaia pravda*, May 24, 1980.

210. Speech at the Twenty-Fourth Party Congress, *Pravda*, April 4, 1971.

211. Speech at the Twentieth Party Congress, *Pravda*, February 21, 1956.

212. Larionov, "Smysl bor'by," *Komsomol'skaia pravda*, June 24, 1970.

213. Peter Grose, "Sholokhov Proud of Role as 'Soviet' Nobel Winner," *The New York Times*, December 1, 1965, p. 13.

214. Speech at the Third All-Union Congress of Collective Farmers, *Pravda*, November 28, 1969.

215. Speech at the Twenty-Third Party Congress, *Pravda*, April 2, 1966.

216. Medvedev, "The Riddles Grow," *Slavic and East European Journal*, no. 1 (1977), pp. 111-112.

217. M. Sholokhov, "Prestupnaia beskhoziaistvennost'," *Pravda*, March 22, 1932; "Rezul'tat neprodumannoi raboty," *ibid*., March 23, 1933; and speech at the meeting of the Rostov Province Party Committee, *Sobranie sochinenii* (1975), 8:290-292.

218. Quoted in V. Koroteev and V. Efimov, "Na Donu," *Izvestiia*, July 1, 1956.

219. Aleksandr Bakharev, "Muzhestvennoe serdtse," in Andriasov, comp., *Mikhail Aleksandrovich Sholokhov*, p. 65.

220. *Pravda*, April 2, 1966.

221. Quoted in Gavrilenko, *S Sholokhovym na okhote*, p. 80.

222. "Iz vystupleniia na zakrytii dekady russkoi literatury v Kazakhstane," *Sobranie sochinenii* (1975), 8:326.

223. Speech at the Twentieth Party Congress, *Pravda*, February 21, 1956. See also Sholokhov's speeches at the Twenty-Second and Twenty-Third Party Congresses in *Pravda*, October 25, 1961, and April 2, 1966, respectively.

224. "Doklad mandatnoi komissii," *Literaturnaia gazeta*, July 1, 1981. The Union's membership has been steadily growing. There were 1,500 members in August 1934; 3,695 in December 1954; 4,801 in May 1959; 6,608 in May 1967; 7,290 in June 1971; and 7,942 in June 1976.

225. *Pravda*, October 25, 1961.

226. Letter to A. Mitrofanov, September 26, 1932, in L. P. Logashova, ed., *"Tikhii Don": Uroki romana* (Rostov-on-Don, 1979), p. 122.

227. Letter to Feliks Kon, I. V. Stalin, *Sochineniia*, vol. 12 (Moscow, 1949), p. 112.

228. Priima, *"Tikhii Don" srazhaetsia* (1975), p. 452.

229. Gura, *Kak sozdavalsia "Tikhii Don,"* pp. 426-427.

230. *Ibid.*, p. 423.

231. This figure and other information about the English translations of *The Quiet Don* can be found in Stewart, *Mikhail Sholokhov*, pp. 203-205, 244.

232. "Tsifry, fakty," *Literaturnaia gazeta*, May 21, 1980.

Chapter II

1. References in the text are made to volume and page numbers of Mikhail Sholokhov, *Sobranie sochinenii*, 8 vols. (Moscow: Pravda, 1975). Each of its first four volumes includes one volume of *The Quiet Don*. Volume 1 of the novel consists of parts 1, 2, and 3, vol. 2 of parts 4 and 5, vol. 3 of part 6, and vol. 4 of parts 7 and 8. Volumes 5 and 6 of *Collected Works* contain, respectively, vols. 1 and 2 of *Virgin Soil Upturned*; vol. 7 includes *They Fought for Their Country: Chapters from the Novel* (pp. 5-220), early stories (pp. 223-573), "The Science of Hatred" (pp. 574-590), and "The Fate of a Man" (pp. 591-622); and vol. 8 comprises sketches, articles, and speeches. References to the 1975 edition are also made in cases when certain passages are missing from it because they were excised in previous editions. Using page and volume numbers of the 1975 edition, one can easily find the corresponding place in other publications of Sholokhov's works. Notes provide references to such publications only in cases when the finding of the cited passages may present difficulties. Above all, this applies to journals that serialized Sholokhov's works or published excerpts from them. My translations from *The Quiet Don* and *Virgin Soil Upturned* are based, respectively, on those in Mikhail Sholokhov, *And Quiet Flows the Don*, trans. Stephen Garry, rev. and completed by Robert Daglish, 4 vols. (Moscow: Progress Publishers, 1967), and *Virgin Soil Upturned*, vol. 1, trans. R. Daglish (Moscow: Progress Publishers [1964]), and vol. 2, trans. Robert Daglish (Moscow: Foreign Languages Publishing House [1961]). In many instances, however, I changed Garry's and Daglish's translations or made my own, especially in passages missing from the above editions. Translations from all other works, unless otherwise noted, are mine.

2. Quoted in Vitalii Zaseev, "U Sholokhova, v Veshenskoi," *V mire knig*, no. 5 (1975), p. 14.

3. This quotation and the word "nonhuman" from the preceding quotation were deleted from the 1953 and 1955 editions.

4. M. Sholokhov, "*Tikhii Don*: Glava iz chetvertoi knigi," *Izvestiia*, March 1, 1936.

5. Quoted in Mikhail Obukhov, "Vstrechi s Sholokhovym (20-30-e gody)," in V. A. Kovalev and A. I. Khvatov, eds., *Tvorchestvo Mikhaila Sholokhova: Stat'i, soobshcheniia, bibliografiia* (Leningrad, 1975), p. 291.

6. *Ibid.*, p. 292. Sholokhov visited Senin in the OGPU office in Millerovo (100 miles from Veshenskaia), probably in 1930.

7. Boris Pasternak, *Doktor Zhivago* (Ann Arbor, Mich.: University of Michigan Press, 1959), p. 348.

8. I. Lezhnev, *Put' Sholokhova: Tvorcheskaia biografiia* (Moscow, 1958), pp. 347-348; Konstantin Priima, "Veshenskie vstrechi: K tvorcheskoi istorii sholokhovskikh proizvedenii," *Pod''em* (Voronezh), no. 5 (1962), pp. 153-154. Erma-

kov's daughter indicated to Lezhnev that her father disappeared in 1927, and a local Communist gave Priima the same year for Ermakov's arrest and execution. A less reliable source asserts that Ermakov was shot in 1925. See N. Botashev, A. Ermakov, and V. Nikolaev, "V gostiakh u Sholokhova," *Sovetskaia Rossiia*, March 18, 1962. The authors of the article—visitors from the Urals—claim to have received this information from Sholokhov. This must be a misunderstanding, for there exists a letter from Sholokhov to Ermakov dated April 6, 1926 (L. P. Logashova, ed., *"Tikhii Don": Uroki romana* [Rostov-on-Don, 1979], p. 113). The information in *Sovetskaia Rossiia* is nonetheless remarkable, because it is the first time that Sholokhov is said to have stated, in plain terms, that Ermakov was executed.

9. Lezhnev, *Put' Sholokhova*, pp. 349-350; V. V. Gura, *Zhizn' i tvorchestvo M. A. Sholokhova*, 2d ed., rev. and enl. (Moscow, 1960), p. 45. For the text of the amnesty see L. Vol'pe's notes in Mikhail Sholokhov, *Sobranie sochinenii*, 8 vols. to date (Moscow: Khudozhestvennaia literatura, 1965-), 5:498. Lezhnev spells Fedor Melikhov's name Melekhov.

10. Nikolai Korsunov, "Vstrechi s Sholokhovym," *Prostor* (Alma-Ata), no. 6 (1975), p. 103. The question was asked at Sholokhov's public appearance in 1969 by a schoolboy who did not agree with his teacher that one should be disgusted with Lushka.

11. "*Tikhii Don*: Otryvok iz 6-i chasti romana Mikh. Sholokhova," *Krasnaia niva*, no. 16 (June 10, 1930), p. 12. Italics are mine. This is the only place in Sholokhov's writings where the word *chekakaiushchie* occurs in combination with "blades." Speaking of the rattling blades of a mowing machine on two other occasions, Sholokhov uses a similar onomatopoeic verb *chechekat'* (*Sobranie sochinenii* [1975], 1:81; 7:511). The phrase *chekakaiushchie nozhi* has been omitted from all subsequent publications of the novel, beginning with the *Oktiabr'* edition where the entire passage appears in a recast version. See *Oktiabr'*, no. 1 (1932), p. 20.

12. V. V. Gura and F. A. Abramov, *M. A. Sholokhov: Seminarii*, 2d ed. enl. (Leningrad, 1962), pp. 26, 27, 67; A. Fadeev, "Staroe i novoe," *Literaturnaia gazeta*, November 11, 1932.

13. Quoted in Gura and Abramov, *M. A. Sholokhov*, p. 67.

14. V. Dobrynin, "Vooruzhennaia bor'ba Dona s bol'shevikami," in Donskaia istoricheskaia komissiia, ed., *Donskaia letopis': Sbornik mater'ialov po noveishei istorii donskogo kazachestva so vremeni russkoi revoliutsii 1917 goda*, vol. 1 (Vienna, 1923), p. 103. Colonel Dobrynin was the chief of Intelligence and Operational Staff of the Don Army.

15. A. I. Denikin, *Ocherki russkoi smuty*, vol. 5 (Berlin, 1926), p. 230.

16. Dobrynin, "Vooruzhennaia bor'ba," p. 130.

17. A. G. Shkuro, *Zapiski belogo partizana* (Buenos Aires, 1961), p. 231.

18. Denikin, *Ocherki*, vol. 5, p. 230. On the numerical strength of the Red Army during the earlier stages of the war (very low, especially in combat units), see John Erickson, "The Origins of the Red Amy," in Richard Pipes, ed., *Rev-*

olutionary Russia (Cambridge, Mass.: Harvard University Press, 1968), pp. 224-256.

19. Iurii Zhdanov, "Tri vershiny v sud'be russkogo romana," in A. M. Suichmezov, ed., *Nash Sholokhov: Slovo o velikom zemliake* (Rostov-on-Don, 1975), p. 50. The author, the son of Andrei Zhdanov, is a corresponding member of the Soviet Academy of Sciences and president of Rostov University.

20. Quoted in I. Eksler, "V gostiakh u Sholokhova," *Izvestiia*, December 31, 1937. See also M. A. Sholokhov, "On ukrashaet zhizn'. . . ," *Don*, no. 9 (1978), p. 4.

21. Quoted in V. G. Vasil'ev, *O "Tikhom Done" M. Sholokhova* (Cheliabinsk, 1963), p. 6. Sholokhov said this in June 1947.

22. L. N. Tolstoi, *Sobranie sochinenii*, ed. N. N. Akopova et al., 20 vols. (Moscow, 1960-1965), 8:177 (hereafter cited in the text by volume and page numbers).

23. Quoted in Roy A. Medvedev, *Problems in the Literary Biography of Mikhail Sholokhov*, trans. A.D.P. Briggs (Cambridge, 1977), p. 10. I made a few changes in Briggs's translation, using the Russian text of Sverdlov's directive in the typescript of Roi A. Medvedev, *Zagadki tvorcheskoi biografii M. A. Sholokhova: K istorii romana "Tikhii Don"* (n. p., 1976), pp. 14-15. According to Roi Medvedev, only less important extracts from the directive have been published in the Soviet Union. Medvedev obtained its full text from the Central Party Archive. The Soviets were compelled to annul the directive after the outbreak of the Upper Don uprising. A particularly vivid picture of the massive extermination of Cossacks based on the documentary evidence of the time is given in Sergei Starikov and Roy Medvedev, *Philip Mironov and the Russian Civil War*, trans. Guy Daniels (New York: Alfred A. Knopf, 1978), pp. 118, 123-128.

24. V. A. Antonov-Ovseenko, *Zapiski o grazhdanskoi voine*, vol. 1 (Moscow, 1924), p. 256.

25. This episode can be found only in Mikh. Sholokhov, "*Tikhii Don*: Otryvki iz 6-i chasti romana," *Na pod''eme* (Rostov-on-Don), no. 6 (1930), p. 16.

26. For Gor'kii's views on women and mothers see Maxim Gorky, *Untimely Thoughts: Essays on Revolution, Culture, and the Bolsheviks, 1917-1918*, ed. and trans. Herman Ermolaev (New York: Paul S. Eriksson, 1968), pp. 207-213.

27. N. V. Gogol', *Sobranie khudozhestvennykh proizvedenii v piati tomakh*, 2d ed., vol. 2 (Moscow: Akademiia nauk SSSR, 1960), p. 162. For comments on digressions in Gogol' and Sholokhov see also D. H. Stewart, *Mikhail Sholokhov: A Critical Introduction* (Ann Arbor, Mich.: University of Michigan Press, 1967), p. 61.

28. Cf. Tolstoi, *Sobranie sochinenii*, 3:211, and *Tikhii Don*, vol. 2 (1975), p. 303.

29. Cf. Tolstoi, *Sobranie sochinenii*, 3:201, and *Tikhii Don*, vol. 2 (1975), p. 32. It is possible that either Tolstoi or Sholokhov exercised a certain influence on the depiction of the dead Red Army soldiers in Grigorii Baklanov's *Iiul' 41 goda* (Moscow, 1965), pp. 152-154.

30. Letter to Mark Kolosov, May 24, 1924, in Viktor Gura, "Vechno zhivoe

slovo (Novye materialy o M. Sholokhove)," *Voprosy literatury*, no. 4 (1965), p. 5.

31. For additional discussion of this relationship see Helen Muchnic, *From Gorky to Pasternak: Six Writers in Soviet Russia* (New York: Random House, 1961), pp. 309-319, 322-324; Stewart, *Mikhail Sholokhov*, pp. 55, 60, 63-68; P. Belov, *Lev Tolstoi i Mikhail Sholokhov* (Rostov-on-Don, 1969). Pavel Belov's book is rather superficial and abounds in strained parallels reflecting the official interpretation of history. Professor Muchnic's perceptive essay on Sholokhov contains, unfortunately, a few factual inaccuracies.

32. Cf. Mikhail Sholokhov, *Deviatnadtsataia godina: Neopublikovannyi otryvok iz "Tikhogo Dona"* (Moscow: Ogonek, 1930), pp. 21-22, and *Oktiabr'*, no. 2 (1932), p. 5. The size of the land allotment mentioned by Grigorii (twelve *desiatinas*) coincides exactly with the size of the average allotment for each adult male Cossack throughout the entire Don region shortly before World War I. Allotments varied from stanitsa to stanitsa, ranging from four to thirty-three *desiatinas* (eleven to ninety-nine acres). See S. Ia. A--n, "Donskie kazaki (Ocherk)," *Russkoe bogatstvo*, no. 12 (1906), pp. 130, 133.

33. In the winter of 1919 Revolutionary committees were set up in the occupied Cossack territories. Staffed with trusted Communists, they represented a dictatorial form of government intended for areas with unfriendly populations. In 1919 the Bolsheviks resolved to forego the formation of the soviets in the Cossack territories for fear that their elected members would not maintain loyalty or would even hold hostilities toward them, as was the case with the soviets organized in the Don region a year earlier. See I. M. Borokhova et al., comps., *Bor'ba za vlast' Sovetov na Donu: Sbornik dokumentov* (Rostov-on-Don, 1957), pp. 31-32, 412-416.

34. Denikin, *Ocherki*, vol. 5, p. 349. See also N. M. Mel'nikov, "Novorossiiskaia katastrofa," *Rodimyi krai* (Paris), no. 35 (July-August 1961), pp. 1-12; I. N. Oprits, *Leib-gvardii Kazachii E. V. polk v gody revoliutsii i grazhdanskoi voiny 1917-1920* (Paris, 1939), pp. 295-297.

35. Telegram of March 11, 1920, V. I. Lenin, *Polnoe sobranie sochinenii*, 5th ed., vol. 51 (Moscow, 1965), p. 159.

36. S. Budennyi, "Babizm Babelia iz 'Krasnoi novi,' " *Oktiabr'*, no. 3 (September-October 1924), pp. 196-197. In its vituperation and nastiness Budennyi's attack foreshadowed Andrei Zhdanov's 1946 diatribes against Mikhail Zoshchenko and Anna Akhmatova. One may wonder whether Babel''s portrayal of the First Cavalry was a contributing factor to his eventual death in a Soviet concentration camp.

37. Lezhnev, *Put' Sholokhova*, p. 333.

38. Cf. *Oktiabr'*, no. 1 (1929), p. 75, and *Tikhii Don*, vol. 3 [1st ed.] (Moscow: Khudozhestvennaia literatura, 1933), p. 22; *Oktiabr'*, no. 3 (1929), p. 54, and *Tikhii Don*, vol. 3 [1st ed.], 1933, p. 78.

39. Quoted in Al. Is., "Chitateli govoriat," *Na literaturnom postu*, no. 7 (April 1929), p. 44. Aleksandr Khvatov, a Soviet scholar, repeatedly asserts that Sholokhov said this in his 1957 conversation with the reporter V. Krupin. Cf. Khvatov, "Obraz Grigoriia Melekhova i kontseptsiia romana 'Tikhii Don,' " *Russkaia li-*

teratura, no. 2 (1965), p. 7; *Khudozhestvennyi mir Sholokhova* (Moscow, 1970), p. 215; 3d ed. (Moscow, 1978), pp. 182, 473; and V. Krupin, "V gostiakh u M. A. Sholokhova," *Sovetskaia Rossiia*, August 25, 1957. In Khvatov's writings the quotation ends with the words "until 1920." The rest is dropped because of the phrase "when an end was put to these vacillations," which indicates that it was the Soviet use of force that brought the Cossacks into obedience after the final occupation of the Don region by the Reds in 1920. According to the official version, the majority of the Cossacks accepted the Bolshevik regime voluntarily.

40. Quoted in Dir [Mikhail Rogov], "Razgovor s Sholokhovym," *Izvestiia*, March 10, 1935.

41. *Ibid.*

42. Quoted in An. Kalinin, "Vstrechi," in S. G. Lipshits, ed., *Mikhail Sholokhov: Literaturno-kriticheskii sbornik* (Rostov-on-Don, 1940), p. 153.

43. Quoted in Vasil'ev, *O "Tikhom Done" M. Sholokhova*, p. 5.

44. Quoted in Lezhnev, *Put' Sholokhova*, p. 343.

45. Quoted in V. Koroteev and V. Efimov, "Na Donu," *Izvestiia*, July 1, 1956. Somewhat surprising here is the ironic use of the sacrosanct shibboleth about "the gleaming heights," even if Sholokhov made his statement during the period of relative liberalization. He must have been strongly irritated by continuing propagandistic distortions of his works in their stage and screen adaptations. The opera *The Quiet Don* (1935) ends, for example, with Grigorii becoming a Red Revolutionary, while the finale of the film *Virgin Soil Upturned* (1939) presents a grand parade of agricultural machines rolling over the fields of the Gremiachii collective farm. The last thing one hears in the opera *Virgin Soil Upturned* (1937) is the chorus singing in praise of the happy Soviet life and Stalin.

46. Korsunov, "Vstrechi s Sholokhovym," *Prostor*, no. 5 (1975), p. 105; Konstantin Priima, "Vstrechi v Veshenskoi," *Don*, no. 5 (1981), p. 139.

47. I therefore disagree with the view that Grigorii's tragic flaw "lies in seeking and supporting justice, and in a stubborn defense of his and others' personal dignity and their right to life and freedom" (Robert F. Price, "Tragic Features in the Character of Grigorij Melexov," *Slavic and East European Journal*, vol. 23, no. 1 [Spring 1979], p. 65). Although these admirable qualities contributed a great deal to his rift with the Bolsheviks and to his physical death at their hands, they played a much lesser role in his real personal tragedy than did his love for Aksin'ia.

48. Quoted in Krupin, "V gostiakh u M. A. Sholokhova," *Sovetskaia Rossiia*, August 25, 1957.

49. "Literatura—chast' obshcheproletarskogo dela: Vystuplenie M. Sholokhova na vechere vstrechi s udarnikami-zheleznodorozhnikami Rostova," *Molot*, October 8, 1934.

50. Aleksandr I. Solzhenitsyn, *The Gulag Archipelago, 1918-1956: An Experiment in Literary Investigation*, parts 1-2, trans. Thomas P. Whitney (New York: Harper & Row, 1974), p. 538. The quick dying out of a thousand families of exiled kulaks is described in G. Andreev [Gennadii Khomiakov], *Trudnye dorogi* (Munich, 1959), pp. 91-93.

51. Solzhenitsyn, *The Gulag Archipelago*, parts 1-2, p. 55.

52. Priima, "Veshenskie vstrechi," *Pod''em*, no. 5 (1962), pp. 155, 156. This information comes from Naum Telitsyn, former chairman of the Bokovskaia Soviet (the Upper Don region), and Evgenii Kuznetsov, one of the two OGPU men who arrested Senin.

53. Quoted in Dir, "Razgovor s Sholokhovym," *Izvestiia*, March 10, 1935.

54. Priima, "Veshenskie vstrechi," pp. 156-158. Sholokhov also changed another detail: in the novel, Polovtsev is arrested near Tashkent, inside a state farm building; actually, Polovtsev's prototype was captured in the open, near a Cossack village. On the other hand, Sholokhov's OGPU men pose as cattle merchants as they did in real life.

55. Gogol', *Sobranie khudozhestvennykh proizvedenii*, 2d ed., vol. 2 (1960), p. 173.

56. Quoted in Mikh. Sokolov, "Velikii pisatel' sovremennosti," *Don*, no. 5 (1975), p. 127.

57. *Ibid.*

58. *Neva*, no. 7 (1959), pp. 61-152, or *Don*, no. 7 (1959), pp. 63-158.

59. A. Iashin, "Rychagi," in *Literaturnaia Moskva*, vol. 2, ed. M. I. Aliger et al. (Moscow, 1956), pp. 502-513; F. Abramov, "Vokrug da okolo," *Neva*, no. 1 (1963), pp. 109-137. Also in English: "Levers," in Hugh McLean and Walter N. Vickery, eds. and trans., *The Year of Protest, 1956: An Anthology of Soviet Literary Materials* (New York: Vintage Books, 1961), pp. 193-208; *One Day in the "New Life"* [translation of "Vokrug da okolo"], trans. David Floyd (New York: Frederick A. Praeger, 1963).

60. *One Day in the "New Life,"* p. 160. Collective farmers worked for virtually nothing. On February 28, 1964, at a conference of the Party and agricultural leaders, Nikita Khrushchev reported that most collective farms had to deliver their products to the state at prices below production costs. As an example he cited eight regions in European Russia in which the payment for one "work day" ranged from 1 to 4 kopecks, while many collective farms paid nothing for years. See I. Vinogradov, "Derevenskie ocherki Valentina Ovechkina," *Novyi mir*, no. 6 (1964), p. 224.

61. *Istoriia Velikoi Otechestvennoi voiny Sovetskogo Soiuza, 1941-1945*, vol. 2 (Moscow, 1961), pp. 101-102; D. F. Grigorovich, *Kiev gorod-geroi* (Moscow, 1962), pp. 46, 67, 68.

62. Basil Dmytryshyn, *USSR: A Concise History*, 2d ed. (New York: Charles Scribner's Sons, 1971), pp. 223-224.

63. Erich v. Manstein, *Verlorene Siege* (Bonn: Athenäum-Verlag, 1955), pp. 178, 246; Paul Carell, *Der Russlandkrieg: Fotografiert von Soldaten* (Frankfort on the Main: Verlag Ullstein, 1967), p. 414; Viktor Nekrasov, "Vzgliad i nechto," *Kontinent*, no. 13 (1977), p. 41.

64. Solzhenitsyn, *The Gulag Archipelago*, parts 1-2, p. 244. For information concerning the fate of returning POWs see pp. 237-251.

65. For a unique description of a screening camp see part 1 of Leonid Semin's short novel *Odin na odin (Face to Face)*, *Neva*, no. 3 (1963), pp. 38-115. Part 2 has not yet appeared.

66. Solzhenitsyn, *The Gulag Archipelago*, parts 1-2, pp. 261-262.

67. For the number of prisoners see Dmytryshyn, *USSR*, 2d ed., p. 223. Stalin's order, dated July 28, 1942, was prompted by his concern for the fighting spirit and discipline of the Red Army, which was retreating without offering serious resistance. To stop any further retreat, Stalin decreed the formation of penal units and "rear security detachments" (*zagraditel'nye otriady*). The latter were to be positioned behind fighting troops, with express orders to shoot on sight anyone retreating without authorization. Actually, the penal units and rear security detachments had already existed in the Red Army. Stalin's order, however, greatly increased their number. To my knowledge, only excerpts from Stalin's order have been published in the Soviet press. Its nearly complete version can be found in Ernst Ott, *Jäger am Feind* (Munich: Kameradschaft der Spielhahnjäger e. V., 1966), pp. 206-209. The order came into German hands via a Soviet commissar who deserted.

68. A. Sofronov, "Bessmertnik," *Ogonek*, no. 31 (July 26, 1964), p. 12.

69. M. F. Lukin " 'My ne sdaemsia, tovarishch general!' " *Ogonek*, no. 47 (November 15, 1964), pp. 27-30.

70. M. V. Shatov, *Materialy i dokumenty osvoboditel'nogo dvizheniia narodov Rossii v gody vtoroi mirovoi voiny (1941-1945)*, vol. 2 (New York, 1966), pp. 114-115.

71. Iurii Lukin, *Dva portreta: A. S. Makarenko, M. A. Sholokhov* (Moscow, 1975), p. 410. Soviet critics refer to Aleksandr Mikhailovich as General Strel'tsov or Strel'tsov, Sr.

72. Korsunov, "Vstrechi s Sholokhovym," *Prostor*, no. 6, p. 99. A 1904 police report describing Stalin's appearance in great detail lists his eyes as "dark brown." See R. A. Medvedev, "Stalin: Nekotorye stranitsy iz politicheskoi biografii," *Dvadtsatyi vek* (London), no. 2 (1977), p. 12. Lana Peters (Svetlana Allilueva) told me that her father's eyes were light brown. Sholokhov, of course, knew the color of Stalin's eyes from his meetings with the dictator.

73. Alexander Solzhenitsyn, *Cancer Ward*, trans. Nicholas Bethell and David Burg (New York: Bantam Books, 1969), p. 507. See also Aleksandr I. Solzhenitsyn, *The First Circle*, trans. Thomas P. Whitney (New York: Bantam Books, 1969), pp. 117, 127.

74. I. Mashbits-Verov, "Mikhail Sholokhov," *Novyi mir*, no. 10 (1928), p. 232; A. Selivanovskii, " 'Tikhii Don,' " *Na literaturnom postu*, no. 10 (May 1929), p. 50.

75. Iu. Lukin, *Mikhail Sholokhov* (Moscow, 1952), p. 41; V. V. Gura, "Istoriia sozdaniia vtoroi knigi romana M. Sholokhova 'Tikhii Don,' " in Vologodskii pedagogicheskii institut, *Uchenye zapiski*, vol. 18 (filologicheskii) (Vologda, 1958), p. 142; L. Iakimenko, *Tvorchestvo M. A. Sholokhova* (Moscow, 1964), p. 339.

76. Stalin's opinion of Kornilov was quoted by the general as having been expressed in a conversation with Red Army commanders.

77. Konstantin Priima, *"Tikhii Don" srazhaetsia*, 2d ed., rev. and enl. (Moscow, 1975), p. 453.

Chapter III

1. *Istoriia russkoi sovetskoi literatury*, vol. 2, ed. L. I. Timofeev and A. G. Dement'ev (Moscow, 1960), p. 159. The autograph begins with "unichtozhat' i razdevat' plennykh" and ends with "blestela na."

2. Cf. Mikh. Sholokhov, *Tikhii Don, Oktiabr'*, no. 3 (1929), p. 55, and " 'Pozhiva': Neopublikovannyi otryvok iz romana M. Sholokhova 'Tikhii Don,' " *Plamia*, no. 7 (April 1929), unpaged. The only noteworthy difference between the two texts is that *Plamia* has the word "army" where *Oktiabr'* and subsequent editions have "division."

3. Examples for each work will be given separately. Information in parentheses pertaining to the journal will include its number, year of publication, and page. The name of the journal and the volume number of the work can be easily established from the following facts of publication: *The Quiet Don*—vol. 1 (*Oktiabr'*, nos. 1-4, 1928), vol. 2 (*Oktiabr'*, nos. 5-10, 1928), vol. 3 (*Oktiabr'*, 1929, 1932), vol. 4 (*Novyi mir*, 1937, 1938, 1940); *Virgin Soil Upturned* (*Novyi mir*, 1932).

4. Description of the Don Cossack dialect can be found in A. V. Mirtov, *Donskoi slovar': Materialy k izucheniiu leksiki donskikh kazakov* (Rostov-on-Don, 1929); Z. V. Valiusinskaia et al., *Slovar' russkikh donskikh govorov*, 3 vols. (Rostov-on-Don, 1975-1976). A considerable number of dialecticisms and colloquialisms from *The Quiet Don* are listed in both Russian and English in "An Introduction and Commentary to Sholokhov's *Tikhiy Don*," edited by A. B. Murphy and published serially in *New Zealand Slavonic Journal* (1975-1977). The usefulness of the "Introduction" is somewhat reduced by ambiguities and factual errors. Furthermore, it fails to take into account all editions from 1931 through 1941. Therefore many corrections made during this period are attributed, implicitly or explicitly, to the 1945 edition. Among other inaccuracies one must point out that the Don Cossacks pronounce the word *kazakí* with the stress on the last syllable (not the second), and that General Kaledin cannot be called a *nakaznyi* (appointed) ataman because he was elected. Incidentally, the Cossacks say Kaledín, not Kalédin.

5. M. Sholokhov, "Za chestnuiu rabotu pisatelia i kritika," *Literaturnaia gazeta*, March 18, 1934.

6. This last *var*, in "the Whirlpool," has remained intact, while the other one (*Oktiabr'*, no. 1 [1928], p. 134) was removed in 1933.

7. The number of the 1956 emendations in both stories is arrived at by comparing their 1956 texts with the texts published in *The Don Stories* (1926).

8. A. I. Matsai, "Na puti bor'by za realizm i samobytnost': O rabote M. Sholokhova nad rasskazami 'Smertnyi vrag' i 'Aleshkino serdtse,' " *Voprosy russkoi literatury* (L'vov), no. 2 (1972), p. 60.

9. Quoted in Konstantin Priima, "Sholokhov v Veshkakh," *Sovetskii Kazakhstan*, no. 5 (1955), p. 82.

10. V. G. Vetvitskii, "Dialektizmy kak sredstvo sozdaniia mestnogo kolorita v romane M. A. Sholokhova 'Tikhii Don,' " in B. A. Larin, ed., *Mikhail Sholokhov: Sbornik statei* (Leningrad, 1956), pp. 185-186. Typically for the Soviet critics of that time, Vetvitskii speaks approvingly of the 1953 edition of *The Quiet Don*. He rationalizes corrections made in it, attributing them to Sholokhov and

Potapov. Ironically, Vetvitskii's article came out at a time when the new edition of the novel, which did not include the bulk of the 1953 corrections, was being completed. For an informative discussion of dialecticisms in *The Quiet Don*, see Olga V. Chebyshowa, "Deviations from the Standard Literary Russian in Sholochov's *Quiet Flows the Don*" (Master's thesis, Stanford University, 1964). The thesis is written in Russian. Based on the 1957 edition of *The Quiet Don*, it does not deal with dialecticisms replaced in previous editions.

11. Two authorial references to old Melekhov's "wadded frock coat," found in an excerpt from the novel published in *Izvestiia*, April 12, 1935, were replaced with a "wadded jacket" in *Novyi mir*, no. 11 (1937), p. 25. The characters, however, continue to call the very same garment a "wadded frock coat" (4:21, 22). Another authorial reference to a "frock coat," in an excerpt printed in the September 27, 1937, issue of *Pravda*, was replaced with a "jacket" in *Novyi mir*, no. 1 (1938), p. 115 (4:219). It is therefore quite possible that a *pidzhak* (later changed to *kurtka*) and a *kurtka*, which appear elsewhere in *Novyi mir* (no. 2-3 [1940], pp. 33, 51), are also editorial substitutions for the original *siurtuk* (4:333, 367).

12. A thorough discussion of the handling of dialecticisms in the 1952 edition can be found in M. I. Privalova, "Iz nabliudenii nad iazykovoi pravkoi 'Podniatoi tseliny,' " in Larin, ed., *Mikhail Sholokhov*, pp. 138-164. Since Privalova compares the 1952 edition only with the first book-form edition of 1932, she erroneously attributes to the 1952 editors a number of corrections made in 1933-1934. Among them are replacements of *zhdetsia* (is expected), *okazyvaia* (showing), *shchepa* (chip), *tsepka* (little chain), *chernet'* (blackness [a noun]). See pp. 151, 152.

13. H. L. Yelland, S. C. Jones, and K.S.W. Easton, *A Handbook of Literary Terms* (New York: Philosophical Library, 1950), pp. 187-188. The first quotation is taken from Joseph T. Shipley, ed., *Dictionary of World Literary Terms* (Boston: Writer, 1970), p. 304. The word "different" is, however, absent from the definition of simile given by Aleksandr Kviatkovskii. According to him, simile is "built on the comparison of two things, concepts, or states which possess a common feature" (*Poeticheskii slovar'* [Moscow, 1966], p. 280).

14. L. N. Tolstoi, *Sobranie sochinenii*, ed. N. N. Akopova et al., 20 vols. (Moscow, 1960-1965), 4:17 (cited hereafter in the text by volume number and page).

15. Aristotle, *Poetics*, trans. Gerald F. Else (Ann Arbor, Mich.: University of Michigan Press, 1967), pp. 57, 61.

16. Aristotle, *The "Art" of Rhetoric*, trans. John Henry Freese (London: William Heinemann; Cambridge, Mass.: Harvard University Press, 1947), p. 397.

17. Quoted in Marsh H. McCall, Jr., *Ancient Rhetorical Theories of Simile and Comparison* (Cambridge, Mass.: Harvard University Press, 1969), p. 229.

18. *Ibid.*, 259.

19. Christine Brooke-Rose, *A Grammar of Metaphor* (London: Secker and Warburg, 1958), p. 14; Max Black, *Models and Metaphors: Studies in Language and Philosophy* (Ithaca, N.Y.: Cornell University Press, 1962), p. 37.

20. Philip Wheelwright, *Metaphor and Reality* (Bloomington, Ind.: Indiana University Press, 1962), p. 71.

21. Philip Wheelwright, *The Burning Fountain: A Study in the Language of Symbolism*, rev. ed. (Bloomington, Ind.: Indiana University Press, 1968), pp. 104-105.

22. See Paul Ricoeur, *The Rule of Metaphor*, trans. Robert Czerny, Kathleen McLaughlin, and John Costello (Toronto: University of Toronto Press, 1977), p. 186.

23. See, e.g., Kviatkovskii, *Poeticheskii slovar'*, p. 281.

24. *Ibid.*, p. 189; A. A. Potebnia, *Iz zapisok po teorii slovesnosti* (Khar'kov, 1905), p. 287; V. I. D'iakonov, "Sravneniia Turgeneva," in N. L. Brodskii, ed., *Turgenev i ego vremia: Pervyi sbornik* (Moscow, 1923), pp. 87-88.

25. T. Hilding Svartengren, *Intensifying Similes in English* (Lund, 1918), pp. v-ix.

26. Carl R. Proffer, *The Simile and Gogol's "Dead Souls"* (The Hague: Mouton, 1967), p. 47. The twelve categories are: man, parts of body, household, food, clothing, animal, insect, nature, mineral, mythology or literature, music, other.

27. I used the following editions of these works: *Bronepoezd No. 14.69* (*Krasnaia nov'*, no. 1, 1922); *Tsement* (*Krasnaia nov'*, nos. 1-6, 1925); *Konarmiia*, 3d ed. (Moscow-Leningrad, 1928), reprint ed., London: Flegon Press, n.d.; *Zavist'*, in *Povesti i rasskazy* (Moscow, 1965); *Piruiushchaia vesna* (Khar'kov, 1929); *Doktor Zhivago* (Ann Arbor, Mich.: University of Michigan Press, 1959). The first two works had to be examined in their earliest journal versions in view of extensive revisions carried out in their later editions. All of the *Konarmiia* thirty-five stories, except "Argamak" (1932), were first published between 1923 and 1926. *Piruiushchaia vesna* is a collection of Veselyi's fiction published between 1923 and 1929. The main works are the story "Reki ognennye" ("Fiery Rivers"), which originally appeared in 1923 as fragments of a novel; the novel *Strana rodnaia* (*My Native Land*, 1925), and parts of an unfinished epic novel, *Rossiia, krov'iu umytaia* (*Russia Washed in Blood*, 1927-). The chronological framework of Veselyi's writings is roughly the same as that of *The Quiet Don*, and at times both authors portray the same events, e.g., disintegration of the tsarist army in 1917 or the retreat of the Volunteer Army from Rostov in February 1918. To save space, all of the above works will be cited hereafter in the text by page numbers. References to *Cement* will also include the numbers of *Krasnaia nov'* issues.

28. A. A. Saburov, *"Voina i mir" L. N. Tolstogo: Problematika i poetika* (Moscow, 1959), p. 583. The assertion is all the more surprising since Saburov, in assigning similes to the man-to-man group (pp. 582-583), appears to apply the same criteria as I do. This group in *War and Peace* is almost four times as large as the man-to-animal group. Saburov's inference is approvingly quoted in Proffer, *The Simile and Gogol's "Dead Souls,"* p. 48.

29. This question is answered in the affirmative in L. Iakimenko, *Tvorchestvo M. A. Sholokhova* (Moscow, 1964), p. 576.

30. Olesha, "Literaturnaia tekhnika," *Povesti i rasskazy*, pp. 416-417.

31. Proffer, *The Simile and Gogol's "Dead Souls,"* p. 28.

32. Aleksei Remizov, ''Chernyi petukh,'' vol. 6 of *Sochineniia* (St. Petersburg, 1910-1912); reprint ed., Munich: Wilhelm Fink Verlag (Slavische Propyläen, no. 79), 1971, pp. 41-44.

33. This anonymous work contains about twenty tropes that can be classified as similes expressed by means of the instrumental case. Professor Justinia Besharov calls the form of these similes ''the instrumental of metamorphosis,'' stating that it is too ambiguous to allow one to tell whether it indicates an actual metamorphosis (usually of man into an animal) or just likeness (*Imagery of the ''Igor' Tale''* [Leiden: E. J. Brill, 1956], p. 72). This may be true of some, but not of the majority, of such cases in *The Tale*. Iaroslavna, for example, might have had a real desire to become a cuckoo and fly to Igor', but it is unlikely that Igor' actually went through successive transformations into an ermine, duck, wolf, and falcon on his flight from the Cuman captivity. V. P. Adrianova-Peretts, for instance, treats the phrase ''polete sokolom'' as a simile (''Frazeologiia i leksika 'Slova o polku Igoreve,' '' in D. S. Likhachev and L. A. Dmitriev, eds., *''Slovo o polku Igoreve'' i pamiatniki Kulikovskogo tsikla* [Moscow-Leningrad, 1966], p. 118); such different translators as Vasilii Zhukovskii, Apollon Maikov, and Nikolai Zabolotskii render it as ''flew like a falcon'' (*''Slovo o polku Igoreve,''* ed. V. P. Adrianova-Peretts [Moscow-Leningrad, 1950], pp. 116, 139, 223). Analogous phrases with ''duck'' and ''wolf'' were translated as plain similes by Zhukovskii and Maikov, while Zabolotskii saw metamorphosis in the case with the ermine. In his translation Igor' ''turned into an ermine-squirrel.'' But such transformations are exceptionally rare. In most cases translators of *The Tale* leave the original instrumental intact; otherwise, they prefer to replace it with typical similes formed with equivalents of ''like'' and ''as.'' Maikov and Zabolotskii did it six times each, in eight different phrases. The presence of instrumental similes in *The Tale* may be taken as an indication that the comparative function of the instrumental grew out of its metamorphic application.

34. The variety of Sholokhov's epithets applied to *tishina* has also been noted in Iakimenko, *Tvorchestvo M. A. Sholokhova*, pp. 619-620.

35. V. G. Vasil'ev, *O ''Tikhom Done'' M. Sholokhova* (Cheliabinsk, 1963), pp. 192-193.

36. S. A. Koltakov, ''Epitet v romane 'Tikhii Don,' '' *Russkaia rech'*, no. 2 (March-April 1970), pp. 37-39, 40.

37. For more details on compound adjectives see *ibid.*, pp. 39-40.

38. Association of *goluboi* with happy memories of the past was also noted by the critic L. Levin. My observations on this point were made independently of Levin, whose pertinent article (''Iz temy o 'Tikhom Done,' '' *Literaturnyi sovremennik*, no. 5 [1941]) is not available to me. Levin's view on the subject is quoted in D. H. Stewart, *Mikhail Sholokhov: A Critical Introduction* (Ann Arbor, Mich.: University of Michigan Press, 1967), p. 117.

39. Used for centuries in conversational language and in nonfictional writings, the word *sin'*, according to a Soviet scholar, came into Russian poetry only at the beginning of the twentieth century. In the 1920s it appeared in prose fiction. Sholokhov was one of the first to use it. See V. N. Zinov'ev, ''Sushchestvitel'noe

sin' i ego sinonimy v russkom iazyke,'' Gor'kovskii gosudarstvennyi universitet, *Uchenye zapiski: Seriia filologicheskaia*, vol. 59 (Gor'kii, 1960), pp. 32-34. Zinov'ev also touches upon a few other color nouns.

40. For color charts of *Red Cavalry* and *Odessa Stories* see Toby W. Clyman, ''Babel' as Colorist,'' *Slavic and East European Journal*, vol. 21, no. 3 (Fall 1977), p. 340. The charts show only color adjectives. The percentage of pure primary colors in *Odessa Stories* is only slightly higher than that in Sholokhov's early stories or in *The Quiet Don*. If we take into account their related hues, the order of frequency of colors in *Red Cavalry* and *Odessa Stories* combined is, according to Clyman, as follows: red, black, blue, yellow, green, and white (p. 333). The corresponding order in both the early stories and *The Quiet Don* begins with black, followed by white, red, yellow, blue, and green.

41. For examples see my article ''Politicheskaia pravka 'Tikhogo Dona,' '' *Mosty* (Munich), no. 15 (1970), pp. 267-268.

42. Koshevoi's list was absent from the earliest publication of this portion of the novel in Mikhail Sholokhov, *Deviatnadtsataia godina: Neopublikovannyi otryvok iz ''Tikhogo Dona''* (Moscow: Ogonek, 1930), p. 10. The author could have added it on request by the *Oktiabr'* editors. The purpose of the list was to justify the Red terror by citing the reasons for the arrest and subsequent execution of a group of the Tatarskii Cossacks.

43. For a somewhat different approach to ornamentalism see Patricia Carden, ''Ornamentalism and Modernism,'' in George Gibian and H. W. Tjalsma, eds., *Russian Modernism: Culture and the Avant-Garde, 1900-1930* (Ithaca, N.Y., and London: Cornell University Press, 1976), pp. 49-64. Perceptive remarks on ornamentalism are contained in Gary L. Browning, ''Russian Ornamental Prose,'' *Slavic and East European Journal*, vol. 23, no. 3 (Fall 1979), pp. 346-352.

44. ''Iz dnevnikov i zapisei I. A. Bunina,'' pub. Militsa Grin, *Novyi zhurnal* (New York), no. 114 (1974), pp. 131-133. While reading volume 2 of *The Quiet Don*, Bunin ''experienced a return of my hatred for Bolshevism'' and dubbed Sholokhov ''a lout and plebian'' (*ibid.*, p. 135). In 1942, upon rereading Babel', Bunin found ''everything florid'' and delivered a bitter harangue against what he called Babel''s ''pathological passion for blasphemy.'' The attack ended with bracketing Babel' and Sholokhov together as ''filthy louts and swine with stinking bodies and vile minds and souls'' (*ibid.*, no. 115, p. 150).

Chapter IV

1. A. I. Denikin, *Ocherki russkoi smuty*, vol. 2 (Paris [1922]), p. 161.

2. N. M. Mel'nikov, *A. M. Kaledin geroi lutskogo proryva i donskoi ataman* (Madrid, 1968), pp. 13-14.

3. I. Sagatskii, ''Radzivillov,'' *Rodimyi krai* (Paris), no. 83 (July-August 1969), p. 25; no. 84 (September-October, 1969), p. 26; no. 85 (November-December, 1969), pp. 27, 30.

4. S. N. Semanov, *''Tikhii Don''—literatura i istoriia* (Moscow, 1977), pp. 32-33.

5. *Strategicheskii ocherk voiny 1914-1918*, part 1, comp. Ia. K. Tsikhovich

(Moscow, 1922), p. 34. The date indicates the capture of Leshniuv by an unidentified unit of the Eleventh Cavalry Division. In *The Quiet Don* Leshniuv is taken by the Cossacks of the Twelfth Regiment at about the same time.

6. Sviatoslav Golubintsev, "Na tikhii Don (Iz starykh vospominanii)," *Novoe russkoe slovo* (New York), January 21, 1968, and letter to the editor, *ibid.*, November 13, 1974.

7. Semanov, *"Tikhii Don,"* p. 71.

8. *Ibid.*, p. 70.

9. Golubintsev, "Na tikhii Don," *Novoe russkoe slovo*, January 21, 1968, and letter to the editor, *ibid.*, November 13, 1974. Sholokhov calls Kamenka-Strumilova Kamenka-Strumilovo.

10. Notes to vol. 2 of Mikhail Sholokhov, *Sobranie sochinenii*, 8 vols. (Moscow: Kudozhestvennaia literatura, 1956-1960), p. 409.

11. Cf. F. Rodin's reminiscences in "Koz'ma Firsovich Kriuchkov," *Rodimyi krai*, no. 56 (January-February 1965), pp. 7-8; "Vostochnyi front," *Novoe vremia*, August 17 (30), 1914; *Neustrashimyi geroi donskoi kazak Kuz'ma Kriuchkov i ego slavnye pobedy nad vragami, kak on odin ubil 11 nemtsev* (Rostov-on-Don, 1914), p. 8.

12. "Vostochnyi front."

13. N. Kaledin's account in "Koz'ma Firsovich Kriuchkov," p. 9.

14. V. V. Zvegintsov, *Russkaia armiia 1914 g.: Podrobnaia dislokatsiia, formirovaniia 1914-1917, regalii i otlichiia* (Paris, 1959), p. 75; N. N. Golovin, *Iz istorii kampanii 1914 goda na russkom fronte: Nachalo voiny i operatsii v Vostochnoi Prussii* (Prague, 1926), p. 144.

15. D. H. Stewart, *Mikhail Sholokhov: A Critical Introduction* (Ann Arbor, Mich.: University of Michigan Press, 1967), p. 211.

16. *Neustrashimyi geroi*, p. 4; Rodin's reminiscences in "Koz'ma Firsovich Kriuchkov," p. 8.

17. For details see A. Iaroshevich, "Volynskaia guberniia," *Novyi entsiklopedicheskii slovar'*, vol. 11 (St. Petersburg: Brokgauz-Efron, n.d. [1913?]), p. 518. According to this source, the national composition of the Volyn' Province in 1897 ranged from Ukrainians (70.1 percent) to Czechs (0.9 percent). Belorussians were not mentioned.

18. E. I. Martynov, *Kornilov: Popytka voennogo perevorota* (Leningrad, 1927), p. 135.

19. Zvegintsov, *Russkaia armiia 1914 g.*, p. 27.

20. *Ibid.*, p. 13. The list of names of Russian regiments is nearly complete in this book. No regiment listed in it has the name *Orshanskii*. In addition to numbers, most Russian regiments had names which frequently were adjectives derived from the names of cities and towns. Sholokhov must have created the 441st Orshanskii Regiment himself, naming it after the town of Orsha. This is why the name of the regiment appears in a substandard form of *Orshevskii* in the 1928-1949 editions of the novel.

21. For the dates of fighting in the Stallupönen region see A. A. Uspenskii, *Na voine: Vostochnaia Prussiia-Litva 1914-1915 g.g.* (Kaunas, 1932), pp. 24-25, 103-

106, 126, 131; *Der Kriegsverlauf, August 1914-Juli 1915* (Berlin: Carl Heymanns Verlag, 1915), pp. 287, 562, 564.

22. Denikin, *Ocherki*, vol. 2, pp. 16-17.

23. Cf. A. Lukomskii, "Iz vospominanii," in I. V. Gessen, ed., *Arkhiv russkoi revoliutsii*, vol. 5 (Berlin, 1922), pp. 105, 106, 107. Lukomskii's "Reminiscences" also appeared in a separate edition (Berlin, 1922). I do not know which edition Sholokhov had; but since he definitely used General Petr Krasnov's memoirs published together with Lukomskii's reminiscences in vol. 5 of *Arkhiv russkoi revoliutsii*, I prefer to cite that source.

24. Cf. Denikin, *Ocherki*, vol. 2, pp. 30-31, and Martynov, *Kornilov*, p. 50.

25. Cf. Lukomskii, "Iz vospominanii," pp. 110-111, and Denikin, *Ocherki*, vol. 1, part 2 (Paris [1921]), pp. 210-211.

26. Cf. Denikin, *Ocherki*, vol. 1, part 2, p. 211.

27. Cf. "Iz vospominanii," p. 105. Lukomskii's phrases begin with "Esli ia ne oshibaius' " ("If I am not mistaken") and Kornilov's with "Vy pravy" ("You are right"). For other parallels cf. *Tikhii Don*, vol. 2, Mikhail Sholokhov, *Sobranie sochinenii* (Moscow: Pravda, 1975), pp. 119-123, and "Iz vospominanii," pp. 104, 105, 107-109.

28. *Ocherki*, vol. 1, part 2, p. 195. See also vol. 2, p. 29.

29. Cf. *Kornilov*, pp. 66-67, and "Prebyvanie v Moskve gen. L. G. Kornilova," *Russkoe slovo*, August 15 (28), 1917. This report was one of the sources for Martynov's account. For Gura's view see his article "Istoriia sozdaniia vtoroi knigi romana M. Sholokhova 'Tikhii Don,' " in Vologodskii pedagogicheskii institut, *Uchenye zapiski*, vol. 18 (filologicheskii) (Vologda, 1956), pp. 143-145.

30. Kaledin's report, quoted in K. Kakliugin, "Voiskovoi ataman A. M. Kaledin i ego vremia," in Donskaia istoricheskaia komissiia, ed., *Donskaia letopis': Sbornik mater'ialov po noveishei istorii donskogo kazachestva so vremeni russkoi revoliutsii 1917 goda*, vol. 2 (Vienna, 1923), pp. 125-126.

31. Denikin, *Ocherki*, vol. 1, part 2, p. 216, and vol. 2, pp. 15-17, 35-43; Lukomskii, "Iz vospominanii," pp. 107-110; Martynov, *Kornilov*, pp. 34-36, 58-59, 70-71.

32. Martynov, *Kornilov*, pp. 71-72; Kakliugin, "Voiskovoi ataman A. M. Kaledin. . . ," pp. 124-128.

33. For details see Kakliugin, "Voiskovoi ataman A. M. Kaledin. . . ," pp. 134-141; P. N. Miliukov, *Istoriia vtoroi russkoi revoliutsii*, vol. 1, part 2 (Sofia, 1921), pp. 272-277; Martynov, *Kornilov*, pp. 127-128; Riabtsev, "Voennaia telegramma o peredvizhenii kazach'ikh voisk po prikazaniiu Kaledina," in Vera Vladimirova, *Kontr-revoliutsiia v 1917 g.: Kornilovshchina* (Moscow, 1924), pp. 222-224.

34. Miliukov, *Istoriia vtoroi russkoi revoliutsii*, vol. 1, part 2, p. 137.

35. "Prebyvanie v Moskve. . . ," *Russkoe slovo*, August 15 (28), 1917; Martynov, *Kornilov*, p. 68.

36. Kaledin's report, in Kakliugin, "Voiskovoi ataman A. M. Kaledin. . . ," p. 126.

37. Kornilov delivered his address early in the afternoon of August 14 (27) and

Kaledin announced his declaration later in the day. After his own, or Kaledin's, speech, Kornilov went straight to the station, where he (apparently in the train) had a long conversation with General Mikhail Alekseev. He departed from Moscow on the same day at 4:20 p.m. ("Prebyvanie v Moskve. . ."; Martynov, *Kornilov*, p. 72). The August 14 (27) session of the State Conference began at 11:45 a.m. Kornilov was the sixth speaker and Kaledin, probably, the eleventh. Before his departure from Moscow, Kornilov gave an interview to reporters on the train. See "Zasedanie 14 avgusta" and "Beseda s generalom Kornilovym," *Rech'* (Petrograd), August 15 (28), 1917.

38. "Iz vospominanii," pp. 118-119. Kornilov's appeal can also be found in Martynov's *Kornilov* (pp. 116-117), but several words in it are not identical with their counterparts in both "Reminiscences" and *The Quiet Don*. Except for an omission of four words and a change in case ending, Sholokhov copied the appeal from Lukomskii verbatim.

39. *Kornilov*, pp. 127-128.

40. *Ibid.*, p. 136.

41. Strictly speaking, Bagration was no longer commander of the Native Division on the day when Romanovskii sent his telegram. On August 22 (September 4) Kornilov ordered the reorganization of the Native Division into the Native Corps and appointed Bagration as commander of the new corps. On the other hand, no real reorganization could have taken place with the troops being in trains en route to Petrograd. In fact, Bagration, though nominally a corps commander, continued to command a division. This may explain why one of the addressees of Romanovskii's telegram was the commander of the Native Division. It is therefore possible that Bagration also received a copy of the telegram. Krymov's case is similar to Bagration's. On August 26 (September 8) Kornilov appointed him commander of a special Petrograd Army. The Third Cavalry Corps, which he had led before this appointment, was given to General Petr Krasnov. But since Krasnov could not assume command of the corps before August 28 (September 10), Krymov was its de facto commander when Romanovskii sent his telegram. For details on appointments see *Kornilov*, pp. 92-93.

42. *Ibid.*, p. 143.

43. "Vozzvanie generala L. G. Kornilova k kazakam," in *Donskaia letopis'*, vol. 2, pp. 297-298; reprinted from *Donskaia volna* (Rostov-on-Don), no. 15 (September 1918), pp. 7-8. The spelling of one word and punctuation in the text of Kornilov's appeal in *The Quiet Don* indicate that Sholokhov was more likely to have copied the appeal from *Donskaia letopis'* than from *Donskaia volna*.

44. *Ocherki*, vol. 2, p. 70. Denikin's plan was also reproduced in Vladimirova, *Kontr-revoliutsiia v 1917 g.*, p. 151. However, a few minor points indicate that Sholokhov used the original source. As a matter of fact, I could not find any evidence that Sholokhov used Vladimirova's book for his representation of the Kornilov movement.

45. Martynov, *Kornilov*, pp. 92, 135, 140-141, 142.

46. Cf. P. N. Krasnov, "Na vnutrennem fronte," in *Arkhiv russkoi revoliutsii*,

vol. 1 (Berlin [1921]), pp. 113, 117, 118. It is possible that Sholokhov used the book-form edition of Krasnov's article, *Na vnutrennem fronte* (Leningrad, 1927).

47. *Kornilov*, p. 143. While copying, Sholokhov apparently overlooked that Martynov calls the station Semrino (correctly), not Somrino.

48. Cf. *Kornilov*, pp. 146, 149, 152, 153, 160-161, 191-193.

49. Cf. "Iz vospominanii," *Arkhiv russkoi revoliutsii*, vol. 5, p. 124. See also p. 123.

50. Cf. *ibid.*, pp. 127-128, 130; Denikin, *Ocherki*, vol. 2, pp. 86-88, 94, 98.

51. Cf. *Ocherki*, vol. 2, p. 77, and "Iz vospominanii," p. 127. Both generals are right: the building that housed the girls' high school was originally a Catholic monastery.

52. Cf. *Ocherki*, vol. 2, pp. 137-139. For other parallels see *ibid.*, pp. 95, 101, 102, 136, 143-144, and *Tikhii Don*, vol. 2 (1975), pp. 170, 171, 172-173.

53. *Ocherki*, p. 144. The words "Krylenko will arrive in . . . which" are no longer in the novel. They were deleted in 1941 because Nikolai Krylenko, the first Bolshevik supreme commander-in-chief, was liquidated in 1938 as an "enemy of the people."

54. Cf. *Ocherki*, vol. 2, pp. 100, 144. Lukomskii also says that the prisoners waited for hours before receiving the news that no train would be dispatched for them ("Iz vospominanii," pp. 131-132). However, according to Lukomskii, this news was brought to prisoners by Kusonskii (a day before he came with the final instructions), who said that Dukhonin had decided to *postpone* the dispatch of the train. In contrast, Denikin speaks of the *cancellation* of the order via a telegram sent by Dukhonin to the prison commandant (p. 144). Sholokhov does not mention the way in which Dukhonin communicated his change of decision, but he follows Denikin in saying that the order was canceled. One must therefore disagree with Brian Murphy's assertion that Sholokhov's reference to Dukhonin's order has its origin in Lukomskii's *Reminiscences* ("Sholokhov and Lukomsky," *Journal of Russian Studies*, no. 19 [Bradford, 1970]), pp. 40-41.

55. Golubintsev, Letter to the editor, *Novoe russkoe slovo*, November 13, 1974; Ivan Sagatskii, "Malen'kaia detal'," *Rodimyi krai*, no. 26 (January-February 1960), p. 8. Sagatskii, however, tells a story of how the officers of the last troop train of the Twelfth Regiment were betrayed by a Cossack and how one of them, his father, was later shot on instructions from the Khar'kov Cheka (p. 9).

56. Cf. Lukomskii, "Iz vospominanii," p. 108.

57. Quoted *ibid.*, p. 120. See also p. 108.

58. Denikin, *Ocherki*, vol. 2, p. 100.

59. "Iz vospominanii," p. 105. The first paragraph begins with "Having said to him that General Romanovskii."

60. Cf. A. A. Frenkel', *Orly revoliutsii* (Rostov-on-Don, 1920), p. 32. Frenkel' reprinted Podtelkov's autobiography from *Donskaia volna*, no. 17 (October 7 [20], 1918), p. 16.

61. Cf. *Orly revoliutsii*, p. 34, and M. Korchin, *Bor'ba za Sovety na Donu* (Rostov-on-Don, 1947), p. 54; quoted in L. Vol'pe's notes to vol. 3 of Mikhail

Sholokhov, *Sobranie sochinenii*, 8 vols. to date (Moscow: Khudozhestvennaia literatura, 1965-), p. 399.

62. Mandel'shtam, "Obryvki vospominanii," in *Proletarskaia revoliutsiia na Donu*, vol. 4, ed. A. A. Frenkel' (Moscow-Leningrad, 1924), p. 156.

63. Cf. V. A. Antonov-Ovseenko, *Zapiski o grazhdanskoi voine*, vol. 1 (Moscow, 1924), pp. 200-201; N. Kakurin, *Kak srazhalas' revoliutsiia*, vol. 1, ed. N. N. Popov (Moscow-Leningrad, 1925), p. 176.

64. Cf. *Ocherki*, vol. 2, pp. 156, 187.

65. Cf. *Orly revoliutsii*, p. 11.

66. *Zapiski*, vol. 1, p. 198.

67. Iv. Ermilov, untitled article under the heading "Frontovoe kazachestvo i Kaledin," in *Proletarskaia revoliutsiia na Donu*, vol. 4, p. 98; S. I. Syrtsov, "Nakanune i vo vremia s"ezda v stanitse Kamenskoi," *ibid.*, p. 121.

68. Cf. G. Ianov, " 'Paritet,' " in *Donskaia letopis'*, vol. 2, p. 188.

69. F. G. Kosov, "Podtelkov v Novocherkasske," in *Donskaia letopis'*, vol. 2, pp. 309, 318. According to Kosov, the Revolutionary Committee's delegation consisted of six members (p. 306). Altogether he mentions five names. One of them, Sverchkov, is incorrect. It should be Skachkov, as it is in " 'Parity' " and *The Quiet Don*. *Donskaia letopis'* reprinted Kosov's record from the journal *Donskaia volna*, no. 27 (December 16 [29], 1918), pp. 6-11. There is no evidence that Sholokhov used *Donskaia volna* as a source for *The Quiet Don*.

70. *Zapiski*, vol. 1, p. 202. The text of the ultimatum cited in Kosov's "Podtelkov v Novocherkasske" (p. 307) and in *Proletarskaia revoliutsiia na Donu*, vol. 4 (pp. 219-220) differs slightly in style from that found in Antonov-Ovseenko and *The Quiet Don*.

71. Cf. "Podtelkov v Novocherkasske," p. 311. The statement begins with "You've got it all wrong! If the Don Government. . . ." This statement and a few other phrases from Kosov's record were reprinted by Frenkel' in *Orly revoliutsii* (p. 35), and Sholokhov might well have taken them from that booklet. Cf. *Tikhii Don*, vol. 2 (1975), pp. 231-232.

72. Cf. "Podtelkov v Novocherkasske," p. 308.

73. *Orly revoliutsii*, p. 36.

74. Cf. " 'Paritet,' " *Donskaia letopis'*, vol. 2, p. 190.

75. Cf. *ibid.*, pp. 189, 190.

76. *Ibid.*, p. 189.

77. The phrase "which covered the sides of the decanter with bubbles" was removed in 1929.

78. *Zapiski*, vol. 1, pp. 202-204. The Don Government's response is also printed in Kosov, "Podtelkov v Novocherkasske" (pp. 315-317) and in *Proletarskaia revoliutsiia na Donu*, vol. 4 (pp. 220-221). A close textual examination reveals that Sholokhov relied on *Zapiski*.

79. Cf. *Zapiski*, vol. 1, pp. 205, 210, 231-232.

80. *Ibid.*, pp. 232, 233-234.

81. Kakliugin, "Voiskovoi ataman A. M. Kaledin. . . ," *Donskaia letopis'*, vol. 2, pp. 159-160.

82. Nikolai Turoverov, "Konets Chernetsova," *Kazach'i dumy* (Sofia), no. 23 (April 15, 1924), p. 19; Dan. Delert, *Don v ogne* (Rostov-on-Don, 1927), pp. 38-39; D. N. Pototskii, "Na Donu," in A. A. fon Lampe, ed., *Beloe delo*, vol. 4 (Berlin, 1928), p. 79.

83. Cf. *Zapiski*, vol. 1, pp. 211-212. The name of one of the members is given as Kopalei both in *Zapiski* and in *The Quiet Don*. It should be Kovalev. See P. Strelianov, "Na Donu," *Novyi mir*, no. 8 (1967), p. 202. The names of all the fifteen members (except for Strelianov's) of the Cossack Revolutionary Committee can be found in S. I. Kudinov, "Imenem revkoma. . . ," in A. N. Ivanov et al., comps. and eds., *Pomniat stepi donskie: Sbornik vospominanii* (Rostov-on-Don, 1967), p. 91.

84. Cf. *Zapiski*, vol. 1, pp. 215, 225.

85. Cf. Denikin, *Ocherki*, vol. 2, p. 220; Ianov, " 'Paritet,' " *Donskaia letopis'*, vol. 2, p. 196; Mel'nikov, "Aleksei Maksimovich Kaledin: Lichnost' i deiatel'nost'," in *Donskaia letopis'*, vol. 1 (Vienna, 1923), p. 39. Ianov and Mel'nikov attended the extraordinary session as members of the Don Government. Denikin's version of the session is based on Mitrofan Bogaevskii's speech at the Don Cossack Parliament meeting on February 7 (20), 1918, and his article "29 ianvaria 1918 g." Both these items can be found in V. Volin, *Don i Dobrovol'cheskaia armiia* (Novocherkassk, 1919), pp. 107-135. The article was originally published in the Novocherkassk newspaper *Vol'nyi Don* for February 8 (21), 1918. Mitrofan Bogaevskii, assistant to Kaledin, was also present at the extraordinary session of the Don Government. There is no indication that Sholokhov read his speech or article.

86. Cf. *Ocherki*, vol. 2, p. 220; Ianov, " 'Paritet,' " p. 196; Mel'nikov, "Aleksei Maksimovich Kaledin," p. 39. In turn, Denikin copied the whole of the statement from Bogaevskii's article. Cf. Volin, *Don i Dobrovol'cheskaia armiia*, p. 129. There is a copy of this book in Denikin's archive at Columbia University.

87. Cf. " 'Paritet,' " pp. 197, 198; "Aleksei Maksimovich Kaledin," p. 40.

88. Cf. Denikin, *Ocherki*, vol. 2, p. 220. Denikin copied the wording of Kaledin's admonition from Mitrofan Bogaevskii's speech of February 7 (20), 1918. Cf. Volin, *Don i Dobrovol'cheskaia armiia*, p. 120. The wording of the admonition is somewhat different in the versions of Bogaevskii's speech published in *Donskaia volna*, no. 3 (June 24 [July 7], 1918), p. 10, and in *Proletarskaia revoliutsiia na Donu*, vol. 4, p. 240.

89. Cf. Ianov, " 'Paritet,' " pp. 196, 197; Mel'nikov, "Aleksei Maksimovich Kaledin," p. 40.

90. Cf. " 'Paritet,' " p. 199. Colin Bearne, a British student of Sholokhov, asserts erroneously that "Sholokhov's version [of Kaledin's suicide] is based, with some divergences, on an article entitled *Alexei Maximovich Kaledin* written by Mel'nikov" ("Sholokhov and His Sources," *Journal of Russian Studies*, no. 22 [Lancaster, 1971], p. 13). In point of fact, Mel'nikov had left the Ataman's Palace before Kaledin shot himself and, unlike Ianov, he says nothing about what happened in the palace at the time of and after Kaledin's suicide ("Aleksei Maksimovich Kaledin," p. 40). Mitrofan Bogaevskii gives essentially the same description of Kaledin's suicide as Ianov. However, unlike Ianov and Sholokhov, he says nothing

about the request for money made by the non-Cossack members of the Don Government and Kaledin's angry reaction to it. See Volin, *Don i Dobrovol'cheskaia armiia*, pp. 121, 122, 131, 132-133.

91. Cf. " 'Paritet,' " p. 198.

92. Cf. K. Kakliugin, "Voiskovoi ataman A. M. Nazarov i ego vremia," in *Donskaia letopis'*, vol. 2, p. 205; Is. Bykadorov, "Vospominaniia o voiskovom atamane Voiska Donskogo generale A. M. Nazarove," *ibid.*, pp. 209, 210, 221. In 1953 the editors of *The Quiet Don* changed the date of Nazarov's election to January 29 (Old Style), apparently thinking that he was elected the day Kaledin died. The wrong date is still in the book.

93. Cf. Denikin, *Ocherki*, vol. 2, p. 220; Volin, *Don i Dobrovol'cheskaia armiia*, p. 39. Since the 1953 edition the age of the Cossacks has been given as "from eighteen to fifty." These figures might have been taken from the chronicle of events in *Proletarskaia revoliutsiia na Donu*, vol. 4, p. 264, or from Ia. N. Raenko, *Khronika istoricheskikh sobytii na Donu, Kubani i v Chernomor'e*, part 1 (Rostov-on-Don, 1939), p. 138.

94. Cf. Antonov-Ovseenko, *Zapiski*, vol. 1, pp. 235-236; Lukomskii, "Iz vospominanii," *Arkhiv russkoi revoliutsii*, vol. 5, p. 149. Neither source mentions the name or rank of the regiment's commander, who is Lieutenant Colonel Tatsin in *The Quiet Don*. Sholokhov might have read a third description of the arrival of the Sixth Regiment, where its commander is said to be Colonel Tatsin. See N. Duvakin, "Voiskovoi ataman general A. M. Nazarov," in *Donskaia letopis'*, vol. 2, p. 226.

95. Cf. *Ocherki*, vol. 2, pp. 227, 235. The source for Sholokhov's portrayal of Kutepov was a passage describing the Volunteer Army twelve days after its retreat from Rostov.

96. *Ibid.*, p. 222. See also p. 218. Since 1955 the date on which Chernov entered Rostov has been given in the New Style (February 22) in most editions, and omitted in some. Similarly, since 1955 most editions have introduced here a footnote stating that all the dates in the novel will be hereafter given in the New Style. This promise has not been kept consistently.

97. Roman Gul', *Ledianoi pokhod* (Berlin [1921]), p. 46. A detachment led by Captain Chernov is also mentioned in Antonov-Ovseenko, *Zapiski*, vol. 1, p. 215.

98. "Iz vospominanii," p. 149. Sholokhov's error might also be partly based upon the inaccurate dating of the Ice March (the first march of the Volunteer Army from the Don region into the Kuban' region) on the map in the Appendix to Kakurin, *Kak srazhalas' revoliutsiia*, vol. 1.

99. *Ocherki*, vol. 2, p. 231. Cf. Lukomskii, "Iz vospominanii," p. 153.

100. P. Popov, "Iz istorii osvobozhdeniia Dona (Zapiski pokhodnogo atamana)," *Donskaia volna*, no. 14 (September 9 [22], 1918), p. 3. Popov's figures for cannons and machine guns are identical with Denikin's and Sholokhov's.

101. "Iz vospominanii," p. 153.

102. Cf. *ibid.*, pp. 153-154.

103. Cf. *Ocherki*, vol. 2, p. 233.

104. Letter to Sergei A. Pahomov [Summer 1952].

105. "Iz vospominanii," p. 153.

106. *Ocherki*, vol. 2, p. 231.

107. "Iz istorii osvobozhdeniia Dona," *Donskaia volna*, no. 14 (1918), p. 3.

108. Letter to Pahomov. Popov was a bachelor.

109. *Ibid.*

110. Cf. *ibid.*; Lukomskii, "Iz vospominanii," p. 155; Denikin, *Ocherki*, vol. 2, pp. 229, 231.

111. Cf. Lukomskii, "Iz vospominanii," p. 153; Denikin, *Ocherki*, vol. 2, p. 231; Popov, "Iz istorii osvobozhdeniia Dona," p. 3.

112. Cf. Antonov-Ovseenko, *Zapiski*, vol. 1, map no. 6 in the Appendix; Duvakin, "Voiskovoi ataman general A. M. Nazarov," *Donskaia letopis'*, vol. 2, p. 227; Bykadorov, "Vospominaniia o voiskovom atamane. . . ," *ibid.*, p. 221; "Chetvertyi Krug," *ibid.*, p. 322.

113. Cf. *Zapiski*, vol. 1, pp. 267-268.

114. Cf. *Orly revoliutsii*, p. 16.

115. Cf. A. Kozhin, "V verkhov'iakh Dona: Bor'ba," *Donskaia volna*, no. 21 (June 9 [22], 1919), pp. 10-13.

116. Cf. *Orly revoliutsii*, pp. 17, 19. Beginning with the 1953 edition, the duration of the Congress has been dated April 10-13. Another source, on the basis of documentary evidence, dates it April 9-14. See I. M. Borokhova et al., comps., *Bor'ba za vlast' Sovetov na Donu, 1917-1920 gg.: Sbornik dokumentov* (Rostov-on-Don, 1957), pp. 284, 310.

117. Cf. *Orly revoliutsii*, pp. 19-24.

118. Cf. *ibid.*, pp. 26, 27. There is a question about Spiridonov's rank. He is a junior captain in *The Quiet Don* and in A. I. Fedortsov, *Riadom s Podtelkovym* (Saratov, 1974), p. 65; an ensign (*praporshchik*) in "Smert' Podtelkova," *Donskaia volna*, no. 8 (July 29 [August 11], 1918), p. 7; and a second lieutenant in K. A. Khmelevskii, *Krakh krasnovshchiny i nemetskaia interventsiia na Donu (aprel' 1918-mart 1919 goda)* (Rostov-on-Don, 1965), p. 44. The last two sources are probably closer to the truth. Since Spiridonov was promoted to ensign only in March 1917, he was unlikely to reach the rank of a junior captain by May 1918. On Spiridonov's promotion and ranks see Gregory P. Tschebotarioff, *Russia, My Native Land* (New York: McGraw-Hill, 1964), pp. 82, 209-210, 254. The author served together with Spiridonov and Podtelkov in 1917.

119. "Smert' Podtelkova," p. 7; Konstantin Priima, "Veshenskie vstrechi: K tvorcheskoi istorii sholokhovskikh proizvedenii," *Pod''em* (Voronezh), no. 5 (1962), p. 153. The detachment of the Karginskaia Cossacks might well have served as a model for the detachment of the Tatarskii Cossacks who are sent against Podtelkov in the novel.

120. Cf. *Orly revoliutsii*, pp. 28-31. For some reason the name of Mikhail Lukin (no. 67) was stricken off the list in 1929 and remains unrestored. According to Frenkel', the two documents were delivered to the Don Bureau of the Bolshevik Party by the chairman of the Revolutionary Committee of Krasnokutskaia Stanitsa, near which the execution took place on April 28 (May 11), 1918. The text of the judges' resolution was reportedly found in a stack of straw (pp. 28, 31).

121. Cf. *Orly revoliutsii*, p. 20.

122. Quoted *ibid.*, p. 22.

123. *Zapiski*, vol. 1, pp. 212, 232.

124. *Ocherki*, vol. 2, p. 227. Sholokhov made an error in his sentence. The column of White troops retreating from Rostov could not have stretched across the Don and moved toward Aksai because both Rostov and Aksai are located on the same bank of the Don. The Volunteer Army crossed the Don at Aksai (Aksaiskaia) and headed toward Ol'ginskaia.

125. Cf. P. N. Krasnov, "Vsevelikoe Voisko Donskoe," in *Arkhiv russkoi revoliutsii*, vol. 5, pp. 192-194, 196-198. In the first book-form edition of volume 3, the number of the Parliament members voting against Krasnov was mistakenly changed from thirteen to thirty. The oversight has not yet been corrected.

126. Cf. "Vsevelikoe Voisko Donskoe," p. 192; G. Ianov, "Osvobozhdenie Novocherkasska i 'Krug spaseniia Dona,' " in *Donskaia letopis'*, vol. 3 (Belgrade, 1924), p. 56.

127. Cf. "Vsevelikoe Voisko Donskoe," pp. 200-201.

128. Cf. *ibid.*, p. 200.

129. Cf. *ibid.*, pp. 200-202; Denikin, *Ocherki*, vol. 3 (Berlin, 1924), p. 155.

130. Cf. "Vsevelikoe Voisko Donskoe," pp. 202-203.

131. Cf. *ibid.*, pp. 209-210.

132. Cf. *ibid.*, pp. 210-212.

133. Cf. *ibid.*, pp. 212, 213-214.

134. Cf. *Tikhii Don*, vol. 3 (1975), pp. 97-100, 102-104, 113-115, and "Vsevelikoe Voisko Donskoe," pp. 269, 270, 271, 272, 273, 274, 276, 278, 291, 292, 293, 295-296, 298-299.

135. Cf. "Vsevelikoe Voisko Donskoe," p. 273. Three insignificant revisions were made, apparently by the editors, in the extract from Krasnov's speech between 1932 and 1957.

136. I. Kalinin, *Russkaia Vandeia* (Moscow-Leningrad, 1926), p. 144.

137. "Vsevelikoe Voisko Donskoe," p. 273.

138. *Ibid.*, pp. 276, 298-299.

139. *Ibid.*, p. 291.

140. Khmelevskii et al., eds., *Iuzhnyi front (mai 1918-mart 1919): Sbornik dokumentov* (Rostov-on-Don, 1962), pp. 321-322, 325-326.

141. Cf. "Vsevelikoe Voisko Donskoe," pp. 292, 298-299.

142. Letter to Ermakov, April 6, 1926, in L. P. Logashova, ed., *"Tikhii Don": Uroki romana* (Rostov-on-Don, 1979), p. 113; or the facsimile of the letter, *ibid.*, between pp. 64 and 65.

143. Quoted in Konstantin Priima, "K tvorcheskoi istorii 'Tikhogo Dona': Kommentarii," in *"Tikhii Don": Uroki romana*, p. 136. Sholokhov said this to Priima in 1974.

144. Cf. Pavel Kudinov, "Vosstanie verkhne-dontsov v 1919 godu (Istoricheskii ocherk)," *Vol'noe kazachestvo* (Prague), no. 80 (May 10, 1931), p. 9. Peripeteia of Kudinov's life might be of some interest. A man of remarkable physical strength, he served in the Twelfth Don Cossack Regiment before and during World War I.

For his valor he earned all four Crosses of St. George and officer's rank. Later, in recognition of his role in the Upper Don uprising and his subsequent service with the White Cossacks, he was promoted to colonel. In emigration he condemned the White movement and became an ardent Cossack nationalist. He also took a conciliatory position toward the Soviet regime. In 1922 the Veshenskaia newspaper *Izvestiia* published his letter attacking General Petr Vrangel' and asking the Cossacks to cooperate with the Soviets in the restoration of their country. However, this attitude did not prevent him from writing about Bolshevik atrocities with indignation in his 1931 article on the Upper Don uprising. In 1938 he was exposed as a Soviet agent and exiled from Sofia to a remote corner of Bulgaria. He took no part in World War II. Upon the occupation of Bulgaria by Soviet troops, he was deported to the USSR and then sent to Siberian concentration camps, where he spent ten or eleven years. In 1955 he wrote Sholokhov a letter from Siberia. He was released in 1956. On his way back to Bulgaria he stopped in Veshenskaia, at the time when Sholokhov was away. In Bulgaria he worked on a collective farm and died in 1967. The money for the monument on his grave came from émigré Cossacks in response to an appeal for help from his poverty-stricken widow. For details see B. Bogaevskii, "Pamiati polkovnika P. N. Kudinova," *Rodimyi krai*, no. 74 (January-February 1968), pp. 39-40; letters of P. I. Kudinova and a letter of Dr. Dmitrov, *ibid.*, no. 75 (March-April 1968), p. 44, and no. 82 (May-June 1969), p. 38; Sagatskii, "Radzivillov," *ibid.*, no. 83 (July-August 1969), p. 28; Z., "Skromnaia rabota bol'shevikov," *Vozrozhdenie* (Paris), September 23, 1938; Graf [Mikhail] Grabbe, "Ot donskogo atamana," *Kazaki zagranitsei* (Sofia), October 17-November 15, 1938, pp. 35-36; Sh[amba] N. Balinov, "Kampaniia lzhi o donskom atamane," *Kazachii golos* (Paris), no. 15-16 (January-February 1939), p. 23; Konstantin Priima, "Sholokhov v Veshkakh," *Sovetskii Kazakhstan*, no. 5 (1955), p. 87, and "Veshenskie vstrechi," *Pod''em*, no. 5 (1962), pp. 150-153.

145. "Vosstanie. . . ," *Vol'noe kazachestvo*, no. 80, p. 9.

146. *Ibid.*, no. 81 (May 25, 1931), p. 7, and no. 82 (June 10, 1931), p. 15.

147. *Ibid.*, no. 83 (June 25, 1931), p. 18.

148. Priima, "Veshenskie vstrechi," p. 153. Kudinov said this to Priima in a telephone interview.

149. "Vosstanie. . . ," *Vol'noe kazachestvo*, no. 82, p. 15.

150. Beginning with the 1955 edition, this date as well as the date of the surrender in Kudinov's letter to Grigorii have been absent from the novel. The Serdobskii Regiment must have gone over to the Cossacks on or about March 28 (April 10). This date is corroborated by documentary evidence in Semanov, *"Tikhii Don"—literatura i istoriia* (Moscow, 1977), pp. 61-62.

151. *Ibid.*, p. 62.

152. "Vosstanie. . . ," *Vol'noe kazachestvo*, no. 82, p. 15. See also Semanov, *"Tikhii Don"—literatura i istoriia*, p. 62.

153. Cf. Zvegintsov, *Russkaia armiia 1914 g.*, p. 8.

154. Cf. Semanov, *"Tikhii Don"—literatura i istoriia*, p. 62. In *The Quiet Don* Vranovskii's place of residence is given as the Smolensk Province. Semanov, on the basis of documentary evidence, states that both Vranovskii and Volkov were

from the town of Serdobsk, in the Penza Province. Semanov also says that the Serdobskii Regiment was manned primarily by the peasants from the Penza Province (p. 61). In the novel this regiment consists of peasants mobilized in the Saratov and Samara Provinces (3:294, 298).

155. "Vosstanie. . . ," *Vol'noe kazachestvo*, no. 83, pp. 17-18.

156. *Ibid.*, p. 17. The date of the airplane's arrival has been missing in *The Quiet Don* since 1955.

157. Sergei Starikov and Roy Medvedev, *Philip Mironov and the Russian Civil War*, trans. Guy Daniels (Alfred A. Knopf: New York, 1978), p. 251. The same date is also given in P. Grigor'ev, "Iz istorii bor'by na severe Dona," *Kazach'i dumy*, no. 4 (June 30, 1923), p. 10. Divergences in dating the arrival of the airplane demonstrate the difficulties in obtaining precise information about the particulars of the Upper Don uprising. This is especially true of local episodes. The same incident can be narrated with different details. Thus a certain Gromov is identified in *The Quiet Don* as an investigator of the Veshenskaia Revolutionary tribunal. At the beginning of the uprising a young Cossack shoots him and then finishes him off with his sword (3:180-181). In another account Gromov is the chairman of the Veshenskaia Revolutionary tribunal and he is sabered by an elderly Cossack, who has no firearms. See E. F. Kochetov, "Vosstanie Verkhne-donskogo okruga," *Kazachii soiuz* (Paris), no. 13-14 (July-October 1952), p. 7. It is virtually impossible to ascertain which of the two versions is correct.

158. Cf. Krasnov, "Vsevelikoe Voisko Donskoe," *Arkhiv russkoi revoliutsii*, vol. 5, p. 312.

159. Cf. Kakurin, *Kak srazhalas' revoliutsiia*, vol. 1, pp. 97-98; Kudinov, "Vosstanie. . . ," *Vol'noe kazachestvo*, no. 83, p. 18. Kudinov is also said to have reported to the Don Army command that in May his forces had 15 cannons, 93 machine guns, and 15,000 rifles (M. Buguraev, "Pokhod k vosstavshim. . . ," *Rodimyi krai*, no. 104 [January-February 1973], p. 16); L. Trotskii, *Kak vooruzhalas' revoliutsiia*, vol. 2, part 1 (Moscow, 1924), p. 455; Grigor'ev, "Iz istorii bor'by. . . ," *Kazach'i dumy*, no. 4 (1923), pp. 10-11. Trotskii's figures are: up to 30,000 men, 6 cannons, and 27 machine guns. Grigor'ev gives 29,455 men, 30 cannons, and about 200 machine guns. Sholokhov also estimates the number of insurgents at 35,000 in chapter 38, pp. 225, 227. The figure appears to be somewhat high.

160. A. Nenarokov, "Istorik grazhdanskoi voiny," *Voenno-istoricheskii zhurnal*, no. 11 (1965), p. 49.

161. Cf. *Kak vooruzhalas' revoliutsiia*, vol. 2, book 1, pp. 174, 186.

162. According to Semanov, "The Uprising in the Rear" was printed in *V puti* (*On the Road*) for May 17, 1919 (*"Tikhii Don"—literatura i istoriia*, p. 232). It is possible that Sholokhov mistook the date of writing the article for the date of its publication. Information printed under the article in *Kak vooruzhalas' revoliutsiia* reads: "May 12, 1919. Kozlov. *On the Road*, no. 44." *V puti* was the bulletin published on the train that served as Trotskii's mobile headquarters during the Civil War.

163. *"Tikhii Don"—literatura i istoriia*, p. 232. Semanov does not conceal

Trotskii's authorship of "The Uprising in the Rear," stating that it gave rise to "furious orders" and "clearly provocative instructions" concerning the behavior of the Red troops toward the insurgents (*ibid.*). Such statements bespeak the growing Soviet trend to put all the blame on Trotskii for the cruel treatment of the Cossacks before and during the Upper Don uprising. This trend must have been the chief reason why the 1980 edition of Sholokhov's *Collected Works* restored the designation of Trotskii's post in his order to the expeditionary forces, which called for the annihilation of all the insurgent Cossacks who would not desert to the Reds with their weapons. It will be interesting to see whether subsequent editions of the novel follow suit.

164. Trotskii, *Kak vooruzhalas' revoliutsiia*, vol. 2, book 1, p. 173.

165. Cf. Kudinov, "Vosstanie. . . ," *Vol'noe kazachestvo*, no. 81, p. 7; Khmelevskii et al., eds., *Iuzhnyi front*, p. 314.

166. See Lenin's and Trotskii's telegrams, in *The Trotsky Papers, 1917-1922*, ed. and annotated Jan M. Meijer, vol. 1 (The Hague: Mouton, 1964), pp. 426, 438, 440, 450, 464, 472; and orders by the commander of the southern front, in *Direktivy komandovaniia frontov Krasnoi Armii (1917-1922 gg.): Sbornik dokumentov*, vol. 2, ed. N. N. Azovtsev et al. (Moscow, 1972), pp. 253, 257.

167. Kudinov, "Vosstanie. . . ," *Vol'noe kazachestvo*, no. 80, p. 8; Grigor'ev, "Iz istorii bor'by. . . ," *Kazach'i dumy*, no. 4 (June 6, 1923), p. 10.

168. Cf. Buguraev, "Pokhod k vosstavshim. . . ," *Rodimyi krai*, no. 104 (January-February 1973), p. 16. In my conversation with Colonel Buguraev on January 12, 1980, he reaffirmed what he had written about the strength and composition of Sekretev's group in his article. He remembered clearly almost all numbers of the batteries and regiments, as well as the names and ranks of their commanders. He also said that Sekretev's force did not include the Ninth Don Regiment, which, according to Sholokhov, was the first unit to make contact with the insurgents (*Tikhii Don*, vol. 4 [1975], p. 40).

169. Krasnov, "Vsevelikoe Voisko Donskoe," *Arkhiv russkoi revoliutsii*, vol. 5, pp. 312, 318.

170. Trotskii, *Kak vooruzhalas' revoliutsiia*, vol. 2, book 1, p. 456; Kakurin, *Kak srazhalas' revoliutsiia*, vol. 1, p. 98; vol. 2, ed. R. P. Eideman (Moscow, 1926), p. 152. Both authors give May 24 as the date of the Sekretev breakthrough and June 7 as the date of the link-up with the insurgents. The same dates are found in V. Dobrynin, "Vooruzhennaia bor'ba Dona s bol'shevikami," in *Donskaia letopis'*, vol. 1, pp. 118, 119. Kudinov also dates the link-up May 25 (June 7) in his "Vosstanie. . . ," *Vol'noe kazachestvo*, no. 84-85 (July 10-25, 1931), p. 13.

171. Sholokhov does not give the date of the conference, but it can be easily established by following the actions of Grigorii Melekhov from May 11 (24). See *Tikhii Don*, vol. 3 (1975), p. 377.

172. "Vosstanie. . . ," no. 84-85, p. 12.

173. N. T. Kuznetsova and V. S. Bashtannik, "U istokov 'Tikhogo Dona,' " *Don*, no. 7 (1978), p. 36.

174. H.N.H. Williamson, *Farewell to the Don*, ed. John Harris (John Day: New York, 1971), p. 70. See also pp. 83-84.

175. *Ibid.*, p. 71.

176. Kuznetsova and Bashtannik, "U istokov 'Tikhogo Dona,' " pp. 35, 36, 37. I. Serdinov, "Nad stranitsami 'Tikhogo Dona,' " *Don*, no. 12 (1978), p. 156.

177. *Farewell to the Don*, p. 95. Here Williamson speaks of a village on the way from Veshenskaia to Migulinskaia. Pleshakov is located near Elanskaia, which the Sidorin party visited before going to Veshenskaia. However, the party might have made a short detour or Williamson might not have remembered the exact order in which every small village had been visited. On the other hand, he describes the itinerary of Sidorin's trip with greater precision than a contemporary newspaper ("Poezdka komanduiushchego armiei," *Zhizn'* [Rostov-on-Don], June 27 [July 10], 1919). His book is based on diaries he kept during his stay in Russia.

178. Denikin, *Ocherki*, vol. 5 (Berlin, 1926), pp. 349, 350.

179. Cf. *Kak srazhalas' revoliutsiia*, vol. 2, p. 251. For other examples cf. chapter 20, pp. 187-190, and *Kak srazhalas' revoliutsiia*, vol. 2, pp. 248, 251-254, 288-291, 293, 295; chapter 23, pp. 210-211, and *Kak srazhalas' revoliutsiia*, vol. 2, pp. 313-315, 323.

180. Cf. *Kak srazhalas' revoliutsiia*, vol. 2, pp. 251, 252-253.

181. *Grazhdanskaia voina, 1918-1921*, vol. 3, ed. A. S. Bubnov et al. (Moscow-Leningrad, 1930), pp. 271-273.

182. K. Voroshilov, *Stalin i Krasnaia armiia* (Moscow: Partizdat TsK VKP[b], 1937), pp. 33-35. In this book and in *Novyi mir* (no. 1 [1938], pp. 110-111) the text of Stalin's memorandum has identical punctuation. In *The Civil War, 1918-1921* the memorandum is occasionally punctuated differently. At the time when Sholokhov dealt with Stalin's memorandum, *The Civil War, 1918-1921* was already banned. Two of its editors, Mikhail Tukhachevskii and Robert Eideman, were executed in June 1937. Their "trial" was widely publicized. The third editor, Andrei Bubnov, was arrested and then shot (in 1940), while Sergei Kamenev, who died in 1936, was consigned to oblivion.

183. Leon Trotsky, *Stalin*, 2d ed., ed. and trans. Charles Malamuth (New York and London: Harper and Brothers, 1946), pp. 314-315.

184. A. Palshkov, "Molodoi Sholokhov," *Don*, no. 8 (1964), p. 162.

185. Priima, "Veshenskie vstrechi," *Pod''em*, no. 5 (1962), p. 154.

186. Starikov and Medvedev, *Philip Mironov and the Russian Civil War*, pp. 184, 215.

187. Filipp Mironov, a former Cossack lieutenant colonel, was a successful Red cavalry commander in the Civil War. However, he was indignant about the Bolshevik mistreatment of the Cossacks and peasants and resented the political control in the Red Army. He was shot in 1921 for plotting an insurrection against the Bolshevik regime, a charge that proved to be false. Well-documented and objective accounts of Mironov's unauthorized march to the front can be found in I. I. Ul'ianov, *Kazaki i sovetskaia respublika* (Moscow-Leningrad, 1929), pp. 76-91, 167-170; Starikov and Medvedev, *Philip Mironov and the Russian Civil War*, pp. 133-184.

188. Cf. Palshkov, "Molodoi Sholokhov," p. 168; S. M. Budennyi, "Proidennyi put'," *Don*, no. 9 (1970), pp. 141, 145. When Budennyi's memoirs were published

in book form, passages about Fomin's detachment and many pages dealing with other anti-Bolshevik formations were omitted (*Proidennyi put'*, vol. 3 [Moscow, 1973], p. 257). This was done to conceal the intensity of the popular resistance, which had to be suppressed by regular troops such as the First Cavalry Army.

189. Reports of December 9 and 10, *Krasnaia gazeta* (Petrograd), December 10 and 11, 1919; report of December 6 (19), *Priazovskii krai* (Rostov-on-Don), December 10 (23), 1919; reports of December 9 (22) and 11 (24), *Vechernee vremia* (Rostov-on-Don), December 11 (24) and 13 (26), 1919.

190. Quoted in I. Eksler, "V gostiakh u Sholokhova," *Izvestiia*, December 31, 1937.

191. Quoted *ibid.*

192. Quoted in V. Ketlinskaia, "Mikhail Sholokhov," *Komsomol'skaia pravda*, August 17, 1934

Chapter V

1. B. B., "Literatura v SSSR," *Poslednie novosti*, May 22, 1930.

2. U. M., Letter to the editor, *Novoe russkoe slovo* (New York), September 18, 1974; Vl. Dordopolo, Letter to the editor, *ibid.*, September 19; P. Kaledin, Letter to the editor, *ibid.*, October 12; G. Gurdzhiian, Letter to the editor, *ibid.*, October 24.

3. N. L'vova, "Zagadki 'Tikhogo Dona,' " *Russkaia mysl'* (Paris), October 10, 1974.

4. Quoted in Gr. Radin, Letter to the editor, *Novoe russkoe slovo*, September 17, 1974.

5. Aleksandr Busygin, *Izbrannoe* (Rostov-on-Don, 1952), pp. 3-4; Vl. Ponedel'nik, "Vysokaia chest'—tvorit' dlia naroda," *Literaturnaia gazeta*, March 29, 1955.

6. Mikhail Gol'dshtein, " 'Tikhii Don' v muzyke," *Novoe russkoe slovo*, November 10, 1974.

7. Andrei Voznesenskii, "Stikhi, prochitannye na dvukhsotom predstavlenii 'Antimirov,' " *Russkaia mysl'*, September 7, 1967. In the original: "Sverkhklassik i satrap, / Stydites', dorogoi. / Chuzhoi roman sodral, / Ne smog sodrat' vtoroi."

8. John Barron, *KGB: The Secret Work of Soviet Secret Agents* (Reader's Digest Press: New York, 1974), pp. 105-106; my telephone conversations with Professor Yakushev on January 21 and 24, 1980. Professor Yakushev chose not to return to the Soviet Union from his trip abroad in 1969.

9. Barron, *KGB*, p. 106.

10. D., *Stremia "Tikhogo Dona": Zagadki romana* (Paris, 1974); Roy A. Medvedev, *Problems in the Literary Biography of Mikhail Sholokhov*, trans. A.D.P. Briggs (Cambridge, 1977).

11. A. Solzhenitsyn, *Bodalsia telenok s dubom: Ocherki literaturnoi zhizni* (Paris, 1975), pp. 429, 456.

12. *Stremia "Tikhogo Dona,"* p. 17 (hereafter cited in the text by page numbers).

13. That is what D. means, though he says that "in the first two volumes the author's text comprises over 95 percent of the entire novel." This is clearly a slip

of the tongue. He also could not mean that the last two volumes contain merely 5 percent of the author's text, for in the same sentence he puts the author's share in these volumes at 68-70 percent.

14. Cf. P. N. Krasnov, "Vsevelikoe Voisko Donskoe," in I. V. Gessen, ed., *Arkhiv russkoi revoliutsii*, vol. 5 (Berlin, 1922), pp. 200-213; N. Kakurin, *Kak srazhalas' revoliutsiia*, vol. 2, ed. R. P. Eideman (Moscow, 1926), pp. 248, 251-254, 288-291, 293, 295.

15. K. Kakliugin, "Stepnoi pokhod v Zadon'e v 1918 godu i ego znachenie," in Donskaia istoricheskaia komissiia, ed., *Donskaia letopis': Sbornik mater'ialov po noveishei istorii donskogo kazachestva so vremeni russkoi revoliutsii 1917 goda*, vol. 3 (Belgrade, 1924), pp. 5-10.

16. Pre-1953 editions of the novel have the word "Mironov" instead of "the Reds" in this passage. The use of a post-1953 edition caused D. to ignore the role of censorship in the textual evolution of the novel. This accounted for some of his errors and omissions.

17. For details see my review article, "Riddles of *The Quiet Don*," *Slavic and East European Journal*, vol. 18, no. 3 (Fall 1974), pp. 306-307. For a discussion of D.'s study see also Medvedev, *Problems*, pp. 110-143.

18. Medvedev, *Problems*, pp. 141-142.

19. D. Mirskii, "Mikhail Sholokhov," *Literaturnaia gazeta*, July 24, 1934.

20. Medvedev, *Problems*, p. 132.

21. V. Gura, *Kak sozdavalsia "Tikhii Don": Tvorcheskaia istoriia romana M. Sholokhova* (Moscow, 1980), p. 427.

22. Aleksandr Solzhenitsyn, afterword to *V kruge pervom*, *Sobranie sochinenii*, vol. 2 (Paris, 1978), n. p.

23. This supposition is expressed in the biographical profile of Kriukov. For the text of Solzhenitsyn's preface in English see *The Times Literary Supplement* (London), October 4, 1974, p. 1056.

24. "Press-konferentsiia A. I. Solzhenitsyna. Stokgol'm 12 dekabria 1974 g.," *Novoe russkoe slovo*, January 25, 1975.

25. Medvedev, *Problems*, p. 17; Gol'dshtein, " 'Tikhii Don' v muzyke," *Novoe russkoe slovo*, November 10, 1974; Popov, Letter to Sergei A. Pahomov [Summer 1952].

26. Information about Kriukov was derived primarily from the following sources: F. Kriukov, "Pervye vybory," *Russkie zapiski*, no. 4 (1916), pp. 160-180; editorial (untitled), *Donskaia volna* (Rostov-on-Don), no. 23 (November 18 [December 1] 1918), p. 1; S. Arefin, "F. D. Kriukov kak politik," *ibid.*, pp. 5-7; S. Filimonov, "Vospominaniia o F. D. Kriukove," *Kazachii put'* (Prague), no. 53 (March 14, 1925), pp. 3-6; D. Vorotynskii, "F. D. Kriukov (Vospominaniia i vstrechi)," *Vol'noe kazachestvo* (Prague), no. 73 (January 25, 1931), pp. 15-17; P. F. Kriukov, "Dva aresta F. D. Kriukova," *Kazachii istoricheskii sbornik* (Paris), no. 8 (June 1959), pp. 19-22; no. 9 (October 1959), pp. 27-30; no. 10 (January 1960), pp. 16-19. The author of the last article is Kriukov's adopted son, Petr. Vorotynskii, who comes from Glazunovskaia, gives valuable details about Kriukov's background and draws a lively portrait of Kriukov as a man. All the above articles seem to be

more reliable than other émigré sources known to me. It is not uncommon to find discrepancies in various sources pertaining to Kriukov. It will suffice to mention that I encountered four different dates for Kriukov's birthday in émigré writings: February 1, 4, 7, and November 2, 1870. The fifth, in Soviet sources, is February 2.

27. Vl. Molozhavenko, "Ob odnom nezasluzhenno zabytom imeni," *Molot* (Rostov-on-Don), August 13, 1965; A. Podol'skii, "Ob odnom nezasluzhenno vozrozhdennom imeni," *Sovetskaia Rossiia*, August 14, 1966. Molozhavenko's article is reprinted in D., *Stremia "Tikhogo Dona"* (pp. 179-189) and published in an English translation in *The Times Literary Supplement*, October 4, 1974, p. 1057. For other Soviet sources on Kriukov see B. N. Dvinianinov, "Pis'ma A. S. Serafimovicha k F. D. Kriukovu," in L. A. Gladkovskaia et al., eds., *A. S. Serafimovich (1863-1963): Materialy mezhvuzovskoi nauchnoi konferentsii* (Volgograd, 1963), pp. 147-157; V. M. Proskurin, "Kriukov, Fedor Dmitrievich," *Kratkaia literaturnaia entsiklopediia*, vol. 3 (Moscow, 1966), pp. 858-859, and "K kharakteristike tvorchestva i lichnosti F. D. Kriukova," *Russkaia literatura*, no. 4 (1966), pp. 179-186. Proskurin's articles are more informative and precise than Molozhavenko's or Dvinianinov's, which contain a few factual errors. However, one point in Proskurin's second article is debatable. He states that it was Filipp Mironov, commander of the Red Cossacks, who released Kriukov after his 1918 arrest by the Bolsheviks (p. 182). According to Petr Kriukov, his father was freed by a certain Kamenov. Fedor Kriukov had met Kamenov during his first confinement, in Petersburg (*Kazachii istoricheskii sbornik*, no. 10, p. 18). Petr lived with his father at the time of his second arrest and release.

28. Medvedev, *Problems*, pp. 81-83.

29. Zhores Medvedev, "O knige Roia Medvedeva," *Novoe russkoe slovo*, January 14, 1975; Roy Medvédev, *Qui a écrit "le Don paisible"?* (Paris: Christian Bourgois éditeur, 1975); Jaurès Medvédev, Foreword to *Qui a écrit*, p. 7. In *Qui a écrit* the text of its manuscript is dated October-December 1974. However, in his preface to *Problems*, Roi Medvedev asserts that he wrote the *Qui a écrit* version between October 1974 and March 1975.

30. R. A. Medvedev, "The Riddles Grow: *A Propos* Two Review Articles," *Slavic and East European Journal*, vol. 21, no. 1 (Spring 1977), pp. 104-116; Herman Ermolaev, "Riddles of *The Quiet Don*," *ibid.*, vol. 18, no. 3 (Fall 1974), pp. 299-310, and "Who Wrote *The Quiet Don*? A review article," *ibid.*, vol. 20, no. 3 (Fall 1976), pp. 293-307.

31. *Problems*, pp. 77, 109 (hereafter cited in the text by page numbers).

32. Vorotynskii, "F. D. Kriukov," *Vol'noe kazachestvo*, no. 73 (January 25, 1931), pp. 16-17; F. Kriukov, "V glubokom tylu," *Russkie vedomosti*, September 21 (October 4), October 26 (November 8), November 2 (15), 1914; "S iuzhnoi storony," *ibid.*, November 6 (19), 1914; "Za Karsom," *ibid.*, February 18 (March 3), February 22 (March 7), 1915; "Pamiati kn. Gelovani," *ibid.*, February 24 (March 9), 1915.

33. F. Kriukov, "U boevoi linii," *Russkie vedomosti*, February 5 (18), 16 (29),

April 6 (19), 10 (23), 1916; "V sfere voennoi obydennosti," *ibid.*, July 2 (15), 1916.

34. F. Kriukov, "Po voennym obstoiatel'stvam," *Russkie vedomosti*, November 15 (28), 1916; "Polzkom," *ibid.*, December 25, 1916 (January 7, 1917). In the first item Kriukov describes problems he had in tracing his undelivered telegram and money order. The story covers a period from January to November 1916.

35. Proskurin, "K kharakteristike. . . ," *Russkaia literatura*, no. 4 (1966), p. 186. Kriukov's nearsightedness is confirmed by himself and Vorotynskii. See Kriukov, "Za Karsom," *Russkie vedomosti*, February 18 (March 3), 1915; Vorotynskii, "F. D. Kriukov," p. 17.

36. General-maior [A. V.] Golubintsev, *Russkaia Vandeia: Ocherki grazhdanskoi voiny na Donu, 1917-1920 gg.* (Munich, 1959), pp. 14, 64. In my article "Who Wrote *The Quiet Don*?" I confused A. V. Golubintsev with Sviatoslav Golubintsev, who was mentioned in chapter 4 in connection with his reminiscences about the Twelfth Don Cossack Regiment.

37. P. F. Kriukov, "Dva aresta. . . ," *Kazachii istoricheskii sbornik*, no. 9 (October 1959), p. 27; P. Skachkov, "Istoricheskaia spravka: K proizvedeniiu F. Kriukova 'Rodimyi krai,' " in *Donskaia letopis'*, vol. 1 (Vienna, 1923), p. 275.

38. K. Kakliugin, "Donskoi ataman P. N. Krasnov i ego vremia," in *Donskaia letopis'*, vol. 3, p. 101; "V Voiskovom Kruge," *Velikaia Rossiia* (Rostov-on-Don), November 6 (19), 1919; "Voiskovoi Krug," *Vechernee vremia* (Rostov-on-Don), November 16 (29), 1919. The item in *Velikaia Rossiia* states that Kriukov requested to be relieved from his duties as secretary of the Don Cossack Parliament; the item in *Vechernee vremia* reports the election of the new secretary, Nikolai Duvakin.

39. "The Riddles Grow," p. 112.

40. Molozhavenko, "Ob odnom nezasluzhenno. . . ," in D., *Stremia "Tikhogo Dona,"* p. 183; Dvinianinov, "Pis'ma A. S. Serafimovicha k F. D. Kriukovu," in Gladkovskaia et al., eds., *A. S. Serafimovich (1863-1963)*, p. 149.

41. F. Kriukov, "Rodimyi krai," in *Donskaia letopis'*, vol. 1, p. 273; Skachkov, "Istoricheskaia spravka," *ibid.*, pp. 275-280.

42. P. Margushin, Letter to the editor, *Novoe russkoe slovo*, September 28, 1974.

43. Proskurin, "K kharakteristike. . . ," *Russkaia literatura*, no. 4 (1966), p. 182.

44. On this date he signed a declaration of the Don Cossack Parliament which, among other things, stated that the Parliament would adjourn until the next session. See *Donskaia letopis'*, vol. 1, pp. 331-332.

45. Proskurin, "K kharakteristike. . . ," p. 183; Filimonov, "Vospominaniia o F. D. Kriukove," *Kazachii put'*, no. 53 (March 14, 1925), p. 5; S. Piontkovskii, *Grazhdanskaia voina v Rossii (1918-1921 g.g.): Khrestomatiia* (Moscow, 1925), pp. 438, 454. It might have been that since this time Kriukov did not plan to continue as secretary of the Parliament. The Don Ataman Bogaevskii mentioned the names of some candidates for the position and asked N. N. Reshetovskii (a

relative of Solzhenitsyn's first wife?) to be in charge of the Parliament's secretariat temporarily. See "Sekretar' Kruga," *Zhizn'* (Rostov-on-Don), July 7 (20) and 16 (29), 1919.

46. Vorotynskii, "F. D. Kriukov," *Vol'noe kazachestvo*, no. 73 (January 25, 1931), p. 17.

47. Proskurin, "K kharakteristike. . . ," p. 183.

48. "Voiskovoi Krug," *Vechernee vremia*, October 19 (November 1) and November 30 (December 13), 1919; "V kuluarakh Kruga," *Parus* (Rostov-on-Don), December 1 (14), 1919; "Bol'shoi Voiskovoi Krug," *Priazovskii krai* (Rostov-on-Don), December 1 (14), 1919; "Otstavka prof. Tarasova," *Velikaia Rossiia*, December 10 (23), 1919.

49. See, e.g., I. Lezhnev, *Put' Sholokhova: Tvorcheskaia biografiia* (Moscow, 1958), pp. 344-348, 353-356; Konstantin Priima, "Veshenskie vstrechi: K tvorcheskoi istorii sholokhovskikh proizvedenii," *Pod''em* (Voronezh), no. 5 (1962), pp. 149-150; Aleksandr Bobrov, "Veshentsy," *Literaturnaia Rossiia*, May 23, 1975, p. 12.

50. E. Kovalev, "Kharlampii Ermakov—geroi 'Tikhogo Dona,' " *Rodimyi krai* (Paris), no. 42 (September-October, 1962), p. 22.

51. See, e.g., notes to vol. 2 of Mikhail Sholokhov, *Sobranie sochinenii*, 8 vols. (Moscow: Khudozhestvennaia literatura, 1956-1960), pp. 408-409; L. Vol'pe, "Primechaniia," in Mikhail Sholokhov, *Sobranie sochinenii*, 8 vols. to date (Moscow: Khudozhestvennaia literatura, 1965-), 2:403-406. Vol'pe erroneously refers to Drozdova as Dudorova and to the Kovalev brothers as the Korol'kov brothers.

52. N. T. Kuznetsova and V. S. Bashtannik, "U istokov 'Tikhogo Dona,' " *Don*, no. 7 (1978), pp. 31, 33, 34, 36.

53. *Ibid.*, pp. 31, 35-36.

54. *Ibid.*, pp. 37-38.

55. *Ibid.*, p. 30.

56. I. Serdinov, "Nad stranitsami 'Tikhogo Dona,' " *Don*, no. 12 (1978), pp. 153-157.

57. *Ibid.*, p. 157.

58. Filimonov, "Vospominaniia o F. D. Kriukove," *Kazachii put'*, no. 53 (March 14, 1925), pp. 3-4.

59. I. Mashbits-Verov, "Sholokhov," *Malaia sovetskaia entsiklopediia*, vol. 10 (1931), p. 87.

60. "The Riddles Grow," p. 109.

61. *Ibid.*, p. 111.

62. F. Kriukov, "Novoe," *Russkoe bogatstvo*, no. 4-5 (1917), p. 292.

63. F. Kriukov, "Siluety," *Russkie zapiski*, no. 11 (1915), p. 180.

64. F. Kriukov, "Dorogie mogily," *Russkie vedomosti*, March 21 (April 3), 1915.

65. F. Kriukov, "V glubokom tylu," *Russkie vedomosti*, September 21 (October 4), 1914; "Novym stroem," *ibid.*, July 6 (19), 1917; "Obval," *Russkie zapiski*, no. 2-3 (1917), p. 373; Vorotynskii, "F. D. Kriukov," *Vol'noe kazachestvo*, no.

73 (January 25, 1931), pp. 16-17; Filimonov, ''Vospominaniia o F. D. Kriukove,'' p. 3.

66. In Russian: *voiskovoi ataman*. On Krasnov's suggestion the Parliament for the Salvation of the Don changed this designation to *donskoi ataman* (the Don ataman) on May 4 (17), 1918. At the same time the term *Bol'shoi Voiskovoi Krug* (the Great Don Cossack Parliament) was replaced by *Donskoi Voiskovoi Krug* (the Don Cossack Parliament, or the Don Parliament). See G. Ianov, ''Osvobozhdenie Novocherkasska i 'Krug spaseniia Dona,' '' in *Donskaia letopis'*, vol. 3, p. 61.

67. Boris Shiriaev, ''Volia k pravde,'' *Chasovoi* (Brussels), no. 476 (February 1966), p. 18.

68. F. Kriukov, *Rasskazy*, vol. 1 (Moscow, 1914), pp. 179-180. Italics and translation are mine. In *Problems* the last two sentences of the first paragraph are omitted (p. 104) and the title ''Zyb' '' is rendered as ''Autumn Furrows.'' The translator might have confused *zyb'* with *ziab'* (land ploughed in autumn).

69. Kriukov, *Rasskazy*, p. 251.

70. *Ibid.*, p. 181.

71. See, e.g., my comparison of descriptions of joy and pride experienced by two fathers upon receiving good news from their sons in Kriukov's ''The Officer's Wife'' and *The Quiet Don* (''Who Wrote *The Quiet Don*?'' p. 302); or compare descriptions of Cossack crowds in festive attire in ''A Cossack Woman'' (*Russkoe bogatstvo*, no. 10 [1896], p. 52) and *The Quiet Don*, vol. 1 (1975), p. 47.

72. F. Kriukov, ''Na tikhom Donu,'' *Russkoe bogatstvo*, no. 10 (1898), p. 116.

73. Geir Kjetsaa, ''Storms on the Quiet Don: A Pilot Study.'' *Scando-Slavica*, no. 22 (1976), pp. 5-24; ''The Battle of *The Quiet Don*: Another Pilot Study,'' *Computers and the Humanities*, vol. 11 (1977), pp. 341-346.

74. ''The Riddles Grow,'' p. 115.

75. *Ibid.*, p. 113. Medvedev gives three versions of how Kriukov's manuscript of volume 1 turned out in Sholokhov's hands. 1. Petr Gromoslavskii, the future father-in-law of Sholokhov, accompanied Kriukov during the retreat in the winter of 1920, took Kriukov's manuscripts, and gave them later to Sholokhov (*Problems*, p. 60). 2. After Kriukov's death his manuscripts were taken by his sister Mariia, who was also retreating with the Whites. She gave the box with manuscripts to a group of Veshenskaia Cossacks who passed it on to Gromoslavskii (*ibid.*, p. 100). 3. Mariia handed the box over to Dem'ian Bednyi; Bednyi to Serafimovich; and Serafimovich, presumably, to Sholokhov (*ibid.*, p. 209). There is no reliable evidence that Gromoslavskii retreated with the Whites. According to Lezhnev, in the winter of 1920 Gromoslavskii was in a Novocherkassk jail, serving an eight-year sentence of hard labor for fighting on the Red side. Advancing Reds released him in January 1920 (*Put' Sholokhova*, p. 32). We also do not know whether Mariia Kriukova was near her brother at the time of his death. A person who was with Kriukov shortly before the latter's death makes no mention of Mariia's presence (Vlad. Mel'nikov, ''Posledniaia stranitsa. . . ,'' *Kazachii put'*, no. 77 [March 19, 1926], pp. 3-4). Other sources state that Kriukov died when he was looking for members of his family among refugees. See P. K., ''Krai rodnoi,'' *Kazachii sbornik* (Berlin), no. 1 (1922), p. 60; S. Serapin, ''Pamiati F. D. Kriukova,''

Rodimyi krai, no. 45 (March-April 1963), p. 22 (reprinted from *Spolokh* [Melitopol'], September 5 [Old Style?], 1920).

76. "The Riddles Grow," pp. 105-106.

77. Shiriaev, "Volia k pravde," *Chasovoi*, no. 476 (February 1966), p. 18. However, eight years earlier General Krasnov, speaking of an eventual reestablishment of a free life for the Cossacks, said: "Again, it must be the real *Quiet Don*, not the one of *Sholokhov's*." To judge by the context, Krasnov refers here not to plagiarism but to the Soviet rule over the Don region, of which Sholokhov approves. See P. N. Krasnov, "Kazaki o kazakakh," *Golos Rossii* (Sofia), April 19, 1938.

78. Popov, Letter to Pahomov; B. Bogaevskii, "Mikhail Aleksandrovich Sholokhov," *Kazachii soiuz* (Paris), no. 20 (April 25, 1954), pp. 7-8; Kaledin, Letter to the editor, *Novoe russkoe slovo*, October 12, 1974.

79. Quoted in Medvedev, "The Riddles Grow," p. 107. This is a written reply to a question by an unidentified Moscow journalist. In a conversation with Professor Geir Kjetsaa on December 20, 1977, Sholokhov also stated that he had not read Kriukov. See Kjetsaa, "Problema avtorstva v romane *Tikhii Don*," *Meddelelser* (Oslo), no. 13 (1978), p. 6.

80. " 'Ein solches Buch wird nicht geklaut,' " *Der Spiegel*, no. 49 (December 2, 1974), p. 173.

81. Mikhail Sholokhov, "S opushchennym zabralom. . . ," *Komsomol'skaia pravda*, March 8, 1951, and Speech at the Second Congress of Soviet Writers, *Literaturnaia gazeta*, December 26, 1954. The controversy over pseudonyms reflected the trend to divulge real names of many Jewish writers. For details see D. H. Stewart, *Mikhail Sholokhov: A Critical Introduction* (Ann Arbor, Mich.: University of Michigan Press, 1967), pp. 189-191.

82. Anatolii Kalinin, "Vremia 'Tikhogo Dona,' " *Izvestiia*, February 22 and 23, 1975. Two months later 100,000 copies of Kalinin's article came out in book form.

83. A. Popov, "Donskoi kinorasskaz," *Komsomol'skaia pravda*, May 24, 1980.

SELECTED BIBLIOGRAPHY

In view of the large number of sources consulted for this study, entries are limited primarily to books cited in footnotes. With the exception of Sholokhov's works, the publisher's name is omitted from all publications in Russian unless it is necessary to indicate a particular edition. Because it had been subjected to prolonged censorship, *The Quiet Don* is represented by a more detailed list of editions than *Virgin Soil Upturned*. Soviet editions of both novels published in places other than Moscow, Leningrad, and Rostov-on-Don are as a rule not included. The category entitled ''Publications Containing Historical Materials Pertinent to Sholokhov's Works'' may contain items used as sources for *The Quiet Don*. Easy-to-understand abbreviations are used for publishers like Foreign Languages Publishing House (FLPH), Khudozhestvennaia literatura, Molodaia gvardiia, Moskovskii rabochii, Progress Publishers, Rostovskoe knizhnoe izdatel'stvo (Rostizdat), and Sovetskii pisatel'.

I. Bibliographies

''Izdanie proizvedenii M. Sholokhova'' and ''Bibliograficheskie materialy o M. Sholokhove.'' Gura, V. V., and F. A. Abramov. *M. A. Sholokhov: Seminarii*. 2d ed. enl. Leningrad, 1962.

Krupyshev, A. M., comp., ''Pis'ma i vystupleniia M. A. Sholokhova, 1966-1973 gody'' and ''Literatura o Sholokhove, 1966-1973 gody''; Stopchenko, N. I., comp., ''M. A. Sholokhov v kritike evropeiskikh stran sotsialisticheskogo sodruzhestva, 1965-1973 gody.'' In Kovalev, V. A., and A. I. Khvatov, eds. *Tvorchestvo Mikhaila Sholokhova: Stat'i, soobshcheniia, bibliografiia*. Leningrad, 1975.

''Mikhail Aleksandrovich Sholokhov.'' In *Russkie sovetskie pisateli prozaiki: Biobibliograficheskii ukazatel'*. Vol. 6, part 2, ed. V. V. Serebriakova. Moscow, 1969. The most comprehensive listing of Sholokhov's fictional works, sketches, articles, speeches, and letters, as well as critical literature about them.

Skorodenko, V. A. ed. *Knigi M. A. Sholokhova na iazykakh narodov mira: Bibliograficheskii ukazatel'*. Moscow, 1975.

II. Sholokhov's Works

1. Stories

Aleshkino serdtse. Moscow-Leningrad: Gosizdat, 1925.
Donskie rasskazy. Moscow: Novaia Moskva, 1926.
———. Moscow: Mosk. rab., *Roman-gazeta*, no. 16, 1929.
———. Moscow: Khud. lit., 1956.
Dvukhmuzhniaia. Ed. F. Berezovskii. Moscow-Leningrad: Gosizdat, 1925.
Krasnogvardeitsy. Moscow-Leningrad: Gosizdat, 1925.
Lazorevaia step': Rasskazy. Moscow: Novaia Moskva, 1926.
Lazorevaia step': Donskie rasskazy, 1923-1925. Moscow: Moskovskoe tovarishchestvo pisatelei, 1931.
"Nauka nenavisti." *Pravda*, June 22, 1942.
O Kolchake, krapive i prochem. Leningrad: Gosizdat [1927?].
Rannie rasskazy. Moscow: Sovetskaia Rossiia, 1967.
"Sud'ba cheloveka." *Pravda*, December 31, 1956; January 1, 1957.
"Veter." *Molodoi leninets*, June 4, 1927.

2. *The Quiet Don*

THE JOURNAL EDITION

Vol. 1, *Oktiabr'*, nos. 1-4, 1928. Vol. 2, *Oktiabr'*, nos. 5-10, 1928. Vol. 3, *Oktiabr'*, nos. 1-3, 1929; nos. 1-8, 10, 1932. Vol. 4, *Novyi mir*, nos. 11, 12, 1937; nos. 1-3, 1938; no. 2-3, 1940.

SEPARATE EDITIONS

Tikhii Don. Vol. 1. Moscow-Leningrad: Mosk. rab., 1928.
———. Vol. 1. Moscow: Mosk. rab., *Roman-gazeta*, nos. 7 (19), 12 (24), 1928.
———. Vol. 2. Moscow: Mosk. rab., *Roman-gazeta*, no. 17, 1928; no. 7, 1929.
———. Vol. 1. 2d ed. Moscow-Leningrad: Mosk. rab., 1928.
———. Vol. 2. Moscow-Leningrad: Mosk. rab., 1929.
———. Vol. 1. 3d, 4th, 5th, 6th eds. Moscow-Leningrad: Mosk. rab., 1929.
———. Vol. 2. 2d, 3d, 4th, 5th, 6th eds. Moscow-Leningrad: Mosk. rab., 1929.
———. 2 vols. Moscow-Leningrad: Gosizdat, 1929.
———. 2 vols. 2d ed. Moscow-Leningrad: Gosizdat, 1929-1930.
———. 2 vols. 3d ed. Moscow-Leningrad: Gosizdat Khud. lit., 1931.
———. Vol. 3. Moscow: Khud. lit., 1933.
———. Vol. 3. Moscow: Khud. lit., Deshevaia biblioteka, 1933.
———. Vol. 3. Moscow: Khud. lit., *Roman-gazeta*, no. 8-9, 1933.
———. 2 vols. Moscow: Khud. lit., 1933.
———. Vol. 1. Moscow: Khud. lit., 1934.
———. 3 vols. Moscow: Khud. lit., 1935.
———. 3 vols. Moscow: Khud. lit. (deluxe ed.), 1935-1937.
———. 3 vols. Moscow: Khud lit., 1936.
———. Vol. 1. Moscow: Khud. lit., 1938.
———. Vol. 4. Moscow: Khud. lit., *Roman-gazeta*, nos. 5, 6, 1938; no. 4-5, 1940.

———. Vol. 4. Moscow: Khud. lit., 1940.
———. 4 vols. Rostov-on-Don: Rostizdat, 1939-1940. All subsequent editions are in four volumes.
———. Moscow: Khud. lit., 1941.
———. Rostov-on-Don: Rostizdat, 1941.
———. Leningrad: Khud. lit., 1945.
———. Moscow: Pravda, 1946.
———. Moscow: Sov. pisatel', 1947.
———. Moscow-Leningrad: Khud. lit., 1947.
———. Leningrad: Khud lit., 1948.
———. Moscow: Khud. lit., 1949.
———. Rev. ed. Moscow: Khud. lit., 1953.
———. Moscow: Detgiz, 1955.
———. Moscow: Khud. lit., 1957.
———. Moscow: Khud. lit., 1959.
———. Rostov-on-Don: Rostizdat, 1962.
———. Moscow: Khud. lit., 1962.
———. Moscow: Voenizdat, 1964.
———. Moscow: Izvestiia, 1964.
———. Rostov-on-Don: Rostizdat, 1965.
———. Moscow: Mol. gv., 1965-1967.
———. Moscow: Khud. lit., Vsemirnaia lit., 1968.
———. Moscow: Khud. lit., 1969.
———. Rostov-on-Don: Rostizdat, 1969.
———. Rostov-on-Don: Rostizdat, 1971.
———. Moscow: Mol. gv., 1971.
———. Moscow: Sovremennik, 1973.
———. Moscow: Khud. lit., 1975.
———. Moscow: Sovremennik, 1975.
———. Rostov-on-Don: Rostizdat, 1978.
———. Moscow: Sov. Rossiia, 1978.
———. Moscow: Khud. lit., 1979-1980.
———. Moscow: Voenizdat, 1980.
———. Moscow: Mol. gv., 1980.

3. Virgin Soil Upturned

THE JOURNAL EDITION

Vol. 1, *Novyi mir*, nos. 1-10, 1932. Vol. 2, *Neva*, no. 7, 1959, and no. 1, 1960; *Don*, no. 7, 1959, and no. 2, 1960; *Oktiabr'*, nos. 2-4, 1960.

SEPARATE EDITIONS

Podniataia tselina. Vol. 1. Moscow: Federatsiia, 1932.
———. 2d ed. Moscow: Federatsiia, 1932.
———. Moscow: Khud. lit., 1933.
———. Moscow: Khud. lit., *Roman-gazeta*, nos. 3-5, 1933.
———. 5th ed. Moscow: Sov. lit., 1933.

Podniataia tselina. Moscow: Khud. lit., 1934.
———. Moscow: Sov. lit., 1934.
———. Moscow: Detgiz, 1934.
———. Rostov-on-Don: Azovo-Chernomorskoe izd., 1935.
———. Moscow: Khud. lit., 1936.
———. Moscow: Khud. lit., 1937.
———. Moscow: Khud. lit., 1945.
———. Moscow: Pravda, 1947.
———. Omsk: Omskoe oblast. izd., 1948. For children of high-school age.
———. Moscow-Leningrad: Detgiz, 1950.
———. Leningrad: Gazetno-zhurnal'noe i knizhnoe izd., 1951. For high-school students.
———. Moscow: Mosk. rab., 1952.
———. Rev. ed. Moscow: Khud. lit., 1952.
———. Rev. ed. Moscow: Khud. lit., 1953.
———. Rostov-on-Don: Rostizdat, 1953.
———. Moscow: Detgiz, 1954.
———. Moscow: Sov. pisatel', 1955.
———. Six eds. Moscow: Uchpedgiz, 1956-1960.
———. Vol. 2. Moscow: Khud. lit., *Roman-gazeta*, nos. 5, 6, 1960.
———. 2 vols. Rostov-on-Don: Rostizdat, 1959-1960. All subsequent editions are in two volumes.
———. Moscow; Mol. gv., 1960.
———. Moscow: Khud. lit., 1960.
———. Moscow: Sov. Rossiia, 1960.
———. Moscow: Khud. lit., 1963.
———. Moscow: Prosveshchenie, 1969.
———. Moscow: Khud. lit., 1970.
———. Moscow: Mosk. rab., 1971.
———. Rostov: Rostizdat, 1972.
———. Moscow: Prosveshchenie, 1973.
———. Moscow: Mosk. rab., 1975.
———. Moscow: Sovremennik, 1976.
———. Leningrad: Lenizdat, 1977.
———. Moscow: Sov. Rossiia, 1977.
Podniataia tselina. Nakhalenok. Sud'ba cheloveka. Moscow: Detskaia lit., 1977.

4. *They Fought for Their Country*

Oni srazhalis' za Rodinu. *Pravda*, May 5-8; November 4, 14, 15, 17, 1943; February 12-14; July 3, 1944; July 28, 29, 30; August 1, 1949; *Literaturnaia gazeta*, October 23, 1954; *Pravda*, March 12-15, 1969.
———. Moscow: Khud. lit., *Roman-gazeta*, no. 1, 1959.
Nauka nenavisti. Oni srazhalis' za Rodinu. Sud'ba cheloveka. Moscow: Sovremennik, 1971.

5. Collected Works

Sobranie sochinenii. 8 vols. Revised by the author. Moscow: Mol. gv., 1956-1960.
———. 8 vols. Moscow: Khud. lit., 1956-1960.
———. 8 vols. Moscow: Pravda, 1962.
———. 8 vols. to date. Moscow: Khud. lit., 1965-.
———. 8 vols. Moscow: Pravda, 1975.
———. 8 vols. Moscow: Pravda, 1980.

6. English Translations

And Quiet Flows the Don. Trans. Stephen Garry [H. C. Stevens]. London: Putnam, 1934. New York: Alfred A. Knopf, 1935; New American Library, 1959. Volumes 1 and 2 of *The Quiet Don*.

———. Trans. Stephen Garry, rev. and completed by Robert Daglish. 4 vols. Moscow: FLPH [1959]; Progress Pub., 1967.

At the Bidding of the Heart: Essays, Sketches, Speeches, Papers. Trans. Olga Shartse. Moscow: Progress Pub., 1973. Abridged translation of *Po veleniiu dushi*, Moscow, 1970.

The Don Flows Home to the Sea. Trans. Stephen Garry. London: Putnam, 1940. New York: Alfred A. Knopf, 1941; New American Library, 1960. Volumes 3 and 4 of *The Quiet Don*.

Early Stories. Trans. Robert Daglish and Yelena Altshuler. Moscow: Progress Pub., 1966.

The Fate of a Man. Trans. Robert Daglish. Moscow: Progress Pub., 1967.

Harvest on the Don. Trans. H. C. Stevens. London: Putnam, 1960. New York: Alfred A. Knopf, 1961. Volume 2 of *Virgin Soil Upturned*.

Hate. Moscow: FLPH, 1942. Translation of "Nauka nenavisti," 1942.

One Man's Destiny and Other Stories, Articles, and Sketches, 1923-1963. Trans. H. C. Stevens. London: Putnam, 1967. Abridged translation of *Slovo o Rodine*, Moscow, 1965.

The Science of Hatred. New York: New Age Publishers [1943].

Seeds of Tomorrow. Trans. Stephen Garry. New York: Alfred A. Knopf, 1935. Volume 1 of *Virgin Soil Upturned*.

The Silent Don. Trans. Stephen Garry. New York: Alfred A. Knopf, 1942. Volumes 1-4 of *The Quiet Don*.

The Soil Upturned. Ed. Albert Lewis. Moscow: Co-operative Publishing Society of Foreign Workers in the U.S.S.R., 1934. Volume 1 of *Virgin Soil Upturned*.

Tales from the Don. Trans. H. C. Stevens. London: Putnam, 1961. *Tales of the Don*. New York: Alfred A. Knopf, 1962.

They Fought for Their Country. Trans. Robert Daglish. *Soviet Literature* (Moscow), nos. 7, 8, 1959; no. 10, 1969.

Virgin Soil Upturned. Trans. Stephen Garry. London: Putnam, 1935.

———. Trans. Robert Daglish. Vol. 1. Moscow: FLPH [1957]; Progress Pub., 1964. Vol. 2. FLPH [1961].

———. Trans. Robert Daglish. 2 vols. Moscow: Progress Pub., 1979.

III. Historical Sources of *The Quiet Don*

Antonov-Ovseenko, V. A. *Zapiski o grazhdanskoi voine*. Vol. 1. Moscow, 1924.

Denikin, A. I. *Ocherki russkoi smuty*. Vol. 1, part 2; vols. 2, 3. Paris, Berlin [1921]-1924.

Donskaia istoricheskaia komissiia, ed. *Donskaia letopis'*. Vol. 2, Vienna, 1923: Bykadorov, Is., "Vospominaniia o voiskovom atamane Voiska Donskogo generale A. M. Nazarove"; "Chetvertyi Krug"; Duvakin, N., "Voiskovoi ataman general A. M. Nazarov"; Ianov, G., " 'Paritet' "; Kakliugin, K., "Voiskovoi ataman A. M. Kaledin i ego vremia" and "Voiskovoi ataman A. M. Nazarov i ego vremia"; Kosov, F. G., "Podtelkov v Novocherkasske"; "Vozzvanie generala L. G. Kornilova k kazakam."

Frenkel', A. A. *Orly revoliutsii*. Rostov-on-Don, 1920.

Gessen, I. V., ed. *Arkhiv russkoi revoliutsii*. Vol. 1, Berlin [1921]: Krasnov, P. N., "Na vnutrennem fronte." Vol. 5, Berlin, 1922: Krasnov, P. N., "Vsevelikoe Voisko Donskoe"; Lukomskii, A., "Iz vospominanii."

Kakurin, N. *Kak srazhalas' revoliutsiia*. Vol. 1, ed. N. N. Popov; vol. 2, ed. R. B. Eideman. Moscow-Leningrad, 1925-1926.

Martynov, E. I. *Kornilov: Popytka voennogo perevorota*. Leningrad, 1927.

Trotskii, L. *Kak vooruzhalas' revoliutsiia*. Vol. 2, part 1. Moscow, 1924.

Voroshilov, K. *Stalin i Krasnaia armiia*. Moscow: Partizdat TsK VKP(b), 1937.

IV. Publications Containing Historical Materials Pertinent to Sholokhov's Works

1. Individual Works

Andreev, G. [Gennadii Khomiakov], *Trudnye dorogi*. Munich, 1959.

Barron, John. *KGB: The Secret Work of Soviet Secret Agents*. Reader's Digest Press: New York, 1974.

Borokhova, I. M. et al., comps. *Bor'ba za vlast' Sovetov na Donu, 1917-1920 gg.: Sbornik dokumentov*. Rostov-on-Don, 1957.

Budennyi, S. M. *Proidennyi put'*. Vol. 3. Moscow, 1973.

Carell, Paul. *Der Russlandkrieg: Fotografiert von Soldaten*. Frankfort on the Main: Verlag Ullstein, 1967.

Delert, Dan. *Don v ogne*. Rostov-on-Don, 1927.

Denikin, A. I. *Ocherki russkoi smuty*. 5 vols. Paris, Berlin [1921]-1926.

Denisov, S. V. *Zapiski: Grazhdanskaia voina na iuge Rossii 1918-1920 g.g.* Book 1. Constantinople, 1921.

Direktivy komandovaniia frontov Krasnoi Armii (1917-1922 gg.): Sbornik dokumentov. Vol. 2, ed. N. N. Azovtsev et al. Moscow, 1972.

Dmytryshyn, Basil. *USSR: A Concise History*. 2d ed. New York: Charles Scribner's Sons, 1971.

Dobrynin, V. *Bor'ba s bol'shevizmom na iuge Rossii: Uchastie v bor'be donskogo kazachestva*. Prague, 1921.

Donskaia istoricheskaia komissiia, ed. *Donskaia letopis': Sbornik mater'ialov po noveishei istorii donskogo kazachestva so vremeni russkoi revoliutsii 1917 goda*. 3 vols. Vienna, Belgrade, 1923-1924.

Fedortsov, A. I. *Riadom s Podtelkovym*. Saratov, 1974.

Golovin, N. N. *Iz istorii kampanii 1914 goda na russkom fronte: Nachalo voiny i operatsii v Vostochnoi Prussii*. Prague 1926.

Golubintsev [A. V.]. *Russkaia Vandeia: Ocherki grazhdanskoi voiny na Donu, 1917-1920 gg.*, Munich, 1959.

Grazhdanskaia voina, 1918-1921. Vol. 3, ed. A. S. Bubnov et al. Moscow-Leningrad, 1930.

Grigorovich, D. F. *Kiev gorod-geroi*. Moscow, 1962.

Gul', Roman. *Ledianoi pokhod*. Berlin [1921].

Ianchevskii, N. L. *Grazhdanskaia bor'ba na Severnom Kavkaze*. Rostov-on-Don, 1927.

Istoriia Velikoi Otechestvennoi voiny Sovetskogo Soiuza, 1941-1945. Vol. 2. Moscow, 1961.

Ivanov, A. N. et al., comps. and eds. *Pomniat stepi donskie: Sbornik vospominanii*. Rostov-on-Don, 1967.

Kalinin, I. *Russkaia Vandeia*. Moscow-Leningrad, 1926.

Khmelevskii, K. A. *Krakh krasnovshchiny i nemetskaia interventsiia na Donu (aprel' 1918-mart 1919 goda)*. Rostov-on-Don, 1965.

Khmelevskii, K. A. et al., eds. *Iuzhnyi front (mai 1918-mart 1919): Sbornik dokumentov*. Rostov-on-Don, 1962.

Kim, M. P., ed. *Istoriia SSSR: Epokha sotsializma (1917-1957 gg.)*. Moscow, 1958.

Korchin, M. *Bor'ba za Sovety na Donu*. Rostov-on-Don, 1947.

Der Kriegsverlauf, August 1914-Juli 1915. Berlin: Carl Heymanns Verlag, 1915.

Kudinov, Pavel. "Vosstanie verkhne-dontsov v 1919 godu (Istoricheskii ocherk)." *Vol'noe kazachestvo* (Prague), nos. 77-85, 1931.

Lapme, A. A. fon, ed. *Beloe delo*. Vol. 4. Berlin, 1928.

Lenin, V. I. *Polnoe sobranie sochinenii*. 5th ed. Vol. 51. Moscow, 1965.

Manstein, Erich v. *Verlorene Siege*. Bonn: Athenäum-Verlag, 1955.

Mel'nikov, N. M. *A. M. Kaledin geroi lutskogo proryva i donskoi ataman*. Madrid, 1968.

Miatezh Kornilova: Iz belykh memuarov. Leningrad, 1928.

Miliukov, P. N. *Istoriia vtoroi russkoi revoliutsii*. Vol. 1, part 2. Sofia, 1921.

Neustrashimyi geroi donskoi kazak Kuz'ma Kriuchkov i ego slavnye pobedy nad vragami, kak on odin ubil 11 nemtsev. Rostov-on-Don, 1914.

Oprits, I. N., *Leib-gvardii Kazachii E. V. polk v gody revoliutsii i grazhdanskoi voiny 1917-1920*. Paris, 1939.

Ott, Ernst. *Jäger am Feind*. Munich: Kameradschaft der Spielhahnjäger e.V., 1966.

Piontkovskii, S. *Grazhdanskaia voina v Rossii (1918-1921 g.g.): Khrestomatiia*. Moscow, 1925.

Pipcs, Richard, ed. *Revolutionary Russia*. Cambridge, Mass.: Harvard University Press, 1968.

Proletarskaia revoliutsiia na Donu. Vol. 2, ed. A. A. Frenkel'. Rostov-on-Don, 1922. Vol. 4, ed. A. A. Frenkel'. Moscow-Leningrad, 1924.

Raenko, Ia. N. *Khronika istoricheskikh sobytii na Donu, Kubani i v Chernomor'e*. Part 1. Rostov-on-Don, 1939.

Semanov, S. N. *"Tikhii Don"—literatura i istoriia*. Moscow, 1977.

Shatov, M. V. *Materialy i dokumenty osvoboditel'nogo dvizheniia narodov Rossii v gody vtoroi mirovoi voiny (1941-1945)*. Vol. 2. New York, 1966.

Shkuro, A. G. *Zapiski belogo partizana*. Buenos Aires, 1961.

Solzhenitsyn, Aleksandr I. *The Gulag Archipelago, 1918-1956: An Experiment in Literary Investigation*. Parts 1-2. Trans. Thomas P. Whitney. New York: Harper & Row, 1974.

Starikov, Sergei, and Roy Medvedev. *Philip Mironov and the Russian Civil War*. Trans. Guy Daniels. New York: Alfred A. Knopf, 1978.

Strategicheskii ocherk voiny 1914-1918. Part 1, comp. Ia. K. Tsikhovich. Moscow, 1922. Part 5, comp. V. N. Klembovskii. Moscow, 1920.

Trotsky, Leon. *Stalin*. 2d ed. Ed. and trans. Charles Malamuth. New York and London: Harper and Brothers, 1946.

The Trotsky Papers, 1917-1922. Ed. and annotated by Jan M. Meijer. Vol. 1. The Hague: Mouton, 1964.

Tschebotarioff, Gregory P. *Russia, My Native Land*. New York: McGraw-Hill, 1964.

Ul'ianov, I. I. *Kazaki i sovetskaia respublika*. Moscow-Leningrad, 1929.

Uspenskii, A. A. *Na voine: Vostochnaia Prussiia-Litva 1914-1915 g.g*. Kaunas, 1932.

Vladimirova, Vera. *Kontr-revoliutsiia v 1917 g.: Kornilovshchina*. Moscow, 1924.

Volin, V. *Don i Dobrovol'cheskaia armiia*. Novocherkassk, 1919.

Williamson, H.N.H. *Farewell to the Don*. Ed. John Harris. New York: John Day, 1971.

Zvegintsov, V. V. *Russkaia armiia 1914 g.: Podrobnaia dislokatsiia, formirovaniia 1914-1917, regalii i otlichiia*. Paris, 1959.

2. *Periodicals from the Civil War Period*

Donskaia volna. Rostov-on-Don.

Donskie vedomosti. Novocherkassk.

Krasnaia gazeta. Petrograd.

Parus. Rostov-on-Don.

Pravda. Petrograd, Moscow.

Priazovskii krai. Rostov-on-Don.

Vechernee vremia. Rostov-on-Don.

Velikaia Rossiia. Rostov-on-Don.

Vol'nyi Don. Novocherkassk.

Zhizn'. Rostov-on-Don.

3. *Russian Émigré Periodicals*

Chasovoi. Brussels.

Golos Rossii. Sofia.

Kazach'i dumy. Sofia.
Kazachii golos. Paris.
Kazachii istoricheskii sbornik. Paris.
Kazachii put'. Prague.
Kazachii sbornik. Berlin.
Kazachii soiuz. Paris.
Kazaki zagranitsei. Sofia.
Novoe russkoe slovo. New York.
Poslednie novosti. Paris.
Rodimyi krai. Paris.
Russkaia mysl'. Paris.
Vol'noe kazachestvo. Prague.
Vozrozhdenie. Paris.

V. Biography, Criticism, Dictionaries

Abramov, F. A., and V. V. Gura. *M. A. Sholokhov: Seminarii*. Leningrad, 1958.
Andreev, D. L., and V. E. Beklemisheva, eds. *Rekviem*. Moscow, 1930.
Andreyev Carlisle, Olga. *Voices in the Snow: Encounters with Russian Writers*. New York: Random House, 1962.
Andriasov, Mikhail. *Veshenskie byli*. Moscow, 1975.
———, comp. *Mikhail Aleksandrovich Sholokhov*. Moscow, 1966.
———, comp. and ed. *Slovo o Sholokhove*. Moscow, 1973.
Aristotle. *The "Art" of Rhetoric*. Trans. John Henry Freese. London: William Heinemann; Cambridge, Mass.: Harvard University Press, 1947.
———. *Poetics*. Trans. Gerald F. Else. Ann Arbor, Mich.: University of Michigan Press, 1967.
Averbakh, L., ed. *Tvorcheskie puti proletarskoi literatury: Vtoroi sbornik statei*. Moscow-Leningrad, 1929.
Bearne, C. G. *Sholokhov*. Edinburgh: Oliver and Boyd, 1969.
Beliaev, N., comp. *Mikhail Kol'tsov, kakim on byl*. Moscow, 1965.
Belov, P. *Lev Tolstoi i Mikhail Sholokhov*. Rostov-on-Don, 1969.
Besharov, Justinia. *Imagery of the "Igor' Tale."* Leiden: E. J. Brill, 1956.
Biriukov, F. *Khudozhestvennye otkrytiia Mikhaila Sholokhova*. Moscow, 1976.
Black, Max. *Models and Metaphors: Studies in Language and Philosophy*. Ithaca, N.Y.: Cornell University Press, 1962.
Britikov, A. F. *Masterstvo Mikhaila Sholokhova*. Moscow-Leningrad, 1964.
Brodskii, N. L., ed. *Turgenev i ego vremia: Pervyi sbornik*. Moscow, 1923.
Brooke-Rose, Christine. *A Grammar of Metaphor*. London: Secker and Warburg, 1958.
Chebyshowa, Olga V. "Deviations from the Standard Literary Russian in Sholochov's *Quiet Flows the Don*." Master's thesis, Stanford University, 1964.
D. *Stremia "Tikhogo Dona": Zagadki romana*. Paris, 1974.
Gavrilenko, Petr. *Sholokhov sredi druzei: Ocherki*. 3d ed., rev. and enl. Alma-Ata, 1975.
———. *S Sholokhovym na okhote: Ocherki*. Alma-Ata, 1965.

Gibian, George, and H. W. Tjalsma, eds. *Russian Modernism: Culture and the Avant-Garde, 1900-1930*. Ithaca, N.Y., and London: Cornell University Press, 1976.

Gladkovskaia, L. A. et al., eds. *A. S. Serafimovich (1863-1963): Materialy mezhvuzovskoi nauchnoi konferentsii*. Volgograd, 1963.

Goffenshefer, V. *Mikhail Sholokhov: Kriticheskii ocherk*. Moscow, 1941.

Gor'kii, Maksim. *Sobranie sochinenii v tridtsati tomakh*. Vol. 26. Moscow, 1953.

Gosudarstvennaia ordena Lenina biblioteka SSSR imeni V. I. Lenina. *Zapiski otdela rukopisei*. Vol. 29. Moscow, 1967.

Gura, V. *Kak sozdavalsia "Tikhii Don": Tvorcheskaia istoriia romana M. Sholokhova*. Moscow, 1980.

———. *Zhizn' i tvorchestvo M. A. Sholokhova*. 2d ed., rev. and enl. Moscow, 1960.

———, and F. A. Abramov. *M. A. Sholokhov: Seminarii*. 2d ed. enl. Leningrad, 1962.

Iakimenko, L. *Tvorchestvo M. A. Sholokhova*. Moscow, 1964; 2d ed., rev. and enl., 1970; 3d ed., 1977.

[———.] Yakimenko, L. *Sholokhov: A Critical Appreciation*. Trans. Bryan Bean. Moscow: Progress Pub., 1973. Abridged translation of *Tvorchestvo M. A. Sholokhova*.

Istoriia russkoi sovetskoi literatury. Vol. 2, ed. L. I. Timofeev and A. G. Dement'ev. Moscow, 1960.

Kalinin, Anatolii. *Vremia "Tikhogo Dona."* Moscow, 1975.

Khigerovich, R. *Put' pisatelia: Zhizn' i tvorchestvo A. Serafimovicha*. Moscow, 1956.

Khrushchev, N. S. *Vysokoe prizvanie literatury i iskusstva*. Moscow, 1963.

Khvatov, A. *Khudozhestvennyi mir Sholokhova*. Moscow, 1970; 3d ed., 1978.

Klimenko, Michael. *The World of Young Sholokhov: Vision of Violence*. North Quincy, Mass.: Christopher Publishing House, 1972.

Kovalev, V. A., and A. I. Khvatov, eds. *Tvorchestvo Mikhaila Sholokhova: Stat'i, soobshcheniia, bibliografiia*. Leningrad, 1975.

Kviatkovskii, Aleksandr. *Poeticheskii slovar'*. Moscow, 1966.

Larin, B. A., ed. *Mikhail Sholokhov: Sbornik statei*. Leningrad, 1956.

Lezhnev, I. *Mikhail Sholokhov: Kritiko-biograficheskii ocherk*. Moscow, 1941.

———. *Mikhail Sholokhov*. Leningrad, 1948.

———. *Put' Sholokhova: Tvorcheskaia biografiia*. Moscow, 1958.

Likhachev, D. S., and L. A. Dmitriev, eds. *"Slovo o polku Igoreve" i pamiatniki Kulikovskogo tsikla*. Moscow-Leningrad, 1966.

Lipshits, S. G., ed. *Mikhail Sholokhov: Literaturno-kriticheskii sbornik*. Rostov-on-Don, 1940.

Literaturnoe nasledstvo. Vols. 70; 72, book 1. Moscow, 1963, 1966.

Logashova, L. P., ed. *"Tikhii Don": Uroki romana*. Rostov-on-Don, 1979.

Lukin, Iurii. *Dva portreta: A. S. Makarenko, M. A. Sholokhov*. Moscow, 1975.

———. *Mikhail Sholokhov*. Moscow, 1952.

McCall, Marsh H., Jr. *Ancient Rhetorical Theories of Simile and Comparison*. Cambridge, Mass.: Harvard University Press, 1969.

Medvedev, Roy A. *Let History Judge: The Origins and Consequences of Stalinism*. Trans. Colleen Taylor, ed. David Joravsky and Georges Haupt. New York: Alfred A. Knopf, 1972.

———. *Problems in the Literary Biography of Mikhail Sholokhov*. Trans. A.D.P. Briggs. Cambridge, 1977.

———. *Qui a écrit "le Don paisible"?* Paris: Christian Bourgois éditeur, 1975.

Medvedev, Zhores A. *Desiat' let posle "Odnogo dnia Ivana Denisovicha."* Rev. ed. London: Macmillan, 1973.

Mirtov, A. V. *Donskoi slovar': Materialy k izucheniiu leksiki donskikh kazakov*. Rostov-on-Don, 1929.

Muchnic, Helen. *From Gorky to Pasternak: Six Writers in Soviet Russia*. New York: Random House, 1961.

Nikitina, N. F., ed. *Mikhail Sholokhov*. Moscow, 1931.

Ortenberg, D. *Vremia ne vlastno: Pisateli na fronte*. Moscow, 1975.

Petelin, Viktor. *Gumanizm Sholokhova*. Moscow, 1965.

———. *Mikhail Sholokhov: Ocherk zhizni i tvorchestva*. Moscow, 1974.

———. *Rodnye sud'by*. 2d ed. enl. Moscow, 1976.

Potebnia, A. A. *Iz zapisok po teorii slovesnosti*. Khar'kov, 1905.

Priima, Konstantin. *"Tikhii Don" srazhaetsia*. Rostov-on-Don, 1972; 2d ed., rev. and enl. Moscow, 1975.

Proffer, Carl R. *The Simile and Gogol's "Dead Souls."* The Hague: Mouton, 1967.

Ricoeur, Paul. *The Rule of Metaphor*. Trans. Robert Czerny, Kathleen McLaughlin, and John Costello. Toronto: University of Toronto Press, 1977.

Saburov, A. A. *"Voina i mir" L. N. Tolstogo: Problematika i poetika*. Moscow, 1959.

Serafimovich, A. S. *Sbornik neopublikovannykh proizvedenii i materialov*. Comp. Iu. A. Krasovskii, ed. A. A. Volkov. Moscow, 1958.

Shipley, Joseph T., ed. *Dictionary of World Literary Terms*. Boston: Writer, 1970.

Simmons, Ernest J. *Russian Fiction and Soviet Ideology: Introduction to Fedin, Leonov, and Sholokhov*. New York: Columbia University Press, 1958.

Sofronov, Anatolii. *Sholokhovskoe*. Moscow, 1975.

Solzhenitsyn, Aleksandr. *Bodalsia telenok s dubom: Ocherki literaturnoi zhizni*. Paris, 1975.

Stalin, I. *Marksizm i voprosy iazykoznaniia*. Moscow, 1950.

———. *Sochineniia*. Vol. 12. Moscow, 1949.

Stewart, D. H. *Mikhail Sholokhov: A Critical Introduction*. Ann Arbor, Mich.: University of Michigan Press, 1967.

Suichmezov, A. M., comp. and ed. *Nash Sholokhov: Slovo o velikom zemliake*. Rostov-on-Don, 1975.

Svartengren, Hilding T. *Intensifying Similes in English*. Lund, 1918.

Toom, Lidiia. *Na krutom perelome: Stat'i*. Moscow, 1930.

Valiusinskaia, Z. V. et al. *Slovar' russkikh donskikh govorov*. 3 vols. Rostov-on-Don, 1975-1976.

Vasil'ev, V. G. *O "Tikhom Done" M. Sholokhova*. Cheliabinsk, 1963.

Vishnevskii, Vsevolod. *Sobranie sochinenii*. 6 vols. Moscow, 1954-1961.

Wheelwright, Philip. *The Burning Fountain: A Study in the Language of Symbolism*. Rev. ed. Bloomington, Ind.: Indiana University Press, 1968.

———. *Metaphor and Reality*. Bloomington, Ind.: Indiana University Press, 1962.

Yelland, H. L.; S. C. Jones; and K.S.W. Easton. *A Handbook of Literary Terms*. New York: Philosophical Library, 1950.

VI. Fictional Works and Sketches (other than Sholokhov's)

Abramov, F. "Vokrug da okolo." *Neva*, no. 1, 1963.

———, Fyodor. *One Day in the "New Life."* Trans. David Floyd. New York: Frederick A. Praeger, 1963.

Babel', Isaak. *Konarmiia*. 3d ed. Moscow-Leningrad, 1928. Reprint. London: Flegon Press, n.d.

Baklanov, Grigorii. *Iiul' 41 goda*. Moscow, 1965.

Busygin, Aleksandr. *Izrbrannoe*. Foreword by M. Sholokhov. Rostov-on-Don, 1952.

Gladkov, Fedor. *Ognennyi kon'*. Vol. 1 of *Sobranie sochinenii*. 2d ed. Moscow-Leningrad: Zemlia i fabrika, 1926.

———. *Tsement*. *Krasnaia nov'*, nos. 1-6, 1925.

Gogol', N. V. *Sobranie khudozhestvennykh proizvedenii v piati tomakh*. 2d ed. Vol. 2. Moscow: Akademiia nauk SSSR, 1960.

Iashin, A. "Rychagi." *Literaturnaia Moskva*. Vol. 2, ed. M. I. Aliger et al. Moscow, 1956.

Ivanov, Vsevolod. *Bronepoezd No. 14.69*. *Krasnaia nov'*, no. 1, 1922.

Kriukov, F. "Dorogie mogily." *Russkie vedomosti*, March 21 (April 3), 1915.

———. "Kazachka." *Russkoe bogatstvo*, no. 10, 1896.

———. *Kazatskie motivy: Ocherki i rasskazy*. St. Petersburg, 1907.

———. "K istochniku istselenii." *Russkoe bogatstvo*, nos. 11, 12, 1904.

———. "Na tikhom Donu." *Russkoe bogatstvo*, nos. 8-10, 1898.

———. "Novoe." *Russkoe bogatstvo*, nos. 4-7, 1917.

———. "Novym stroem." *Russkie vedomosti*, July 6 (19), 1917.

———. "Obval." *Russkie zapiski*, no. 2-3, 1917.

———. "Ofitsersha." *Russkoe bogatstvo*, nos. 4, 5, 1912.

———. "Pamiati kn. Gelovani." *Russkie vedomosti*, February 24 (March 9), 1915.

———. "Pervye vybory." *Russkie zapiski*, no. 4, 1916.

———. "Polzkom." *Russkie vedomosti*, December 25, 1916 (January 7, 1917).

———. "Po voennym obstoiatel'stvam." *Russkie vedomosti*, November 15 (28), 1916.

———. *Rasskazy*. Vol. 1. Moscow, 1914.

———. "Rodimyi krai." Donskaia istoricheskaia komissiia, ed. *Donskaia letopis'*. Vol. 1. Vienna, 1923.

———. "Shkval." *Russkoe bogatstvo*, nos. 11, 12, 1909.
———. "Siluety." *Russkie zapiski*, nos. 11, 12, 1915.
———. "S iuzhnoi storony." *Russkie vedomosti*, November 6 (19), 1914.
———. "U boevoi linii." *Russkie vedomosti*, February 5 (18), 16 (29), April 6 (19), 10 (23), 1916.
———. "V glubokom tylu." *Russkie vedomosti*, September 21 (October 4), October 26 (November 8), November 2 (15), 1914.
———. "V kamere No. 380." *Russkoe bogatstvo*, no. 6, 1910.
———. "V sfere voennoi obydennosti." *Russkie vedomosti*, July 2 (15), 1916.
———. "Za Karsom." *Russkie vedomosti*, February 18 (March 3), February 22 (March 7), 1915.
McLean, Hugh, and Walter N. Vickery, eds. and trans. *The Year of Protest, 1956: An Anthology of Soviet Literary Materials*. New York: Vintage Books, 1961.
Olesha, Iurii. *Povesti i rasskazy*. Moscow, 1965.
Pasternak, Boris. *Doktor Zhivago*. Ann Arbor, Mich.: University of Michigan Press, 1959.
Remizov, Aleksei. *Sochineniia*. Vol. 6. St. Petersburg, 1910-1912. Reprint. Munich: Wilhelm Fink Verlag (Slavische Propyläen, no. 79), 1971.
Semin, Leonid. *Odin na odin*. *Neva*, no. 3, 1963.
Slovo o polku Igoreve. Ed. V. P. Adrianova-Peretts. Moscow-Leningrad, 1950.
Solzhenitsyn, Aleksandr I. *The First Circle*. Trans. Thomas P. Whitney. New York: Bantam Books, 1969.
———. *V kruge pervom*. Vols. 1 and 2 of *Sobranie sochinenii*. Paris, 1978.
———, Alexander. *Cancer Ward*. Trans. Nicholas Bethell and David Burg. New York: Bantam Books, 1969.
Tolstoi, L. N. *Sobranie sochinenii*. Ed. N. N. Akopova et al. 20 vols. Moscow, 1960-1965.
Trifonov, Iurii. *Starik*. *Druzhba narodov*, no. 3, 1978.
Troepol'skii, G. *Chernozem*. Moscow, 1962.
Veselyi, Artem. *Piruiushchaia vesna*. Khar'kov, 1929.
Zalygin, S. *Na Irtyshe*. *Novyi mir*, no. 2, 1964.

INDEX

LIBRARY OF CONGRESS CATALOGING IN PUBLICATION DATA

Ermolaev, Herman.
Mikhail Sholokhov and his art.

Bibliography: p.
Includes index.
1. Sholokhov, Mikhail Aleksandrovich, 1905-
Tikhiĭ Don. I. Title.
PG3476.S52T57 891.73′42 81-47123
ISBN 0-691-07634-0 AACR2